The Swashbucklers

By James Robert Parish

AS AUTHOR

THE FOX GIRLS*
THE PARAMOUNT PRETTIES*
THE SLAPSTICK QUEENS
GOOD DAMES
THE RKO GALS*
HOLLYWOOD'S GREAT LOVE TEAMS*
ELVIS
THE GREAT CHILD STARS

AS CO-AUTHOR

THE EMMY AWARDS: A PICTORIAL HISTORY
THE CINEMA OF EDWARD G. ROBINSON
THE MGM STOCK COMPANY: THE GOLDEN ERA*
THE GREAT SPY PICTURES
THE GEORGE RAFT FILE
VINCENT PRICE UNMASKED
FILM DIRECTORS GUIDE: THE U.S.
FILM DIRECTORS GUIDE: WESTERN EUROPE
THE GLAMOUR GIRLS*
THE DEBONAIRS*
HOLLYWOOD PLAYERS: THE FORTIES*
THE GREAT GANGSTER PICTURES
THE GREAT WESTERN PICTURES
LIZA!
THE GREAT MOVIE HEROES

AS EDITOR

ACTORS' TELEVISION CREDITS: 1950-1972

AS ASSOCIATE EDITOR

THE AMERICAN MOVIES REFERENCE BOOK
TV MOVIES

By Don E. Stanke

THE GLAMOUR GIRLS (CO-AUTHOR)*
THE DEBONAIRS (CO-AUTHOR)*

* Published by Arlington House

The Swashbucklers

James Robert Parish
& Don E. Stanke

EDITOR

T. ALLEN TAYLOR

RESEARCH ASSOCIATES

EARL ANDERSON □ JOHN ROBERT COCCHI
MICHAEL R. PITTS □ FLORENCE SOLOMON

ARLINGTON HOUSE·PUBLISHERS
NEW ROCHELLE, NEW YORK

Manufactured in the United States of America

Library of Congress Cataloging in Publication Data

Parish, James Robert.
  The swashbucklers.

  Includes index.
  1. Moving-picture actors and actresses—Biography.
I. Stanke, Don E., joint author. II. Title.
PN1998.A2P413   791.43'028'0922   76-4540
ISBN 0-87000-326-7

For MAUREEN O'HARA
The Loveliest Swashbuckler of Them All

Contents

Acknowledgments

RESEARCH CONSULTANT:
  Doug McClelland

John R. Adams
Jack Barnich
Richard Bojarski
Richard Braff
Bruco Enterprises
Mrs. Loraine Burdick
Kingsley Canham
Ellen Corby
Bill Culp
Howard Davis
Jeff Donnell
Morris Everett, Jr.
Alice Faye
Filmfacts
Film Fan Monthly
Films and Filming
Films in Review
Connie Gilchrist
Pierre Guinle
Mrs. R. F. Hastings
John Hill
Richard Hudson
Ken D. Jones
Peg Koken
Miles Kreuger
William T. Leonard

David McGillivray
Gregory Mank
Albert B. Manski
Alvin H. Marill
Jim Meyer
Mrs. Earl Meisinger
Peter Miglierini
Norman Miller
Monthly Film Bulletin
Movie Poster Service
  (Bob Smith)
Movie Star News
  (Paula Klaw)
Pat Nix
Morris Read
Screen Facts
  (Alan G. Barbour)
Don Shay
Charles Smith
Mrs. Peter Smith
Roz Starr Service
Charles K. Stumpf
TV Guide
  (San Francisco Office)
Theatre 80 (Howard Otway)
J. Cotton Walp
Cornel Wilde

And special thanks to Paul Myers, curator of the Theatre Collection at the Lincoln Center Library for the Performing Arts, and his staff: Monty Arnold, David Bartholomew, Rod Bladel, Donald Fowle, Maxwell Silverman, Dorothy Swerdlove, Betty Wharton; and Donald Madison, Photographic Services.

Foreword

by Hal B. Wallis

It is a pleasure to write a preface to a book devoted to cinema stars who have excelled in the swashbuckling field. The genre appeals to me, both as a viewer and as a film producer.

A few yesterdays ago, when I entered the film business as a Los Angeles theatre manager and, later, as a Warner Bros. publicist, we were all captivated by the adventurous Douglas Fairbanks, Sr. His reckless nature so completely suited the excitement of costumed drama that it was difficult to think of anyone else ever matching his array of gymnastics or exuding as much infectious charm as he did in silent photoplays.

While Doug was cavorting on screen over at United Artists, I had my initial personal experience with sword and plume movies at Warner Bros. I had moved from First National to the spot vacated by Darryl Zanuck, when he formed Twentieth Century Pictures with Joe Schenck. I was made executive producer in charge of all production at Warner Bros. Studios. Our company had done well with rough-and-tumble gangster films—thanks to Edward G. Robinson and James Cagney—but we realized that the public needed something different to help shake away the depression blues. The British had proved that intelligent historical drama (*The Private Life of Henry VIII*) and exciting period pictures (*The Count of Monte Cristo*) interested moviegoers.

We worked on a deal to import Robert Donat from England to star in a new version of *Captain Blood*. Complications arose, and we settled on using one of our own contract players to assume the lead in the expensive production. Both director Michael Curtiz and I were convinced that a young Australian had what it took to carry the Sabatini tale. We were right, and Errol Flynn went on to become a major screen star.

Over the years, I personally supervised several of Errol's costume films, including *The Charge of the Light Brigade, The Adventures of Robin Hood, The Sea Hawk,* and *They Died with Their Boots On.* The mention of these titles brings back vivid memories and the satisfaction of having created entertainment that has stood the test of time.

World War II brought about a great change in public taste. The popularity of swashbuckling films declined. Pictures produced on a grand scale became too expensive, and the public preferred contemporary stories which dealt with present-day problems. Occasionally there was a revival of the form, but it was left largely to the Italians, who produced cloak-and-sandal epics hastily assembled for the action markets.

My interest, however, did not wane, and in 1964 I produced the screen version of the Jean Anouilh play, *Becket.* It co-starred Peter O'Toole and Richard Burton and recreated the fascinating years of King Henry II's reign over Great Britain. We no longer dealt with a light-hearted look at the period (interspersed with the swordplay of an Errol Flynn or the petite, lady-fair femininity of an Olivia de Havilland), but with a thoughtful study of the problems of the times. My later productions, *Anne of the Thousand Days, Mary Queen of Scots,* and *The Nelson Affair,* placed greater stress on characterization and dramatic situation than on the interplay of cross-swords or rapiers.

I was heartened to see the enthusiasm placed in a new rendering of Alexandre Dumas' *The Three Musketeers,* but I fear our succeeding generations will never again see the likes of a Fairbanks or a Flynn. Through the pages of this book their excitement lives again.

Hal Wallis

KEY TO THE FILM STUDIOS

AA	Allied Artists Picture Corporation
AVCO/ EMB	Avco Embassy Pictures Corporation
CIN	Cinerama Releasing Corporation
COL	Columbia Pictures Industries, Inc.
EMB	Embassy Pictures Corporation
FN	First National Pictures, Inc. (later part of Warner Bros.)
FOX	Fox Film Corporation
LIP	Lippert Pictures, Inc.
MGM	Metro-Goldwyn-Mayer, Inc.
MON	Monogram Pictures Corporation
PAR	Paramount Pictures Corporation
RKO	RKO Radio Pictures, Inc.
REP	Republic Pictures Corporation
20th	Twentieth Century-Fox Film Corporation
UA	United Artists Corporation
UNIV	Universal Pictures, Inc.
WB	Warner Bros. Inc.

SWASHBUCKLERS ON THE SCREEN

BY EDWARD CONNOR

The *American College Dictionary* defines "swashbuckler" as "swaggering swordsman or bully."

The latter part of that definition would certainly come as a surprise to the person whose idea of the swashbuckler as a hero has been colored by romantic novels (especially those by Rafael Sabatini) and the motion pictures derived from them.

If the average movie enthusiast were asked to name the greatest swashbuckler of silent films he would almost certainly say Douglas Fairbanks, Sr., because of the half-dozen famous films the star made in the twenties. Actually, in his period of greatest productivity (1915-1920), he played the same screen role over and over again: an idealized average American boy, devil-may-care, athletic, living and enjoying life to the fullest. It was for a change in pace that, in 1920, Fairbanks, Sr. decided to take on his first feature-length costume drama: Johnston McCulley's *The Curse of Capistrano,* retitled *The Mark of Zorro.* He had a field day showing off his athletic prowess and ability at swordplay as he portrayed the wealthy, foppish Don Diego Vega who disguised himself as the heroic Zorro (Spanish for "fox") and went about avenging the wrongs done the peons of California when that territory was a Spanish colony.

So successful was that film that Fairbanks decided to continue in this swashbuckling mold. Indeed, he ended his acting career with the tongue-in-cheek, yet very bitter sweet, *The Private Life of Don Juan* (1934), which was shot in England. Like the hero of the celluloid piece, Doug had grown old with his boots on, and hardly knew which way to turn professionally.

But even before the illustrious Fairbanks, Sr., there had been swash-bucklers on the screen, especially in films based on the Robin Hood legend. *Robin Hood and His Merry Men* had been filmed in England as early as 1909, and the one-reel *Robin Hood—Outlawed,* also made in England, had been released in 1913. During that same year in the United States, Eclair produced a three-reel *Robin Hood* featuring Robert Frazer, while Thanhouser released a four-reel film with the same title and featuring William Russell. It seemed that movie viewers enjoyed vicariously reliving bygone days when men were gallant, women were gracious and charming, and disagreements were settled with the rapier or sword.

Always enthusiastic about the classics, the British filmed Sir Walter Scott's *Ivanhoe* twice in 1913. The first was a four-reeler directed by Herbert Brenon, a craftsman who would later migrate to Hollywood. King Baggott was the hero, Leah Baird played Rebecca, and Brenon appeared as Isaac. The second *Ivanhoe* (titled *Rebecca the Jewess* in the United States) was made by Zenith and featured Lauderdale Maitland, Edith Bracewell, and Hubert Carter in the respective roles.

Another writer whose romantic works have often appealed to the filmmaker was Alexandre Dumas, *pere.* Back in 1909 Selig produced a version of *The Count of Monte Cristo* with Hobart Bosworth in the leading role. Famous Players remade it in 1913 with James O'Neill (father of Eugene), and John Gilbert starred in the 1922 version, which was titled *Monte Cristo.* Later versions in 1934 and 1962 starred Robert Donat and Louis Jourdan respectively. For the 1975 television season, Richard Chamberlain bounced onscreen as the latest interpreter of that well-loved story.

Ruritanian romance and adventure films were long a popular staple of the movies, and one of the most enduring tales of all times is Anthony Hope's *The Prisoner of Zenda,* first picturized in 1913 with James K. Hackett. Remakes followed in 1922 (with Lewis Stone), 1937 (with Ronald Colman), and 1952 (with Stewart Granger). Little is known or written about the first film production, but expert swordplay and lush mountings were displayed in the other three.

So successful was the 1922 edition of *The Prisoner of Zenda,* that a sequel, *Rupert of Hentzau,* was prepared a year later. Even though that role had been portrayed memorably by Ramon Novarro in the first film, Lew Cody was chosen to play the part in the sequel. (In 1923, Novarro was busy acting in another swashbuckler, *Scaramouche,* based on the novel by Rafael Sabatini. This historical romance took place during the era of the French Revolution. It would be remade in Hollywood in 1952 with Stewart Granger heading the MGM production.)

Another Sabatini novel, *The Sea Hawk,* was given a lavish production in 1924. Milton Sills starred as the wealthy baronet who suffers at the hands of both his half-brother and the Spaniards, who capture him and make him a galley slave. He is so embittered that, when he escapes to North Africa, he becomes both a Moslem and later the infamous pirate called "the Scourge of Christendom." Perhaps because of the sensitivity of the religious aspects of the original script, *The Sea Hawk,* starring Errol Flynn in 1940, had a completely different plot line.

Nineteen hundred twenty-six was a vintage year for swashbucklers. In addition to *The Black Pirate,* it also saw the release of John Gilbert's *Bardelys the Magnificent,* ° Ricardo Cortez' *Eagle of the Sea,* and John Barrymore's *Don Juan.* The lengthy duel between Barrymore and villain Montagu Love at the climax of the latter epic is, perhaps, unequaled in film history.

To backtrack a bit: the 1922 *Captain Fly-By-Night* with Johnnie Walker had elements of *The Mark of Zorro* (each was written for the screen by Johnston McCulley), as did *The Californian* (1937) with Ricardo Cortez.

Nineteen hundred twenty-two also saw the release of the famous *When Knighthood Was in Flower,* with Marion Davies ("she never looked lovelier") and William Powell telling the romantic troubles of Mary Tudor, sister of Henry VIII. It was filled with pomp and circumstance, delighting and impressing filmgoers. The plotline material would be used again by Walt Disney in his "live" feature, *The Sword and the Rose* (1953), with Richard Todd and Glynis Johns.

Rudolph Valentino indulged himself in enough swaggering swordplay to qualify as a French swashbuckler in *Monsieur Beaucaire* (1924), and as a Russian in *The Eagle* (1925).

Also in 1925, Western film star Tom Mix traded in his lasso for a sword to make Fox's *Dick Turpin,* but the results were so uninspired that he returned to sagebrush outings, permanently. That same year Ernest Torrence made an impressive, swaggering Captain Hook in the Betty Bronson version of *Peter Pan.*

The Vagabond King—with Dennis King playing Francois Villon in the 1930 version and Oreste Kirkop in the leading role in the 1956 edition—might be considered a swashbuckling operetta; the nonmusical doings of Villon were enacted by Johnny Barrymore in *Beloved Rogue* (1927) and by Ronald Colman in *If I Were King* (1938).

In 1921 Douglas Fairbanks, Sr. had romped through *The Three Musketeers,* and in 1929 he made *The Iron Mask,* a film with sound effects, in which he again played D'Artagnan. Over the decades there would be several new editions of both *The Three Musketeers* and the book's

°Also based on a Sabatini novel.

sequel, *20 Years After*. *The Three Musketeers* would pop up on the Hollywood production scene in 1935 (with Walter Abel as a lacklustre D'Artagnan), in 1936 (with Don Ameche as a singing D'Artagnan), in 1948 (with Gene Kelly as an agile D'Artagnan), and in 1974 (with Michael York playing the role as a wide-eyed, country bumpkin hero).

Further details of the life, family, and property of the illustrious Count of Monte Cristo were seen in *The Son of Monte Cristo* (1941, with Louis Hayward), *The Return of Monte Cristo* (1946, with Louis Hayward), *The Wife of Monte Cristo* (1946, with Lenore Aubert), *The Countess of Monte Cristo* (1948, with Sonja Henie), *The Treasure of Monte Cristo* (1949, with Glenn Langan), *The Sword of Monte Cristo* (1951, with George Montgomery), *and The Secret of Monte Cristo* (1961, with Rory Calhoun).

Dapper, charming Louis Hayward almost made a complete career playing in low-budget swashbucklers. Besides the films mentioned above, he was starred in *The Man in the Iron Mask* (1939), *The Black Arrow* (1949), *The Pirates of Capri* (1949), *The Fortunes of Captain Blood* (1950), *The Lady and the Bandit* (1951), and two 1952 entries, *Captain Pirate* and *The Lady in the Iron Mask*.

It was no surprise to the film colony when Douglas Fairbanks, Jr., who had been highly praised for his Rupert of Hentzau in *The Prisoner of Zenda* (1937), decided to emulate his famous father still further. The younger Fairbanks starred in four swashbucklers in the forties, all with middling results: *The Corsican Brothers* (1941), *Sinbad the Sailor* (1947), *The Exile* (1947), and *The Fighting O'Flynn* (1949). On the surface, at least, like father, like son. If one wanted to make other comparisons, beyond the Fairbanks, *pere et fils,* one has only to contrast Doug, Jr.'s *The Corsican Brothers* with the flabby remake (1960), which starred Geoffrey Horne. It seemed that even the middling performance of Doug, Jr. was better than the other later actors could contribute to the genre.

Besides the eight stars so diligently examined in this volume, there were many other performers who contributed to the genre known as swashbuckling films on an occasional basis, such as Robert Donat's appearance in *The Count of Monte Cristo,* Basil Rathbone's string of villains in a host of thirties and forties features, and the more frequent intriguing (and certainly fetching) caperings of Maureen O'Hara, Patricia Medina, and Yvonne De Carlo in a flock of colorful, if low-budget, entries in the forties and fifties. (These trio of damsels excelled with rapier in hand, proving in their screen entries that the sword was mightier than the pen for exercising their own version of women's liberation.) Other leading players such as Richard Greene and John Payne, both berthed at Twentieth Century-Fox at one time or another, would turn to modestly budgeted cloak-and-sword feature-making

18

when filmmakers needed "names" to bolster their lightweight adventure entries.

Over the years, however, studios sometimes could conceive of the swashbuckler as big-budgeted productions. Paramount seemed to spare no expense in bringing Daphne du Maurier's *Frenchman's Creek* (1944) to the screen with Joan Fontaine, Arturo de Cordova, Basil Rathbone, and "glorious" color. However, money expended does not necessarily make a hit, as the studio learned with this ultimately lethargic feature. On a more limited budget, RKO made out somewhat better with *The Spanish Main* (1946) starring Paul Henreid, Maureen O'Hara, and Walter Slezak. Henreid was another star who, when his matinee idol days were over, made several action entries: *The Last of the Buccaneers* (1950), *The Chief of Damascus* (1952), and *The Pirates of Tripoli* (1952).

For source material, movie producers have often relied on the perennial favorite by Robert Louis Stevenson, *Treasure Island.* That exciting pirate story has been made into films no less than five times (1917, 1920, 1934, 1950, and 1972). While most people have forgotten who played Long John Silver the first time around, the role was handled in the four remakes by Charles Ogle, Wallace Beery, Robert Newton, and Orson Welles respectively. The fourth entry had a sequel in *Long John Silver* (1955), also with Newton.

The other major Stevenson favorite, *Kidnapped,* was filmed by Fox in 1938 (with Warner Baxter as the Scotch swashbuckler-hero Alan Breck), by Monogram in 1948 (with Dan O'Herlihy), by Buena Vista in 1960 (with Peter Finch), and by American International in 1971 (with Michael Caine).

Quite naturally, there are endless films with the pirate theme. The 1938 and 1958 versions of *The Buccaneer* detailed the exploits of Jean Lafitte as played by Fredric March and Yul Brynner respectively. Another famous pirate was treated in *Captain Kidd* (1945) by Charles Laughton, and later in *Captin Kidd and the Slave Girl* (1954) by Anthony Dexter. *Blackbeard the Pirate* was fleshed out for the cameras by Robert Newton in 1952, by Murvyn Vye in *The Boy and the Pirate* (1960), and by Peter Ustinov in Walt Disney's *Blackbeard's Ghost* (1968).

If moviemakers could spoof other genres, they could also poke fun at the swashbuckler. Usually, it was the pirate story that came in for the rib-tickling treatment. Charles Laughton was on hand to join the famous comedy team in *Abbott and Costello Meet Captain Kidd* (1952), while in *Double Crossbones* (1951), starring Donald O'Connor, Alan Napier was the famous Kidd. Bob Hope joined in the fun when he made *The Princess and the Pirate* (1944), with Virginia Mayo and Victor McLaglen in the respective title roles. And then there was Frank

Morgan as the bumbling town mayor trying to cope with an onslaught against law and order in *The Dancing Pirate* (1935).

Other swashbuckling features not covered per se in the body of this book would include *The Pirates of Monterey* (1947, with Maria Montez and Rod Cameron), the high-budgeted musical fiasco, *The Pirate* (1948, with Gene Kelly and Judy Garland), the almost equally lavish *Captain Horatio Hornblower* (1951 with Gregory Peck), and *The Crimson Pirate* (1952, with Burt Lancaster). There were also *The Prince of Pirates* (1952, with John Derek), *Rob Roy* (1954, with Richard Todd), *Prince Valiant* (1954, a dreadful recreation of the comic strip favorite, with Robert Wagner), *The Saracen Blade* (1954, with Ricardo Montalban), *The Black Knight* (1954, with Alan Ladd), *The Black Pirates* (1955, with Anthony Baxter), *The Pirates of Tortuga* (1961, with Ken Scott and Letitia Roman), and *The Guns of the Black Witch* (1961, with Don Megowan and Silvana Pampini). Also to be mentioned are *The Pirates of Blood River* (1962, with Kerwin Mathews), *The Son of Captain Blood* (1964, with Sean Flynn following in father Errol's footsteps), and *The King's Pirate* (1967, a remake of 1952's *Against All Flags,* with Doug McClure and Jill St. John taking over for Errol Flynn and Maureen O'Hara). *The Decameron Nights* (1953), filmed in Spain, featured four stories, each starring Louis Jourdan and Joan Fontaine, with the second episode titled *Paganino the Pirate.*

Almost qualifying for the pirate category are *The Brigand* (1952) with Anthony Dexter and Anthony Quinn, and the same year's *Mutiny* with Mark Stevens and Angela Lansbury. In the former, Dexter plays a dual role in a story of intrigue in the Spanish royal court, while the latter is concerned with blockade-running in the War of 1812.

The nearest multi-talented Frank Sinatra came to a swashbuckling yarn, if one excludes the lumbering *The Pride and the Passion* (1957) with Cary Grant and Sophia Loren, was MGM's *The Kissing Bandit* (1949), which did a lot to ruin the crooner's early boxoffice image. Similar bad luck plagued John "The Duke" Wayne when he made *The Conqueror* (1956), in which the star played a Genghis Khan more interested in conquering Susan Hayward than the world. *Cyrano de Bergerac* (1950) won José Ferrer an Oscar. Jean-Paul Belmondo was swaggered, in the Gallic fashion, in the tongue-in-cheek *Cartouche* (1964).

Other swashbucklers of the forties and fifties include *The Fighting Guardsman* (1945, with Willard Parker), *The Swordsman* and *The Gallant Blade* (1947 and 1948 respectively, both with Larry Parks), *The Flame and the Arrow* (1950, with Burt Lancaster), *The Mark of the Renegade* (1951, with Ricardo Montalban), *Hurricane Island* (1951, with Jon Hall), plus a colorful trio: *The Golden Horde* (1951, with David Farrar), *The Golden Hawk* (1952, with Sterling Hayden and Rhonda Fleming), and *The Golden Blade* (1953, with Rock Hudson).

Meanwhile, the legendary Robin Hood was continuing his exciting exploits in front of the camera. *The Adventures of Robin Hood* (1938, with Errol Flynn) stands supreme. However, less ambitious attempts on this theme include *The Bandit of Sherwood Forest* (1946, with Russell Hicks as the aging Robin and Cornel Wilde as his son Robert), *The Prince of Thieves* (1948, with Jon Hall), *The Rogues of Sherwood Forest* (1950, with John Dered as Robin, Jr.), *The Tales of Robin Hood* (1952, with Robert Clarke), *The Men of Sherwood Forest* (1956, with Don Taylor), and *The Son of Robin Hood* (1959, with a daughter, actually, Deering Hood, played by June Laverick). Richard Green, who had been playing Robin in a British TV series, portrayed him again in *The Sword of Sherwood Forest* (1961). In 1975 there was the British-made *Robin Hood Junior* with Keith Chegwin in the title role.

More expensive than any of these was Walt Disney's *The Story of Robin Hood* (1952) with Richard Todd. Although it hardly qualifies as a swashbuckler, there is also the 1973 Disney cartoon feature, *Robin Hood,* in which all of the traditional characters are played as animals. However, there is plenty of "animated" swordplay in it (as well as in the earlier Disney feature cartoons, *Peter Pan* [1953] and *The Sword in the Stone* [1963].)

Robin Hood films (as well as MGM's lavish *Ivanhoe* [1952], with Robert Taylor as the title character) concern themselves with the problems facing England when its monarch, Richard the Lion-Hearted, was off with the Third Crusade trying to deliver the Holy Land from the Moslems. However, the Crusade itself was treated in such films as *Richard the Lion-Hearted* (with Wallace Beery recreating the Richard role he had done so memorably in the 1922 version of *Robin Hood*), the Cecil B. DeMille epic, *The Crusades* (1935, with Henry Wilcoxon as Richard), and *King Richard and the Crusaders* (1954, with George Sanders). In these costumed pictures, Saladin, leader of the Moslems, was presented as an even greater swashbuckler than Richard, and was played by Ian Keith in 1935 and by Rex Harrison in 1954.

For the record, the first color CinemaScope swashbuckling film was *The Knights of the Round Table* (1954), featuring Robert Taylor. MGM, also with Taylor starred, turned out *Quentin Durward* (1955) based on the Sir Walter Scott novel. Taylor's co-star was Kay Kendall.

The widescreen process seemed made for swashbuckling ventures, and 1955 was a banner year for the genre. There was *Moonfleet* (Stewart Granger), *The Purple Mask* (Tony Curtis), *The King's Thief* (Edmund Purdom), *The Shadow of the Eagle* (Richard Greene), and *The Warriors* (Errol Flynn), as well as the aforementioned *Long John Silver* and *Quentin Durward.*

By 1959, movie swashbucklers were in a pretty sad state. There was Robert Stack posturing most unconvincingly in the title role of *John Paul Jones,* a belabored feature which in all respects represented War-

21

ner Bros.'s decline from its former golden era of Errol Flynn actioners.

Moving into a new decade, Allied Artists' *El Cid* (1961), with Charlston Heston and Sophia Loren, gave every indication of being the most costly swashbuckler since *Robin Hood* (1922) and *The Sea Hawk* (1924). However, it failed to provide even half as much entertainment. This dud had the unique distinction of being preceded by its sequel, *The Son of El Cid* (1956), with Mark Damon, as well as being followed by *The Sword of El Cid* (1964, with Roland Carey).

Swashbuckling elements were also to be found on other such historical films as the British-made *Fire Over England* (1935, with Laurence Olivier, Vivien Leigh, and featuring Flora Robson as Queen Elizabeth), *The Private Lives of Elizabeth and Essex* and *The Virgin Queen,* 1939 and 1955 respectively, both with Bette Davis, and *Cromwell* (1970, with Richard Harris). In the 1936 version of *Mary of Scotland,* directed by John Ford, the swaggering Lord Bothwell was energetically played by Fredric March, while in the 1971 edition of *Mary, Queen of Scots,* the role was somewhat less flamboyantly done by Nigel Davenport.

While silent serials did not employ the swashbuckling theme (though one chapter of the Pearl White chapterplay, *The Perils of Pauline,* had a pirate setting), several talkies did. Best of all was Republic's *Zorro's Fighting Legion* (1939), which had Reed Hadley as the title character, masquerading as the foppish Diego, and goes into action with sword, whip, and pistol. Expert duels were fought along the way, especially an extremely well-staged one in a cantina in chapter one, ending with Zorro carving the letter "Z" on his opponent's forehead. It is amusing to note the Hays office passed this sequence, but forbade it a year later in the Tyrone Power super-production, *The Mark of Zorro.* Obviously, what was okay for the kiddie trade was considered too much for their parents! (And what would the censors have thought, had they foreseen that in 1972, as part of the sexploitation film cycle, along would come *The Erotic Adventures of Zorro,* in which the hero makes his mark in the boudoir.)

Columbia Pictures attempted several swashbuckling serials and achieved some merit with *The Desert Hawk* (1944, with Gilbert Roland playing twin brothers, one good and one evil). But the others— *The Son of the Guardsman* (1946, with Robert Shaw), *The Adventures of Sir Galahad* (1949, with George Reeves), and *The Great Adventures of Captain Kidd* (1953, with Richard Crane)—were, in a word, deplorable.

Widescreen camera processes were but one gimmick used for the swashbuckling genre. Back in 1925, the stereoscopic short, *Zowie,* found a pirate shooting a blunderbuss at the audience. Three years earlier, the first 3-D feature, *The Power of Love* (made in the anaglyph process with the viewer wearing red and blue glasses), found Elliott

Sparling, Barbara Bedford, and Noah Beery involved in swordplay in early nineteenth-century California. Contemporary reviews commented on the extreme effectiveness of swordplay in the 3-D process. However, in the 1950's revival of 3-D features (in the Polaroid process) the closest to a swashbuckler was the low-budget Pine-Thomas *Sangaree* (1953), a pirate drama with Fernando Lamas and Arlene Dahl.

Just like the gangster and the Western film, the swashbuckling feature has gone through many changes over the decades. Unlike these other two formats, little has been done with the swashbuckler on television. Economics is the chief reason. Using full-rigged vessels (or even mock-ups or miniatures) and the other elaborate appurtenances of the genre's sets, of its action on the high seas or in the elaborate castle sets, would be just too costly for a teleseries. A rare exception was the TV special *The Count of Monte Cristo* (NBC-TV, 1975) filmed in Europe, and starring Richard Chamberlain, with Tony Curtis (as a villain!) and Louis Jourdan in the supporting cast.

Good news for the action film fans came in mid-1975 when, in the wake of Twentieth Century-Fox's successful *The Three Musketeers* (1974) and its sequel, *The Fourth Musketeer* (1975), Universal Pictures announced that it was scheduling *Blarney Cock* with Robert Shaw and Peter Boyle starred, and that in 1976 it would film the life story of Errol Flynn. Meanwhile in Europe, Alain Delon was filming the latest variation of *Zorro* and Michael Sarrazin was performing on camera as the new Scavamouche.

Thus it seems the swashbuckling genre will perhaps go on and on and on. . . .

23

5' 10"
145 pounds
Gray eyes
Black hair
Gemini

Douglas Fairbanks, Sr.

Part of twentieth-century American folklore is the recurring image of athletic Douglas Fairbanks, Sr. capering across the screen as the cinema's zestful and constantly smiling perfect swashbuckler. For a rare change, legend reflects the truth.

There were several reasons for Doug's pre-eminence in the genre. First of all, he was the founding star of the form. There had been other swashbuckling films before Doug's major entries in the Twenties, but never—not even in the area of serials—had one star of the screen been almost totally associated with the sword-and-cloak type of picture. Thus Fairbanks, as an innovator, could set the standards by which others would have to follow. His competitors and successors would have a tough battle to equal or beat Doug, because Fairbanks was naturally acrobatic and effervescent. He brought a bounce and a heartiness to even the simplest of character action. Combined with this, he had a chivalrous approach to life both oncamera and off. It certainly did not hurt his status that he was married to Mary Pickford, "America's Sweetheart." In fact, it automatically infused his screen presence with even more gallantry.

Another reason for Doug's success as a screen swordsman was that most of his major work occurred in the silent picture era.

Moviegoers then had to rely upon their imagination to "hear" the unspoken dialogue and the array of sound effects that did *not* accompany the screen action. Most film viewers, possessed of a fertile imagination, would automatically enlarge upon any and every aspect of the picture they were watching, including the attributes of the hero.

Then too, during the Twenties when Fairbanks' landmark swashbuckling films were issued by United Artists—including *The Mark of Zorro* (1920), *The Three Musketeers* (1921), *Robin Hood* (1921), *The Thief of Bagdad* (1923), and *The Black Pirate* (1926)—Doug was not only producing and starring in these vehicles, but was often scripting them as well. As a co-founder of United Artists Corporation, he was in the unique position of making every one of his movie vehicles a total showcase for all his best screen qualities. It was a situation that could only—and did—enhance his appeal to the public.

The coming of sound brought many changes to Hollywood, among them the decline of Douglas Fairbanks, Sr.'s career. Talkies somehow did not suit the star's style, which was flamboyant and unsubtle. Also, by 1930, he was forty-seven years old and hard living had taken its physical toll. Gone were the verve and snap of his peak filmmaking years. Soon he found himself relegated to the sidelines as other, younger players captured the pre-eminence in the field. It must have been tough enough for him to observe Errol Flynn usurping his genre throne, but to see his son, Douglas Fairbanks, Jr., scampering through *The Prisoner of Zenda* (United Artists, 1936) and *Gunga Din* (RKO, 1939) must have caused the venerated film hero great pangs of envy.

The future star was born Douglas Elton Ulman on Wednesday, May 23, 1883, in Denver, Colorado. His mother, nee Ella Adelaide Marsh, was a Southern belle whose first husband was wealthy John Fairbanks, owner of sugar mills and extensive plantations near New Orleans where the young couple resided. They were comparatively well-to-do. Shortly after the birth of a son, John, named after his father, John Fairbanks Senior died. Not long afterward, the late businessman's partner swindled the widowed Mrs. Fairbanks out of her inheritance by selling the firm and absconding with all the money.

Despite the subsequent legal efforts of her husband's attorney, H. (Hezekiah) Charles Ulman,[1] none of the estate was recovered, and the

---

[1]Born on September 15, 1833, in Berrysburg, Pennsylvania, Ulman had served as an officer during the Civil War after having been admitted to the bar in 1856. Returning to his law practice after the war, he was one of a group of judges and attorneys who founded the United States Law Association, forerunner of all American bar associations.

young widow was forced to apply for help to her sister, then living in Georgia. It was there that she impetuously married Edward Wilcox, who turned out to be an abusive alcoholic. Shortly after their son, Norris, was born, Ella again sought out Ulman's aid. This time she requested that he help her to obtain a divorce from Wilcox. When Ella turned to him for a second time, he was president of the United States Law Association and head of the New York firm of Ulman, Gazzam, and Remington.

Their marriage soon after the divorce was something that simply was "not done." Rather than submit to petty censure, Ulman sold his interests in the law firm and the bar association and headed for Denver, encouraged by an associate who was already practicing law there. His bride and her first son,[2] John, accompanied him. Arriving in Denver in the spring of 1881, Ulman invested his entire stake in various mining enterprises. They soon had two sons of their own, Robert, born March 13, 1882, and Douglas, born the following year.

Douglas was born with a swarthy olive complexion which, he later admitted to an interviewer, made his mother quite reluctant to show the new baby to her friends. During his first years he never smiled, and he rarely spoke to anyone except his brother Robert. However, he immediately displayed the athleticism which later would bring him fame and fortune. On his third birthday he climbed a vine-covered lattice to the roof of the barn beside the house. He came down without hazard to face a whipping from his angered mother.

Six months later, when the family was spending the summer in Jamestown, Colorado, little Douglas tried the same stunt again. This time, however, he fell to the ground and was knocked unconscious. When he opened his eyes on the couch in the sitting room he asked his mother, "What did I do?" She replied that he had fallen off the roof. The boy thought it very funny and broke into a broad smile followed by hilarious laughter. It was the first time the family had ever seen him either smile or laugh. The Fairbanks smile would later become world famous, and in 1917 Fairbanks wrote a book, *Laugh and Live.*

Denver was a boom town in the 1880s, made rich by the wealth found in the silver mines nearby, a wealth which continued to elude Ulman. Richest and most flamboyant of the new millionaires was H. A. W. Tabor. In 1881, the year the Ulmans arrived, the Tabor Grand Opera House was built. It housed all the great touring companies on their way to San Francisco. Both of the Ulmans shared an interest in the theatre and the boys were exposed to its culture at an early age.

Charles Ulman's mining ventures collapsed in 1888 and he left his family to accept a position as campaign speaker for Benjamin Harri-

---

[2]Norris was left behind in Georgia with a paternal aunt, Lottie Barker. Although his mother intended to return for him when things were more settled, she never did. Years later he would be employed by the New York office of United Artists Corporation.

son, the Republican Presidential candidate. The occasional letters and checks which he would send Ella stopped after the election. By Christmas of 1888 she found herself deserted, without funds, and with three sons to raise. The boys never saw their father again.[3]

The resourceful Ella opened a boarding house, divorced Ulman on the grounds of desertion, resumed the name Fairbanks, and had her three sons baptized in the Roman Catholic faith. She exacted from Douglas a temperance pledge which he continued to observe until as long as the late 1920s, long after her death.

As a youngster Douglas (or Doug as he was more often called) heard his father speaking lines from Shakespeare, who was a staple of many of the touring companies which passed through Denver. Later, as punishment for his frequent pranks in school, his teachers would assign him a Shakespearean soliloquy to memorize. This was excellent training for the future actor, and not the punishment they supposed.

When he was twelve, Doug made his first stage appearance, as an Italian newsboy, supporting Steve Brodie, who was appearing in Denver in *On the Bowery*. The family did not learn about Doug's debut until it was over. Years later he could not remember his first show business wages but he thought they must have been about fifty cents.

Approximately the same time, the would-be gymnast tackled a more impressive stunt; with brother Robert, he climbed the highest building in Denver and proceeded to hang from a cornice, holding on by his toes.

At school, Doug remembered "I might have been a good student, but I wouldn't apply myself. I liked spelling, grammar, and geography, and, later, history became my favorite study. But mathematics I detested, and schooling as such didn't appeal to me a bit. I wouldn't stop fooling."

After two years at Jarvis Military Academy, where Robert and Douglas were sent with the help of John, and where they learned something about physical fitness, erect posture, and personal neatness, Ella enrolled Douglas in a dramatic school. His teacher, Margaret Fealy, perceived within him a genuine talent. Touring actor Frederick Warde saw him in one of Miss Fealy's productions and informed the teacher, "That dark-haired youngster has more vigor than virtuosity."[4]

When Douglas scaled the outside wall of the theatre to gain access to Warde's dressing room, the star offered him a job as an extra in crowd scenes with the proviso that he help clean the stage after each performance. Doug accepted.

---

[3]To his credit, Mr. Ulman never approached his children for money, even later when Douglas had established himself on the stage, Robert had become a prosperous electrical engineer, and John was an executive with the Morey Mercantile Company. Ulman died in 1915.

[4]Warde was a touring performer who never played on Broadway but had gained great popularity by bringing the classics to the hinterlands in one night stands.

Warde listened to the teenage boy's professional ambitions. After he finished his last year in high school, Douglas wanted to go to New York and become an actor. Perhaps giving in to the energy with which Douglas explained his hopes, Warde informed him that if he could manage to get to New York the next year he would attempt to find a spot for him in his company.

Ella was less than enthusiastic about the idea, but Douglas' next prank turned the tide. Before an assembly in the school auditorium took place on St. Patrick's Day, Doug decorated the busts of the American heroes with funny hats and large green ties. He was promptly expelled. Mrs. Fairbanks sold everything she owned and raised the money for their fares to New York. As a parting gift, Robert gave his younger brother the twenty-three dollars he had saved. Mother and son arrived in New York in the late spring of 1900.

Warde may have been surprised to see the eager young man from Denver, but he kept his word. Douglas made his first stage appearance in Warde's company as Florio, a lackey, in *The Duke's Jester* (better known as the opera *Rigoletto*) at the Academy of Music, Richmond, Virginia, on September 10, 1900. The problem with the new young actor was that he never played the role the same way twice. His natural exuberance demanded continual improvisation. When the company arrived at Duluth the actor who was playing Cassio and Laertes became ill, and Warde reluctantly gave the parts to Douglas. He squirmed his way through the part of Laertes in *Hamlet* and the next day received his first brief newspaper review: "Mr. Warde's supporting company was bad but worst of all was Douglas Fairbanks as Laertes." Years later Warde described Douglas' acting with him as "a catch-as-catch-can encounter with the immortal bard."

At the end of the season Warde told Douglas that he required more experience in the world before he could successfully pursue a theatrical career. In January, 1901, Fairbanks enrolled at Harvard to try to make up the credits requisite to his enrolling as a freshman in the fall. The excellent gymnasium at the university proved more fascinating than studying Latin, French, and English literature.

After five months he embarked with two Harvard friends as hay stewards on a cattle boat bound for Liverpool. They received eight shillings each for their twelve-day voyage plus tickets back to New York. Two weeks later the three boys had run through their savings and the other two returned. Douglas remained, eventually working his way to Belgium and northern France. The trip ended with his first visit to Paris, which he promised himself to see again.

Back in New York he worked as a clerk in a hardware store, followed by nearly six months in the Wall Street brokerage house of De Coppet and Doremus. On February 24, 1902, he returned to the theatre in the minor role of Glen Masters, supporting Effie Shannon and Herbert

Kelcey in *Her Lord and Master* at the Manhattan Theatre. When the play closed in May he was "at liberty" through the summer until he appeared as Phillippe in *A Rose o' Plymouth Town*.[5] Then came *Mrs. Jack*, starring Alice Fisher, a play which toured for most of 1903. For his practical jokes played on fellow performers, Douglas was asked to resign from the cast.

Thinking he might follow in the footsteps of his father, Fairbanks took a job in the law offices of E. M. Hollander. However, he became too restless in the post and decided to make a trip to the Orient. He got as far as London before his funds ran out and he had to return to Manhattan. Once in New York, he began his theatrical association with William A. Brady, a very important professional liaison.

Fairbanks' first role for producer Brady was in a dramatization of Frank Norris' *The Pit* (Lyric Theatre: February 10, 1904, 77 performances). In a minor role, Doug, for the first time was called upon to display his athletic prowess by leaping over the actors in a crowd scene. Next came *Two Little Sailor Boys*, which lasted for thirty-two performances.

The following January he appeared for Sam S. Shubert in the musical *Fantana* (Lyric Theatre: January 14, 1905, 298 performances). Douglas may have been off-key in the musical numbers, but actress Grace George, Brady's second wife, saw the show and told her husband, "He's not good looking but he has a world of personality—just worlds of it. His name is Douglas Fairbanks."

Brady remembered the impression Fairbanks had made the year before in *The Pit* and signed him to a contract. The first appearance was to be in *A Case of Frenzied Finance* (Savoy Theatre: April 3, 1905, 8 performances). For the first time Douglas saw his name in lights over the marquee. Despite the show's short run, Brady saw the makings of a star in his discovery if he were cast in juvenile comedy leads suitable to his frenetic personality. Brady would recall of Fairbanks, "He was an odd young man, running over with energy to such an extent that it fatigued me even to look at him sitting down—and he seldom sat."

The producer cast him next as Lute Ludlam, a "jack of all trades," in Reverend John Snyder's melodrama *As Ye Sow*. Brady wisely toured the show all over the country during the 1905-1906 season, with a thirty-four-performance run in New York (Garden Theatre: December 25, 1905) in the middle of the tour.

Back in New York, Brady cast Fairbanks in the juvenile lead of *Clothes* (Wallack's Theatre: September 11, 1906, 113 performances), starring Miss George. The actor received fifty dollars a week. Before the run of *Clothes* was completed, Brady replaced Fairbanks in the cast

---

[5]The play opened on September 29, 1902, at the Manhattan Theatre and ran for 21 performances. Years later, the star, Minnie Dupree, would describe the young actor with these words: "I thought he had a bad case of St. Vitus's dance."

and starred him as Perry Carter Wainwright in George Broadhurst's *The Man of the Hour* (Savoy Theatre: December 4, 1906, 479 performances). The play was Doug's greatest success to date.

A year later *The Man of the Hour* was still running when Gladys Smith, her name changed by David Belasco to Mary Pickford, made her Broadway debut at the age of fourteen as Betty Warren in *The Warrens of Virginia.*

Douglas' happiness in his success as a Broadway star was sweetened by having fallen in love with Anna Beth Sully, the eldest daughter of Daniel J. Sully, the "Cotton King." Sully was not swayed by Fairbanks' stardom. The only condition under which he would give his permission for Doug to wed Anna Beth was that Fairbanks must quit the stage and set up in a respectable business which the older man would specify and finance.

The charms of Miss Sully were sufficiently alluring that Douglas consented to these rather unreasonable terms. Brady reluctantly agreed to allow him to break his contract.[6] The young lovers married on July 11, 1907, and two weeks later Douglas was an employee of Buchan's Soap Corporation at 225 Fifth Avenue. He received a letter there from Joseph Grismer, who had been co-producer with Brady on *As Ye Sow.* What Grismer said must have sunk in, because it was one of the few mementos[7] of the early days that Fairbanks saved.

In Richard Schickel's book *His Picture in the Papers* (1974), the author quotes Douglas Fairbanks, Jr. as saying that Sully's insistence on a proper business venture was only to ensure the couple of a proper income during the short period the star could not find suitable roles on Broadway. The fact that Doug left the cast of *The Man of the Hour* during a successful run would seem to belie this statement.

In any event, the soap business soon failed, and within a year the balance of Sully's fortune was wiped out. Douglas returned to the stage, which he should never have left in the first place.

Brady's new play for Douglas, written by Rupert Hughes, was appropriately titled *All for a Girl* (Bijou Theatre: August 22, 1908, 33 performances). The moment that *All for a Girl* opened, rehearsals were

[6]Brady would recall: "I argued with [him] until I was black in the face along the lines . . . that once you get grease paint on your face, you have no business anywhere but the theatre, particularly when you're going great guns. But Doug was willing to do anything to get the girl, so we parted. I reminded him that, so long as he stayed out of the theatre, it was all right. But, if he ever tried to come back to the stage, our contract still had some years to run and I'd make him complete it if I had to have him shanghaied from Timbuktu."

[7]Grismer wrote: "I cannot at length tell you how much I regret your decision to retire from the stage whether temporary or permanent. Whether I ever see you act again or not, I want to be on record as saying that I think you are making a great mistake abandoning a professional career, which indicates so bright a future for you, for any other occupation or career. 'What do you care for the vulgar money' and even if you do, there will be as much money in the theatrical business in the future as in any other business and easier to get. Better think it over some more for your own sake."

begun for *A Gentleman from Mississippi* (Bijou Theatre: September 29, 1908, 407 performances), which began its run directly after the earlier play folded. During the long run of this production, Douglas Fairbanks, Jr. was born on December 9, 1909.

In the play that followed, *The Cub* (Comedy Theatre: November 1, 1910, 32 performances), Douglas made further use of his athletic abilities. Instead of running upstairs on stage to save the heroine's life—it was a two-level set—he suggested jumping. There was a twelve-foot gap between the floors. Doug took a running jump, caught the edge of the upper floor, then pulled himself up. It was all done with the ease of a cat in action and made a tremendous hit with audiences.

On May 1, 1911, Brady revived an old play, *The Lights o' London* (Lyric Theatre), which only had a thirty-two-performance run despite its star-studded cast, which included the young Marguerite Clark before she entered films. *Gentleman of Leisure,* the last phrase in the world one would use to characterize Fairbanks, followed on August 24, 1911, at the Playhouse Theatre. After its seventy-six-performance engagement, which was disappointing to Brady who was then in financial straits, the producer asked his star to cancel his contract. At the time, neither of them could have anticipated the impact the movies would soon have on both of their careers.

The next morning, Doug dropped in on Cohan and Harris, a new producing team who were only a few years older than he. Cohan exclaimed, "I've always wanted to write a play for you. The typical young American, winning fame, fortune, and female over insurmountable odds." When the promised play was not ready a month later, restless Doug set out with a friend to walk across Cuba from Havana to Santiago, sailing from there to Yucatan, where he explored the Mayan ruins.

When he returned to New York, to find that Cohan still had not completed the play ("I've got the young man in the drawing room and I can't get him out"), Doug accepted a short engagement in a vaudeville sketch entitled *A Regular Businessman.* He followed that with a long and prosperous season on the road in *Officer 666.*

As a result of a meeting in Chicago with the great English actor Lewis Waller, Douglas suggested to Cohan and Harris that they revamp and retitle a play that had been done in London by Waller. *Hawthorne of the U.S.A.* opened on Broadway at the Astor Theatre on November 4, 1912.

When Cohan, whose full name was George M. Cohan, did find a way to extricate the hero from the drawing room, he decided that the vehicle *Broadway Jones* was so good, he would play it himself. So Doug next found himself in the juvenile lead of a revised version of an 1887 play, *The New Henrietta* by Bronson Howard. The revamped production, starring the grand old actor William H. Crane, Doug, and Patricia

Collinge, played on the road for some months before it opened in New York at the Knickerbocker Theatre (December 22, 1913, 48 performances).*

Doug's next and possibly best stage role was in *He Comes up Smiling* (Liberty Theatre: September 16, 1914, 61 performances). It was the prototype of a character role that would establish him shortly as a major film star. It was about a young vagabond who could see no point in chaining himself to a dull job in a bank. Life was to be enjoyed. Eventually he inadvertently lands in the midst of high finance and a love affair, and becomes both a husband and a financier. The reviewer for *Everybody's* Magazine said Doug played it "so gaily [that] one almost overlooks the fact that he is getting to be more than a mere pleasant personality and is doing some real acting."

During the run of *He Comes up Smiling,* Doug was strolling in Central Park with his wife and Doug, Jr. when he was recognized by a passing motion picture cameraman who asked him to pose. Doug obliged by making a few jumps over a park bench. The footage was viewed by Harry E. Aitken, then one of the partners in Triangle Films. Aitken offered Fairbanks a contract to go to Hollywood to make films for Triangle, the producing company that released the work of D. W. Griffith, Thomas Ince, and Mack Sennett. The enterprising Aitken had recently concluded contracts to work in films with such diverse stage personalities as William Collier, Billie Burke, Raymond Hitchcock, Sir Herbert Beerbohm Tree, Eddie Foy, Weber and Fields, Mary Anderson, Texas Guinan, Dustin Farnum, Frank Keenan, Willard Mack, and DeWolf Hopper. (Other stage performers were being just as ardently wooed by Famous Players-Lasky.)

The salaries being offered to the would-be movie stars were so enormous that they were regarded as the inventions of a crazed press agent. Douglas was offered two thousand dollars a week but he was reluctant to exchange his hard-won status as an established Broadway performer for even this princely sum. His friend, Frank Case, the proprietor of the Algonquin Hotel where the Fairbanks family resided, pointed out that two thousand dollars was not a figure to be tossed aside lightly. Furthermore, Fairbanks had made his stage success as an athletic juvenile. If thirty-one-year-old Fairbanks rejected the offer and remained on Broadway, the onset of middle age would make suitable plays harder to find. The deciding factor proved to be Fairbanks' innate restlessness. Hollywood would be a new world to conquer.

On New Year's Eve, 1914, he opened on Broadway in James Forbes' *The Show Shop* (Hudson Theatre). It was to prove to be his last stage appearance. Patricia Collinge was again the leading lady in a cast that

---

*The play would be transferred to the screen as *The Saphead* with Crane repeating his role, and the Metro release of 1921 featured young Buster Keaton.

featured Ned Sparks and George Sidney. When the show closed on May 15, 1915, Douglas and his family embarked for Hollywood. His heart was already there, since, a month earlier, Griffith's *The Birth of a Nation* had opened in New York at legitimate theatre prices (two dollars a ticket), and he had perceived the unlimited possibilities offered by the new medium.

Doug's first picture, *The Lamb* (Triangle-Fine Arts, 1915), was shot in six weeks. Except for a few days' shooting in the Sunset Boulevard studio, it was done on location in the San Fernando Valley and on the beach above Santa Monica. The five-reel feature was directed by W. Christy Cabanne, with Seena Owen cast as the leading lady. It was the classic tale of an effete Eastern snob invited to a house party in the Wild West, where he turns from a lamb into a lion, and saves the girl from marauding Indians. Douglas was given little help during the production work. Griffith, who had supplied the basic story and who was the project's producer-supervisor, was totally unimpressed by the extrovert behavior of the star. He felt Doug might be more at home with the Keystone unit than with his, and he let his star know it. The makeup man deliberately did a poor job, and the stunts (fighting with a lion, letting a rattlesnake crawl over him, performing jiu-jitsu fighting with Indians) had to be performed by the new cinema star.

Aitken had arranged that the new Knickerbocker Theatre in New York would open with a product from Triangle. It was the first time that three dollars would be charged for admission to a film. Griffith was absorbed with completing *Intolerance,* so *The Lamb* had to serve as the premiere attraction. The picture opened on September 23, 1915, to enthusiastic reviews before a distinguished audience which included Ignace Jan Paderewski, Howard Chandler Christy, Rupert Hughes, and Irvin S. Cobb. Fairbanks was surprised. He had liked the film as little as Griffith and the other Triangle executives. Perhaps, after all, a successful film career would be his.

Before he went East for the festivities of *The Lamb, Double Trouble* (Triangle-Fine Arts, 1915), also directed by Cabanne under the disapproving supervision of Griffith, had been completed.

In the aftermath of the successful showing of *The Lamb,* two fateful meetings occurred with Mary Pickford which would eventually alter the balance of Doug's life.

The popular musical comedy star, Elsie Janis, and her mother, Mrs. Bierbower, had bought Phillipse Manor near Tarrytown, New York. On a Sunday in early November, 1915,[8] Elsie invited Doug and Beth

---

[8]Some film historians place the "historic" meeting during the autumn of 1914, but Miss Pickford in her autobiography, *Sunshine and Shadows* (1955), says it took place in November 1915. As further testimony, Elsie Janis in her autobiography, *So Far, So Good* (1932), indicates that she was in England in the fall of 1914 and did not buy the Tarrytown property until late 1915.

and her friends, Mary Pickford[9] and her husband Owen Moore, to come up to spend the day. During the afternoon, Elsie proposed a walk around the grounds. Not content with merely strolling, Doug suggested they play "Follow the Leader." Eventually the party reached a stream over which everyone except Beth Fairbanks and Mary Pickford had leaped. Beth decided to return to the house while Mary, undecided whether to ruin her new outfit by a possible plunge in the water or to follow Mrs. Fairbanks' lead, waited. Fairbanks made her decision for her by sweeping her in his arms and, in one hop, carrying her across the brook. By the time they returned to the house Mary's new shoes were ruined, but they were on a first name basis, no longer "Mrs. Moore" and "Mr. Fairbanks."

Shortly afterward, the second meeting between Doug and Mary occurred at a dinner dance at the Algonquin Hotel. Doug had arrived early, without Beth. When Mary entered the room she complimented him on the success of *The Lamb*, and they spent the balance of the evening together. The mutual attraction they felt for one another was apparent to everyone present.

A few days later Doug escorted Mary to meet his mother for high tea, Mary being properly chaperoned by Charlotte Pickford. The two stage mothers had a great deal in common: each had raised several children alone after a husband had either died or deserted her. There were several more such teas where the two stage-screen personalities had an opportunity to meet and become more deeply involved before Doug had to return to Hollywood. (Miss Pickford's features at that time were being made in the East.)

When Fairbanks returned to California it was fortunate for his film career that Griffith was so deeply involved with *Intolerance*. For, despite his genius as a film director, Griffith was inclined to be a puppet master with his performers. Many of the important creative figures of the silent cinema began with Griffith but made their contributions to the screen after they were removed from his iron control.

Doug was assigned to director John Emerson, a former Broadway actor. Both the Emerson and Fairbanks options with Triangle were soon to expire, so Emerson was given permission to go ahead with *His Picture in the Papers* (Triangle-Fine Arts, 1916), written by twenty-two-year-old Anita Loos. Emerson and Miss Loos wove the storyline around the personality of the star, rather than chaining Doug within a pre-conceived format.

In the course of the picture, the hero Peter Prindle runs an automo-

[9]By this point, Mary Pickford was already the most important star of motion pictures. She had entered the movies at the age of sixteen in 1909, had impetuously married her leading man, Owen Moore, two years later, and through the financial acuity of her mother, Charlotte, was already enjoying a salary of $4,000 a week plus fifty percent of the profits per film of Famous Players, the producing organization which released her pictures.

35

In *His Picture in the Papers* (1916)

bile over a cliff, engages in a six-round bout with a professional boxer, jumps off an ocean liner and swims to a distant shore, mixes in a brawl with half a dozen gunmen, and twice leaps from fast-moving trains. What made this picture different from the first two was the wit of Miss Loos' subtitles. Griffith watched the preview in silence, suggesting at the end that if the subtitles were cut, perhaps the five-reel film could be released as a two-reeler.

According to Miss Loos' autobiography, *A Girl Like I* (Viking Press, 1966), everyone was so busy at the studio that the picture was sent to New York before Griffith et al. had a chance to tamper with it. One night at the Strand Theatre the scheduled feature did not arrive, and the manager showed *His Picture in the Papers* in its stead. The next day the reviews were ecstatic, saying that films had grown out of their infancy, and satire was now possible. This favorable reception solidified the impression that Fairbanks had already made on film audiences.

As a result, Triangle picked up the options on Emerson and Fairbanks, and Miss Loos was put to the well-nigh impossible task of writing the titles for *Intolerance*.

During 1916 Doug appeared in eleven pictures, all feature-length five-reel productions except the two-reeler *The Mystery of the Leaping Fish*. His next two, *The Habit of Happiness* and *The Good Bad Man*, were directed by Allan Dwan, with whom he was to have a long, constant association. In *The Habit of Happiness* he was in a fight scene with five gangsters which he set about to enact so conscientiously that his hands were swollen for a week and his face so bruised that shooting was delayed even longer. *The Good Bad Man,* with a scenario by Fairbanks, was a Western.

One measure of Doug's growing popularity in films was the fact that the *New York Times* reviewed nine of the ten feature-length Triangle-Fine Arts films at a time when they did not have a policy of reviewing that many films. Of *The Good Bad Man,* the anonymous critic stated: "[It] might have been designed by Penrod Schofield with flashes by a sentimental chambermaid, but it is full to the brim with Fairbanks. His expressive face, radiant, toothsome smile, immense activity, and apparent disposition to romp all over the map make him a treasure to the cinema. No deserter from the spoken drama is more engaging in the new work than [he]. May his shadow never grow less."

Flirting with Death (Triangle-Fine Arts, 1916) finds Doug in a moment of oncamera despondency, and he engages a professional assassin to kill him. Repenting of his decision, he spends the balance of the photoplay bounding all over the landscape in quest of a place of safety. In the short subject, *The Mystery of the Leaping Fish* (Triangle-Fine Arts, 1916), he played a hero who was in effect a human submarine whose aquatic skills defeat a group of Japanese opium smugglers.

The Half-Breed (Triangle-Fine Arts, 1916), with a scenario by Anita Loos based on a Bret Harte story, was lensed in Calaveras County in one of California's national parks among the redwoods. It led the *New York Times'* critic to comment that California must have been made and then set aside for the advent of motion pictures. Doug's costume for this entry was the briefest of breech-clouts, which gave film audiences an extended look at the athletic body. As the *Times* reported: "[He] has infrequent opportunities here for his talented smile but his muscles are starred and, from the way he bounds about, you realize that he can, whenever he leaves the movies, become a pugilist or represent us at the Olympics games. That is, if they don't kill him."

Allan Dwan, the director, remembered Beth being unhappy about this picture in which her husband played "a dirty, filthy character and so greasy," living in a tree trunk. The objection was overcome by having the hero, Lo Dorman, dive into a river early in the film, swim across, and then dry himself with leaves. If he was shown as being properly hygienic, it would remove some of the onus of his living so primitively with hardly any clothes.

The remaining quartet of 1916 films showed the star fully attired but still involved in more than his share of madcap adventures. In *American Aristocracy* (Triangle-Fine Arts) he played Cassius Lee, a hero who vaulted some dozen walls and fences, swung from the branches of trees, and flew in a hydroplane. A typical Anita Loos touch in this film occurs when Cassius Lee, after having scaled innumerable walls, prepares to enter a building by leaping at a window far above the ground, then finds a basement window available and climbs in through it instead. A contemporary critic labeled *Manhattan Madness* "really nothing more than St. Vitus's dance set to ragtime."

The Americano (Triangle-Fine Arts, 1916), from yet another Anita Loos scenario, proved to be the last film Fairbanks did for Triangle. It was shot at the San Diego Exposition and across the border at Tijuana. In those days of *al fresco* shooting, it is unlikely that Triangle had obtained any official permission from the authorities to stage scenes for their production on Mexican soil. Whether or not official arrangements had been made, the local Tijuana militia was apparently not informed; the sight of a group of armed men in front of the local jail suggested incipient revolution to the patriotic Mexican soldiers, and Doug and several others from the company spent several unpleasant hours in jail before the situation was cleared up.

After a year and a half in films, Doug, who had become one of the medium's major stars, was convinced that he was being underpaid for his efforts which now brought him ten thousand dollars a week. He was living in a rented mansion on Hollywood Boulevard, where he had installed the first swimming pool constructed in Hollywood. It galled him that most of Triangle's profits were unquestionably due to the success of his pictures. He sought professional advice from his half-

**With Bessie Love
in *The Americano* (1916)**

38

With Carl Stockdale in *The Americano*

brother, John, who had risen to an executive position with the Morey Mercantile Company in Denver. After repeated entreaties, John came to Hollywood and observed what life was like for anyone residing in that climate (before smog) and making ten thousand dollars a week (in a day before income taxes made any appreciable dent). His initial pragmatic suggestion to his younger brother was to live on a mere two thousand dollars per week and bank the balance for a rainy day.

Before long Doug was able to convince John that he should become his business manager[10] and that there was a way to make even more money, and faster. John agreed to go east to negotiate a contract with Famous Players-Lasky, for them to serve as a distribution outlet for future Fairbanks films. They would be distributed separately under the Artcraft-Paramount label, as were those of Mary Pickford.

Ironically, the same day in December, 1916, that Doug received word of the new contract's closing, a telegram arrived from Beth. She, too, had gone east, alerted by the illness of Ella Fairbanks. Her communication notified Fairbanks that Ella had been stricken with pneumonia. Doug hastened east, but when he arrived in Buffalo he received the message that his mother had died. She had died in Beth's arms.

---

[10]John never returned to his old job with the Morey Mercantile Company. He remained as Doug's business manager until he was stricken with paralysis, and died, in 1926.

Whatever conflict had existed between his wife and his mother earlier had been dispelled.

A few days after the funeral Douglas called Mary Pickford, who agreed to drive with him around Central Park. During the drive, as he was talking about all he had loved and admired in his mother, he stopped the car and crumpled over the wheel sobbing. Mary noticed that the clock on the dashboard had stopped the moment he began to cry. Perhaps coincidentally, the clock stopped at exactly the same time that Ella Fairbanks had died a few days before. In future years, Mary and Doug would use the phrase "by the clock" as a symbol of that moment of utter sincerity they experienced together.

After his mother's funeral Doug returned to California with his wife and son to make films for Artcraft-Paramount. During the previous years he had made friends with Charlie Chaplin, the most popular male figure on the screen, who, many years later, was to remember Doug in his *Autobiography* (Simon and Schuster, 1964) as his *best* friend. Doug had also begun to assemble an entourage who would remain with him during the next productive decade. One of these people was a spectacularly unattractive actor, Bull Montana, born Luigi Montagna in Italy four years after Doug, while another was the redoubtable Benny Zeidman, who had accompanied him east for Ella's funeral. Benny would come in very handy during the year ahead. If the star explained to his wife that he had gone on a fishing trip or a duck hunt, Benny had the foresight to round up the fish or the ducks so that Fairbanks' jaunt would seem credible when he did return home.

Another important friend was a writer, Tom Geraghty, whose imagination supplied Doug with ideas for his insatiable appetite for practical jokes. Perhaps most important was Kenneth Davenport, a former actor who had appeared with Doug in *The Pit.* Shortly after that film was made, Davenport contracted tuberculosis. Doug later explained that he was at fault because he had borrowed Kenneth's overcoat, when there was only one between them, and had kept it all winter. Davenport became Fairbanks' ghost writer and during 1917-1918 wrote the series of books that appeared under Doug's name, *Laugh and Live, Make Life Worthwhile, Whistle and Hoe-Sing as We Go,* and others. (Don't they all sound like the titles of Gracie Fields films of the 1930s?)

One of the inspired inventions of the Fairbanks-Davenport-Geraghty team was the creation of the totally fictitious Charlie Fuhr. Articles giving details of Fairbanks' life and thoughts over that signature were created by Geraghty and/or Davenport and are still quoted today.

By far the most important addition to his creative company was the team of director John Emerson and writer Anita Loos, which was responsible for four of the five 1917 Fairbanks films. These were the celluloid entries which solidified Doug's reputation, made him the undisputed idol of millions, and culminated in a unique distinction for a motion picture performer: Mount Fairbanks in Alaska was named after Doug, who seemingly could scale any obstacle.

Miss Loos' film scripts for Doug continued to satirize particular foibles in American life. Publicity, psychiatry, pacifism, Couéism ("every day in every way I'm getting better and better") were all fair game. In his role in *In Again, Out Again* (Artcraft-Paramount, 1917), which premiered two weeks after the United States entered the war, Doug is suspected of being the anarchist who has been blowing up munitions factories. Naturally, he ultimately discovers the real villains. Bull Montana made his film debut in this picture as a burglar, and Erich von Stroheim was its assistant director. In its topicality—making fun of pacifists—it hit a responsive chord with filmgoers. Audiences enjoyed the fact that in the course of the film, Doug climbed the façades of three different buildings. The persistent tongue-in-cheek quality was evident throughout *In Again, Out Again*, as when Doug finally weds the jailer's daughter, and they agree to fit out a room in their home complete with bars (to look just like the cell in which they had fallen in love).

Early in 1917 Mary Pickford came to California to make two films directed by Cecil B. DeMille (*Romance of the Redwoods* and *The Little American*), for the Artcraft-Paramount unit. What was to be a temporary sojourn proved to be a permanent move.

In order to see Mary, Doug often told Beth that he had to be away from the house to work with Anita Loos at the Hollywood Hotel on the

In *In Again-Out Again* (1917)

scenarios of forthcoming films. Finally, a suspicious Mrs. Fairbanks insisted that they could work at their house in the future. Later Doug took to sleeping on an outdoor porch, well removed from the bedrooms. After the family had gone to sleep he would slide down a pillar, coast his car down the incline, and visit Mary. The problem came on the return trip when he had to cut off his car's engine so he would not be heard. Pushing the car up an incline to the garage and climbing back up the pillar to the porch were other obstacles Doug had to conquer on his return trips home.

Two of the 1917 Artcraft-Paramount films, *Wild and Woolly*[11] and *The Man from Painted Post,* were Westerns, permitting Doug his customary acrobatics in an outdoor setting. *Down to Earth* (Artcraft-Paramount, 1917) was a satire on hypochondria; *Reaching for the Moon* (Artcraft-Paramount, 1917), a spoof concerning a young man who learns he is of royal blood, only to awaken from his dreams in the last scene after five reels of typical "Fairbanksian" adventures. Eileen Percy was leading lady for four of the films, three of which were lensed by Victor Fleming who later became a noted director. By the time *Reaching for the Moon* was completed, John informed Doug that he had accumulated one million dollars.

During 1918, Mary Pickford (chaperoned by her mother), Charlie Chaplin, and Doug, the three foremost stars in the movies, as well as Marie Dressler, embarked on a cross-country bond-selling tour. It was a welcome opportunity for the lovers to be together and, at the same time as they increased their boxoffice appeal, be thoroughly patriotic.

In *Wild and Woolly* (1917)

---

[11]Perhaps the most charming of the early series of Doug's features, this entry finds the star cast as the son of a railroad magnate who is so enamored of what he imagines the West to be like that he lives in a tepee in one of the rooms of his father's New York mansion. When a town in Arizona is hopeful of gaining a spur railroad line, they pander to representative Fairbanks, by converting the environs into what he imagines it had been like there in bygone frontier days. He is delighted to see gun battles in the street, all performed with blank cartridges. He wants to pitch right in, but there is the imposing problem of his having real bullets. Later, the villain stirs up the Indians, but Doug enthusiastically quells the uprising, wins the girl, and is happy to think that the West is what he thought it would be all along. The five-reel film handled the story expediently without any padding.

Advertisement for *The Man from Painted Post* (1917)

Publicity pose, 1918

The four of them did more for the war effort than any other entertainers in the country. Ironically, Miss Dressler and Miss Pickford were both Canadian-born, Chaplin was British and never became an American citizen. Only Fairbanks was American.

The tour ended in Washington at the office of the Secretary of the Navy. The Assistant Secretary was the handsome and personable Franklin D. Roosevelt. Doug thought the dynamic young man could have a great career in films, but Roosevelt declined the opportunity.

Beth was waiting for Doug at the Algonquin Hotel in New York at the conclusion of the bond tour. When Doug arrived in New York he checked into the Sherry-Netherland. This was Mrs. Fairbanks' first recognition that he intended to break up the marriage. If Beth was aware that Doug's affair with Mary had been an open secret in Hollywood, she behaved with great dignity. Hedda Hopper, not yet then a columnist but the fifth wife of actor DeWolf Hopper and a film player herself, later recalled walking with Beth in Beverly Hills and passing the house in which Doug and Mary often trysted. Beth thought it was a charming house and Hedda decided it might be advisable to take a different route on their future walks.

In 1918 a certain stigma was still attached to divorce. Then, too, Doug was not unaware of the heartache that a broken home could bring upon the child or children involved. Fairbanks' brothers attempted to dissuade him, pointing out that, if Beth would consent to a divorce, an eventual marriage to the Queen of the Movies most likely would spell the end of their cinema careers.

But Doug was determined and he was prepared to make a settlement with Beth, giving her half of his fortune. Junior received $100,000 in trust and Beth $350,000. Counting everything, it cost Doug, Sr. more than $625,000 to be rid of his domestic obligations.

Beth filed for divorce in White Plains, New York, in November, 1918, and obtained her final decree on March 5, 1919. A week later she wed James Evans, a Pittsburgh stock broker, a marriage which would end in divorce a year later.

Doug's Artcraft-Paramount features for 1918 were essentially reworks of the themes that had proven popular earlier. Anita Loos and John Emerson had moved to New York to work on films for Constance Talmadge, but Allan Dwan remained on hand to direct five of the 1918 films, in four of which the winsome Marjorie Daw was the heroine. (In the early part of his movie career Doug had been reluctant to appear more than twice with the same leading lady, for fear that they might be mistaken as a cinema team. But by now it had been firmly established that Doug was the unmistakable star and that the woman was merely the attractive cipher who represented the ultimate achievement in the photoplay.)

Perhaps because Mary Pickford had taken a giant step forward in making a thoughtful film (*Stella Maris,* Artcraft-Paramount, 1918),[12] Doug was emboldened to include two films among his 1918 releases which included the usual Fairbanks acrobatics but which subordinated them to the films' main themes. One such production was a version of his play *He Comes up Smiling* (Artcraft-Paramount, 1918), and the other was a film version of Augustus Thomas' play *Arizona* (Artcraft-Paramount, 1918).

Of *He Comes up Smiling,* the *New York Times* recorded: "The distinctly minor part which physical action plays in the picture . . . leads one to the hope that the star may finally leave this field behind him and devote himself to more subtle comedy. Like Chaplin he has something of a genius for small comedy touches, and now that he is established high in the popular favor he should be able to hold his public easily—even to find an additional public—by the selection of subjects which call for a treatment more delicate than a blow from an axe."

Of *Arizona,* the *Times'* critic wrote: "Fairbanks can take the most farfetched story of melodrama or the most slushy of sentimental scenes and without burlesque, by spontaneous reality in the midst of unreality, save them from theatrical banality. That is why it is such a relief to see him occasionally—even if he is not the most subtle actor on the screen and takes the same character into every part. With Fairbanks in the leading role, [*Arizona*] has become an enjoyable comedy in which the athletic stunts of the star play a conspicuous and entertaining, though by no means monopolizing, part."

Doug might not have been another William S. Hart, Tom Mix, or Harry Carey, but he showed that as with his comedies and adventure films, he could make a remarkable impression in other genres as well, in this case the sagebrush tale.

On November 11, 1918, Mary had established herself as an independent producer of her films, which were distributed by First National. Her *basic* salary jumped to $675,000 a year, or $350,000 a picture. In addition, fifty percent of the gross receipts per film was to be paid to her account. Chaplin had signed an earlier million-dollar contract with First National which guaranteed him the same return for the gross. In return, he was to guarantee to the First National Corporation eight films of unspecified length.

Mary suggested that the most popular artists on the screen could do even better than this. In fact, they were victims of the system. If they would unite and found their own distributing corporation, they could reap one hundred percent of the profits. A series of meetings, which included the popular Western star, William S. Hart, took place. Hart

---

[12]Many regard *Stella Maris* as Miss Pickford's finest screen achievement. In it she plays a dual role, one the attractive heroine of the title and the other, a deformed waif, Unity Blake. The film parallels the lives of the two girls until the unattractive one is killed off and Mary can finish the film with a happy ending.

was satisfied to leave well enough alone, but on February 5, 1919, the United Artists Corporation, a distributing organization, was formed with D. W. Griffith (who a few years earlier had entertained doubts about Doug's screen future), Charlie Chaplin (Doug's best friend), and Mary and Doug as the founders. When he heard the news, Richard Rowland, the head of Metro, made his famous pronouncement: "The lunatics have taken over the asylum."

Having founded the innovating corporation, the next problem was to provide products. Doug's final film under the Artcraft-Paramount banner was *The Knickerbocker Buckaroo* (1919), again with Marjorie Daw as leading lady. The *New York Times* was enthusiastic: "[He] has found new stunts . . . and he performs them, apparently, with all of the ease and eclat with which the average man crosses Fifth Avenue with the traffic policeman's permission. It is not only his performance of amazing feats that makes Fairbanks delightful, however. It is his manner and the personality, and the fun he seems to get out of doing things that are fun for others. He is always refreshing, and especially [here]."

Griffith was the first of the United Artists' partners to be able to contribute a product. *Broken Blossoms* had cost only $88,000 to produce. It cost another $250,000 to pay Adolph Zukor to free the film for United Artists distribution in 1919. Mary had to complete *Daddy Long-Legs, The Hoodlum,* and *The Heart o' the Hills* for First Nation-

In *The Knickerbocker Buckaroo* (1919)

al before she was free. Chaplin, working as slowly as he did, did not complete his obligation until 1922.

Thus, Doug's *His Majesty, the American* (United Artists) was the first film made by one of the new company's founders. But it would be released after *Broken Blossoms,* in September, 1919.) It was followed by *When the Clouds Roll By* (United Artists, 1919), directed by Victor Fleming, a film involving the bursting of a dam and a consequent flood. Doug and the leading lady, Kathleen Clifford, are married on the roof of a house when a minister comes floating past, clinging to the steeple of his church.

During the summer of 1919, Charlotte Pickford had purchased a house on the Nevada side of Lake Tahoe, which would enable Mary to claim that she was a Nevada resident and had fulfilled the six-month residency requirement before obtaining a divorce from Owen Moore. Despite the very real risk that a divorce could destroy her film career, she determined to go ahead as planned. She and Moore had been separated for almost three years, but he was unwilling to legally sever his relationship with America's Sweetheart. Moore threatened to shoot Fairbanks, "that climbing monkey," and issued a statement to the press that he would "leave the case to the judgment of the American public, morally sound, and always possessing a keen instinct for justice."

Mary found unsuspected allies in the persons of the movie moguls who warned Moore that if he persisted in creating trouble they would see to it that he never worked in films again. Both of his brothers, Tom Moore and Matt Moore, had established themselves in films by this time and presumably, the tacit warning included them as well. Moore decided to accept the inevitable, *if* he received a settlement from Mary. Charlotte went to the bank in Los Angeles with a bundle of bonds to cash in to pay him off. At the bank, she encountered Moore's mother who said, "Oh, sure, Mrs. Pickford, poor Owen must have something." The amount of the settlement was never disclosed.

Mary and her mother, accompanied by her attorney, Dennis O'Brien, went to live on a farm in a town called Genoa, near Minden, Nevada. Mary wore flat-heeled shoes with her curls falling down her back. The farmer must have been the sole person in America who had never seen Mary Pickford in similar guise in her motion pictures. Eventually, however, the newspapers became aware that Mary was somewhere in Nevada for the purpose of obtaining a divorce. On March 2, 1920, she slipped into Minden with her mother and O'Brien and obtained the divorce. When the reporters caught up with her she informed them that she would wait a full year before wedding anyone else. She had reckoned without considering Fairbanks' impetuous nature.

For a time before the divorce, Doug had rented the imposing thirty-six-room home built by Syl Spaulding, the sporting goods maker. Fairbanks talked about trying to purchase it, but Mary considered it "too big and brown." Instead, he acquired the hunting lodge and surrounding acreage across from the Spaulding house, had it enlarged, and added a swimming pool as well as a wall to encircle the property.

Every force—major and small—in Hollywood warned the lovers that if they married they ran the grave risk of destroying their careers. They were certainly not ordinary movie stars. The roles they played on the screen had built up a special picture of them both. Mary writes in *Sunshine and Shadow* (Doubleday, 1955) that she asked Doug, "What if the world doesn't approve? Will your love be strong enough? If we both lose our careers, will our love be sufficient for our future happiness together?"

He replied, "I can't speak for you, Mary, but I know that my feeling for you is not of the moment. It has nothing to do with your career or your fame, or how other people feel about you. I love you for yourself."

On March 28th, Doug held a formal dinner party in the converted hunting lodge. Mary, dressed in a formal white tulle dress edged in apple green with a green spray at the waist, was accompanied by her mother. Other guests included the resourceful Benny Zeidman, Carlyle Robinson, Marjorie Daw (the leading lady of a number of Doug's recent films and a cast member of Mary's *Rebecca of Sunnybrook Farm*), and Robert Fairbanks and his wife. Also attending the gathering were R. S. Sparks, the Los Angeles County marriage license clerk, and the Reverend Dr. J. Whitcomb Brougher of Temple Baptist Church in Los Angeles. Sparks issued a license, and about 10:30 the party adjourned to Brougher's house in Glendale where he married Mary and Doug in a double ring ceremony. Robert was best man and Marjorie Daw was the bridesmaid. The bride was twenty-six; the groom was thirty-six.

Doug took his new bride home to the house, which was christened "Pickfair," and presented it to her as a wedding present. Presumably, there was a bit of last-minute persuasion on Doug's part, because neither Mary's sister Lottie nor brother Jack had been included in the party, and not even Charles Chaplin had been notified.

Two days later the same dinner guests were invited back to Pickfair where the announcement was made to the press. It was a logical ending for the All-American "boy" to marry the All-American "girl," America's sweetheart.

After the wedding Owen Moore challenged his divorce on the grounds of "fraud and collusion" and the fact that Mary had not fulfilled the six-month residency requirement. In addition, there were rumors that Mary was pregnant. If the state of Nevada invalidated the decree, what would the baby's name be: Moore, Fairbanks, or Pickford? The Nevada Attorney General filed a seven-thousand-word complaint against Mary, and accused both Fairbanks and Moore as fellow lawbreakers on charges of "wholesale collusion, conspiracy, fraud and untruthful testimony with the object of defeating the California and Nevada laws on marriage and divorce."

While the newspapers were having the time of their lives with the scandal, Mary was quietly completing *Suds* (United Artists, 1920), and Doug was making *The Mollycoddle* (United Artists, 1920). In this film, Fairbanks once again used a natural disaster in the climax of the picture. This time it was a landslide, considered the most spectacular landslide ever shown on the screen.

On May 31, 1920, the Nevada Supreme Court upheld the Pickford divorce decree, and the newlyweds set out for Europe aboard the *Lapland* for a belated honeymoon, which turned into a royal progression. During their entire stay in England they were mobbed by crowds seeking a quick look at the lovers and if they were lucky, autographs. At a garden party in Kensington Gardens, Doug had to carry Mary on his shoulders to get out of the crowds.

After a week in London they crossed to Holland, where the crowds in Amsterdam may have been smaller but no less demonstrative. They decided to try resting in Germany, where their films had not been shown due to the War. From Cologne to Wiesbaden no one recognized them. After such anonymity, they decided it was preferable to be somewhere they were known and loved rather than so unknown. In Basel, Switzerland, Doug bought a Fiat, engaged a chauffeur, and they pro-

With Ruth Renick in *The Mollycoddle* **(1920)**

49

ceeded into Italy. As they pulled into Lugano that first morning at seven A.M., a small boy recognized them and went shouting through the streets, *"Maria e Lampo, artisti della cinema!"* Doug was called "Lampo," or Lightning, by his Italian fans.

They next motored into France via the Italian Riviera. In Paris they stayed at the Hotel Crillon in a suite adjoining that of General Pershing. When they returned to America on the *Olympic* a big crowd of admirers were waiting, including Jack Dempsey, and a welcoming committee from the Friars' Club with two big motor buses headed by William A. Brady, James J. Corbett, and many other prominent people of the theatrical and sporting worlds. Whatever doubt there might have been about the public's opinion of their marriage had been effectively dispelled, both at home and abroad.

Doug had now appeared in twenty-nine films, each following closely the pattern of the preceding ones. The only noticeable differences were in technical improvements and a greater assurance on the part of the star. In addition to the popularity he gained from his films, there were the articles in *Boy's Life* Magazine and the books ghost-written by Kenneth Davenport. Doug was quoted as feeling that, in addition to standard rules for achieving success, one needed "clean and regular living, industry and hard work, steady application and perseverance," as well as the most vital ingredient, "enthusiasm."[13]

For his thirtieth film, *The Mark of Zorro* (United Artists, 1920), he made a considerable departure from the formula that had succeeded so well. As frequently occurs in film history when a major step takes place, conflicting accounts emerge as to who was responsible. A story by Johnston McCulley, *The Curse of Capistrano,* had appeared in the August 9, 1919 issue of the pulp magazine, *All-Story Weekly.*

In *Douglas Fairbanks: The Fourth Musketeer* (Henry Holt, 1953), the biography of her uncle, Letitia Fairbanks says Robert Fairbanks suggested that Doug take a look at this story after his return from Europe. Knowing how to arouse Doug's interest, he told the star, "It's not bad once you get past the title." Two years later Mary wrote that she had begged Doug all during the European trip to read a story that had been submitted for his approval. She had read it going over on the *Lapland.* Accepting her enthusiasm, he cabled the studio to buy the

[13]Fairbanks said: "All children have [enthusiasm] . . . but when they grow up they often lose it, and that's one of the world's tragedies. To be successful you must be happy; to be happy you must be enthusiastic; to be enthusiastic you must be healthy; and to be healthy you must keep mind and body active." In order to retain enthusiasm he recommended "fresh air and regular daily exercise. . . . These are the only sure medicine for driving away the doubts and fears that are the greatest enemies of accomplishment. The moment you begin to entertain any doubts of your ability to do a thing is the moment when your failure begins. And these doubts usually come from a sluggish circulation or an improper care of the body." Once he voiced the thought that instead of having age instruct youth on how to succeed, it ought to be the other way around, that middle age should humbly ask youth for its secret.

story, prepare the script and the sets, and make the costumes. He finally read the property for the first time on the return train trip from New York. Richard Schickel, in his biography of Fairbanks, states that a play agent, Ruth Allen, was the individual who brought the story to the attention of the Fairbanks studio. All three—Miss Allen, Miss Pickford, and Robert Fairbanks—probably have legitimate claims to influencing Doug in his major decision to break with the tried-and-true formula which had worked so well for five years.

It was not that much of a break as the contemporary *New York Times* carefully points out, but it was a costume picture and such vehicles had been a dubious financial proposition since the commercial failure of Griffith's *Intolerance* four years earlier. The story, set in Spanish California in the 1840s, concerns a young dilletante from a good family who returns from his studies in Spain to find California in the grip of a dictatorial governor (George Periolat). Continuing to pose as a fop, the hero enters a double life as "Zorro," (the word translates as "fox") righting the wrongs of the governor, and with his expert swordsmanship, cutting a wide swath among the enemies of the people. Every time Zorro is the victor in a dazzling display of swordplay he carves a "Z" in the face or shoulder of his opponent. Sometimes out of pure deviltry he carves it in a wall.

The *Times* reported: "The program says it is 'from' a story . . . called

With Marguerite De La Motte and Robert McKim in *The Mark of Zorro* (1920)

51

The Curse of Capistrano but one who has not read [the] story imagines that is pretty far from it. There's too much Fairbanks in it for anyone to have written it without the athletic comedian definitely in mind. . . . All of which means that *The Mark of Zorro* is more enjoyable than *The Curse of Capistrano* could ever hope to be. . . . The settings of the picture are picturesquely, and some of them magnificently, Spanish, and they often contrast amusingly with the emphatically non-Spanish appearance of some of the players, including, of course, Fairbanks himself."

The preview at the Beverly Hills Hotel did not engender very much enthusiasm, so to hedge his bet on *Zorro,* Douglas quickly made *The Nut* (United Artists, 1921), a romantic farce very much in the old Fairbanks mold. Marguerite de la Motte was again the leading lady as she had been in *Zorro,* with the "too beautiful" Barbara La Marr as the other woman. He was not to make another film in a contemporary setting for ten years. *The Nut* was a commercial failure, and *The Mark of Zorro*[14] was the biggest success of his career.

Publicity pose for *The Nut* (1921)

[14]The success of Fairbanks' *The Mark of Zorro* would encourage later filmmakers to try their hand with the swashbuckling tale. Republic would produce three serials which tangentially dealt with *Zorro* and/or the concept: *Zorro Rides Again* (1937), *Zorro's Fighting Legion* (1939), *Zorro's Black Whip* (1944). Tyrone Power, the 1940s' "answer" to Fairbanks, tried his hand at *The Mark of Zorro* (Twentieth Century-Fox, 1940). There would be a 1950s Walt Disney teleseries on "Zorro," a 1963 Italian feature, *Zorro the Avenger,* a 1972 offshoot exploitation feature *The Erotic Adventures of Zorro,* a 1974 ABC "Movie of the Week" telefeature, *The Mark of Zorro* with Frank Langella, and a 1974 European co-production *Zorro* (Titanus), starring Alain Delon.

With Willis Roberts and Marguerite De La Motte in *The Three Musketeers* (1921)

Doug's favorite character from childhood had been D'Artagnan, the hero of Dumas' *The Three Musketeers* (1844). Late in 1917, under Allan Dwan's direction he had made a contemporary version about a young man who roams the country in a Model T Ford, helping people in need. In *A Modern Musketeer* (Artcraft-Paramount, 1918) he rescues a family stranded with car trouble and takes them on to the Grand Canyon. Encouraged by the reception of *The Mark of Zorro*, Fairbanks determined to go ahead with a full dress film version of Dumas' opus.

He engaged Edward Knoblock, an established British playwright, to write the scenario, hired Professor H. J. Uyttenhove, former world's champion fencer, to coach the cast in fencing, had Edward M. Langley, art director for the Fairbanks Company, make detailed drawings of the sets before they were constructed, and employed Willie Hopkins, a noted sculptor, to model busts and statuary for the palace sets. Louis F. Gottschalk, a descendant of the famous American composer and pianist, who had been the musical director of the first American production of *The Merry Widow*, was engaged to write a special musical score for the film.

Fred Niblo was the director, as he had been for *The Mark of Zorro*, and Marguerite De La Motte and Barbara La Marr reappeared as Constance and Milady de Winter. Knoblock had considerably altered the

53

Dumas original so that Constance would be the niece of Bonacieux (Sidney Franklin) rather than his wife, thereby making possible the discreet love scenes[15] between Doug and his blonde leading lady without offending any filmgoing patron. Adolphe Menjou, who had appeared as little more than an extra in some of the earlier Fairbanks features, made a major impression in his role as King Louis XIII.

According to Hedda Hopper, Doug had told Mary that during the first year he expected he might be referred to as "Mr. Mary Pickford," but after that year she would be "Mrs. Douglas Fairbanks" and she had better not forget it. The New York premiere of *The Three Musketeers* (United Artists, 1921) took him a giant step further toward that goal.

The critic of the *New York Times* was unbounded in his enthusiasm for *The Three Musketeers.* "The world of the motion picture celebrated its fullest and most satisfying night of the year last evening [August 21st] at the Lyric Theatre. . . . Here plainly is a D'Artagnan that not even Dumas ever dreamed of. He is the personification of all the dashing and slashing men of Gascony that ever fought their way through French novels. . . . He makes *The Three Musketeers* a stirring, even thrilling, picture. . . . If you like Douglas Fairbanks, and it is impossible to believe that you don't, you are certain to devour [this film]."

James Quirk, the editor of *Photoplay* Magazine, selected it as the best picture of the month (November, 1921): "A great picture: one that the whole world will enjoy, today and tomorrow. . . . It is one of the finest photoplays ever produced, a real classic. . . . Some of the street scenes are obviously f.o.b. Hollywood; and Doug is an American D'Artagnan despite his French mustache. But considering everything—it's great. . . . Don't miss this!"[16]

There had been ovations at the New York premiere to which the star, accompanied by Mary and Charlie Chaplin from the world of films and Jack Dempsey from the world of sports, responded before the film, during the interval, and at the end. A more introspective man than Doug might have wondered how he could top this. But the man of action did top it—twice!

During the second Fairbanks-Pickford trip to Europe, which is remarkably undocumented in comparison to their first trip, they were

---

[15]Particularly in *The Mark of Zorro,* the love interest had been on a very idealistic plane. Romance in a Fairbanks movie was apt to be more courtly than ardent, which kept the censors and the lower-brow public happy.

[16]Inspired by the success of the Fairbanks' versions, there were many subsequent versions of *The Three Musketeers:* RKO, 1935 with Walter Abel, Paul Lukas; Twentieth Century-Fox, 1939 with Don Ameche, the Ritz Brothers; MGM, 1948 with Gene Kelly, Van Heflin, Gig Young; French 1954, with Bourvil, George Marchal; Twentieth Century-Fox, 1974 with Michael York, Oliver Reed, Richard Chamberlain (and the Fox sequel, *The Four Musketeers,* 1975). There have also been many spinoffs, ranging from the Mascot serial, *The Three Musketeers* (1933) with John Wayne, to the Republic Western series, *The Three Mesquiteers,* to the 1951 Hal Roach, Jr. feature, *The Sword of D'Artagnon* with Robert Clarke, John Hubbard, Mel Archer.

presented at court in Sweden, met the Prince of Wales and his cousin, Lord Louis Montbatten in England, and were the guests of honor at a reception hosted by the American ambassador in Paris. (Mary Pickford had made *Little Lord Fauntleroy* (United Artists, 1921) playing dual roles. She rushed the film to completion so she could make this European trek with her husband.)

In their absence a gigantic set had been constructed for Doug's next film. A choice had had to be made between *Ivanhoe* and *Robin Hood,* and the latter won, being deemed a more commercial prospect for United Artists' 1922 season. The set, constructed on the company's new lot on Santa Monica Boulevard which Mary and Doug had bought, was ninety feet high, the biggest set since Griffith had reconstructed ancient Babylon for *Intolerance.* In the interim, there had been a recession in film production and the banks had refused to grant the Fairbanks' company a loan to finance the *Robin Hood* production. Against the advice of his brother John, Doug decided to invest his own money in the picture, which would also give him outright ownership of the film.

When Doug returned to Hollywood and saw the set, he decided that it would be impossible to act against such a background without feeling dwarfed. Even though it had cost $250,000 of his own money, he refused to do the picture and it was shelved—or so it seemed. Director

In *Robin Hood* (1922)

Allan Dwan thereupon employed a clever trick to re-elicit Fairbanks' enthusiasm. Doug was informed that there was a possibility to rent the set to another company so that Fairbanks' investment would not be a complete loss.

As Dwan explained it, the hero of the alleged "other" picture would climb a flight of stairs to confront his enemies on a balcony, while being hotly pursued by another group following him up the stairs. The hero would escape by sliding down a curtain. Hidden behind the curtain was a slide. After Dwan demonstrated the action, Doug was as eager as a schoolboy to try it and there was no further doubt on anyone's part that the projected picture would now be made. Australian-born Enid Bennett, the wife of Fred Niblo who had directed *The Three Musketeers,* appeared as Lady Marian, Alan Hale was cast as Little John, a role he would repeat on several other film occasions, and Wallace Beery portrayed King Richard the Lion-Hearted. Beery had appeared as a villain in earlier Fairbanks films, and this represented the first important break-through in his career.

In a gesture no more crude or less commercial than the current pre-fabricated "studio tours" of 1970s Hollywood, bleachers were built on the Fairbanks-Pickford lot for the large audience which came every day to watch the shooting. In addition, Doug also had constructed a gymnasium in which he spent most of his time when he wasn't before the camera, and in which he entertained most of the famous visitors to the studio. Doug was also one of the first male stars to install a barber's chair in his dressing room for the sessions with his full-time makeup man.

Robin Hood cost more than the million dollars that had been budgeted, but it netted Fairbanks five million in return. The film had its premiere in New York at the Capitol Theatre on October 30, 1922. It was the world's largest film emporium at the time, and the picture played to 101,000 people the first week, breaking all records for theatre attendance anywhere. So great was the demand for tickets to the opening that there had to be a double premiere. The second showing started at midnight so that Doug's professional pals could attend after their own shows.

James Quirk in *Photoplay* selected Mary's new version of *Tess of the Storm Country* (United Artists, 1922) as the best picture of the month, with *Robin Hood* relegated to second place that month. He reasoned: "*Robin Hood* left us with just an edge of disappointment. We can't say what it is that is missing but the void is there. [It] is curiously divided into two parts, one showing the departure of Richard the Lion Hearted and his knights to the Crusades and the other presenting the tyranny of John in England along with the appearance of Robin Hood in Sherwood Forest to combat the usurper. The first is of measured tempo, the second moves with super-Fairbanks speed. . . . Curiously, in the first half, Wallace Beery . . . fairly runs away with the spectacle. The second half is all Doug, however, the gymnastic Doug of *Zorro* and *The Three Musketeers.* Yet Fairbanks is always a twentieth century swashbuckler, for all his massive and atmospheric surroundings. Somehow, he does not achieve the personal glory of either his *Zorro* or his *D'Artagnan.* He is rather swallowed up in the massiveness." *Photoplay* selected Beery as the best actor of the month.

For the *Robin Hood*[17] opening, Doug brought to New York the bow and arrow he had used in the film. When a reporter doubted that Doug

Antic pose, 1923

[17]*Robin Hood* has been one of the more popular heroes utilized oncamera. There had been at least three British (1909, 1912, 1913) and two American Robins (1912, 1913) before Fairbanks' rendition. In 1938 there was *The Adventures of Robin Hood* (Warner Bros.) in color and with Errol Flynn, followed by Cornel Wilde's *Bandit of Sherwood Forest* (Columbia, 1946), in which he was the outlaw's son. Jon Hall did *Prince of Thieves* (Columbia, 1948). John Derek was Robin Hood's son in *Rogues of Sherwood Forest* (Columbia, 1950), Robert Clarke appeared in *Tales of Robin Hood* (Lippert, 1951), and Richard Todd graced *The Story of Robin Hood* (RKO, 1953). The character of Robin was played by Harold Warrender in *Ivanhoe* (MGM, 1952). Don Taylor was the lead in *Men of Sherwood Forest* (Astor, 1956). It was actually June Laverick who was the *Son of Robin Hood* (Twentieth Century-Fox, 1959). Richard Greene was the star of teleseries on "Robin Hood" and the lead in *Sword of Sherwood Forest* (Columbia, 1961). Barrie Ingham starred in *A Challenge for Robin Hood* (Twentieth Century-Fox, 1967). A modern rendition of the Robin Hood theme was used by Frank Sinatra and the Rat Pack in *Robin and the Seven Hoods* (Warner Bros., 1964). In 1973 Buena Vista released *Robin Hood,* a full-length animated version featuring Brian Bedford as the voice of Robin. Most recently, there appeared *Robin Hood Junior* (Children's Film Foundation) a British-made entry starring Keith Chegwin in the title role. In 1976, Warner Bros. released *Robin and Marian,* with Sean Connery and Audrey Hepburn.

had actually performed all the feats of archery, the star and a group of reporters moved to the roof of the Ritz Hotel where Doug aimed at a gargoyle a hundred yards away. A second arrow was shot "to see how far it would go." It went through an open window where a Polish furrier, recently arrived in this country, was bending over to retrieve a scrap of mink. The furrier was willing to forget his wounded derriere for five thousand dollars, the opportunity to meet Fairbanks, and two tickets to the premiere of *Robin Hood.*

Although United Artists was product-starved, Doug made no film in 1923. The time he didn't spend at the studio, in the pool, the gymnasium, or at the steam bath, was taken up with the preparation for a new spectacle which would hopefully top the *Robin Hood* success.

Meanwhile, Mary was having professional problems. She had imported Ernst Lubitsch to direct her in a vehicle, *Rosita* (United Artists, 1923), a film that was popular but not as publicly acclaimed as more typical Mary Pickford films. She has always called this rendition of the French play, *Don Cesar de Bazan,* her worst screen appearance.

But Doug was more troubled by the screen debut of his son in *Stephen Steps Out* (Paramount, 1923). Jesse Lasky, head of Paramount, had realized the boxoffice potential of the Fairbanks name and signed the thirteen-year-old boy for that single film. Doug and Mary first learned the news in Paris during the European trip which followed the premiere of *Robin Hood.* Fairbanks was furious, threatening to cut his son out of his will, give him no help whatsoever, and oppose all his son's theatrical efforts.

Junior was adamant, and he and his mother[18] arrived in Hollywood on June 18, 1923, to make his debut picture which was to be directed by Joseph Henabery who had helmed some of Doug's early movie successes.

The senior Fairbanks, at the top of his craft and painfully reminded that he had reached forty, was furious at the potential threat to his own career. He is reported as saying: "He's too young and doesn't really know what he's doing. I wanted him to have the best education possible, but I don't think that's possible now. You can't work in pictures and attend a university at the same time. He should have been permitted to wait until his education was completed before he took up a career. The boy's management is in his mother's hands, though, and she ought to know what's best for him."

For a man of his abundant energy, it was difficult to have to sit out 1923 because his son was doing something of which he strongly disapproved. It seemed advisable not to have father and son competing for

---

[18]Beth Fairbanks, after her divorce from James Evans, had lost most of her settlement from Doug through poor investments. They were living in Paris where the exchange rate at that time was more favorable than at home, and they were the sole support of grandfather Sully, the one-time "Cotton King."

publicity which would surely rake up the skeletons of the pair of divorces which led to the "perfect union."

To Doug Senior's immense relief, *Stephen Steps Out* was not the success Lasky had hoped for, and Junior and his mother returned to Paris. Doug saw his son there the following year when he and Mary returned to Europe to attend the 1924 Olympic Games. Although there was no further talk about cutting the boy out of his will, he was not happy to learn that his son fully intended to continue his film career when he was a little older.

Nevertheless, the year away from the screen had benefited Doug. When he eventually started work on his next and probably best feature, *The Thief of Bagdad* (United Artists, 1924), he had a deep tan, was considerably slimmer, and looked younger than he had in any of his earlier films. William Cameron Menzies had had the opportunity to take his time in designing elaborate, fantastic sets that are still a marvel to see fifty years later. These sets covered four acres. Directed by Raoul Walsh, his only essay into fantasy, the film is fourteen reels, two reels longer than *Robin Hood,* which had in the meantime won the *Photoplay* Gold Medal as the best picture of 1922. Brunette Evelyn Brent had originally been scheduled to play "The Princess," but she was replaced by blonde Julanne Johnston in her first important role. Miss Johnston was attractive but rather vapid and her career subsequent did not amount to very much. More vivid was the teenaged Anna May

As *The Thief of Bagdad* (1924)

Pose for *The Thief of Bagdad*

Wong in her first important role as the Mongol slave. The critics were enthusiastic about *The Thief of Bagdad*. The *New York Times* evaluated: "It is an entrancing picture, wholesome and beautiful, deliberate but compelling, a feat of motion picture art which has never been equaled and one which itself will enthrall persons time and again. You can see this film and look forward to seeing it a second time."[19]

The poet Vachel Lindsay went even further. He thought it was worth seeing ten times, the first three "just to enjoy the story and the splendor," several times "for reminiscences of *Intolerance*," another time to observe how the new production had digested both "the glories and the mistakes of *Intolerance*," and "at least once to watch the sea." Robert E. Sherwood wrote, "Fairbanks has gone far beyond the mere bound of possibility, he has performed the super-human feat of making his magic seem probable."

James Quirk, in *Photoplay* wrote: "Here is magic. Here is beauty. Here is the answer to the cynics who give the motion picture no place in the family of the arts. . . . It is a work of rare genius, and the entire industry, as well as the public, owes [Fairbanks] a debt of gratitude. . . . Go see this picture at the earliest opportunity." This time Fairbanks topped the list of the six best performances of the month.[20]

Photoplay's second best picture of the month would be D. W. Griffith's *America* (1924), which was to be that director's penultimate film for United Artists. Although a press statement was issued on March 28, 1924, by the partners in the United Artists Corporation that they were all renewing their contracts, Griffith was deeply in debt and signed an

---

[19]In his autobiography, *Each Man in His Time* (Farrar, Straus, & Giroux 1974), Walsh recalls: "Everyone followed the script, and all I did was keep my eyes open and marvel at the ease with which Fairbanks turned into a human fly and went up city and palace walls without apparent effort. Doug got around in baggy pants, slippers, and his skin. This outfit showed off his athletic ruggedness to perfection. It is a tossup whether the princess responded to his vehement declarations of love or his physical comeliness. . . . I purposely heightened the action so that the build-up to the fanatastic finale would not drag and become tedious. The rival princes got more than the script called for. Toward the end, I had them running all over the palace searching for the imposter and demanding his head on a platter. The idea of making the thief invisible was my own. I trust my blatant ad-libbing did not cause the clever Scheherazade to turn over in her grave."

[20]In a *Films and Filming* (1973) piece on Douglas Fairbanks, Gordon Gow assesses: "Ahmed, the hero-thief [of *The Thief of Bagdad*] rates very high among Doug's characterisations: for he did make each of them a separate individual, although his own blithe personality shone through them all. Masculinity gleamed from the thief's naked torso, the chest and arms and back trimly muscled, the legs lightly clad in transparent trousers which gave place discreetly to thicker material in the hip region, the curly hair partly bound back by a head scarf, the moustache pencil-slim above a smile that disclosed impeccably white teeth, and the big golden ear-rings completing an image of pagan grace. Furthermore, a star and a crescent moon were painted on one of his biceps. Daring stuff, aided by the customary virile exploits."

There would be two subsequent, very different versions of *The Thief of Bagdad*. Zoltan Korda's 1940 United Artists version with Sabu and Conrad Veidt, and a 1961 Italian rendition with Steve Reeves and Giorgia Moll.

60

unfortunate contract with Paramount to release his next film productions.

Meantime, Mary, ever anxious to keep pace with her famous husband, had starred in *Dorothy Vernon of Haddon Hall* (United Artists, 1924), directed by Marshall Neilan. A splendid costume picture, it was considered to be very slow-moving and lacking spontaneity of performance. A very concerned Mary then requested the readers of *Photoplay* Magazine to name properties in which they would like to see her. The results, published in the October, 1925 issue, were rather disheartening. The tabulation of more than 20,000 letters indicated in order of preference: *Cinderella,* in which she had appeared earlier; *Anne of Green Gables,* in which Mary Miles Minter had already appeared; *Alice in Wonderland,* which Mary later seriously considered making as a co-production with Walt Disney; *Heidi; The Little Colonel;* and *Sara Crewe,* which she had already filmed as *The Little Princess.*

Meanwhile, Doug had his problems when Junior and his mother returned from Paris, this time determined that they would seriously pursue a screen career for the boy. At fourteen and a half he was already taller than his father and looked several years older than his real age. Relations with his father were resumed on a level of strained formality. Occasionally, he would be invited to come for a swim in the pool at Pickfair or for dinner. Over a period of years he remained to

With Charles Chaplin and Mary Pickford at the Fairbanks' home in Beverly Hills, August, 1924

watch a film and to stay overnight only three times. The visits were extremely irregular. During this period Mary let it be known that young Fairbanks was always welcome at Pickfair. If she observed that father and son were engaged in friendly conversation, she would busy herself elsewhere so that they could get to know each other better.

During the summer of 1924, Doug and Mary returned to Europe where they were presented to the Kings and Queens of Norway and Spain. On their return, Doug turned to *Don Q, Son of Zorro* (United Artists, 1925) as his next project. It took him six weeks to master the Australian stock whip which was used throughout the film to disarm an enemy swordsman, to put out a lighted candle, to cut in two the contract for a forced marriage, to break a bottle, to capture a wild bull, to snap a cigarette out of the villain's mouth, to bring down and tie up another, lesser villain, and to use as a swing to mount a dungeon's walls and escape from the villain. As Letitia Fairbanks later wrote, "Let parents of two-gun smallfry be thankful Don Q doesn't ride today. His contemporary imitators broke more windows, vases, and chandeliers with popping whips than they do today with popping toy guns."

The Donald Crisp-directed feature finds Doug in dual roles. He is both Zorro (thirty years after the time of the original story, hence

With Mary Astor in *Don Q, Son of Zorro*

62

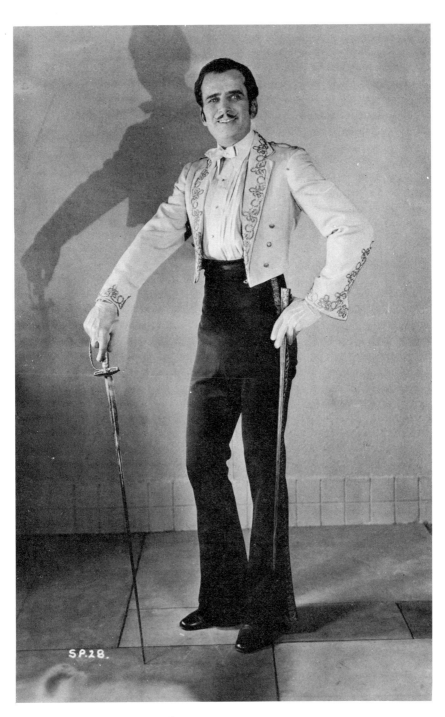

As *Don Q, Son of Zorro* (1925)

decked out in a gray wig) and his son, Don Cesar de Vega. The latter has also gone to Spain for "study and relaxation," where he meets the beautiful Dolores (Mary Astor), daughter of the Lord Chamberlain. There is even a film clip of the swordfight from *The Mark of Zorro* to tie in the prior feature to this happy sequel, filled with romantic balcony scenes, feats of derring-do, and combats between the good and the evil (as represented by Jean Hersholt).

Of Doug's performance, *Photoplay* said: "In Spanish clothes doing a Spanish dance, [he] is a sight to behold. In fact, in all his pantomime, he's really more of a dancer than actor." The *New York Times,* noting that the star had not attended the premiere, liked the film: "Mr. Fairbanks appears to have trained down to a very slender figure for the part which is an ideal one for him. . . . This is a photoplay which creates no end of mirth and sustains the interest all through. It will probably prove to be a far more satisfactory box office asset than even *The Thief of Bagdad.* Those who enjoyed *The Mark of Zorro* will find this brimful of the same satisfying gallantry and courage, in which the villains have backed off the screen."

Young Mary Astor recalled later that the shooting of *Don Q* was frequently interrupted by the various distinguished visitors, royal and otherwise, who visited the set. Mary and Doug were the undisputed social leaders of Hollywood. One wag said that their annual trips to Europe were for the purpose of booking their guests for the next year.

Doug had briefly considered doing a pirate story after *Robin Hood.* He had put the idea aside then because he could not conceive of pirates in tones of gray. In 1924, Paramount had released a two-tone Technicolor film, *Wanderer of the Wasteland,* starring Jack Holt and Billie Dove, which was considered the most successful use of the process up to then. Doug determined to use the process for *The Black Pirate* (United Artists, 1926), a story he had written under his pseudonym Elton Thomas. In its final form, it incorporated bits and pieces of all the pirate stories ever told. Since Miss Dove had photographed so fetchingly before, she was engaged as Doug's leading lady. Swedish artist Carl Oscar Borg was hired to design the production. He used only those colors which registered with reasonable fidelity in the process. The palette for the most part was kept limited. Red was only included to depict the blood on a man's hands or on his sword. The story began slowly. Fairbanks gave the audience time to enjoy the color effects before making his entrance ten minutes later.

Mordaunt Hall's review in the *New York Times* was characteristic of the general enthusiasm for this adventure tale set on the Spanish high seas: "With its excellent titles and wondrous colored scenes this picture seems to have a Barriesque motif that has been aged in Stevensonian wood. . . . As for Mr. Fairbanks, he seems more active than ever. He goes through his fighting stunts with the same cheerfulness he did in

As *The Black Pirate* (1926)   In *The Black Pirate*

other productions. . . . This is a production which marks another forward stride for the screen, one that the boy and his mother will enjoy and one that is a healthy entertainment for men of all ages."

The best remembered scene of this swashbuckling yarn, which greatly benefited from Donald Crisp's oncamera comedy bits as an old Scot, was the one in which the hero, Michel, descends from the heights of the ship's riggings by digging a knife into the sails and ripping them from top to bottom as he comes down. This scene and a number of other action scenes are still effective for today's audience.[21] Unfortunately, only black and white prints are currently available, the same fate that has befallen too many original color celluloid productions.

With the release of *The Black Pirate*, forty-two-year-old Douglas Fairbanks was at the zenith of his film career. Hollywood had yet to produce a rival of equal proportions to Doug. The late Wallace Reid may have been more contemporaneous in his dashing appeal, Ramon Novarro more erotic in his Metro spectacles, and the soon-to-die Rudolph Valentino more exotic in his Latin Lover "Sheik" prototype. However, Fairbanks was as unique to the swashbuckling romantic adventure film of the 1920s as Tom Mix was to the Western or Charles

---

[21]On September 17, 1974, when the American Film Institute inaugurated its fall program of film screenings (focusing on fourteen Douglas Fairbanks features), *The Black Pirate* was the picture screened at the Kennedy Center in Washington, D.C. Douglas Fairbanks, Jr. was among the guests present.

Chaplin to comedy. Solid Richard Dix, devil-may-care John Gilbert, and debonair Ronald Colman were each extraordinarily popular with moviegoers of the Roaring Twenties, but, like the up-and-coming wholesome Charles Farrell, their boxoffice appeal lay in their roles as romantic leading men, rather than as super-athletic screen heroes. For the time being, Doug, Sr. still had the field pretty much to himself.

With *The Black Pirate* and Mary's latest film, *Sparrows* (United Artists, 1926) (the last in which she would play a little girl), successfully running as a double feature at road show prices at Hollywood's Egyptian Theatre, the two stars again left the country in April, 1926. Intending a trip around the world, they were accompanied by Mr. and Mrs. Robert Fairbanks. On May 4th, they were presented onstage in Berlin during an engagement of *Little Annie Rooney* (United Artists, 1925), with "The Star Spangled Banner" played in Germany the first time since World War I. In Rome, a week later, they were received by Il Duce, Benito Mussolini, and exchanged autographs. After an enthusiastic welcome in Warsaw, they continued into Russia.

They were continually filmed during their week in Moscow; most of their time there seems to have been spent in the Russian film studios. Many movie fans later have wondered what ever happened to those thousands of feet of film, during which Mary was persuaded to kiss Igor Ilinsky, the leading Soviet comedian, and Doug offered some of his acrobatics for the camera. The Soviet movie industry had figured out a method for employing the two most important and highest paid stars in the world and not having to pay them a cent. Directed by S. Komarov, *The Kiss of Mary Pickford,* starring Ilinsky and with A. Sudakevich as his leading lady, was released by Gosfilmofond in 1927. Seen recently at the Pacific Film Archive, it proved to be a delightful comedy about a cinema doorman who is rejected by his girlfriend until he is kissed by Mary Pickford. Miss Pickford, especially, receives much more footage than a star normally gets in what is called today a "cameo" role.

In August, the Fairbanks and party were called back from Russia by the news that Charlotte Pickford's health had worsened. She had injured her breast when a trunk lid had fallen while she was searching for old clothes that might have been suitable for Mary's use in *Little Annie Rooney*. The redoubtable architect of Mary's career lived in deteriorating health until March 22, 1928, when she died from cancer.

During 1927, Doug filmed *The Gaucho* (United Artists) in which, for the first time, he permitted his screen character to age. Real-life events were the direct cause of this situation. Beginning with *Stella Dallas* (United Artists), released in November, 1925, Douglas, Junior had begun to establish himself as an attractive cinema juvenile lead. Mary had embarked on a modern Cinderella story written by Kathleen Norris, *My Best Girl* (United Artists, 1927), in which she was an eighteen-

As *The Gaucho* (1928)

year-old shop girl who falls in love with the boss' son, not knowing at first, of course, who he is. For the leading man, she chose Charles "Buddy" Rogers, age twenty-three, who had just finished filming *Wings* (1927) for Paramount.

One day Doug visited the set where she was filming a love scene with Buddy. After watching a few minutes he left abruptly, telling his brother that "it's more than jealousy. I suddenly felt afraid."

Brother John died in November, 1926, while sets for *The Gaucho* were under construction; on the other hand, Charlotte Pickford was enduring a painful, lingering death. No wonder intimations of his own mortality began to creep into Doug's screen work.

Of *The Gaucho*, which featured relative newcomer Lupe Velez as the "Mountain Girl" heroine, the *New York Times* commented: "Dashing heroes and unalloyed cheer have been the outstanding feature of all Douglas Fairbanks's productions . . . therefore it is not a little surprising to find in his latest film adventure a rather gruesome undertone to an otherwise gay symphony. . . . Mr. Fairbanks is no less agile than he has been in other productions; perhaps he has even more chances here to display his agility."

The gimmick this time was the use of the *boleadoras,* or bolas, used by the Argentine cowboy. This whiplike device is made of three leather thongs tied together in the form of a Y, with the ends fastened to stone or metal balls about the size of apples. Doug used this with the same dexterity as he had the whip in *Don Q,* but even *Photoplay* noted that it was an older Doug. Perhaps this was more noticeable because his leading lady was only eighteen years old. Mary made some cameo appearances in *The Gaucho* as "The Madonna," her first appearance in the same film as Doug, if the previously mentioned Russian venture is excluded.

On May 4, 1927, a group of thirty-six industry leaders, including Mary, Doug, and Louis B. Mayer, whose idea it was in the first place, got together to form the Academy of Motion Picture Arts and Sciences. Its purpose was to encourage the arts and sciences of the movies by awards of merit for distinctive achievement. Doug was elected the Academy's first president. It was unquestionably an honor befitting his position as the screen's most popular male star (with the exception of Chaplin), but it was also a sign that his youth was far behind him.

On October 17, 1927, a month before *The Gaucho* was released, Doug, Jr. opened at the Majestic Theatre in Los Angeles in the leading role of John van Druten's *Young Woodley.* Mary and Doug were present, as was a young MGM contract player, Joan Crawford[22], accompanied by Paul Bern, a Metro executive.

---

[22]A whirlwind romance developed between Doug, Jr. and the six-years-older Joan. On December 31, 1927, he proposed. While waiting for the next year and a half, until June 3, 1929, when they were finally wed, they acted in public in a very extroverted fashion,

During the months that followed the release of *My Best Girl,* Mary had gone into seclusion to care for her mother. When Charlotte died she left the bulk of her estate, estimated at three million dollars, to Mary with bequests of $200,000 each to her other children, Jack and Lottie, and to Lottie's daughter, Gwynne. After the funeral, Doug and Mary took a short trip to Europe.

On their return, on June 21, 1928, Mary took an impetuous and fatal step. Without telling Doug, she went to the salon of Charles Bock, accompanied by a girlfriend and a photographer, and had the famous Pickford curls cut. Six curls left the salon with her, two for a case in Pickfair, and two each for the museums of San Diego and Los Angeles. Doug is quoted in Letitia Fairbanks' book as responding to Mary's question if he liked it with, "I don't know. I guess no man wants to see any change in the woman he loves."

The Gaucho had competed in the boxoffice sweepstakes with *The Jazz Singer* (Warner Bros., 1927), the first feature-length motion picture with talking sequences. By the time Pickford and Fairbanks had returned to Hollywood, most of the pictures in production had accepted the latest development. He embarked on the production of *The Iron Mask* (United Artists, 1929), a sort of valedictory to D'Artagnan, with Marguerite De La Motte repeating her earlier role as Constance and

---

making no secret of their mutual attraction and attachment. With the release of *Our Dancing Daughters* (1928), Joan became a full-fledged MGM star.

A "civilian" pose, 1928

Leon Barry as his Athos. Eugene Pallette had grown too corpulent to appear at all, so that, this time, Gino Corrado played Aramis. Stanley J. Sandford appeared here as Porthos. Doug brought to this film the same meticulous care that he had shown with his earlier movies: Maurice Leloir, an illustrator of Dumas' books, was imported for $40,000 to prepare the costumes, and Allan Dwan, the director of *Robin Hood,* was recalled for the production. Dwan later remembered: "Doug seemed to be under some sort of compulsion to make this picture one of his best productions. He had always meticulously supervised every detail of his pictures, but in this one I think he eclipsed himself. It was as if he knew this was his swan song."

With its talking sequences, sound effects, and music score, the eleven-reel *The Iron Mask*[23] gave the account of the birth of twin sons to Louis XIII of France and his wife, Anne of Austria. Cardinal Richelieu (Nigel De Brulier) has the unwanted twin smuggled into Spain. Years later, D'Artagnan (Fairbanks) and his three comrades (Leon Barry, Corrado, and Sandford) give up their lives to rescue the real new king, Louis XIV, and restore him to the throne. The monarch then orders the "Pretender" to suffer the remainder of his life in an iron mask.

[23]Louis Hayward would star in *The Man in the Iron Mask* (United Artists, 1939), and Patricia Medina in *The Lady in the Iron Mask* (Twentieth Century-Fox, 1952). In 1974 a new rendition of *The Man in the Iron Mask* was shot in Europe with Claude Dauphin, Jean-Pierre Aumont and Fausto Tozzi as the Musketeers—thirty years after. Besides Cornel Wilde-Maureen O'Hara's *At Sword's Point* (RKO, 1952), which dealt with the original musketeers' offsprings, there were George Montgomery's *The Son of D'Artagnan*

In *The Iron Mask* (1929)

Of this first picture in which Doug died oncamera, *Photoplay* report-ed: "Action, action, action—more action! It is adroit. It is imaginative. It is resplendent. . . . There is the characteristic Fairbanks breadth and sweep and stunts. And it is his best job of story-telling. . . . Fairbanks gives us D'Artagnan artistically done, particularly the aged D'Artagnan. Don't miss it." The *New York Times* was equally approving, noting that Fairbanks looked, even in the earlier episodes, a little older, but none the less ingratiating: "and when he adopts a sort of middle-aged make-up one is impelled to think that Fairbanks can go on for years and years and still appeal to the thousands who like to see a production that is a picture with charm and good taste."

Shortly afterward, Mary filmed *Coquette* (United Artists, 1929) her first talkie, with John Mack Brown as her male lead and former broth-er-in-law Matt Moore in a secondary role.

Sources vary as to who actually suggested that a film version of *The Taming of the Shrew* (United Artists, 1929)* might be an ideal vehicle to finally team the King and Queen of Hollywood. Ten days after the successful premiere of *Coquette* (April 12, 1929), the news was announced.

The ambitious production was fraught with difficulties. The lax practices of Fairbanks when he was his own producer had not con-cerned Mary. Now that they were embarked in a co-production, it was her concern when he lingered in the gymnasium while cast and crew (and Miss Pickford!) waited. Whoever actually did decide upon the final joint co-production, Miss Pickford later wrote, "I was talked into it against my better judgment."

Having made her sound film debut with *Coquette* (she would win an Academy Award for her performance), Mary was expecting a brand new (well almost!) career in the cinema of talking pictures. If her histrionically mature performance in *Coquette* was any indication, her future in movies still had a good way to go. But *The Taming of the Shrew* was no boon to her career status. She considered it one of her worst performances; she had been jumpy and nervous from morning to night during the shooting. "And the strange new Douglas acting oppo-site me was being another Petruchio in real life, but without the humor or the tongue-in-cheek playfulness of the man who broke Katherine's shrewish spirit."

When Doug did show up on the set, he would not know his lines, which had to be chalked on enormous blackboards. He would object when Mary wanted to retake a scene. Mary wrote later, "The making of that film was my finish. My confidence was completely shattered, and I

(1960) and the 1974-1975 *The Three Musketeers* and *The Four Musketeers* with Michael York, Richard Chamberlain, Frank Finlay, Oliver Reed, et al.

*The husband-and-wife team of Richard Burton and Elizabeth Taylor would make their version of *The Taming of the Shrew* (Columbia, 1967), and, of course, there was the MGM musical *Kiss Me, Kate* (1953) based on the stage musical by Cole Porter.

With Mary Pickford in *The Taming of The Shrew* (1929)

was never again at ease before the camera or microphone. All the assurance of *Coquette* was gone."

Photoplay Magazine noted that, although the filmed *The Taming of the Shrew* had little to do with Shakespeare, it was "splendidly acted, picturesquely mounted [and] a lot of fun in addition. Doctor Mack Sennett couldn't have done a better job." The less enthusiastic *New York Times* wrote: "Mr. Fairbanks does not permit any Shakespearean vehicle to stay him from vaulting here and there and demonstrating what he can do on horseback. He is likeable and well-spoken. Miss Pickford is delightful."

Despite its elaborate mounting, the picture suffers from serious miscasting in the supporting roles and is much too short at sixty-five minutes to do justice to the original Elizabethan play. The biggest but accidental laugh occurs in the credits when the following line appears on the screen: "Additional Dialogue by Sam Taylor."

As it emerged, *The Taming of the Shrew* could not have come at a worse time. Doug had relied so much on youth and vitality for his screen image, and he could no longer even kid himself that he wasn't very middle-aged. Facing reality was never one of his fortés, and it distressed him deeply that life could not or would not go on as before. The restrained response to his initial talking film, while not nearly as fatal as sound films would prove to other well-established silent cinema names, gave him pause to wonder just where his screen career could lead him in the years to come. The practical solution would have been to modify his once flamboyant swashbuckling image and turn himself into a talking film light comedian or character leading man. But Doug could not, or would not, commit himself to such a path at this time, at least not with any serious conviction. He would wait and see, as if the passage of a few more months could reverse an inevitable trend.

On September 4, 1929, the Fairbankses seemed to have resolved their domestic differences sufficiently to set out on another trip; this time they did go around the world. In October it was rumored that Mary would return while Doug remained in Europe. However, November fourteenth found them both in Cairo. In December, their stay in Shanghai was shortened to one day because of a threatened boycott of them on the grounds that a Chinese sequence in *The Thief of Bagdad* had been derogatory to the Chinese. The couple arrived back in Los Angeles on January 4, 1930.

In May, Doug surprised Hollywood by going to Europe alone to view the Walker Cup matches. Mary and Doug's togetherness had been so constant that they were always seated next to each other at dinner, whether at home or dining out in society. He had objected if she even danced with another man. This was the first time since their marriage that they had been apart. After his return they issued a joint denial that they had any plans to separate, but the rumors were to persist during the next several years as he was more and more frequently away on extended trips.

Anxious to fill her days and to erase the unpleasant memories of *The Taming of the Shrew*, Mary embarked on a talking version of an old Norma Talmadge silent, *Secrets* (First National, 1924), to be called *Forever Yours*. Marshall Neilan was director and Kenneth MacKenna the leading man. For reasons never satisfactorily explained, she abandoned production midway and burned the negative at a cost of $300,000.

Upon his return from Europe, Doug decided that his next vehicle would be a modern dress feature, his first in almost ten years. Edmund Goulding, who had scripted and directed Gloria Swanson in her first sensationally successful sound film, *The Trespasser* (United Artists, 1929), was selected to try to work a similar miracle for Doug. It was to be a musical and Irving Berlin was engaged to compose an original score. The leading lady was Bebe Daniels, who had been a kind of distaff athletic version of Fairbanks during the 1920s. The year before she had made a triumphant sound film debut in *Rio Rita* (RKO), 1929). For *Reaching for the Moon* (United Artists, 1930), which bore no relation to the silent film except for the title, Bebe became a blonde. The plot was light and frothy, as befits a musical. Unfortunately, by the time the picture was released musicals were temporarily out of fashion

With Bebe Daniels in *Reaching for the Moon* (1931)

and all the musical numbers, save one, "High Up and Low Down," were deleted.

Most of the film's action took place on an ultra-modern trans-Atlantic liner, and a great deal of it concerned the curious effects on the principals when they drank a cocktail known as "Angel's Breath." The on-camera effect on Fairbanks caused him to leap into the air, climb up walls, and do other stunts that demand no mean agility. The *New York Times* noted that the star (at age forty-seven) was just as active as he had been in the early days of pictures, and continued. "Mr. Fairbanks occasionally looks as if he aspired to be the great lover in film comedies, for he is not satisfied with changing his clothes frequently, appearing in outing or lounge suits, a swallow tail suit, a dinner jacket, a dressing gown, but also stripped to the waist. He is quite all right as the comedian, but even when he tells [the heroine] that he never thought of going down on his knees to any other woman but his mother until he met the girl in the case, one is hardly convinced that he means what he says."

For the first time since Doug had been his own producer, a Fairbanks film failed to place in the best-of-the-month list in *Photoplay*. Their critic considered, "If anybody but Doug Fairbanks played in this, you might not like it. But Doug, with the vitality of a kid, leaps merrily through a dizzy hodgepodge of gags good and bad, old and new."

It was a time of indecision on Doug's part, and his remedy was to play and play and play. After entertaining the Duke of Sutherland during December, Fairbanks embarked for the Orient on January 2, 1931, for a big game hunting expedition to Cambodia, Siam, French Indochina, and India. He was accompanied by director Victor Fleming and co-cameraman Chuck Lewis, and during the course of the trip he was entertained by the Emperor of Japan, the King of Siam (who had been a visitor to Pickfair several years earlier), and the Maharajahs of Rajputna and Baroda. The publicized reason for the trip was to shoot location footage for a picture. The *real* reason was to get away from Hollywood where he now felt caged. The plan was to shoot a kind of documentary of the trip and call it *Around the World in 80 Minutes with Douglas Fairbanks*. When Fleming wondered how certain scenes would fit into the narrative, Doug told him that they could worry about that tiny problem when they returned to Hollywood.

During this period Mary had gone to New York, but the January 16, 1931 newspapers reported that she and Doug had spoken together over ship-to-shore radio telephone—he was on the *S.S. Belgenland* near Honolulu, a distance of some 7,400 miles from Manhattan.

The movie star finally arrived in England in late April where Mary joined him in Reading on May 17, after the couple had been apart for four and a half months. Before leaving New York, she confirmed the reports that she had ordered all her motion pictures to be destroyed after her death, because her sole aim was to bring joy to the present generation. (Fortunately, such good friends as Lillian and Buddy Rogers convinced her later to change her mind.) She said that when she retired she hoped to realize four ambitions: to take care of Rancho Zorro (which Doug had bought in 1927 in San Diego County), to take up interior decoration, to study music, and to manufacture cosmetics. She denied reports of an estrangement, saying, "For eleven years, Doug and I have had to deny reports of our divorce. No one can say how long a happy marriage can exist. But at present Doug and I are as happy as anyone ever was." Her latest film, *Kiki* (United Artists, 1931), a remake of Norma Talmadge's 1924 silent version, had not been very successful. She confided to the press that she felt Hollywood had taken a step backward with sound.

Around the World in 80 Minutes with Douglas Fairbanks (United Artists, 1931) had an intelligent narration written by Robert E. Sherwood. Before its release Doug said, "I am now completing a travel picture of my experiences in my recent tour of the world, and I believe it will be far superior in entertainment than any fictional romance I could make. As to the future, I plan to appear only in films recording my travels."

The best brother Robert could say about this venture was, "At least there was film in the camera." In spite of some witty touches within this feature, it still smacked somewhat of a deluxe home movie. Since it had not cost much, it turned a profit, but it was a far cry from Doug's earlier, carefully crafted film productions.

In Hollywood, during the summer of 1931, while the footage to *Around the World* was being assembled, Doug and his son established a really warm relationship for the first time. Since being called "Dad" made him feel too old, Doug was called "Pete" and Douglas, Jr. was called "Jayar." Joan Crawford, Doug. Sr.'s daughter-in-law, called him "Uncle Douglas" and he addressed her as "Billie."

In September it was announced that Doug was contemplating a fifteen-thousand-mile air venture into the wilds of South America and the headwaters of the Amazon for a new travelogue, and that Mary *might* accompany him. Two months later the plans were abruptly changed, and he sailed for Europe, accompanied by brother Robert, director Lewis Milestone, and humorist Robert Benchley. They sailed on November 16, and three weeks later the party was in St. Moritz where Doug undertook his first skiing lessons. On December 16, the plans were again altered as he and his party sailed back to the States in order to spend Christmas in Hollywood. He only just managed it by flying from New York without his luggage. To insure greater comfort, all ten seats on the plane were purchased so that Fairbanks' party would not have to mingle with strangers.

Less than a month after Christmas, it was announced that peripatetic Doug had chartered producer Joseph Schenck's 136-foot yacht, *Invader,* for a cruise to the South Seas to film *Mr. Robinson Crusoe* (United Artists, 1932). Included in the party, which sailed on February 9, was an attractive young Spanish actress, Maria Alba, with two or three unimportant credits behind her, actors William Farnum and Earle Browne, and director Edward Sutherland.

The plot, which featured Miss Alba as "Saturday," concerned one Steve Drexel (Fairbanks) who, while on a cruise to the South Seas with two friends, swims ashore followed by his dog, "Rooney," to win a bet that he can spend two months on the island as the original Robinson Crusoe did. Of course, the original Mr. Crusoe did not have the Fairbanks' prop men. In short order, he is joined by a monkey and a parrot. In a confrontation with a native, which he wins, he acquires the radio tubes which adorn the native's neck and constructs a radio. Shortly after that, he gains the companionship of a pretty native girl (Alba). Drexel constructs a fairly elaborate dwelling, trains a turtle to pump water and the monkey to milk a goat, and has hot and cold running

With Maria Alba in *Mr. Robinson Crusoe* (1932)

water pouring from bamboo faucets. One of his contrivances flings a fishing net into the sea and another is a unique trap for animals.

The oncamera devices were reminiscent of Rube Goldberg at his best, and the whole picture has an ingenuous charm. The viewer willingly believes that one man, unaided, could accomplish so much. The *New York Times* verified: "The film is done in Mr. Fairbanks' best vein. It is artful, jolly and imaginative, and one never thinks while watching the laughable incidents that the lone man on the island was always accompanied by a camera crew."

The feature was shot silent, then dubbed for sound after Doug's return to Hollywood in May. Because it was shot in the silent-film technique, its strength lies in its visual effects. It was yet another indication that Doug, like United Artists' partner Charles Chaplin, was really unwilling to concede that talkies were here to stay.

During the summer of 1932, the Olympic Games were held in Los Angeles, with Mary and especially Doug very much in evidence as ex-officio hosts. The athletes were entertained at Pickfair, and Doug, as the movies' favorite athlete, was in his element. Before the Games were over, Mary had had enough of it all and proceeded by plane to Albuquerque and thence by train to New York, ostensibly to "shop for plays." Late July hardly seemed the most appropriate time to be in New York for that purpose. The press noted that she had been seen publicly with Buddy Rogers on several occasions, including a speed boat ride down the Hudson. However, the only comment Mary would make about Mr. Rogers was, "He's a nice boy."

If Pickford's New York visit was intended to give Fairbanks a dose of his own medicine and make him jealous, it failed. Doug sailed in late August on the S. S. *Chichibu Maru* to hunt long-haired tigers in Manchuria, and ostensibly to make another film. Mary was dutifully on hand, as always, to bid him an affectionate farewell. When he returned to New York in late December, after having gone westward across Asia through Europe, he told newsmen that unsettled conditions in Manchuria had thwarted his plans for the big hunt. Later, his party was forbidden entrance to Tibet to hunt a giant panda, but he had gone through Indochina with his own safari. He was planning a screenplay about China, because he thought it was now the most colorful country in the world, a place where there was always something exciting happening.

While Doug was away on this trip, Mary resolutely turned again to the idea of a sound remake of *Secrets* (United Artists, 1933). Leslie Howard was cast as her leading man and Frank Borzage directed. The film was still shooting when Doug thoughtfully returned home for Christmas, accompanied by Lady Millicent Hawes, Dowager Duchess of Sutherland, who had traveled back on the boat with him from England.

A month later, while Mary was completing *Secrets* and recovering from the grief of her thirty-six-year-old brother Jack's death in Paris, Doug returned to Europe. His destination was St. Moritz. It was the first time that he traveled alone (or almost alone—his valet accompanied him). The customary entourage of friends was left behind. It was rumored that he was planning to enjoy the winter sports with a lady whom he had met in London before Christmas.

In February Mary joined him in Naples, where they presented the same united front to the public that they had a decade earlier. *Secrets* opened during her absence in twenty-five major cities—as fate would have it, on the day of the 1933 Bank Holiday. The notices for her picture were respectable enough, but the public stayed away. While on the trip Mary was faced with the irrefutable evidence that Doug was infatuated with another woman. She sailed home two weeks later, and Doug followed on the next boat. He arrived in time for his fiftieth birthday, but Mary had left for New York the day before without informing him of her departure. Doug flew to Albuquerque to meet Mary's train, then went on to New York where he sailed again for England to attend another golf tournament. He was accompanied this time by Tom Geraghty and Doug, Jr.

When he reached London, Doug issued a statement that he intended to remain abroad indefinitely and refused comments about the state of his marriage. He sent Mary a cable, informing her that he intended to stay abroad, and that she should remain at Pickfair or not as she chose. Mary confided in her old friend, Frances Marion, the scenarist for many of Mary's best silent films, as well as the script for *Secrets.* Ever the pragmatist, Miss Marion, who had been wed four times (thrice divorced), arranged to lunch with Mary the next day at the Vendome. She was accompanied by the redoubtable Louella O. Parsons.

The ardent reader of cinema history is recommended to turn to the pages that deal with this memorable lunch as recorded by Mary (in her book *Sunshine and Shadow*), Miss Marion (in *Off with Their Heads!,* Macmillan, 1972), Louella Parsons (in *The Gay Illiterate,* Garden City Publishing, 1944) and George Eels' admirable synthesis of the conflicting versions (*Hedda and Louella,* G. P. Putnam, 1972). They all agree that Mary did show Parsons the most recent cable and did confirm the persistent rumors that Pickford and Fairbanks were separated. Mary was apparently even more naive than some of her oncamera teenage characters if she thought that such a voracious columnist as Parsons would regard her confidences "with discretion."

The next day, Sunday, July 2, 1933, the news made banner headlines in the Hearst press across the nation: "PICKFORD AND FAIRBANKS SPLIT: PERFECT COUPLE SEPARATE." Pages of copy recounted the details of the marriage, the previous divorces, and the exhaustive accounts of their careers and social successes. All this greeted Mary as she emerged from church that morning. It was the biggest news that had come out of Hollywood in years and can only be equated with the similar headlines and subsequent articles that followed the abdication of Edward VIII, or the resignation of President Nixon.

Meanwhile, in England, father and son[24] formed a bond between themselves that ended only with Doug, Sr.'s death. Impressed by Alexander Korda's *The Private Life of Henry VIII* (1933), which they saw in a rough cut, they contracted Korda to become a producer-owner of United Artists. There was talk that father and son would appear together in something called *Zorro Rides Again* or *Zorro and Son,* but nothing came of it.

While Doug, Jr. began a close personal and professional relationship with Gertrude Lawrence, who was eleven years his senior, and appeared for Korda as mad Grand Duke Peter in *Catherine the Great* (United Artists, 1934), Doug, Sr. was too deeply involved in his infatuation with Lady Ashley[25] to consider any professional activity. She was twenty years younger than he. One of Doug's old friends thought it was her title more than anything else which attracted him. If she had been simply Miss Hawkes, their affair would not have gotten so far.

In February, 1934, Doug was named co-respondent in a divorce suit filed in London by Lord Ashley. Doug called Mary, who was in Boston on a personal appearance tour to ask what her responses would be to Ashley's charges. She assured him she would not escalate the scandal, at least publicly. Lord Ashley's action had backed the movie star into a difficult corner. He admitted privately to intimates that he hoped a reconciliation with Mary could be accomplished, and she seems to have been willing to consider it.

At the nadir of his popularity in America, Doug proceeded to make for Korda in England what would be his last film, *The Private Life of Don Juan* (United Artists, 1934). Despite a sometimes witty script by Frederick Lonsdale and Lajos Biro, elaborate production values, and a strong cast which included Merle Oberon, Binne Barnes, Benita

[24]The marriage of Doug, Jr. and Joan Crawford had been on shaky footing for several years. In 1932 they had gone to England together to attempt to mend the problems, but the trip solved nothing. Joan consulted her father-in-law and told him how hollow the marriage had become. He replied, "Billie, when two people are this unhappy, they shouldn't stay together." The younger Fairbankses were divorced in March, 1933.

[25]Born Sylvia Hawkes c. 1903, she had begun her career as a mannequin (an underwear model, one unkind source says) before becoming a chorus girl in *Midnight Follies Primrose* (1924) and *Tell Me More* (1925). She left the stage when she married Anthony, Lord Ashley, son of the Earl of Shaftesbury. She and Ashley had separated in 1928, and as one of London's reigning beauties, she devoted most of her time to being a leader of cafe society.

Hume, and some excellent character actors, the tongue-in-cheek rendition of the legendary lover did not come off quite as planned. André Sennwald (*New York Times*) reported: "Nor is Douglas Fairbank's performance in the principal part of any vast assistance. The bounding one's current return to the screen has about it a lamentable air of anachronism. For fleeting moments, in a spirited bit of swordplay, in the arrogant way he crosses a floor or mounts a balcony, he is the Fairbanks of the blessed *Zorro* and *The Three Musketeers.* But the microphone is ruthlessly unkind to him. Neither in voice nor theatrical skill is he gifted to read lines. He whom we loved for his reckless swagger and airy movement now finds himself trapped and forced to play the actor. It is a poor fate for one who was once so free, and it is not always pleasant to watch."

While Doug was making this career-concluding film, the much younger Robert Donat was in Hollywood making *The Count of Monte Cristo* (United Artists, 1934), a quite popular feature that would help to inaugurate the new cycle of swashbuckling features which would gain a great momentum at Warner Bros. in the later 1930s with Errol Flynn.

During the shooting of *The Private Life of Don Juan,* Doug rented an historic house, North Mymms Park, where he and Sylvia Ashley shut themselves away. None of Doug's old friends nor his son was ever invited to visit him there, but on weekends the house parties continued with new faces willing to live solely for pleasure.

With Benita Hume, Merle Oberon, Joan Gardner and (seated) Elsa Lanchester in ***The Private Life of Don Juan*** **(1934)**

81

Mary filed for divorce on December 8, 1934, the day before *Don Juan* opened in New York. During the year, both Mary and Doug had turned to Beth, who since 1929 had been happily married to the years-younger musical comedy star Jack Whiting. One day Mary asked Beth, "Can you imagine? My husband running off with another woman!" Beth offered no comment. Doug sent his first wife a two-hundred-word cablegram asking her to intercede for him with Mary, which she did, but to no avail.

Doug himself returned to California to try to persuade Mary not to go through with the divorce suit. On December 29, 1934, he sailed for Europe again, and on January 10, 1935, Mary was awarded an interlocutory decree in a three-minute proceeding.

During the spring of 1935 Doug and Lady Ashley traveled in a chartered yacht from the Virgin Islands to the South Seas and eventually to Shanghai. Lady Ashley was left behind in Shanghai, while Doug sailed to Canada on the *Empress of Canada,* flying from there to Hollywood. The four-month cruise had cost nearly $100,000. *The Private Life of Don Juan* had been a boxoffice failure, like all Doug, Sr.'s talking films which preceded it. In July, 1932, the Los Angeles County Assessor's Office had revealed that Chaplin stood first in the film colony with wealth estimated at $7,687,570; Mary stood second with stocks

With producer Samuel Goldwyn, Mary Pickford, and Charles Chaplin at the Hollywood stockholders' meeting of United Artists, July 1935

and bonds worth $2,316,940; and Doug stood third with assets worth $1,384,690. But Doug's high living was taking its toll on his personal fortune.

In October, 1935, fifty-two-year-old Doug asked Robert Fairbanks to come to England to advise him on the contracts and financing of *Marco Polo,* which he planned to co-produce with Korda. After a study of the contracts and financial arrangements, Robert realized that it was not a good deal for either party. Privately, Korda was deeply relieved to be let off the hook. Doug eventually sold the property to Samuel Goldwyn, who produced it with Gary Cooper. The result, *The Adventures of Marco Polo* (United Artists, 1938), proved to be a costly dud for Goldwyn.

The day after Mary received her final divorce papers, Doug again appeared in Hollywood to beg her, literally on bended knees, to set the divorce aside. The once dashing, confident cavalier proposed, "Let's put ourselves on the shelf. We're no longer important to the world and I don't think anyone really cares about us any more. Why don't we go away together and live in peace, perhaps in Switzerland, or if you like we can build on the rancho [Rancho Zorro] as we've always planned."

However much Mary still loved him—and she did—she was not ready to go into retirement from public life with a man who had caused her so much public anguish during the previous six years. Doug went to New York where he asked Doug, Jr. to meet him. Fairbanks continued to press his suit via long wires which went unanswered. On the night of February 25, 1936, father and son went to see Richard Barthelmess in the opening of his new play, *The Postman Always Rings Twice.* They had an appointment for lunch the next day.

The next morning Doug, Jr. learned from Frank Case, the Algonquin Hotel manager, that he had seen Doug, Sr. off at eight o'clock that morning for England. Doug, Sr. had asked that his son go to the Waldorf and collect any messages that might be there and send them to him by ship's radio. One of the messages was a telegram from Mary indicating a willingness to reconcile and a suggestion that he return to California. A new clerk at the hotel had inadvertently put the telegram in the wrong box, and Doug left without receiving it.

"Jayar" phoned his father on the ship, and even Mary phoned. She explained that she had tried to reach him by telephone all night, but Doug had left the night clerk instructions that he was not to be disturbed. As Letitia Fairbanks writes:

"Was it for the reason I wanted more than anything to hear?" he asked.
"Yes, it was, Douglas," she said.
He remained silent for several seconds.
"It's too late," he said finally. "It's just too late." He had already telephoned Lady Ashley and asked her to marry him.
They were married in Paris on March 7, 1936.

With Douglas Fairbanks, Jr. in Hollywood, February, 1936

For a man who had been so eager to be away from Hollywood before, it seems rather curious that he should have been so eager now to return there with Sylvia. Once in California, they resided in the beach house, while Mary remained at Pickfair. As part of the divorce settlement, Doug received Rancho Zorro. Always impressed by his bride's title, Doug introduced his new wife as "Lady Ashley" to his old friends. Sylvia's warmth and graciousness made a favorable impression, and soon they were in the thick of social activities with Doug looking like a very tired, sick, balding old man.

Doug could not avoid seeing Mary at meetings of United Artists, of which they remained principal stockholders. One corporate meeting occurred in Mary's bedroom when she was ill. Samuel Goldwyn, disagreeing over some company matter, became so excited and angry that he began shaking his fist at Mary. Doug threw him out of the room, shouting, "How dare you talk to my wife like that!"

If Doug could remarry, so could Mary. On June 26, 1937, at the home of Mr. and Mrs. Louis D. Lighton (the screenwriter-producer), Mary wed Buddy Rogers. Hope Lighton had been the person who had brought Buddy around ten years earlier to audition for the part in *My Best Girl.* At the end of that film the onscreen newlyweds had embarked on a cruise for a Honolulu honeymoon. In a case of life imitat-

With the former Lady Sylvia Ashley (Mrs. Fairbanks, Sr.), Norma Shearer, and Irving Thalberg in Los Angeles, June, 1936

With Kay Francis at a New York party, January, 1937

ing art, Mr. and Mrs. Rogers sailed for Honolulu for their real-life honeymoon. It was all rather like a typical film happy ending. On the ship with them were Jeanette MacDonald and Gene Raymond on their own honeymoon. A crowd of some five thousand fans jammed the Honolulu waterfront for the arrival of these romantic couples.

After their marriage, Doug and Sylvia spent most of their time in Hollywood, although there were frequent trips to London where he bought Sylvia a house.

Doug had always been an early riser. He continued his daytime athletic activities, which were generally followed in the evening by some kind of social activity with Sylvia. However, Doug was exhausting himself, burning the candle at both ends. He told brother Robert, 'The greatest luxury in life, for me, would be to get enough sleep." To his accountant he said, "I have a weariness that will never be rested. This life I'm forced to live is killing me."

On April 22, 1939, the semi-retired film star proudly served as best man for his son's wedding to the former Mary Lee Epling Hartford. Doug ruminated on the problems of the past: "It was something of a problem for a while. There's no doubt my son was a little annoyed at the thought professionally of merely being my son. He wanted to be somebody on his own, and to that end he carefully avoided doing the kind of pictures I had done. Now he's all right, he's arrived, he's an actor in his own right. I like his work. I was just thinking how funny it would be if one day I got to be known as Douglas Fairbanks, Jr.'s father—or no, maybe that wouldn't be funny."

When World War II began, Doug and Sylvia were in London. He sent Sylvia and her sister and her two children back to California while he stayed behind. Eventually, almost reluctantly, he got a ticket on the *Clipper* through a cable to Jock Whitney, and returned.

He seemed pleased to learn that Mary Lee, wed to Doug, Jr., was expecting a child. He would now be a grandfather. On December 9, Jayar's birthday, a party was given but the next day Doug was ill. He reluctantly consented to have a doctor examine him, at which point it became clear that he had suffered a coronary thrombosis. Now he was faced with at least six months of semi-invalidism. On December 11, 1939, he saw Robert and told him that if anything happened, Robert was to convey to Mary the message, "by the clock." Doug confessed to not being afraid of death but, instead, of being an invalid chained to a bed.

On the night December 11, Sylvia was away at a Red Cross meeting. A few doors away, Norma Shearer was entertaining with a midnight supper to which the Fairbankses had been invited. Doug was alone in the house except for his bull mastiff, Polo, and a male nurse who took up his station in the hall outside.

Shortly after midnight Doug asked the male nurse, "Please open the

With Elsa Maxwell in San Francisco, February, 1939

window and let me hear the sea." The nurse obliged, asking his patient how he felt. Doug replied with the D'Artagnan grin, "I've never felt better," and fell quickly asleep. It was 12:45 A.M. on the morning of December 12, 1939.[26] At fifty-six, the man who had seemed indestructible on screen and off was dead.

Norma Shearer was notified. She removed their placecards from the table and said nothing further. Her guests, most of whom old friends of Doug, learned the news the following day in the morning paper.

Mary was awakened in Chicago at 4 A.M. She was with Buddy, who had an engagement with his band at the Drake Hotel. They spent the balance of the early morning talking about everything but Douglas. Only the next day, en route to New York alone, did she break down. Mary issued a statement saying that obligations would prevent her from attending the funeral. "I am sure it will prove a consolation to us all to recall the joy and the glorious spirit of adventure he gave to the world.[27] He has passed from our mortal life quickly and spontaneously as he did everything in life, but it is impossible to believe that that vibrant and gay spirit could ever perish."

Mrs. Basil Blech (sister of Lady Ashley), Mrs. Fairbanks, Sr., and Douglas Fairbanks, Jr. at funeral rites for Douglas Fairbanks, Sr. at Glendale, Calif., December 16, 1939

[26]Ironically, Doug died on Owen Moore's birthday. Moore had died six months to the day earlier, on June 12th.

[27]Scenes from *Wild and Woolly* would be included in *Days of Thrills and Laughter* (Twentieth Century-Fox, 1961), a compilation feature of excerpts from silent film comedies and thrillers.

Under the terms of his will, half of Doug's fortune, not to exceed one million dollars in value, was left to Sylvia. Doug, Jr was to receive twelve-fortieths, not to exceed six hundred thousand dollars, brother Robert two-fortieths, not to exceed a hundred thousand dollars, and Norris Wilcox, his half-brother, one-fortieth, not to exceed fifty thousand dollars. His four nieces, the daughters of John and Robert, were each left the same amount in trust, and another fortieth was left for distribution by his son to various friends and charities in accordance with his instructions.

At the twelfth annual Academy Award ceremonies held in early 1940, Douglas Fairbanks, Sr., the first president of the Academy of Motion Pictures Arts and Sciences, was posthumously given a commemorative award. It was in recognition of his unique and outstanding contribution to the international development of the motion picture.

After Doug's death, Sylvia married Lord Stanley, but after their divorce she returned to Hollywood as Lady Ashley, and in 1949 married Clark Gable, who had been the "King" of Hollywood during the 1930s and 1940s, just as Doug had been during the previous decade and a half. Their marriage was short-lived (they divorced in 1952), and she disappeared from the Hollywood scene as abruptly as she had arrived.

Doug, Jr. has had an active career on stage and screen and television for a half-century. Although he has an attractive personality and possibly is a better actor than his father ever was, his work lacks the charisma of Douglas Fairbanks, Sr. in his prime. "Jayar" has been awarded the CBE (Companion of the British Empire) by Great Britain for his wartime diplomatic service. His social success on the international scene is impeccable.

Mary Pickford still lives at Pickfair, where she came as a bride some fifty-four years ago. Today, she is a total recluse. Although she has been married to Buddy Rogers since 1937, and he has made considerable efforts, especially during recent years, to insure that Mary's immense contributions to the screen become known to a latter-day audience, the results have not been completely successful.

Nevertheless, in the twenties, Hollywood was Camelot. Douglas Fairbanks and Mary Pickford remain enshrined in many people's memories and fixed in that time and place, as the King and Queen of that legendary city.

Feature Film Appearances

THE LAMB (Triangle-Fine Arts, 1915), five reels.
Producer-supervisor, D. W. Griffith; director, William Christy Cabanne; based on the story *The Man and the Test* by D. W. Griffith (Granville Warwick); screenplay, Cabanne; camera supervisor, G. W. Bitzer; camera, William E. Fildew.

Douglas Fairbanks, Sr. (Gerald the Lamb); Seena Owen (Mary); Lillian Langdon (Her Mother); Monroe Salisbury (Her Cousin); Kate Toncray (The Lamb's Mother); Alfred Paget (Bill Cactus); William E. Lowery and Eagle Eye (Yaqui Indian Chiefs); Julia Faye (Woman), Charles Stevens (Lieutenant).

DOUBLE TROUBLE (Triangle-Fine Arts, 1915), five reels.
Producer-supervisor, D. W. Griffith; director, William Christy Cabanne; based on the novel by Herbert Quick; screenplay, Griffith; adaptor, Cabanne; camera, William E. Fildew.

Douglas Fairbanks, Sr. (Mr. Amidon/Mr. Brassfield); Margery Wilson (His Fiancée); Tom Kennedy (Judge Blodgett); and Richard Cummings, Olga Grey, Gladys Brockwell, Monroe Salisbury, William E. Lowery, Kate Toncray, Lillian Langdon.

HIS PICTURE IN THE PAPER (Triangle-Fine Arts, 1916), five reels.
Producer-supervisor, D. W. Griffith; director, John Emerson; screenplay, John Emerson, Anita Loos.

Douglas Fairbanks, Sr. (Peter Prindle); Clarence Handysides (Proteus Prindle); Rene Boucicault (Pansy Prindle); Jean Temple (Pearl Prindle); Charles Bulter (Cassius Cadwalader); Homer Hunt (Melville); Loretta Blake (Christine Cadwalader); Helena Rupport (Olga).

THE HABIT OF HAPPINESS (Triangle-Fine Arts, 1916), five reels.
Producer-supervisor, D. W. Griffith; director, Allan Dwan; based on a story by Griffith; screenplay, Dwan, Shannon Fife.

Douglas Fairbanks, Sr. (Sunny Wiggins); George Fawcett (Jonathan Pepper); Dorothy West (Elsie Pepper); George Backus (Mr. Wiggins); Macey Harlan (Foster); Grace Rankin (Clarice Wiggins); William Jefferson (Jones); Adolphe Menjou (Bit).

THE GOOD-BAD MAN (Triangle-Fine Arts, 1916), five reels.
Producer-supervisor, D. W. Griffith; director, Allan Dwan; story-screenplay, Douglas Fairbanks, Sr.; camera, Victor Fleming.

Douglas Fairbanks, Sr. (Passin' Through); Sam De Grasse (Bud Frazer/The Wolf); Pomeroy Cannon (Bob Evans the Marshal); Joseph Singleton (The Weazel); Bessie Love (Amy); Mary Alden (Jane Stuart); George Beranger (Thomas Stuart); Fred Burns (The Sheriff).

REGGIE MIXES IN (Triangle-Fine Arts, 1916), five reels.
Producer-supervisor D. W. Griffith; director, William Christy Cabanne; screenplay, Roy Somerville; camera, William E. Fildew.

Douglas Fairbanks, Sr. (Reginald Morton); Joseph Singleton (His Valet); Bessie Love (Agnes Fleming); William E. Lowery (Tony Bernard the Gangster); Wilbur Higby (The Cafe Proprietor); Frank Bennett (His Assistant); A. D. Sears (Admirer of Agnes).

MANHATTAN MADNESS (Triangle-Fine Arts, 1916), five reels.
Producer, S. A. Lynch Enterprises; supervisor, D. W. Griffith; director, Allan Dwan; story, E. V. Durling; screenplay, Charles T. Dazey.

Douglas Fairbanks, Sr. (Steve O'Dare); Jewel Carmen (The Girl); Ruth Darling (The Maid); Eugene Ormonde (Count Marinoff); Macey Harlan (The Villain); George Beranger (The Butler); Warner P. Richmond (Jack Osborne); John Richmond (Cupid Russell); Albert MacQuarrie, Adolphe Menjou, and Norman Kerry (Bits).

FLIRTING WITH FATE (Triangle-Fine Arts, 1916), five reels.
Producer-supervisor, D. W. Griffith; director, William Christy Cabanne; story, Robert M. Baker; screenplay, Cabanne; camera, William E. Fildew.

Douglas Fairbanks, Sr. (Augy Ainsworth); Howard Gaye (Roland Dabney); Jewel Carmen (Gladys Kingsley); William E. Lawrence (Augy's Friend); George Beranger (Automatic Joe); Dorothy Haydel (Phyllis); Lillian Langdon (Mrs. Kingsley); Wilbur Higby (Landlord); J. P. McCarty (Detective); Lillian Gish (Bridesmaid).

THE MYSTERY OF THE LEAPING FISH (Triangle-Fine Arts, 1916), two reels.
Producer-supervisor, D. W. Griffith; director, John Emerson; story-screenplay, Granville Warwick (Griffith), Tod Browning.

Douglas Fairbanks, Sr. (Coke Ennyday); Bessie Love (The Little Fish Blower); A. D. Sears (Gent Rolling in Wealth); Alma Rubens (His Female Accomplice); Charlie Stevens, George Hall (Japanese Accomplices). Tom Wilson (Chief of Police I. M. Keene).

INTOLERANCE (Wark Distributing, 1916), 210 min.
Director-screenplay, D. W. Griffith; assistant directors, Erich von Stroheim, W. S. Van Dyke II, Tod Browning, George Seigmann, Joseph Henabery, Elmer Clifton, Edward Dillon; music arrangers, Joseph Carl Breil, Griffith; camera, G. W. Bitzer, Karl Brown.

Lillian Gish (The Woman Who Rocks the Cradle).

The Modern Story:
Mae Marsh (The Girl); Fred Turner (Her Father); Robert Harron (The Boy); Sam de Grasse (Jenkins); Vera Lewis (Mary T. Jenkins); Mary Alden, Pearl Elmore, Lucille Brown, Luray Huntley, and Mrs. Arthur Mackley (Uplifters); Tom Wilson (The Policeman); Walter Long (Musketeer of the Slums); Lloyd Ingraham (The Judge); Ralph Lewis (The Governor); Monte Blue (Striker); Max Davidson (Friendly Neighbor); Reverend A. W. McClure (Father Farley); Marguerite Marsh (Debutante); Tod Browning (Owner of Car); Edward Dillon (Chief Detective); Clyde Hopkins (Jenkins' Secretary); William Brown (The Warden); Alberta Lee (Wife of the Neighbor).

91

The Judean Story:
Howard Gaye (The Nazarene); Lillian Langdon (Mary the Mother); Olga Grey (Mary Magdalene); Erich von Stroheim and Gunther von Ritzau (Pharisees); Bessie Love (Bride of Cana); George Walsh (Bridegroom).

Medieval French Story:
Margery Wilson (Brown Eyes); Eugene Pallette (Prosper Latour); Spottiswoode Aitken (Her Father); Ruth Handforth (Her Mother); Frank Bennett (King Charles IX); A. D. Sears (The Mercenary); Maxfield Stanley (Duc d'Anjou); Josephine Crowell (Catherine de Medici); Constance Talmadge (Marguerite de Valois); W. E. Lawrence (Henry of Navarre); Joseph Henabery (Admiral Coligny); Douglas Fairbanks, Sr. (Man on White Horse—Huguenot).

Babylonian Story:
Constance Talmadge (The Mountain Girl); Elmer Clifton (The Rhapsode); Alfred Paget (Belshazzar); Seena Owen (Princess Beloved); Carl Stockdale (King Nabonidas); Tully Marshall (High Priest of Bel); George Seigmann (Cyrus the Persian); Elmo Lincoln (The Mighty Man of Valor); George Fawcett (Judge); Kate Bruce (Old Woman); Loyola O'Connor (Slave); James Curley (Charioteer); Howard Scott (Babylonian Dandy); Alma Rubens, Ruth Darling, Margaret Mooney (Girls of the Marriage Market); Mildred Harris, Pauline Starke, and Winifred Westover (Favorites of the Harem); Eve Southern, Carmel Myers, Jewel Carmen, Colleen Moore, Natalie Talmadge, Carol Dempster, Ethel Terry, Daisy Robinson, Anna Mae Walthall, and The Denishawn Dancers (Entertainers at Belshazzar's Feast); William Dark Cloud (Ethiopian Chieftain); Charles Eagle Eye (Barbarian Chieftain).

THE HALF-BREED (Triangle-Fine Arts, 1916), five reels.
    Producer-supervisor, D. W. Griffith; director, Allan Dwan; based on the story *In the Carquinez Woods* by Bret Harte; screenplay, Anita Loos.
Douglas Fairbanks, Sr. (Lo Dorman); Alma Rubens (Teresa); Sam De Grasse (Sheriff Dunn); Tom Wilson (Curson); Frank Brownles (Winslow Wynn); George Beranger (Jack Brace); Jewel Carmen (Nellie).

AMERICAN ARISTOCRACY (Triangle-Fine Arts, 1916), five reels.
    Producer-supervisor, D. W. Griffith; director, Lloyd Ingraham; story-screenplay, Anita Loos.

    Douglas Fairbanks, Sr. (Cassius Lee); Charles de Lima (Leander Hicks); Jewel Carmen (Jewell Hicks); Albert Parker (Percy Horton); Arthur Ortego (Delgado).

THE MATRIMANIAC (Triangle-Fine Arts, 1916), five reels.
    Producer-supervisor, D. W. Griffith; director, Paul Powell; story-screenplay, Octavus Roy Cohen and J. C. Giesy.

    Douglas Fairbanks, Sr. (Jimmy Conroy); Constance Talmadge (Marna Lewis); Wilbur Higby (Theodore Lewis); Clyde Hopkins (G. Walter Henderson); Fred Warren (Rev. Tobias Tubbs); Winifred Westover (Maid).

THE AMERICANO (Triangle-Fine Arts, 1916), five reels.
    Producer-supervisor, D. W. Griffith; director, John Emerson; based on the story *The Dictator* by Richard Harding Davis; screenplay, Anita Loos and Emerson; camera, Victor Fleming.

Douglas Fairbanks, Sr. (Blaze Derringer—The Americano); Alma Rubens (Juana de Castalar); Lillian Langdon (Señora de Castille); Tote Du Crow (Alberto de Castille); Carl Stockdale (Salsa Espada); Spottiswoode Aitken (Presidente de Castalar); Charles Stevens (Colonel Gargaras); Tom Wilson (Hartod Armitage White); Mildred Harris (Stenographer).

IN AGAIN-OUT AGAIN (Fairbanks-Artcraft-Par 1917), five reels.
Producer, Douglas Fairbanks, Sr.; director, John Emerson; Assistant director-art director, Erich von Stroheim; story-screenplay, Anita Loos; camera, Victor Fleming.

Douglas Fairbanks, Sr. (Teddy Rutherford); Arline Pretty (Janie Dubb); Walter Walker (Sheriff Dubb); Arnold Lucy (Amos Jennings); Helen Greene (Pacifica Jennings); Homer Hunt (Henry Pinchit); Albert Parker (Jerry); Bull Montana (Quenton Auburn, the Burglar); Ada Gilman (His Mother); Spike Robinson (The Trustee); Betty Tyrel (The Nurse); Erich von Stroheim (Officer); Frank Lalor (Pinkie, the Duggist).

WILD AND WOOLLY (Fairbanks-Artcraft-Paramount, 1917), five reels.
Producer, Douglas Fairbanks, Sr.; director, John Emerson; story, Horace B. Carpenter; screenplay, Anita Loos; camera, Victor Fleming.

Douglas Fairbanks, Sr. (Jeff Hillington); Walter Bytell (Collis J. Hillington); Joseph Singleton (Judson, The Butler); Eileen Percy (Nell Larabee); Calvert Carter (Tom Larabee, Hotel Keeper); Forest Seabury (Banker); Charles Stevens (Pedro); Sam De Grasse (Steve Shelby, the Indian Agent); Tom Wilson (Casey, Engineer); J. W. Jones (Lawyer); Bull Montana (Bartender); Monte Blue ('A Badman').

DOWN TO EARTH (Fairbanks-Artcraft-Paramount, 1917), five reels.
Producer, Douglas Fairbanks, Sr.; director, John Emerson; story, Fairbanks; screenplay, Anita Loos; camera, Victor Fleming.

Douglas Fairbanks, Sr. (Billy Gaynor); Eileen Percy (Ethel Forsythe); Gustav von Sefferytitz (Dr. Jollyem); Charles P. McHugh (Dr. Samm); Charles Gerrard (Charles Riddles—Ethel's Lover); William H. Keith (Mr. Carter); Ruth Allen (Mrs. Fuller Jermes); Fred Goodwins (Jordan Jinny); Herbert Standing (Mr. S. D. Dyspeptic); Bull Montana (Wild Man); Florence Mayon (Mrs. Phattison Oiles); David Porter (Mr. Coffin).

THE MAN FROM PAINTED POST (Fairbanks-Artcraft-Paramount, 1917), five reels.
Producer, Douglas Fairbanks, Sr.; director, Joseph Henabery; based on the story *Silver Slippers* by Jackson Gregory; screenplay, Fairbanks; camera, Victor Fleming.

Douglas Fairbanks, Sr. (Fancy Jim Sherwood); Eileen Percy (Jane Forbes the School Teacher); Frank Clampeau (Bill Hecht); Herbert Standing (Warren Bronson); William E. Lowery (Charles Ross); Rhea Haines (Wah-Na Madden); Charles Stevens (Toby Lopez); Monte Blue ("Slim" Carter).

REACHING FOR THE MOON (Fairbanks-Artcraft-Paramount, 1917), five reels.

Producer, Douglas Fairbanks, Sr.; director, John Emerson; story-screenplay, Anita Loos and Emerson; camera, Victor Fleming.

Douglas Fairbanks, Sr. (Alexis Caesar Napoleon Brown); Eileen Percy (Elsie Merrill); Frank Clampeau (Black Boris); Richard Cummings (Old Bingham the Boss); Eugene Ormonde (Sergius Badinoff the Prime Minster of Vulgaria); Millard Webb (Mr. Mann); Charles Stevens (Boris' Lieutenant); Erich von Stroheim (Prince Badinoff's Aide).

A MODERN MUSKETEER (Fairbanks-Artcraft-Paramount, 1917), five reels.

Producer, Douglas Fairbanks, Sr.; director, Allan Dwan; based on the story *D'Artagnan of Kansas* by E. R. Lyle, Jr.; screenplay, Dawn; camera, Victor Fleming.

Douglas Fairbanks, Sr. (Ned Thacker); Marjorie Daw (Dorothy Moran); Katherine Kirkham (Mrs. Moran); Frank Campeau (Navajo); Eugene Ormonde (Raymond Vandeteer); Tully Marshall (Philip Marden); ZaSu Pitts (Bit).

HEADIN' SOUTH (Fairbanks-Artcraft-Paramount, 1918), five reels.

Producer, Douglas Fairbanks, Sr.; supervisor, Allan Dwan; director, Arthur Rosson; story-screenplay, Dwan; camera, Hugh C. McClung, Harry Thorpe.

Douglas Fairbanks, Sr. (Headin' South); Frank Campeau (Spanish Joe); James Mason (His Aide); Katherine MacDonald (The Girl); and: Hoot Gibson, Art Acord, Edward Burns, Tommy Grimes and Johnny Judd.

MR. FIX-IT (Fairbanks-Artcraft-Paramount, 1918), five reels.

Producer, Douglas Fairbanks, Sr.; director, Allan Dwan; story, Ernest Butterworth; screenplay, Dwan; camera, Frank C. McClung.

Douglas Fairbanks, Sr. (Dick Remington); Wanda Hawley (Mary McCullough); Marjorie Daw (Marjorie Threadwell); Katherine MacDonald (Georgiana Burroughs); Frank Campeau (Uncle Harry Burroughs); Leslie Stuart (Reginald Burroughs); Ida Waterman (Aunt Agatha Burroughs); Alice Smith (Aunt Priscilla Burroughs); Margaret Landis (Olive Van Tassell); Fred Goodwin (Gideon Van Tassell); and: Mrs. H. R. Hancock and Mr. Russell.

SAY! YOUNG FELLOW (Fairbanks-Artcraft-Paramount, 1918), five reels.

Producer, Douglas Fairbanks, Sr.; director-story-screenplay, Joseph Henabery; camera, Hugh C. McClung.

Douglas Fairbanks, Sr. (The Reporter); Marjorie Daw (The Girl); Frank Campeau (The Villain); Edythe Chapman and James Neill (The Old Folks).

BOUND IN MOROCCO (Fairbanks-Artcraft-Paramount, 1918), five reels.

Producer, Douglas Fairbanks, Sr.; director-story-screenplay, Allan Dwan; camera, Hugh C. McClung.

Douglas Fairbanks, Sr. (George Travelwell); Pauline Curley (Ysail); Tully Marshall (Ali Pah Shush); Edythe Chapman (Ysail's Mother); Frank Campeau (Basha El Harib); Jay Dwiggins (Kaid Mahedi El Menebhi); Fred Burns (Bandit Chief); and: Marjorie Daw.

HE COMES UP SMILING (Fairbanks-Artcraft-Paramount, 1918), five reels.
Producer, Douglas Fairbanks, Sr.; director, Allan Dwan; based on the novel by Charles Sherman and the play by Byron Quigley, Emil Mytray; screenplay, Frances Marion; camera, Hugh C. McClung.

Douglas Fairbanks, Sr. (Jerry Martin the "Watermelon"); Marjorie Daw (Betty); Herbert Standing (Mike, a Hobo); Bull Montana (Baron Bean, a Tramp); Albert MacQuarrie (Batchelor, a Stock Broker); Frank Campeau (John Bartlett—Betty's Father); Jay Dwiggins (General); Kathleen Kirkham (Louise).

ARIZONA (Fairbanks-Artcraft-Paramount, 1918), five reels.
Producer-director, Douglas Fairbanks, Sr.; based on the play by Augustus Thomas; screenplay, Fairbanks; camera, Hugh C. McClung, Hugh Carlyle, Glen MacWilliams.

Douglas Fairbanks, Sr. (Lieutenant Denton); Theodore Roberts (Canby); Kate Price (Mrs. Canby); Frederick Burton (Colonel Benham); Frank Campeau (Keller); Kathleen Kirkham (Estralita); Marjorie Daw (Benita); Marguerite de La Motte (Lena); Raymond Hatton (Thomas); Robert Boulder (Doctor); Albert MacQuarrie (Lieutenant Hatton); Harry Northup (Captain Hodgeman).

THE KNICKERBOCKER BUCKAROO (Fairbanks-Artcraft-Paramount, 1919), five reels.
Producer, Douglas Fairbanks, Sr.; director, Albert Parker; story-screenplay, Fairbanks; camera, Hugh C. McClung, Glenn MacWilliams.

Douglas Fairbanks, Sr. (Teddy Drake); Marjorie Daw (Mercedes); William A. Wellman (Her Brother, Henry); Frank Campeau (The Crooked Sheriff); Edythe Chapman (Mercedes' Mother); Albert MacQuarrie (Manual Lopez, the Bandit); Ted Reed (New York Clubman).

HIS MAJESTY, THE AMERICAN (United Artists, 1919), eight reels.
Producer, Douglas Fairbanks, Sr.; director, Joseph Henabery; story-screenplay, Henabery, Elton Banks (Fairbanks); camera, Victor Fleming.

Douglas Fairbanks, Sr. (William Brooks); Lillian Langdon (Princess Marguerite); Marjorie Daw (Felice, the Countess of Montenac); Frank Campeau (Grand Duke Sarzeau); Boris Karloff (The Spy); Sam Sothern (King Phillipe IV); Jay Dwiggins (Emile Meitz).

WHEN THE CLOUDS ROLL BY (United Artists, 1919), six reels.
Producer, Douglas Fairbanks, Sr., directors, Victor Fleming and Ted Reed; original story and screenplay, Fairbanks, Lewis Weadon, and Tom Geraghty; camera, Harry Thorpe, William C. McGann; art director, Edward Langley.

Douglas Fairbanks, Sr. ([Sense of Humor] Daniel Boone Brown); Kathleen Clifford (Lucette Bancroft); Ralph Lewis (Curtis Brown); Frank Campeau (Mark Drake); Daisy Robinson (Bobby De Vere); Albert MacQuarrie (Hobson); Herbert Grimwood (Dr. Ulrich Metz); Bull Montana (The Nightmare); Babe London (Switchboard Operator); Victor Fleming, Tom J. Geraghty, Harry Thorpe, William McGann (Themselves).

THE MOLLYCODDLE (United Artists, 1920), six reels.
Producer, Douglas Fairbanks, Sr.; director, Victor Fleming; story, Harold McGrath; screenplay, Fairbanks, Tom Geraghty; camera, William C. McGann.

Douglas Fairbanks, Sr. (Richard Marshall); Wallace Beery (Henry Von Holkar); Ruth Renick (Virginia Hale); Charles Stevens (Yellow Horse—a Bad Indian); Betty Boulton (Mollie Warren); George Stewart (Ole Olsen); Albert MacQuarrie (Driver of the Desert Yacht); Paul Burns (Samuel Levinski); Morris Hughes (Patrick O'Flannigan); Adele Farrington (Mrs. Warren); Lewis Hippe (First Mate).

THE MARK OF ZORRO (United Artists, 1920), seven reels.
Producer, Douglas Fairbanks, Sr.; director, Fred Niblo; based on the story *The Curse of Capistrano* by Johnston McCulley; screenplay, Elton Thomas (Fairbanks); camera, William C. McGann, Harry Thorpe.

Douglas Fairbanks, Sr. (Zorro/Don Diego Vega); Marguerite de La Motte (Lolita); Robert McKim (Captain Juan Ramon); Noah Beery (Sergeant Pedro); Charles H. Mailes (Don Carlos Pulido); Claire McDowell (Donna Catalina); George Periolat (Governor Alvarado); Walt Whitman (Fra Felipe); Sidney de Grey (Don Alejandro Pulido); Tote du Crow (Bernardo).

THE NUT (United Artists, 1921), six reels.
Producer, Douglas Fairbanks, Sr.; director, Theodore Reed; story, Kenneth Davenport; screenplay, William Parker and Lotta Woods; camera, William McGann, Harry Thorpe.

Douglas Fairbanks, Sr. (Charlie Jackson); Marguerite de La Motte (Estrell Wynn); William Lowery (Philip Feeney); Gerald Pring (Gentleman George); Morris Hughes (Pernelius Vanderbrook, Jr.); Barbara La Marr (Claudine Dupree).

THE THREE MUSKETEERS (United Artists, 1921), 11,700 feet.
Presenter, Douglas Fairbanks, Sr.; director, Fred Niblo; based on the novel *Les Trois Mousquetaires* by Alexandre Dumas, pere: adaptor, Edward Knoblock; screenplay editor, Lotta Woods; art director, Edward M. Langley; technical director, Frank England; music, Louis F. Gottschalk; assistant director, Doran Cox; costumes, Paul Burns; camera, Arthur Edeson; editor, Nellie Mason.

Douglas Fairbanks, Sr. (D'Artagnan); Leon Barry (Athos); George Siegmann (Porthos); Eugene Pallette (Aramis); Boyd Irwin (de Rochefort); Thomas

Holding (George Villiers, Duke of Buckingham); Sidney Franklin (Bonacieux); Charles Stevens (Planchet, D'Artagnan's Lackey); Nigel de Brulier (Cardinal Richelieu); Willis Robards (Captain de Treville); Lon Poff (Father Joseph); Mary MacLaren (Queen Anne of Austria); Marguerite de La Motte (Constance Bonacieux); Barbara La Marr (Milady de Winter); Walt Whitman (D'Artagnan's Father); Adolphe Menjou (Louis XIII, King of France); Charles Belcher (Bernajoux); Douglas Fairbanks, Jr. (Boy).

ROBIN HOOD (United Artists, 1922), 10,680 feet.
Presenter, Douglas Fairbanks, Sr.; director, Allan Dwan, story, Elton Thomas; screenplay editor, Lotta Woods; supervising art director, Wilfred Buckland; art directors, Irvin J. Martin and Edward M. Langley; technicall director, Robert Fairbanks; research director, Arthur Woods; literary consultant, Edward Knoblock; costumes, Mitchell Leisen; trick camera, Paul Eagler; camera, Arthur Edeson.

Douglas Fairbanks, Sr. (Robert, The Earl of Huntingdon/Robin Hood); Wallace Beery (Richard the Lion-Hearted); Sam De Grasse (Prince John); Enid Bennett (Lady Marian Fitzwalter); Paul Dickey (Sir Guy of Gisbourne); William Lowery (The High Sheriff of Nottingham); Roy Coulson (The King's Jester); Billie Bennett (Lady Marian's Serving Woman); Merrill McCormick, Wilson Benge (Prince John's Henchmen); Willard Louis (Friar Tuck); Alan Hale (Little John); Maine Geary (Will SCarlett); Lloyd Talman (Allan-a-Dale).

THE THIEF OF BAGDAD (United Artists, 1924) 12,933 feet
Presenter, Douglas Fairbanks, Sr.; director, Raoul Walsh; story, Elton Thomas; screenplay editor, Lotta Woods; art director, William Cameron Menzies; consulting art director, Irvin J. Martin; technical director, Robert Fairbanks; assistant director, James T. O'Donohoe; music, Mortimer Wilson; costumes, Mitchell Leisen; consultant, Edward Knoblock; research director, Arthur Woods; director of mechanical effects, Hampton Del Ruth; associate artists, Anton Grot, Paul Youngblood, H. R. Hopps, Harold Grieve, Park French, William Utwich, and Edward M. Langley; camera, Arthur Edeson; assistant camera, P. H. Whitman and Kenneth MacLean; editor, William Nolan.

Douglas Fairbanks, Sr. (The Thief of Bagdad); Snitz Edwards (His Evil Associate); Charles Belcher (The Holy Man); Julanne Johnston (The Princess); Anna May Wong (The Mongol Slave); Winter-Blossom (The Slave of the Lute); Etta Lee (The Slave of the Sand Board); Brandon Hurst (The Caliph); Tote du Crow (The Soothsayer); Sojin (The Mongol Prince); K. Nambu (His Counselor); Sadakichi Hartmann (His Court Magician); Noble Johnson (The Indian Prince); Mathilde Comont (The Persian Prince); Charles Stevens (His Awaker); Sam Baker (The Sworder); Jess Weldon, Scott Mattraw and Charles Sylvester (Eunuchs).

DON Q, SON OF ZORRO (United Artists, 1925), 10, 264 feet.
Presenter, Douglas Fairbanks, Sr.; director, Donald Crisp; based on the novel *Don Q's Love Story* by Hesketh Prichard, Kate Prichard screenplay, Jack Cunningham; screenplay editor, Lotta Woods; supervising art director, Ed-

ward M. Langley; assistant art directors, Frances Cugat, Anton Grot, and Harold Miles; consulting artist, Harry Oliver; research director, Arthur Woods; technical effects, Ned Mann; music, Mortimer Wilson; assistant director, Frank Richardson; wardrobe, Paul Burns; lighting effects, William S. Johnson; camera, Henry Sharp; additional camera, E. J. Vallejo; editor, William Nolan.

Douglas Fairbanks, Sr. (Don Cesar de Vega/Zorro); Mary Astor (Dolores de Muro); Jack McDonald (General de Muro); Donald Crisp (Don Sebastian); Stella De Lanti (The Queen); Warner Oland (The Archduke); Jean Hersholt (Don Fabrique); Albert MacQuarrie (Colonel Matsado); Lottie Pickford Forrest (Lola); Charles Stevens (Robledo); Tote du Crow (Bernado); Martha Franklin (The Duenna); Juliette Belanger (Dancer); Roy Coulson (Her Admirer); Enrique Acosta (Ramon).

THE BLACK PIRATE (United Artists, 1926), C- 8,490 feet.
Presenter, Douglas Fairbanks, Sr.; director, Albert Parker; story, Elton Thomas; adaptor, Jack Cunningham; screenplay editor, Lotta Woods; art director, Carl Oscar Borg; associate artists, Edward M. Langley and Jack Holden; music, Mortimer Wilson; Marine technical advisor, P. H. L. Wilson; research director, Arthur Woods; consultants, Dwight Franklin and Robert Nichols; Technicolor consultants, Arthur Ball and George Cave; camera, Henry Sharp; editor, Willian Nolan.

Douglas Fairbanks, Sr. [The Black Pirate (Michel) Duke of Arnaldo]; Billie Dove (The Princess); Anders Randolf (Pirate Leader); Donald Crisp (Scotty McTavish); Tempe Pigott (Duenna); Sam De Grasse (Lieutenant); Charles Stevens (Powder Man); Charles Belcher (Chief Passenger); and: Fred Becker, John Wallace, E. J. Ratcliffe (Bits) Barry Norton (Youth).

POTSELUI MARY PICKFORD (THE KISS OF MARY PICKFORD) (Mezhrabpom-Rus & Sovkino, 1927) 62½ min.
Director, Sergei Komarov; screenplay, Komarov and Vadim Shershenevich; decors, Sergei Kozlovsky and D. Kolupayev, from designs by Ju. A. Merkulov; camera, Ge. Alekseyev.

With: Igor Ilinsky, Anna Sudakevich, M. Rosenshtein, N. Sizova, Ya. Lents, A. Glinsky V. Malinovskaya, N. Rogozhin, Abram Room, and: Douglas Fairbanks, Sr., Mary Pickford (Themselves).

THE GAUCHO (United Artists, 1928), 9,358 feet.*
Producer, Douglas Fairbanks, Sr.; director, F. Richard Jones; story, Elton Thomas; screenplay, Lotta Woods; supervising art director, Carl Oscar Borg; associate artists, Harry Oliver, Jack Holden, Frances Cugat, Edward M. Langley, and Mario Larrinaga; assistant directors, Lewis R. Foster and William J. Cowen; costumes, Paul Burns; consultants, Wallace Smith and Eugene P. Lyle, Jr.; research director, Arthur Woods; main titles, Joseph B. Harris; camera, Antonio Gaudio; associate camera, Abe Scholtz; editor, William Nolan.

---

*Color sequences

Douglas Fairbanks, Sr. (The Gaucho); Lupe Velez (The Mountain Girl); Geraine Greear (Girl of the Shrine); Eve Southern (Girl of the Shrine—As a Child); Gustav von Seyffertitz (Rutz the Usurper); Michael Vavitch (Ruiz's First Lieutenant); Charles Stevens (The Gaucho's First Lieutenant); Nigel De Brulier (The Padre); Albert MacQuarrie (Victim of the Black Doom); Mary Pickford (Our Lady of the Shrine).

SHOW PEOPLE (MGM, 1928), 7, 453 feet.

Director, King Vidor; treatment, Agnes Christine Johnston, Laurence Stallings; continuity, Wanda Tuchock; titles, Ralph Spence; sets, Cedric Gibbons; wardrobe, Henrietta Frazer; song, William Axt and David Mendoza; camera, John Arnold; editor, Hugh Wynn.

Marion Davies (Peggy Pepper); William Haines (Billy Boone); Dell Henderson (Colonel Pepper); Paul Ralli (Andre); Tenen Holtz (Casting Director); Harry Gribbon (Comedy Director); Sidney Bracy (Dramatic Director); Polly Moran (Maid); Albert Conti (Producer); John Gilbert, Mae Murray, Charles Chaplin, Douglas Fairbanks, Sr., Elinor Glyn, William S. Hart (Themselves)

THE IRON MASK (United Artists, 1929), 8,855 feet.

Director, Allan Dwan; based on *Les Trois Mousquetaires* and *Le Vicomte de Bragelonne ou dix ans plus tard* by Alexandre Dumas, pere; story, Elton Thomas; screenplay editor, Lotta Woods; interior decorator, Burgess Beall; production designer, Maurice Leloir; music arranger, Hugo Riesenfeld; song, Ray Klages and Louis Alter; assistant directors, Bruce Humberstone, Vinton Vernon, and Sherry Shourds; wardrobe, Maurice Leloir and Gilbert Clark; makeup, Fred C. Ryle; advisors, Earle Browne, Arthur Woods and Jack Cunningham; artists, Ben Carre, H. W. Miles, David S. Hall, Edward M. Langley, William Buckland, and Jack Holden; technical director, Willard M. Reineck; camera, Henry Sharp; additional camera, Warren Lynch; editor, William Nolan.

Douglas Fairbanks, Sr. (D'Artagnan); Belle Bennett (The Queen Mother); Marguerite de La Motte (Constance); Dorothy Revier (Milady de Winter); Vera Lewis (Madame Peronne); Rolfe Sedan (Louis XIII); William Bakewell (Louis XIV/Louis XIV's Twin); Gordon Thorpe (The Young Prince/The Young Prince's Twin); Nigel De Brulier (Cardinal Richelieu); Ullrich Haupt (Rochefort); Lon Poff (Father Joseph); Chalres Stevens (Planchet, D'Artagnan's Servant); Henry Otto (The King's Valet); Leon Barry (Athos); Stanley J. Sandford (Porthos); Gino Corrado (Aramis).

THE TAMING OF THE SHREW (United Artists, 1929), 6,117 feet.

Director, Samuel Taylor; based on the play by William Shakespeare; adaptor, Taylor; art directors, William Cameron Menzies and Laurence Irving; production assistants, Earle Browne, Bruce Humberstone, Walter Mayo, Constance Collier, and John Craig; sound, David Forrest; camera, Karl Struss; editor, Allen McNeil.

Mary Pickford (Katherine); Douglas Fairbanks, Sr. (Petruchio); Edwin Maxwell (Baptista); Joseph Cawthorn (Gremio); Clyde Cook (Grumio); Geoffrey Wardwell (Hortensio); Dorothy Jordan (Bianca); Charles Stevens (Servant).

99

REACHING FOR THE MOON (United Artists, 1921), 90 min.
Director, Edmund Goulding; story, Goulding and Irving Berlin; screenplay, Goulding; dialog, Goulding and Elsie Janis; song, Berlin, sound, Oscar Laegerstrom; camera, Ray June, Robert Planck; editors, Lloyd Nosler and Hal C. Kern.

Douglas Fairbanks, Sr. (Larry Day); Bebe Daniels (Vivian Benton); Edward Everett Horton (Roger the Valet); Claud Allister (Sir Horace Partington Chelmsford); Jack Mulhall (Carrington); Walter Walker (James Benton); June MacCloy (Kitty); Helen Jerome Eddy (Larry's Secretary), Bing Crosby (singer); Bud Geary (Flier); Bill Elliott, Dennis O'Keefe (Dancers on deck); Larry Steers (Captain); Lloyd Whitlock (Associate); Alphonse Martel (Warden).

AROUND THE WORLD IN 80 MINUTES WITH DOUGLAS FAIRBANKS (United Artists, 1931), 80 min.
Directors, Victor Fleming, and Douglas Fairbanks, Sr.; screenplay Robert E. Sherwood; sound-camera, Henry Sharp and Chuck Lewis.

With: Douglas Fairbanks, Sr., Sessue Hayakawa.

MR. ROBINSON CRUSOE (United Artists, 1932), 70 min.
Director, Edward Sutherland; story-screenplay, Tom J. Geraghty; sound, Walter Pahlman; camera, Max Dupont; editor, Robert Kern.

Douglas Fairbanks, Sr. (Steve Drexel); William Farnum (William Belmont); Earle Browne (Professor Carmichale); Maria Alba (Saturday).

THE PRIVATE LIFE OF DON JUAN (United Artists, 1934), 90 min.
Producer-director, Alexander Korda; based on the play by Henri Bataille; screenplay, Lajos Biro and Frederick Lonsdale; song "Don Juan's Serenade" by Michael Spolianski; song, Arthur Wimperis and Arthur Benjamin; camera, George Perienal; editor, Stephen Harrison.

Douglas Fairbanks, Sr. (Don Juan); Merle Oberon (Antonia); Benita Hume (Dolores); Binnie Barnes (Rosita); Joan Gardner (Carmen); Melville Cooper (Leporello); Athene Seyler (Theresa); Owen Nares (Actor); Patricia Hilliard (Girl in Castle); Gina Malo (Pepita); Heather Thatcher (Actress); Claud Allister (Duke); Barry MacKay (Roderigo); Lawrence Grossmith (Guardian); Edmond Breon (Arthur); Clifford Heatherley (Pedro); Diana Napier (Would-Be Wife); Gibson Gowland (Don Ascanio) Hay Petrie (Manager of the Golden Pheasant); Natalie Paley (Wife); Bruce Winston (Cafe Manager); Edmund Willard (Prisoner); Hindle Edgar (A Husband); Florence Wood (A Cook at the Inn); Annie Esmond (Dolores' Duenna); Morland Graham (The Cook in Don Juan's Kitchen); William Heughan (Statue); Veronica Brady (One of Don Juan's Early Loves); Betty Hamilton (An Actress); Margaretta Scott (Tonita a Dancer); Natalie Lelong and Rosita Garcia (Wives of Tired Business Men); Nancy Jones (Woman); Elsa Lanchester (Maid).

5′ 11″
165 pounds
Black hair
Brown eyes
Aquarius

Ronald Colman

"**A**ctors should be expected to interpret life, but cannot observe objectively when everybody's eyes are on them. Their every move is noticed, reported, and blared through the world, yet everyone demands better acting, giving the actor no opportunity to really study things objectively. It's particularly tough on the young people in the business who succeed to early fame, thus having no chance of study, concentration, and observation, so essential to the improvement of the art." So analyzed Ronald Colman *the* heartthrob *par excellence* for three decades of moviegoers.

Since he was so very British, one should hardly imagine that Ronald would make his first major impact in the cinema as an imitation Rudolph Valentino Latin lover. But in the silent cinema nearly anything was possible! Teamed with Vilma Banky, Ronald and his leading lady were turned by producer Samuel Goldwyn into arch rivals of such other Twenties' love teams as Janet Gaynor and Charles Farrell, and Greta Garbo and John Gilbert.

Since Colman, was fortunate to have, in addition to good breeding, intelligence and charm, an admirably modulated speaking voice, he had no difficulty in making the transition to the talkies. In fact he became an even bigger star. Taking their cue from his very popular *Beau Geste* (Paramount, 1926) success, producers in the Thirties frequently starred Colman in elaborate action epics, where he was always cast as the idealistic hero. Whether as the brave Sydney Carton in *A Tale of Two Cities* (MGM, 1935) or as the super humanistic Robert Conway in *Lost Horizon* (Columbia, 1937), well-dictioned Mr. Colman was eminently well-received by moviegoers.

We may never enjoy the likes of Ronald Colman again. Fortunately, he left a legacy of fine film performances for future generations to study and enjoy.

The life of the man whose voice and acting would delight radio and motion picture fans for almost forty years began on Monday, February 9, 1891. He was born in Richmond, a small town on the River Swale in Surrey, England, to silk importer Charles Colman and his wife, Marjory Fraser Colman. Dark-haired, brown-eyed Ronald Charles, fifth of six children,[1] had three sisters and one brother, Eric. Although, as Ronald once said, "There is no proof that there ever was an actor in the family before my time," he was descended from George Colman, an eighteenth-century producer-playwright, and George Colman the younger, who was England's Censor of Plays.

With his sisters and brother, Ronald attended the local Richmond elementary school with more than an occasional paternally enforced excursion to the Colman silk-imported offices. It was the wish of the elder Colman that his two sons should one day enter the business. Although Ronald "liked the smell and color of what I saw" and found something romantic about silk, the busy docks, and the valuable-cargoed ships, he could not envision that type of future for himself. Charles Colman also paid frequent visits to the nickelodeons, and, after viewing one particular presentation with Ronald, said, "This invention has a future, so—watch it. It is going to make the fortunes of a great many people."

As Ronald grew older, he expressed a desire to become an engineer and enrolled at Hadley School in Littlehampton, Sussex, preparatory to higher education at Cambridge University. Suddenly, in 1907, his plans were drastically altered with the death of his father. The Colman importing business collapsed and with it went most of the family finances. There was but one course to follow—to get a job. After the family had transferred to a small house on the outskirts of London, Ronald set out to look for work. This was no easy task for a sixteen-year-old youth with no letters of recommendation for a clerk's job, the only work of which he thought himself capable.

---

[1] The sixth Colman child, Freda, would be born in 1895.

He threw his inexperience on the mercy of potential employers and waited. During this period of nonactivity he discovered amateur theatricals and joined a group called the Bancroft Amateur Dramatic Society. "I thought it would be fun to act," he once remembered. "So I played juvenile roles, atrociously, I am sure, in such pieces as *Charley's Aunt, The Admirable Crichton, The Private Secretary,* and others. It was amusing, but I had not the slightest idea of becoming an actor. There was in my mind an instinctive barrier against such an idea. I think my father would have hated it had he known."

At last, he was hired by the Briton Steamship Company to work as an office boy for 10 shillings ($2.50) a week. "I was shy with girls until I was past sixteen," he confessed. "But when I became an office boy, I discovered that it was more comfortable to do as the Romans did, to be one of the fellows. And, to be one of the fellows, a chap had to talk about girls and dates." He attended subscription dances and also went to dances in the homes of girls.

"The chief profit and pleasure I derived from these excursions, I must ungallantly admit, is that it gave me the right to talk like the other fellows." At the age of seventeen, to earn extra money, he played a banjo at a Masonic smoker with a group who called themselves "The Mad Medicos," and frequently read from the works of great authors for pennies in gaslit salons. When he was eighteen he joined the London Scottish Regiment, a type of national guard outfit, and, in 1910, after three years with the steamship company, Ronald was promoted to the position of junior accountant earning a salary of $12.50 a week. ("I congratulated myself on such stirring progress.")

In spite of the fact that "I joined the London Scottish Regiment more to get away from the office than because of the fighting spirit which I did not have," his unit went to France in September, 1914. As one of Lord Kitchener's "famous contemptibles," he spent six weeks in the trenches and participated in the muddy battle of Ypres. During the advance at Messines, an exploding shell hurled him into a front-line trench with a fractured ankle. "My wound was an unheroic injury," he later explained. "It could have happened stepping off a bus at Charing Cross. The war was for me a very bad, a very messy business."

He ended up in a field hospital, where it was determined that he also suffered from a lung infection. He became impressed with the skill of the doctors and, later, hobbling in and out of London military hospitals, he thought that he would like to pursue the study of medicine. On his discharge from the Regiment in 1916, however, he had no funds to devote to a medical education and he turned to other avenues of endeavor.

After a few weeks of floundering in uncertainty, he was told that Lena Ashwell, whom he described as "a short of English prototype of Ethel Barrymore," needed a dark, young man for a small part in her

103

production of *The Maharanee of Arakan*.[2] He applied for and won the part, mainly because there was a shortage of young men in wartime London. For six pounds a week he played an Indian herald in darkface who tooted a horn and toted a flag. Lena Ashwell then took him under her wing and introduced him to Sir Gerald Du Maurier and Sir Charles Wyndham, two great personages of the English theatre. Gladys Cooper then chose Ronald for a small part in her starring vehicle, *The Misleading Lady* (Playhouse Theatre: September 6, 1916, 231 performances). The London *Times* was unimpressed with the production, although it admitted that it is only fair to say that the public last night swallowed the cocktail . . . with every sign of the liveliest enjoyment." For her part, the star, Miss Cooper, thought Ronald "very clumsy indeed."

It was at about this time that an uncle in the government came forth with an offer for Ronald in the consulate field. Now faced with a career decision, Colman pondered the prospects of government versus the stage. He graciously declined the uncle's offer, and then played the juvenile lead in the controversial play, *Damaged Goods*[3] (St. Martin's Theatre: March 17, 1917, 281 performances), which dealt with the taboo subject of veneral disease. Mary Gray as the mother and J. Fisher White as the doctor headed the cast, which was directed by James Bernard Fagan.

In 1919 Ronald acted in his first film, a two-reel comedy entitled *The Live Wire*. "This was my foretaste of Hollywood's opulence," he once said, but the film was not released. A London casting office listed him as "does not screen well," but that same year was, nevertheless, chosen by director Tom Watts to play the part of Bob, the adopted selfish son of a fisherman's widow in the five-reeler, *The Toilers* (Neville Bruce, 1919). *Bioscope,* the trade journal, reviewed the production in its March 27, 1919 issue and considered it "a weak story." However, the review continued, "It is not Ronald Colman's fault that one can feel very little interest in Bob." He then had minor film roles in *A Daughter of Eve* (Walturdaw, 1919) and *Snow in the Desert* (Walturdaw, 1919), and also during this period, his pre-moustache era, he was on stage in *The Little Brother (1918)* and *The Great Day* (1918). In the cast of the latter play was an actress—a year older then Ronald named Thelma Victoria Maud Dawson (Thelma Raye) whom Colman lived with and then married on September 18, 1919, at St. George's Registry Office in London.

[2]Lena Ashwell, born September 28, 1872, abandoned the West End stage early in 1916 to organize several companies to entertain the troops in France and at home. She engaged some six hundred artists in the course of her work: when the Armistice was declared, there were twenty-five companies in France.

[3]Richard Bennett, the father of Barbara, Constance, and Joan, starred in the American production of *Damaged Goods* on Broadway and on the road, as well as in a film version in 1915.

Ronald continued to intersperse screen acting with stage work, and began 1920 with the substantial role of Maurice, a Jewish prizefighter, in *A Son of David* (Walturdaw). *Bioscope* of February 5, 1920 found "Ronald Colman as the older Maurice, Poppy Windham as the older Esther and Robert Vallis all act very cleverly, but it would have been wiser to cast players of a distinctive Jewish type for these roles." This vehicle was followed by a woman's picture, *Anna the Adventuress* (National, 1920), in which Ronald had little to do, but *The Black Spider* (Butcher, 1920) provided him with the title role. Filmed at Monte Carlo, the latter picture film has him as the seemingly respectable Vicomte de Beauvais who is revealed later to be an international crook. *Bioscope* of May 13, 1920 found the film "so involved as to be difficult to follow," but added, "Ronald Colman makes the bold, bad Vicomte a romantic figure in the short glimpses we have of him." This flashy part foreshadowed the swashbuckling roles that were to lie ahead for Colman.

Then, in 1920, with the post-war depression causing rampant unemployment throughout England, Ronald decided to seek work in the United States. His wife agreed that she would remain in London until he could establish himself, and Ronald took a second-class steamship berth to New York. He arrived with three clean shirt collars, two letters of introduction, and about thirty-five dollars in cash. His initial step was to secure lodgings in a Brooklyn boarding house, where he survived on a diet of soup and rice pudding while pounding the New York

Publicity pose *c.* 1923

pavements in search of a job. Just as his funds were about to give out, he landed a role in a tour of *The Dauntless Three,* starring Robert Warwick. In Act One of the play, Ronald was a Turkish police chief, and then he disappeared until Act Three when he returned as a bearded Russian spy. He had a bit in *The Nightcap* (39th Street Theatre: August 15, 1921, 96 performances), and he had a walk-on in a George Arliss vehicle, *The Green Goddess* (Booth Theatre: January 18, 1921, 440 performances). Still later he took on the supporting role of a rich playboy gambler in a Lewis J. Selznick film, *Handcuffs or Kisses* (Select, 1921), starring Elaine Hammerstein. Some fifteen years later, Ronald would be under contract to Selznick's son, David.

Finding himself a commercial commodity, Ronald joined the touring company of *East Is West* in support of Fay Bainter, but was back in New York in 1922 for the part of Alain Sergyll, the other man in a love triangle with Ruth Chatterton and Henry Miller, in *La Tendresse (The Tenderness)* (Henry Miller Theatre: September 25, 1922, 64 performances).

Co-workers and other striving actors along Manhattan's Great White Way liked Ronald and respected his gentlemanly manners. He was everyone's friend and took particular delight in establishing a rapport with another novice actor, William Powell. It was to be the beginning of a lifetime comradeship.

At that time, movie director Henry King and his star, Lillian Gish, were hunting for an actor to play the part of the Italian prince in *The White Sister* (Metro, 1923). Inspiration Pictures (headed by Charles H. Duell and Boyce Smith), the producing company, had booked passage to Italy where the film would be photographed. As the sailing date came closer, the search for a dark-haired actor became frantic. Then, photographer James Abbé told King that he had seen *La Tendresse* and that there was a young Englishman in the cast who would be perfect as the prince.

After seeing the play, King and Miss Gish went backstage and asked Ronald if he would make a test for them the next morning. Miss Gish has said in her autobiography, *The Movies, Mr. Griffith, and Me* (Prentice-Hall, 1969), "Once we had run the test we knew our search was over. Ronald Colman was perfect for the part." Miss Gish sent Henry Miller, the star-producer of *La Tendresse,* a note begging him to release Ronald from the run-of-the-play contract, "and that gracious gentleman, knowing what an opportunity it was for Mr. Colman, let him sail with us forty-eight hours later."

Since *The White Sister* was the first of the big American films to be made in Italy, there was a paucity of adaptable studio facilities and equipment. Needed items had to be purchased and rushed from Germany, while the company sought locations. During this period, Ronald sent for his wife. She joined him in his quarters at the Excelsior Hotel

With Charles Lane, J. Barney Sherry, Lillian Gish, and Gail Kane in *The White Sister* (1923)

in Rome, but the move was a mistake. (Mrs. Colman was given a small part in the feature to keep her occupied.) Their marriage was never too successful and the squabbles that came with their reunion were either witnessed or heard about by the entire company. Miss Gish wrote in her book, "Once Thelma Colman ran down the hotel corridor crying, 'He's dead! He's dead!' Some of the company ran in to find Ronnie on the floor. When he came to, he said, 'I must have fallen and hit my head.' " A short time later they had another fierce quarrel at a party that resulted in Thelma's immediate departure for England.

For one scene in the film, Ronald, as the prince, was required to kidnap his love (Gish), who had become a nun after thinking that he had been killed in Africa. "To get him to play with the passion and abandon necessary for the kidnapping scene, Henry King plied him with whiskey. Ronnie actually said 'damn' during the scene. It was a great surprise to all of us." They worked all night on the scene, but the next day Ronald was not able to remember what had happened. According to Miss Gish, "Ronnie looked like an aristocrat; he could make you believe that he was a prince. But he had all the reserve of an English gentleman."

The White Sister premiered at New York's Forty-fourth Street Theatre on September 5, 1923. Its thirteen reels of 13,147 feet of film were cut to ten reels and 10,055 feet for its February, 1924 national release and was subsequently edited to nine reels and 9,361 feet for its general release.[4] The critics were enthusiastic about the film and its cast.[5] The *New York Times* rated Ronald "splendid," but like many another viewer of the spectacular picture, wondered just why the script had to introduce the rather incongruous flood scenes, which led to Colman's death by drowning. For many it seemed a very overtly artificial manner of providing a means for Lillian Gish's nun to remain true to her vows.

Ronald remained in Rome to take a bit part, without billing, in a Samuel Goldwyn presentation, *The Eternal City* (Associated First National, 1923), a film dealing with the current political struggle in Italy between the Communists and Mussolini's Fascists. Meanwhile, with the release of *The White Sister,* he was hailed as a new Valentino, and was immediately signed by Inspiration Pictures for a key role in *Romola* (Metro-Goldwyn, 1924), again with Henry King directing and Lillian Gish starring. This film was made in Florence, where an entire replica of the fifteenth-century city was reconstructed. Also in the cast were Dorothy Gish and William Powell. The latter appeared as the villain whose acting overshadowed Ronald's more modulated performance as the overly virtuous sculptor who adores the heroine (Lillian Gish).

Before *Romola* was released, however, Samuel Goldwyn, who had recently formed his own company in Hollywood and had seen *The White Sister,* cabled Ronald with an offer of the male lead in a film opposite May McAvoy. Colman accepted, and, on returning to New York, found that he had just enough time to take a role in a Selznick comedy starring George Arliss, an actor whom he greatly admired. In *$20 a Week* (Selznick Distributing, 1924), Ronald was cast as Arliss' son, who challenges the older man to a bet that he cannot live on twenty dollars a week. The father takes the wager by procuring a job in a steel plant which he saves from financial ruin by uncovering an in-house embezzler. The father is taken into the firm as a partner while the son marries the daughter (Edith Roberts) of the plant's owner (Taylor Holmes).

---

[4]*The White Sister* was remade in 1933 by MGM, with Helen Hayes. Clark Gable was in the role originally played by Ronald.

[5]While David Robinson in *Hollywood in the Twenties* (Tantivy Press, 1968) would state of *The White Sister* and director King, "Outside his familiar American atmosphere, his romanticism tended to reveal clichés of sentimentality," other historians would be kinder to the film and the director. In *Hollywood Professionals: Vol. II* (Tantivy Press, 1974), Clive Denton re-examines the first *The White Sister:* "King, in his very impressive original, takes the story at face value but deepens it by character exploration and decorates his scenes with many details which reinforce conviction of the social time and place. The indolent pleasures of aristocratic Italian life before the 1914 war are captured with scenes of fox hunts . . . and trysts at the garden wall. . . . The superbly framed and lit convent scenes suggest, through ritual and resignation, religion's dual face of serenity and fear. Most remarkably of all, King brings to his climactic scenes a sweep and fury which also gain from the leisurely tempo of all that has gone before."

Publicity pose for *Romola* (1924)

The Goldwyn film, shot in Hollywood, was *Tarnish* (Associated First National, 1924), based on Gilbert Emery's play of the same title which had starred Ann Harding and Tom Powers. As Emmett Carr, Ronald works with a girl (McAvoy) who must support her parents because of the philandering father (Albert Gran). The showdown comes when one of papa's girlfriends (Marie Prevost) blackmails him, and the daughter demands the return of the payments that have been made. She finds Emmett in the girl's apartment, but soon realizes that he, too, has been trying to help the family cause. All is cleared up, with Emmett and the daughter finding blissful happiness. Samuel Goldwyn was extremely pleased with Ronald, both professionally and personally, perhaps because Ronald was the complete antithesis to Goldwyn's pushy, earthy ways. A contract was drawn and signed, thereby making Ronald one of the first actor contractees on the Goldwyn payroll.

His next assignment was on loanout to Constance Talmadge for her production of the comedy, *Her Night of Romance* (First National, 1924), with Miss Talmadge also starring. Ronald, her leading man, plays an impoverished English nobleman posing as a doctor in order to meet and woo an heiress (Talmadge) whom he has never seen. When they do meet, he does not know she is the target of his intentions since she has taken a false identity. As could be expected, the two do fall in love, and everything turns out well.

With the official release in December, 1924, of *Romola*, Ronald had three films being run on silent screens across the nation. The reviewers

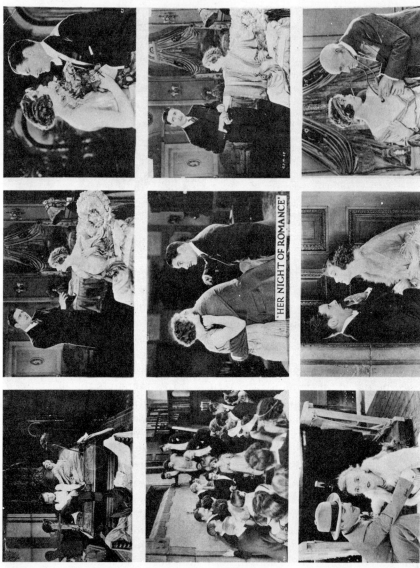

With Constance Talmadge in a series of shots from *Her Night of Romance* (1924)

heartily endorsed the screen's new heart-throb ("Suits well the role of the noble and picturesque artist," said the *Chicago Daily Tribune*). American women became very aware of the dark-haired, suave man with the thin moustache, and shrewd Samuel Goldwyn understood the appeal of his new actor. He took immediate steps to aid this appeal by casting Ronald opposite some of the most adored female stars in the business.

In *A Thief in Paradise* (First National,[6] 1925), with Doris Kenyon, Ronald is a beachcomber on a Samoan island earning a living by diving for pearls with Charles Youree, the disinherited son of a San Francisco millionaire (Claude Gillingwater). When Youree is killed by a shark, Ronald is persuaded to assume the dead man's identity, and he goes to San Francisco where he falls in love with the dead man's childhood sweetheart (Kenyon). They marry, but a spiteful wench (Aileen Pringle) exposes him as a fraud. When Kenyon deserts him, he attempts suicide, but she returns to nurse him back to health and happiness. Obviously, films such as *A Thief in Paradise* were constructed as audience-pleasers and not as enduring examples of artistic integrity.

In *His Supreme Moment* (First National, 1925), which boasted some color sequences, Blanche Sweet is his leading lady. Colman appears as mining engineer John Douglas who lives platonically (!) with an actress (Sweet) in South America. Their arrangement, a trial brother-sister relationship prior to marriage, fails miserably, but once they are back in New York, they honestly fall in love after the actress almost sacrifices herself by wedding a rich man (Cyril Chadwick) in order to obtain sufficient backing for Ronald's mineral mine.

In *The Sporting Venus* (Metro-Goldwyn, 1925), directed with dispatch by that *bon vivant*, Marshall Neilan, Ronald is reunited with Blanche Sweet, who was wed to Neilan. In the film Colman and Blanche are lovers from different social levels whose relationship is discouraged by the girl's father (Edward Martindel). Ronald, first a medical student, then a World War I soldier, finally becomes a wealthy physician, but by that time, the once-rich girl loses her fortune. With their social roles now reversed, he rescues her from poverty and a raging storm in order to claim her as his wife. Mordaunt Hall, in reviewing this film for the *New York Times*, took occasion to inform his readers, "Mr. Colman is quite effective in many of the scenes, but his performance is not as sincere and thorough as the one he gave in *His Supreme Moment*." Filming of this Metro release required Colman to go on location to Scotland for a bit; it would be the last such filming he would do out of the United States.

In *Her Sister from Paris* (First National, 1925) Ronald is asked to make love to two Constance Talmadges, one as his wife and the other

---

[6]Goldwyn's features were then distributed by First National Pictures.

as his wife's twin sister. He is Joseph, an author who has lost interest in his wife, Helen. She encounters her twin sister, Lola, a Parisian vamp, and asks her to help win back her husband. Lola suggests to Helen that she impersonate her (Lola) and vamp Joseph into re-loving her. It works! Eventually, Helen confesses that she is not Lola, but by this time, Joseph is so erotically and emotionally aroused that he accepts the return of his wife with hungry arms. If the plot seems very familiar, that is because it was used for *Moulin Rouge* (United Artists, 1933) and for *Two-Faced Woman* (MGM, 1941).

At this point, Goldwyn made an industry move that would prove to be a major coup for legendary Hollywood. He teamed Ronald (in top billing) with the blonde vamp from Hungary, Miss Vilma Banky.[7] It was the beginning of a love team liaison that would bring incredible profits to the great producer and elevate the two film personalities to the highest ranks of silent screen stardom.

Their initial appearance as a screen team was in *The Dark Angel* (First National, 1925), adapted from the play by H. B. Trevelyan. The

[7]She was born Vilma Baulsy in Budapest on January 9, 1898. The 5′ 6″ actress made her film debut in the 1920 Hungarian feature, *Im Letzten Augenblick*, and thereafter made twelve additional pictures before coming to America. They included: *Tavaszi Szerelem* (Hungarian, 1921), *Kauft Mariett-Aktien* (German, 1922), *Die Letzte Stinde (Hotel Potemkin* (Austrian, 1924), *Das Schöne Abenteurer (The Lady from Paris)* (German, 1925), and *Sollman Heiraten* (German, 1925).

With Blanche Sweet
in *The Sporting Venus* (1925)

With Vilma Banky
in *The Dark Angel* (1925)

time is the World War I period, the place is England, and the characters are Captain Alan Trent and Kitty Vane. Alan and Kitty are in love but do not have time to obtain a marriage license, because Allan has been called back suddenly into action. They spend their last night together at an inn where they declare undying (if not pure) love. Later, Alan, blinded in battle and taken prisoner by the Germans, is reported dead, but Kitty *must* go on living. Captain Shannon (Wyndham Standing), Alan's best friend, offers consolation and romance to the distraught miss. After the war, Shannon finds Alan living anonymously and blind, the author of children's books.

Colman displays his noble character by begging Shannon not to bring Kitty to see him, but Shannon insists that he owes her an explanation. They agree that Kitty should not learn of his affliction. Alan memorizes newspaper articles and carefully locates the furniture in his room so that he will make no telltale errors. When she appears, he tells her that he had not contacted her after the war because he had stopped loving her. She believes him, but as she rises to leave, she puts out her hand to him which he does not acknowledge. As the truth leaps out at her she weepingly embraces him, saying that she loves him no matter what.

The Dark Angel[8] may seem a heart-tugger of the worst order by the standards of the 1970s, but in 1925 it was considered a "beautiful screen conception" (*New York Times*). Mordaunt Hall of the *Times* took elaborate pains to credit the accomplishments of each artist involved with the winning production: "This is by all means the best picture George Fitzmaurice[9] has to his credit. He demonstrates his ability as a director in more ways than one. . . . When Mr. Fitzmaurice has an idea he pictures it with sincerity, but does not shout about it." As for veteran scripter Frances Marion,[10] Hall judged, "[She] also deserves much praise, for, although the ending is changed, it has been accomplished with a certain subtlety which will not offend those who saw the play."

As far as the two stars of *The Dark Angel* were concerned, the *Times'* film critic was exultant in his praise. "Vilma Banky . . . is a young

[8]Goldwyn would remake the film in 1935 with Fredric March as the blinded lover and Merle Oberon as Kitty.

[9]Fitzmaurice, who had directed three of Colman's previous films (*Tarnish, A Thief in Paradise,* and *His Supreme Moment*), had been schooled as a painter before becoming a film director. As David Robinson would note in *Hollywood in the Twenties* "there always remained a strong pictorial sense about his films, allied to his complete technical assurance and a firm grasp on commercial values. He was at his best with frankly romantic themes."

[10]In *Off with Their Heads* (1972), autobiographist Frances Marion recalls, "As the picture progressed, it was fascinating to watch the scenes between Vilma and Ronnie Colman. He spoke his lines in a deep, rich voice and with the authority of an actor schooled in the theatre. Hesitant in speech, struggling to master our difficult language, Vilma responded in a mixture of pidgin English and Hungarian. When we saw them together on the screen we realized how clever Sam had been to sign this lovely blonde girl and to team her with his dark-eyed star."

person of rare beauty, a girl who might be American or English with soft, fair hair, a slightly retroussé nose and lovely eyes which have the suggestion of a slant. Her acting is sincere and earnest, and her tears seem very real." As for Ronald, Hall penned, "[He] is most sympathetic and capable. A strong man might well be excused for weeping at some of the scenes in this delightful romance, especially when Trent decides to end it all and changes his mind through the cheerful note of a youngster's voice."

The Dark Angel and Ronald's next film were Goldwyn's top money makers of 1925. *Stella Dallas* (United Artists,[11] 1925) was adapted for the screen by Frances Marion[12] from the 1923 novel by Olive Higgins Prouty. The resultant film is a tearjerker of the highest order. Ronald received top billing as Stephen Dallas, a wealthy socialite who marries Stella (Belle Bennett) out of remorse over the suicide of his father. Stella is a flamboyantly crude soul and definitely not a part of her husband's esteemed social stratum. He deserts her after a daughter is born, but she steadfastly refuses him a divorce. Years later, when daughter Laurel (Lois Moran), called "Lolly Baby" by her mother, is grown up, Stella knows that the girl will benefit more from living opulently with Stephen than with her.

She consents to a divorce so that Stephen may marry Helen Morrison (Alice Joyce), thereby providing a proper home for Laurel. Stella makes Laurel believe that she does not want her around and sends her to Stephen's richly appointed mansion. Later, as Laurel is married to socialite Richard Grosvenor (Douglas Fairbanks, Jr.) in the parlor of Stephen's home, Stella watches the ceremony from the street.

For years to come, *Stella Dallas*[13] would mark the watershed between casual soap operas and the real McCoy, a four-handkerchief film. As Palmer Smith in the *New York Evening World* would pro-

---

[11]Goldwyn's features were now being released through United Artists.

[12]Marion in her autobiography recalls being told by her new employer Goldwyn, "Your first assignment will be *Stella Dallas*. It's a beautiful woman's story. I'm starring Ronald Colman in it." Spunky Marion could not resist replying, "As a female impersonator?"

[13]Goldwyn would remake the landmark feature in 1937 with John Boles as Stephen, Barbara Stanwyck as Stella, and Anne Shirley as Laurel. Beginning on October 25, 1937, NBC radio would offer its serialized version of *Stella Dallas*. Anne Elstner played Stella with the part of Stephen falling through the eighteen-and-one-half-year tenure of the show to Arthur Hayes, Carleton Young, and Frederick Tozere.

In promoting *Stella Dallas* (1925), Goldwyn's advertisements proclaimed, "She married above her class. Was she a millstone to her child's happiness and her aspiring husband? What should she do? As a novel this smashing story startled millions of readers. . . . [It] is as great as the book." Goldwyn also acquired testimonials from V.I.P. show business performers, whose endorsements were touted to the public.

Ethel Barrymore: "I cried as I have hardly ever cried in a theatre, certainly as I have never cried at a picture. It is a magnificent achievement and I do most profoundly congratulate you." *Harold Lloyd:* "You have literally taken a slice of life and transferred it to the screen in a highly entertaining and artistic manner." *Cecil B. DeMille:* "*Stella Dallas* is one of the few great screen achievements and will appeal strongly to all classes and all intellects. I am proud of you for having made it."

claim: "If any heart fails to throb to the screen version of *Stella Dallas* the trouble is with the heart, not with the picture. Not a dry eye was to be seen. . . . It is the most tender, the most emotionally artistic film offering of its kind that I have ever seen. The picture is real and it's human." The *New York Times* said, "The acting of all players is unusually telling." Another New York critic applauded the "sound, sincere performance by Ronald Colman," while John Rosenfield, Jr. of the *Dallas News* wrote of Colman that "[He] happily portrays the manliness, dignity and breeding of Stephen."

Offcamera, Ronald and his wife (of whom the public was deliberately told little) were going through another domestic transition. In February, 1925, she applied for separate maintenence (she was then living on the Riviera and elsewhere in Europe) and in August of 1926 Colman filed for divorce. However, both these actions eventually were dropped.

Professionally, though, Ronald was much in the news and many Hollywood observers were wondering why Goldwyn was not promoting his chief attraction in the same manner as Metro-Goldwyn (-Mayer) was with its John Gilbert in *The Merry Widow* and *The Big Parade.* Allegedly, Goldwyn's response to questions on this subject, such as, "Aren't you afraid that Gilbert will beat him to the draw?" led the filmmaker to remark, "Ever hear the fable about the tortoise and the hare? It's no fable. The one who runs too fast loses his breath."

Therefore, for his final film of 1925, Goldwyn loaned Colman's services to Warners as Lord Darlington in *Lady Windermere's Fan,* taken from Oscar Wilde's comedy written in 1892.[14] The film was directed by Ernst Lubitsch, and the European craftsman attempted the near impossible, that is, to film Wilde's well-known story without utilizing one of the author's famed epigrams. As the *New Yorker* Magazine's Ted Shane reassured his readers: "Oscar Wilde will have no cause to turn over in his grave. Dr. Herr Lubitsch has done magnificently, if somewhat Germanically, by the Gifted Magpie of the perfumed sayings. . . . . . . He has attempted and succeeded in transfilming a Wilde without use of a single tinseled Wildean epigram from the play, rather trusting to his own great sense of cinematic wit and the dramatic."

Lady Windermere's Fan emerged as one of the year's most popular photoplays. Spiced with light malice it is an adult study in misunderstanding and suspected marital infidelity as Lady Windermere (May McAvoy), certain that her husband (Bert Lytell) is having an affair with the sentimental, mysterious Mrs. Erlynne (Irene Rich) disappears from her own party to initiate a little romance with handsome *bon vivant* Lord Darlington. She leaves her fan in his apartment, which is found

---

[14]First presented on Broadway in 1893 with Maurice Barrymore in the Darlington role, it was revived on the New York stage in 1914 and in 1946. In 1949, Twentieth Century-Fox remade the play as *The Fan* with George Sanders as Lord Darlington.

With Bert Lytell and May McAvoy in *Lady Windemere's Fan* (1925)

With Neil Hamilton and Ralph Forbes in *Beau Geste* (1926)

by her spouse, but Mrs. Erlynne quickly claims it as her own. The upshot of the whole affair is that Mrs. Erlynne is actually the Lady's mother, long-lost and believed to be dead, and she has an attraction for another man (Edward Martindel), rather than for her son-in-law. One would have thought that Colman would have been quite adept at this type of polished drawingroom fare, but the august *New York Times* decided that he "is not convincing, being a somewhat halting admirer who hardly believes in himself." Nevertheless, it was a prestige film and re-emphasized Ronald's growing position in the film colony as a man of very high professional stature.

Nineteen twenty-six began for Ronald with *Kiki*,[15] produced by and starring Norma Talmadge, for First National distribution. Ronald is the manager of a Parisian theatre who switches his affections from the witchy Gertrude Astor to the gamine Talmadge.[16] In this bit of *frou frou*, perhaps a bit too Americanized in its interpretation of the Gallic ambiance, Ronald received his usual good notices.[17] The *New York Times* credited him for offering "a restrained and charming performance."

Through the Hollywood grapevine, Ronald learned that Paramount's Adolph Zukor owned the screen rights to P. C. Wren's novel, *Beau Geste.* It was an escapist adventure story, which Ronald found appealing. Besides, he felt that it would provide him with an excellent escape hatch from romantic yarns. He was tired of emulating the Adolph Menjou type of screen dandy.

Zukor had toyed with the idea of filming the Wren work, but he was not sure that the public would accept the concept of three brothers fighting the Arabs while striving to survive against the neurotic demands of a psychotic top sergeant. The story had no romance, no spot for a leading dramatic actress. Who would want to pay to see uniformed men die on the screen? Ronald met with the Paramount executives and fought for the picture as he had never done before. He argued that the material was new and fresh and that the studio could afford to gamble. Furthermore, he astounded them by stating that he wanted the title role. One wonders how the conversations must have gone, but no matter, since Ronald won.

Thus, his next screen role, and his favorite up to that time, was *Beau*

---

[15]Based on Andre Picard's play, presented on Broadway in 1921, with Lenore Ulric and Sam Hardy. Mary Pickford and Reginald Denny starred in the 1931 United Artists' remake of the play, and in 1937 it was announced that Lily Pons would star in yet another film version. (The RKO plans came to naught.)

[16]The ads proclaimed: "Kiki with the soul of a child and the wit and wiles of a gamine." Producer-star Talmadge claimed, "I have never made a picture I like better."

[17]Out-of-town reviewer Eleanor Barnes (*Los Angeles Illustrated*) reported that Ronald "has one of the most interesting parts of his popular career. His handsome, irregular features make a fine contrast to the whimsical, wistful face of Norma, and he plays a convincing role."

Geste (Paramount, 1926). The movie opens with the arrival of a relief detachment of the French Foreign Legion to Fort Zinderneuf in the African desert. The garrison is found to be manned by a bastion of dead men. As the Arabs attack, the scene shifts in flashback to England. The Geste Brothers, Beau (Ronald), John (Ralph Forbes), and Digby (Neil Hamilton), are aware that their aunt (Alice Joyce) owns a priceless sapphire, but only Beau knows that she intends to replace it with an imitation. He steals it and leaves her a note telling of his guilt. The other brothers, not wishing him to sacrifice himself, also leave notes. All three join the Foreign Legion. Beau and John are assigned to the post which is run by the brutal Sergeant Lejaune (Noah Beery), while Digby is made a trumpeter at another garrison. Lejaune has his spies, among them a scheming rat, Boldini (William Powell), who discovers that Beau carries the gem. Lejaune is determined to get it, but his avaricious plans are thwarted by the revolt of the entire post.

Then the Arabs attack: four thousand against forty Legionnaires. Hated as he is, Lejaune has respect from his men for being a resourceful soldier; as the men are killed, he places their corpses into positions atop the walls to make the enemy believe that the fort is still well-defended. When Beau is killed, John refuses to allow Lejaune to place the body into position and shoots the heinous sergeant. Digby arrives with the replacements and, on finding Beau's body, conducts a Viking-type funeral, but, he too dies from an Arab's bullet. Only John survives to return to England. He returns to explain that Beau had stolen the sapphire so that their aunt could not sell it for an amount less than its value. John then turns to Isabel (Mary Brian), who was tossed into the plotline for romantic reasons.

Zukor and the Paramount staff had to retract their previous misgivings as *Beau Geste* became a major cinematic success. The Sahara Desert never looked more beautiful as photographed by J. Roy Hunt and his associates, who substituted the white sands of the desert near Yuma, Arizona, for the real thing. It is impossible at this point to say whether or not Ronald Colman was psychic in his insistence that *Beau Geste*[18] should be his, but, because of it, his screen image was quickly changed from one of a passive, interesting lover to that of aggressive, worldly, interesting adventurer-lover. Now there were many moviegoers who were comparing Ronald Colman not only to John Gilbert, but to the 1920s' great celluloid swashbuckler, Douglas Fairbanks.

Fully realizing that he had a top star under contract, Goldwyn set a policy of using Ronald exclusively in Goldwyn films, with no further loanouts to be sanctioned.

[18]In January, 1929, Laurence Olivier starred in a dramatized version at His Majesty's Theatre in London with Madeleine Carroll as his co-star. It was a flop. The 1939 Paramount film remake found Gary Cooper in the Colman role, while in the 1966 Universal version, Guy Stockwell would portray Beau.

In the Western romantic drama, *The Winning of Barbara Worth* (United Artists, 1926), he was opposite Vilma Banky in their second joint outing.[19] Ronald is an eastern engineer in charge of reclaiming the imperial Valley by damming the Colorado River in an enormous irrigation project. Abe Lee (Gary Cooper), another engineer, discovers that the dam is faulty, but no one listens to him until the structure is about to burst. Ronald then routs the town and averts a catastrophe, but Abe loses his life. Ronald wins Banky, who plays the landowner's (Charles Lane) daughter.[20]

The film was shot largely on location in the barren Black Rock Desert of Nevada, where a town was constructed and to which the company's drinking water had to be carted from two hundred miles away. Novice Gary Cooper's admiration for Ronald was almost boundless, and in his death scene in which he laid in Ronald's arms, Colman advised: "Easy does it, old boy. Good scenes make good actors. Actors don't make a scene. My own feeling is that all you have to do is take a nap, and every woman who sees the picture is going to cry her eyes out."

---

[19]Since their last picture together, Banky had co-starred twice with Rudolph Valentino: in *The Eagle* (United Artists, 1925) and *The Son of the Sheik* (United Artists, 1926), the latter released after the star's untimely death.
[20]Miss Banky was in a dual role: as the mother who dies and as the woman's daughter.

With Vilma Banky in *The Winning of Barbara Worth* (1926)

119

From the "finely handled spectacle" of *Barbara Worth*,[21] Ronald went to the excesses of *The Night of Love* (United Artists, 1927), his first real swashbuckling film, with Miss Banky again as his leading lady. This George Fitzmaurice-directed feature was to prove that Colman, could be as much a Latin lover as John Gilbert or Ramon Novarro and that he could outsheik the late sheik, Rudolph Valentino.

Within the film, set in the Spain of the Middle Ages, he is a son of a gypsy leader who chooses a bride. The feudal lord (Montagu Love), however, exercises his right by demanding that the bride spend a night at his castle prior to the wedding. Rather than accede to the lord's demands, she commits suicide. Ronald then embarks on a career of revenge; when the lord marries Princess Marie (Banky), Colman kidnaps them. Marie falls in love with him, but remains faithful to her husband out of fear and tradition. Ronald later sets them free, but the lord then has his one-time captor taken prisoner. Our hero is condemned to die at the stake, but before the fires are set, the mob kills the evil lord. Ronald is liberated and is promptly engulfed in Banky's arms. As an added cast attraction, to keep the men in the audience happier, Miss Sally Rand, without her fans, danced as a fiery gypsy maiden.

When Ronald and Banky had first been teamed in 1925, they had had the field of screen love teams almost to themselves, but by 1927 there was fierce competition from two other studios. Fox offered Janet Gaynor and Charles Farrell in *Seventh Heaven* and MGM had teamed Greta Garbo with John Gilbert in *Flesh and the Devil*. Both these new cinema duos would soon outstrip the earlier performances of Colman and Banky. But for now, Goldwyn found it commercially feasible to re-team his star players in yet another opus, this time, *The Magic Flame* (United Artists, 1927). It was another first for Ronald, for in this Henry King-directed picture he performed his first dual role: as a circus clown and as the skirt-chasing, murderous Crown Prince of a mythical European nation. As the clown, Tito, he loves and is loved by Bianca (Banky), a high-flyer in the circus. He pushes the dastardly prince to a watery death while protecting Bianca's virtue and then assumes the prince's identity. Bianca, however, believes that the prince has killed Tito and seeks revenge by attempting to assassinate him. Tito reveals his true identity in time and they rejoin the circus. Bliss, so we can assume, will be theirs.

By 1928, Ronald was considered the screen's number one romantic

---

[21]There were some reviewers, such as the *New York Times'* Mordaunt Hall, who had severe reservations about the film. "The story of this photoplay has its degree of interest without any more dramatic value than is to be expected from the film version of one of Mr. Wright's literary efforts." As for Colman's interpretation, Hall offered, "[He] acquits himself competently, and to the casual observer there is no reason why his love for Barbara should not have been reciprocated long before it is."

lead; only John Gilbert continued to give him any kind of stiff competition. The team of Colman-Banky was accepted by swooning fans as the personification of romantic love, always tinged with adventure and excitement. The film titles meant little; it was sufficient to know that the cinema team could be seen together and that they would be in each other's arms at the fadeout.

Offscreen, Banky had shattered her fans' illusions about her and Colman by her much publicized wedding to actor Rod La Rocque in 1927. Ronald was one of four ushers at the church wedding. As for Colman, he was a mystery man, called a "male Madame X" by fan magazine authors.

In a town with few genuine secrets, no one really knew much about him. Few people knew he was still married and that his estranged wife resided in England. He never attended premieres, and once argued, "You get writer's cramp signing autograph books, and a stiff collar is uncomfortable for a whole warm evening in a picture house, when you can see the same film in a nice projection room." Soon after the release of *The Dark Angel*, a Goldwyn Press agent spread the word that Ronald was aloof and silent. No writers could refute these adjectives, because he seldom gave interviews, and the description stuck.

His friends, chief among whom were William Powell and Richard Barthelmess, all told of his good character and nice human traits, none of which made for spicy reading. He lived a bachelor's life in a house that was small by Hollywood standards, and entertained at dinner two or three times a week. When he went out, it was to a friend's home for a party or to an out-of-the-way restaurant. At one time he pleaded his ignorance of the way a star was expected to live, with the rationale: "I didn't know that a star had to make certain gestures, so I didn't make them. I didn't know that I was supposed to go to dull places and meet dull people just because I happened to be making a living by wearing grease paint and loving beautiful women on the screen."

He admitted a love for caviar, tennis, and horseback riding. His weekly salary was reported to be $6,500, which was low when compared to that of John Gilbert ($13,000) or Richard Barthelmess ($8,-750). Only a few people in Hollywood addressed him or referred to him by the less-than-dignified name of Ronnie.

To add to their reputation as a volatile screen couple, Goldwyn next placed Ronald and Vilma in *Two Lovers* (United Artists, 1928), taken from a novel by the Baroness Orczy, whose most famous work was undoubtedly *The Scarlet Pimpernel*. With a musical score by Hugo Riesenfeld and sound effects, the film presented Ronald as Mark Van Rycke, a close friend and bodyguard of the Flemish Prince William of Orange (Nigel De Brulier), attempting to rid his country of the Spanish conquerors. Miss Banky is a Spanish damsel forced to marry Ronald so

With Vilma Banky in *Two Lovers* (1928)

that she might spy on the silent William. She learns to love the Dutch people, however, and to understand their political position. Through her newly gained compassion for the oppressed, she finds genuine love for her husband.

Even before *Two Lovers* had been released, Goldwyn had decided that it was time to split up his famous celluoid couple. He announced to the trade, who in turn alerted the public, that *Two Lovers* would be the final offering of the Colman-Banky team. They would be on their own in separate productions.

Much to the producer's consternation, neither Colman nor Banky clicked in their subsequent feature films with their new oncamera partners.[22] Colman was a little more fortunate than Banky in *The Rescue* (United Artists, 1929), which had the benefit of the Joseph Conrad book as the story base and the fine work of director Herbert Brenon, who made the best of Ronald's onscreen features as he guided the star through his paces. Along with music and sound effects, *The Rescue* brought Colman together with curvaceous Lily Damita[23] in what would be his last silent feature. He is a sea captain stranded in the Java Sea on a bit of real estate which abounds with unfriendly natives. The plot thickens considerably when the yacht of a wealthy English couple (Damita and Alfred Hickman) is wrecked on the same island. He falls for the English woman, but sends her away with the decision that, in his life, duty to his stranded crew comes before love.

Goldwyn's publicists went all out to promote *The Rescue*. "A love surging with the force of the storm-tossed ocean—sweeping man and woman to new heights of admiration! Vivid! Colorful! Colman's supreme romance."

Unfortunately, *The Rescue* met with mixed critical and public reaction,[24] leading Goldwyn to deduce that Miss "Hotcha" Damita was not the proper catalyst for further Colman vehicles.

[22]Miss Banky floundered in *The Awakening* (United Artists, 1928) with Walter Byron as her vis-a-vis. The excitement was also missing from *This Is Heaven* (United Artists, 1929), in which James Hall was her unsatisfying screen partner. By this point, it was obvious that sound films were here to stay, and since Vilma's guttural accent showed no signs of diminishing, Goldwyn decided it was wiser to settle her contract (for a reported one million dollars) and be done with his Hungarian discoverery. In *The Movie Stars* (Doubleday & Co., 1970). Richard Griffith reports: "Vilma Banky was another whose beauty alone put across her rather empty films. Her public might have been happy to watch them even longer than it did, in spite of the guttural Hungarian speech which the talkies revealed, were it not for the fact that as the aforementioned Mrs. Goldwyn warned her husband, Miss Banky's real interest was in the pork chops Budapest which she secretly cooked in her dressing room in spite of his dietary ukases."

[23]Parisian-born Miss Damita had gained fame as a dancer at the Casino de Paris. She later appeared in several German, French, and British films before coming to America in 1928 to co-star with Colman in *The Rescue*. Perhaps her greatest achievement on the Hollywood scene was snaring Errol Flynn into marriage in 1935. Their divorce in 1942 provided her with a very hefty community property settlement and a monthly alimony that outranked some players' screen salaries.

[24]The reviews were far from enthusiastic in their cautious tone: "While nothing more

With Lily Damita in *The Rescue* (1929)

By the latter part of 1928, the film studios of Hollywood were hives of confusion in the hectic rush to convert their productions to all sound. The microphone would cause a major revolution in filming techniques as the industry watched to see which actors could and would survive. Goldwyn, afraid that Americans were not ready to accept Ronald's British voice (after all, he had been promoted for some time as a "Latin Lover"), carefully searched for an appropriate story for the star's first all-talking film venture.

Finally, settling on a character devised by the English writer Sapper (Cyril McNeile), Goldwyn put scenarists Wallace Smith and Sidney Howard to the task of making *Bulldog Drummond* (United Artists,

---

than an entertaining programme picture of not more than average merit, nevertheless justifies the action of Samuel Goldwyn in raising Colman to the realm of stardom. . . . [He] portrays his character with praiseworthy restraint" (*Philadelphia Inquirer*). "Exquisitely beautiful scenic effects and a highly exciting plot make *The Rescue* an extremely worthwhile film" (*Boston Globe*). "Throughout the picture he has one set expression—a cross between anguish and worry which he (Colman) never varies. . . . smiles or deep emotions are apparently at a premium with him" (*Brooklyn Times*). "Considering the inevitable limitations imposed upon a director in reducing a Conrad story to a swift flow of animated photographic scenes, Herbert Brenon has done valiant work in his pictorial transcription. . . . Even though Ronald Colman may not answer Conrad's description of Tom Lingard, his performance is so earnest and sensitive that in spite of his coal-black hair, his clean-shaven chin and small mustache he is not only far from a disappointment but reflects the spirit of 'King' Tom" (*New York Times*).

1929)[25] urbane, suave, and brittle. Sapper's original Drummond was an angry man who did nothing to register sympathy from readers. With Drummond set as Ronald's voice debut on film, the next chore was to find a suitable leading lady. Both Vilma Banky and Lily Damita were out of the question. The quest began in New York, where there were performers with stage-trained voices. Goldwyn sent executive Joseph Schenck east to find an ingenue to play the part of Phyllis, a young American, in Ronald's film. Schenck wanted Joan Bennett to test, but she turned him down because of two previous unsuccessful tries. He kept looking, but returned to Miss Bennett and agreed to cast her without a test.

As detailed in the ninety-minute feature, Bulldog Drummond is a London civilian who is bored after having seen action in World War I. Seeking excitement, he runs an advertisement which is answered by Phyllis Benton, who enlists his aid in rescuing her uncle (Charles Sellon) from an insane asylum. The uncle is held captive by the sadistic Dr. Larkington (Lawrence Grant), who tortures the man in an effort to force him to sign over his fortune to the physician and his accom-

---

[25]The work was also adapted for the stage. It was first played by Sir Gerald Du Maurier at Wyndham's Theatre in London (March 29, 1921). On the Broadway stage (Knickerbocker Theatre: December 26, 1921, 162 performances), A. E. Matthews had the lead, with H. B. Warner later taking the play on tour.

With Joan Bennett in *Bulldog Drummond* (1929)

plice (Montagu Love). Within the action drama, Drummond becomes involved in plenty of excitement before he "kidnaps" the uncle and earns the love of Miss Benton.

Directed on a fast time schedule by F. Richard Jones, the cast of *Bulldog Drummond* often worked long hours, as much as from nine o'clock in the morning until three o'clock the following morning. This was before the formation of the many protective unions. Ronald finally rebelled at the long working day. Since he was a star, there was not much that Jones could do about it, but the lesser actors were severely admonished when they followed Ronald's example of ignoring an early call after having worked through the previous night.

Goldwyn was overwhelmed by audience reaction to *Bulldog Drummond.* The critics[26] raved about Ronald's "clipped correct English voice," "his English poise," and his "Chesterfieldian manner," while people stood in lines in New York (at $2.00 a seat) and in London to see and hear the screen's matinee idol. Such popularity resulted in his next successes: *Condemned* (United Artists, 1929), in which he is a debonair jewel thief sent to Devil's Island where he is assigned to be a servant to the warden (Dudley Digges) and his wife (Ann Harding); Ann Harding hates the island and falls in love with Ronald. *Raffles* (United Artists, 1930),[27] in which he is the clever, debonair safecracker

---

[26]Mordaunt Hall of The *New York Times* reported: "Mr. Colman is as ingratiating when he talks as when he was silent. He has served his time on the stage and therefore the microphone holds no terrors for him. His performance in this part is matchless so far as talking pictures are concerned." The *Times'* Hall also included a recapitulation of the film's opening at the Apollo Theatre on May 2nd, 1929: "In the audience last night was the bashful Mr. Colman, who escorted Mrs. Samuel Goldwyn to a box, which was soon the cynosure of all eyes. He bowed before the film was screened and he bowed afterward. He was not in any bulldoggish mood, for if there is one feature of the motion picture game to which Mr. Colman is averse it is a crowd interested in him."

Ann Silver (*Brooklyn Herald*) wrote: "Because of his work in other pictures, we had dubbed Mr. Colman the one-expression man. We can't ever recall his smiling or looking pleased. Rather, it seemed to us that he wore a constant and never-changing pained look. *The Rescue* is a good illustration of our point. Last night, however, we discovered that the slightly detached Mr. Colman had a lovely smile, twinkling eyes and some of the most ingratiating manners ever to come from the male element of Hollywood. And his voice—well, it was just as big a surprise as the rest. Mr. Colman, as we have always admitted before, is one of the best screen actors of the day—but he seems ever so much more so to us now."

In retrospect, William K. Everson in *The Detective in Film* (Citadel, 1972) notes: "Colman's flawless diction, his beautiful timing, and the sense of fun he brought to the role not only dominated the film, but influenced the tongue-in-cheek playing of the rest of the film. The Drummond had nothing whatsoever in common with the surly Drummond of the books, it was a debonair and sophisticated interpretation, a Drummond who was really a twentieth-century D'Artagnan. In fact, there was a good deal of Fairbanksian flair in Colman's performance, and the character shared a great many of the qualities that had made up the Fairbanks 'image' in his modern silent comedies—good society connections, an educated background, and an unstressed but apparently unlimited private income."

[27]The role of *Raffles* was originated on the stage by Kyrle Bellew in 1903. It was first made as a film by Universal in 1925 with House Peters. The property would be remade by Goldwyn in 1940 with the upcoming David Niven as the new "Amateur Cracksman."

who successfully eludes Scotland Yard but falls in love with Lady Gwen (Kay Francis) and decides to go straight. *The Devil to Pay* (United Artists, 1930), in which he is the son of an English lord (Frederick Kerr) who talks to his dog and has a fun-filled, witty time at Epsom Downs where he enlarges greatly a loan from his father by betting on the winning horses; with his wildest oats fairly well sown, he is then ready to settle into marriage with Loretta Young, the girl of his choice. The screenplay, by Frederick Lonsdale, was written especially for Ronald. *The Unholy Garden* (United Artists, 1931),[28] in which he is an English (what else?) thief of considerable charm who escapes to a port near the Sahara Desert, the one spot on earth where all criminals have immunity. There, he is romanced by two beauties (Fay Wray and Estelle Taylor), but he is too busy being clever in his quest for wealth. This film was said to be Ronald's least favorite of those in which he had appeared.

Although Goldwyn was often accused of being blinded to reality wherever the career of Ronald Colman was concerned, the magnate realized the star's drawing power was in danger of a decline. Something had to be done to recoup the status Colman enjoyed when he was Oscar-nominated[29] for his performances in *Bulldog Drummond* and *Condemned*. With typical perspicacity, Goldwyn reached into the production barrel and, on December 6, 1931, revealed one of his production masterpieces. It was *Arrowsmith* (United Artists), based on the Pulitzer Prize-winning novel by Sinclair Lewis. Mr. Lewis and playwright-scenarist Sidney Howard had persuaded Goldwyn that the episodic nature of the novel and its unusual thematic material could be made into a film, and that audiences could be made to empathize with the turmoil of the midwestern doctor who sacrifices personal needs for the cause of medicine. Directed by John Ford,[30] the film is one of the best[31] to come from Hollywood in the early 1930s, although it and its sterling cast were ignored when it came to handing out awards for the 1931-1932 cinema season.

---

[28]Goldwyn's publicists pushed hard with this vehicle, labeling it "A great star's greatest achievement! Now giving you the thrill of a lifetime in a sensational drama of sinners, sirens, and strange adventure."

The *London Times* was not impressed, judging, "The makers of this film have not troubled to do more than their bare duty." As for Colman, the same paper, reported, "[He] plays the part easily and well, tumbling excitingly from one scrape to another, double-crossing his associates with a coolness which compels our admiration and making love with the regretful tenderness of a man whose past must always stand between him and a happiness he has glimpsed too late. For him, good actor that he is, the part is only too simple."

[29]George Arliss won the Oscar in 1929-1930 for his performance in *Disraeli*. Other nominees had included Arliss (*The Green Goddess*), Wallace Beery (*The Big House*), Maurice Chevalier (*The Love Parade, The Big Pond*), and Lawrence Tibbett (*The Rogue Song*).

[30]This was Ford's first film away from Fox since 1921. The director says, "It was a good story and I think it's still a very modern picture."

[31]In *Hollywood in the Thirties* (1968) John Baxter evaluates *Arrowsmith* as "among the

With Fay Wray
in *The Unholy Garden* **(1931)**

With Helen Hayes
in *Arrowsmith* **(1931)**

Some said that Ronald, with his very distinctive British accent, was all wrong to portray the very midwestern Martin Arrowsmith. However, after screening the completed film, author Lewis wrote Colman, saying, "I want to thank you for *Arrowsmith;* it completely carried out everything I tried to do in the novel." Martin Arrowsmith, M.D. is an idealist when he hangs out his shingle in a small Wisconsin town with his selfless wife, Leora (Helen Hayes), at his side. He is vastly disappointed on learning that his serum discovery for combatting a virus that was killing cattle had been earlier discovered in France. Going to

best films of its time," citing its "literary adaptation and pertinent social comment." He adds, "Ford's direction and restrained acting from Ronald Colman as the idealistic Doctor Martin Arrowsmith and Helen Hayes as his wife Leora give an intensity to the film that few of its contemporaries attain."

In his booklet *Samuel Goldwyn: The Producer and his Films* (Museum of Modern Art, 1956), Richard Griffith responds to the inherent problems of making *Arrowsmith.* "The conflict between long-term experimental research and immediate piteous human needs is not understood by any large section of the public even today. To make such a conflict of ideas and levels of knowledge the heart of a film drama was unheard of in 1931. *Arrowsmith* was an early forerunner of what came to be known in the late thirties as 'message pictures.' . . . This is a script which, as well as any single instance, exemplifies the meaning of the 'Goldwyn touch': in its elusion of the incidental and highlighting of the genuinely thematic elements of the plot, an editorial task which was the joint responsibility of producer and writer. . . . *Arrowsmith* stands alone in a year whose typical productions otherwise were *The Public Enemy* and *Frankenstein.*"

the West Indies, he fights the bubonic plague, which takes the life of his Leora, but he continues his scientific work up to the film's end.[32]

With the career-satisfying success of *Arrowsmith* to reconfirm that Colman was still at the peak of his boxoffice prowess,[33] the star decided that he could well afford to take a leisurely holiday away from picture-making. Let Lowell Sherman, Adolph Menjou, and Ronald's good friend William Powell wear themselves to a frazzle making one film after another. The public response to *Arrowsmith* proved that Colman had nothing to fear from his competitors. (Such former competitors as John Gilbert already were in sharp professional decline, leaving even a clearer field for the champion from the Goldwyn lot.

When Ronald did return to filmmaking, it was in *Cynara* (United Artists), his sole 1932 picture. There had been those critics who had complained[34] that *Arrowsmith* was a bit of miscasting from the usual run-of-roles offered by the urbane Colman. But *Cynara* put Ronald into a drawingroom drama in which he was perfectly at ease. Granted, the premise of the film was a bit strange, for it insisted that a thought-ful, kindly soul who indulges in marital indiscretions will cause a good deal of pain to those around him. As Richard Watts, Jr. would state in the *New York Herald-Tribune*, "Good intentions are bound to result in general unhappiness." It required a more indulgent filmgoer to agree with the view expressed by *Variety* concerning this plot premise: "[The] story really is a romantic tragedy, built out of a minor bit of philandering. A Frenchman would have made it into high comedy but this serious and sympathetic handling gives it powerful appeal for the women fans and therein lies its prospect for commercial success. That and the genuinely moving sincerity of its acting."

With its special moral standard, *Cynara* (from Ernest Dowson's poe-try line, "I have been faithful to thee Cynara, in my fashion") recounts, through some clumsy flashbacks, the story of an English barrister[35] in London who is wed to Kay Francis. When his wife is forced to go to Venice on family matters, he becomes involved, innocently at first, with Phyllis Barry. As the symbol of shaken British austerity, however,

---

[32]Spencer Tracy would portray the dedicated Arrowsmith in the "Lux Radio Theatre" abridgement broadcast on October 25, 1937.

[33]The London *Times* championed: "It is Mr. Colman who in the best performance we have yet seen him give, threads together the short, rapid scenes so that they fall into a satisfying unit."

[34]The *New York Herald-Tribune* criticized of *Arrowsmith* that "it undeniably suffers from the fact that the pleasant Englishman [Colman], despite his histrionic virtues, is not quite the type. In the first place, he is too definitely British for the part, and, in addition to that, he is perhaps a bit too dashing and romantic-looking for the role of an eager-eyed zealot with a religious passion for scientific research."

[35]The stage edition of *Cynara* was first presented at the Playhouse in London on June 26, 1930, with Sir Gerald du Maurier and Gladys Cooper starred. On Broadway it played at the Morosco Theatre (November 2, 1931, 210 performances) with Philip Merivale and Phoebe Foster starred.

Colman's Jim Warlock has the plight of a man with no gift for unfaithfulness[36] (despite his remark to his mistress, "Doris dear, don't you see you don't know what you're doing? I do"). The affair ends tragically with Miss Barry killing herself.

As cinema historian Richard Griffith would later reassess, "[In *Cynara*] Ronald Colman . . . finds a role which gives full expression to his sensitive talent. That may have been what Mr. Goldwyn had in mind in supplying him with so unorthodox a vehicle." Most critics[37] of the day found Colman up to his usual standard of efficient playing. The *New York Times* reported: "Mr. Colman is always on the *qui vive* to avoid any suggestion of awkwardness, and if Warlock is talking, Mr. Colman invariably finds something to occupy his hands. There is a pleasing sincerity about his acting, which evidently has been helped by Mr. Vidor's imaginative direction."

Ronald's performance in his next film, *The Masquerader* (United

---

[36]At one point in the film, Colman says to Francis, "This sex business is just so much nonsense."

[37]One leading source found unfavorable aspects to Ronald's performance. "Mr. Colman is efficient, Mr. Colman is dexterous, but a great deal more than efficiency and dexterity are needed to make Jim a sufficiently interesting character decisively to win the struggle between an imaginative and a stereotyped interpretation of the story." (*London Times*).

With Al Jolson, Douglas Fairbanks, Sr., Mary Pickford, Samuel Goldwyn, and Eddie Cantor on the United Artists lot (1932)

With Kay Francis in *Cynara* (1932)

With Elissa Landi in *The Masquerader* (1933)

131

Artists, 1933), was much more interesting. He performed in a dual role (his second), although he hated doing so and swore never to do so again. He said, "If an actor is good, a doubleheader characterization will add nothing to his stature." He begins the picture as Sir John Chilcote,[38] a drug-addicted member of the English Parliament. His cousin, journalist John Loder, identical in looks, is persuaded to fill in for him when he has a "spell" and gives a compelling speech in the House of Commons. Ronald's leading lady is Elissa Landi as Sir John's estranged wife.

Goldwyn's press crew manufactured a rather specious publicity compaign for *The Masquerader*, with billboards blazoning the slogan, "His own wife couldn't tell these two men apart! But his mistress could! Why?" The thrust of the advertisement could perhaps be justified by the tenor of reviews. *Variety* reported, "Classiest of class productions, treatment and casting failed to blow the breath of life into this noted synopsis." As for Colman's performance, the *New York Sun* recorded, "Somehow or other, though, the film never permits his personality to come through at its best." A large portion of the *New York Times'* review was devoted to the technical aspects of the trick photography. "The double exposures in which the drug-wrecked Chilcote is beheld conversing with the debonair Loder are set forth with great artistry and Mr. Colman seizes his opportunity to give emphatically different natures to the two individuals."

Above and beyond the merits and/or deficiencies of *The Masquerader*, the film had some other built-in publicity value that might well have been exploited to the hilt had Goldwyn been sure how the matter would terminate. In the late summer of 1932, Goldwyn, through his publicity department, had stated in passing that Ronald "looks better for pictures when moderately dissipated than when completely fit." Goldwyn asserted that Colman was generally drunk on the set and performed his best celluloid love scenes while in that condition. Ronald sued his employer in mid-September, 1932, for two million dollars, charging the corporation caused statements to be issued which "reflected upon my character and my ability as an actor." The star swore that he would never again work for the iconoclastic Goldwyn.

Goldwyn's calm reply, through his attorneys, was that Ronald could not work for anyone else until his contract expired two years hence. While the legal brains battled and jockeyed for top positioning, *Cynara* and *The Masquerader* were released. The studio could have easily publicized *The Masquerader* as Colman's "last film for the duration."

In early 1933, while the legal hassles were progressing, Ronald's name was briefly linked with that of Lupe Velez, but no one took

[38]Portrayed on Broadway (Lyric Theatre: September 3, 1917, 160 performances) by Guy Bates Post, who also took the dual roles in the 1922 film version released by Associated First National.

seriously the possibility of a romance between the man who epitomized the cultured and dignified Britisher and the girl known as "The Mexican Spitfire." As the undisputed leader of the British film colony in Hollywood, Ronald remained, outwardly at least, unattainable and a recluse. *Vanity Fair* Magazine, in 1933, reproduced a Steichen photograph of him with this description: "His unobtrusive, self-confident British charm, his casual preciousness, his reticent manner, which are entirely refuted by the intensive pride that crackles in his brown eyes —these saving qualities have done much to make him so popular on the screen."

When it seemed that his *contretemps* with Goldwyn might continue indefinitely, Ronald took a vacation trip around the world. During a twelve-month period he visited Japan, China, Spain, Italy, France, and England. In London he became re-acquainted with an English film actress, Benita Hume (she had tested for a role in *Cynara*), and he initiated divorce proceedings from his long-estranged wife.

The threat of preventing Ronald from making a movie for two years (which would mean a loss of about $500,000 in salary income for the star) led to rumors that Colman might go to England to star in pictures for Alexander Korda. Instead, it was Darryl F. Zanuck of the newly-formed Twentieth Century Studios (releasing through United Artists) who came to the rescue of Ronald's career.[39] After Goldwyn settled out of court with his ex-star, the contract was sold to Zanuck and the actor resumed film making. This, of course, ended any possibility of Colman appearing with Goldwyn's new import, Anna Sten, in *Nana* or *We Live Again,* both 1934 United Artists releases.

On August 1, 1934, Ronald officially became a man free of marital connections (a *decree nisi* was entered for Thelma Raye in the undefended divorce suit), and, on August fourteenth, his first Twentieth Century production was unveiled at Manhattan's Rivoli Theatre. Semantically at least, *Bulldog Drummond Strikes Back* (United Artists) was an appropriate title for his initial film away from Goldwyn.

This time, the amateur sleuth[40] is accused by Scotland Yard of pestering the poor, beleagued Oriental Prince Achmed (Warner Oland),

---

[39]A popularity contest held in 1934 requested fifty Hollywood actresses (including Jeanette MacDonald, Norma Shearer, Madge Evans, Loretta Young, Bette Davis, Irene Dunne, Dolores Del Rio, Ginger Rogers, Claudette Colbert, Barbara Stanwyck, Ann Harding, and Ethel Merman) to pick their ten favorite male stars. The final tally in order of preference listed: Ronald Colman, Fredric March, Clark Gable, Nils Asther, Joel McCrea, Francis Lederer, James Cagney, Richard Arlen, and Randolph Scott.

[40]Among the actors to have played Bulldog Drummond oncamera have been (besides Colman): Carlyle Blackwell in the British *Bulldog Drummond* (Astra-National, 1923), Jack Buchanan in the English *Bulldog Drummond's Third Round* (Astra-National, 1925), Kenneth MacKenna in *Temple Tower* (Fox, 1930), Ralph Richardson in the British *The Return of Bulldog Drummond* (Wardour, 1934), John Lodge in the English *Bulldog Drummond at Bay* (Wardour, 1937). Paramount revitalized the property as a series, first with Ray Milland as the sleuth in *Bulldog Drummond Escapes* (1937), and

133

With Loretta Young in *Bulldog Drummond Strikes Back* (1934)

but in reality the Far Eastern royal figure is a fur smuggler. Drummond pursues the villain through many exciting sequences, which are happily interspersed with comic performances by Charles Butterworth (as Algy Longsworth), Una Merkel (Butterworth's fianceé), and C. Aubrey Smith (Inspector Neilsen). Loretta Young, who had been lured away from First National-Warner Bros. to Twentieth by Zanuck, was seen as Lola Field, the gal beloved by the amateur detective.

There is much to recommend this follow-up Colman-Drummond film. In particular, the jocular element that made the 1929 entry so endearing was also present in the new adventure, even, if this time, only the good guys had humorous overtones to their characterizations. Ronald was in capital form as the sophisticated gentleman thief, using his comedy flair with precision timing. Two particular moments stand out as highlights of this joshing film. At one point the ever optimistic Colman, undaunted by an especially perilous situation, exclaims to his sidekick, "Think of it, Algy! . . . Alone . . . unarmed . . . surrounded by villains . . . locked in a cellar . . . from that, to complete mastery of the situation in ten minutes. *If* we can do that, we'll be magnificent!" (As, of course, the intrepid duo were.) Later on in the eighty-three-minute film, directed with dispatch by Roy Del Ruth, Colman looks front-

---

then, for the seven remaining entries in the series, with John Howard starred. Howard's first in the programmer series was *Bulldog Drummond Comes Back* (Paramount, 1937).

view-right into the camera, shrugs his noble shoulders, arches his eyebrows, and waits with refined resignation for the next set of calamities to befall him.

As Mrs. Goldwyn could have attested, her husband Sam had been obsessed with presenting Colman in a variety of guises to delight filmgoers. Ronald's new boss, Darryl F. Zanuck, a man who would be more noteworthy in his efforts to promulgate female star attractions (Loretta Young, Alice Faye, Betty Grable, Gene Tierney, June Haver) and a moppet superstar (Shirley Temple), was almost as determined as Goldwyn to promote Colman as the greatest star attraction of the 1930s. Zanuck assigned Ronald to *Clive of India* (United Artists, 1935). If Robert Donat could shine in *The Count of Monte Cristo* (United Artists, 1934) and Errol Flynn could charm in *Captain Blood* (First National, 1935), and Clark Gable flaunt masculinity in *Mutiny on the Bounty* (MGM), then Colman could reinstate his *Beau Geste* image for the greater glory of Zanuck's Twentieth Century firm.[41]

For *Clive of India,* forty-four-year-old Ronald shaved his moustache, a trademark that had endeared him to feminine fans for more than ten years. Robert Clive (1725-1774), who began his career at

[41]The play (Wyndhan's Theatre, London: January, 1934, 409 performances), which starred Leslie Banks as Clive, was purchased by Zanuck for $75,000. In early 1975 it was producer Gene Corman, who planned to make a new, more elaborate study of *Clive of India.* At one point, Sean Connery was considered for the title role in the five-million-dollar roadshow entry.

As *Clive of India* (1935)

twenty-one as a clerk with the East India Company, had too full a life to be totally recorded on film. Many of the dramatic events of this dedicated man's existence were covered with only a mention or a subtitle denoting the occurrence. Historically exaggerated (but nothing compared to later Zanuck paeans to momentous personages and events), the screenplay by W. P. Lipscomb and Rubeigh James Minney takes the young man through his conquest of southern India, to his position as one of England's richest men at age thirty-four, and into Parliament. With each passing decade his hair became whiter. Through his spectacular eighteenth-century achievements, he is married to Margaret (Loretta Young), but relinquishes his family ties for India. "India is a sacred trust," he says. "I must keep faith." Clive died a broken man.

Perhaps the costliest ($30,000) scene of the film was the depiction of The Black Hole of Calcutta, a sequence which was onscreen for perhaps fifteen seconds at most. Into the dungeon, eighteen feet by fourteen feet, the Indians in June, 1756, placed 146 English prisoners from Fort William in Calcutta. After one night in the small, dark space only twenty-three prisoners were still alive.

Ronald told a Hollywood writer in January, 1935, "If *Clive* has a big success I will be extremely happy because it will open still further possibilities for worthwhile stories on the screen. I have enjoyed playing this historic Englishman more than any role on the screen. If I do another historical film soon I would like to play an American historical character." His statement, obviously aimed at aiding his boxoffice potential, was anything but prophetic, since all studios in the mid-thirties were aiming their salvos at the historical drama which had found sudden popularity with moviegoers.

Otis Ferguson (*The New Republic*) may have labeled *Clive of India* "dilly-dally biography with elephants and Ronald Colman," but Thornton Delehanty (*New York Evening Post*) was more in accord with public response when he wrote, "Its prodigious use of men and materials are justifiable not merely in their eye-filling quality, but as proper accoutrements for the epic style of the subject." There is no denying that *Clive of India* exhibited the usual drawback of a Darryl F. Zanuck production: an overconcerted effort to pander to the most popular of tastes, omitting any obtrusive fact that hindered the flow of the narrative or prevented the intrusion of a tidy domestic sequence.[42] (After all, the $2,000 weekly salary paid to Miss Young had to be justified by having her appear oncamera sometime, and she certainly was not to be found in the battle of Plassey scene or the other action bits.)

---

[42]André Sennwald of the *New York Times* felt duty-bound to note that, midway into the picture, "the film divides its attentions—fatally, in the opinion of this reporter— between Clive's public triumphs and defeats and his intermittent quarrels with his wife, who want him to settle down to the life of an English country gentleman. . . . The drama

How did the British react to Colman's interpretation of an empire builder? *Today's Cinema* reported, "He infuses the character with just the right air of mad adventure and makes of Clive a believable and highly interesting figure." The American press was only a little less generous to Ronald's impersonation: "Suppressing the debonair manner which has made him one of our finest light comedians, [he] enacts the title role with vigor and conviction, providing a touching portrait of a man with consuming passion for power. Certainly this is one of his best screen achievements." (*New York Times*) Today *Clive of India* may seem anachronistic and corny, not to mention cliché-ridden, but in 1935 it was received with the same enthusiasm that greeted a typical Cecil B. DeMille spectacle; it was seen to be a rousing, mindless tribute to adventure.[43] At least a Zanuck's product could boast of its Anglophile patriotism which infused the storyline, and a heady interpretation of a visionary zealot by Mr. Colman.

The ladies of the world were able to relax after seeing Ronald's next film. His moustache was back, an indication that all was right with their handsome hero. *The Man Who Broke the Bank at Monte Carlo*

concludes, not with his collapse and suicide, but, more optimistically, in his wife's arms following their long separation."

[43]In late 1974, producer Gene Corman made plans to film a roadshow version of Robin Garton's book *Clive of India*, with Sean Connery mentioned as a contender for the lead part.

With Joan Bennett in a publicity pose for *The Man Who Broke the Bank at Monte Carlo* (1935)

137   ·

(1935), released through Zanuck's newly reorganized Twentieth Century-Fox, presented Ronald as an expatriate Russian nobleman employed by a Parisian cafe. He does just as the film title[44] says, and then is pursued by the casino's Joan Bennett, who is hired to bring him back with his loot. It is the casino's hope that he will lose it at the gambling tables. She lures him back, but in the process falls in love with him. He gambles and loses, whereupon she tears up her paycheck and dashes after him. Andre Sennwald (*New York Times*) thought Ronald "handsome and debonair, though somewhat less sprightly than is his custom."

Realizing that his new forte lay in interpreting adventurers with noble souls, Ronald eagerly requested a loanout to MGM when that studio's David O. Selznick acquired the screen rights from Warner Bros. of Charles Dickens' *A Tale of Two Cities* (1935). Warners sold the property after its proposed star, Leslie Howard, refused the dual role of Sydney Carton/Charles Darnay. Ronald was signed[45] for the picture, in spite of his past denunciation of dual roles. He saw no reason why one performer should enact both characters. In Dickens' classic novel about the French Revolution, Carton and Darnay resemble each other, but are *not* identical in looks. Ronald won the argument, with Donald Woods commissioned to play Darnay to his Carton.

Carton, as all Dickens readers know, is a lonely London barrister in love with Lucie Manette (Elizabeth Allan). She, however, considers him no more than a friend, and marries Darnay, the nephew of the most hated aristocrat in all of France, the Marquis St. Evremonde

---

[44]The Fox film's title attained a good deal of publicity for its tie-in with the popular song "The Man That Broke the Bank at Monte Carlo" (1892) by Fred Gilbert. A law suit entailing the film's use of the title (unfair competition was the cause of action) occurred, with the plaintiff winning his case.

[45]In *Memo from Donald O. Selznick* (Viking Press, 1972) Rudy Belhmer includes correspondence from the producer to Nicholas M. Schenck of MGM in New York. The October 3, 1935 memo states (in part): "I should like also to call to your attention the danger of treating this picture as just another Colman starring vehicle. Granted that Colman is a big star; that any picture with him achieves a good gross. *A Tale of Two Cities*, even badly produced, would completely dwarf the importance of any star, and certainly it does any picture that Colman has appeared in since *Beau Geste*. The picture is beautifully produced. If I do not say this, no one else in the organization will. It has been splendidly directed by Jack Conway; and Colman is at his very top. Further, bear in mind that the book *A Tale of Two Cities* would without Colman have a potential drawing power equaled only by *David Copperfield, Little Women*, and *The Count of Monte Cristo* among the films of recent years because only these books have an even comparable place in the affections of the reading public."

In the same memo, Selznick took pains to mention: "Can you imagine if it were made by Zanuck? Just think back to the ballyhoo attendant upon *Clive of India* [1935] and how the whole trade was led to believe that this dreadful picture was a masterpiece. If *Clive of India* had been even a passable picture, its gross after its buildup would have been fabulous. As it is, I think whatever gross it did attain can be attributed largely to the loyalty of the Zanuck organization to its product, the excitement of Twentieth Century and United Artists executives about it, and the publicity campaign that accompanied every step of its production and release."

With Isabel Jewell in *A Tale of Two Cities* (1935)

(Basil Rathbone). Darnay, a compassionate young man, had fled to England to escape his uncle's tyranny. With the start of the revolution in France, all members of the St. Evremonde family are murdered except Darnay, who has returned to France. But he is also condemned to die. Because Carton cannot stand the thought of his beloved Lucie going through the torment of losing her husband to the guillotine, he persuades Darnay that he will change places with him.

As Darnay, Lucie, and their child (Fay Chaldecott) face freedom, Carton ascends the steps leading to the guillotine. "It is a far, far better thing I do now than I have ever done. It is a far, far better rest that I go to than I have ever known." His resonant, hopeful words echo from the screen as the camera moves away from the fanatical mob, the deadly instrument of death, and the man who gives his life for the only woman he has ever loved, and focuses on the cloudless calm sky above.

A Tale of Two Cities[46] was an enormous crowd-pleaser and confirmed once again that in his chosen arena, Colman was without a peer. It is difficult to imagine any of the other contemporary swashbuckler

---

[46]Other screen versions of the Dickens novel have included: Vitagraph, 1911, with Maurice Costello; Fox, 1917, with William Farnum; W. C. Rowden, 1922, with Clive Brook; British First National, 1925, as *The Only Way*, with John Martin Harvey; and J. Arthur Rank, 1958, with Dirk Bogarde. CBS-TV's "DuPont Show of the Month" on March 27, 1958, telecast a video version starring James Donald, Denholm Elliott, and Rosemary Harris.

leading men—whether Robert Donat (*The Count of Monte Cristo*), Leslie Howard (*The Scarlet Pimpernel*), Clark Gable (*Mutiny on the Bounty*), Errol Flynn (*Captain Blood*), Douglas Fairbanks, Sr. (*Private Life of Don Juan*), or Gary Cooper (*The Lives of a Bengal Lancer*)—investing the potentially sticky characterization[47] of Carton with the proper sense of recognition, humanitarianism, and, most of all, decency. The *London Times* extolled Ronald's performance as "subtle—Dickens created in Carton the most psychologically complicated of all his characters and Mr. Colman, who has never acted so well before, has realized it." For the second time in his screen career, Ronald shaved his moustache in order to play a screen role.

On March 22, 1936, The House Ways and Means Committee in Washington, D.C., reported the salaries of movie stars and moguls of industry. It was revealed that Ronald's earnings for 1934 had amounted to $108,000. Also in 1936, Ronald's pal, William Powell, told *Photoplay* Magazine of his delight over Ronald's relationship with Benita Hume. "I hope they will marry," he said. "Benita is good for Ronnie." This was also the era of Louella O. Parsons' CBS Radio show, "Hollywood Hotel," one of the first to emanate from the West Coast. Louella reportedly collected $2,500 a week for hostessing the broadcasts, but the stars appeared on the program without payment. The only three invited guests to refuse the "honor" of appearing without remuneration were Ronald Colman, Ginger Rogers, and Ruth Chatterton. For their effrontery, the stars were excommunicated for years from Louella's syndicated newspaper column. (A few years later, when the Screen Actors Guild decreed that Louella must simply pay her guests, the show folded within a thirteen-week period.)

Under Two Flags (1936) was to be Ronald's final film under his contract with Twentieth Century-Fox. As directed by Frank Lloyd, the film is filled with action as Sergeant Victor[48] (Ronald), a dashing French Foreign Legionnaire, is sent into the Arab-controlled desert by his commandant (Victor McLaglen). It seems that the high officer loves Cigarette[49] (Claudette Colbert), a café girl, who, instead, loves Sergeant Victor. The latter, in turn, loves Lady Venetia (Rosalind Rus-

---

[47]In *Hollywood in the Thirties* (Tantivy Press, 1968), John Baxter writes of Colman and the influence of director Jack Conway on the film. "His direction of Ronald Colman . . . seems, because of the aptness of the Sydney Carton character to Conway's approach, especially effective; nobody has captured so accurately Carton's melancholy fatalism or the moral necessities which can drive a man to self-destruction. If only for the scene where Carton waits in the snow at Christmas time and watches the carollers and churchgoers hurry past to the warmth of the home which he does not possess, *A Tale of Two Cities* must be considered one of the most successful films of the period."

[48]Played by Herbert Heyes in the 1916 Fox version and by William Farnum in the 1922 Universal remake.

[49]Simone Simon, a Fox contractee, had originally begun filming the part, but after ten days of shooting, it was deemed necessary to replace her. Former "It" Girl Clara Bow was among those considered for the role before Claudette was borrowed from Paramount.

140

With Marc Lawrence, Claudette Colbert, and Francis McDonald in *Under Two Flags* (1936)

sell),[50] but the commandant thinks that Victor loves Cigarette. So, he sends him on the dangerous mission, hoping he will not return. Cigarette saves the day as she boisterously leads the Chasseurs to Victor's rescue. The battle is won, but she dies in Victor's arms. The production cost over $1 million and was expansive and sweeping but hardly "so truly great . . . no claim can exaggerate its glory" (as the Fox publicity department extolled). Ronald, who was commended for his easy, smooth portrayal, received quite a bit of publicity during the picture's filming in Yuma, Arizona, when Yaqui Indian knife thrower Steve Clements missed his mark and nicked Colman in the chest.

Now at liberty, Ronald decided to freelance rather than to sign another restrictive contract with Fox. Zanuck did not push the point, for he had become suddenly intrigued with the potentials of a young player on the Fox lot named Tyrone Power, who would make his mark in

---

[50]Not long ago, Miss Russell recalled, "Ronald Colman was charming, but he never would kiss you on the mouth. He always got over on the corner of your mouth because of the better camera angle.

"He knew the camera better than any actor I have known.

"He also played a little bit to your ear, never looking you in the eyes, so that his face would be more turned toward the camera.

"That was always a little disconcerting. After I couldn't find his eyes, I asked, 'What is he doing?' And I learned something from him. That was the way he worked with everyone. He couldn't have been more polite. He was the essence of good manners."

141

the swashbuckling field with *Lloyds of London* (Twentieth Century-Fox, 1937). Power was a good two decades younger than Colman and his salary—at that time—was a good deal less.

It was also in 1936 that David O. Selznick began his search for stars to portray the larger-than-life characters of Margaret Mitchell's Civil War novel, *Gone with the Wind.* Among those mentioned as possibilities for the role of Rhett Butler were Colman, Gary Cooper, Preston Foster, Basil Rathbone, and Clark Gable. Ronald, who was never one to make a quick decision (and a man who dearly loved his privacy and especially his leisure time), studied the pros and cons of the matter after Selznick had painstakingly discussed the plum role with him. The largest concern on the part of the producer was whether Ronald could simulate a proper Southern accent, and he took his time making up his mind. Meanwhile, he said to *Photoplay* Magazine, "I should say that, on the whole, the casting of Clark Gable as Rhett might meet with the approval of the greatest number of people." So true; Gable seemed to have been born to the characterization. It is odd that Ronald was not considered for the part of Ashley Wilkes (which went to Leslie Howard), for which he seemed more temperamentally suited.

It was not a case of Ronald being cavalier in his interest in the potential role of Rhett Butler; he was also busy with other film projects, such as *Lost Horizon* (Columbia, 1937).

Screenwriter Robert Riskin worked with director Frank Capra for

With Benita Hume and Theodore Von Eltz at Beverly Hills Tennis Club (July, 1937)

142

In _Lost Horizon_ (1937)

almost two years in adapting the James Hilton novel (1933) for the screen. On Columbia's ranch in Burbank rose a huge never-never land of sprawling lawns, gushing fountains, and milky white buildings. The entire production cost two million dollars, one-half the expense of Columbia's entire lineup of films for a year. (Ronald's salary for the picture was $162,500.)

When the elaborate production was completed, Capra had twenty-six reels of showable film. He cut this to fourteen reels and premiered it at Santa Barbara. However, the audience reaction was disastrous. The moviegoers laughed! In desperation, he edited two more reels off the top (which set the stage for the flashback) and premiered it a second time, now at Wilmington, California. In its new format it was received heartily. The director personally burned the two reels that had contained the preliminary introductions to the characters.

While the subsequent appearance of a horrendous musical remake[51] of _Lost Horizon_ (Columbia, 1973), with Peter Finch and Liv Ullman, makes the original version seem even better than it is, a close analysis of the thirties' edition indicates that Colman's strong portrayal of Robert Conway is a mixture more of professionalism than inspired acting. This is not to downgrade Colman's contributions to the feature, for such a blend of performance ingredients was standard practice for stars of the day.

[51]A short-lived stage musical of _Lost Horizon_ (Winter Garden Theatre: June 19, 1956, 21 performances) with book and lyrics by James Hilton, Jerome Lawrence, and Robert E. Lee, music by Harry Warren, starred Dennis King in the Colman role.

The *Lost Horizon* scripters make sure that protagonist Robert Conway (in the book called Hugh "Glory" Conway) blends into the accepted screen image *then* so closely allied to the Colman celluloid persona, that of a visionary humanitarian of the highest debonair order. As the story[52] opens, Colman's Conway is identified as "England's Man of the East," a very important figure who, we are led to believe, can help save the world from self-destruction. The time is July 7, 1936[53] and the place is the strife-torn Chinese city of Baskul.

Conway, a former soldier-turned-diplomat, is suddenly plunged into an adventure of romance and mysticism. The city is about to be occupied by the Japanese, and Conway must evacuate the bastion with as many Caucasians (no natives were to be rescued) as possible. Aboard this last plane to freedom, which is headed for Shanghai, are Conway and four other "foreigners": Conway's impulsive brother George (John Howard), Lovett, the pristine paleontologist (Edward Everett Horton), Barnard, the backslapping businessman-freebooter (Thomas Mitchell), and Gloria Stone, a rather hysterical tart (Isabel Jewell).

We soon learn that Conway is a man of courage and resourcefulness. Throughout the aerial ordeal, he remains calm, in marked contrast to the others. As the adventure tale progresses, the plane makes a crash landing and the passengers are eventually rescued from their mountain peak resting spot by a caravan of natives, led by one called Chang (H. B. Warner). After a treacherous descent they are led into the Valley of the Blue Moon where lies the gleaming lamasery of Shangri-la, set far below the Himalayas, "with the chance delicacy of a flower petal impaled upon a crag."

Here the wayfarers learn that time has little meaning and that the people truly love one another. Almost at once, Conway is at peace with the world ("Did you ever go to a totally strange place and feel you'd been there before?"). He soon becomes taken by Sondra (Jane Wyatt) and is informed by the high lama (Sam Jaffe[54]) that he has been chosen, because of his efforts toward global peace, to succeed him.[55]

[52]Interestingly it took author Hilton only some six weeks to write the novel while Capra was involved with the film project for two years.

[53]Later in the film, when the story shifts to the enchanted city, Edward Everett Horton's character writes in his diary, "Second day at Shangri-la—March 13th [!]" This is obviously one of the technical boners in the picture.

[54]Both Henry B. Walthall and A. E. Anson who had been considered for the role died before filming began. Charles Laughton was another contender for the role, and actually, at Harry Cohn's insistence, Walter Connelly re-did all of Jaffe's scenes. However, Capra prevailed in using the Jaffe footage for the final release print.

[55]It is during one of the philosophical discussions between the elder of Shangri-la and Conway that a rather discomforting realization creeps up on the viewer (especially when seen today). Jaffe's lama, who is supposed to be approximately two hundred and six years old, says to Colman's Conway (Colman, in real life, was approaching the professionally "dangerous" age of fifty), "You are a relatively youngish man. . . . in normal life you could expect twenty or thirty years of gradually diminished activity." It was also a rather prophetic statement concerning Ronald's own cinema future!

As *Lost Horizon* unwinds its mystical plot, Conway feels it is his duty to help George reach the outer world, regardless of the fact that in Shangri-la he (Conway) has found "the answer to the bewilderment and confusion of a lifetime." Before leaving, they are warned that Maria, (Margo) the alleged eighteen-year-old girl with whom George has fallen in love, will die of "old age" once out of Shangri-la. However, George takes no notice of this advice, and the three set off through the mountain passes and over the treacherous snow trails. As predicted, Maria becomes weak and, before she dies, she admits that she is really over sixty years old. George is later killed, and Robert, alone, makes his way out of the mountains. (In the course of Conway's trek back to civilization, the long shots—which seem to be stock footage—reveal a man with a very shaggy beard and hair. In the close-ups for this sequence, Colman's Conway has rather closely trimmed facial hair.) Later, back in civilization, he finds that he is no longer happy and dreams of returning to Shangri-la, the unbelievable refuge from reality. The closing shots find "the man who was not human" approaching the mountain entrance to the wondrous city. Peace on earth is to be his.

When *Lost Horizon* premiered at the Globe Theatre on March 3, 1937, for a two-a-day showing it was declared a hit by the critics and by the public.[56] "[It] is a grand adventure film, magnificently staged, beautifully photographed and capitally played." (*New York Times*) Frank S. Nugent of the *Times* had "nothing but unqualified endorsement here of Mr. Colman's Conway," but it is significant to note that in this year when Spencer Tracy (of *Captains Courageous*) won the Best Actor Oscar, Ronald's performance was not even nominated.[57]

Shangri-la was to receive further acknowledgment a few years later during World War II with the first American raid on Tokyo. When asked what base General Doolittle's bombers had used, President Franklin D. Roosevelt said, with a chuckle, "Shangri-la."[58] He referred to it later in a radio broadcast as well. This inspired Columbia to reissue the film in the fall of 1942 as *Lost Horizon of Shangri-la.*[59] In 1946,

[56]There were dissenters, however. One of them was hard-to-please Otis Ferguson (*The New Republic*), who said of *Lost Horizon,* "It strikes me as little more than moxie and noodles, being in total mawkish, muffed, and as mixed up as the only figures by which you could describe the general effect—e.g., by saying in one breath that the Master's hand was not steady on the throttle because in diving off the deep end he has landed on the horns of a dilemma and laid a pretty terrific egg."

[57]Other nominees for the category were Charles Boyer (*Conquest*), Fredric March (*A Star Is Born*), Robert Montgomery (*Night Must Fall*), and Paul Muni (*The Life of Emile Zola*).

[58]The actual base was the aircraft carrier Hornet.

[59]In his *Screen Facts* Magazine article, *Revisiting Lost Horizon* (1963), Edward Connor reveals that between the "roadshow engagement" and the September, 1937, general release of the picture, twelve minutes of film was deleted (including the famous sequence in the aviary). More footage disappeared for the fall 1942 reissue and even more (especially that pertaining to Isabel Jewell) vanished from the 1952 reissue print. What

Ronald would record a six-part adaptation of *Lost Horizon* on three seventy-eight RPM records for the Decca label, with a supporting cast and musical score by Victor Young.[60]

At this time Ronald was contracted by David O. Selznick, some 15 years after he had worked for the producer's father Lewis. At one point, Selznick publicized that he was preparing a new screen version of *Julius Caesar* to be lensed in color, and that Ronald would portray Brutus. Then it was announced that Colman, as part of his seven-year and two-picture-per-annum deal, would appear in *Sometimes It's Fun.* Instead, the Colman-Selznick team came out with a blockbuster. It is one of the finest films ever to come out of the industry. Metro made *The Prisoner of Zenda* in 1922 with Lewis Stone starring, and when Selznick acquired the property it was prepared solely with Ronald in mind. However, this was not done before producer and star had lengthy discussions regarding the necessity of his playing the dual roles of Rassendyll and King Rudolf. Colman relented and portrayed both parts.

Preliminary training for the swashbuckling role of Rassendyll included fencing instructions from a master, Ralph Faulkner, who also took the part of an adversary in the film. For the remainder of the cast, Selznick chose a handful of actors possessing some of the most famous voices available: Madeleine Carroll, Douglas Fairbanks, Jr., C. Aubrey Smith, Raymond Massey, and Mary Astor. The film, released by United Artists, was previewed in Huntington Park, California, in August, 1937, where, strangely, it bombed. Back to the drawing board with Selznick in command. A new beginning to the picture was devised, an Alfred Newman score was added, and several of the dueling scenes were re-photographed by cinematographer James Wong Howe, who interspersed the action with imposing shadows of the duelers against the stone walls of the castle where the king was held prisoner. (W.S. Van Dyke II directed the rousing duel scenes used toward the close of the film.)

Satisfied that he now had a winner, Selznick premiered his adventure film at Manhattan's Radio City Music Hall on September 2, 1937. He was right! As William Boehnel (*New York World-Telegram*) would judge for the majority opinion: "[It] is a film so gay, so witty, so exciting, so thoroughly enjoyable that it definitely ranks among the exceptional pictures of the year." Ronald, sporting a goatee for this rousing actioner, plays both the actor Rudolf Rassendyll and Rassendyll's

---

has appeared on television showings are even more butchered versions.
[60]Also in 1946 Ronald recorded for Decca a rendition of Dickens' *A Christmas Carol,* for which he was Ebenezer Scrooge, and shortly after that, he recorded a condensed version of *A Tale of Two Cities* for the same label.

cousin, King Rudolf of Ruritania. King Rudolf is drugged by his enemies (Massey and Fairbanks, Jr.) in an attempt to keep him off the
throne. But the king's allies have Rassendyll pose as King Rudolf to
cover up the latter's indispostion. When the king's enemies discover

With Douglas Fairbanks, Jr. in *The Prisoner of Zenda* (1937)

the substitution, the real monarch is abducted. Things are further complicated when Rassendyll falls in love with the king's lady, Flavia (Carroll), and tells her, "I love you. With my whole heart and soul I love you." But honor comes between them, and when the king is rescued he leaves her. King Rudolf, safely returned to the throne, tells Rassendyll, "You taught me how to be a king."

Of this "hokum of the 24-carat variety" (*Variety*), Ronald stood out as the guiding force. "[He] has the ability to make a full dress court uniform appear as comfortable as a suit of pajamas. He never trips over his sword, or loosens his collar for air. No matter how ridiculous the costumes, he can make love in a moonlit garden as though he means it." Howard Barnes (*New York Herald-Tribune*) was even more enthusiastic about the veteran star. "The quiet ease of his portrayal would persuade one into accepting far more fantastic happenings than occur in *The Prisoner of Zenda*. . . . Mr. Colman knows how to conjure up sympathy and suspense in a fancy costume without adding too much flourish to the impersonation and he has used the gift to magnificent effect."

At the time, no one was quite aware of it, but *Lost Horizon* and *The Prisoner of Zenda*[61] were the peak films of Ronald's long career. After those pictures, he turned down the lead roles in Selznick's projected productions of *Intermezzo, The Paradine Case, Rebecca,* and *Jane Eyre,*[62] saying the parts were not right for him. He was released from his contractual obligations when he and Selznick were unable to find a suitable vehicle. Although relatively wealthy and not really anxious to work, Colman could not bring himself to stay away from filmmaking for long and he soon signed a two-picture deal with Paramount.

The first vehicle chosen for him was *If I Were King* (1938), directed by Frank Lloyd from the play by Justin Huntley McCarthy.[63] In the lighthearted tale of a fifteenth-century French rascal who becomes Louis XI's Grand Marshal for a few days, Ronald was never more

---

[61]Fifteen years later, MGM would repurchase the screen rights from Selznick and remake it, using much of the dialogue from the Selznick film. Stewart Granger would portray the dual roles in the 1952 color version. There have been at least two musical editions of the story. *Princess Flavia* (Century Theatre: November 2, 1925, 152 performances) had book and lyrics by Harry B. Smith and music by Sigmund Romberg. Harry Welchman and Evelyn Herbert were the stars. *Zenda,* with an updated book by Everett Freeman and music by Vernon Duke, was premiered at the Curran Theatre in San Francisco in August, 1963. Alfred Drake played the dual role leads in this pre-Broadway fizzle.

[62]The parts would be taken, respectively, by Leslie Howard, Gregory Peck, Laurence Olivier, and Orson Welles.

[63]*If I Were King* was first presented on Broadway in 1901 and was revived in 1916, both times with E. H. Sothern as star. In 1925 it became a musical known as *The Vagabond King* and starred Dennis King. Onscreen, William Farnum was François Villon in the Fox film version of 1920, while Dennis King starred in the Paramount musical adaptation in 1930. In 1956, Paramount would again bring *The Vagabond King* to the screen with Oreste featured.

With Ellen Drew and C. V. France in *If I Were King* (1938)

effervescent nor as winsome than as François Villon. He begins his career in Paris in the slums, where it is a matter of every thief for himself. He makes his way to the palace of the eccentric king (Basil Rathbone), where he falls for a lady-in-waiting (Frances Dee). For this visually outstanding picture, that slum quarter of medieval Paris known as the Court of Miracles was reconstructed on 75,000 square feet of Paramount backlot with fifteen buildings on the premises and a slice of the "Seine River" in view.

As the rather tattered, mangy-bearded poet-adventurer who wears baggy tights, long boots, ragged jerkin and cape, and a rakishly angled feathered cap, Colman sparkled as the beguiling rogue. He moves with gusto, acts with charm, and talks with sensitive conviction. In many ways, Ronald's performance was more satisfying than the similarly spirited one of Errol Flynn in the sixteenth-century England of *The Prince and the Pauper* (Warner Bros., 1937).

On September 30, 1938, Ronald and Benita Hume[64] were secretly married on the San Ysidro Ranch near Santa Barbara, California. The bride was thirty-two; Ronald was forty-seven. Attendants at the wed-

[64]Born in London on October 14, 1906, the 5 ft. 5 in. black-haired actress had trained at the Royal Academy of Dramatic Art in London. She had appeared in several British silent features, including *The Happy Ending* (Gaumont, 1925), *Second to None* (Gaumont, 1926), and *The Constant Nymph* (Woolf & Freedman Film Service, 1928). Her British talkie pictures included, *Reserved for Ladies* (Paramount-British, 1931), *Men of*

ding were actress Heather Thatcher and Western actor Colonel Tim McCoy. The Colmans moved into a large, rambling house of white-painted brick in Beverly Hills, where, among others, their neighbors were Jack Benny and his wife Mary Livingstone. Both Ronald and Benita often appeared as guests on Benny's CBS radio show and Ronald's other radio work of the period included "The Screen Guild Theatre" (CBS) on which he was given the opportunity to speak his 1925 silent screen role of the blinded lover in *The Dark Angel*. His co-stars on that occasion were Merle Oberon and Donald Crisp. Ronald was also heard as a master of ceremonies for a panel discussion program called "The Circle," a forerunner of television's talk shows, which did not meet with audience approval. On June 5, 1939, Cecil B. De-Mille presented *The Prisoner of Zenda* on his "Lux Radio Theatre" with Ronald and Douglas Fairbanks, Jr. repeating their screen roles. Benita took the Madeleine Carrol role.

Ronald's second film within the Paramount pact was *The Light that Failed* (1939). In the era of the "woman's picture," this picture was intended for the men, with Ronald as Dick Heldar of the Rudyard Kipling novel.[65] Heldar is an artist who loses his eyesight and retreats to the Sudan, leaving behind him the Cockney girl (Ida Lupino) who would marry him out of pity, and who vengefully destroys his canvas masterpiece when he rejects her.

The production history of this version of *The Light that Failed* was filled with cross purposes. Originally, Paramount had intended it as either a Gary Cooper or a Ray Milland vehicle, and at one point announced it would be lensed in Technicolor. After Colman was signed to the picture, William Wellman, never noted for helming this type of production, was assigned to the project. Almost at once the star and the director clashed. As Wellman would later explain, "Ronald Colman was a gentleman—well, so am I, but I'm a different kind of a gentleman." The feud erupted over the casting of the part of Bessie Broke. Ronald had promised the part to Vivien Leigh, but Wellman had become convinced that Ida Lupino was the proper one for the pivotal part.

According to Wellman, the star stormed into the Paramount executive offices demanding that Wellman be dropped from the picture ("Who the hell is William Wellman?" he allegedly said to the brass).

Steel (Langham, 1932), *Lord Camber's Ladies* (B.I.P., 1932), and *The Private Life of Don Juan* (United Artists-British, 1934). She made her Hollywood film debut in the starring role of *The Worst Woman of Paris?* (Fox, 1933). The picture was a dud and thereafter she obtained only supporting roles in American movies: *The Garden Murder Case* (MGM, 1936), *Tarzan Escapes* (MGM, 1936), *Rainbow on the River* (RKO, 1936), and *The Last of Mrs. Cheyney* (MGM, 1937). Ronald and Hume had met again in Hollywood at a dinner party given by Colman's business manager, William Hawks.

[65]Among the other versions of the Kipling work have been the 1916 Pathé version, and the 1923 Paramount edition, the latter with Percy Marmont.

The studio hierarchy stood firmly by Wellman and suggested to Ronald that if he were unhappy he could walk off the lot and then be sued.

What transpired on *The Light that Failed* set would have made its own telling film story. When it came time to shoot the crucial scene between Colman's artist and Lupino's street urchin, Colman continually blew his line. As director Wellman recalls vividly:

I said, "Cut!" I said to Lupino, "Do you mind doing it again?" "No," she says, "but you must take it now, while I'm still in the mood. . . ." So we do it again, and in the very same place, Colman blows his line. I said, "Cut! Everybody take a break." I say to Colman, "Mr. Colman" . . . it was all "Mr." Colman and "Mr." Wellman, and we were outwardly being very friendly and gentlemanly about the whole thing . . . "Mr. Colman, let's take a walk around the block . . ." So we did, and I said, "Look, I *know* what you're trying to do, and if you want my opinion, I don't think it's worthy of you . . ."—He was trying to undermine the kid's confidence—"Now," I said, "I'm *behind* the camera, and this is what I'll do. You play the scene with Lupino or I'll make a character man out of you. You've got that lovely face, and when I'm through it's gonna look kinda fuzzy—that's what I can do. So how about it . . . ?" So we go back and do the scene, and it's perfect.

Now we come to Colman's big scene. I know he's going to play it beautifully: Colman had this beautiful face, and this lovely voice—well, you know the voice, it was very famous—and he was a *magnificent* actor, so I knew the scene would be great. So I spent the whole time looking at my feet, just listening to that voice. When it's over I say, "Cut!" So Colman comes up. "Well, Mr. Wellman, how was it? How did it go?" "I didn't see it." "Didn't see it?" He looked at me kinda funny. "Nope. I was just listening to the most beautiful voice I ever heard in my life . . ." and Colman sort of backs away with his mouth hanging open.

As far as Colman and Lupino's future professional relationship was concerned, it all ended happily, since Ida was picked several times by Ronald to co-star with him on radio programs.

Although there were many who felt that this edition of *The Light that Failed,* which eschewed the happy ending tacked on to the two earlier versions, was too morose and cynical, the majority opinion was that the film benefitted greatly from "a directness of approach and clarity of thought . . . [and] is essentially the last defiant blaze of the torch of man's freedom from woman. (Naturally it fails, but it's none the less gallant for a 'that.')" (*New York Times*) As for Ronald's performance, Frank S. Nugent of the *Times* decided, "Mr. Colman has rarely handled a role with greater authority or charm, manfully underplaying even the sure-fire melodramatics of the sequence in which he goes blind—a heaven-sent infirmity for 99 out of 100 hard-pressed actors."

After the popular but not sure-fire *The Light that Failed,* Ronald's business manager William Hawks negotiated an agreement with United Producers Corporation which stated that Colman would star in five pictures to be released in the 1940-1943 period through RKO. The star was in no rush to pick his initial vehicle. He carefully waded through the offered projects, being very choosy about the scripts, directors, and leading ladies. It was said that he generally liked only about one out of every twenty-five scripts offered. He decided to put himself onto a more leisurely schedule than had been the case in the late 1930s.

Uppermost in his mind was a good story, and he stated, "A man is sunk unless he retains the amateur in himself. You cannot get too professional—too intent on making money. You have got to have some of the enthusiasm, some of the eagerness of the amateur. And may I modestly say that I have this."

The choice of his next two films, both directed by Lewis Milestone, half contradicted his proclamation. In the first, *Lucky Partners* (RKO, 1940), he is extremely debonair as a Greenwich Village artist who brings luck and love to a dark-haired mousy bookshop woman (Ginger Rogers), much to the consternation of her rather screwy fiancé (Jack Carson). This film, which might have benefitted even more from the presence of a Cary Grant rather than a Ronald Colman, should be credited to the plus side of Ronald's judgment. On the other side of the scale there is *My Life with Caroline* (RKO, 1941), an unimpressive, unfunny comedy. Publisher Ronald marries flighty Anna Lee, who later believes herself to be smitten with love for Reginald Gardiner. Most of the "action" centers around Ronald talking his screen wife out of her crush on sculptor Gardiner (not to mention Latin lover Gilbert Roland). The studio had so little faith in this "modern, romantic comedy" that it played off release engagements around the country for some two to three months before it was brought into New York for bigtime critical appraisal.

Rightfully aware of his professional ranking, Ronald was reluctant to accept the role of Professor Michael Lightcap in Columbia's *The Talk of the Town* (1942), because he considered the role a subservient one and because the character loses the housekeeper (Jean Arthur) to suspected arsonist Cary Grant. Producer-director George Stevens argued that Ronald would nevertheless steal the show with a last reel speech in which he defends Grant. Stevens was right, and Ronald's down-to-earth, humane performance overshadowed those of both Arthur and Grant, each a past master at comedy timing. After distrusting and disliking the arsonist, the professor proves the man's innocence, but loses his housekeeper (Arthur) to him. The idea that an attractive man could consider his attractive housekeeper only in a platonic sense could only occur in a 1942 screenplay.

After reviewing the success of *Mrs. Miniver* (MGM, 1942), the film that would make a true star of Greer Garson, Metro was eager to follow

With Ginger Rogers in a publicity pose for *Lucky Partners* (1940)

With Jean Arthur and Cary Grant in *Talk of the Town* (1942)

it up with another such vehicle that would insure her status. Producer Sidney Franklin ordered a scenario (by Claudine West, George Foreschel, and Arthur Wimperis) based on the popular James Hilton novel, *Random Harvest* (MGM, 1942). For such a British story with an already-cast British actress, Franklin and his director Mervyn LeRoy would settle for nothing less than an English star. Ronald, who already had had success with another James Hilton-based picture (*Lost Horizon*), enthusiastically accepted their offer of the key role.

In top billing as Charles Rainier, he is an amnesiac soldier of World War I who, on the night of the Armistice, is comforted and given a home by a showgirl, Paula (Garson). They soon marry and live happily. But then, miles away from home and wife, he is struck by an automobile. The blow he suffers in this accident restores his memory and during the remainder of the feature, Paula is devoted to helping him remember. As director LeRoy would later say, "Between the two of them [Colman and Garson], the English language was never spoken more beautifully on film."

It was inevitable that Ronald, now in his fifty-first year, should find himself judged differently by the critics due to his age. As *Variety* phrased it, "Colman gives a fine performance, but is not quite the romantic type that he was years ago. In fact, he looks older than he should have been for film expediency." Nevertheless, for his generally

With Greer Garson in *Random Harvest* (1942)

authoritative performance, Ronald received his second Academy Award nomination, but lost to James Cagney for his portrayal of George M. Cohan in *Yankee Doodle Dandy* (Warner Bros.).

As the rest of the world went to war again in 1940-1941, Ronald joined Charles Boyer and Douglas Fairbanks, Jr. in founding the Franco-British War Relief, an organization devoted to sending money abroad to aid refugees. Throughout the war[66] Colman was a member of the Hollywood Victory Committee and gave of his time and services to the American Red Cross. It was reported that his contributions to war relief agencies averaged twenty-eight percent of his net income, and his net income per film was said to be $150,000.

On July 24, 1944, a daughter was born to the Colmans in Hollywood. The baby's father was fifty-three, her mother was thirty-seven. "I wanted to name her Miranda," Benita had said, "I thought it was a cute name, but Ronnie said, 'Suppose she grew up ugly. She couldn't be called Miranda.' So, then he suggested Juliet, after Shakespeare's Juliet." And the blonde little girl was named Juliet.

A month after he became a father for the first and only time, Ronald was seen in Technicolor as the turbaned, be-whiskered knave, Haifiz,[67]

---

[66]In the spring of 1944 Ronald had been heard on the radio show "Everything for the Boys" as host of the program.

[67]Playwright Edward Knoblock's rascally gent was created on the New York stage by Otis Skinner in 1911. The actor starred in two film versions, a 1920 silent edition for Robertson-Cole, and a talkie in 1930 for First National. In 1953, Alfred Drake would be seen in a stage musical version, and in 1955 Howard Keel would star in the MGM musical movie.

**With Juliet and Benita Hume Colman
in Hollywood (August, 1944)**

155

With Marlene Dietrich in a pose for *Kismet* **(1944)**

in the fairytale-like *Kismet* (MGM, 1944). The rather stodgy tongue-in-cheek story tells of Haifiz' romantic pursuit of Jamilla (Marlene Dietrich) while instructing the Caliph (James Craig) in the art of making love to the girl of his intentions (Joy Ann Page), not realizing that the girl is his daughter. The gaudy but pedestrian film[68] received most of its publicity for the dance performed by Dietrich in which she slithered about with her famed legs encased in several coats of gold paint. Despite his usual light touch, Ronald seemed rather tired in the essentially character role.

Wisely deciding it was time to take stock of his career and his life, Ronald took a two-and-a-half-year absence from the motion picture screen. He returned in Twentieth Century-Fox's *The Late George Apley* (1947), a project which Fox mogul Darryl F. Zanuck insisted would be the ideal film to return Ronald to full prominence in filmdom. To the viewer who had neither read the novel by John P. Marquand nor seen the 1944 stage version with Leo G. Carroll, the film presented Mr. Apley (Ronald) as nothing more than a narrow-minded Bostonian Brahmin who undergoes a mental metamorphosis regarding the care of his two grown children (Peggy Cummins and Richard Ney). Whereas the original Apley was staunchly aloof, arrogant, and immovable, the Philip Dunne scenario transforms him into a charming, cute old-timer. Accordingly, Bosley Crowther (*New York Times*) found the story "botched on the screen—but good!"

Time Magazine of February 23, 1948 commented about Colman's next film, "Ronald Colman's role is a wonderfully rich present to an actor who is celebrating his twenty-fifth [sic] year in movies." That film was *A Double Life* (Universal, 1947[69]), in which he had the role of Anthony John, one he had earlier rejected because he felt unworthy of it.

"An original, created by three such superb writers, terrified me," he explained. "Just think—Ruth Gordon, Garson Kanin *and* William Shakespeare."[70] He changed his mind about the offer, and permitted the makeup department to darken his now white hair. When the writers saw the initial George Cukor-directed rushes they were ecstatic. A hit was predicted and a hit they got.[71]

---

[68]The film was budgeted at over three million dollars, a large amount considering the existing wartime restrictions on movie projects. One NY reviewer said of the opulent settings, "After *Kismet*, God had better give up trying to compete with M-G-M."

[69]Although not officially released until January 6, 1948, the film was shown in Los Angeles during the required period in 1947 to qualify for that year's Academy Awards.

[70]The plot situation of *A Double Life*, however, was "borrowed" from *Men Are Not Gods* (United Artists, 1936), a British-filmed entry in which Sebastian Shaw played the actor starring onstage in Othello, with Gertrude Lawrence as his "almost" victim and Miriam Hopkins starring as Miss Fix-it.

[71]The studio advertisements proclaimed: "Cheered by the world—but consumed by the fires of his own greatness! So inspired an actor that when he portrayed the role of a man

With Richard Haydn and Edna Best in *The Late George Apley* (1947)

Accepting his *A Double Life* Oscar
from Olivia de Havilland (March, 1948)

In *A Double Life* (1947)

Within the 104-minute black-and-white feature, Anthony John is a stage actor of powerful ability[72] who takes on the personality of the character he is portraying onstage. During a production of *Othello* he goes beyond reality and becomes a murderer for real when he strangles a waitress, played by Shelley Winters,[73] with whom he has had a maddening affair. On stage, opposite his ex-wife (Signe Hasso) who is playing Desdemona, it is suspenseful touch-and-go as to whether he will kill her, too.[74] *Time*'s critique included,"his performance is a pleasure in itself, but the real delight is to watch his delight in his job. Colman is not a great actor, but he gives an arresting demonstration of what a good actor can do with great material when he cares enough for it." Some other reviewers were more ecstatic. *Cue* Magazine insisted that "in the "Jekyll-Hyde role of matinee idol and madman [he] gives the greatest performance of his long and distinguished career on stage and screen."

Ronald proclaimed that *A Double Life* was now his favorite film. "Yes, yes," he said, "it is my favorite part since it has come off so well. That makes a difference, you know. It was most exhausting because it was so difficult and such good material." He admitted to never having been "a very good stage actor" and praised the work of Walter Hampden, who had coached him for his *Othello* scenes. When asked if his mood, when playing a tormented actor onscreen, extended into his homelife, Benita said, "He was very ugly at home. I finally said I was going to the studio to see his rushes. I did and was knocked sideways by them. I said, 'Darling, you can be as ugly as you like.'"

As was expected, Ronald was nominated for an Oscar. Also in competition that year[75] was his buddy, William Powell, for *Life with Father* (Warner Bros.). Although Powell had been named Best Actor by the New York Film Critics, it was Ronald who was handed the Oscar

who killed for love, his real-life self could not resist a mad impulse that destroyed his soul!'

[72]In *On Cukor* (G. P. Putnam's, 1972), the director told Gavin Lambert: "Colman had so much equipment for a screen actor, he was photogenic, he could move, he could give the impression of movement and yet remain perfectly still, he had this plastic quality, he'd studied Chaplin and Fairbanks. For the death scene, I was shooting from a high angle, and I told him, 'When you die, all your life, everything that's happened, should come into your eyes for a brief moment.' Well, he did it—or told me he did it—but I couldn't see it when we shot it. Next day, in the rushes, it was all there. He knew how to let the quality of *thought* come out. But, yes, I question whether he had the danger and the madness for a great Othello, on the stage or in real life. Some can be scary, some can't, and Colman was a most gifted actor who didn't have a sense of the demonic."

[73]Due to Miss Winters' temperament, the producer (Michael Kanin) and director Cukor were all for releasing her from the part, but it was because of Ronald's insistence that she stayed.

[74]Just as *Random Harvest* had plot similarities to *Kisses for Breakfast* (WB, 1941) and *I Love You Again* (MGM, 1940), so there were parallels between *A Double Life* and John Loder's *The Brighton Strangler* (RKO, 1945).

[75]Other nominees that year included John Garfield (*Body and Soul*), Gregory Peck (*Gentleman's Agreement*), and Michael Redgrave (*Mourning Becomes Electra*).

by Olivia de Havilland (the previous year's Best Actress) on the stage of the Shrine Auditorium in Los Angeles the evening of March 20, 1948. One can only imagine how his possessive ex-boss, Samuel Goldwyn, must have felt about this long-delayed victory for the perennially popular star.

In the summer of 1948, Ronald returned to England for the first time since 1934. The occasion was a gigantic British premiere of *A Double Life.* This was followed by a second premiere in Brussels, after which he went back to London to revisit the scenes of his childhood.

Among Hollywood's major talents, Ronald was one of the first stars to consider the potentials of television. His pride would never allow him to gracefully age into a character player (as had Herbert Marshall and others), and it seemed that the video medium, more interested in established names than youthful lead performers, would be the salvation and solution for the cinema's one-time debonair swashbuckler. In mid-1948, producer Ben Finney announced to the trade papers that he had contracted Ronald for twenty-six half-hour telefilms, each to be budgeted at $13,500. Thirteen would be based on Robert Louis Stevenson material, with another thirteen derived from Charles Dickens' works. Finney also talked of having Colman narrate twenty-six additional segments based on O. Henry stories.

While none of the Finney plans came to realization, Ronald did accept the lead in a new radio series, "The Halls of Ivy," which co-starred him and his wife (then retired from screen acting) as Dr. and Mrs. William Todhunter Hall of Ivy College. The half-hour program (with a $21,000 budget for each weekly installment) debuted at eight o'clock in the evening on NBC network on January 6, 1950, and soon became a popular Friday evening entry. Set on a small college campus, Ronald's character was the type of civilized, sonorous soul who said, "You people are children callously pulling the wings off butterflies. The chief purpose of education is to impart an understanding of the butterfly's viewpoint." (Those involved with the show would later relate how Ronald and Benita would continually vie for laughs on the program. Miss Hume, as in other areas of her marriage with Colman, would give in to her spouse.)

The critics—like the listening audiences—were rather kind to the Colmans' series venture. John Crosby (*New York Herald-Tribune*) predicted, "In fact, I see no clear reason why Ronald and Benita, who are already well known to radio audiences through their work on the Jack Benny show, shouldn't become one of America's favorite radio couples." Crosby went on to analyze: "The Colman personality, a mixture of urbanity, charm and culture with just a hint of Raffles still there, is too overwhelming to fit any such precise category. Colman is always Colman in addition to his acquired characteristics."

160

At the end of his review of *A Double Life,* the *New York Times'* Bosley Crowther had asked, "Now, what does Mr. Colman do for an encore?" His question was answered two years later with *Champagne for Caesar* (United Artists, 1950), a satire on the popular radio guessing-game shows. Ronald is Beauregard Bottomley, a knowledgable fellow who is refused a job with the Milady Soap Company. He seeks revenge as a contestant on the soap company's quiz show, "Masquerade for Money." When he pushes his prize money up to $40,000 by his correct answers, the company's overbearing owner (Vincent Price) sends a young woman (Celeste Holm) into his life to find out what Colman does not know. What he cannot remember on the next show (a rather contrived plot gimmick, at that) is his Social Security number, thereby causing him to lose the big prize money. However, he does win the girl. The Caesar of the title is his pet and friend, a parrot. The moderately budgeted feature proved once again—in case there was anyone of even the new generation who needed such confirmation —that Ronald was a very droll farceur. *Champagne for Caesar* was one of the first features sold to television early in that medium's history, and it became a staple of the late show circuit. Much more so than *A Double Life,* it served to substantiate Colman's place in the cinema field with latter-day movie watchers.

Now past sixty years old with most of his contemporaries retired, dead, or trying to cover up for fading careers, Ronald still believed that he remained a top-drawing commodity on the motion picture market. He did admit, "The older you get the harder you are to cast and the harder to please." He was especially firm when he said: "I won't do another motion picture role unless it adds a feather to my cap or is a lot

With Celeste Holm and detectives in *Champagne for Caesar* (1950)

of fun, something that tickles one's fancy. . . . But just to go and sit in those uncomfortable chairs on a movie set at nine and hope they get to you by quarter to six, oh no. It's such a waste of time. . . . I was set for two or three pictures the past year [1953], but they never got off the ground."

About television, Ronald was less stringent in his working demands. He was a frequent guest on the CBS-TV show, "Four Star Playhouse," often at a low salary to help out his friend David Niven, one of the show's creators. Then, on October 19, 1954, the Colmans brought "The Halls of Ivy" to television. About this half-hour CBS series, *Variety* reported, "The addition of sight to the dulcet Ronald Colman & Co. tones appears to rob the show of much of its comfortable warmth, and that, above everything else, was the quality that made the show on radio." Jack Gould (*New York Times*) was a little friendlier in his appraisal. "The Colmans moved smoothly through their assignments —a warm, gay and witty couple who were a veritable godsend after the many absurd caricatures of husband and wife on TV." The series also featured Mary Wickes as the housemaid, and lasted one season for thirty-nine episodes.

In 1955[76] the Colmans moved to Santa Barbara, and also purchased a home in Switzerland, while maintaining their Hollywood apartment. Although Ronald had been in the United States for over twenty-five years, he was still a British subject. (In 1975, the Colmans' daughter, Juliet Benita Colman, would write her biography, *Ronald Colman: A Very Private Person,* (William Morrow & Co.), a lovingly perceptive, detailed and warm study of her actor-father's last years.) As she recalls, it was a period in which he varied from good spirits to dark depressions, the moods inspired by his enforced retrenchment from his acting craft. "Upon return from school I would usually find him in his study, patio, or studio, and if he were ominously quiet or morose, I'd go and find Benita—most often in the garden—to share the latest news and giggles. If, on the other hand, he were lighthearted, we might go off for a drive in his Jag with the top down, into the evening hills. There were domino and Scrabble games. . . . Or we might walk up the street hill to his studio to have a look at his latest paintings, he pausing often to catch his breath."

His first theatrical feature in over six years was *Around the World in 80 Days* (United Artists, 1956), the Mike Todd super extravaganza boasting some fifty top internationl stars, most of whom turned up in what Todd called "cameo" roles. Ronald is an official, British, of course, on the Great Peninsular Railroad in India on which Phileas Fogg (David Niven) and entourage (Shirley MacLaine, Cantinflas, and

---

[76]The Colmans with their daughter took a trip to Europe in mid-1955. There was mentioned a possibility of Ronald making a film in Berlin that fall—possibly a version of George Bernard Shaw's *Back to Methuselah*—but it never materalized.

With Cecil B. DeMille, Jesse L. Lasky, Mary Pickford, Henry King, Mae Marsh, Frank Borzage, and General O. L. Solbert (director of the Memorial) at the George Eastman House Memorial Ceremony for Silent Film Celebrities (December, 1955)

With Benita Hume Colman rehearsing for CBS-TV's "The Halls of Ivy" (October, 1954)

Robert Newton) flag a ride. A reporter asked him about his salary for the virtual walk-on: "Did you really get a Cadillac for one day's work?" a reporter inquired. "No," said Colman, "For the work of a lifetime."

After making an appearance on "G.E. Theatre" in the episode *The Chess Game* (CBS-TV, December 16, 1956), Ronald made what would prove to be his last film appearance.[77] He undertook a major role, as the defender of mankind at a heavenly tribunal in *The Story of Mankind* (Warner Bros., 1957). Known as The Spirit of Man, he debates with the Devil (Vincent Price) over the merits and future of the human race. The rest of the cast of this picture (which relied a good deal on stock footage) must surely have been chosen for "camp" appeal: Hedy Lamarr as Joan of Arc, Dennis Hopper as an anemic Bonaparte, Reginald Gardiner as Shakespeare, Harpo Marx as Isaac Newton, etc.

Vincent Price later recalled the filming of this dud, and his reactions to Ronald: "He was a marvelous gentleman, quiet and charming and with a delicious humor. We knew during the filming that the picture was heading downwards; the script was bad to begin with and it worsened with daily changes. I remember one puzzled visitor asking Ronnie: 'Is this picture based on a book?' and he replied in that beautiful,

---

[77]About this time (1956), Ronald was approached to play Captain Vere in a projected film version of Herman Melville's *Billy Budd*. According to DeWitt Bodeen, who scripted the screen property, Colman was very anxious to participate in the venture, which would have been funded and released through Twentieth Century-Fox. However, upon checking with his physicians, Ronald had to bow out reluctantly. His doctors feared that the shipboard location filming might induce complications in the star's precarious health, leading to a possible heart attack. The film would be eventually made in 1962 with Peter Ustinov, co-producing, directing, co-scripting (with Bodeen), and starring as Captain Vere. Allied Artists released the underrated venture. One can only regret that Colman had not been able to tackle the tailor-made role of the gentlemanly sea captain.

With Sir Cedric Hardwicke, David Niven, and Cantinflas in *Around The World in 80 Days* (1956)

With Vincent Price in *The Story of Mankind* (1957)

soft diction of his, 'Yes, it is. But they are using only the notes on the dust jacket.' "

Finding himself very much at professional leisure, Ronald took his family back to London again, a town that Benita dearly loved. When they returned, Ronald set about recording an LP album of Shakespeare's sonnets. There was occasional mention of acting roles—he very much wanted to film Shaw's *Man and Superman.* Sometimes he would speak seriously of setting to work on his autobiography. However, the thought of the huge effort continually discouraged him from such writing. For diversion, the Colmans rented a house at Palm Springs.

In mid-March, 1957, Ronald was hospitalized for two weeks at St. John's Hospital in Santa Monica for pneumonitis. Apparently he recovered from this lung infection (due, it was thought, to his World War I injuries). But in the spring of 1958 he became ill again. His physician suggested Colman be hospitalized. After Benita and Juliet visited Ronald that evening, they returned home. The next morning his condition worsened and he died. The day was May 19, 1958, and he was then sixty-seven years old.

The actor who was the idol of three generations of movie fans was buried by his lifelong friends, William Powell and Richard Barthelmess. At the fifteen-minute funeral service held at All Saints by the Sea Episcopal Church, Easter hymns were played, but no eulogy was given—Colman had always hated gloom. Others who attended the rites beside his widow and daughter were George Sanders,[78] Joseph Cotten, Patricia Medina, Jack Benny, Vincent Price, Gladys Cooper, Herbert Marshall, and George Cukor. He was buried at the Santa Barbara cemetery. Benita had had engraved on his black marble tombstone Prospero's speech from Act IV, scene 1 of *The Tempest:* "Our revels now are ended. . . . We are such stuff As dreams are made of, and our little life Is rounded with a sleep." The bulk of Colman's estate was left to Benita and Juliet.

One of the persisting rumors in the last years of Colman's life was that he had become embittered at having been edged out of the matinee idol arena because of his age. Not long before Colman died, Benita Hume took occasion to reply by letter to one film fan magazine which had printed a rather sensational account of Colman languishing by the fireside. She responded, "It is perfectly apparent to him, if not to you, that people are born, they live, they grow old and they die, and Mr. Colman has not cornered the market in this respect. . . . Nor are his diverse interests in life contingent upon remaining 35 for all eternity. . . . Ronald Colman is not and never will be the less magical for being mortal."

---

[78]In 1959 Benita would wed actor George Sanders; she would die on November 1, 1967, of cancer.

Feature Film Appearances

THE TOILERS (Diamond Super, 1919), 5,000 feet.
Producer, Neville Bruce; Director, Tom W. Watts; screenplay, Eliot Stannard.

Manora Thew (Rose); George Dewhurst (Jack); Gwynne Herbert (Mother); Ronald Colman (Bob); Eric Barker (Jack as a Child); John Corrie (Lighthouse Keeper); Mollie Terraine (Merchant's Daughter).

A DAUGHTER OF EVE (Walturdaw, 1919), 5,000 feet.
Producer-director, Walter West.

Violet Hopson (Jessica Bond); Stewart Rome (Sidney Strangeways); Cameron Carr (Charles Strangeways); Ralph Forster (John Bond); Edward Banfield (Sir Hugh Strangeways); Vesta Sylva (Jessica as a Child); Ronald Colman (Bit).

SNOW IN THE DESERT (Walturdaw, 1919), 7,000 feet.
Director Walter West; based on the novel by Andrew Soutar; screenplay, Benedict James.

Violet Hopson (Felice Beste); Stewart Rome (William B. Jackson); Sir Simeon Stuart (Sir Michael Beste); Ronald Colman (Rupert Sylvester); and: Poppy Wyndham, Mary Masters, and A. B. Caldwell.

A SON OF DAVID (Walturdaw, 1920), 4,700 feet.
Producer, Walter West; director, Hay Plumb; story, Charles Barnett; screenplay, Benedict James.

Poppy Wyndham (Esther Raphael); Ronald Colman (Maurice Phillips); Arthur Walcott (Louis Raphael); Constance Backner (Miriam Myers); Robert Vallis (Sam Myers); Joseph Pacey (Maurice as a Child); Vesta Sylva (Esther as a Child).

ANNA THE ADVENTURESS (National, 1920), 6,280 feet.
Director, Cecil M. Hepworth; based on the novel by E. Phillips Oppenheim; screenplay, Blanche McIntosh.

Alma Taylor (Anna/Annabel Pelissier); James Carew (Montagu Hill); Gerald Ames (Nigel Ennison); Gwynne Herbert (Aunt); Christine Rayner (Mrs. Ellicote); Ronald Colman (Brendan); James Annand (Sir John Ferringhall); Jean Cadell (Mrs. White).

THE BLACK SPIDER (Butcher, 1920), 5,800 feet.
Producer, Edward Godal; director, William J. Humphrey; based on the novel by Carlton Dawe; screenplay, Humphrey.

Lydia Kyasht (Angela Carfour); Bertram Burleigh (Archie Lowndes); Sam Livesey (Reginald Conway); Ronald Colman (Vicomte de Beauvais); Hayden

167

Coffin (Lord Carfour); Adeline Hayden Coffin (Lady Carfour); Mary Clare (Coralie Mount); Dorothy Cecil (Marjorie West).

HANDCUFFS OR KISSES (Select, 1921), 6 reels.
Presenter, Lewis J. Selznick; director, George Archainbaud; based on the story *Handcuffs and Kisses* by Thomas Edgelow; screenplay, Lewis Allen Browne; camera, Jules Cronjager.

Elaine Hammerstein (Lois Walton); Julia Swayne Gordon (Mrs. Walton); Dorothy Chappell (Violet); Robert Ellis (Peter Madison); Alison Skipworth (Miss Strodd); Florence Billings (Miss Dell); Ronald Schabel (Leo Carstairs); George Lessey (Elias Pratt); Ronald Colman (Lodyard).

THE WHITE SISTER (Metro, 1923), 13,147 feet.
Presenter, Charles H. Duell; director, Henry King; based on the novel by Francis Marion Crawford; screenplay, George V. Hobart and Charles E. Whittaker; titles, William M. Ritchey and Don Bartlett; art director, Robert M. Haas; camera, Roy Overbaugh; assistant camera, William Schurr and Fernando Risi; editor, Duncan Mansfield.

Lillian Gish (Angela Chiaromonte); Ronald Colman (Captain Giovanni Severini); Gail Kane (Marchesa di Mola); J. Barney Sherry (Monsignor Saracinesca); Charles Lane (Prince Chiaromonte); Juliette La Violette (Madame Bernard); Signor Serena (Professor Ugo Severini); Alfredo Bertone (Filmore Durand); Ramon Iblañez (Count del Ferice); Alfredo Martinelli (Alfredo del Ferice); Carloni Talli (Mother Superior); Giovanni Viccola (General Mazzini); Antonio Barda (Alfredo's Tutor); Giacomo D'Attino (Solicitor to the Prince); Michele Gualdi (Solicitor to the Count); Giuseppe Pavoni (The Archbishop); Francesco Socinus (Professor Torricelli); Sheik Mahomet (The Bedouin Chief); James Abbe (Lieutenant Rossini); Duncan Mansfield (Commander Donato): Thelma Raye (Bit).

THE ETERNAL CITY (Associated First National, 1923), 7,929 feet.
Presenter, Samuel Goldwyn; director, George Fitzmaurice; based on the novel by Hall Caine; screenplay, Ouida Bergéré; camera, Arthur Miller.

Barbara La Marr (Donna Roma); Bert Lytell (David Rossi); Lionel Barrymore (Baron Bonelli); Richard Bennett (Bruno); Montagu Love (Minghelli); Ronald Colman (Bit), Betty Bronson and Joan Bennett (pages).

$20 A WEEK (Selznick Distributing, 1923), 5,990 feet.
Director, Harmon Weight; based on the novel *The Adopted Father* by Edgar Franklin; screenplay, Forrest Halsey; camera, Harry A. Fischbeck.

George Arliss (John Reeves); Taylor Holmes (William Hart); Edith Roberts (Murial Hart); Walter Howe (Henry Sloane); Redfield Clarke (George Blair); Ronald Colman (Chester Reeves); Ivan Simpson (James Pettison); Joseph Donohue (Little Arthur); William Sellery (Clancy the Restaurant Keeper); George Henry (The Harts' Butler).

TARNISH (Associated First National, 1924), 6,831 feet.
Presenter, Samuel Goldwyn; director, George Fitzmaurice; based on the play by Gilbert Emery; screenplay, Frances Marion; technical director, Ben Carré; camera, William Tuers and Arthur Miller; editor, Stuart Heisler.

May McAvoy (Letitia Tevis); Ronald Colman (Emmett Carr); Marie Prevost (Nettie Dark); Albert Gran (Adolf Tevis); Mrs. Russ Whytall (Josephine Tevis); Priscilla Bonner (Aggie); Harry Myers (The Barber); Kay Deslys (Mrs. Stutts); Lydia Yeamans Titus (Mrs. Healy); William Boyd (Bill); Snitz Edwards (Mr. Stutts).

ROMOLA (Metro-Goldwyn, 1924), 12,974 feet.
Producer-director, Henry King; based on the novel by George Eliot; screenplay, Will M. Ritchey; art director, Robert M. Haas; shipbuilder, Tito Neri.

Lillian Gish (Romola); Dorothy Gish (Tessa); William H. Powell (Tito Melema); Ronald Colman (Carlo Buccellini); Charles Lane (Baldassarre Calvo); Herbert Grimwood (Savonarola); Bonaventure Ibanez (Bardo Bardi); Frank Puglia (Adolfo Spini); Amelia Summerville (Brigida); Angelo Scatigna (Bratti); Edulilo Mucci (Nello); Tina Rinaldi (Monna Ghita); Alfredo Bertone (Piero de Medici); Alfredo Martinelli (Tournabuoni); Ugo Ucellini (Bishop of Nemours); Guiseppe Zocchi (Executioner); Thelma Raye (Bit).

HER NIGHT OF ROMANCE (First National, 1925), 7,211 feet.
Presenter, Joseph M. Schenck; director, Sidney A. Franklin; screenplay, Hans Kraly; camera, Ray Binger, Victor Milner; editor, Hal Kern.

Constance Talmadge (Dorothy Adams); Ronald Colman (Paul Menford); Jean Hersholt (Joe Diamond); Albert Gran (Samuel C. Adams); Robert Rendel (Prince George); Sidney Bracey (Butler); Joseph Dowling (Professor Gregg); Templar Saxe (Dr. Wellington); Eric Mayne (Dr. Scott); Emily Fitzroy (Nurse); Clara Bracey (Housekeeper); James Barrows (Old Butler); Claire de Lorez (Artist).

A THIEF IN PARADISE (First National, 1925), 7, 355 feet.
Presenter, Samuel Goldwyn; director, George Fitzmaurice; based on the novel *The Worldlings* by Leonard Merrick; adaptor, Frances Marion; camera, Arthur Miller.

Doris Kenyon (Helen Saville); Ronald Colman (Maurice Blake); Aileen Pringle (Rosa Carmino); Claude Gillingwater (Noel Jardine); Alec Francis (Bishop Saville); John Patrick (Ned Whalen); Charles Youree (Philip Jardine); Etta Lee (Rosa's Maid); Lon Poff (Jardine's Secretary).

HIS SUPREME MOMENT (First National, 1925), 6,500 feet.°
Presenter, Samuel Goldwyn; director, George Fitzmaurice; based on the novel *World Without End* by May Edginton; adaptor, Frances Marion; camera, Arthur Miller.

°Technicolor sequences

Blanche Sweet (Carla King); Ronald Colman (John Douglas); Kathleen Myers (Sara Deeping); Belle Bennett (Carla Light); Cyril Chadwick (Harry Avon); Ned Sparks (Adrian); Nick De Ruiz (Mueva).

THE SPORTING VENUS (Metro-Goldwyn, 1925), 5,938 feet.

Presenter, Louis B. Mayer; director, Marshall Neilan; based on the story by Gerald Beaumont; screenplay, Thomas J. Geraghty; assistant director, Thomas Held; wardrobe, Ethel P. Chaffin; art director, Cedric Gibbons; camera, David Kesson; editor, Blanche Sewell.

Blanche Sweet (Lady Gwendolyn); Ronald Colman (Donald MacAllan); Lew Cody (Prince Carlos); Josephine Crowell (Countess Van Alstyne); Edward Martindel (Sir Alfred Grayle); Kate Price (Housekeeper); Hank Mann (Carlos' Valet); Arthur Hoyt (Detective); George Fawcett (Father).

HER SISTER FROM PARIS (First National, 1925), 7,255 feet.

Presenter, Joseph M. Schenck; director, Sidney Franklin; screenplay, Hans Kraly; art director, William Cameron Menzies; assistant director, Scot R. Beal; wardrobe, Adrian; camera, Arthur Edeson.

Constance Talmadge (Helen Weyringer/Lola); Ronald Colman (Joseph Weyringer); George K. Arthur (Robert Well); Margaret Mann or Gertrude Claire (Bertha).

THE DARK ANGEL (First National, 1925), 7,341 feet.

Presenter, Samuel Goldwyn; director, George Fitzmaurice; based on the play by H. B. Trevelyan; screenplay, Frances Marion; camera, George Barnes.

Ronald Colman (Captain Alan Trent); Vilma Banky (Kitty Vane); Wyndham Standing (Captain Gerald Shannon); Frank Elliott (Lord Beaumont); Charles Lane (Sir Hubert Vane); Helen Jerome Eddy (Miss Bottles); Florence Turner (Roma).

STELLA DALLAS (United Artists, 1925), 10,157 feet.

Presenter, Samuel Goldwyn; director, Henry King; based on the novel by Olive Higgins Prouty; adaption, Frances Marion; camera, Arthur Edeson; editor, Stuart Heisler.

Ronald Colman (Stephen Dallas); Belle Bennett (Stella Dallas); Alice Joyce (Helen Morrison); Jean Hersholt (Ed Munn); Beatrix Pryor (Mrs. Grovesnor); Lois Moran (Laurel Dallas); Douglas Fairbanks, Jr. (Richard Grovesnor); Vera Lewis (Miss Tibbets); Maurice Murphy, Jack Murphy, and Newton Hall (Morrison Children); Charles Hatten, Robert Gillette, and Winston Miller (Morrison Children—Ten Years Later).

LADY WINDEMERE'S FAN (Warner Bros., 1925), 79 min.°

Director, Ernst Lubitsch; based on the play by Oscar Wilde; adaption, Julian

---

°Blue tint scenes

Josephson; assistant director, George Hippard; camera, Charles Van Enger; assistant camera, Willard Van Enger.

Ronald Colman (Lord Darlington); Irene Rich (Mrs. Erlynne); May McAvoy (Lady Windemere); Bert Lytell (Lord Windemere); Edward Martindel (Lord Augustus); Helen Dunbar, Carrie Daumery, and Billie Bennett (Duchesses); Larry Steers (Guest-Admirer); Wilson Benge (Butler); Mrs. Cowper-Cowper (Lady Plymdale).

KIKI (First National, 1926), 8,279 feet.
Presenter, Joseph M. Schenck; director, Clarence Brown; based on the play by André Picard; screenplay, Hans Kraly; camera, Oliver Marsh.

Norma Talmadge (Kiki); Ronald Colman (Renal); Gertrude Astor (Paulette); Marc MacDermott (Baron Rapp); George K. Arthur (Adolphe); William Orlamond (Brule); Erwin Connelly (Joly); Frankie Darro (Pierre); Mack Swain (Pastryman).

BEAU GESTE (Paramount, 1926), 129 min.°
Presenters, Adolph Zukor and Jesse L. Lasky; producer-director, Herbert Brenon; based on the novel by Percival Christopher Wren; screenplay, Paul Schofield; adaptors, Brenon and John Russell; art director, Julian Boone Fleming; music score, Hugo Riesenfeld; assistant director, Ray Lissner; camera, J. Roy Hunt.

Ronald Colman (Michael "Beau" Geste); Neil Hamilton (Digby Geste); Ralph Forbes (John Geste); Alice Joyce (Lady Patricia Brandon); Mary Brian (Isobel); Noah Beery (Sergeant Lejaune); Norman Trevor (Major de Beaujolais); William Powell (Boldini); George Regas (Maris); Bernard Siegel (Schwartz); Victor McLaglen (Hank); Donald Stuart (Buddy); Paul McAllister (St. Andre); Redmond Finlay (Cordere); Ram Singh (Prince Ram Singh); Maurice Murphy ("Beau" as a Child); Philippe De Lacey (Digby as a Child); Mickey McBan (John as a Child).

°Technicolor sequences

THE WINNING OF BARBARA WORTH (United Artists, 1926), 8,757 feet.
Producer, Samuel Goldwyn; director, Henry King; based on the novel by Harold Bell Wright; screenplay, Frances Marion; art director, Carol Oscar Borg; titler, Rupert Hughes; music score, Ted Henkel; camera, George Barnes and Gregg Toland; editor, Viola Lawrence.

Ronald Colman (William Holmes); Vilma Banky (Barbara Worth); Charles Lane (Jefferson Worth); Paul McAllister (The Seer); E. J. Ratcliffe (James Greenfield); Gary Cooper (Abe Lee); Clyde Cook (Tex); Erwin Connelly (Pat); Sam Blum (Blanton); Edwin Brady (Cowboy).

THE NIGHT OF LOVE (United Artists, 1927), 7,600 feet.
Producer, Samuel Goldwyn; director, George Fitzmaurice; based on the play by Pedro Calderon de la Barca; adaptation-screenplay, Lenore J. Coffee; art director, Carl Oscar Borg; camera, George Barnes and Thomas Brannigan.

Ronald Colman (Montero); Vilma Banky (Princess Marie); Montagu Love (Duke de la Garde); Natalie Kingston (Donna Beatriz); John George (Jester); Bynunsky Hyman, Gibson Gowland (Bandits); Laska Winter (Gypsy Bride); Sally Rand (Gypsy Dancer).

THE MAGIC FLAME (United Artists, 1927), 8,308 feet.

Producer, Samuel Goldwyn; director, Henry King; based on the play *König Harlakin* by Rudolph Lothar; adaptation, Bess Meredyth; continuity, June Mathis; titles, George Marion, Jr. and Nellie Revell; art director, Carl Oscar Borg; assistant director, Robert Florey; theme song, Sigmund Spaeth; camera, George Barnes.

Ronald Colman (Tito the Clown/The Count); Vilma Banky (Bianca the Aerial Artist); Agostino Borgato (The Ringmaster); Gustav von Seyffertitz (The Chancellor); Harvey Clark (The Aide); Shirley Palmer (The Wife); Cosmo Kyrle Bellew (The Husband); George Davis (The Utility Man); André Cheron (The Manager); Vadim Uraneff (The Visitor).

TWO LOVERS (United Artists, 1928), 8,817 feet.

Producer, Samuel Goldwyn; director, Fred Niblo; based on the novel *Leatherface: A Tale of Old Flanders* by Emmuska Orczy; adaptation, Alice D. G. Miller; titles, John Colton; assistant director, H. Bruce Humberstone; music, Hugo Riesenfeld; songs, Wayland Axtell and Abner Silver; camera, George Barnes; editor, Viola Lawrence.

Ronald Colman (Mark Van Rycke); Vilma Banky (Donna Leonara de Vargas); Noah Beery (The Duke of Azar); Nigel De Brulier (The Prince of Orange); Virginia Bradford (Grete); Helen Jerome Eddy (Inez); Eugenie Besserer (Madame Van Rycke); Paul Lukas (Ramon de Linea); Fred Esmelton (Meinherr Van Rycke the Bailiff of Ghent); Harry Allen (Jean); Marcella Daly (Marda); Scotty Mattraw (Dandermonde Innkeeper); Lydia Yeamans Titus (Innkeeper's Wife).

THE RESCUE (United Artists, 1929), 7,980 feet.

Presenter, Samuel Goldwyn; director, Herbert Brenon; based on the novel by Joseph Conrad; screenplay, Elizabeth Meehan; titles, Katherine Hilliker and H. H. Caldwell; art director, William Cameron Menzies; assistant director, Ray Lissner; music, Hugo Riesenfeld; camera, George Barnes; editors, Marie Halvey, Hilliker, and Caldwell.

Ronald Colman (Tom Lingard); Lily Damita (Lady Edith Travers); Alfred Hickman (Mr. Travers); Theodore von Eltz (Carter); John Davidson (Hassim); Philip Strange (D'Alacer); Bernard Siegel (Jorgensen); Sojin (Daman); Harry Cording (Belarab); Laska Winters (Immada); Duke Kahanamoku (Jaffir); Louis Morrison (Shaw); George Regas (Wasub); Christopher Martin (Tenga).

BULLDOG DRUMMOND (United Artists, 1929), 90 min.

Presenter, Samuel Goldwyn; producer-director, F. Richard Jones; based on the play by H. C. McNeile ("Sapper") and Gerald du Maurier; screenplay, Wallace Smith and Sidney Howard; continuity, Smith; dialog, Howard; art director, William Cameron Menzies; song, Jack Yellen and Harry Akst; assistant director, Paul Jones; associate director, A. Leslie Pearce; camera, George Barnes and Gregg Toland; editors, Viola Lawrence and Frank Lawrence.

Ronald Colman (Bulldog Drummond); Joan Bennett (Phyllis Benton); Lilyan Tashman (Erma Peterson); Montagu Love (Carl Peterson); Lawrence Grant (Dr. Lakington); Wilson Benge (Danny); Claud Alister (Algy Longworth); Adolph Milar (Marcovitch); Charles Sellon (John Travers); Tetsu Komai (Chong); Donald Novis (Singer); Gertrude Short (Barmaid); Tom Ricketts (Colonel).

CONDEMNED (United Artists, 1929), 91 min.
Producer, Samuel Goldwyn; director, Wesley Ruggles; suggested by the book *Condemned to Devil's Island* by Blair Niles; screenplay, Sidney Howard; dialog director, Dudley Digges; settings, William Cameron Menzies; song, Jack Meskill and Pete Wendling; camera, George Barnes and Gregg Toland; editor, Stuart Heisler.

Ronald Colman (Michel Oban); Ann Harding (Madame Vidal); Dudley Digges (Warden Jean Vidal); Louis Wolheim (Jacques Duval); William Elmer (Pierre); William Vaughn (Vidal's Orderly); Albert Kingsley (Felix); Henry Ginsberg, Bud Somers, Stephen Selznick, Baldy Biddle, John George, Arturo Kobe, and Emil and John Schwartz (Inmates); Constantine Romanoff (Brute Convict).

RAFFLES (United Artists, 1930) 6,509 feet.
Producer, Samuel Goldwyn; directors, Harry D'Abbadie D'Arrast, George Fitzmaurice; based on the novel *The Amateur Cracksman* by Ernest William Hornung and the play *Raffles, the Amateur Cracksman* by Hornung and Eugene Wiley Presbrey; screenplay, Sidney Howard; art directors, William Cameron Menzies and Park French; assistant director, H. Bruce Humberstone; technical directors, Gerald Grove and John Howell; camera, George Barnes and Gregg Toland; editor, Stuart Heisler.

Ronald Colman (Raffles); Kay Francis (Lady Gwen); Bramwell Fletcher (Bunny); Frances Dade (Ethel); David Torrence (McKenzie); Alison Skipworth (Lady Melrose); Frederick Kerr (Lord Melrose); John Rogers (Crawshaw); Wilson Benge (Barraclough).

THE DEVIL TO PAY (United Artists, 1930), 72 min.
Producer, Samuel Goldwyn; director, George Fitzmaurice; based on the play by Frederick Lonsdale; screenplay, Benjamin Glazer; dialog, Lonsdale; dialog stager, Ivan Simpson; camera, George Barnes and Gregg Toland; editor, Grant Whytock.

Ronald Colman (Willie Leeland); Loretta Young (Dorothy Hope); Florence Britton (Susan Leeland); Frederick Kerr (Lord Leeland); David Torrence (Mr. Hope); Mary Forbes (Mrs. Hope); Paul Cavanagh (Grand Duke Paul); Craufurd Kent (Arthur Leeland); Myrna Loy (Mary Caryle).

THE UNHOLY GARDEN (United Artists, 1931), 85 min.

Producer, Samuel Goldwyn; director, George Fitzmaurice; screenplay, Ben Hecht and Charles MacArthur; music, Alfred Newman; set designers, Willy Pogany and Captain Richard Day; camera, George Barnes and Gregg Toland; editor, Grant Whytock.

Ronald Colman (Darrington Hunt); Fay Wray (Camille de Jonghe); Estelle Taylor (Eliza Mowbry); Tully Marshall (Baron de Jonghe); Ulrich Haupt (Colonel Von Axt); Henry Armetta (Nick the Goose); Lawrence Grant (Dr. Shayne); Warren Hymer (Smiley Corbin); Mischa Auer (Prince Nicolai Poliakoff); Morgan Wallace (Captain Krugor); Kit Guard (Kid Twist); Lucille La-Verne (Lucie Villars); Arnold Korff (Lautrac); Charles Mailes (Alfred de Jonghe); Nadja (Native Dancer); and: Henry Kolker, William Von Brincken.

ARROWSMITH (United Artists, 1931), 108 min.

Producer, Samuel Goldwyn; director, John Ford; based on the novel by Sinclair Lewis; screenplay-dialog, Sidney Howard; music, Alfred Newman; set designer, Richard Day; sound, Jack Noyes; camera, Ray June; editor, Hugh Bennett.

Ronald Colman (Martin Arrowsmith); Helen Hayes (Leora Tozer); Richard Bennett (Dr. Gustav Sondelius); A. E. Anson (Professor Max Gottlieb); Claude King (Dr. Tubbs); Russell Hopton (Terry Wickett); Myrna Loy (Joyce Lanyon); Bert Roach (Bert Tozer); Charlotte Henry (The Pioneer Girl); James Marcus (The Old Doctor); DeWitt Jennings (Mr. Tozer); Beulah Bondi (Mrs. Tozer); John M. Qualen (Henry Novak); Adele Watson (Mrs. Novak); Sidney DeGrey (Dr. Hesselink); David Landau (State Veterinary); Alec B. Francis (Twyford); Florence Britton (Miss Twyford); Lumsden Hare (Sir Robert Fairland); Clarence Brooks (Oliver Marchand); Ward Bond (Cop); Raymond Hatton (Drunk); Theresa Harris (Native Mother); George Humbert (Italian Uncle); Erville Alderson (Pioneer); Pat Somerset and Eric Wilton (Ship's Officers).

CYNARA (United Artists, 1932), 78 min.

Producer, Samuel Goldwyn; director, King Vidor, based on the novel *An Imperfect Lover* by Robert Gore Brown and the play by Brown and H. M. Harwood; adaptation, Frances Marion and Lynn Starling; camera, Ray June.

Ronald Colman (Jim Warlock); Kay Francis (Clemency Warlock); Phyllis Barry (Doris Lea); Henry Stephenson (John Tring); Viva Tattersall (Milly Miles); Florine McKinney (Garla); Clarissa Selwyn (Onslow); Paul Porcasi (Joseph); George Kirby (Mr. Boots); Donald Stewart (Henry); Wilson Benge (Merton); C. Montague Shaw (Constable); Charlie Hall (Court Spectator).

THE MASQUERADER (United Artists, 1933), 77 min.

Producer, Samuel Goldwyn; director, Richard Wallace; based on the novel by Katherine C. Thurston and the play by John Hunter Booth; adaptation, Howard Estabrook; dialog, Moss Hart; camera, Gregg Toland; editor, Stuart Heisler.

Ronald Colman (Sir John Chilcote/John Loder); Elissa Landi (Eve Chilcote); Juliette Compton (Lady Joyce); Halliwell Hobbes (Brock); David Torr-

174

ence (Fraser); Creighton Hale (Lakely); Helen Jerome Eddy (Robbins); Eric Wilton (Alston); Montague Shaw (Speaker of the House).

BULLDOG DRUMMOND STRIKES BACK (United Artists, 1934), 83 min.

Producer, Samuel Goldwyn; director, Roy Del Ruth; based on the novel by H. C. McNeile ("Sapper"); adaptation, Henry Lehrman; screenplay, Nunnally Johnson; camera, Peverell Marley; editor, Allen McNeil.

Ronald Colman (Captain Hugh Drummond); Loretta Young (Lola Field); C. Aubrey Smith (Inspector Neilsen); Charles Butterworth (Algy Longworth); Una Merkel (Gwen); Warner Oland (Prince Achmed); George Regas (Singh); Mischa Auer (Hassan); Kathleen Burke (Jane Sothern); Arthur Hohl (Dr. Sothern); Ethel Griffies (Mrs. Field); H. N. Clugston (Mr. Field); Douglas Gerrard (Parker); William O'Brien (Servant at Banquet); Vernon Steele, Creighton Hale, and Pat Somerset (Men at Wedding); Gunnis Davis (Man with Harsh Voice); Charles Irwin (Cockney Drunk on Street); Halliwell Hobbes, E. E. Clive, and Yorke Sherwood (Bobbies); Wilson Benge (Neilsen's Valet); Lucille Ball (Girl); Bob Kortman (Henchman); Doreen Monroe (Woman in Hotel Room).

CLIVE OF INDIA (United Artists, 1935), 90 min.

Presenter, Joseph M. Schenck; producer, Darryl F. Zanuck; associate producers, William Goetz and Raymond Griffith; director, Richard Boleslawski; based on the play by W. P. Lipscomb and R. J. Minney; screenplay, Lipscomb, Minney; music, Alfred Newman; costumes, Omar Kiam; camera, Peverell Marley.

Ronald Colman (Robert Clive); Loretta Young (Margaret Maskelyne Clive); Colin Clive (Lieutenant Johnstone); Francis Lister (Ed Maskelyne); Vernon P. Downing (Stringer); Peter Shaw (Miller); Neville Clark (Vincent); Ian Wolfe (Kent); Robert Greig (Pemberton); Montagu Love (Governor Piget); Phyllis Clare (Miss Smythe); Leo G. Carroll (Manning); Etienne Girardot (Warburton); Lumsden Hare (Sergeant Clark); Wyndham Standing (Colonel Townsend); Douglas Gerrard (Lieutenant Walsh); Connie Leon (Ayah); Ann Shaw (Mrs. Clifford); Doris Lloyd (Mrs. Nixon); Mischa Auer (Suraj Ud Dewlah); Cesar Romero (Mir Jaffur); Ferdinand Munier (Admiral Watson); Gilbert Emery (Sullivan); C. Aubrey Smith (Prime Minister); Ferdinand Gottschalk (Old Member); John Carradine (Drunken-Faced Clerk); Emmett O. King (Merchant); Pat Somerset (Official in Margaret's Room/Officer); Olaf Hytten (Parson at Hasting); Don Ameche (Black Hole of Calcutta Prisoner).

THE MAN WHO BROKE THE BANK AT MONTE CARLO (20th Century-Fox, 1935), 67 min.

Producer, Darryl F. Zanuck; associate producer, Nunnally Johnson; director, Stephen Roberts; based on the play by Illia Surgentchoff and Frederic Albert Swanson; screenplay, Johnson, Howard Smith; camera, Ernest Palmer.

Ronald Colman (Paul Gallard); Joan Bennett (Helen Beckeley); Colin Clive (Bertrand Beckeley); Nigel Bruce (Ivan); Montagu Love (Director); Ferdinand Gottschalk (Office Man); Frank Reicher, Lionel Pape (Assistant Directors); Leonid Snegoff (Nick the Chef); Sam Ash (Guard); Charles Coleman (Head

Waiter); Vladimir Bykoff (Helen's Guide); John Percoria (Patron); Lynn Bari (Flower Girl); Charles Fallon (Croupier); Georgette Rhodes (Check Room Girl); Ramsey Hill, Milton Royce (Ushers); Bruce Wyndham (Excited Man); Dora Clemant, Cecil Weston (Women); Frederic Sullivan (Pompous Man); Alphonse Martel (Chasseur); John Spacey and William Stack (Directors); Don Brodie (Photographer); E. E. Clive, Bob De Coudic, and Joseph De Stefani (Waiters); Will Stanton (Drunk Waiter); Christian Rub (Gallard's Guide); I. Miraeva (Singing and Dancing Cook); Tom Herbert (Man at Table).

A TALE OF TWO CITIES (MGM, 1935), 121 min.

Producer, David O. Selznick; director, Jack Conway; based on the novel by Charles Dickens; screenplay, W. P. Lipscomb and S. N. Behrman; music, Herbert Stothart; revolution sequences, Val Lewton and Jacques Tourneur; camera, Oliver T. Marsh; editor, Conrad A. Nervig.

Ronald Colman (Sydney Carton); Elizabeth Allan (Lucie Manette); Edna May Oliver (Miss Pross); Blanche Yurka (Madame DeFarge); Reginald Owen (Stryver); Basil Rathbone (Marquis St. Evremonde); Henry B. Walthall (Dr. Manette); Donald Woods (Charles Darnay); Walter Catlett (Barsad); Fritz Leiber, Sr. (Gaspard); H. B. Warner (Gabelle); Mitchell Lewis (Ernest DeFarge); Claude Gillingwater (Jarvis Lorry); Billy Bevan (Jerry Cruncher); Isabel Jewell (Seamstress); Lucille LaVerne (La-Vengeance); Tully Marshall (Woodcutter); Fay Chaldecott (Lucie the Daughter); Lawrence Grant (Prosecuting Attorney in Old Bailey); Tom Ricketts (Tellson, Jr.); Donald Haines (Jerry Cruncher, Jr.); Ralf Harolde (Prosecutor); Ed Peil Sr. (Cartwright); Richard Alexander (Executioner); Nigel De Brulier, Sam Flint, and Winter Hall (Aristocrats); Walter Kingsford (Victor the Jailer); Rolfe Sedan (Condemned Dandy); Robert Warwick (Tribunal Judge); Billy House (Border Guard); Jimmy Aubrey (Innkeeper); Montague Shaw (Chief Registrar); Dale Fuller (Old Hag).

UNDER TWO FLAGS (20th Century-Fox, 1936), 111 min.

Producer, Darryl F. Zanuck; associate producer, Raymond Griffith; director, Frank Lloyd; based on the novel by Ouida; screenplay, W. P. Lipscomb and Walter Ferris; music director, Louis Silvers; assistant directors, Ad Schaumer and A. F. Erickson; technical director, Jamiel Hassen; ballistic expert, Lou Witte; camera, Ernest Palmer; editor, Ralph Dietrich.

Ronald Colman (Corporal Victor); Claudette Colbert (Cigarette); Victor McLaglen (Major Doyle); Rosalind Russell (Lady Venetia); J. Edward Bromberg (Colonel Ferol); Nigel Bruce (Captain Menzies); Herbert Mundin (Rake); Gregory Ratoff (Ivan); C. Henry Gordon (Lieutenant Petaine); John Carradine (Cafard); William Ricciardi (Cigarette's Father); Lumsden Hare (Lord Seraph); Fritz Leiber (French Governor); Onslow Stevens (Sidi Ben Youssiff); Louis Mercier (Barron); Francis McDonald (Husson); Thomas Beck (Pierre); Harry Semels (Sergeant Malines); Frank Lackteen (Ben Hamidon); Jamiel Hasson (Arab Liaison Officer); Frank Reicher (French General); Gwendolen Logan (Lady Cairn); Hans Von Morhart (Hans); Tor Johnson (Bidou); Marc Lawrence (Grivon); George Regas (Keskerdit); Rolfe Sedan (Mouche); Hector Sarno (Arab Merchant); Gaston Glass (Adjutant); George Ducount (Soldier).

LOST HORIZON (Columbia, 1937), 118 min.

Producer-director, Frank Capra; based on the novel by James Hilton; screenplay, Robert Riskin; art director, Stephen Goosson; set decorator, Babs Johnstone; music, Dmitri Tiomkin; music director, Max Steiner; costumes, Ernst Dryden; technical advisor, Harrison Foreman; assistant director, C. C. Coleman; special camera effects, E. Roy Davidson and Ganahl Carson; camera, Joseph Walker; aerial camera, Elmer Dyer; editors, Gene Havlick and Gene Milford.

Ronald Colman (Robert Conway); Jane Wyatt (Sondra); Edward Everett Horton (Alexander P. Lovett); John Howard (George Conway); Thomas Mitchell (Henry Barnard); Margo (Maria); Isabel Jewell (Gloria Stone); H. B. Warner (Chang); Sam Jaffe (High Lama); Hugh Buckler (Lord Gainsford); John Miltern (Carstairs); Lawrence Grant (Man); Max Rabinowitz (Seiveking); Willie Fung (Bandit Leader); Wyley Birch (Missionary); Hall Johnson Choir (Voices); Richard Loo (Shanghai Airport Official); Chief Big Tree, Delmer Ingraham, Ed Thorpe, and Harry Lishman (Porters); Noble Johnson (Leader of Porters); Neil Fitzgerald (Radio Operator); Leonard Mudie (Foreign Secretary); Boyd Irwin (Assistant Foreign Secretary); Dennis D'Auburn (Aviator).

THE PRISONER OF ZENDA (United Artists, 1937), 101 min.°

Producer, David O. Selznick; directors, John Cromwell and W. S. Van Dyke II; based on the novel by Anthony J. Hope and the play by Edward Rose; screenplay, John Balderston, Wells Root, and Donald Ogden Stewart; art director, Lyle Wheeler; set decorator, Casey Roberts; music, Alfred Newman; costumes, Ernest Dryden; assistant director, Frederick A. Spencer; technical advisors, Prince Sigvard Bernadotte and Colonel Ivar Enhorning; sound, Oscar Lagerof; special effects, Jack Cosgrove; camera, James Wong Howe; editors, Hal C. Kern and James E. Newcom.

Ronald Colman (Rudolph Rasendyll/King Rudolf V); Madeleine Carroll (Princess Flavia); Douglas Fairbanks, Jr. (Rupert of Hentzau); Mary Astor (Antoinette De Mauban); C. Aubrey Smith (Colonel Zapt); Raymond Massey (Black Michael); David Niven (Captain Fritz von Tarlenheim); Eleanor Wesselhoeft (Cook); Byron Foulger (Johann); Montagu Love (Detchard); William Von Brincken (Kraftstein); Ian MacLaren (Cardinal); Torben Meyer (Michael's Butler); Lawrence Grant (Marshal Strakencz); Howard Lang (Josef); Ben Webster (British Ambassador); Evelyn Beresford (British Ambassador's Wife); Charles K. French (Bishop); Al Shean (Orchestra Leader); Charles Halton (Passport Officer); Spencer Charters (Porter); Francis Ford (Man.)

°Sepia sequences

IF I WERE KING (Paramount, 1938), 100 min.

Producer, Frank Lloyd; associate producer, Lou Smith; director, Lloyd; based on the play by Justin Huntly McCarthy; screenplay, Preston Sturges; art directors, Hans Dreier and John Goodman; music director, Boris Morros; music, Richard Hageman; special camera effects, Gordon Jennings; camera, Theodor Sparkuhl; editor, Hugh Bennett.

Ronald Colman (François Villon); Basil Rathbone (King Louis XI); Frances Dee (Katherine de Vaucelles); Ellen Drew (Huguette); C. V. France (Father Villon); Henry Wilcoxon (Captain of the Watch); Heather Thatcher (The Queen); Stanley Ridges (de Reoneo Montigny); Bruce Lester (Neal le Jolya);

Walter Kingsford (Tristan L' Hermite); Alma Lloyd (Colette); Sidney Toler (Robin Turgis); Ralph Forbes (Oliver Le Dain); John Miljan (Thibaut D'Aussigny); William Haade (Guy Tabarie); Adrian Morris (Colin De Gayoulx); Montagu Love (General Dudon); Lester Matthews (General Saliere); William Farnum (General Barbozier); Paul Harvey (Burgundian Herald); Francis McDonald (Gasin Cholet); Russ Powell (Ruffian); Harry Wilson (Beggar); John George (Dwarf Beggar); Stanley King (Captain of Archers); Henry Brandon (Soldier); Ethel Clayton (Old Woman); Judith King and Cheryl Walker (Girls).

THE LIGHT THAT FAILED (Paramount, 1939), 97 min.
Producer-director, William A. Wellman; based on the novel by Rudyard Kipling; screenplay, Robert Carson; art directors, Hans Dreier and Robert Odell; music, Victor Young; camera, Theodor Sparkuhl; editor, Thomas Scott.

Ronald Colman (Dick Heldar); Walter Huston (Terpenhow); Muriel Angelus (Maisie); Ida Lupino (Bessie Broke); Dudley Digges (The Nilghai); Ernest Cossart (Beeton); Ferike Boros (Madame Binat); Pedro de Cordoba (Monsieur Binat); Colin Tapley (Gardner); Fay Helm (Red-haired Girl); Ronald Sinclair (Dick as a Boy); Sarita Wooten (Maisie as a Girl); Halliwell Hobbes and Colin Kenny (Doctors); Charles Irwin (Soldier Model); Francis McDonald (George); George Regas (Cassavetti); Wilfred Roberts (Barton); Clyde Cook and James Aubrey (Soldiers); Major Sam Harris (Wells); Connie Leon (Flower Woman); Harry Cording (Soldier); Cyril Ring (War Correspondent); Barbara Denny (Waitress); Pat O'Malley (Bullock); Clara M. Blore (Mother); George Chandler and George H. Melford (Voices); Leslie Francis (Man with Bandaged Eyes); Barry Downing (Little Boy); Harold Entwistle (Old Man with Dark Glasses).

LUCKY PARTNERS (RKO, 1940), 102 min.
Producers, Harry E. Edington and George Haight; director, Lewis Milestone; based on the story *Bonne Chance* by Sacha Guitry; screenplay, Allan Scott and John Van Druten; art director, Van Nest Polglase; music, Dmitri Tiomkin; special effects, Vernon L. Walker; camera, Robert de Grasse; editor, Henry Berman.

Ronald Colman (David Grant); Ginger Rogers (Jean Newton); Jack Carson (Freddie Harper); Spring Byington (Aunt); Cecilia Loftus (Mrs. Sylvester); Harry Davenport (Judge); Billy Gilbert (Charles); Hugh O'Connell (Niagara Clerk); Brandon Tyman (Mr. Sylvester); Leon Belasco (Nick #1); Edward Conrad (Nick #2); Olin Howland (Tourist); Benny Rubin and Tom Dugan (Spielers); Walter Kingsford (Wendell); Otto Hoffman (Clerk); Lucile Gleason (Ethel's Mother); Helen Lynd (Ethel); Dorothy Adams (Maid in Apartment); Fern Emmett (Hotel Maid); Grady Sutton (Reporter); Nora Cecil (Club Woman); Lloyd Ingraham (Chamber of Commerce Member); Edgar Dearing (Desk Sergeant); Al Hill (Motor Cop); Murray Alper (Orchestra Leader); Jane Patten (Bride); Bruce Hale (Bridegroom); Frank Mills (Bus Driver).

MY LIFE WITH CAROLINE (RKO, 1941), 81 min.
Producer-director, Lewis Milestone; based on the play *Train to Venice* by Louis Verneuil, Georges Barr; screenplay, John Van Druten, Arnold Belgard; camera, Victor Milner.

178

Ronald Colman (Anthony Mason); Anna Lee (Caroline Mason); Charles Winninger (Bliss); Reginald Gardiner (Paul Martindale); Gilbert Roland (Paco Del Valle); Katherine Leslie (Helen); Hugh O'Connell (Muirhead); Matt Moore (Walters the Butler); Murray Alper (Jenkins the Chauffeur); Richard Carle (Dr. Curtis); Clarence Straight (Bill the Pilot); Dorothy Adams (Rodwell); Nicholas Soussanin (Pinnock); Jeanine Crispin (Delta); James Farley (Railroad Conductor); Billy Mitchell (Railroad Porter); Gar Smith (Radio Announcer); Jack Mulhall (Man); Frances Kellogg (Stunt Double).

THE TALK OF THE TOWN (Columbia, 1942), 118 min.

Producer, George Stevens; associate producer, Fred Guiol; director, Stevens; based on a story by Sidney Harmon; adaptation, Dale Van Every; screenplay, Irwin Shaw and Sidney Buchman; music, Frederick Hollander; music director, Morris W. Stoloff; art director, Lionel Banks; camera, Ted Tetzlaff; editor, Otto Meyer.

Cary Grant (Leopold Dilg); Jean Arthur (Nora Shelley); Ronald Colman (Michael Lightcap); Edgar Buchanan (Sam Yates); Glenda Farrell (Regina Bush); Charles Dingle (Andrew Holmes); Emma Dunn (Mrs. Shelley); Rex Ingram (Tilney); Leonid Kinskey (Jan Pulaski); Tom Tyler (Clyde Bracken); Don Beddoe (Chief of Police); George Watts (Judge Grunstadt); Clyde Fillmore (Senator James Boyd); Frank M. Thomas (District Attorney); Lloyd Bridges (Forrester); Billy Benedict (Western Union Boy); Bud Geary (Man); Lee "Lasses" White (Hound Keeper); Al Ferguson (Detective); Jack Gardner (Cameraman); Dewey Robinson (Jake); Leslie Brooks (Secretary); Robert Walker (Deputy Sheriff); Bill Lally (Sergeant); Joe Cunningham (McGuire); Alan Bridge (Desk Sergeant); Clarence Muse (Doorkeeper); Lelah Tyler (Woman).

RANDOM HARVEST (MGM, 1942), 125 min.

Producer, Sidney Franklin; director, Mervyn LeRoy; based on the novel by James Hilton; screenplay, Claudine West, George Froeschel, and Arthur Wimperis; music, Herbert Stothart; art director, Cedric Gibbons; sound, Douglas Shearer; camera, Joseph Ruttenberg; editor, Harold F. Kress.

Ronald Colman (Charles Ranier); Greer Garson (Paula); Philip Dorn (Dr. Jonathan Benet); Susan Peters (Kitty); Reginald Owen ("Biffer"); Edmund Gwenn (Prime Minister); Henry Travers (Dr. Sims); Margaret Wycherly (Mrs. Deventer); Bramwell Fletcher (Harrison); Arthur Margetson (Chetwynd); Jill Esmond (Lydis Chetwynd); Marta Linden (Jill); Melville Cooper (George); Alan Napier (Julian); David Cavendish (Henry Chilcotte); Norma Varden (Julia); Ann Richards (Bridget); Elisabeth Risdon (Mrs. Lloyd); Charles Waldron (Mr. Lloyd); Ivan Simpson (Vicar); Rhys Williams (Sam); Henry Daniell (Heavy Man); Helena Phillips Evans (Ella the Charwoman); Marie de Becker (Vicar's Wife); Montague Shaw (Julia's Husband); Lumsden Hare (Sir John); Frederick Worlock (Paula's Lawyer); Hilda Plowright (Nurse); Arthur Space (Trempitt); Ian Wolfe (Registrar); Terry Kilburn (Boy); Reginald Sheffield (Judge); Arthur Shields (Chemist); Kay Medford (Wife); Olive Blakeney (Woman); Cyril McLaglen (Policeman); Leonard Mudie (Old Man); Peter Lawford (Soldier); Lowden Adams (Clerk); George Kirby (Conductor); Major Sam Harris (Member of House of Commons).

179

KISMET (MGM, 1944), C-100 min.

Producer, Everett Riskin; director, William Dieterle; based on the play by Edward Knoblock; screenplay, John Meehan; songs, Harold Arlen and E. Y. Harburg; music, Herbert Stothart; orchestrator, Murray Cutter; art directors, Cedric Gibbons and Daniel B. Catheart; set decorators, Edwin B. Willis and Richard Pefferle; assistant director, Marvin Stuart; sound, Douglas Shearer and James Z. Flaster; special effects, Warren Newcombe; camera, Charles Rosher; editor, Ben Lewis.

Ronald Colman (Haifiz); Marlene Dietrich (Jamilla); James Craig (Caliph); Edward Arnold (Mansur the Grand Vizier); Hugh Herbert (Feisal); Joy Ann Page (Marsinah); Florence Bates (Karsha); Harry Davenport (Agha); Hobart Cavanaugh (Moolah); Robert Warwick (Alfife); Beatrice and Evelyne Kraft (Court Dancers); Victor Kilian (Jehan); Barry Macollum (Amu); Charles Middleton (The Miser); Harry Humphrey (Gardener); Nestor Paiva (Police Captain); Eve Whitney (Cafe Girl); Minerva Urecal (Retainer); Cy Kendall (Herald); Dan Seymour (Fat Turk); Dale Van Sickel (Assassin); Pedro de Cordoba (Meuzin).

THE LATE GEORGE APLEY (20th Century-Fox, 1947), 98 min.

Producer, Fred Kohlmar, director, Joseph L. Mankiewicz; based on the novel by John P. Marquand and the play by Marquand and George S. Kaufman screenplay, Philip Dunne; art directors, James Basevi and J. Russell Spencer; set decorators, Edwin B. Willis and Paul Fox; music, Cyril J. Mockridge; music director, Alfred Newman; orchestrator, Maurice de Packh; assistant director, F. E. Johnston; sound, Bernard Freericks and Roger Heman; special camera effects, Fred Sersen; camera, Joseph LaShelle; editor, James B. Clark.

Ronald Colman (George Apley); Peggy Cummins (Eleanor Apley); Vanessa Brown (Agnes); Richard Haydn (Horatio Willing); Charles Russell (Howard Boulder); Richard Ney (John Apley); Percy Waram (Roger Newcombe); Mildred Natwick (Amelia Newcombe); Edna Best (Catherine Apley); Nydia Westman (Jane Willing); Francis Pierlot (Wilson); Kathleen Howard (Margaret); Paul Harvey (Julian Dole); Helen Freeman (Lydia); Theresa Lyon (Chestnut Vendor); William Moran (Henry Apley); Clifford Brooke (Charles); David Bond (Manager of Modiste Shop); Diana Douglas (Sarah); Ottola Nesmith (Mme. at Modiste Shop); Wyndham Standing and Stuart Hall (Gentlemen); Mae Marsh (Maid); Cordelia Campbell (Child Skater). Richard Shaw (Man).

A DOUBLE LIFE (Universal, 1947), 104 min.

Producer, Michael Kanin; director, George Cukor; based on *Othello* by William Shakespeare; screenplay, Ruth Gordon and Garson Kanin; art directors, Bernard Herzbrun and Harvey Gillett; set decorators, Russell A. Gausman and John Austin; music, Miklos Rosza; assistant director, Frank Shaw; advisor on *Othello* sequences, Walter Hampden; sound, Leslie I. Carey and Joe Lapis; special effects, David S. Horsley; camera, Milton Krasner; editor, Robert Parrish.

Ronald Colman (Anthony John); Signe Hasso (Brita); Edmond O'Brien (Bill Friend); Shelley Winters (Pat Kroll); Ray Collins (Victor Donlan); Philip Loeb (Max Lasker); Millard Mitchell (Al Cooley); Joe Sawyer (Pete Bonner); Charles LaTorre (Stellini); Whit Bissell (Dr. Stauffer); John Drew Colt (Stage Manager); Peter Thompson (Assistant Stage Manager); Elizabeth Dunne (Gladys); Alan Edmiston (Rex); Art Smith and Sid Tomack (Wigmakers); Wilton Graff (Dr. Mervin); Harlan Briggs (Oscar Bernard); Claire Carleton (Waitress); Betsy Blair, Janet Warren, and Marjorie Woodworth (Girls in Wig Shop); *Othello* sequence: Guy Bates Post, Leslie Denison, David Bond, Virginia Patton, Thayer Roberts, Percival Vivian, Boyd Irwin, Fay Kanin, Frederick Worlock, Arthur Gould-Porter; *A Gentleman's Gentleman* sequence: Elliott Reid, Georgia Caine, Mary Young, Percival Vivian; Curt Conway (Reporter); Paddy Chayefsky (Photographer); Nina Gilbert (Woman); John Derek (Police Stenographer); Buddy Roosevelt (Fingerprint Man); Fred Hoose (Laughing Man); Bruce Riley and Wayne Treadway (Men at Party); Pete Sosso (Tailor); Mary Worth (Woman in Audience).

CHAMPAGNE FOR CAESAR (United Artists, 1950), 99 min.

Executive producer, Harry M. Popkin; producer, George Moskov; director, Richard Whorf; story-screenplay, Hans Jacoby and Fred Brady; music, Dmitri Tiomkin; art director, George Van Marter; assistant directors, Ralph Stosser and Leon Chooluck; camera, Paul Ivano; editor, Hugh Bennett.

Ronald Colman (Beauregard Bottomley); Celeste Holm (Flame O'Neil); Vincent Price (Burnbridge Waters); Barbara Britton (Gwenn Bottomley); Art Linkletter (Happy Hogan); Gabriel Heatter and George Fisher (Announcers); Byron Foulger (Gerald); Ellye Marshall (Frosty); Vici Raaf (Waters' Secretary); Douglas Evans (Radio Announcer); John Eldredge, Lyle Talbot, George Leigh, and John Hart (Executives); Mel Blanc (Caesar's Voice); Peter Brocco (Fortune Teller); Brian O'Hara (Buck-T Man); Jack Daly (Scratch-T Man); Gordon Nelson (Lecturer); Herbert Lytton (Chuck Johnson); George Meader (Mr. Brown).

AROUND THE WORLD IN 80 DAYS (United Artists, 1956), C-168 min.

Producer, Michael Todd; associate producer, William Cameron Menzies; director, Michael Anderson; based on the novel by Jules Verne; screenplay, S. J. Perelman; music, Victor Young; choreography, Paul Godkin; art directors, Ken Adams and James W. Sullivan; camera, Lionel Lindon; editors, Gene Ruggiero and Paul Weatherwax.

David Niven (Phileas Fogg); Cantinflas (Passepartout); Robert Newton (Mr. Fix); Shirley MacLaine (Aouda); Charles Boyer (Monsieur Gasse); Joe E. Brown (Stationmaster); Martine Carol (Tourist); John Carradine (Colonel Proctor); Charles Coburn (Clerk); Ronald Colman (Official of Railway); Melville Cooper (Steward); Noël Coward (Hesketh-Baggott); Finlay Currie (Whist Partner); Reginald Denny (Police Chief); Andy Devine (First Mate); Marlene Dietrich (Barbary Coast Saloon Hostess); Luis Miguel Dominguin (Bullfighter); Fernandel (Coachman); Sir John Gielgud (Foster); Hermione Gingold (Sportin' Lady); Jose Greco (Dancer); Sir Cedric Harwicke (Sir Francis Gromarty); Trevor Howard (Fallentin); Glynis Johns (Companion); Beatrice Lillie (Revivalist); Evelyn Keyes (Flirt); Buster Keaton (Conductor); Peter Lorre (Steward); Edmund Lowe (Engineer); Victor McLaglen (Helmsman); Colonel Tim McCoy (Commander); A. E. Mathews (Club Member); Mike Mazurki (Character); John Mills (Cabby); Alan Mowbray (Consul); Robert Morley (Ralph); Edward R. Murrow (Narrator); Jack Oakie (Captain); George Raft (Barbary Coast Saloon Bouncer); Cesar Romero (Henchman); Gilbert Roland

181

(Achmed Abdullah); Frank Sinatra (Barbary Coast Saloon Pianist); Basil Sydney, and Ronald Squire (Members); Harcourt Williams (Hinshaw); Ava Gardner (Spectator).

THE STORY OF MANKIND (Warner Bros., 1957), C-100 min.

Producer, Irwin Allen; associate producer, George E. Swink; director, Allen; based on the book by Hendrik van Loon; screenplay, Allen and Charles Bennett; art director, Art Loel; music, Paul Sawtell; assistant director, Joseph Don Page; costumes, Marjorie Best; camera, Nick Musuraca; editor, Gene Palmer.

Ronald Colman (Spirit of Man); Hedy Lamarr (Joan of Arc); Groucho Marx (Peter Minuit); Harpo Marx (Isaac Newton); Chico Marx (Monk); Virginia Mayo (Cleopatra); Vincent Price (Devil); Peter Lorre (Nero); Charles Coburn (Hippocrates); Sir Cedric Hardwicke (High Judge); Cesar Romero (Spanish Envoy); John Carradine (Khufu); Dennis Hopper (Napoleon); Marie Wilson (Marie Antoinette); Helmut Dantine (Anthony); Edward Everett Horton (Sir Walter Raleigh); Reginald Gardiner (Shakespeare); Marie Windsor (Josephine); Cathy O'Donnell (Early Christian Woman); Franklin Pangborn (Marquis de Varennes); Melville Cooper (Major Domo); Francis X. Bushman (Moses); Henry Daniell (Bishop of Beauvais); Jim Ameche (Alexander Graham Bell); Dani Crayne (Helen of Troy); Anthony Dexter (Columbus); Austin Green (Lincoln); Bobby Watson (Hitler); Reginald Sheffield (Caesar); Nick Cravat (Apprentice); Alexander Lockwood (Promoter); Melinda Marx (Early Christian Child); Bart Mattson (Cleopatra's Brother); Don Megowan (Early Man); Marvin Miller (Armana); Nancy Miller (Early Woman); Leonard Mudie (Chief Inquisitor); Major Sam Harris (Nobleman in Queen Elizabeth's Court); Abraham Sofaer (Indian Chief).

Tyrone Power

In 1948, Tyrone Power told the press, "I'm extremely fond of my work. Well, I suppose it's in my blood. I've been on the stage since I was eight and my father and grandfather were actors before me. While a picture is being filmed, I think of little else. Certainly I have no time for social life."

While this statement may be an austere, even self-serving, version of his professional life, Tyrone Power was a very dedicated craftsman. Ironically, it was to his detriment that he was so handsome, charming, and appealing in almost every way. It made it so easy for his home lot, Twentieth Century-Fox, and the public to demand so little from him. It seemed all he had to do to earn his pay was to parade through a series of poses in front of the camera. But beneath the facile exterior, Power was always striving to better himself in his craft. One has only to observe the progression of his screen performances over the decades to realize the achievements and untapped potential within the man.

Had not Twentieth Century-Fox's colorful *The Mark of Zorro* (1940) and *Blood and Sand* (1941) so indelibly targeted him as Errol Flynn's major swashbuckling competitor of the Forties, he might have done more films like *Nightmare Alley* (Twentieth

Century-Fox, 1947) or *Abandon Ship!* (Columbia, 1957). His stage work in the Fifties revealed Tyrone as much more than a glib mannequin; he was a consummate artist. How ironic that the man who wanted so much to be accepted as mature actor, should die while making yet one more costumed picture, *Solomon and Sheba* (United Artists, 1959).

The name Tyrone Power, a celebrated one in the theatre since 1827, was given to a frail, dark-eyed boy child born in Cincinnati, Ohio, on Tuesday, May 5, 1913. His London-born father, Frederick Tyrone Edmond Power, and his mother, Helen Emma Reaume Power, were Shakespearean stage actors known, on the stage as Tyrone Power and Patia Power. The child's great-grandfather, the first Tyrone, had been a popular comedian on the Dublin stage and later at London's Drury Lane. The boy's grandfather, Frederick, apparently chose a profession other than the stage for there is no record of his having been in any plays. Up to two months before her son's birth, Patia Power was active on the stage, but she left her career; she and her husband moved to her family's Cincinnati home, where Tyrone, Jr. was born in 1913, and a daughter, Ann, was born in 1915. Because of Tyrone, Jr.'s frail health, Tyrone and Patia moved to sunny San Diego, California, in 1917.

Tyrone, Jr. saw his first play at the age of three. In John Steven McGroarty's annual mission play at San Gabriel, California, he watched his father perform as Junipero Serra. Four years later, he went on the same stage in the part of Pablo, a neophyte monk in the mission's drama of 1921.

In 1923, the Power family returned to Cincinnati. While Tyrone, Sr. toured in Shakespearean drama, Patia taught voice and dramatic expression at the Schuster-Martin School of Drama. Their son obtained his elementary schooling at The Sisters of Mercy Academy and at St. Xavier Academy in Cincinnati, and, from 1928 to 1929, he attended the Preparatory School of The University of Dayton in Dayton, Ohio. During these years, his mother Patia "taught him everything I could, and then, of course, his own talents took him on."

These talents were first observed at Purcell High School in Cincinnati where he played the lead in the senior class play, *Officer 666*. Until his graduation from high school in 1931, Tyrone Jr. worked part-time as a drugstore soda jerk and as a theatre usher. His parents argued over his future education. It was decided by his father that young Tyrone learn acting through application rather than in college. His father took him to a resort in Quebec, Canada, for a summer of intensive Shakespearean coaching. Then in September, 1931, Tyrone, Jr. accompanied his father to Chicago, where the elder Power had been signed for the autumnal season to play Shakespearean repertoire.

In *The Merchant of Venice*, Tyrone, Jr. acted with his father in the small part of an old man, friend of the Doge. During one performance, Fritz Leiber, who played Shylock, misjudged his mark and stuck a huge knife into the scenery next to Tyrone Jr.'s head. His father calmly muttered to his shaken son, "You're not hurt, boy. Keep on playing."

Young Tyrone supplemented his education of the drama with a few minor parts on NBC radio's Chicago-based show, "The Little Theatre off Times Square," starring Don Ameche and June Meredith. On November 19, 1931, the Chicago Civic Shakespeare Company, starring Tyrone, Sr., performed in *Hamlet* at the Royale Theatre in New York, with Tyrone, Jr. appearing in the production as a page.

From New York, father and son went to Hollywood after the former agreed to appear as the Patriarch in Paramount's sound film remake of *The Miracle Man* (1932), starring Sylvia Sidney and Chester Morris. Tyrone, Jr. was given the verbal promise of a small part in the same film, but this was forgotten when his father took ill in the early days of production and collapsed on the set. He died of a heart attack in the arms of his eighteen-year-old son at four A.M. on December 30, 1931. The role of the Patriarch was assumed by Hobart Bosworth, but the movie was an "unsatisfactory attempt to repeat in talkie form a film which was a landmark in the history of the silent screen." (*Film Weekly*).

Patia Power then moved to Santa Barbara, California, with her daughter Ann. Tyrone, Jr. remained in Hollywood, where he haunted the various casting offices. The skinny, hollow-cheeked youth managed to obtain the small part of John, one of the tyrannical school boys in *Tom Brown of Culver* (Universal, 1932), but he spent most of his time sitting around in dressing rooms with older actors who liked to reminisce about his famous father.

On May 16, 1933, at the Pasadena Playhouse, Tyrone, Jr. was featured in a revue known as *Lo and Behold,* which, ten months later, would be seen at New York's Fulton Theatre under the title *New Faces.* Also in the Pasadena cast were, among others, Leonard Sillman, Kay Thompson, June Sillman, Chuck Walters, and Eunice Quedens (Eve Arden). To pay for his room and board with screenwriter Arthur Caesar, a friend of Tyrone's father, he chauffeured his host about Hollywood as the latter peddled his stories. Only one other film job came the youth's way, and that was as an extra (a cadet) in *Flirtation Walk* (First National, 1934), starring Dick Powell and Ruby Keeler.

Discouraged by Hollywood's apparent lack of interest in him, he decided to return to New York. Stopping in Chicago enroute, to visit the Century of Progress Exposition, he decided to stay there and work with the Circuit Theatre and to do several radio shows. In November 1934, he got the part of Fred Livingstone in an eight-week revival of *Romance,* with Eugenie Leontovich, at the Blackstone Theatre. At the

185

close of that auspicious engagement, he continued on to New York where Michael Strange, the former wife of John Barrymore (and the mother of Diana) and a friend of Tyrone, Jr.'s mother, put him up in her elaborate guest room.

Another Power family friend, actress Helen Mencken, introduced him to producer Guthrie McClintic, Katharine Cornell's husband. McClintic hired him to understudy Miss Cornell's leading man, Burgess Meredith, in *The Flowers of the Forest,* which proved to be an unsuccessful venture at its opening at the Martin Beck Theatre (April 8, 1935).

He spent the summer of 1935 in a season of stock at West Falmouth, Massachusetts, after which he returned to Broadway at the request of McClintic, to play the part of Benvolio in *Romeo and Juliet,* a revival which opened at the Martin Beck on December 23, 1935, for fifteen performances. The production starred Katharine Cornell, Maurice Evans, Florence Reed, Ralph Richardson, and Orson Welles, who played Mercutio. Later, in 1948, when a bit player dropped his sword while filming *Macbeth* at Republic, Welles recalled, "I had a *good* sword carrier once. Young fellow by the name of Tyrone Power." In March, 1936, Tyrone played Bertrand de Poulengy in Miss Cornell's revival of *St. Joan,* with Maurice Evans as The Dauphin. Tyrone's salary was sixty dollars a week.

Joe Pincus, a talent scout representing the recently merged Twentieth Century-Fox, made a screentest of Tyrone in New York and sent the results to studio head Darryl F. Zanuck in Hollywood. The executive's initial order at seeing the test was, "Take it off. He looks like a monkey." Like his father, Tyrone's hairline was low on his forehead and his thick, bushy eyebrows grew in an almost continuous wide line above his nose. Zanuck's perceptive wife Virginia, also in the projection room for the test viewing, saw an appealing quality in the novice which her husband had overlooked. She suggested astutely that his eyebrows could be shaved and his hairline raised slightly. Zanuck agreed that the young man, with these alterations, could be made attractive.

Pincus was ordered to arrange for Tyrone's passage to California, where a second test was shot with studio star-in-the-rising Alice Faye, who volunteered her services because of an intuitive belief that the young actor would prove to be big boxoffice material.[1] "I thought he was without a doubt the handsomest man I had ever met," Miss Faye admitted in a recent letter. She asked that he be cast in her upcoming production, *Sing, Baby, Sing* (1936), and Zanuck agreed. Tyrone rehearsed for the part of newspaperman Ted Blake in the musical-with-a-story and posed for studio stills. After completing a few scenes, Zan-

---

[1]Miss Faye shared the same Taurus birthday as Tyrone—May 5.

186

uck changed his mind and replaced Tyrone with a better known performer, contract player Michael Whalen.

Tyrone then debuted for Twentieth in the last scene of *Girls' Dormitory* (1936), in which, in his only line of dialogue in the picture, he asked Simone Simon, "Could I have this dance?" The film also marked Miss Simon's debut in an American film. The vehicle also co-starred Herbert Marshall and Ruth Chatterton. When a sneak-preview audience was asked for comments on the film, most people wrote that they liked best the good-looking fellow in the final scene.

In seventh billing for *Ladies in Love* (Twentieth Century-Fox, 1936), his role as the romance in Loretta Young's life was larger. Set in Budapest, it was one in the long line of Fox films dealing with three girls (in this case, Janet Gaynor, Young, and Constance Bennett) who pool money and brains in an endeavor to snare husbands, preferably of the wealthy sort.[2] Don Ameche, also a Twentieth contract star-in-the-making, received top male billing as Gaynor's oncamera love. This was the last feature Tyrone would make in which the "junior" would appear on his credit line.

Zanuck now realized that he had a potentially hot star attraction on his payroll.[3] He made the decision to take a big chance and star Tyrone (in place of originally-scheduled Don Ameche) in the million-dollar 1936 production, *Lloyds of London* (Twentieth Century-Fox). Zanuck favorite Loretta Young rebelled at taking the lesser assignment of Lady Elizabeth in order to build up Fox's new-found pet, and British-born Madeleine Carroll filled the role. Englishman George Sanders was assigned to portray her callous, imperious husband, Lord Everett Stacy, establishing for himself and Hollywood a new pattern of cinema villainy.

Based on a story by Curtis Kenyon and directed by Henry King, the 117-minute *Lloyds of London* is a sprawling, semi-fictional accounting of the early-nineteenth-century beginnings of the group of insurance brokers who formed the now famous syndicate. Tyrone is Jonathan Blake,[4] a fictional boyhood friend of Horatio Nelson (Douglas Scott), who went on to become England's greatest naval hero. Blake is instrumental in behind-the-scenes tactics of making Lord Nelson's Trafalgar victory possible. Blake's daring for business does not extend into his

---

[2]Such other girl trio features made at Fox were *Three Blind Mice* (1938), *Moon Over Miami* (1941), *Three Little Girls in Blue* (1946), and *How to Marry a Millionaire* (1953).

[3]Besides Warner Baxter, Fox's top male star, the studio roster included Don Ameche, Eddie Cantor, Lon Chaney, Jr., Brian Donlevy, Jack Haley, Robert Kent, Allan Lane, Peter Lorre, Robert Lowery, Victor McLaglen, Tony Martin, Warner Oland, Jed Prouty, Bill Robinson, The Three Ritz Brothers, George Sanders, Slim Summerville, and Michael Whalen.

[4]Interestingly, although Tyrone had the principal role in *Lloyds of London,* he was billed fourth after Freddie Bartholomew, Madeleine Carroll, and Sir Guy Standing. Bartholomew played Jonathan Blake as a child; Power played Blake as an adult. Tyrone's wigs were all blond, in sharp contrast to the brunette look of Bartholomew.

With Loretta Young in *Ladies in Love* (1936)

With Madeleine Carroll
in *Lloyds of London* (1936)

private life, however, and he is fatally wounded by the irate husband (Sanders) of his paramour (Carroll). Said the *New York Times* critic: "Tyrone Power plays a much more varied role than any he has had previously for the screen. Where sheer action and character delineation are concerned, he is excellent. That he is required by the frequently lofty script to utter occasional passages which seem addressed to a hearkening posterity, is, of course, beyond his control."

With the film's release on November 25, 1936, Twentieth Century-Fox and Darryl F. Zanuck had themselves a first-rate star, and Tyrone's salary was increased appreciably. Heralded as a rival to MGM's Robert Taylor and Warner Bros.' Errol Flynn, Tyrone, at the age of twenty-two, stood an even six feet in height, weighed 155 pounds, and, as the studio publicity department pointed out, "Like many sensitive young actors, he makes an intelligent effort to keep up on artistic matters, likes to discuss literature and painting." To liven up his personality, it was "revealed" that he had several girlfriends (including Janet Gaynor and Loretta Young)—all conveniently Fox stars—liked swimming and tennis, and that he drove a sleek black Cord Phaeton.

Rebellious Loretta Young was forced to honor her studio contract and join Tyrone in *Love Is News* (Twentieth Century-Fox, 1937), but she received second billing after him in this Tay Garnett-directed feature. In the screwball comedy tradition of the middle-to-late 1930s, Loretta appeared as Tony Gateson, a bouncy heiress whose newspaper publicity, originated by a brash reporter (Tyrone), is far from compli-

189

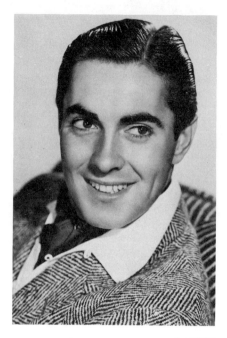

In 1937

Advertisement for *Love Is News* (1937)

mentary. She retaliates by announcing her engagement to him. He is fired by his managing editor (Don Ameche in third (!) billing), skirmishes with the girl, and both of them end up in jail—for the film's most delightfully wacky sequence. Eventually, he falls in love with her, as she does with him. Such fine supporting players as Slim Summerville, Walter Catlett, Jane Darwell, Stepin Fetchit, and George Sanders (as Count de Guyon, Loretta's jilted fiancé) gave the seventy-eight-minute comedy a good deal of entertaining stability. So facile was the Harry Tugend-Jack Yellen scenario that it would be rehashed in 1943 for *Sweet Rosie O'Grady* (with Robert Young and Betty Grable) and in 1948 as *That Wonderful Urge* (with Tyrone and Gene Tierney). Of Tyrone's work in *Love Is News*, *Time* Magazine found that he "gives surprisingly mature restraint to a role which might easily have slipped into frantic mugging."

So pleased was Zanuck by the public response to the screen teaming of Tyrone and Loretta—called by some the screen's most handsome couple, or the cinema's prettiest twosome—that he immediately ordered the duo to the sets of *Café Metropole* (Twentieth Century-Fox, 1937). This time Miss Young was given priority billing over Tyrone, although debonair Adolphe Menjou had the actual lead part. Zanuck's pal and contractee, Gregory Ratoff, wrote the whimsical story and also appeared in the film in a supporting character role. By now Tyrone had learned to relax a great deal more on screen than before, and he could handle his part of a poor but outspoken Princeton playboy with a good degree of professionalism. As Alexis, the bogus Russian prince, he is maneuvered by Monsieur Victor (Menjou), the manager of the Café Metropole, into charming rich American Laura Ridgeway (Young) out of her money. Naturally, love wins out in this confectionary caper, but not before boy delights, angers, romances, apologizes, and re-woos girl.

Sidney Lanfield's direction of *One in a Million* (Twentieth Century-Fox, 1936) had been of major importance in making a major screen personality of blonde Sonja Henie, who had starred in that successful film. He was again called upon to direct *Thin Ice* (Twentieth Century-Fox, 1937), in which Power had second billing under the new Scandanavian skating star. In this elaborate diverson, Tyrone plays the part of Prince Rudolf, prince of a small country located high in the Alps. Sonja Henie, who plays a local hotel skating instructress, mistakes the prince for a newspaperman. For reasons unknown to her—but actually because of her friendship with the prince—she becomes popular and famous in the skating world. Their love blooms on the white ski slopes and on the glistening ice rinks. The end result was Zanuck's most successful film of 1937.

Offscreen, the studio publicists worked overtime at convincing the public through fan magazine articles that Tyrone and Sonja were the

With Sonja Henie and Christian Rub in *Thin Ice* (1937)

With Stuart Erwin and Marjorie Weaver in *Second Honeymoon* (1937)

biggest romantic duo in tinseltown. Although the two screen favorites dated and had lunch together during the filming of *Thin Ice*, the affair was merely a ploy by the home lot to stir up added popularity for two of its already popular personalities.

In *Second Honeymoon* (Twentieth Century-Fox, 1937), Tyrone's third film with Loretta Young, he is very rich with a surfeit of suits, yachts, planes, and ingratiating charm. He has a wife (Young) but cannot keep her because of his idling ways. She spitefully weds ultra-conservative Lyle Talbot, but deserts him also because of his finicky ways, and returns to her ex-husband. Directed by Walter Lang, the feature lacks the originality and the charm of its chief comedy competition of the year, RKO's *The Awful Truth* (with Cary Grant and Irene Dunne).

Desirous of a cinematic spectacle to match MGM's earthquake destruction in *San Francisco* (1936) and Samuel Goldwyn's island holocaust in *The Hurricane* (United Artists, 1937), Zanuck had decided on portraying the Chicago fire of October, 1871. When the Niven Busch novel, *We, the O'Leary's*, was brought out, Zanuck pounced on it and ordered Lamar Trotti and Sonya Levien to devise an appropriate screenplay. Zanuck wanted to surpass all other disaster films in both spectacle and drawing power. For months he negotiated with Louis B. Mayer for the loan of Clark Gable, who was finally pronounced "unavailable." Jean Harlow had been signed for the feminine lead, but illness (the illness that was to take her life in June, 1937) made her loan an impossibility. Although Tyrone was not quite an equal match for the boxoffice draw of Gable, Zanuck assigned him to play the male lead, while director Henry King insisted on Alice Faye for the part of Belle Fawcett, the saloon singer. Don Ameche, who was fast becoming an also-ran in billing to Tyrone, was cast in the third slot. Not so long ago, when Miss Faye was asked if Tyrone had changed very much between the time she tested with him and when they worked together in this epic, the actress responded, "Just better looking." She considers him "a very special person, and very special to work with."

Although no one ever really unearthed the actual cause of the Chicago fire, the legend about Mrs. O'Leary's cow, as created by newsman Michael Ahern, was adopted by Zanuck and his associates, and the proper cow was selected to portray Mrs. O'Leary's "Daisy," whose right hind hoof would overturn the kerosene lamp. The $1,800,-000-budget production centered on Mrs. O'Leary (Alice Brady), a widow in Chicago's poor section called "The Patch." She takes in washing to raise her three sons, Dion (Tyrone), Jack (Ameche), and Bob (Tom Brown). Bob is soon paired off with Gretchen (June Storey), which leaves the remainder of the plot to focus on the older brothers. Dion opens a saloon in competition with Gil Warren (Brian Donlevy) and steals the latter's girl (Faye). Jack becomes a noted politician, winning the mayoralty election with Dion's unconventional method of obtaining the needed votes. When Dion marries Belle (Faye) so that she cannot testify against him and his unique electioneering methods, Jack fights with him in the mayor's office. Widow O'Leary, on hearing of the fight, dashes from her barn to stop it. In her haste, she forgets to place the wooden bar between Daisy's active legs, and the animal kicks over the fateful lantern.

In recreating the two-thirds of Chicago that burned in the $200 million fire, Zanuck constructed, on a far-removed portion of the studio lot, replicas of those buildings. The onscreen fire lasted twenty-five minutes, five minutes longer than *The Hurricane*, the recordholder for filmed devastation up to that time. During the three days that it took to shoot the fire scene, at a cost of $750,000, men wearing long skirts, wigs, and bonnets, filled in as oncamera women. Memorable shots included the scramble of humans to the safety of the Chicago River and of bellowing steers bursting their stockyard pens to stampede through the city's street (killing, among others on screen, Gil Warren). The monumental film received two Academy Awards in the 1937 sweepstakes:[5] Alice Brady for Best Supporting Actress and Robert Webb for Assistant Director (the last time this particular award was given). Nominated as Best Picture of the year, it lost to *The Life of Emile Zola* (Warner Bros.)

In the course of the 115-minute *In Old Chicago*, Alice Faye offered a dazzling array of vocal selections, ranging from the lilting "In Old Chicago," to "I've Taken a Fancy to You," and "Carry Me Back to Old Virginny," the latter number featuring Alice in stage tights and wearing the well-publicized $1,500 pair of jeweled stockings that she had first worn onscreen in *On the Avenue* (Twentieth Century-Fox, 1937). Ameche was his usual stentorian self, inclined to solemn dramatics, as when he voiced the belief to his oncamera brothers, "The only thing that matters is we are together and thinking alike." Brady, bespeaking her years as a stage and screen trouper, gave substance and warmth to what could have been a one-dimensional role as the washerwoman mother of the fighting Irish brood.

As for Tyrone, he revealed in this feature what many filmgoers knew and what most of the critics suspected: he was fine when it came to celluloid romancing or being feisty, but his cinema artistry at handling strongly emotional scenes left a good deal to be desired. Two sequences within *In Old Chicago* demonstrate this. In the first, Tyrone has been knocked down in a skirmish with Gil Warren's men. Ameche rushes over to his semi-unconscious brother, forgetful for the moment that his main concern is to have the dynamite lit, so, as General Sheridan (Sidney Blackmer) advises, they can fight fire with fire. Injured

[5]Although released in January, 1938, after a delay for careful editing of the sound effects, the film was included in the 1937 balloting.

With Alice Faye in *In Old Chicago* (1938)

Tyrone, cradled in Ameche's arms, unconvincingly shouts out in his best martyr's tone, "Jack, light 'em . . . light 'em . . . it's just a scratch . . . light 'em!"

Later on, when Tyrone somehow has been reunited with Alice Brady, Tom Brown, and June Storey, at the Chicago River waterfront, he is asked to deliver a very trying bit of business. Brady, thankful to find Tyrone alive, wants to know about her son the mayor.

Brady: "And Jack?"

Tyrone: (burying his head in her shoulder): "Ah, Ma . . ." Power's handling of this sequence, granting its over-maudlin and clichéd tones, was far less than satisfactory.

Moments later in the film story, both Brady and Tyrone had regained their composure (after all, the movie must end on an optimistic note— didn't *San Francisco*?). Tyrone is then required to utter a bit of dialog that, when heard, defies logic. "He'll [late brother Jack] have his dream, Ma. Nothing can lick him any more than it can lick Chicago." The music swells up, and the end titles flash on the screen.

Whatever their histrionic shortcomings, the popularity of Power, Faye, and Ameche was cinched in *In Old Chicago*, and they were summarily reunited oncamera in *Alexander's Ragtime Band* (1938). Again, while being acclaimed by Zanuck and critics alike as "the fastest rising star in America," Tyrone received top billing. At an overall

195

production cost of two million dollars, it required nearly two years for writers Lamar Trotti and Kathryn Scala to devise the script. In a rather unusual policy decision for a Fox film, Gwen Wakeling was given monetary leeway to design flavorful costumes of the 1911-1938 era for this nostalgic survey musical. Thomas Little was permitted a strong touch of the opulent in designing his eighty-five sets, one of which contained (according to publicity releases) some seven and three-quarters tons of cut glass chandeliers imported from Czechoslovakia. *Time* Magazine called the finished product "easily the best cinemusical of 1938," and *Liberty* decided it "makes for color, gaiety, romance, and movement and adds up to a great evening's entertainment."

Boasting thirty of Irving Berlin's then canon of six hundred published songs, the film traces the dramatic account of Roger Grant (Tyrone), of San Francisco's Nob Hill, who forsakes classical music for ragtime, of the type heard along the Barbary Coast. He forms a band with piano player Charlie Dwyer (Ameche) and changes his name to Alexander after acquiring a songstress named Stella Kirby (Faye), who introduces him to the new tune, "Alexander's Ragtime Band." Tyrone sternly tells his attentive band members, "If you fellows want to stick with me and go places . . . like New York . . . you're going to have to work." The group does work, and hard, and soon they are being featured at San Francisco's fashionable Cliff House Restaurant, where a

With Alice Faye in *Alexander's Ragtime Band* (1938)

196

musical trap is set for the famous New York producer, Charles Dillingham (Joe King). Stella beguiles him into listening to the band and, later, Alexander kisses her, saying, "That's for all the times I've wanted to break your neck. . . ."

But it is Stella whom Dillingham wants in a big New York revue show, not the band. Noble Charlie persuades her to go East, much to Alex's consternation, and the potential lovers quarrel bitterly (all according to tried and true screen tradition). Alex joins the army at the outbreak of World War I, while Charlie becomes a success at composing songs, and Stella emerges as a smash success on stage. She marries Charlie, and, after the war, Alex finds temporary solace with brassy Jerry Allen (Ethel Merman). Stella later divorces Charlie, although Alex does not know it. He has, by this time, formed a new band, which is the rage of Paris. When he returns to New York for a big 1938 radio broadcast at Carnegie Hall, Stella dramatically appears backstage. They are reunited in love and song.

Time Magazine recorded, "Both look much younger than at their first meeting," and the *New York Times* observed, "Miss Faye and Tyrone Power go through the years without a gray hair or a wrinkle." Nominated for six Oscar nominations, including Best Picture, the film was awarded only one: to Alfred Newman for his Best Scoring.

Tyrone was loaned to MGM in 1938 in exchange for the services of Spencer Tracy (For Twentieth's forthcoming *Stanley and Livngstone*, 1939). The occasion was the reign and decapitation of Queen *Marie Antoinette* (1938). From the instant that Marie, an Austrian Archduchess (Norma Shearer[6]), learns that she is to marry King Louis XVI (Robert Morley) of France, a man she has never met, and exclaims to her mother, "Oh Maman, I'm to be the Queen of France," the 160-minute film belongs to her.

Marie Antoinette is the embroidered account of a fun-loving, misunderstood, compassionate woman whose marriage is one of companionship rather than of love. Although Tyrone received second billing in the ambiguous role of Swedish Count Axel de Fersen, the one passionate love in the Queen's relatively short life, he is lost amid the MGM opulence. In his rather drab outfits designed by Gile Steele, he is overshadowed by the swirling, glistening feminine creations of Adrian, by Cedric Gibbon's dazzling set decorations, and by William H. Daniels' camera which, under W. S. Van Dyke II's cagey direction, always gives careful attention to Miss Shearer, then reigning queen of the Culver City studio. (She was also then recently widowed as a result of the untimely death of Thalberg.)

[6]Back in 1933 a battle royale occurred on the MGM lot between Norma (aided by her Metro executive producer husband Irving Thalberg) and Marion Davies (supported by her media magnate lover, William Randolph Hearst) over who would have the *Marie Antoinette* project, as well as the lead in *The Barretts of Wimpole Street* (1934). Miss Shearer won both vehicles for herself.

With Norma Shearer in *Marie Antoinette* (1938)

The star-crossed film romance commences with a masked ball when the queen dashes out of the ballroom jokingly in quest of a Russian aristocrat. Finding Fersen, she takes him back to the ball and laughingly presents him to her fine friends as a Russian. He is insulted by their tart remarks and sarcastically informs the coquettish ruler, "Mademoiselle is charming and, I've not doubt, talented; I'm sure mademoiselle excels in the role of soubrette, she has the appearance, the manners and the temperament." But forty minutes of celluloid later, he confesses that he loves her with, "I've been saying it with every word and I've no right." In the tradition of the Scarlet Pimpernel, he helps the royal family to escape the palace, but they are discovered by the revolutionaries and his efforts to obtain last-minute help from other European sovereigns are fruitless. Miss Shearer, Mr. Morley, and the film itself were nominated for Academy Awards, but none were bestowed on the expensive *Marie Antoinette*.

The world premiere of the film took place on July 12, 1938, at Hollywood's Cathay Circle where Los Angeles NBC-affiliated radio stations KFI and KECA refused MGM's request to donate air time for the "historical" event. It was demanded that the studio pay regular commercial rates. On August 16, 1938, the spectacle film made its East Coast debut at the Astor Theatre, playing on a two-a-day performance basis. The *New York Times* reported, "The splendors of the French monarchy in its dying days have not simply been equaled, they have been surpassed by Metro-Goldwyn-Mayer's film biography." As for Tyrone's performance, the same paper recorded, "Only Tyrone Power as the romantically rather far-fetched Count Axel de Fersen is permitted to approach the luminous bounds of that divinity which hedges the Shearer throne, and he does so timidly, with due deference, and with the tender consciousness not so much of love as of second-billing in his eyes." Enough said!

When Tyrone returned to the sanctity of the Pico Boulevard sound-stages of Twentieth Century-Fox, an enraged Darryl F. Zanuck swore that his prize male lead[7] would never again be loaned out to another film company. It was felt, and justifiably, that Power had not been shown to good advantage by MGM. Zanuck did not wish to risk another chance with his number one contract star, and let it further be known that Tyrone would henceforth have the pick of both his scripts and his co-players. The mighty mogul even went so far as to extend to Tyrone the use of his private steam room located in the basement of one of the studio's buildings. No other player on the studio lot was afforded that unique privilege.

Previously, Zanuck had been able to exercise his mania for historical drama by casting Ronald Colman as the swashbuckling hero, but now with the younger, more conventionally handsome Tyrone Power on the lot, he had a new protagonist for his oversized cinema spectacles. *Suez* (Twentieth Century-Fox, 1938) depicted the sepia-tinted story (not altogether a true one) of Ferdinand de Lesseps (1804-1895), the French engineer credited with constructing the canal that extends from the Red Sea to the Mediterranean. In a bit of more astute casting than had been the case with *Marie Antoinette,* Tyrone appears as the legendary builder, whose vision and determination to accomplish the near impossible is only equalled by the beauty of his face in repose or his dashing romanticism with the women who enter his hectic life. Loretta Young, nearing her final breach with Zanuck and Fox, plays the stately Empress Eugenie, whom Tyrone loves unrequitedly and the French gamine, Annabella, is Toni Pellerin, who gives him his grand inspiration. Two hundred fifty thousand dollars was spent in filming what the Arabian desert folk term a "zobah-hah," a combination cyclone and dust storm. At the height of the howling cinematic storm, Tyrone falls unconscious. Feather-weighted Annabella ties him to a large pole stuck in the sand before the gargantuan wind whips her away to her death in the choking sands. Of his performance, *Time* Magazine snide-

[7]Although Warner Baxter, with a salary at over $300,000 annually, was technically still Fox's top male star, Tyrone had supplanted the older leading man both in executive and film fan favoritism.

With J. Edward Bromberg and Michael Visaroff in *Suez* (1938)

ly suggested, "In the brief interval since he played the orchestra leader in *Alexander's Ragtime Band,* Tyrone Power has not had time to make major changes in his technique."

A month after the release of the big-budgeted *Suez,* certain descendants of de Lesseps complained publicly because the film did not reveal that their forefather had married happily, so happily, in fact, that he had sired seventeen children. Their legal action, brought in France, was dismissed by that country's courts on the grounds that *Suez* heaped such honors on France and its countrymen that to allow any course of action against the film was out of the question.

In January, 1939, *Motion Picture Herald,* in its annual poll of ten thousand independent U.S. theatre owners, declared that Tyrone was the number ten boxoffice attraction. All of the ten, interestingly, were from Twentieth and MGM (five from each studio). That same month, three of Tyrone's releases were listed by *Film Daily* in its yearly poll of 536 newspapers, syndicates, and magazine critics as among the ten best of 1938: *Alexander's Ragtime Band, Marie Antoinette,* and *In Old Chicago.* Tyrone Power was fast approaching the zenith of his fame at Twentieth, in Hollywood, and with the moviegoing public.

Tyrone's first movie in Technicolor was *Jesse James* (1939), a purified 105-minute insight into the morally corrupt crook of the 1870s. Henry King, in his fourth professional association with the young star, directed Tyrone in his debut screen Western. Power and his oncamera

With John Carradine and Charles Tannen in *Jesse James* (1939)

brother Frank (Henry Fonda)[8] rob Western trains with a charming, almost debonair manner. Jesse treats his wife (Nancy Kelly) with tenderness, and is shot on April 3, 1882, by the weasel-like Bob Ford (John Carradine) as he places an embroidered sampler reading, "God Bless Our Home," on a wall in his house.

Clive Denton, writing of director Henry King in *The Hollywood Professionals: Volume 2* (Tantivy Press 1974) says of *Jesse James*, "It possesses a magnificent forward-pressing attack, a surge of images, not always present in his work, together with those moments of calm and reflection that are native to him." King had scheduled filming for the Western in Liberty, Missouri. However, on learning that the real home of the James Brothers had been torn down, he flew over the Ozarks searching for a village where an old courthouse still stood. He found one in Pineville, Missouri, where he constructed false fronts over the modern stores to make them appear old, covered the concrete streets with dirt, and hired dozens of the town's citizens to act as extras.

Pineville's Mill Creek Church, the scene of Jesse's marriage to his "gun-moll," was further immortalized on postal cards which delighted tourists who traveled to the town to take a look at the ground where famous movie stars had walked. Of the two-million-dollar production,

---

[8]A sequel, *The Return of Frank James* (Twentieth Century-Fox) with Fonda would be filmed in 1940, using a brief film clip of Tyrone as brother Jesse.

a descendant of the outlaw brothers, Miss Jo Frances James, a bank executive in Los Angeles, said, "About the only connection it had with fact was that there was once a man named James and he did ride a horse."[9]

There were many Old West and Western film purists who complained that the Fox movie whitewashed the truth and, more to the point, turned the real-life outlaw into a Robin Hood of the Old West. Then, too, in his characterization of the famed lawbreaker, Tyrone was altogether too handsome and charming as the ill-fated bandit, leading the *New York Times* to report of his performance as the often unshaven bank robber, he "makes out an excellent melodramatic case against himself as Jesse." Nevertheless, the public heartily endorsed *Jesse James* and its noble star, leading to Power's selection as number two boxoffice star in the nation for the year 1939.[10] (Mickey Rooney was in the top spot in this annual survey.)

Since his rise to screen stardom, there had been much speculation regarding Tyrone's romantic vis-a-vis of the moment. Then, in 1938 during the filming of *Suez,* Power became amorously interested in co-star Annabella.[11] She also was under contract to Twentieth Century-Fox and had been wed to French actor Jean Murat, her third husband, since 1934. However, on October 31, 1938, she publicly announced that her marriage was heading toward a divorce. When knowing reporters asked her if Tyrone's presence in her life might have had something to do with her domestic restructuring, she mysteriously stated, "Tyrone Power? He is a nice boy. But that is all."

Throughout 1938, both Tyrone and Annabella played a shell game with the eager press. When he arrived in Rio de Janiero on November 28, he insisted it was merest coincidence that she was in the Brazilian city to meet him. On December 23, he arrived in New York City from

[9]In February, 1939, Sydney H. Coleman, president of the American Humane Society, charged that Twentieth went to "incredible lengths of inhuman cruelty to horses. He stated that a blindfolded horse was chuted down a greased slide over the top of a seventy-foot cliff into a lake and was killed. His allegation included proof, he said, as recorded on 16mm. film by an unnamed on-the-spot amateur. Coleman reported the incident to the Hays Office for action.

[10]Coincidentally it was also in 1939 that Warner Bros.' James Cagney and Errol Flynn, in *The Oklahoma Kid* and *Dodge City* respectively, each made their Western film debut. And, of course, 1939 marked the year of John Wayne's *Stagecoach* (United Artists). From this time onward, the Western genre was back in good standing at the major studios. In 1940 MGM would launch Robert Taylor in the Western genre with *Billy the Kid.*

[11]She was born Suzanne Georgette Charpentier in Paris on July 17, 1909. Trained for the theatre, she later made her film debut in Abel Gance's *Napoleon* (1927), followed by Gremillon's *Maldonne* (1928). It was Rene Clair's *Le Million* (1931) which made her a star. This was followed by *Le Quatorze Juillet* (1933) and other pictures. After a talking film remake of Dupont's *Variety* (1937), she appeared in England in three Twentieth Century-Fox features: *Under the Red Robe* (1936), with Conrad Veidt, *Dinner at the Ritz* (1937), with Paul Lukas, and *Wings of the Morning* (1937), in Technicolor with Henry Fonda. Her first Hollywood film was Fox's *The Baroness and the Butler* (1938), with William Powell.

Rio. When asked about you-know-who, he responded, "Fantastic. We are merely good friends." Sharp reporters were quick to note that the French actress just happened to be booked at the Pierre Hotel as well. On April 18, 1939, the famous couple opened their secret and actually applied for a marriage license in Los Angeles. They were wed in Hollywood on April 23, 1939, in the garden of the home of Charles Boyer and his wife Pat Paterson. At the age of twenty-nine, Annabella was four years her groom's senior. Louella Parsons wrote in her Hearst-syndicated column soon after the wedding, "Frankly, and if I can judge by the batch of letters that have come to this desk recently, the youngsters are brokenhearted over the marriage of their hero, Ty Power. Mildred and Harold Lloyd told me their two daughters practically went into a decline when they heard."

The newlyweds honeymooned in Rome.

Tyrone's first picture in release as a married man was, nevertheless, a success, indicating that the ladies of America still loved him on the silver screen. In *Rose of Washington Square* (Twentieth Century-Fox), he is billed above Alice Faye in their third and final film together, although it has more of Faye than of Power. Strongly denied by Twentieth that it was a parody on the life story of Fanny Brice[12] and her

[12]Viewers are invited to compare the presentation of "Fanny Brice" in *Rose of Washington Square* with the 1964 Broadway musical *Funny Girl* and the two films thereafter, *Funny Girl* (Columbia, 1969) and *Funny Lady* (Columbia, 1975). Barbra Streisand was the Funny Girl/Lady, while Omar Sharif recreated the role of Nicky Arnstein that had been handled on the stage by Sidney Chaplin.

**With Alice Faye
in *Rose of Washington Square* (1939)**

203

husband Nicky Arnstein, the film is concerned with Ziegfeld star, Rose Sargent (Faye), whose good name is sullied by her con-artist husband, Bart (Tyrone), when he flees from justice in a bond scandal. She sings several songs, including a song called "My Man" in a tremulous voice pleading for him to give himself up to the law and face the charges. He does just that and is given five years at Sing Sing prison, while she promises, "I'll be waiting."

Adding sparks to the publicity surrounding *Rose of Washington Square* was a legal suit filed by Miss Brice against the studio claiming that it *was* her life depicted in the musical movie. The case was settled out of court.

Tyrone continued to take second billing to Norway's former skating champ, dimpled Sonja Henie, as they plowed through another joint movie, this time, Irving Berlin's *Second Fiddle* (Twentieth Century-Fox, 1939). With Rudy Vallee and Edna May Oliver in support, Tyrone appeared as Jimmy Sutton, an ambitious press agent for Consolidated Productions, who devises a romance between the studio's new skating find from Minnesota and an established star (Vallee). However, the plan backfires when she falls for the agent instead. Neither the film nor its Irving Berlin songs (including "An Old-Fashioned Tune Always Is New," "Song of the Metronome," and "I Poured My Heart into a Song") left much of an impression with devout moviegoers.

With Edna May Oliver, Sonja Henie, and Rudy Vallee in *Irving Berlin's Second Fiddle* (1939)

With Don Ameche, Lionel Barrymore, and Pat O'Brien for NBC Radio's "All American Broadcast" (June, 1939)

Meanwhile, Darryl Francis Zanuck popped up with yet another historical epic, this one containing four catastrophes: earthquake, fire, flood, and plague. Written for the screen by Philip Dunne and Julien Josephson from Louis Bromfield's popular novel *The Rains Came* (Twentieth Century-Fox, 1939) the feature presented Tyrone with tinted skin as Major Rama Safti,[13] a graduate surgeon of Johns Hopkins Medical School. He returns to his native town of Ranchipur in India where he works tirelessly in behalf of his impoverished people, until the bored Lady Esketh (MGM's Myrna Loy) arrives in town followed by Cognac-soaked Tom Ransome (Warner Bros.' George Brent), her ex-lover. The good lady falls for the surgeon while a missionary's daughter (Brenda Joyce in her movie debut) makes a shameless play for Tom. Mother Nature lowers the boom on these British despots who, through their harrowing experiences, find a new set of life's values. Of Tyrone, whose teeth sparkled against his darkened skin, *Newsweek* Magazine noted that he was "persuasive and sincere," while sour-penned Frank S. Nugent of the *New York Times* wrote, "He is still Mr. Power—young, impetuous and charming, with all the depth of a coat of skin-dye."

---

[13]Richard Burton would enact the role in the 1955 Fox remake, entitled *The Rains of Ranchipur,* filmed in CinemaScope and color.

With the completion of this major film, the Powers went to Europe. With the threat of war hovering over the continent, Annabella arranged to have her parents flown from France, first to England, and then on to California via trans-Atlantic clipper. Tyrone and Annabella resided in Brentwood in a modern Georgian house at 139 Saltair, to which they had moved immediately after their marriage. Especially designed for Tyrone in 1938, the house featured broad windows, terraces, and wide verandas that overlooked long stretches of lawn. His in-laws discovered that Tyrone's hobby was collecting model railroad engines.

Along with spectacles, marital farce was extremely popular with moviegoers of the late thirties, and Tyrone had another opportunity at screwball comedy with *Daytime Wife* (Twentieth Century-Fox, 1939), directed by Gregory Ratoff. As the executive of a roofing firm, he plays platonic attention to his secretary (Wendy Barrie), while his wife (Linda Darnell[14]) waits at home on the night of their wedding anniversary. To even the score, she obtains a job as secretary to his friend and customer (Warren William). The film was described by one critic as "merely a harmless piece of frothy, theatrical fiction."

Like many other performers whose screen success was undeniably

---

[14]Loretta Young had been selected for the part, but she and Fox were severing professional relations by the time of this production.

With Linda Darnell in *Day-Time Wife* (1939)

due more to good looks than acting acumen, Tyrone bridled at each passing year that saw him enacting more cardboard screen characterizations. He had an earnest desire to prove that he was his father's son, and that his histrionic prowess was real. Thus, he persuaded his studio mentor, Zanuck, to allow him to go dramatic. The vehicle selected was *Johnny Apollo* (Twentieth Century-Fox, 1940). The director was Henry Hathaway, who later would helm five Tyrone Power pictures, and the supporting cast included Edward Arnold as Power's Wall Street embezzler-father, Lloyd Nolan as a mobster, and Lionel Atwill as Arnold's gentleman lawyer. For boxoffice insurance, Fox relied on the visual-vocal services of Paramount's Dorothy Lamour who dropped her sarong long enough to cavort as "Lucky" Dubarry, a rather old-fashioned gangster's moll; Lamour proved she has a way with a song (such as "This Is the Beginning of the End" and "Dancing for Nickels and Dimes"), if not with a straight dramatic scene. Tyrone was Bob Cain, who, after graduating from college, turns to a career of crime while disgusted with the dishonest methods employed by his father (Arnold). The *New York Times'* B. R. Crisler generously complimented Tyrone for maintaining "a nice balance between Harvard and the Tenderloin." Other critics were more direct in their appraisal of Tyrone's contra-casting. "In spite of all the cracks that have been made about his looks, there is a quality in his face which takes him out of the pretty-

With Lloyd Nolan, Dorothy Lamour, and Charley Grapewin in *Johnny Apollo* (1940)

pretty class and makes him just right for the part. . . ." (William Boehnel, *New York World-Telegram*) If he saw Herbert Cohn's report in the *Brooklyn Daily Eagle,* Tyrone must have leaped for joy at the confirmation of his own beliefs. "For the first time in his career, the pride of the Zanuck lot has shown traces of the dramatic skill that has been a family tradition for more than a century."

Henry Hathaway was in the captain's chair, also for *Brigham Young —Frontiersman* (Twentieth Century-Fox, 1940). Tyrone received top billing, for obvious boxoffice reasons, but his role was actually secondary to that of Dean Jagger (as Young) and Brian Donlevy (as Angus Duncan, the rival leader of the Mormon sect). Tyrone appears as earnest, romantic Jonathan Kent, a follower of Young's Mormon beliefs, who treks by covered wagon with the group to the promised land at the edge of the Great Salt Lake. Linda Darnell was the comely girl in his life on the way to Utah, and the elaborate film proved to be only a marginal success.

The year 1940 came to a glorious finish for Tyrone in one of the films for which he is best remembered. As Don Diego Vega, he played his first real swashbuckling screen role in *The Mark of Zorro* (Twentieth Century-Fox), directed by the esteemed craftsman, Rouben Mamoulian. Vega, the only son of the richest Spanish hidalgo in California of the 1820s, is a pampered fop from sunrise until sunset. But, at night, he covers his face with a black mask and rides his horse Tornado through the countryside, performing great deeds of daring in his goal to rid the land of its tyrannical military aide (Basil Rathbone) and corrupt Spanish overseer (J. Edward Bromberg).

From the pages of Johnston McCulley's story, *The Curse of Capistrano* (1919), written in six days, the property was first put to film in 1920 by United Artists with Douglas Fairbanks as Zorro. Critics such as Bosley Crowther of the *New York Times* stated that "Tyrone Power is no Douglas Fairbanks, and any resemblance which he may bear to his late predecessor in the title role is purely coincidental."

However, each film star had his own individual style, with Fairbanks excelling in acrobatic élan, while Tyrone, the more handsome of the two, was both romantic and dashing. His swordplay, although lacking Fairbanks' finesse and nimbleness, was convincing, and his leaps from balcony to horse were more exciting due to the accompanying sound effects. There was no denying that a new screen swashbuckler was born in the person of Tyrone Power, whose lengthy climactic duel with the heinous Rathbone was just as good as any performed by the sword-and-smile champion, Errol Flynn. J. Edward Bromberg's bit of film dialog spoken to Zorro within the film sums up Power's special skill: "You handle a sword like a devil from hell."

Even the most casual re-viewing of *The Mark of Zorro* reveals aspects of Tyrone's acting that few critics of the day or screen historians

With Basil Rathborne in *The Mark of Zorro* (1940)

of the present generation care to recall—that Power was adept with comedy lines. Throughout this dashing feature, an abiding tone of mock-seriousness courses like an elixir, a remedy utilized by director Mamoulian to insure that this resurrection of an old warhorse melodrama would be taken as entertainment and not as a historical relic.

As the dandy of old Los Angeles who strides about in frilled outfits, toying with a monocle, a lace handkerchief, and a quotient of snuff, Tyrone's bogus character is forever registering mock terror at the very mention of Zorro's name. "Heaven help me," he proclaims, "My blood chills at the very thought [of him]." Everyone seems to accept Power's dandy as the real thing, even his father who proclaims with disgust, "Zorro is a man, this is my worthless offspring."

Even Power's romantic scenes are tinged with comedy, a mood made all the more delightful with the luscious, young Linda Darnell as the heroine. For example, when she goes to the chapel of her uncle's house, she prays to the Blessed Virgin, "Send one to take me from this place. Let him be kind and handsome and brave." Who should pop out of the shadowy corner but Tyrone, disguised in a cleric's garment, and at the moment more bent on escaping the Spanish soldiers than in conversing with this young lady. But, in a send-up of the romantic tradition, he is almost immediately captivated by her charms. "Why you're more radiant, more lovely than a morning in June," he tells her. Thereafter the two would-be lovers launch into a sequence of comedy byplay as they sit on a chapel bench. She naively tries to discern who is actually beneath the religious garb. She darts her frame to and fro, suddenly bending this way or that, hoping for a glimpse of the face hidden by the shadows of the cleric's hood. However, the nimble Tyrone is always one move ahead of her in this amusing bit of shadow boxing.

Later, Power experiences a mock romantic sequence with the vain wife (Gale Sondergaard) of bumbling Bromberg. Sitting by the side of a stream, flirtatious Sondergaard confesses, "Talking with you is like drinking cool water in the desert." Power responds with a subtle double take, as if measuring how far he can lead this self-deluded courtesan on a merry path. Almost imperceptibly, he shrugs his shoulders, and in a lampoon of a gallant gesture, he takes her extended hand, peels back the white glove, kisses her wrist, and then allows the glove to fall back in place. The audience, if not Sondergaard's character, fully appreciates the satire.

Perhaps the biggest intentional laugh of *The Mark of Zorro* occurs, not when rotund Father Felipe (Eugene Pallette) skirmishes agilely with Rathbone, but when Tyrone arrives late to Bromberg's dinner, at which time he is to seal the bargain to wed Darnell. Bromberg, Sondergaard, Darnell, and Rathbone are impatiently waiting the fop's entrance. Power minces into their presence and immediately launches into an apology, complaining that his bath was drawn too early, and by the time he was ready to submerge in it, it had grown tepid, and then there was the matter of adding the proper amount of salts to the water. Darnell sits back in disgust, wondering what married life to this lily-livered dandy will be like. Rathbone smirks and confides to Sondergaard, "Poor Lolita [Darnell]. I'm afraid her married life will be the same [as the bath water].

Yet another example of Tyrone's felicity with a wry line occurs when he announces to his parents that he intends to wed the niece (Darnell) of the tyrannical Spanish law enforcer (Bromberg). Montagu Love's Don Alejandro Vega storms out of the room, leaving a baffled Janet Beecher to plead with her son to show some sense and respect his father's advice. Power sits back and explains with mock seriousness, "I had no say in my father's marriage, so why should he in mine?"

Since the resurrection of *Zorro* had proven so successful, Twentieth chose to remake another film classic of the 1920s, a feature based on Vincente Blasco Ibanez' 1908 novel *Sangre y Arene, Blood and Sand* (1941),[15] with Mamoulian again at the helm. The director's masterful touch for realism was exploited by the Technicolor camera work of Ray Rennahan and Ernest Palmer, which helped to make the new version a film very much worth remembering. Filmed on the Fox backlot and in Mexico, the picture is about a Spanish peon (Tyrone) who feels he was

[15]Filmed originally in 1922 by Paramount with Rudolph Valentino.

With Nazimova in *Blood and Sand* (1941)

born to be a matador like his late father, despite the fears of his hard-working mother (the famed silent screen vamp Nazimova). He eventually marries his childhood sweetheart (Linda Darnell), whose marital joy is threatened by the appearance of a temptress, Dona Sol (Rita Hayworth), who practically ruins the handsome, ambitious young matador. The wordy script by Jo Swerling, and the director's penchant for creating living tapestries and exploiting symbolic possibilities through the use of color, allowed little time for action, but Tyrone was a knock-out in his bullring wardrobe.[16]

The public responded happily to the richly mounted *Blood and Sand* and accepted Power's interpretation of the fiery youth who grows to be a swaggering matador and who dies in the ring. If the actor fell short in capturing the passion of a dedicated bullfighter, he excelled in his fourth oncamera romancing with Miss Darnell and was especially convincing as the puppy dog suitor of the beguiling, materialistic Dona Sol. Said *Newsweek* Magazine, "Tyrone Power, who recently in *The Mark of Zorro* tried Douglas Fairbanks's shoes on for size and found them a little roomy, tackles an even more difficult job in following Valentino, and is persuasive enough."

After three consecutive costume films, the Fox hierarchy decided to

---

[16]Years later, he would be immortalized in wax at the Hollywood Wax Museum wearing the splashy outfit of a matador.

With Betty Grable in *A Yank in the R.A.F.* (1941)

return their pride and joy[17] to the contemporary era, and teamed him with Alice Faye's fast-rising rival, Betty Grable, in *A Yank in the R.A.F.* (1941). Filmed in Hollywood, it has a London setting during the Dunkirk episode of World War II, and it utilized actual on-the-scene background shots of the Royal Air Force in action. As Tim Baker, Tyrone is a cocky, brash American flier who finds a former girl friend (Grable) also American, in the floor show of a London nightclub. He joins the R.A.F. for adventure's sake, and to be near her, and in the process is caught up in some exciting air exercises. The original script[18] (called *The Eagle Flies Again*) ordained that the American flier be killed, but Zanuck changed it to a happy ("lovers united") ending at the unoffical request of the British. Under Henry King's workmanlike direction, Grable was given two songs ("Another Little Dream Won't Do Us Any Harm" and "Hi-Ya Love") to please her growing retinue of devoted fans. The film emerged a solid boxoffice hit.

Hal B. Wallis wanted Tyrone for the major role of Parris Mitchell, in his Warner Bros. production of Henry Bellamann's novel of turn-of-the-century Americana, *Kings Row* (1941), but Zanuck, still smarting from the abuse Tyrone received at the hands of MGM, staunchly re-

[17]The complexion of the male player roster at Fox had changed with the coming of the new decade. Among the newer crop of contract performers were Dana Andrews, Richard Greene, John Loder, Victor Mature, George Montgomery, John Payne, and John Sutton, many of whom were, or would be, competing for parts that were once Tyrone's province.
[18]Written by Darryl F. Zanuck, using the pseudonym of Melville Crossman.

fused. Robert Cummings was given the role and performed well. Tyrone's disappointment at not playing Drake McHugh was partially assuaged when Zanuck allowed him time off to appear on stage at Westport, Connecticut, with a summer stock rendition of *Liliom*. Annabella was his co-star.

In his first of three films of 1942, *Son of Fury* (Twentieth Century-Fox), Tyrone is the Benjamin Blake of Edison Marshall's novel of eighteenth-century England. Born a bastard (resulting from his wealthy father's indiscretion with a maid), his rightful legacies are taken over by his cruel Uncle Arthur (George Sanders), who reminds him periodically of his illegitimacy. After one beating too many, Benjamin runs away to a South Pacific island where he meets Eve (Gene Tierney). He also finds a goodly number of pearls which he brings back to England as payment to a London lawyer (Dudley Digges), who clears his name and helps him remove Uncle Arthur from the family estates. Benjamin then returns to the island paradise for Eve.

There was very little with which to carp in *Son of Fury*,[19] since the escapist entertainment drew upon all the standard ploys to insure audience approval. Tyrone appeared as the idealistic, robust, adventurous hero; Miss Tierney, in her tropical garden, was exotically alluring;

---

[19]Fox would remake the film, almost scene for scene as *Treasure of the Golden Condor* (1953) with Cornel Wilde in the lead role.

With Gene Tierney in *Son of Fury* (1942)

213

Frances Farmer as Sanders' consort was icily beautiful; and Sanders, who had excelled as Power's mighty opponent in *Lloyds of London* (and in a more conventional sense in *Love Is News*), was resolutely dastardly as the conniving villain. Under director John Cromwell's astute guidance, the final product was 102 minutes of smooth-flowing filmfare, with each scene full of engaging, supporting players, plush scenery, and Alfred Newman's fitting music score.

In *This Above All* (Twentieth Century-Fox, 1942), written for the screen by R. C. Sherriff from Eric Knight's novel of England at war and that country's resultant social problems, Tyrone is seen as Clive Briggs, a lower middle-class Englishman. He deserts from the British army because he feels that he should not risk his life for the upper classes unless he can be certain of social equality after the war is won. During a London blackout he just happens to encounter Prudence Cathaway (Joan Fontaine), a WAAF of gentle breeding, and through his growing love for her he begins to understand the meaning of God and country. *Time* Magazine recorded, "Although Tyrone Power gives the performance of his cinematic career . . . it is not good enough. His handsome, unlined face contradicts the profound words he is asked to utter. He does not for a moment look as if he had either thought or lived them." The film, which had its world premiere at New York's Astor Theatre on May 12, 1942, was directed by Anatole Litvak and hit a popular note with the public.

With Joan Fontaine and Nigel Bruce in *This Above All* (1942)

Publicity pose in 1946

In *The Black Swan* (Twentieth Century-Fox, 1942), the studio played it safe with their high-priced commodity: Tyrone was put into a costume adventure picture directed by Henry King. The Technicolor feature was further bolstered by the appearances of red-headed Maureen O'Hara, red-bearded George Sanders, and such solid types as Laird Cregar, George Zucco, as well as Thomas Mitchell's telling performance (his presence had added to the credibility of *This Above All*). Tyrone is Jamie Waring, an adventurer of the seventeenth century and a swashbuckler of great style. The multi-hued product, due to the set decoration of Richard Day and and James Basevi, and Leon Shamroy's photography, was as the *New York Times* pointed out, one of the "season's prettiest adventures." Pirates, gold, brocades, swords, Miss O'Hara, and the Spanish Main are all colorfully depicted.

On August 24, 1942, twenty-eight-year-old Tyrone enlisted in the U.S. Marine Corps as a private. Zanuck enthusiastically offered to get him into an officer's uniform, but Tyrone stuck to his belief that his status as a screen star should in no way entitle him to special military treatment. Zanuck did arrange with the Marines to place Tyrone on the inactive rolls until he was able to finish a war film about the U.S. Navy. (Contrary to popular thought, Tyrone, who was then earning about $5,000 weekly, was not leaving Hollywood a wealthy man. Despite his new contract, which provided for even "bigger" money, he had had the misfortune of allying with a business manager who grossly mismanaged his assets, and it was predicted that it would take several seasons of picture making to take Tyrone out of the financial red.)

Crash Dive (Twentieth Century-Fox, 1943) was the film, competently directed by Archie Mayo. But Jo Swerling's screenplay devoted too much time to a love triangle involving a submarine lieutenant (Tyrone), his commanding officer (Dana Andrews) and the latter's girl (Anne Baxter). The momentum picks up greatly when the boys go to their North Atlantic battlefield to raid a secret Nazi base. Otis L. Guernsey, Jr., in the *New York Herald-Tribune*, found that Tyrone's "latest vehicle is . . . generally effective, and it is hoped, in passing, that Mr. Power's career as an officer in the Marine Corps will be as brilliant as that portrayed in his new screen offering."[20] (Ty sang "Don't Sit Under the Apple Tree" within the film.)

Tyrone was sent to Camp Elliot at San Diego, California, where he received his basic training as a Marine. At the end of the rugged eight-week course, and, prior to going on to officer's candidate school, he appeared in a ten-minute short entitled *Hollywood in Uniform* (1943). This joint studio product, released through Columbia, showed several of the industry's uniformed male stars who had answered their nation's

---

[20]Obviously, no one alerted Mr. Guernsey, Jr. to the fact that Tyrone's rank was to be that of a private, initially.

call. While Tyrone was at flight training school at Corpus Christi, Texas, as a second lieutenant in mid-1944, wife Annabella took to the Broadway stage in *Jacobowsky and the Colonel,* a comedy with Louis Calhern, Oscar Karlweis, and J. Edward Bromberg.

Jacobowsky had a long run at the Martin Beck Theatre. It produced a telling incident, which Annabella chose to share with the press. "After our play opened, he [Tyrone] came to New York on a few days' leave, and you should have seen how happy he was to be in a theatre again. The first evening he saw the play from the front, and the next he was backstage with us. The whole company told him if he stayed longer he would walk right out on the stage and start acting.

"He looked around my dressing room and said he remembered coming into it to talk with Katharine Cornell when he was in her company. He came to tell her he had a chance to go into pictures. He did not know if it would be a good thing for him, but he would like to try."

In February, 1945, Tyrone was sent to the Pacific as a pilot. He was based at Kwajalein, Saipan, Okinawa, and Guam, and was among the first airmen to fly supplies into Iwo Jima during the battle there. In November, 1945, he returned to the States and was discharged as a first lieutenant on January 14, 1946. At Twentieth Century-Fox, he signed a new contract calling for him to star in two films a year.

Tyrone and Annabella had been famous in Hollywood for their house parties at which they delighted in making up games for their celebrated guests to play. On May 20, 1946, they hosted a party in honor of David Niven's wife, Primula, who had arrived in America only five weeks before. During a game called "Sardines"—a hide-and-seek in the dark—Primula opened a door thinking it led to a closet where she might hide. Instead, she tumbled down a flight of steps to the cement basement floor. She died on May twenty-first without ever having regained consciousness.

Adding to the stress of the traumatic event was Annabella's decision to portray the lesbian onstage in Sartre's *No Exit.* But she insisted, and departed for New York to assume the Broadway role. It was from Manhattan on October 24, 1946, that she announced her separation from Tyrone because of their "incompatibility of careers."

Meanwhile, Zanuck had engineered a spectacular return vehicle to reintroduce Tyrone to moviegoing audiences. Taking a lesson from MGM's misdeed in starring returning serviceman Clark Gable in a dull, conventional love story, *Adventure* (1945), the Fox executive decided to spare no company expense to showcase Power. As a basis for this blockbuster, Zanuck acquired the screen rights to Somerset Maugham's powerful novel, *The Razor's Edge* (1944), hired a battery of screen writers (including Maugham) to transform the romantic but highly philosophical novel to the screen, and maneuvered with gentlemanly director George Cukor to supervise the production. Eventually, it was Lamar Trotti's rather pedestrian scenario that was used for the 146-minute feature, and it was Edmund Goulding who stepped in to fill the breach when Cukor decided he could not come to terms with Zanuck.

Having approved a whopping expenditure for the elaborate and varied settings for *The Razor's Edge* (Twentieth Century-Fox, 1946), which transports the viewer from 1919 Chicago, to the smart and Bohemian sections of Paris, to a coal mine in Germany, then on to India and, finally, back to the French Riviera, Zanuck craftily stocked the feature with a sure-fire cast. The film featured two veterans from the celebrated *Laura* (Twentieth Century-Fox, 1944), Gene Tierney and Clifton Webb, and each—she as the domineering, selfish Isabel, he as the waspish, witty, social-climbing Elliott Templeton—laced the movie with fascinating portrayals. There was also John Payne (in a thankless straight man's part as Tierney's beau and later husband), Anne Baxter (as Sophie, the childhood friend of Larry Darrell/Power, who meets a tragic end), Lucile Watson (Tierney's stately, wise, and witty mother), Elsa Lanchester (in a marvelous cameo as the romantic Scottish spinster social secretary), and, recapping his appearance from *The Moon and Sixpence* (United Artists, 1942), debonair, subtle Herbert Marshall as Mr. Somerset Maugham, the narrator of this gargantuan photoplay.

With Herbert Marshall, Gene Tierney, and John Payne in *The Razor's Edge* **(1946)**

Just as many literary critics have passed off Maugham as merely a competent storyteller (can there be any finer compliment for a novelist?), so most film reviewers, past and present, have only grudgingly acknowledged the depth of focus that lies behind the filmed odyssey of one Larry Darrell (Tyrone), a Chicago-bred youth who loses his innocence on the battlefields of France when a compatriot deliberately sacrifices his life to save Larry's. If *The Razor's Edge* seems to some viewers to lack persuasiveness, it is most likely because the film glides so smoothly along its chronicle path (like the original book), that one mistrusts the very ease of the storytelling; many of the sequences contain an anticlimactic quality, rising to crescendos and then tumbling the onlooker into the next scene, creating a continuity at the expense of the reader's feelings.

Just as Biblical films portraying Christ have always had great problems in showing the godliness of the Jesus characterization on film, so in *The Razor's Edge* there is an inherent problem in establishing the sincerity of Larry Darrell's motives behind his attempt to find out the real meaning of life. Power's credibility level is not aided by Trotti's screenplay, which continually emphasizes the ambiguity of the hero's quest. At one point Larry tells an amazed Isabel, "I don't think I'll ever find peace until I make up my mind about things . . . you keep asking yourself what life is all about—is there any meaning or is it a stupid blunder." Later in the story, Isabel again begs Larry to explain what he is really doing with his life, and for once to be concrete and precise with her. He mumbles rather apologetically, "It's rather difficult to explain—if I try you'll only be angry with me." Further on in the film, he makes another major effort to convey his soul-searching dream to Isabel. "I want to learn as, for example, Gray wants to earn money . . . I know it sounds vague and trivial . . . I know I'm being difficult." And finally, well into the picture, Larry does blurt out his big ambition, which, if taken on a mercenary value, hardly makes him more than a dimestore visionary, "It may be when I am through I will have found something to give people."

It is not until near the very end of this lengthy two-hour feature, with all its diverting subplots and intricate changes of locales, costumes, and times, that Larry—thankfully, for the viewer's sake—believes he has made some headway in life's mission. "The wonderful thing about life is to get a second chance. I got a second chance." With his soul recharged and his mind clear, he plans to return to New York (working his way across the Atlantic on a freighter). Later, perhaps, he will become a taxi driver so he can always be on the go and meet new people, hopefully sharing his discoveries of life with countless strangers, making an impression on them, as ripples in a stream spread out to greater stretches.

For the above reasons, it is no wonder that Bosley Crowther (*New*

York Times) complained that Power "tries exceeding hard to play a 'good' man on little more than frequent statements that he is. His face glows like Mr. Sunshine's and he affects a sublime serenity. But the quality of 'goodness' that is in him must depend for demonstration on no more."

Another problem which faced Tyrone in portraying Larry Darrell was that, at age thirty-two, he was about ten years too old to play the ethereal do-gooder, and without doubt the war period had matured the actor's face so that he now looked every one of his years.

While Power could never be considered an ensemble player—even with such frequent co-stars as Loretta Young, Linda Darnell, and Gene Tierney (he was always acting to them and not with them)—in *The Razor's Edge* he revealed a maturity of acting style which at least made him seem more cognizant, for a change, of his fellow players. And there are at least two memorable scenes where Power fully captures the elusive qualities of the benign Larry. One occurs on a fling-on-the-town spree with Isabel, who has agreed that Darrell is not the man to marry her. Like the spider she is, however, she decides to weave a "spell" on the naive soul and seduce him, so that, should she still want him after she has returned to Chicago from Paris, she can easily make him feel guilty enough to comply with the code of gentlemanly behavior. They are sitting in a booth at a Parisian nightclub, enjoying a moment's rest from their evening's club-hopping, and as Tyrone leans his head against the padded back of the booth, his spiritual isolation from the very earthly Isabel and their surroundings is dramatically evident. Later, in the India interlude, when the Holy Man (Cecil Humphreys) comes to visit Power on the mountaintop retreat, Power is required to deliver a long monologue explaining how he became one with God. In this simplistic, rather logically suspect speech, he manages to be entirely convincing and to display a sense of inner calm that any level-headed person could only envy.

Despite its faults and, most likely, because of its virtues, *The Razor's Edge* garnered distributors' domestic grosses of five million dollars, a tidy profit on its one-million-dollar-plus production cost. Anne Baxter received an Oscar for Best Supporting Actress and Zanuck earned the *Look* Magazine Achievement Award as Producer of the Year, but Tyrone was not even Oscar-nominated for his performance in the smash hit film.[21]

The great Zanuck and the great David O. Selznick, in 1947, considered it would be a lucrative venture to combine their greatest assets, Tyrone Power and Jennifer Jones, in a film to be directed by Otto Preminger. Tentatively titled *The Dark Wood,* the project never passed

---

[21]*The Razor's Edge* was promoted with the rather misleading campaign slogan: "Theirs was a Hunger No Earthly Love Could Satisfy."

beyond the planning stage, for the producers could not overcome scripting difficulties.

Edmund Goulding also directed Tyrone in his next feature, *Nightmare Alley* (Twentieth Century-Fox, 1947), in a role he had asked to do. Produced by George Jessel (another Zanuck crony) and based on a novel by William Lindsay Gresham, it is a sorid tale of avarice that begins in a lurid second-class carnival. Stanton Carlisle (Tyrone) is a barker who works with "mind-reader" Zeena (Joan Blondell) and her dipsomaniac husband, Pete (Ian Keith). Among the side show attractions is the "Geek," who kills and eats live chickens for a bottle of booze every day and a place where he can sleep off his hangover. Stan's curiosity about the Geek prompts him to observe, "I can't understand how anyone can get so low." Forgetting the Geek, he tells of his love for carnival life: "It gives you a superior feeling as though you were on the inside in the know and they are looking in." He acquires Zeena's blindfold code and with Molly (Coleen Grey), whom he has wed, leaves the carnival to become a successful mind reading act in a high-toned Chicago supper club.

Later in the film, Stan becomes confident that he can fool all the people all the time. He sets himself up as a spiritualist with the help of a cool psychiatrist (Helen Walker), who has a wealthy clientele. They plan to maneuver industrialist Ezra Grindle (Taylor Holmes) into building a temple in Stan's honor and to give them a hefty bonus fee as well. Their scheme includes convincing Grindle that the spirit of his long-dead-mistress has returned to earth. The plan collapses when Molly, impersonating the mistress' spirit, breaks down and cries when she sees the old man on his knees praying to the vision. Stan then puts Molly on a train back to the carnival and visits the psychiatrist to split whatever take they have gotten, but she smartly double-crosses him by playing dumb to the plan and confusing him. His reputation shot, he turns to alcohol for solace and sinks to the depths. At a carnival, he begs for work, any kind, and is given a job as the local Geek. He accepts ruefully, after a couple of drinks, exclaiming, "I was meant for the job."

"Tyrone Power . . . steps into a new class as an actor," reported James Agee (*Time* Magazine) of his *Nightmare Alley* performance. Beyond a doubt, it was Tyrone's best cinema acting job. His scenes with Helen Walker are flawless and his cunning in convincing Grindle of his spiritualistic powers is superior. Ironically, whatever hopes Zanuck and Tyrone might have shared with regards to an acting award were not realized, nor did Tyrone (just as in the case of *The Razor's Edge*) receive so much as a nomination. Moreover, due to its sordid, offbeat theme, the film was not popular with the public.

Unlike such prefabricated 1930s romances as Tyrone and Loretta Young, Tyrone and Sonja Henie, Tyrone and Alice Faye, the much-publicized offscreen romance between Tyrone and Lana Turner was very real in the mid-1940s. However, it ran its course when their unofficially announced engagement (since Power was still technically wed to Annabella) failed to culminate in marriage. "They were such an unbelievably handsome pair," Louella Parsons later wrote, "and they had so much to give each other. Ty, with his gentleness and his well-bred ways. Lana with her verve, her loveliness, her almost childlike sensuality." Earlier, Tyrone and another MGM luminary, Judy Garland had been the principals in a hush-hush affair that ended very abruptly.

While Ty was conducting his active private life, he found occasion to offer a few ideas to his movie-going public. In an interview in 1947 he said, "If the moviegoers like a new type of picture or a new actor, they should say so in a letter. Studios are extremely sensitive to the mail they receive about their films. Most people don't know this and hesitate about writing a constructive letter. The producers and directors are conscious of the fact that they must keep a hand on the pulse of their customers."

Through just such letters and the paltry box-office receipts of the carnival film Darryl F. Zanuck fully appreciated that the public did not care to see Tyrone Power in strong dramatic fare such as *Nightmare Alley*. Thus he returned the star to a metier in which he always excelled: the swashbuckling adventure tale. The vehicle in question was a gloriously Technicolored version of Samuel Shellabarger's sweeping novel, *Captain from Castile* (Twentieth Century-Fox, 1947), directed by Henry King. Pedro De Vargas (Tyrone) is a dashing young Spaniard from sixteenth-century Castile who joins Cortez (Cesar Romero) in his amazing conquest of Mexico. For the most part, the 140-minute feature lacked the bloody action of the novel, but it proved to be exceedingly commercial at the boxoffice.

In Hollywood, and later in Rome, Tyrone became acquainted with Linda Christian,[22] the daughter of a Dutch petroleum engineer. Born in Mexico, Linda, described as "a league-of-nations beauty," (she was of Dutch, German, French, and Spanish descent) was christened Blanca Rosa Welter. Along with extensive world-wide travel, her professional sights were focused on screen acting; she had appeared in *Holiday in Mexico* (MGM, 1946) and in *Green Dolphin Street* (MGM, 1947). Publicists, with a strong nudge from her agent, had dubbed her the "Anatomic Bomb."

During Tyrone's latest headline-creating period, Annabella, who had appeared in *13 Rue Madeleine* (Twentieth Century-Fox, 1946), went to Europe to star in *The Eternal Conflict* (1947). Regarding her pending divorce from Tyrone, the usually laconic Annabella announced in terms that would do justice to any press conference, "Ty-

[22]Born in Tampico, Mexico, on November 13, 1923.

rone is a closed chapter. Although we were married seven years, Tyrone was away for four of those years in the Marine Corps and it is inevitable that the attitudes of people, who are separated for long periods of time, change. Tyrone changed considerably, and I did, too, I suppose. We decided that we had come to the parting of the ways and the separation, by mutual agreement, was a very amicable one. We are still very good friends and I am happy that it is this way."

On January 18, 1948, Annabella sued for divorce[23] from Tyrone, an action granted on January 26. Under the divorce settlement, she was to receive $85,000 a year from the actor. (Tyrone's earnings for 1947, as disclosed by the U.S. Treasury Department, were $231,027.)

Power's next two films were comedies, neither of which did a thing for his declining star status. In *The Luck of the Irish* (Twentieth Century-Fox, 1948), he is a New York executive who gives up marriage to the boss' daughter (Jayne Meadows) in order to court and wed a rather plain but beguiling Irish lass (Anne Baxter). It was a pretty sad state of affairs when the creative geniuses at Fox could think of nothing better for Tyrone to do than to star in a remake of *Love Is News*. In *That Wonderful Urge* (Twentieth Century-Fox, 1948), Gene Tierney inherited the Loretta Young role, even though Power's preference for the part was Paramount's Wanda Hendrix. (Zanuck thought her lacking in box-office drawing power. He was right.)

In June, 1948, Ty was pictured in the *Lakeland* (Fla.) *Tribune*, being on his way to receive an honorary degree of doctor of humanities from Tampa University. A local reporter asked him the question of the day: "What Is the Greatest Fault of the American Woman Today?" The star's replay was, "Do they have any faults? I have always tried to look for the good features in women and disregard their faults if possible. I don't deny that women do have some faults, but they are not so great they cannot be overlooked. I would rather look for the good side of a woman rather than look for her faults." It would seem that Power missed his calling—he should have been a diplomat instead.

Meanwhile, Tyrone's relationship with Linda Christian extended to a three-continent[24] love affair when she accompanied him to Rome, where he went into the production of *Prince of Foxes* (Twentieth Century-Fox, 1949). A spokesman for the couple announced the postponement of their planned August, 1948, wedding because, "They will have

---

[23]As Annabella filed for divorce in Los Angeles, Tyrone met Linda Christian at the local airport. When photographers tried to take their picture together he said, "It would not be in good taste at this time."

[24]In 1947, Ty, Cesar Romero, and four others had embarked on an 18-country, 32,-000-mile trip. During the five week trek, which began on September 1, they flew from Los Angeles to Miami, to Natal, Brazil, then to Leopoldville in the Belgian Congo. They circled Africa, stopped in Athens and Rome, and, from Italy, flew to London and Dublin. Back in the U.S., Ty told the press, "Anybody who isn't happy in America wouldn't be happy in heaven."

With Anne Baxter in *The Luck of the Irish* (1948)

With Gene Tierney in *That Wonderful Urge* (1948)

more time for their honeymoon when the studio work is over." The spokesman failed to point out that Annabella's divorce would not be recognized as final until the following January.

For *Captain from Castile*, the Fox publicity campaign had boasted, "A whole new world of adventure and romance lay before their swords." This new film venture, also based on a Samuel Shellabarger novel, was conceived on a far smaller scale, with house director Henry King assigned to supervise the black-and-white feature. At this juncture even Zanuck had to admit that fair-haired boy Tyrone, at age thirty-four, was in a delicate career position. With the exceptions of *The Razor's Edge* and *Captain from Castile*, his post-war features had failed to regenerate the star's once great audience interest. Even in the field of swashbucklers, Power, like Warners' Errol Flynn, was facing two problems: each was growing a bit too mature to handle such youthful capering, and, secondly, there was now serious competition from other marquee favorites in the adventure genre. Although none of these rivals would ever gain the followings that both Tyrone and Flynn once enjoyed, they did cut into the established stars' domain. There were Douglas Fairbanks, Jr., ex-Fox player Cornel Wilde (now at Columbia), Paul Henreid, Larry Parks, and Universal's once hot star, Jon Hall.

Milton Krim's screenplay for *The Prince of Foxes* was an overly

With John Sutton in *Captain from Castile* (1947)

With Wanda Hendrix in *Prince of Foxes* (1949)

wordy one. Although it sported some of filmdom's and radio's more famous voices (Orson Welles, Everett Sloane) it provided little space for action. As Bosley Crowther observed in the *New York Times,* "Tyrone Power as the bold adventurer swashes as much as he can, but the tempo and mood of the picture perceptibly hold him down." Loaded with palaces and with scenery of Florence, Rome, and San Marino, Italy, the film is a monochromatic picture postcard. This time Tyrone did have Wanda Hendrix for his co-star, but she was clearly out of her depth as the young spouse of the old duke (Aylmer) whom the Prince of Foxes is ordered by Cesare Borgia (Welles) to conquer. Instead, the adventurer allies himself with the duke against the scheming Borgia. Tyrone arranged for Linda Christian's sister, Ariadne, to play a bit part in the feature, but it failed to generate an acting career for the young lady.

Twentieth Century-Fox publicists called the Power-Christian nuptials, "The Wedding of the Century." It took place at the medieval church of Santa Francesca Romana in Rome on January 27, 1949. While Monsignor William Hemmick of Washington, the U.S. representative at St. Peter's, pronounced Tyrone and Linda man and wife, the crowds outside screamed "Ty il magnifico" and "Viva Linda." Never had Rome seen such a wedding, whose opulence surpassed even that of Rita Hayworth and Aly Kahn. The couple knelt on a carpet of

With Linda Christian in 1949

With Jack Hawkins in ***The Black Rose*** **(1950)**

white lilacs as they exchanged vows before an altar built especially for them and used to better accommodate the flood of photographers. One invited guest suffered a broken finger and another lost his suit coat to the one, or perhaps more, of the ten thousand grasping Italian bobby-soxers (known as "tifosi") lined up at the church entrance. Policemen on white horses guarded the couple's exit from the church and their subsequent drive to the Vatican for a closed session with Pope Pius. It was explained by a Catholic spokesman that Tyrone's civil marriage to Annabella was not recognized by the church. (At the hour Tyrone was being married to Linda, he was still legally married to Annabella, since the termination of their marriage was fifty minutes away.)

Tyrone and Linda (he was thirty-five and she, twenty-five) honeymooned in the snows of the Italian Dolomites, from which they traveled through Italy, Austria, and Switzerland. They then went to North Africa, where Tyrone resumed his cinema career with *The Black Rose* (Twentieth Century-Fox, 1950).

Shot in Morocco and England and based on Thomas B. Costain's action-packed novel of the same title, the picture is burdened with far too much dialog, except for one rambunctious scene of swordplay near the film's beginning. Filmed in a high level quality of Technicolor, it relates the tale of the Saxon, Walter of Gurnie (Tyrone), who runs away from Oxford University ("How can you fight the Normans with books?").[25] Unwilling to accept the authority of the Normans, who have ruled England for two hundred years, he and Tristram (Jack Hawkins) exile themselves to Cathay. Enroute, they encounter a brutal, foreboding Tartar general (Orson Welles), who takes them into his caravan after Hawkins displays his mastery of archery. One disgruntled reviewer suggested that the adventure film should have been titled "The Rover Boys in Far Cathay." The usually generous *Variety* complained, "It is awe-inspiring in much of its physical beauty. Frequently that beauty eclipses the narrative value."

After so many years of filmmaking, many fans were surprised when on July 19, 1950, Tyrone was to be found starring at the Coliseum Theatre in London as *Mister Roberts,* with Jackie Cooper playing the role of Ensign Pulver. As the star explained the circumstance, "I was at a party . . . in New York and Nedda Harrigan, Josh[ua] Logan's wife, walked up to me and said, 'Why don't you take six months off and play *Mister Roberts* in London?' Well, I had six months at the time and I said, yes. It was as simple as that."

Before the play's West End opening, Tyrone stated, "The play—my first for nine years—is now in its third year on Broadway. I have a six-month contract and a three-month labor permit. I hope to get an extension if the play succeeds here."[26] The opening-night audience of two

---

[25]The film was narrated by Michael Rennie who also appears in the film as King Edward I.

[26]*Mister Roberts* had originally opened on Broadway on February 19, 1948.

With Russell Collins, Hildy Parks, Jackie Cooper, and George Mathews of the London cast of *Mister Roberts* (July 1950)

thousand gave the cast a standing ovation. Beaming, Tyrone comment-ed, "There's nothing in films to match those two minutes before the last line and the start of that reception. I've never heard anything like it." Patia Power, on her first trip to Europe, sat beside Linda during the London debut and said later, "This is the first time I've seen my son's name on a theatre. It looks good." John Barber wrote from London for the *New York Herald-Tribune,* "He gives the performance of his life as Mister Roberts, his quietness redeeming the character from goody-goodiness." The British, however, were only moderately impressed with the comedy that had kept New Yorkers laughing for more than two years. The show, playing a 2,200-seat theatre, lasted for six months.

Nineteen hundred fifty could be considered a demarcation point in Tyrone's film career. Not only was he *not* among the top ten boxoffice attractions in the U.S. (only Betty Grable and Clifton Webb from Fox were in that heady group in 1950), but for the first time since Tyrone rose to prominence in the late 1930s, his home studio had a new male lead who was getting the prime vehicles. That lucky guy was another ex-McClintic-Cornell veteran, Gregory Peck, the former David O. Selz-nick player who, in 1950, would appear at Fox in two sterling features, *Twelve O'Clock High* and *The Gunfighter.* Other Twentieth male leads besides Peck and Webb included Victor Mature, Paul Douglas, Rich-ard Widmark, Dan Dailey, Dana Andrews, James Stewart, Hugh Mar-lowe, Gary Merrill, and William Lundigan.

Tyrone's only 1950 release proved to be *American Guerrilla in the Philippines* (Twentieth Century-Fox), which even its director, Fritz Lang, passed off as hack work. It was done because, as he later bluntly said, "Even a director has to eat." Location work was done in the Pacific on some actual sites, and France's Micheline Presle played a rather bland heroine in the feckless production. As the U.S. soldier stranded on that World War II warfront, Tyrone did his best in a disjointed film, but the results were negligible. In *Rawhide* (Twentieth Century-Fox, 1951), directed by Henry Hathaway, he and Susan Hay-ward are held captive at a stage coach relay station in Arizona by a gang led by Hugh Marlowe. The outlaws, after gold, mistake their hostages to be married to each other, although they are strangers. The feisty Miss Hayward gave the eighty-six minute feature its only redeeming drive.

While his movie career was sagging, Tyrone did receive an uplift from the domestic side of his life. On October 2, 1951, a six-pound, eleven-ounce daughter was born to Linda Christian Power in Holly-wood. The child was named Romina Francesca, in honor of the city and the church where her parents had been married.

Tyrone's second contract obligation of 1951 was *I'll Never Forget You,* filmed by Twentieth Century-Fox in Denham, England. Based on the play and the 1933 Fox film, *Berkeley Square,* both of which had

With Micheline Presle (left) in *American Guerrilla in the Philippines* (1950)

With Susan Hayward in a publicity shot for *Rawhide* (1951)

229

starred Leslie Howard, it partakes of a time-travel theme. A modern-day nuclear physicist, Peter Standish (Tyrone), becomes so curious about an old house he has inherited that he suddenly finds himself transported to the London of 1784 where he is sickened by the existing social conditions. He has his portrait painted by Sir Joshua Reynolds (Ronald Simpson) and falls in love with his comely cousin, Helen (Ann Blyth). In his efforts to aid the plight of the ignorant eighteenth-century inhabitants in London, he established a laboratory where he creates a camera, a steamboat, storage batteries, and a light bulb. He is considered mad in that century, and returns to the present day, where he meets Martha (Blyth), an exact double of the girl from the past. Unfortunately, *I'll Never Forget You* was not of the same calibre of *Berkeley Square* (nor of Tyrone's own rousing costumer, *Lloyds of London*), and 1951 filmgoers, who had the alternatives of free television to entertain them, wanted something more contemporary from their outings to the movies.

Lydia Bailey (1952) was next on his Fox agenda, but Tyrone balked at doing yet another costume film. Suspensions from salary were customarily associated with a studio's errant stars, and Tyrone, once the light of Zanuck's eyes, chose that way out of the immediate situation. He was replaced in the period· adventure tale, based on the novel by Kenneth Roberts, by Dale Robertson.

While Linda was voted the "Hollywood Sweater Queen of 1952," Tyrone emoted in *Diplomatic Courier* (Twentieth Century-Fox, 1952), a spy story hampered by an uneven script (written by Casey Robinson and Liam O'Brien). Narrated in part by Hugh Marlowe, the complex film tells of a U.S. State Department messenger (Tyrone) who scampers all over Trieste in his desperate attempts to retrieve the secret time table of the Russian invasion of Yugoslavia. And in what better place to hide such a master plan than in a watch? In his plight, he crosses paths with an American tourist (blonde Patricia Neal), whom he thinks is on his team, but who turns out to be a member of the other side. Then he meets a mysterious girl (Hildegarde Neff), whom he believes is a Soviet spy, but who, the script would have it, is as good as gold. In the annals of espionage films, *Diplomatic Courier* does not have a very high ranking.

In the early 1950s, Tyrone seemed to pass from one undistinguished film to another. Joseph M. Newman, who would usually be associated with the lesser celluloid product at Fox, was the director of *Pony Soldier* (1952), a glorified Western with little historical flavor. At least in *Diplomatic Courier,* Tyrone had an attractive adversary (Neal), while in this Saskatchewan-set yarn, it is Cameron Mitchell who proves to be Power's most deadly opponent. All of which makes it difficult for Canadian Northwest Mountie Tyrone to return migrating Cree Indians to

With Patricia Neal in *Diplomatic Courier* (1952)

their reservation. Tyrone seemed to be ill at ease even in his colorful costume.

Long gone were Tyrone's days as Fox's fair-haired boy, and with his current crop of pictures being so indifferently received by the public, he deemed it wise to try a change. At Universal, for a producer friend, Ted Richmond, he traded in his swords for dueling pistols as Mark Fallon, surrounded by lovely ladies—one willing (Julia Adams), the other not so pliable (Piper Laurie)—in *The Mississippi Gambler* (1953). If anything, this conventional action tale revealed that Tyrone was indeed losing his looks.

Unwilling to try his luck in the television medium, Tyrone then returned to his original love, the theatre. After a successful cross-country tour of *Don Juan in Hell*,[27] Charles Laughton teamed up with producer Paul Gregory as director of a sixty-city, twenty-eight-state tour of the dramatic reading of Stephen Vincent Benet's epic Civil War poem, *John Brown's Body*. Like *Don Juan in Hell* it was played on a barren stage, but with the innovation of a choral group of five women and fifteen men. Said producer Gregory of the vehicle, "It takes you places—into Lee's tent and Lincoln's room, to Bull Run, Gettysburg and Harpers Ferry. Not having any physical scenery to compete with, the audience paints its own, building far better sets in the mind."

---

[27]The show's complement included Charles Laughton, Charles Boyer, Agnes Moorehead, and Sir Cedric Hardwicke.

231

With Andre Charlot, Dayton Lummis, and George Eldredge in *Mississippi Gambler* (1953)

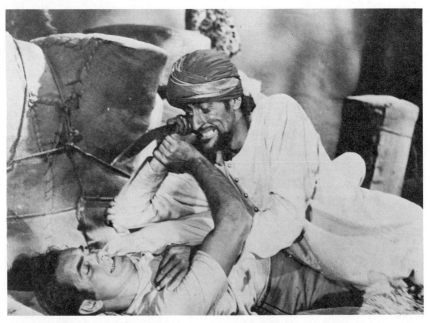

With Guy Rolfe in *King of the Khyber Rifles* (1954)

After Gregory had signed Tyrone to speak the lines of Jack Ellyat, the symbolic Northern soldier, and Clay Wingate, the "typical" Southern soldier, Tyrone said, "The moment he suggested that I participate in *John Brown's Body*, there was nothing further to discuss. I was eager to get back on the stage, and, having seen *Don Juan*, I knew it would be a great opportunity."

During the two-hour poetry recitation, only one prop was used by the cast, an "acting bar," a three-foot-high rail against which the actors (Tyrone, Judith Anderson, Raymond Massey) in formal dress, sat or leaned. In its tour, the show opened for a limited engagement at the Century Theatre in New York on February 14, 1953 (and was recorded by Columbia Records).

Tyrone returned to his old stamping grounds, Twentieth Century-Fox, for *King of the Khyber Rifles*, a remake of John Ford's *The Black Watch* (Fox, 1929), which had starred Victor McLaglen. In the new edition, directed by Henry King and lensed in grand CinemaScope on location in India, Tyrone played Captain King, the half-caste son of a British officer and a Moslem girl. He is sent to the northwest frontier to quell a native uprising led by a childhood friend, Guy Rolfe. Bosley Crowther of the *New York Times* called the film "the best in Cinemascope we've seen." Tyrone's co-star in this adventure fluff was Terry Moore, whose popularity at Fox, some said, lay more in her friendship with Darryl F. Zanuck's daughter Virginia, than in her display of acting talent.

A second daughter, Taryn, was born to the Powers on September 13, 1953, at Los Angeles' Cedars of Lebanon Hospital. In January, 1954, it was revealed that Tyrone's investment in personal automobiles amounted to more than $30,000. While in Hollywood he had his choice of either a Mark Seven Jaguar or a Deusenberg or a 1900 c.c. Alpha Romeo, depending on his mood of the day. On his visits in Rome he traveled in his sleek 2500 c.c. Alpha Romeo. None of this expensive mode of motor transportation, however, was enough to keep worldly Linda Christian content. On October 18, 1954, Tyrone announced their marital separation, alleging "career incompatibility" as the cause of the domestic dissention. Miss Christian, on the other hand, asserted that he was perpetually "cool and distant." When she received her legal divorce from him in 1955, she collected a reputed million-dollar settlement from the one-time Twentieth Century-Fox star.

After a year's absence from the screen, Tyrone returned in Columbia's *The Long Gray Line* (1955) as Marty Maher, an old-time West Point athletic instructor. A true story, based on Nardi R. Campion's biography of Maher, (*Bringing up the Brass*), the film encompasses the man's life from the time of his arrival in the United States from Ireland, when he takes a job as a waiter at the military academy, through

233

With Maureen O'Hara in *The Long Gray Line* (1955)

his marriage (to spunky Maureen O'Hara), and on into his autumn years of white hair and matching mustache.

"Duty, pride and honor are the virtues that glow warmly in this film, which might better be titled 'The Long Green Line'—especially when the customers start flocking in." (*New York Times*) Against a cost of $1,748,000, *The Long Gray Line* grossed $5,635,000 in distributors' domestic rentals, giving Tyrone his first boxoffice hit in some time. Directed by John Ford (who abhored being forced to use the Cinema-Scope process), the 138-minute film is at times mawkish and full of blarney (how could one avoid this with such shamrock-festooned performers as Donald Crisp and Ward Bond on hand?). Thanks to Power's thoughtful interpretation, however, the movie emerged as a humane study. Both he and Miss O'Hara had developed far richer screen personalities since their last joint film work (*The Black Swan*), and the filmgoer could find believable moments throughout their ensemble scenes. Tyrone had nearly come of age as a mature cinema actor.

Henry King again directed Tyrone in South Africa for *Untamed* (Twentieth Century-Fox, 1955), a woman's picture containing man-sized scenery. Power is Paul Van Riebeck, a Dutchman who saves a wagon train of settlers from a Zulu attack. Among the passengers is Katie O'Neill (Susan Hayward), whose husband (John Justin) has been killed. Paul and Katie fall in love, but he has no time to settle down since he is more intent on establishing a Dutch free state. He leaves her with a farm which is manned by Kurt (Richard Egan), who is wildly in love with her. She has Paul's baby and waits for his return. Miss Hayward, then very much in her acting prime, riveted audience attention to her performance and there was little room for moviegoer interest in the other players.

Tyrone found consolation for his middle-aged blues by again going onstage. In the theatre he had found respect and inspiration. On February 9, 1955, he was reunited, after eighteen years, with Katharine Cornell at the ANTA Theatre in Manhattan in Christopher Fry's play, *The Dark Is Light Enough*.[28] Although modestly successful in its pre-Broadway showings in Buffalo, Toronto, and Cleveland, it failed to generate public or critical interest. "Like the great nineteenth-century country house in which it takes place, the play has obscure corners and half-lit passages," said John Beaufort (*Christian Science Monitor*) In a cast that included such solid stage performers as Miss Cornell, Christopher Plummer, and John Williams, the movie star found the going tough. As *Variety* explained: "Tyrone Power, wearing chin whiskers, has perhaps the most thankless co-starring role of recent seasons. . . . Try to act that hodgepodge of a role with conviction—yet Ty Power does just that. It's uphill all the way, with practically no help from the script, but he gets there—the dark is light enough." Other critics such as Rowland Field (*Newark Evening News*) were less generous. "[He] seems quite stilted and ineffectual at times in the brash, semi-swashbuckling portrayal of the rather disagreeable Gettner. It is a hurried and generally disappointing version of the rakish renegade that this popular film actor presents." The costume drama closed on April 23, 1955, after only sixty-nine performances. Obviously, neither star's remaining boxoffice draw was powerful enough to keep the show on a profit margin.

Not yet willing to abandon the theatre after this unsuccessful venture, Tyrone agreed to star for the Playwrights' Company in Julian Colman's new play, *A Quiet Place*, staged by Delbert Mann. In this romantic drama of a "modern" marriage, Tyrone was cast as young American musician Oliver Lucas. The setting was the Amalfi coast of Italy in a villa high above the Mediterranean. Leora Dana was cast as his wife, with Frederick Worlock and Susan Kohner in supporting roles. The production opened at the Shubert Theatre in New Haven on November 23, 1955. The pre-Broadway fiasco closed at the National Theatre in Washington, D.C., on December 31, 1955.

At this unsatisfactory juncture, Tyrone's wobbling acting career received rejuvenation with his performance as pianist Eddy Duchin in *The Eddy Duchin Story* (Columbia, 1956). In Technicolor, the film is a

---

[28]The play had first been presented at the Aldwych Theatre, London on April 30, 1954, with Edith Evans and James Donald in the leads.

In *The Eddy Duchin Story* (1956)

With Mai Zetterling and Moira Lister in *Abandon Ship!* (1957)

236

glossy accounting of Duchin's life in the 1930s and 1940s. With Carmen Cavallero substituting on the actual keyboard, Power reenacts the highlights of the musician's life as he reaches success as a bandleader-pianist of popular ballads. He marries the girl of his dreams, beautiful Kim Novak, only to lose her when she dies giving birth on Christmas Eve. He refuses to have anything to do with the son (Rex Thompson) who innocently caused the wife's death until he remarries (Victoria Shaw) and learns to forgive. A short time later, Duchin learns that his end is near.

Tyrone's glamorous love scenes with the very boxoffice-worthy Miss Novak did not reflect his offcamera distaste for her unprofessional manner on the set. Her persistent tardiness and delays caused the usually taciturn star to comment, "Confusion between temperament and bad manners is unfortunate."

Variety named *The Eddy Duchin Story* as the third most popular film in the U.S. during the month of August, 1956 (three months after its official release). The picture went on to gross $5,300,000 in distributors' domestic rentals, proving once again that audiences enjoy shedding tears. Filmgoers with long memories (or addicted to late, late TV shows) found it interesting to compare Tyrone's performance in this slick, surface-deep feature with his earlier bandleader characterization in *Alexander's Ragtime Band.* If his youth had been sacrificed over the years, the consequent life and acting experience permitted him to play the Eddy Duchin tearjerker lead with a knowing quality that was reassuring.

In 1956, Tyrone attempted yet another stage appearance that proved disastrous. At the Opera House in Manchester, England, he played in George Bernard Shaw's *The Devil's Disciple,* with his vis-á-vis, Dorothy Bromiley, a young English unknown. The show was later moved to the West End's Winter Garden Theatre (November 8, 1956) for a brief run. *Plays and Players'* reviewer was on hand to report, "[Tyrone adopts a slightly Hollywoodish romanticism, coupled with clear delivery and an avoidance of over-flamboyance. He should not have been made a 'star', however, for no Shaw play is a one-man play."

While in England, he formed an independent producing company with Ted Richmond, which they named Copa Productions. Their initial product was *Abandon Ship!* (Columbia, 1957), also known as *Seven Waves Away.* Tyrone starred as the executive officer of a luxury liner on a world cruise. The liner blows up when it hits a derelict mine in the South Atlantic, and the remainder of the story takes place on a lifeboat.

The lifeboat is designed to carry fourteen persons, but it is loaded with seventeen survivors, many of whom are seriously wounded. Eleven additional passengers, in the water wearing life jackets, are tied to the sides of the boat. Before dying, seaman Kelly (Lloyd Nolan) tells

Tyrone that he will have to sacrifice the weak and wounded if any are to survive the ordeal. "You've got to evict some of the tenants," Kelly insists. "Anyone who can't pay the rent." With a storm on the horizon, Tyrone realizes that Kelly was right and at gunpoint he orders twelve of his passengers to drop out of the boat. "I want only the strong," he yells above the wind, "who can row 1,500 miles to Africa and walk ashore alive. I want the strong who won't fall faint when the food gives out and the water runs dry. I want only those who can make it and not those who can't."

When those remaining in the boat make it through the raging storm, he is praised for his decision, but when they are about to be rescued, their tone of commendation changes to castigation. Only Mai Zetterling, as a nurse who loves him and Mora Lister, a married but bored playgirl, who eyes him through the film as though he were a delectable piece of creamy cake, stick by him. A narration at the film's end informs us that what we have seen is based on a true story; that the character portrayed by Tyrone was tried and convicted of murder and had served six months in prison. Copa Productions had put together an absorbing film with clearly defined characterizations, graced by a steely performance from once-glamour-boy Tyrone Power. The realistic little film was a far contrast from such later overblown maritime disaster "epics" as *The Poseidon Adventure* (Twentieth Century-Fox, 1972) or *Juggernaut* (United Artists, 1974).

Offscreen, Tyrone and the Swedish-born Miss Zetterling[29] (bearing a resemblance to Annabella) were fodder for the gossip columns of Europe as they conducted a discreet romance at several resort beach areas of Italy and France. Meanwhile, Linda obtained her final divorce decree in London on August 7, 1956.

In August, 1957, Tyrone narrated the introduction of a film produced in Ireland by the Four Provinces Production Company under the direction of John Ford. With an Irish cast and featuring the Abbey Theatre Players, the film was entitled *The Rising of the Moon* (Warner Bros., 1957), with screenplay by Frank S. Nugent, formerly of the *New York Times,* a journalist who at one time had been one of Tyrone's severest critics.

Zanuck, who had resigned as production head for Twentieth Century-Fox in 1956, formed his own producing company known as DFZ Productions. He requested Tyrone as the star of the second film[30] under his independent banner (released through Twentieth), a Technicolor distortion of Ernest Hemingway's *The Sun Also Rises.* The picture was photographed in Pamplona, Spain, Paris, Biarritz, and Mexico, at a reputed cost of five million dollars. Directed by Henry

[29]She and Tyrone had appeared in 1956 on British TV in a well-regarded adaptation of Strindberg's *Miss Julie.*

[30]The first was *Island in the Sun* (Twentieth Century-Fox, 1957).

With Eddie Albert in *The Sun Also Rises* (1957)

King, the film seeks to capture the feeling of futility carried by the "Lost Generation" principals as they travel to bars, hotels, and bullfights in search of enjoyment. These 1920s expatriates are Jake (Tyrone), who is impotent due to a World War I wound, Brett (Ava Gardner), who loves him, and Robert (Mel Ferrer) who loves her. They are joined by Mike (Errol Flynn in a supporting role), Brett's fiancé, and by Bill (Eddie Albert) who is along for the fun of it.

It is hard to say what aspect of this eleventh and final Henry King-Tyrone Power association is more disappointing: the lacklustre scripting of Peter Viertel, the inability of the very middle-aged cast to cope with their roles of discouraged but youthful souls, or the inability of the production to instill the proceedings with either a glow of nostalgia or of sharply-etched emotions, ambiance, and twenties' lifestyles.

Since bachelor Ty was being seen in public with his ex-wife Annabella, columnist Louella A. Parsons felt obliged to ask the star if he had thoughts of rewedding the actress. "It's funny that you should mention Annabella now, because I just talked with her today and she wants to come and see the children before they return home. But as for marriage, that's not for me. I have had two and that's enough. I see Annabella often and we are good friends but you can take my word for it, I am not marrying anyone." Power would go back on his word a year later.

If a great number of people in Hollywood thought that Tyrone was well on the way toward being washed-up, director Billy Wilder felt otherwise. He agreed to the casting of Tyrone opposite Marlene Dietrich and Charles Laughton in *Witness for the Prosecution* (United

Artists, 1958), shot on the Goldwyn lot (with side excursions to London for location work) between June and August, 1957. Based on Agatha Christie's tingling courtroom drama, which had been a London and Broadway stage hit, producers Edward Small and Arthur Hornblow, Jr. believed the vehicle was just the type of gimmicky suspense yarn that would draw in potential moviegoers. They were correct.

Within the well-mounted production, Leonard Vole (Tyrone) is a handsome, married man who has a decided way with older women, one in particular, a wealthy widow (Norma Varden). When she is found murdered, he is suspected of the deed because she had bequeathed him 80,000 pounds in her will. The only witness who can testify to his innocence is his wife Christine (Dietrich). The famous barrister, Sir Wilfrid Robarts (Laughton), takes the case for the defense, although he is a recent heart attack victim and is followed everywhere by a flibberty nurse (Elsa Lanchester). Through flashbacks, the viewer is shown how Vole and Christine met[31] and were married, which provides relief to what had been on the stage, a continual courtroom trial, albeit fast-moving.

While a good deal of attention in *Witness for the Prosecution* was paid to Laughton's outrageous but effective mugging, Dietrich's surprising in-depth acting, and, of course, to the new twists added to Christie's adroit plot by crafty Wilder, Tyrone as "the smooth rogue" received his fair share of plaudits. Robert Downing (*Films in Review*) applauded his playing "with such skillful ambivalence the audience is never certain of his guilt or innocence." At long last Tyrone had won the battle of separating his gilt-edged screen image with this portrayal. Characterization was the victor. The picture grossed $3.75 million in distributors' domestic rentals.

In the winter of 1957, after appearing on television in October with Kay Thompson and Jimmy Durante on the "NBC Standard Oil Show," Tyrone toured with Faye Emerson in *Back to Methuselah,* a condensation of the George Bernard Shaw work, now reduced to a two-hour outing with one intermission. The show was brought into New York for a limited (twenty-nine performances) run at the Ambassador Theatre on March 26, 1958. Although the revamped drama received only modest accord from the critics, some reviewers had perceptive, kind words to say of Tyrone's chores in the herculean offering. "Mr. Power is exceptionally good whether he be Adam, a toothy rector, an archbishop or a gray ghostly, almost pure spirit dotard from a remote time ahead of us."

Then, on May 7, 1958, Tyrone, who was not often without the company of an attractive woman, wed brunette Mrs. Deborah Montgomery Minardos in the chapel of the Tunica (Mississippi) Presbyterian

---

[31]This Hamburg nightclub sequence was geared to show off Dietrich's still shapely legs and to allow her to sing "I May Never Go Home Anymore!"

Church. Pastor Reverend Dr. T. T. Williams officiated at the ceremonies. Deborah[32] was twenty-six; Tyrone was forty five.

He then went to Madrid to star as King Solomon in an epic directed by King Vidor, *Solomon and Sheba* (United Artists, 1959). Gina Lollobrigida was cast as the captivating Sheba, with Tyrone's old cinematic adversary, George Sanders, as his villainous brother. On November 15, during a difficult dueling scene with Sanders, Tyrone asked for a rest period and retired to his dressing room. There, he mentioned a pain in his arms and chest but said that he had had it before. He insisted that it would pass and referred to it as bursitis. He was rushed to the local hospital at 11:30 A.M., but died there within an hour from the heart attack.[33] Like his father, Tyrone Power was struck down on the set, commited to the work he loved—acting.

The star's body was transferred from the hospital to U.S. Torrejon Air Force Base, and then flown back to California to Hollywood's Chapel of the Psalms for burial at Hollywood Memorial Park Cemetery. The crowd, with box lunches, began to line up at dawn on Friday, November 21, the day of the funeral services. Inside, dressed in black, Deborah sat beside the open casket, holding Tyrone's hand while an organist played "I'll Be Seeing You." Commander Thomas M. Gibson a Navy chaplain, conducted the services for the Marine veteran. Cesar Romero delivered the eulogy. After reading from Thomas Wolfe's "The Promises of America," he spoke the following, "He constantly gave of himself until one day he gave a little too much. He was a beautiful man. He was beautiful outside and he was beautiful inside. Rest well, my friend."

Loretta Young entered the chapel wearing Oriental makeup for a role on her television series, and Yul Brynner, who was signed to replace Tyrone in *Solomon and Sheba,* was cheered loudly by the outside crowd. Linda Christian,[34] who had caused a scene the previous year at the Italian burial of her good friend, auto racer Alfonso de Portago, was discouraged from attending by Deborah, who wired her, saying, "It is my express wish that you do not come to California with the children to attend the funeral." Deborah explained to newsmen that she was afraid Linda's presence "might result in an emotional scene such as had occurred at recent funerals of other prominent persons."

Among other people once close to Tyrone who were also not present

---

[32]The daughter of Mr. and Mrs. Rice Hungerford III of Greenwood, Mississippi, she had attended the University of Mississippi. In 1954 she wed actor Nico Minardos; they were divorced two years later. She had a daughter by this union.

[33]Ironically in the summer of 1958, he had appeared in a short subject film sponsored by the American Heart Association in which he spoke of the necessity of averting overwork because "time is the most precious thing we have."

[34]Miss Christian had earned herself the sobriquet, "Star of stage, screen, and funerals." In 1958 she would be the alleged reason for actor Edmund Purdom's divorce, his then wife claiming that Purdom and Christian had been privately wed and divorced in Mexico in 1956.

The casket of Tyrone Power
(November 21, 1958)

Deborah Minardos Power and Tyrone
William Power (February, 1959)

at the funeral was Power's mother, who had had a stroke several years
before and was not even told of her son's death. (She would die on
October 7, 1959, at the age of seventy-seven at the home of her daughter Anne in Canterbury, New Hampshire.) From Saint-ee-sur-Nivelle,
in the lower Pyrenees, Annabella confided to the press, "I was horribly
sad to learn that he had left us so suddenly. Only last week we were
together in Madrid, where he was shooting. . . . He had invited me. He
absolutely wanted to introduce me to his new little wife, whom he
adored. For me, he is an irreplaceable friend who has disappeared."

When the services[35] were over, an honor guard of six Marine officers
carried the mahogany coffin[36] to its grave site, not too distant from the
resting places of Rudolph Valentino, Douglas Fairbanks, Sr., Marion
Davies, and Norma Talmadge. That evening, Linda and Tyrone's
daughters, who had flown in from Paris, placed a five-foot cross of
white gardenias at the grave site. When Deborah heard of the visit, she
commented, "I feel no anger toward anyone. Ty belongs to me now."
Linda was quoted with saying in rebuttal, "I am happy if she can find
peace in that belief."

On January 22, 1959, at Cedars of Lebanon Hospital in Hollywood,
Deborah Power gave birth to a son. The five-pound, twelve-ounce boy
was named Tyrone William, "after his father and our friend William
Wyler," explained Deborah. Describing her child to the press, she

[35]Deborah had even requested that the funeral services not be carried over the loud-
speakers for the benefit of the mulling crowd outside.
[36]Tyrone had requested that his eyes be left to a medical foundation for the transplanting
of the corneas to the blind.

exclaimed, "He's beautiful. Black hair and he has a dimple in his chin exactly like Tyrone. He looks exactly like his father."

Linda, in February, 1959, sought $200,000 from Tyrone's estate on behalf of their daughters, and in April, a court granted the estate executors' plea to cut allowances to the widow, the ex-wife, and the children because of various claims against the estate. (In November, 1962, at the Plaza Art Gallery on New York's East 79th Street, some of Tyrone's estate (once valued at $800,000) went under the auction gavel.)

On September 30, 1959, Deborah married Arthur Loew, Jr. During the course of their brief union, Arthur Loew, Jr., adopted Deborah's two children. Just before his death, Tyrone had written his daughters, then ages seven and five: "I miss you both and I do so look forward to the time we can be together again. . . . Be good girls and work well in school so that mummy and daddy can be proud of you." Both girls have followed the Power tradition of acting. Romina has appeared in Italian films, but retired for a time during her marriage to singer Al Bano, by whom she had two children. In 1974, during Taryn's stage stint in *The Importance of Being Earnest*, at the Goldini Theatre, Rome, rumor had it that the young woman was engaged to fellow actor Carlo De Majo, the son of Alida Valli. She made her American TV acting debut in the January, 1975 NBC network version of *The Count of Monte Cristo*, starring Richard Chamberlain. (Chamberlain had become her new romantic interest, and because of their "affair" there was renewed interest in her father, Tyrone.) Of her father, Taryn says, "My memories of him are from the screen. I related to him mostly as a young, goodlooking man in films like *Marie Antoinette*. He did set a high standard for the men in my life. They don't have to be fantastic looking, but they have to have something. I'm easily seduced by gentlemanly behavior like sending flowers."

In the summer of 1974 both of Tyrone and Linda's girls came into an inheritance from their father's estate, amounting to a reported two million dollars each.

Although television re-showings and art house revivals of his most famous movies continue to keep the legend of Tyrone Power alive, few visitors[37] make pilgrimages anymore to his grave at Hollywood Memorial Park, where a white marble bench serves as an unobtrusive marker. The bench, which overlooks a shimmering pool nearby, is inscribed[38] with a stanza from Hamlet: "Good night, sweet prince, and flights of angels sing thee to thy rest."

---

[37]On November 15, 1975, a memorial service for Tyrone was held at Hollywood Memorial Park. Francis Lederer was the main speaker while Captain Monty Tennes and a Marine Color Guard presented a tribute from the U.S. Marine Corps. Also participating in the service were Pilton Potter, chaplain of the Trouper's Club, and Ray Sepastion, Power's former makeup man.

[38]The quotation is also to be found on the tomb of Douglas Fairbanks, Sr.

Feature Film Appearances

TOM BROWN OF CULVER (Universal, 1932), 82 min.
Director, William Wyler; story, George Green and Dale Van Every; screenplay, Tom Buckingham; camera, Charles Stumar.

Tom Brown (Tom Brown); H. B. Warner (Dr. Brown); Slim Summerville (Slim); Richard Cromwell (Bob Randolph); Ben Alexander (Ralph); Sidney Toler (Major Wharton); Russell Hopton (Doctor); Andy Devine (Call Boy); Willard Robertson (Captain White); Norman Phillips, Jr. (Carruthers); Tyrone Power, Jr. (John).

FLIRTATION WALK (First National, 1934), 97 min.
Producer, Robert Lord; director, Frank Borzage; screenplay, Delmer Daves, Lou Edelman; art director, Jack Okey; choreography, Bobby Connolly; music director, Leo F. Forbstein; songs, Mort Dixon and Allie Wrubel; costumes, Orry-Kelly; camera, Sol Polito and George Barnes; editor, William Holmes.

Dick Powell (Dick "Canary" Dorcy); Ruby Keeler (Kit Fitts); Pat O'Brien (Sergeant Scrapper Thornhill); Ross Alexander (Oskie); John Arledge (Spike); John Eldredge (Lieutenant Robert Biddle); Henry O'Neill (General Jack Fitts); Guinn "Big Boy" Williams (Sleepy); Frederick Burton (General Paul Landacre); John Darrow (Chase); Glen Boles (Eight Ball); University of Southern California and Army Polo Teams (Polo Players); Lieutenant Joe Cummins (Cadet); Gertrude Keeler (Dancer); Colonel Tim Lonergan (General); Tyrone Power, Jr., Carlyle Blackwell, Jr., and Dick Winslow (Cadets); Maude Turner Gordon (Dowager); Frances Lee (Blonde); Avis Johnson (Redhead); Mary Russell (Girl); William J. Worthington (Civilian); Cliff Saum, Paul Fix (Soldiers); Sol Bright (Native Leader).

GIRLS' DORMITORY (Twentieth Century-Fox, 1936), 66 min.
Producer, Darryl F. Zanuck; associate producer, Raymond Griffith; director, Irving Cummings; based on a play by Ladislaus Fodor; screenplay, Gene Markey; art director, Hans Peters; music director, Arthur Lange; camera, Merritt Gerstad; editor, Jack Murray.

Herbert Marshall (Dr. Stephen Dominki); Ruth Chatterton (Professor Anna Mathe); Simone Simon (Marie Claudel); Constance Collier (Professor Augusta Wimmer); J. Edward Bromberg (Dr. Spindler); Dixie Dunbar (Luisa); John Qualen (Toni); Shirley Deane (Fritzi); Tyrone Power, Jr. (Count Vallais); Frank Reicher (Dr. Hoffenreich); George Hassell (Dr. Wilfinger); Lynne Berkeley (Dora); June Storey (Greta); Christian Rub (Forester); Rita Gould (Emma Kern); Lillian West (Professor Josephine Penz); Symona Boniface (Professor Clotilde Federa); Lynn Bari (Student).

LADIES IN LOVE (Twentieth Century-Fox, 1936), 97 min.
Producer, B. G. DeSylvia; director, Edward H. Griffith; based on the play by Ladislaus Bus-Fekete; screenplay, Melville Baker; music director, Louis Silvers; camera, Hal Mohr; editor, Ralph Dietrich.

Janet Gaynor (Martha Kerenye); Loretta Young (Susie Schmidt); Constance Bennett (Yoli Haydn); Simone Simon (Marie Armand); Don Ameche (Dr. Rudi Imre); Paul Lukas (John Barta); Tyrone Power, Jr. (Karl Lanyi); Alan Mowbray (Paul Sandor); Wilfrid Lawson (Ben Horvath); J. Edward Bromberg (Brenner); Virginia Field (Countess Helena); Frank Dawson (Johann); Egon Brecher (Concierge); Vesey O'Davoren (Fritz); Jayne Regan (Mrs. Dreker); John Bleifer (Porter); Eleanor Wesselhoeft (Charwoman); William Brisbane (Chauffeur); Lynn Bari (Clerk); Helen Dickson (Woman); Paul Weigel (Waiter); Tony Merlo (Assistant Stage Manager); Paul McVey (Actor); Maxine Elliott Hicks (Girl in Audience); Edward Peil, Jr. (Boy in Audience); Hector Sarno (Turkish Waiter).

LLOYDS OF LONDON (Twentieth Century-Fox, 1936), 117 min.

Producer, Darryl F. Zanuck; associate producer, Kenneth Macgowan; director, Henry King; story, Curtis Kenyon; screenplay, Ernest Pascal and Walter Ferris; music director, Louis Silvers; camera, Bert Glennon; editor, Barbara McLean.

Freddie Bartholomew (Young Jonathan Blake); Madeleine Carroll (Lady Elizabeth Stacy); Sir Guy Standing (John Julius Angerstein) Tyrone Power (Jonathan Blake); C. Aubrey Smith (Old "Q"); Virginia Field (Polly); Montagu Love (Hawkins); Gavin Muir (Sir Gavin Gore); Arthur Hohl (First Captain); J. M. Kerrigan (Young Horatio Nelson); Lumsden Hare (Captain Suckling); Charles Coleman, Leonard Mudie, and Charles McNaughton (Waiters at Lloyds'); Miles Mander (Jukes); Murray Kinnell (Reverend Nelson); Una O'Connor (Widow Blake); Will Stanton (Smutt); Forester Harvey (Percival Potts); George Sanders (Lord Everett Stacy); E. E. Clive (Magistrate); Robert Greig (Lord Drayton); John Burton (Lord Nelson); Ivan F. Simpson (Old Man); Holmes Herbert (Spokesman); May Beatty (Lady Masham); Hugh Huntley (Prince of Wales); Charles Croker-King (Willoughby); Georges Renavent (French Lieutenant); Lester Mathews (Captain Hardy); Reginald Barlow (Second Captain); Rita Carlyle (Pawn Seller); D'Arcy Corrigan (Chimney Sweep); Yvonne Severn (Ann); Yorke Sherwood (Dr. Sam Johnson); William Wagner (Boswell); Captain John Blood (Doorman); Leonard Walker (Fiddler); Cecil Weston (Woman); Jean De Briac (Fisherman); Thomas A. Braiden (Chaplain); Olaf Hytten (Telescope Man).

LOVE IS NEWS (Twentieth Century-Fox, 1937), 78 min.

Producer, Darryl F. Zanuck; associate producers, Earl Carroll and Harold Wilson; director, Tay Garnett; story, William Lipman, Frederick Stephani; screenplay, Harry Tugend and Jack Yellen; song, Sidney Mitchell and Lew Pollack; camera, Ernest Palmer.

Tyrone Power (Steve Leyton); Loretta Young (Tony Gateson); Don Ameche (Marty Canavan); Slim Summerville (Judge); Dudley Digges (Cyprus Jeffrey); Walter Catlett (Johnson); Jane Darwell (Mrs. Flaherty); Stepin Fetchit (Penrod); George Sanders (Count de Guyon); Pauline Moore (Lois Westcott); Frank Conroy (Finlay); Charles Coleman (Bevins); Elisha Cook, Jr. (Eggleston); Paul McVey (Alvord); Julius Tannen (Logan); Ed Dearing (Motor Cop); Frederick Burton (J. D. Jones); George Offerman, Jr. (Copy Boy); Art Dupuis (Tony's Chauffeur); Charles Tannen, Sidney Fields, Arthur Rankin, Jack Byron, Sterling Campbell, Dick French, Paul Frawley, Ray Johnson, Al Jenson (Reporters); Richard Powell (Insurance Salesman); Jack Mulhall (Yacht Salesman); Sam Ash (Tailor).

CAFÉ METROPOLE (Twentieth Century-Fox, 1937), 83 min.

Producer, Nunnally Johnson; director, Edward H. Griffith; story, Gregory Ratoff, screenplay, Jacques Duval; assistant director, William Forsyth; music director, Louis Silvers; camera, Lucien Andriot; editor, Irene Morra.

Adolphe Menjou (Adolph); Loretta Young (Laura Ridgeway); Tyrone Power (Alexis Penayev [Alexander Brown]); Charles Winninger (Ridgeway); Gregory Ratoff (Paul); Christian Rub (Leroy); Helen Westley (Margaret); Georges Renavent (Maitre d'Hotel); Ferdinand Gottschalk (Monnett); Hal K. Dawson (Thorndyke); Leonid Kinsky (Artist); Louis Mercier (Courtroom Attendant); Jules Raucourt, Albert Pollet, Gino Corrado, and Eugene Borden (Waiters); Rolfe Sedan (Flower Clerk); Albert Morin and Charles De Ravenne (Page Boys); Leonid Snegoff and Octavio J. Giraud (Porters); Fred Cavens (Train Guard); Jean De Briac and Jean Perry (Gendarmes); Andre Cheron (Croupier); Jean Masset, Mario Dominici, and George Herbert (Players); George Andre Beranger (Hat Clerk); Paul Porcasi (Police Official); Jacques Lory (Elevator Operator); Fredrik Vogeding (Attendant).

THIN ICE (Twentieth Century-Fox, 1937), 78 min.

Producer, Darryl F. Zanuck; associate producer, Raymond Griffith; director, Sidney Lansfield; based on the novel *Der Komet* by Attilla Orbok; screenplay, Boris Ingster and Milton Sperling; songs, Sidney Mitchell and Lew Pollack, and Mack Gordon and Harry Revel; choreography, Harry Losee; music director, Louis Silvers; camera, Robert Planck and Edward Cronjager; editor, Robert Simpson.

Sonja Henie (Lili Heiser); Tyrone Power (Prince Rudolph); Arthur Treacher (Nottingham); Raymond Walburn (Uncle Dornik); Joan Davis (Orchestra Leader); Sig Rumann (Prime Minister); Alan Hale (Baron); Leah Ray (Singer); Melville Cooper (Krantz); Maurice Cass (Count); George Givot (Alex); Torben Meyer (Chauffeur); George Davis (Waiter) Lon Chaney, Jr. (American Reporter); Rudolph Anders (German Reporter); Alphonse Martell and Walter Bonn (Officers of Prime Minister); Elsa Janssen (Woman); Greta Meyer (Martha); Egon Brecher (Hans the Janitor); Alberto Morin (Attendant); Iva Stewart, Dorothy Jones, June Storey, June Gale, Clarice Sherry, June Wilkins, Monica Bannister, Bonnie Bannon, Pauline Craig, Ruth Hart, Wanda Perry, Doris Davenport, Diane Cook, and Margaret Lyman (Members of Girls' Band), Christian Rub (Man).

SECOND HONEYMOON (Twentieth Century-Fox, 1937), 79 min.

Producer, Darryl F. Zanuck; associate producer, Raymond Griffith; director, Walter Lang; story, Philip Wylie; screenplay, Kathryn Scola, Darrell Ware; art directors, Bernard Herzbrun and David Hall; music director, David Buttolph; camera, Ernest Palmer; editor, Walter Thompson.

Tyrone Power (Raoul); Loretta Young (Vicki); Stuart Erwin (McTavish); Claire Trevor (Marcia); Marjorie Weaver (Joy); Lyle Talbot (Bob); J. Edward

246

Bromberg (Herbie); Paul Hurst (Huggins); Jayne Regan (Paula); Mary Treen (Elsie); Hal K. Dawson (Andy); William Wagner (Dr. Sneed); Robert Kellard, Lon Chaney, Jr., Charles Tannen, Arthur Rankin, Robert Lowery, and Fred Kelsey (Reporters); Major McBride (Croupier); Sarah Edwards (Woman in Airplane); Wade Boteler, Stanley Blystone (Policemen); Joseph King (Lieutenant); Herbert Fortier (Lawyer); Henry Roquemore, Alex Novinsky (Bondsmen); Harry Burkhardt, Thomas Pogue, and Arthur Stuart Hull (Lawyers); Troy Brown (Piano Player); Phillipa Hilbere and Lillian Porter (Telephone Operators).

IN OLD CHICAGO (Twentieth Century-Fox, 1938), 115 min.

Producer, Darryl F. Zanuck; associate producer, Kenneth Macgowan; director, Henry King; based on the novel *We the O'Learys* by Niven Busch; screenplay, Lamar Trotti and Sonya Levien; art directors, William Darling and Rudolph Sternad; set decorator, Thomas Little; assistant director, Robert Webb; costumes, Royer; music director, Louis Silvers; songs, Mack Gordon and Harry Revel; James A. Bland; sound, Eugene Grossman and Roger Heman; special effects, Fred Sersen, Ralph Hammeras, and Louis J. White; special effects director, H. Bruce Humberstone; camera, Peverell Marley; editor, Barbara McLean.

Tyrone Power (Dion O'Leary); Alice Faye (Belle Fawcett); Don Ameche (Jack O'Leary); Alice Brady (Molly O'Leary); Andy Devine (Pickle Bixby); Brian Donlevy (Gil Warren); Phyllis Brooks (Ann Colby); Tom Brown (Bob O'Leary); Sidney Blackmer (Phil Sheridan); Berton Churchill (Senator Colby); June Storey (Gretchen O'Leary); Paul Hurst (Mitch); Tyler Brooke (Specialty Singer); J. Anthony Hughes (Patrick O'Leary); Gene Reynolds (Dion as a Boy); Bobs Watson (Bob as a Boy); Billy Watson (Jack as a Boy); Madame Sul-Te-Wan (Mattie); Spencer Charters (Beavers); Rondo Hatton (Rondo); Thelma Manning (Carrie Donahue); Ruth Gillette (Miss Lou); Eddie Collins (Drunk); Harry Stubbs (Fire Commissioner); Francis Ford (Driver); Gustav Von Seyffertitz, and Russell Hicks (Men in Jack's Office).

ALEXANDER'S RAGTIME BAND (Twentieth Century-Fox, 1938), 105 min.

Producer, Darryl F. Zanuck; associate producer, Harry Joe Brown; director, Henry King; screenplay, Kathryn Scola and Lamar Trotti; adaptor, Richard Sherman; music director, Alfred Newman; new songs, Irving Berlin; choreography, Seymour Felix; art directors, Bernard Herzbrun and Boris Leven; set decorator, Thomas Little; costumes, Gwen Wakeling; sound, Arthur von Kirbach and Roger Heman; camera, Peverell Marley; editor, Barbara McLean.

Tyrone Power (Alexander [Roger Grant]); Alice Faye (Stella Kirby); Don Ameche (Charley Dwyer); Ethel Merman (Jerry Allen); Jack Haley (Davey Lane); Jean Hersholt (Professor Heinrich); Helen Westley (Aunt Sophie); John Carradine (Taxi Driver); Paul Hurst (Bill); Wally Vernon (Himself); Ruth Terry (Ruby); Douglas Fowley (Snapper); Chick Chandler (Louie); Eddie Collins (Corporal Collins); Joseph Crehan (Dillingham's Stage Manager); Robert Gleckler (Dirty Eddie); Dixie Dunbar (Specialty Performer); Joe King (Charles Dillingham); Grady Sutton (Babe); Stanley Andrews (Colonel); Lon Chaney, Jr. (Photographer); Selmer Jackson (Manager of Radio Station); Paul McVey (Stage Manager); King's Men (Quartet); Tyler Brooke (Assistant Stage Manager); Robert Lowery (Reporter); Charles Williams (Agent); James Flavin (Captain); Edward Keane (Major); Kay Griffith, Lynne Berkeley (Autograph Seekers); Sam Ash, Edwin Stanley (Critics); Cecil Weston (Woman); Pop Byron (Conductor).

MARIE ANTOINETTE (MGM, 1938), 160 min.

Producer, Hunt Stromberg; director, W. S. Van Dyke II; story, Stefan Zweig; screenplay, Claudine West, Donald Ogden Stewart, and Ernest Vajda; music supervisor, Herbert Stothart; choreography, Albertina Rasch; costume designers, Adrian and Gile Steele; makeup, John Dawn; art director, Cedric Gibbons; technical adviser, George Richelavie; sound, Douglas Shearer; special effects camera, Slavko Vorkapich; camera, William Daniels; editor, Robert J. Kern.

Norma Shearer (Marie Antoinette); Tyrone Power (Count Axel de Fersen); John Barrymore (King Louis XV); Gladys George (Mme. DuBarry); Robert Morley (King Louis XVI); Anita Louise (Princess DeLamballe); Joseph Schildkraut (Duke of Orleans); Henry Stephenson (Count Mercy); Reginald Gardiner (Artois); Peter Bull (Gamin); Albert Dekker (Provence); Barnett Parker (Prince DeRohan); Joseph Calleia (Drouet); Holmes Herbert (Herald); Walter Walker (Doctor); Henry Kolker (Court Aide); Horace McMahon (Rabblerouser); Robert Barrat (Citizen); Scotty Beckett (Dauphin); Alma Kruger (Empress Marie Theresa); George Zucco (Governor of Conciergerie); Ian Wolfe (Herbert the Jailer); Mae Busch (Mme. La Motte); Cecil Cunningham (Mme. DeLerchenfeld); Ruth Hussey (Mme. LePolignac); Victor Kilian (Guard in Louis' Cell); Harry Cording (Executioner); John Merton (Soldier Announcing Birth); Lionel Royce (Guillaume); Barry Fitzgerald (Peddler); Kathryn Sheldon (Mrs. Tilson); Lawrence Grant (Old Nobleman at Birth of Dauphin); Harry Davenport (Monsieur de Cosse); Dick Alexander (Man with Pike); Trevor Bardette and John Butler (Municipals); Buddy Roosevelt and Lane Chandler (Revolutionary Officers); Carl Stockdale (National Guard); Dorothy Christy (Lady in Waiting to Mme. DuBarry); Henry Daniell (LaMotte), George Houston (Marquis De St. Priest).

SUEZ (Twentieth Century-Fox, 1938), 104 min.

Producer, Darryl F. Zanuck; associate producer, Gene Markey; director, Allan Dwan; story, Sam Duncan; screenplay, Philip Dunne and Julien Josephson; art directors, Bernard Herzbrun and Rudolf Sternad; set decorator, Thomas Little; costumes, Royer; special effects, Fred Sersen; camera, J. Peverell Marley; editor, Barbara McLean.

Tyrone Power (Ferdinand De Lesseps); Loretta Young (Empress Eugenie); Annabella (Toni); J. Edward Bromberg (Said); Joseph Schildkraut (La Tour); Henry Stephenson (Count De Lesseps); Sidney Blackmer (Du Brey); Maurice Moscovich (Mohammed Ali); Sig Rumann (Sergeant Fellerin); Nigel Bruce (Sir Malcolm Cameron); Miles Mander (Benjamin Disraeli); George Zucco (Prime Minister); Leon Ames (Louise Napoleon); Rafaela Ottiano (Maria De Teba); Victor Varconi (Victor Hugo); Jacques Lory (Millet); Odette Myrtil (Duchess); Frank Reicher (General Chagarnier); Carlos J. de Valdez (Count Hatzfeld); Albert Conti (Fevier); Brandon Hurst (Liszt); Marcelle Corday (Mme. Paquineau); Egon Brecher (Doctor); Alphonse Martel (General St. Arnaud); C. Montague Shaw (Elderly Man); Leonard Mudie (Campaign Manager); Jean Perry (Umpire); Robert Graves (Official); Christina Mantt (Maid); Anita Pike (Julia); Louis LaBey (Servant); Frank Lackteen (Swami); Alberto

Morin (Achmed); Michael Visaroff, Louis Vincenot, and Fred Malatesta (Jewel Merchants); Denis d'Auburn, Jerome De Nuccio, and Tony Urchal (Wrestlers); Jean De Briac (Engineer); George Sorel (Assistant); Jacques Vanaire (Old Engineer).

JESSE JAMES (Twentieth Century-Fox, 1939), C-108 min.
Producer, Darryl F. Zanuck; associate producer, Nunnally Johnson; director, Henry King, based on historical data assembled by Rosaline Schaeffer and Jo Frances James; screenplay, Johnson; Technicolor director, Natalie Kalmus; art directors, William Darling and George Dudley; music director, Louis Silvers; camera, George Barnes; Technicolor camera, W. H. Greene; editor, Barbara McLean.

Tyrone Power (Jesse James); Henry Fonda (Frank James); Nancy Kelly (Zee [Zerelda] Cobb James); Randolph Scott (Will Wright); Henry Hull (Major Rufus Cobb); Slim Summerville (Jailer); J. Edward Bromberg (George Runyon the Pinkerton Man [George Remington]); Brian Donlevy (Barshee); John Carradine (Bob Ford the Killer); Donald Meek (McCoy); John Russell (Jesse James, Jr.); Jane Darwell (Mrs. Samuels); Charles Tannen (Charles Ford); Claire Du Brey (Mrs. Ford); Willard Robertson (Clark); Paul Sutton (Lynch); Paul Burns (Hank); Spencer Charters (Preacher); Arthur Aylsworth (Tom); Charles Halton (Heywood the Banker); George Chandler (Roy the Printer); Erville Alderson (Old Marshal); Harry Tyler (Farmer); George Breakston (Farmer's Boy); Virginia Brissac (Boy's Mother); Lon Chaney, Jr. (One of Jesse's Gang); Don Douglas (Infantry Captain); Leonard Kibrick (Boy); Tom London (Soldier); Eddy Waller (Deputy); Charles Middleton (Doctor).

ROSE OF WASHINGTON SQUARE (Twentieth Century-Fox, 1939), 86 min.
Producer, Darryl F. Zanuck; associate producer, Nunnally Johnson; director, Gregory Ratoff; story, John Larkin and Jerry Horwin; screenplay, Johnson; art directors, Richard Day and Rudolph Sternad; set decorator, Thomas Little; costumes, Royer; music director, Louis Silvers; songs: Mack Gordon and Harry Revel; James F. Hanley and Ballard MacDonald; Harry Carroll and Joe McCarthy; Maurice Yvain, A. Willemetz, and Jacques Charles with English lyrics by Channing Pollack; Gus Kahn and Ernie Erdman; Al Piantadosi and Henry Fink; N. J. Clesi; Byron Gay; B. G. DeSylva, Joseph Meyer, and Al Jolson; Joe Young, Sam Lewis, and Walter Donaldson; Tony Jackson and Egbert Van Alstyne; Bob Carleton; Jean Schwartz, Sam M. Lewis, and Joe Young; and Noble Sissle and Eubie Blake; choreography, Seymour Felix; sound, Eugene Grossman and Roger Heman; camera, Karl Freund; editor, Louis Loeffler.

Tyrone Power (Bart Clinton); Alice Faye (Rose Sargent); Al Jolson (Ted Cotter); William Frawley (Harry Long); Joyce Compton (Peggy); Hobart Cavanaugh (Whitney Bourne); Moroni Olsen (Russell); E. E. Clive (Barouche Drive); Louis Prima (Himself); Charles Wilson (Mike Cavanaugh); Paul Burns, Hal K. Dawson (Chumps); Ben Welden (Toby); Horace McMahon (Irving); Paul Stanton (District Attorney); Harry Hayden (Dexter the Apartment Owner); Charles Lane (Kress the Booking Agent); Chick Chandler (Master of Ceremonies); Igor and Tanya (Specialty Performers); Edgar Dearing (Lieutenant); Murray Alper (Candy Butcher); Ralph Dunn (Officer); Robert Shaw and Charles Tannen (Reporters); Paul Irving (Publisher); James Flavin (Guard); Leonard Kibrick (Newsboy).

IRVING BERLIN'S SECOND FIDDLE (Twentieth Century-Fox, 1939), 86 min.

Producer, Gene Markey; director, Sidney Lanfield; story, George Bradshaw; screenplay, Harry Tugend; songs, Irving Berlin; music director, Louis Silvers; camera, Leon Shamroy; editor, Robert Simpson.

Sonja Henie (Trudi Hovland); Tyrone Power (Jimmy Sutton); Rudy Vallee (Roger Maxwell); Edna May Oliver (Aunt Phoebe Hovland); Mary Healy (Jean Varick); Lyle Talbot (Willie Hogger); Alan Dinehart (George "Whit" Whitney); Minna Gombell (Jenny); Stewart Reburn (Skating Partner); Spencer Charters (Joe Clayton); Brian Sisters (Specialty); George Chandler (Taxi Driver); Irving Bacon (Harvey Vaughan, the Justice of the Peace); Maurice Cass (Alex Blank the Justice); A. S. Byron (Bit); Lillian Porter (Jimmy's Girl); Robert Lowery (Orchestra Leader); Charles Lane (Voice of the Chief of the Studio); John Hisstand (Announcer); Minerva Urecal (Miss Bland the School Principal); Cyril Ring (Florist); Dale Van Sickel (Musician); Ralph Brooks (Dining Extra); Gertrude Sutton and Fern Emmett (Women); Frank Coghlan, Jr. (Call Boy); Purnell Pratt (Abbott the Editor); Dick Redman (Freddie the Boy Skater); Leyland Hodgson (Henry the Maitre d'Hotel); Don Douglas (Director); King Sisters Quartette (Themselves); Harold Goodwin (Photographer).

THE RAINS CAME (Twentieth Century-Fox, 1939), 104 min.°

Producer, Darryl F. Zanuck; associate producer, Harry Joe Brown; director, Clarence Brown; based on the novel by Louis Bromfield; screenplay, Philip Dunne and Julien Josephson; music, Alfred Newman; songs, Mack Gordon and Harry Revel; and Lal Chand Mehra; sets, Thomas Little; costumes, Gwen Wakeling, special effects, Fred Sersen; camera, Arthur Miller; editor, Barbara McLean.

Myrna Loy (Lady Edwina Esketh); Tyrone Power (Major Rama Saft); George Brent (Tom Ransome); Brenda Joyce (Fern Simons); Nigel Bruce (Lord Albert Esketh); Maria Ouspenskaya (Maharani); Joseph Schildkraut (Mr. Bannerjee); Mary Nash (Miss Mac Daid); Jane Darwell (Aunt Phoebe Smiley); Marjorie Rambeau (Mrs. Simon); Henry Travers (Reverend Homer Smiley); H. B. Warner (Maharajah); Laura Hope Crews (Lily Hoggett-Egbury); William Royle (Raschid Ali Khan); Montagu Shaw (General Keith); Harry Hayden (Reverend Elmer Simon); Herbert Evans (Bates); Abner Biberman (John the Baptist); Mara Alexander (Mrs. Bannerjee); William Edmunds (Mr. Das); Adele Labansent, Sonia Charsky (Princesses); Rita Page (Maid); Pedro Regas (Official); Major Sam Harris (Officer).

°Filmed in Sepia

DAY-TIME WIFE (Twentieth Century-Fox, 1939), 71 min.

Producer, Darryl F. Zanuck; associate producer, Raymond Griffith; director, Gregory Ratoff; story, Rex Taylor; screenplay, Art Arthur and Robert Harari; art directors, Richard Day and Joseph C. Wright; music director, Cyril J. Mockridge; camera, Peverell Marley; editor, Francis Lyons.

Tyrone Power (Ken Norton); Linda Darnell (Jane); Warren William (Dexter); Binnie Barnes (Blanche); Wendy Barrie (Kitty); Joan Davis (Miss Applegate);

Joan Valerie (Mrs. Dexter); Leonid Kinsky (Coco); Mildred Gover (Melbourne); Renie Riano (Mrs. Briggs); Robert Lowery and David Newell (Bits); Otto Han (House Boy); Marie Blake (Western Union Girl); Mary Gordon (Scrubwoman); Alex Pollard (Waiter); Frank Coghlan, Jr. (Office Boy).

JOHNNY APOLLO (Twentieth Century-Fox, 1940), 93 min.

Producer, Darryl F. Zanuck; associate producer, Harry Joe Brown; director, Henry Hathaway; story, Samuel G. Engel and Hal Long; screenplay, Philip Dunne and Rowland Brown; songs, Frank Loesser and Lionel Newman; Loesser and Alfred Newman; and Mack Gordon; camera, Arthur Miller; editor, Robert Bischoff.

Tyrone Power (Bob Cain); Dorothy Lamour ("Lucky" Dubarry); Edward Arnold (Robert Cain, Sr.); Lloyd Nolan (Mickey Dwyer); Charley Grapewin (Judge Emmett F. Brennan); Lionel Atwill (Jim MacLaughlin); Marc Lawrence (Harry Bates); Jonathan Hale (Dr. Brown); Russell Hicks (District Attorney); Fuzzy Knight (Cellmate); Charles Lane (Assistant District Attorney); Selmer Jackson (Warden); Charles Trowbridge (Judge Penrose); George Irving (Mr. Ives); Eddie Marr (Harry the Henchman); Anthony Caruso (Joe the Henchman); Harry Rosenthal (Piano Player); Wally Albright (Office Boy); Milburn Stone (Reporter); Tom Dugan (Tom the Prisoner); James Flavin (Guard); Walter Miller (Guard in Solitary); Robert Shaw, (Clerk); Ed Gargan (Detective).

BRIGHAM YOUNG—FRONTIERSMAN (Twentieth Century-Fox, 1940), 114 min.

Producer, Darryl F. Zanuck; associate producer, Kenneth Macgowan; director, Henry Hathaway; story, Louis Bromfield; screenplay, Lamar Trotti; art directors, William Darling, Maurice Ransford; music, Alfred Newman; camera, Arthur Miller; editor, Robert Bischoff.

Tyrone Power (Jonathan Kent); Linda Darnell (Zina Webb); Dean Jagger (Brigham Young); Brian Donlevy (Angus Duncan); Jane Darwell (Eliza Kent); John Carradine (Porter Rockwell); Mary Astor (Mary Ann Young); Vincent Price (Joseph Smith); Jean Rogers (Clara Young); Ann Todd (Mary Kent); Willard Robertson (Heber Kimball); Moroni Olsen (Doc Richards); Stanley Andrews (Hyrum Smith); Frank Thomas (Hubert Crum); Fuzzy Knight (Pete); Dickie Jones (Henry Kent); Selmer Jackson (Caleb Kent); Russell Simpson (Major); Arthur Aylsworth (Jim Bridges); Cheif Big Tree (Big Elk); Claire Du Brey (Emma Smith); Tully Marshall (Judge); Ralph Dunn (Jury Foreman); George Melford (John Taylor); Frederick Burton (Mr. Webb); Lee Shumway and Charles Middleton (Mobsters); Eddy Waller and Harry Tyler (Bits); Blacke Whiteford (Bit in Court); Cecil Weston (Woman).

THE MARK OF ZORRO (Twentieth Century-Fox, 1940), 93 min.

Producer, Darryl F. Zanuck; associate producer, Raymond Griffith; director, Rouben Mamoulian; based on the story *The Curse of Capistrano* by Johnston McCulley; adaptors, Garrett Fort and Bess Meredyth; screenplay, John Tainton Foote; assistant director, Sidney Bowen; art directors, Richard Day and Joseph C. Wright; set decorator, Thomas Little; music; Alfred Newman; costumes, Travis Banton; sound, W. D. Flick and Roger Heman; camera, Arthur Miller; editor, Robert Bischoff.

Tyrone Power (Don Diego Vega); Linda Darnell (Lolita Quintero); Basil Rathbone (Captain Esteban Pasquale); Gale Sondergaard (Inez Quintero); Eugene Pallette (Father Felipe); J. Edward Bromberg (Don Luis Quintero); Montagu Love (Don Alejandro Vega); Janet Beecher (Señora Isabella Vega); Robert Lowery (Rodrigo); Chris-Pin Martin (Turnkey); George Regas (Sergeant Gonzales); Belle Mitchell (Maria); John Bleifer (Pedro); Frank Puglia (Cafe Proprietor); Eugene Borden (Officer of the Day); Pedro de Cordoba (Don Miguel); Guy d'Ennery (Don Jose); Ralph Byrd (Soldier); Michael (Ted) North (Bit); Jean Del Val (Sentry); Hector Sarno (Peon at Inn); Frank Yaconelli (Servant); Gino Corrado (Caballero).

BLOOD AND SAND (Twentieth Century-Fox, 1941), C-123 min.

Producer, Darryl F. Zanuck; associate producer, Robert T. Kane; director, Rouben Mamoulian; based on the novel *Sangre y Arena* by Vincente Blasco Ibanez; screenplay, Jo Swerling; assistant directors, Robert Webb and Sidney Bowen, Henry Weinberger; Technicolor director, Natalie Kalmus; art directors, Richard Day and Joseph C. Wright; set decorator, Thomas Little; costumes, Travis Banton; toreador costumes, Jose Dolores Perez Martinez; choreography of fiesta scenes: Hermes Pan; dance "El Torero' conceived by Budd Boetticher, executed by Geneva Sawyer; sound, W. D. Flick and Roger Heman; camera, Ernest Palmer and Ray Rennahan; editor, Robert Bischoff.

Tyrone Power (Juan Gallardo); Linda Darnell (Carmen Espinosa); Rita Hayworth (Dona Sol); Nazimova (Señora Augustias); Anthony Quinn (Manolo de Palma); J. Carrol Naish (Garabato); John Carradine (Nacional); Laird Cregar (Natalio Curro); Lynn Bari (Encarnacion); Vincente Gomez (Guitarist); Monty Banks (Antonio Lopez); George Reeves (Captain Pierre Lauren); Pedro de Cordoba (Don Jose Alvarez); Fortunio Bonanova (Pedro Espinosa); Victor Kilian (Priest); Michael (Adrian) Morris (La Pulga); Charles Stevens (Pablo Gomez); Ann Todd (Carmen as a Child); Cora Sue Collins (Encarnacion as a Child); Russell Hicks (Marquis); Maurice Cass (El Milquetoast); Rex Downing (Juan as a Child); John Wallace (Francisco); Jacqueline Dalya (Gachi); Cullen Johnson (Manolo as a Child); Larry Harris (Pablo as a Child); Ted Frye (La Pulga as a Child); Schuyler Standish (Nacional as a Child); Harry Burns (Engineer); Francis McDonald (Friend); Kay Linaker (Woman); Alberto Morin (Attendant); Paul Ellis (Ortega).

A YANK IN THE R.A.F. (Twentieth Century-Fox, 1941), 98 min.

Producer, Darryl F. Zanuck; associate producer, Lou Edelman; director, Henry King; story, Melville Grossman (Zanuck); screenplay, Darrell Ware and Karl Tunberg; songs, Leo Robin and Ralph Rainger; art directors, Richard Day and James Basevi; camera, Leon Shamroy; editor, Barbara McLean.

Tyrone Power (Tim Baker); Betty Grable (Carol Brown); John Sutton (Wing Commander Morley); Reginald Gardiner (Roger Phillby); Donald Stuart (Corporal Harry Baker); Morton Lowry (Squadron Leader); Ralph Byrd (Al); Richard Fraser (Thorndyke); Denis Green (Redmond); Bruce Lester (Richardson); Gilchrist Stuart (Wales); Lester Mathews (Group Captain); Frederick Worlock (Canadian Major); Ethel Griffies (Mrs. Fitzhugh); Stuart Robertson and Dennis Hoey (Intelligence Officers); Lynne Roberts (Nurse at Boat); Fortunio Bonanova (Headwaiter at Regency); James Craven (Instructor); G. P. Huntley, Jr. (Radio Operator); Otto Reichow and Kurt Kreuger (German Pilots); Lillian Porter (Chorus Girl); Claud Allister (Officer); Hans Von Morhart (German Sergeant); Bobbie Hale (Cab Driver); Craufurd Kent (Group Captain; Maureen Roden-Ryan (Barmaid); Gil Perkins (Sergeant).

SON OF FURY (Twentieth Century-Fox, 1942), 102 min.
Producer, Darryl F. Zanuck; associate producer, William Perlberg; director, John Cromwell; based on the novel *Benjamin Blake* by Edison Marshall; screenplay, Philip Dunne; music director, Alfred Newman; camera, Arthur Miller; editor, Walter Thompson.

Tyrone Power (Benjamin Blake); Gene Tierney (Eve); George Sanders (Sir Arthur Blake); Frances Farmer (Isabel Blake); Roddy McDowall (Ben as a Boy); John Carradine (Caleb Greene); Elsa Lanchester (Bristol Isabel); Harry Davenport (Amos Kidder); Kay Johnson (Helen Blake); Dudley Digges (Bartholomew Pratt); Halliwell Hobbes (Purdy); Marten Lamont (Kenneth Hobart); Arthur Hohl (Captain Greenough); Pedro de Cordoba (Feanou); Dennis Hoey (Lord Tarrant); Robert Greig (Judge); Ray Mala (Marnoa); Clifford Severn (Paddy); Heather Thatcher (Maggie Martin); Lester Mathews (Prosecutor); Charles Irwin (Captain); Ethel Griffies (Matron); Mae Marsh (Mrs. Purdy); Harry Cording (Turnkey); Olaf Hytten (Court Clerk); Leonard Carey (Pale Tom); Igancio Saenz (Native Boy); Clive Morgan (Lord St. George).

THIS ABOVE ALL (Twentieth Century-Fox, 1942), 110 min.
Producer, Darryl F. Zanuck; director, Anatole Litvak; based on the novel by Eric Knight; screenplay, R. G. Sherriff; art director, Thomas Little; camera, Arthur Miller; editor, Walter Thompson.
Tyrone Power (Clive); Joan Fontaine (Prudence); Thomas Mitchell (Monty); Henry Stephenson (General Cathaway); Nigel Bruce (Ramsbottom); Gladys Cooper (Iris Cathaway); Philip Merivale (Roger); Sara Allgood (Waitress in Tea Room); Alexander Knox (Rector); Queenie Leonard (Violet); Melville Cooper (Wilbur); Jill Esmond (Nurse Emily); Arthur Shields (Chaplain); Dennis Hoey (Parsons); Miles Mander (Major); Rhys Williams (Sergeant); John Abbott (Joe); Carol Curtis-Brown (Maid); Holmes Herbert (Dr. Mathias); Denis Green (Dr. Ferris); Thomas Louden (Vicar); Mary Forbes (Vicar's Wife); Forrester Harvey (Proprietor); Harold de Becker (Conductor); Billy Bevan (Farmer); Aubrey Mather and Lumsden Hare (Headwaiters); Heather Thatcher and Jean Prescott (Nurses); Rita Page and Clare Verdera (Corporals); Brenda Forbes (Mae the Singer); Virginia McDowall (Girl); Olaf Hytten (Proprietor); Cyril Thornton (Station Master); Mary Field (Maid); Will Stanton (Bartender); Herbert Clifton (Secretary); Colin Campbell (Man).

THE BLACK SWAN (Twentieth Century-Fox, 1942), C-85 min.
Producer, Robert Bassler; director, Henry King; based on the novel by Rafael Sabatini; screenplay, Ben Hecht and Seton I. Miller; music, Alfred Newman; art directors, Richard Day and James Basevi; camera, Leon Shamroy; editor, Barbara McLean.

Tyrone Power (James Waring); Maureen O'Hara (Margaret Denby); Laird Cregar (Henry Morgan); Thomas Mitchell (Blue); George Sanders (Leech); Anthony Quinn (Wogan); George Zucco (Lord Denby); Edward Ashley (Ingraham); Fortunio Bonanova (Don Miguel); Stuart Robertson (Captain Gra-

253

ham); Charles McNaughton (Fenner); Frederic Worlock (Speaker); Willie Fung (Chinese Cook); Charles Francis (Captain Higgs); Arthur Shields (Bishop); Keith Hitchcock (Major-Domo); John Burton (Captain Blaine); Cyril McLaglen (Captain Jones); Clarence Muse (Daniel); Olaf Hytten (Clerk); David Thursby, Charles Irwin, and Frank Leigh (Sea Captains); Arthur Gould-Porter, C. Montague Shaw, Boyd Irwin, and George Kirby (Assemblymen); Rita Christiani (Dancer); Bryn Davis, Jody Gilbert (Women); Billy Edmunds (Town Crier)

CRASH DIVE (Twentieth Century-Fox, 1943), C-105 min.

Producer, Milton Sperling; director, Archie Mayo; story, W. R. Burnett; screenplay, Jo Swerling; technical adviser, M. K. Kirkpatrick, Commander U.S.N.; art directors, Richard Day and Wiard B. Ihnen; set decorators, Thomas Little and Paul Fox; music, David Buttolph; music director, Emil Newman; assistant director, John Johnston; sound, Roger Heman; special camera effects, Fred Sersen; camera, Leon Shamroy; editors, Walter Thompson and Ray Curtiss.

Tyrone Power (Lieutenant Ward Stewart); Anne Baxter (Jean Hewlitt); Dana Andrews (Lieutenant Commander Dewey Connors); James Gleason (McDonnell); Dame May Whitty (Grandmother); Henry Morgan (Brownie); Ben Carter (Oliver Cromwell Jones); Frank Conroy (Captain Bryson); Minor Watson (Admiral Bob Stewart); Kathleen Howard (Miss Bromley); Charles Tannen (Harmond); Florence Lake (Doria); John Archer (Curly); Frank Dawson (Henry the Butler); Edward McWade (Crony); Paul Burns (Simmons the Clerk); Gene Rizzi (Sailor); Thurston Hall (Senator from Texas); Trudy Marshall (Telephone Operator); Chester Gan (Lee Wong); Bruce Wong (Waiter); Cecil Weston (Woman); Lionel Royce (Captain of Q Boat); Hans Moebus (German Officer).

THE RAZOR'S EDGE (Twentieth Century-Fox, 1946), 146 min.

Producer, Darryl F. Zanuck; director, Edmund Goulding; based on the novel by W. Somerset Maugham; screenplay, Lamar Trotti; art directors, Richard Day and Nathan Juran; set directors, Thomas Little and Paul S. Fox; music, Alfred Newman; song, Mack Gordon and Goulding; choreography, Harry Pilcer; Miss Tierney's costumes, Oleg Cassini; assistant director, Saul Wurtzel; sound, Alfred Bruzlin and Roger Heman; special camera effects, Fred Sersen; camera, Arthur Miller; editor, J. Watson Webb.

Tyrone Power (Larry Darrell); Gene Tierney (Isabel Bradley); John Payne (Gray Maturin); Anne Baxter (Sophie); Clifton Webb (Elliott Templeton); Herbert Marshall (Somerset Maugham); Lucile Watson (Mrs. Louise Bradley); Frank Latimore (Bob MacDonald); Elsa Lanchester (Miss Keith); Fritz Kortner (Kosti); John Wengraf (Joseph); Cecil Humphreys (Holy Man); Harry Pilcer (Speciality Dancer); Cobina Wright, Sr. (Princess Novemali); Albert Petit (Albert); Noel Cravat (Russian Singer); Isabelle Lamore (Maid); Andre Charlot (Bishop); Renee Carson (Sophie's Friend); Jean Del Val (Police Clerk); Walter Bonn (Butler); Robert Laurent (Singer); Marie Rabasse (Flower Woman); Bess Flowers (Matron); Barry Norton (Escort of Princess); Helen Fasquelle (Proprietress); Mayo Newhall (Kibitzer); Stanislas Bielski (Man at Bar); Peggy O'Neill, Betty Lou Volder, Mary Brewer, Blanche Taylor, Dorothy Abbott, and Marge Pemberton (Show Girls); Ruth Miles and Edward Kover (Adagio Team);

Richard (Shaw) Sisson (Interne); Greta Granstedt (Hospital Telephone Operator); Major Fred Farrell and Albert Pollet (Men); Lilian Stanford (Customer in Sulka's); Marcel De La Brosse (Conductor); George Sorel (French Surete Man); Dr. Gerald Echeverria (Doctor); Eddie Das and Hassan Khayyam (Hindus).

NIGHTMARE ALLEY (Twentieth Century-Fox, 1947), 111 min.

Producer, George Jessel; director, Edmund Goulding; based on the novel by William Lindsay Gresham; screenplay, Jules Furthman; art directors, Lyle Wheeler and J. Russell Spencer; set decorators, Thomas Little and Stuart Reiss; music, Cyril Mockridge; orchestrator, Earle Hagen; music conductor, Lionel Newman; assistant director, Gaston Glass; sound, E. Clayton Ward and Roger Heman; special effects, Fred Sersen; camera, Lee Garmes; editor, Barbara McLean.

Tyrone Power (Stan Carlisle); Joan Blondell (Zeena); Coleen Gray (Molly); Helen Walker (Lilith Ritter); Taylor Holmes (Ezra Grindle); Mike Mazurki (Bruno); Ian Keith (Pete); Julia Dean (Mrs. Peabody); James Flavin (Hoatley); Roy Roberts (McGraw); James Burke (Town Marshall); Maurice Navarro (Fire Eater); Leo Gray (Detective); Marjorie Wood (Mrs. Prescott); Harry Cheshire (Mr. Prescott); Eddy Waller (Old Farmer); Nina Gilbert (Worried Mother); June Bolyn (Maid in Grindle Home); Florence Aver (Housekeeper); Al Herman (Cabby); George Chandler (Cab Driver); George Chandler, Emmet Lynn, Oliver Blake, George Lloyd, and Jack Raymond (Hobos); John Wald (Radio Announcer).

CAPTAIN FROM CASTILE (Twentieth Century-Fox, 1947), C-140 min.

Producer, Lamar Trotti; director, Henry King; based on the novel by Samuel Shellabarger; screenplay, Trotti; Technicolor director, Natalie Kalmus; assistant directors, William Eckhart and Henry Weinberger; art directors, Richard Day and James Basevi; set decorator, Thomas Little; music director, Alfred Newman; orchestrator, Edward Powell, sound, Winston H. Leverett and Roger Heman; special effects, Fred Sersen; camera, Charles Clarke and Arthur E. Arling; editor, Barbara McLean.

Tyrone Power (Pedro De Vargas); Jean Peters (Catana Perez); Cesar Romero (Hernand Cortez); Lee J. Cobb (Juan Garcia); John Sutton (Diego De Silva); Antonio Moreno (Don Francisco De Vargas); Thomas Gomez (Father Bartolome Romero); Alan Mowbray (Professor Botello); Barbara Lawrence (Luiza De Caravajal); George Zucco (Marquis De Caravajal); Roy Roberts (Captain Alvarado); Marc Lawrence (Corio); Robert Karnes (Manuel Perez); Fred Libby (Hernand Soler); Virginia Brissac (Dona Maria De Vargas); Jay Silverheels (Coatl); John Laurenz (Cermeno); Dolly Arriaga (Mercedes); Reed Hadley (Escudero); Stella Inda (Donna Marino); Chris-Pin Martin (Sancho Lopez); Edward Mundy (Crier); Robert Adler (Reyes); Gilberto Gonzales (Aztec Ambassador); Harry Carter (Captain Sandoval); Mimi Aguglia (Hernandez); Willie Calles and Ramon Sanchez (Aztecs); Harry Carter (Captain Sandoval); Bud Wolfe (Sailor); David Cato (Singer); Julian Rivero (Marquis' Servant).

THE LUCK OF THE IRISH (Twentieth Century-Fox, 1948), 104 min.

Producer, Fred Kohlmar; director, Henry Koster; based on the novel by Guy and Constance Jones; screenplay, Philip Dunne; art directors, Lyle Wheeler

255

and J. Russell Spencer; set decorators, Thomas Little and Paul S. Fox; music, Cyril Mockridge; music director, Lionel Newman; assistant director, Joseph Behm; makeup, Ben Nye and Harry Maret; wardrobe director, Charles Le Maire; costumes, Bonnie Cashin; sound, George Leverett and Roger Heman; special effects, Fred Sersen; camera, Joseph La Shelle; editor, J. Watson Webb, Jr.

Tyrone Power (Stephen Fitzgerald); Anne Baxter (Nora); Cecil Kellaway (Horace); Lee J Cobb (D. C. Augur); James Todd (Bill Clark); Jayne Meadows (Frances); J. M. Kerrigan (Taedy); Phil Brown (Higginbotham); Charles Irwin (Cornelius); Louise Lorimer (Augur's Secretary); Tim Ryan (Clancy); Harry Antrim (Senator Ransom); Margaret Wells (Mrs. Augur); John Goldsworthy (Butler); Douglas Gerrard (Receptionist); Tito Vuolo (Greek Vendor); Tom Stevenson (Gentleman's Gentleman); Bill Swingley (Terrance); Hollis Jewell (Cab Driver); Eddie Parks (Pickpocket); John Roy (Subway Guard); J. Farell MacDonald (Captain); George Melford (Doorman); John Davidson, Wilson Wood, Don Brodie, Gene Garrick, Robert Adler, and Robert Karnes (Reporters); Jimmy O'Brien (Singer); Marion Marshall (Secretary); Frank Mitchell (Irish Dancer); Norman Leavitt (Milkman).

THAT WONDERFUL URGE (Twentieth Century-Fox, 1948), 82 min.
Producer, Fred Kohlmar; director, Robert B. Sinclair; based on *Love Is News* by William R. Lipman and Frederick Stephani; screenplay, Jay Dratler; music, Cyril Mockridge; orchestrator, Maurice de Packh; music director, Lionel Newman; art directors, Lyle Wheeler and George Davis; set decorators, Thomas Little and Walter M. Scott; assistant director, Jerry Bryan; makeup, Ben Nye and Allen Snyder; costumes, Oleg Cassini and Fred A. Picard; sound, Eugene Grossman and Roger Heman; special effects, Fred Sersen; camera, Charles C. Clarke; editor, Louis Loeffler.

Tyrone Power (Thomas Jefferson Tyler); Gene Tierney (Sara Farley); Reginald Gardiner (Count Andre de Guyon); Arleen Whelan (Jessica Woods); Lucile Watson (Aunt Cornelia Farley); Gene Lockhart (Judge Parker); Lloyd Gough (Duffy); Porter Hall (Attorney Ketchell); Richard Gaines (Mr. Whitson); Taylor Holmes (Attorney Rice); Chill Wills (Homer Beggs, the Justice of the Peace); Hope Emerson (Mrs. Riley, the Apartment House Keeper); Frank Ferguson (Findlay); Charles Arnt (Mr. Bissell); Francis Pierlot (Barret); Joe Haworth (Ski Patrolman); Hal K. Dawson (Passerby); Norman Phillips (Western Union Boy); Mickey Simpson and Robert Foulk (Workmen); Charles Woolf (Freddie, the Copy Boy); Edwin Randolph (Waiter); Gertrude Michael (Mrs. Whitson); Isabel Randolph (Mrs. Vickers); Forbes Murray (Butler); Wilson Wood (Court Clerk); David Newell (Reporter); Robert B. Williams (Special Policeman); Marjorie Wood (Woman); David Thursby (Bailiff); Eddie Parks (Artist); Bess Flowers (Party Guest); Charles (Chuck) Hamilton (Chauffeur); Eula Guy (Mrs. Beggs).

PRINCE OF FOXES (Twentieth Century-Fox, 1949), 111 min.
Producer, Sol C. Siegel; director, Henry King; based on the novel by Samuel Shellabarger; screenplay, Milton Krims; art directors, Lyle Wheeler and Mark-Lee Kirk; set decorator, Thomas Little; assistant director, Joe Behm; music-music director, Alfred Newman; costumes, Vittorio Nino Novarese; sound, Charles Hisserich and Roger Heman; special effects, Fred Sersen; camera, Leon Shamroy; editor, Barbara McLean.

Tyrone Power (Orsini); Orson Welles (Ceasare Borgia); Wanda Hendrix (Camilla Varano); Marina Berti (Angela); Everett Sloane (Belli); Katina Paxinou (Mono Zoppo); Felix Aylmer (Count Varano); Leslie Bradley (Esteban); Joop van Hulzen (D'Este); James Carney (Alphonso E'Este); Eduardo Ciannelli (Art Dealer); Rena Lennart (Lady in Waiting); Guiseppe Faeti (Priest); Njntsky (Specialty Dancer); Ves Vanghielova (Tonia); Eva Breuer (Fabio); Ludmilla Durarowa (Vittoria) Albert Latsaha, Adriano Ambrogi (Townsmen).

THE BLACK ROSE (Twentieth Century-Fox, 1950), C-120 min.
Producer, Louis D. Lighton; director, Henry Hathaway; based on the novel by Thomas B. Costain; screenplay, Talbot Jennings; music, Richard Addinsell; music conductor, Muir Mathieson; art directors, Paul Sheriff and W. Andrews; Technicolor consultant, Joan Bridge; camera, Jack Cardiff; editor, Manuel Del Campo.

Tyrone Power (Walter of Gurnie); Orson Welles (Bayan); Cecile Aubry (Miriam); Jack Hawkins (Tristram); Michael Rennie (King Edward I); Finlay Currie (Alfgar); Herbert Lom (Anemus); Mary Clare (Countess of Lessford); Bobby Blake (Mahmoud); Alfonso Bedoya (Lu Chung); Gibb McLaughlin (Wilderkin); James Robertson Justice (Simeon Beautrie); Henry Oscar (Friar Roger Bacon); Laurence Harvey (Edmond); Torin Thatcher (Harry); Hilary Pritchard (Hal the Miller); Ley on (Chinese Captain); Madame Phang (Empress of China); Carl Jaffe (Mongolian Officer); Peter Drury (Young Man); Ben Williams (Guard); George Woodbridge (Warder); Valery Inkijinoff (Chinese Minister); Alexis Chesnakov, Alan Tilvern, Thomas Gallagher, and John Penrose (Mongolians).

AMERICAN GUERRILLA IN THE PHILIPPINES (Twentieth Century-Fox, 1950), C-105 min.
Producer, Lamar Trotti; director, Fritz Lang; based on the novel by Ira Wolfert; screenplay, Trotti; art directors, Lyle Wheeler and J. Russel Spencer; set decorators, Thomas Little and Stuart Reiss; costumes, Travilla; music, Cyril Mockridge; second unit director, Robert D. Webb; assistant director, Horace Hough; special camera effects, Fred Sersen; camera, Harry Jackson; editor, Robert Simpson.

Tyrone Power (Ensign Chuck Palmer); Micheline Presle (Jeanne Martinez); Tom Ewell (Jim Mitchell); Bob Patten (Lovejoy); Tommy Cook (Miguel); Juan Torena (Juan Martinez); Jack Elam (The Speaker); Robert Barrat (General Douglas MacArthur); Carleton Young (Colonel Phillips); Maria Del Val (Señora Martinez, the Aunt); Eddie Infante (Colonel Dimalanta); Chris De Vera, Eduardo Rivera (Japanese Officers); Fred Gonzales and Arling Gonzales (Radio Operators); Captain Slim Martin (Colonel Benson); Miguel Anzures, Erlinda Cortez, Rosa del Rosario and Hati Ruby (Bits).

British release title: **I SHALL RETURN.**

RAWHIDE (Twentieth Century-Fox, 1951), 86 min. (TV title: **DESPERATE SIEGE.**)
Producer, Samuel G. Engel; director, Henry Hathaway; story-screenplay, Dudley Nichols; art directors, Lyle Wheeler and George W. Davis; music, Sol Kaplan; music director, Lionel Newman; camera, Milton Krasner; editor, Robert Simpson.

Tyrone Power (Tom Owens); Susan Hayward (Vinne Holt); Hugh Marlowe (Zimmerman); Dean Jagger (Yancy); Edgar Buchanan (Sam Todd); Jack Elam (Tevis); George Tobias (Gratz); Jeff Corey (Luke Davis); James Millican (Tex Squires); Louis Jean Heydt (Fickert); William Haade (Gil Scott); Milton Corey, Sr. (Dr. Tucker); Ken Tobey (Wingate); Dan White (Gilchrist); Max Terhune (Miner); Robert Adler (Billy Dent); Judy Ann Dunn (Callie); Vincent Neptune (Mr. Hickman); Walter Sande (Flowers); Si Jenks (Old Timer); Dick Curtis (Hawley); Walter Sande (Flowers); Edith Evanson (Mrs. Hickman).

I'LL NEVER FORGET YOU (Twentieth Century-Fox, 1951), C-91 min.
Producer, Sol C. Siegel; director, Roy Baker; based on the play *Berkeley Square* by John L. Balderston; screenplay, Ranald MacDougall; music, William Alwyn; music director, Muir Mathieson; art director, C. P. Norman; sound, Buster Ambler; camera, George Perinal; editor, Alan Obiston.

Tyrone Power (Peter Standish); Ann Blyth (Helen Pettigrew/Martha Forsyth); Michael Rennie (Roger Forsyth); Dennis Price (Tom Pettigrew); Beatrice Campbell (Kate Pettigrew); Kathleen Byron (Duchess of Devonshire); Raymond Huntley (Mr. Throstle); Irene Browne (Lady Anne Pettigrew); Robert Atkins (Dr. Samuel Johnston); Ronald Adam (Ronson); Gibb McLaughlin (Jacob); Hamlyn Benson (Magistrate) Ronald Simpson (Sir Joshua Reynolds); Felix Aylmer (Sir William, the Physician); Diane Hart (Dolly); Tom Gill (Macaroni); Alexander McCrindle (James Boswell); Jill Clifford (Maid); Peter Drury (Policeman); Victor Maddern (Geiger Man); Alec Finter (Throstle's Coachman); Anthony Pelly (Footman); Catherine Carlton (Girl); Richard Carrickford (Bow Street Runner); Rose Howlett (Woman); Arthur Denton (Loonies' Driver).

British title: **THE HOUSE IN THE SQUARE**

DIPLOMATIC COURIER (Twentieth Century-Fox, 1952), 97 min.
Producer, Casey Robinson; director, Henry Hathaway; based on the novel *Sinister Errand* by Peter Cheyney; screenplay, Robinson, Liam O'Brien; music, Sol Kaplan; music director, Lionel Newman; orchestrator, Edward Howell; makeup, Ben Nye; art directors, Lyle Wheeler and John De Cuir; set decorators. Thomas Little and Stuart Reiss; wardrobe, Charles Le Maire; costumes, Eloise Janssen; sound, W. D. Flick and Roger Heman; special camera effects, Ray Kellogg; camera, Lucien Ballard; editor, James B. Clark.

Tyrone Power (Mike Kells); Patricia Neal (Joan Ross); Stephen McNally (Colonel Cagle); Hildegarde Neff (Janine); Karl Malden (Ernie); James Millican (Sam Carew); Stefan Schnabel (Platov); Herbert Berghof (Arnov); Arthur Blake (Max Ralli); Helene Stanley (Airline Stewardess); Michael Ansara (Ivan); Sig Arno (Chef de Train); Alfred Linder (Cherenko) Lee Marvin (M.P. at Trieste); Tyler McVey (Watch Officer); Peter Coe (Zinski); Dabbs Greer (Intelligence Clerk); Carleton Young (Brennan); Charles La Torre (French Ticket Agent); Tom Powers (Cherney); Monique Chantal (French Stewardess); Lumsden Hare (Jacks); Russ Conway (Bill).

PONY SOLDIER (Twentieth Century-Fox, 1952) C-82 min.

Producer, Samuel G. Engel; director, Joseph M. Newman; based on the story by Garnett Weston; screenplay, John C. Higgins; music, Alex North; music director, Lionel Newman; art directors, Lyle Wheeler and Chester Gore; set decorators, Thomas Little and Fred J. Rode; assistant director, Horace Hough; camera, Harry Jackson; editor, John McCafferty.

Tyrone Power (Duncan MacDonald); Cameron Mitchell (Konah); Thomas Gomez (Natayo); Penny Edwards (Emerald); Robert Horton (Jess Calhoun); Anthony Earl Numkena (Comes Running); Adeline DeWalt Reynolds (White Moon); Howard Petrie (Inspector Frazer); Stuart Randall (Standing Bear); Richard Shackleton (Bryan Neeley); James Hayward (Tim Neeley); Muriel Landers (Poks-Ki); Frank De Kova (Gustin); Louis Heminger (Crier); Grady Galloway (Shemawgun); Nipo T. Strongheart (Medicine Man); Carlow Loya (Katatatsi); Anthony Numkena, Sr., John War Eagle, Chief Bright Fire, and Richard Thunder-sky (Indians).

British release title: **MACDONALD OF THE CANADIAN MOUNTIES.**

THE MISSISSIPPI GAMBLER (Universal-International, 1953), C-98½ min.
Producer, Ted Richmond; director, Rudolph Maté; story-screenplay Seton I. Miller; music, Frank Skinner; choreography, Gwen Verdon; camera, Irving Glassberg; editor, Edward Curtiss.

Tyrone Power (Mark Fallon); Piper Laurie (Angelique Duroux); Julia Adams (Ann Conant); John McIntire (Kansas John Polly); John Baer (Laurent Duroux); Paul Cavanagh (Edmund Duroux); Ron Randell (George Elwood); William Reynolds (Pierre); Guy Williams (Andre); Robert Warwick (Paul O. Monet); Ralph Dumke (Caldwell); Hugh Beauont (Kennerly); King Donovan (Spud); Gwen Verdon (Voodoo Dancer); Alan Dexter (Man); Al Wyatt, Dale Van Sickel, Michael Dale, and Bert LeBaron (Henchmen); Dennis Weaver (Julian Conant); Marcel De La Brosse (Maitre d'); Frank Wilcox (Judge); Edward Earle (Duroux Lawyer); Dorothy Bruce and Angela Stevens (Girls); Rolfe Sedan and Saul Martell (Tailors); Maya Van Horn (Mme. Lesanne); Tony Hughes (Teller); Fred Cavens (Emile); George Hamilton (Elwood Butler); David Newell (Helmsman); Eduardo Cansino, Jr., Buddy Roosevelt, and Jon Shepodd (Bits); Anita Ekberg, Renate Hoy, Jackie Loughery, and Jeanne Thompson (Bridesmaids), Paul Bradley (Gambler); Le Roi Antienne (Singer).

KING OF THE KHYBER RIFLES (Twentieth Century-Fox, 1953), C-99 min.
Producer, Frank P. Rosenberg; director, Henry King; based on the novel by Talbot Mundy; screenplay, Ivan Goff and Ben Roberts; art directors, Lyle Wheeler and Maurice Ransford; music, Bernard Herrman; choreography, Asoka; assistant director, Henry Weinberger; camera, Leon Shamroy; editor, Barbara McLean.

Tyrone Power (Captain King); Terry Moore (Susan Maitland); Michael Rennie (Brigadier General Maitland); John Justin (Lieutenant Heath); Guy Rolfe (Karram Khan); Richard Stapley (Lieutenant Baird); Murray Matheson (Major MacAllister); Frank de Kova (Ali Nur); Argentina Brunetti (Lali); Sujata (Native Girl); Frank Lackteen (Ahmed); Gilchrist Stuart (Officer of the Week); Karam Dhaliwal (Pal-Singh); Aly Wassil (Ismael); John Farrow (Corporal

Stuart); Richard Peel (Sergeant Fowler); Aram Katcher (Napur); Gavin Muir (Major Lee); Patrick Whyte (Lieutenant White); David Cota (Singer); Naji Cabbay and Mohinder Bedi (Native Servants).

THE LONG GRAY LINE (Columbia, 1955) C-138 min.

Producer, Robert Arthur; director, John Ford; based on the book *Bringing up the Brass* by Marty Maher with Nardi Reeder Campion; screenplay, Edward Hope; art director, Robert Peterson; set decorator, Frank Tuttle; assistant directors, Wingate Smith and Jack Corrick; music adaptor, George Duning; gowns, Jean Louis; camera, Charles Lawton, Jr.; editor, William Lyon.

Tyrone Power (Marty Maher); Maureen O'Hara (Mary O'Donnell); Robert Francis (James Sundstrom, Jr.); Donald Crisp (Old Martin); Ward Bond (Captain Herman J. Koehler); Betsy Palmer (Kitty Carter); Phil Carey (Charles Dotson); William Leslie (Red Sundstrom); Harry Carey, Jr. (Dwight Eisenhower); Patrick Wayne (Cherub Overton); Sean McClory (Dinny Maher); Peter Graves (Corporal Rudolph Heinz); Milburn Stone (Captain John Pershing); Erin O'Brien Moore (Mrs. Koehler); Walter D. Ehlers (Mike Shannon); Willis Bouchey (Major Thomas); Don Barclay (McDonald); Martin Milner (Jim O'-Carberry); Chuck Courtney (Whitney Larson); Major Philip Kieffer (Superintendent); Norman Van Brocklin (Gus Dorain); Diane DeLaire (Nurse); Donald Murphy (Army Captain); Lisa Davis (Eleanor); Dona Cole (Peggy); Robert Roark (Cadet Pirelli); Robert Ellis (Cadet Short); Ken Curtis (Specialty Bit); Jack Pennick (Recruiting Sergeant); Mimi Doyle (Nun); James Sears (Knute Rockne); Fritz Apking, Mary Benoit, Raoul Freeman, Jack Mower, Jack Ellis, and Leon McLaughlin (Bits).

UNTAMED (Twentieth Century-Fox, 1955) C-111 min.

Producers, Bert E. Friedlob and William A. Bacher; director, Henry King; story, Helga Moray; screenplay, Talbot Jennings, Frank Fenton, and Michael Blankfort; adaptors, Jennings and William A. Bacher; art directors, Lyle Wheeler and Addison Hehr; music, Franz Waxman; orchestrator, Edward B. Powell; camera, Leo Tover; editor, Barbara McLean.

Tyrone Power (Paul Van Riebeck); Susan Hayward (Katie O'Neill); Richard Egan (Kurt); John Justin (Shawn Kildare); Agnes Moorehead (Aggie); Rita Moreno (Julia); Hope Emerson (Maria De Groot); Brad Dexter (Christian); Henry O'Neill (Squire O'Neill); Paul Thompson (Tachaka); Alexander D. Havemann (Jan); Louis . Mercier (Joubert); Emmett Smith (Jantsie); Jack Macy (Simon); Trude Wyler (Madame Joubert); Louis Polliman Brown (Bani); Tina Thompson, Linda Lowell, Bobby Diamond, Gary Diamond, and Brian Corcoran (Maria's Children); Edward Mundy (Grandfather Joubert); John Dodsworth (Captain Richard Eaton); Kevin Corcoran (Young Paul); Eleanor Audley (Lady Vernon); Cecil Weston (Woman); Forest Burns (Commando); Leonard Carey (Hansen); Nya Van Horn and Robin Hughes (Couple at Irish Ball).

THE EDDY DUCHIN STORY (Columbia, 1956), C-123 min.

Producer, Jerry Wald; associate producer, Jonie Taps; director, George Sidney; story, Leo Katcher; screenplay, Samuel Taylor; art director, Walter Holscher; music supervisor-conductor, Morris Stoloff; piano recordings, Carmen Cavallaro; incidental music, George Duning; assistant director, Seymour Friedman; gowns, Jean Louis; camera, Harry Stradling; editors, Viola Lawrence and Jack W. Ogilvie.

Tyrone Power (Eddy Duchin); Kim Novak (Marjorie Oelrichs); Victoria Shaw (Chiquita); James Whitmore (Lou Sherwood); Rex Thompson (Peter Duchin at Age Twelve); Mickey Mags (Peter Duchin at Age Five); Shepperd Strudwick (Mr. Wadsworth); Frieda Inescort (Mrs. Wadsworth); Gloria Holden (Mrs. Duchin); Larry Keating (Leo Reisman); John Mylong (Mr. Duchin); Gregory Gay (Philip); Warren Hsieh (Native Boy); Jack Albertson (Piano Tuner); Carlyle Mitchell (Doctor); Richard Sternberg and Andy Smith (Boys); Lois Kimbrell (Nurse); Oliver Cliff (Man); Ralph Gamble (Mayor Walker); Kirk Alyn and Richard Walsh (Young men); Howard Price (Range Recorder Operator); Richard Crane and Brad Trumbull (Seamen); Arline Anderson (Guest); Jacqueline Blanchard (Girl); Butler Hixson (Butler); Peter Norman (Waiter); Gloria Ann Simpson (Mrs. Rutledge).

ABANDON SHIP! (Columbia, 1957), 100 min. (a.k.a., **SEVEN WAVES AWAY.**)
Executive producer, Ted Richmond; producer, John R. Sloan; director-screenplay, Richand Sale; assistant director, Basil Keys; music, Sir Arthur Bliss; art director, Ray Simm; camera, Wilkie Cooper; editor, Ray Poulton.

Tyrone Power (Alec Holmes); Mai Zetterling (Julie); Lloyd Nolan (Frank Kelly); Stephen Boyd (Will McKinley); Moira Lister (Edith Middleton); James Hayter ("Cookie" Morrow); Marie Lohr (Mrs. Knudsen); Moultrie Kelsall (Daniel Cane); Noel Willman (Aubrey Clark); Gordon Jackson (John Merritt); Clive Morton (Major General Barrington); Laurence Naismith (Captain Darrow); John Stratton ("Sparks" Clary); Victor Maddern (Willy Hawkins); David Langton (John Hayden); Ferdy Mayne (Solly Daniels); Jill Melford (Mrs. Kilgore); Orlando Martins (Sam Holly); Ralph Michael (George Kilgore); David Langton (John Hayden); and: John Gray, Meurig Wyn-Jones, Colin Broadley, Derek Sidney, Clare Austin, and Danny Green.

THE RISING OF THE MOON (Warner Bros., 1957), 81 min.
Producer, Michael Killanin; director, John Ford; based on the story *The Majesty of the Law* by Frank O'Conner and the plays *The Rising of the Moon* by Lady Gregory and *A Minute's Wait* by Michael J. McHugh; screenplay, Frank S. Nugent; art director, Ray Simm; costumes, Jimmy Bourke; music, Eamonn O'Gallagher; camera, Robert Krasker; editor, Michael Gordon.

Tyrone Power (Introduction). *The Majesty of the Law:* Noel Purcell (Dan O'Flaherty); Cyril Cusack (Inspector Michael Dillon); Jack MacGowran (Mickey J.); Eric Gorman and Paul Farrell (Neighbors); John Cowley (The Gombeen Man). *A Minute's Wait:* Jimmy O'Dea (Porter); Tony Quinn (Railroad Station Chief); Paul Farrell (Chauffeur); J. G. Devlin (Guard); Michael Trubshawe (Colonel Frobisher); Anita Sharp Bolster (Mrs. Frobisher); Maureen Potter (Barmaid); Godfrey Quigley (Christy); Harold Goldblatt (Christy's Father); Maureen O'Connell (May Ann McMahon); May Craig (May's Aunt); Michael O'Duffy (Singer); Ann Dalton (Fisherman's Wife). *921:* Dennis O'Dea (Police Sergeant); Eileen Crowe (His Wife); Maurice Good (P. C. O'Grady); Frank Lawton (Major); Edward Lexy (R.Q.M.S.); Donal Donnelly

261

(Sean Curran); Joseph O'Dea (Chief of Guards); Dennis Brenna and David Marlowe (Black and Tan Officers); Doreen Madden and Maureen Cusack (False Nuns); Maureen Delaney (Old Woman); and Members of the Abbey Theatre Company.

THE SUN ALSO RISES (Twentieth Century-Fox, 1957), C-129 min.

Producer, Darryl F. Zanuck, director, Henry King; based on the novel by Ernest Hemingway; screenplay, Peter Viertel; music Hugo Friedhofer; music conductor, Lionel Newman; orchestrator, Maurice de Packh; Spanish music, Alexander Courage; orchestrators, Bernard Mayers and Arthur Morton; guitar music, Vicente Gomez; art directors, Lyle R. Wheeler and Mark-Lee Kirk; set decorators, Walter M. Scott, Paul S. Fox, and Jack Stubbs; executive wardrobe designer, Charles LeMaire; Miss Gardner's wardrobe, Fontana Sisters; make-up, Jack Obringer; assistant director, Stanley Hough; bullfight sequences stage by Miguel Delgado; brass bands director, Ramon Hernandez; sound, Bernard Freericks and Frank Moran; camera, Leo Tover; editor, William Mace.

Tyrone Power (Jake Barnes); Ava Gardner (Lady Brett Ashley); Mel Ferrer (Robert Cohn); Errol Flynn (Mike Campbell); Eddie Albert (Bill Gorton); Gregory Ratoff (Count Mippipopolous); Juliette Greco (Georgette); Marcel Dalio (Zizi); Henry Daniell (Doctor); Bob Cunningham (Harris); Danik Patisson (The Girl); Robert Evans (Pedro Romero); Eduardo Noriega (Mr. Braddock); Jacqueline Evans (Mrs. Braddock); Carlos Muzquiz (Montoya); Rebecca Iturbi (Frances); Carlos David Ortigos (Romero's Manager).

WITNESS FOR THE PROSECUTION (United Artists, 1958), 116 min.

Producer, Arthur Hornblow, Jr.; director, Billy Wilder; based on the play by Agatha Christie; adaptor, Larry Marcus; screenplay, Wilder and Harry Kurnitz; assistant director, Emmett Emerson; art director, Alexander Trauner; music, Matty Malneck; song, Ralph Arthur Roberts and Jack Brooks; music conductor, Ernest Gold; sound, Fred Lau; camera, Russell Harlan; editor, Daniel Mandell.

Tyrone Power (Leonard Vole); Marlene Dietrich (Christine Vole); Charles Laughton (Sir Wilfrid Robarts); Elsa Lanchester (Miss Plimsoll); John Williams (Brogan-Moore); Henry Daniell (Mayhew); Ian Wolfe (Carter); Una O'-Connor (Janet McKenzie); Torin Thatcher (Mr. Meyers) Francis Compton (Judge); Norma Varden (Mrs. French); Philip Tonge (Inspector Hearne); Ruta Lee (Diana); Molly Roden (Miss McHugh); Ottola Nesmith (Miss Johnson); Marjorie Eaton (Miss O'Brien); Pat O'Malley (Shorts Salesman).

6'
175 pounds
Brown hair
Brown eyes
Gemini

Errol Flynn

Like his close friend John Barrymore, Errol Flynn's bigger-than-life personality usually carried over into his motion picture work. Like "the Great Profile," Errol's worst enemy was always himself.

A vivid exploit-maker in private life, Flynn created his own prototype for the screen heroes he portrayed so agilely for the cameras. His success as a screen swashbuckler was always being compared to that of his predecessor, Douglas Fairbanks, Sr. And his cinema feats were always being matched against the head-lines that followed Flynn the explorer, the lover, the sailor, the writer, the wanderer, and the family man.

Describing himself as "a bit of color in a dull world," Errol represented for several generations of filmgoers the epitome of the devil-may-care hero, usually in the guise of a swashbuckler. Unlike many of his actor contemporaries, Flynn never seemed to break free of his screen stereotype. However, he *did* survive the careers of many actors who had a far greater variety of parts.

In his latter years, Errol once lamented that he had become a "male Mae West" in the eyes of America's women, a hounded male sex symbol often challenged to prove his supposed consid-erable virility. Privately he seemed tired of the image which haunted him till his untimely death. Yet publicly he generally fulfilled the pose of the eternal playboy, chasing, catching, and discarding one female after another. Errol Flynn was indeed a complex man.

On Sunday, June 20, 1909, Errol Leslie Thomson Flynn was born in Hobart, the seaport capital of Tasmania. His parents were Theodore Thomas Flynn, a marine biologist, and Marcelle Young Flynn, the daughter of a sea captain alleged to have been descended from Midshipman Young of the *H. M. S. Bounty.* At the time of Errol's birth, Mr. Flynn was on a biological expedition to the South Pole. (Upon his return to the island, he would become a biology lecturer at the University there.)

Tasmania, a state of the Commonwealth of Australia, is over 26,000 square miles in size, and is located near the southeast tip of Australia. In "this strange cold little land to the south of Australia," the boy led an active childhood. He soon developed a dislike for his mother, who, he would claim, never seemed to understand him. But he maintained a deep admiration for his professor father. Because of the senior Flynn's occupation, the child grew to know much about marine life and lore, and he cultivated a lifelong love of the ocean. In fact, in the last days of his life, Errol would say, "the only real wives I have ever had have been my sailing ships." At home, one of the family treasures was a sword that once belonged to Fletcher Christian (of the *Bounty*), and the young boy was captivated by stories of the famous Mutiny which would eventually lead him to make his first theatrical film appearance and be the springboard for worldwide fame.

Perhaps the roots of Errol's restlessness, his passionate but persistently short relationships with women, were developed at this early age in his life because of the strained relationship with his mother. At seven he first ran away from home, after being caught in a compromising position, the first of many, with a neighbor's daughter. His mother was furious, and, although he was found three days later, he already had begun to develop the deep desire to remove himself from maternal influence.

While still an adolescent, Errol moved with his parents to England. His father, who had attained a great deal of recognition in the field of marine biology, had been invited there for a lecture tour of several universities. The boy was enrolled at South West London College, but at the age of fifteen he was expelled. He was also dismissed from a second British school, but the family relocated to Sydney, Australia, where Errol was enrolled at the Northshore School. Already restless and opposed to any form of authority, the youth did not take well to the cerebral side of education, although he excelled in boxing and swimming.

By this time there was another child in the Flynn family, Rosemary,

264

who accompanied her parents on another English lecture tour while Errol remained in Sydney. He was expelled from Northshore and at age seventeen was forced to seek employment on his own. He worked as an office boy, but was fired for raiding the petty cash box to bet on horses. Disgusted with life in Sydney, he headed for New Guinea to seek his fortune, and perhaps his fame.

The year was 1926 and Errol was admitted to government service as a cadet in New Guinea and trained as a constable. The job was of little interest to him, and he spent more of his time in pursuit of the comely local girls than in his work, resulting in his dismissal from government service and a reputation as an incompetent civil service worker. He then worked as an overseer of a copra plantation for forty pounds a month. The job of supervising the daily routine of 120 native workers was difficult, and the main satisfaction from the job came as a result of saving a young girl's life after a salt raid. She gratefully became his servant and his mistress.

Next, the adventurous Errol teamed with a pal named Dusty Miller in the joint ownership of a small schooner, the *Maski,* which hauled freight and sometimes passengers. Not long after starting out on this adventure, he was introduced to an American named Joel Swartz, who hired him as a guide for the filming of a documentary in New Guinea. The film was designed to be a travelog of the island, with special interest centering on the headhunters of the Sepik River, which Flynn called "a human graveyard." Near the voyage's end, Swartz told Flynn the filming was not altogether for theatrical purposes, as both the United States and Britain required films of the river's mouth in case trouble ever developed with Japan.

During the arduous trek, Errol noticed the cameraman occasionally moved away from focusing on the scenery to include him on celluloid as captain of the *Maski.* The documentary was eventually issued in America in 1932 as *Dr. H. Erbin's New Guinea Expedition.* Errol had quite a bit of footage in the finished product, which was to lead to his first feature film offer.

At the end of the assignment, early in 1929, Errol returned to the copra plantation to find he had long since been permanently relieved of his official duties. His mistress was returned to her family, now a rich girl by native standards. Errol was now intent on "making some money," his only real ambition at this time—the trip up the Sepik River had whetted his gold fever. He sold out his interest in the *Maski* to Miller and booked passage on a steamer bound for the east coast of the New Guinea mainland. "I realized there was no good reason for being in New Guinea other than to strike it rich," he later said.

With a group of native boys Flynn headed inland for a week's march to the famed Edey Creek gold fields. The journey was a rough one, and Errol found existence even tougher once he reached the mineral deposits. Unequipped to endure the strain of the climate and the competitive life of a gold hunter, he soon returned to the coast, a poorer but wiser young man.

Back on the coast he entered into partnership with an elderly schooner captain, Ed Bowen, who owned a vessel called the *Matupi.* The team decided to search for gold along the New Guinea coast or perhaps to trail the birds of paradise for their luxurious feathers. Instead the duo ended up "recruiting" natives who were, in turn, sold for plantation work. Errol Flynn, the slave trader, is one segment of his steamy life that everyone who knew of it would prefer to forget in later years.

While involved in his jungle "recruiting," Flynn's party was attacked by a group of natives and he was forced to kill one of them in self defense. The incident resulted in his arrest and he was tried for murder. He claimed self defense and was later acquitted.

Following the trial escapade, Errol went into partnership with a woman who owned a stake in land at Edey Creek, but before he could commence panning the claim, he came down with the "black pox," or gonorrhea. At first he thought it was recurring malaria, an ailment which would plague him all his adult life. However, after a series of ineffective treatments, he went to Sydney for a prolonged cure and faced near-starvation. To stave off complete impoverishment, he accepted a job as a bottle sniffer, which had him whiffing bottles for contents before they were reused. While at this profession he learned his initial gold claim at Edey Creek was between two strikes and he was able to sell the claim for five thousand dollars. The sale represented what was to become a typical aspect of Flynn's see-sawing life: down-and-out one day, rich the next.

With four thousand dollars of the money from the sale, he purchased a yacht, the *Sirocco,* and after paying off several debts, he and three seafaring friends set out on a three-thousand-mile trip to the mainland of New Guinea. The trip required several months and proved particularly difficult when navigating the waters of the Great Barrier Reef. The voyage occurred in 1930 and seven years later Errol was to make this adventure the theme of his first book, *Beam Ends.*

After the trip, mercurial Flynn sold the *Sirocco* and with the money he started a tobacco plantation. The venture proved to be interesting, but the bulk of work on all levels was done by cheaply paid natives, leaving owner Flynn with little to do. "I was alone, too much alone, the only white man for miles around, and sometimes I got tired of reading books and was restless." He took care of this situation by buying the daughter of his foreman.

Besides filling his idle hours with his new mistress (she was somewhere over the age of twelve), Errol also began to write a series of articles which he sold to the *Sydney Bulletin.* The freelance pieces dealt with life in New Guinea and showed that the young Flynn had a knack for story-telling.

Joel Swartz came back into Flynn's life with an intriguing offer for him to appear in a motion picture about the *H.M.S. Bounty*. Ironically, Flynn was scheduled to portray Fletcher Christian,[1] who had been with his ancestor, Midshipman Young. Leaving the plantation in the hands of his boss boy, Flynn took a ship to Tahiti where he worked in the film *In the Wake of the Bounty* (Expeditionary Films, 1933) for three weeks. Most of the footage was shot at Maatavi Bay, where 140 years earlier Captain Bligh had anchored the *Bounty*.

"The experience came swiftly and it seemed to go swiftly," Flynn later recalled. "But it was different than anything I had ever done before: so much at variance with digging earth, selling Kanakas [natives] the idea of becoming workers, carrying guns for real in the gold fields. I had touched on something that the world called an art form and it affected me deeply."

Following his initial feature film experience, Errol returned briefly to his tobacco plantation, and then, finding himself still bored with the occupation, he took a post as an overseer at a copra plantation at Laloki. Here he continued his writing and he developed a strong interest in law and literature, reading as many books as he could unearth. Later in life, he recalled that at the time to be a lawyer appealed "to me more than anything in life."

In a combined business venture and publicity stunt, Flynn returned to Sydney with a company of Papuans in an effort to make stock flotations in tobacco. By the time he maneuvered the Papuans back on board ship for New Guinea, he realized his venture into big business was a flop. A new turn took place, however, when his film, *In the Wake of the Bounty*, opened in Sydney and Errol was requested to make a personal appearance.[2]

Through Joel Swartz,[3] Flynn had obtained the part of Fletcher Christian in the film after producer-director-scenarist Charles Chauvel

---

[1]Clark Gable would play Mr. Christian in *Mutiny on the Bounty* (MGM, 1935), with Marlon Brando interpreting the part in Metro's 1962 version. In 1956, Twentieth Century-Fox released *Women of Pitcairn Island*, with James Craig, Lynn Bari, and Arleen Whelan, a film detailing how the widows and children of survivors of the *Bounty* existed on a desolate island.

[2]In his autobiography (*My Wicked, Wicked Ways*, G. P. Putnam's Sons, 1959) Errol recalls: "The manager made an announcement before the picture was flashed on the screen. He said that Errol Flynn, who would appear as Fletcher Christian in the picture, was here in person. I was decked out in a bizarre out-of-date British uniform. There were only two actors' wigs in Sydney they could find and they stuck one of them on me. It was parted in the middle and it came down in a pigtail in the back, blonde, tied with a bow...."

[3]In *The Films of Errol Flynn* (Citadel Press, 1969), authors Tony Thomas, Rudy Behlmer, and Clifford McCarty suggest that Joel Swartz did not really exist. They credit Dr. Herman F. Erben with offering Flynn the job of leading his expedition on the Sepik River. They reason it was Flynn who confused Swartz, a character in his book *Show-*

267

saw him in the Erben documentary. Topped off with an ill-fitting blonde wig, Flynn had little to do in the catch-as-catch-can film in which he was second-billed to Mayne Lynton's Captain Bligh. Most of Errol's scenes were with Lynton and *Variety* reported the performances were, at best, "rather patchy." The feature was a mixture of melodrama and documentary style, with scenes of Pitcairn Island and Tahiti and a soundtrack of sea chanties and Hawaiian music. (In 1935, MGM would purchase the rights to this film when the studio was producing its *Mutiny on the Bounty.* Footage from the Flynn entry was used for two promotional short subjects called *Primitive Pitcairn* and *Pitcairn Island Today,* which the studio issued in 1935.)

With no new film offers, Errol worked on a sheep ranch but was removed from the post after being caught in a compromising situation with the "farmer's daughter." Prior to that, the devil-may-care Flynn had stolen diamonds from an older woman with whom he had an affair, but then found he could not sell the "hot" stones. After a trek across a desert to escape his stormy way of life, this typically lucky guy learned that he had won a gold claim in New Guinea.

But the gold fields proved no more lucrative this time for Errol than before, and he was soon back "recruiting" natives. Things became so risky for Flynn, however, that he decided to call it quits with New Guinea and board a ship for Manila (he was still in possession of his cache of stolen diamonds.) On the trip he met a Dr. Gert H. Koets, who would become a lifelong friend. After a stay in the Philippines, the duo headed for Hong Kong and Macao, the latter known as Portugese China. It was while on board the Macao-bound boat that Errol first tried opium, which a girl he picked up insisted would stimulate their sexual encounter. In his autobiography, Errol said, "Today I'm told that the effect of opiates removes sexual desire in the man in inverse ratio to the female, who becomes more excited. Dr. Flynn can tell you that such is not the case. I made love to Ting Ling [the girl in question] in ways and manners that I would never believe myself capable of. Next day I put it all down to a dream."

After this same native girl left him, Flynn proceeded to Hong Kong with Koets where, for lack of funds, he joined the Royal Hong Kong Volunteers, a group organized to aid Britain and China against the Japanese. Errol fully appreciated the romantic image of a soldier, but he and Koets soon grew weary of digging ditches, one of the menial tasks the service offered them, instead of fighting. They both deserted.

Next, the friends headed for Ceylon, and then on to India. A trip on a French boat to the East Coast of Africa ended rather abruptly when Flynn slugged the aide of an important French official in Djibouti, the

---

down (Sheridan Press, 1946), with Erben. In further support of their thesis, they add that Swartz was not listed in the production credits of *In the Wake of the Bounty* and that Charles Chauvel was solely responsible for hiring Flynn for the picture.

capital of French Somaliland. Errol and Dr. Koets went to Ethiopia, up through the Suez Canal, crossed the Mediterranean, and then landed at last in Marseilles. After having traveled more than eight months together, Flynn and Koets parted, although they would be reunited when Errol became a Hollywood star.

From Marseilles, Errol went to England to join his family, whom he had not seen for several years. His father was then a lecturer at Heidelberg University and was incapable of giving much moral or practical support to his adventurous son. Thus, a financially broke Errol spent weeks in London trying to find a job. Finally, in a burst of desperation and imagination, he spent twenty pounds for an advertisement in local papers which stated he was a "smash hit" and a "genuine hit" in four films, all of which, except *In the Wake of the Bounty,* were fakes. But the bluff did not lead to an actual show business job. Later he landed an acting job with the Northampton Repertory Company. While in this theatre group, Errol would hone and develop his natural flamboyance into a workable acting style.

During the eighteen months he spent in Northampton, Errol played a wide variety of parts, from Shakespearean roles to Bulldog Drummond. He even wrote a play entitled *Cold Rice,* a satire on imperial British India. That Errol had been initially hired by the Northampton group because of his extraordinary handsomeness and his alleged ability to play cricket (the group's manager was a sports fiend who fancied

In 1934

269

himself a cricket coach) was one thing. That he managed to stay on in the theatre for a year and a half is an indication that even in this apprenticeship period he radiated an aura of excitement about his person which compensated for his inexperience.

After leaving the Northampton company, Errol appeared in two productions at the Stratford-on-Avon Festival, presentations chosen to play London's West End. Both shows flopped but, since he still had a strong desire to break into films, Errol saw to it that several casting agents for the studios saw him onstage. Two of the film industry men who "spotted" Errol were Irving Asher, then head of Warner Bros. Pictures in England, and his studio manager, Doc Solomon. They offered him a part in *Murder at Monte Carlo* (First National, 1935).

Directed by veteran Ralph Ince, *Murder at Monte Carlo* found a very self-conscious Errol second-billed to popular leading lady Eve Gray in a journeyman story by Tom Van Dycke. The seventy-minute programmer was nothing more than a standard murder mystery with Errol as a newspaper writer who travels to Monte Carlo to unfold an exposé of the roulette system, only to find the system's inventor (Paul Graetz) has been murdered. Miss Gray, in a part that would have fitted Joan Blondell, played Errol's girlfriend, who, coincidentally is also a news reporter for a rival paper. Of this quota production, the British *Kinematograph Weekly* reported that Errol, now in his third film, contributed "a high pressure portrayal."

Although *Murder at Monte Carlo* was nothing more than a quickie B production, the film was brought to the attention of Jack L. Warner, the mogul in charge of the overall Warner Bros. operations. Warner and/or his executive assistants were smart enough to sense a screen-potentiality in Flynn and signed him on to a six-month contract at $150 a week. The English-based Australian was ordered to Hollywood.

On board the ship *The Paris* to New York, Errol met Merle Oberon, Louis Hayward, Russian princess Naomi Tiarovitch, and the French star, Lili Damita,[4] who later was to become his wife. Arriving in Holly-

[4]Born Liliane-Marie-Madeleine Carré in Bordeaux on July 19, 1901. She was educated in private schools in Vienna and Berlin before the war, and at sixteen appeared in revues. When she was twenty she entered a magazine contest as Damita del Rojo and as a result was asked to appear in several films. (She was billed as Lily Deslys in these productions.) In 1923 she made her first screen appearance under the name of Lili Damita in *La Voyante*. In 1926 she followed Mistinguett as the star of the Casino de Paris, with which company she later went on tour to Germany. There she left the company to become a film star for Deutscher Film Gesellschaft, appearing first in Michael Curtiz' *Das Spielzeug Von Paris* (1926). She was brought to Hollywood by Goldwyn to replace Banky as Ronald Colman's new co-star, and appeared with him in *The Rescue* (United Artists, 1928). One of her more memorable film appearances was in *The Cock-eyed World* (Fox, 1929), the follow-up to *What Price Glory*. By the early 1930s her RKO features were behind her, and Lupe Velez, the "Mexican Spitfire" had demonstrated that she was the more volatile, enduring screen figure of the two. In 1935, Lili was returning to Hollywood to appear in *The Frisco Kid* at Warner Bros. (Many at the time agreed that Lili had not looked so well on screen in a long time, and she might have had a whole new career, had not her private life taken a new turn.)

wood early in 1935 he posed for publicity pictures at the studio but did little else except meet a number of other industry newcomers who also were not working, including Jerry Wald. Through a friend of Wald's, director Michael Curtiz, Errol landed the strictly perfunctory part of a corpse in *The Case of the Curious Bride* (First National, 1935). "Some people claim it was my best role," the actor later wrote.

Actually, Errol was seen but not heard in the film, as he was on-camera both as the corpse and, later, in a brief one-minute flashback, he appears as the about-to-be murdered man. Curtiz directed the film, the second of four Perry Mason features which Warners ground out from Erle Stanley Gardner novels about the larger-than-life courtroom lawyer. Warren William, then still a top Warner Bros. star, played the articulate advocate and Margaret Lindsay was on tap as an old friend of Mason's whom he helps after she is accused of murdering her first husband (Flynn). During one scene, cinema fledgling Errol had to slap Miss Lindsay and, so engrossed was he in playing the business realistically, he accidentally knocked her out.

Although it was discussed whether to cast Errol for a part in *A Midsummer Night's Dream* (Warner Bros., 1935), Errol next landed a part in a Robert Florey-directed cheapie, *Don't Bet on Blondes* (Warner Bros., 1935) which also starred urbane Warren William. Given eighth billing, Flynn did a turn as a society playboy who has set his mark on Claire Dodd, the daughter of a wealthy Kentucky colonel (Guy Kib-

With Margaret Lindsay in *The Case of the Curious Bride* (1935)

271

bee). Errol, of course, loses out in the love contest to successful gambler William.

Despite two small parts in two quickly forgotten films, Errol's personal life was a rousing success. Always quick to adapt to a new social scene, Errol found himself soon ensconced as a firm part of the Hollywood night life. Many people who had come to know chameleon-like Errol during his short stay in Hollywood were more than surprised when he began dating the fiery Miss Damita in earnest. The couple (he was twenty-six, she was nearly thirty-four) were married in June, 1935, which many of Errol's critics would insist over the year proved how mercenary Flynn was in striving for his screen success. Because rambunctious, radiant Lili was such a close friend of Michael Curtiz, and, in turn, of the Warner Bros. hierarchy, a good word from her could help enormously in advancing Errol's screen career in a big hurry. Thus, when a bitter Errol later insisted that it was Damita who badgered him into the nuptials, the only sensible conclusion to be reached is that at this point in life, career did come first.

As has now been frequently documented, Warner Bros. was set to star Robert Donat and Jean Muir in *Captain Blood* (First National, 1935), from the novel by Rafael Sabatini, which Vitagraph had filmed in 1923 with J. Warren Kerrigan and Jean Paige. Britisher Donat backed out of the project at the last minute and Jack Warner took a gamble on starring an unknown in the part. He finally decided on

With Lili Damita Flynn at their Hollywood home (June, 1935)

272

With Olivia de Havilland in *Captain Blood* (1935)

contractee Errol after seeing both his brief work for Warners and a test specially made for the coveted part. Warner also decided to co-star nineteen-year-old Olivia de Havilland in the part originally designated for Miss Muir. However, the supporting cast was filled with tried-and-true veterans, including Basil Rathbone, Lionel Atwill, Guy Kibbee, Ross Alexander, and Henry Stephenson.

During the filming of the Michael Curtiz-directed *Captain Blood*, Flynn suffered a recurrence of malaria but nonetheless, he was accused of drinking on the set, a charge which greatly upset the still moderate-drinking actor. He was paid three hundred dollars a week for his leading part but later said, "I could have used a little more. Lili was expensive."

Captain Blood was Errol's second feature with "hardboiled" Curtiz, who would direct ten other of his starring vehicles. The exciting plot has Peter Blood (Flynn), a doctor, treating a rebel during the reign of England's James II and being convicted of treason and sent to Jamaica as a slave. There he treats the governor's gout and earns privileges and meets and falls in love with a lovely but high-spirited daughter (de Havilland) of a plantation owner (Atwill). After the Spanish attack the island, Blood and several slaves escape and become free-booting pirates, raiding the Caribbean. Blood has an exciting duel with a French pirate (Rathbone) and wins de Havilland's love. Later, James II is dethroned by William of Orange and Blood receives a naval commission and defeats two French galleys. For his extraordinary heroism he is appointed governor of Jamaica and is now free to wed de Havilland. All this within 119 minutes.

Released[5] some six weeks after MGM's *Mutiny on the Bounty,* in December, 1935, *Captain Blood* was an immediate success. The film was to stereotype Errol Flynn in the one type of role for which the moviegoing public would always prefer and remember him. For the next two decades, with some variation, he would play the hero swashbuckler with shining smile and swinging sword. The duel scene in the film between Rathbone and Flynn would be the first of many for the actor (although his coach Fred Cavens often doubled oncamera for him) and he proved to be good with the blade. The very professional and meticulous Rathbone commented in later years, however, that he did not like to duel with Errol because the latter was so careless.

Captain Blood also provided another first—beyond being the first of seven Flynn films that Erich Wolfgang Korngold would score—it was the first of many of Errol's co-starring features with Miss de Havilland. Thirty-seven years later she admitted she fell in love with him during the shooting. "Yes, I loved him and it lasted three years and I didn't tell him," she recently said. (Interestingly, a discreet sexual decorum between Flynn and de Havilland always existed in their joint films; whenever his character would become too overly familiar, she would put him in his place promptly with a searing look or a slap to his face.)

Apparently, Warners did not immediately recognize Flynn's boxoffice potential, for he was permitted to appear in an MGM short called *Pirate Party on Catalina Isle,* released early in 1936.[6] It was Errol's sole appearance onscreen with Lili Damita and the two-reeler featured a number of MGM personalities, as well as Cary Grant and Charles "Buddy" Rogers and his band doing the Al Jolson song, "Avalon." The short would be Flynn's only film away from the Warner Bros.' lot until 1945 when he was in a Columbia "Screen Snapshots" short. (His first feature away from the Burbank lot did not come until 1949 when he was in MGM's *That Forsyte Woman.*)

The *New York Times* had tagged Errol "a spirited and criminally good-looking Australian" (for *Captain Blood*), but the studio thought it

---

[5]In 1951 Warner Bros. would re-issue *Captain Blood,* but by that time it had taken a back seat in filmgoers' esteem to other Flynn swashbucklers, including *The Adventures of Robin Hood* and *The Sea Hawk.*

[6]An ironic fact, since Curtiz carefully structured *Captain Blood* to showcase Errol. As George Morris points out in *Errol Flynn* (Pyramid, 1975), "When Flynn and his fellow slaves from Port Royal take over the Spanish pirate ship, the unfurling of the sails is accompanied by the men's singing lustily as the anchor of the vessel is lifted. Flynn strides boldly around the deck, giving the necessary orders, and in an extraordinary series of close-ups Curtiz presents us with the emergence of a star."

more advantageous to publicize their new find as a free-spirited Irishman, probably thinking that such a heritage would account for his proclivities for drinking and wenching. As Errol's distinguished, reserved father would later admit, "[Errol] thought all publicity was good publicity. Sometimes we protested but it was no good. He would laugh it off." Thus, with little encouragement from the studio publicity department, Errol would elaborate tall tales for the edification of the willing press and the gullible public. Sometimes, when he would get carried away, he would actually recount true, but astounding adventures from his past, feats which were often ignored by incredulous newsmen. In Belfast, Errol's parents, who were now residing there, were asked about their suddenly famous son. On one occasion the rather jealous Mrs. Flynn insisted, "He was a nasty little boy." Errol's wife Lili, who generally maintained a veil of secrecy about their stormy marriage (unlike her counterpart Lupe Velez who delighted in relating minute details of domestic skirmishes with hubby Johnny Weissmuller), did become candid (or so it seemed) on one occasion when she "revealed" in a magazine piece, "[Errol] loves to annoy people in childish ways. He knows their weak points and plays on them. He is a liar, too. You never know when he is telling the truth." To re-emphasize this particular point, she added, "He lies for the fun of it."

While Lili temporarily abandoned her blissless home life for film-making in France (*L'Escadrille de la Chance* [1936]), Warner Bros. had decided that Errol was indeed the new Douglas Fairbanks, Sr., and that he could well be the Burbank studio's answer to MGM's Clark Gable. If, due to health and other reasons, Robert Donat insisted on remaining in England, then Jack Warner would push Errol into the dashing image that the company had been preparing for the well-established Mr. Donat. The Warners studio already had a full complement of tough-guy stars (James Cagney, Paul Muni, Edward G. Robinson, and, soon, Humphrey Bogart), such genteel leading men as George Brent and Ian Hunter, a fast-talking hero (Pat O'Brien), a resident crooner (Dick Powell) and, to round out the stable, two bucolic "young" leads (Dick Foran and Wayne Morris) would soon be added to the roster. *If* the swashbuckling vogue could become a long-enduring screen cycle—and Warners now intended it to be so—then there was every reason (and only little competition) for Errol to become the latest progenitor of the costumed, derring-do school of screen adventure. After all, how long could aging ex-Samuel Goldwyn star Ronald Colman continue turning out exhausting adventure films like *A Tale of Two Cities* (MGM, 1935) or *Clive of India* (United Artists, 1935)?

Despite its enormous million-dollar-plus outlay on *Captain Blood*

Warner Bros. had economized wherever possible on the budget.[7] Now, the studio decided to spare no expense in making *The Charge of the Light Brigade* (Warner Bros., 1936). Flynn would call this Michael Curtiz-directed vehicle "the toughest picture I ever made." The star would claim that the director had little regard for his cast and "he didn't care if you hated him." Often during the location filming,[8] the cast had to spend hours waiting in the freezing cold sitting on horses for scenes to be shot (and reshot). Flynn said, "As for the treatment of horses in this film, I myself complained to the Society for the Prevention of Cruelty to Animals." Flynn also performed many of his own stunts, in this his second starring role, which was "stupid of me and stupid of Warner Brothers to let me do it."

Released in October, 1936, nearly one year after *Captain Blood*'s debut, the film reunited swaggering Errol with leading lady Olivia de Havilland and featured Patric Knowles[9] as Flynn's younger brother. Unlike the later *The Charge of the Light Brigade* (United Artists, 1962), which was more historically precise, politically bitter, and restrictively enjoyable, the Warners' edition was a free-wheeling adaptation[10] of the title and theme of Alfred Lord Tennyson's poem about the Crimean War. Everything in the Michel Jacoby-Rowland Leigh screenplay was aimed at building to the climax of the film, the final charge of the Cavalry Lancers ("into the Valley of Death rode the 600"), where the British horsemen ride against an army of 25,000 Russians allied with the villainous Surat Khan. This spectacular climax was directed by second unit director, B. Reeves "Breezy" Eason, and it is one of the best examples of such battle scenes in the annals of the cinema, not to mention that it becomes the rousing highpoint of the film.

In *Warner Brothers Presents* (Arlington House, 1972) Ted Sennett calls the spectacle a "lavish and robust adventure film, it was squarely in the tradition of Hollywood's Anglophile tradition of the thirties," and it "was an unabashed testimonial to the courage and tenacity of

---

[7]Use of miniatures, footage extracts from the 1923 versions, and screen titles to indicate transitions never shown had been some of their budget-cutting devices.

[8]The British fort was built at Agoura, California, with several exteriors shot at Lone Pine, and the leopard hunt lensed at Lake Sherwood. Other locales were Chatsworth and Sonora.

[9]A pal of Flynn's from their British First National-Warner Bros. days, it is alleged that it was Errol who suggested the somewhat similarly structured Knowles for the sibling role in *The Charge,* the first of four films in which they would play together.

[10]In the 1850s, Surat Khan (C. Henry Gordon) loses an annuity from England, leading the India chieftain to enter into an alliance with Russia, the latter country having difficulties in the Balkans. The story then focuses on a young major (Errol) with the British 27th Cavalry who is sent to Arabia to purchase horses for the British. In Calcutta he stops to see his fiancée (de Havilland) and his brother (Knowles) who have secretly fallen in love. Later Khan destroys the 27th Cavalry fort, but the major and his fiancée escape and thereafter the Cavalry Lancers are transferred to the Crimea. In the climactic charge, the major throws a lance, killing Khan before the hero is himself killed, leaving the way open for his fiancée and brother to wed.

With Olivia de Havilland in *The Charge of the Light Brigade* (1936)

British soldiers in far-flung outposts." Made at a cost of $1.2 million, the film's cinematographer, Tony Gaudio, received an Academy Award for his lush photography.[11]

The Charge solidified Flynn's reputation for being able convincingly to combine heroics and romance with the proper dash of stiff-upper lip, charm, and, most importantly, dash and aplomb. With Miss de Havilland as his obliging lady fair, Errol commanded a focal point in the 116 minutes of sweeping action, but he was not the chief facet of attention in the scope of this tumultuous adventure yarn. Although the studio frequently would return Errol to the swashbuckler mode in which he fitted so neatly, never again would the impact of a Warner Bros. costume film starring Flynn outshine the star himself.

Since his sudden rise to commercial status with *Captain Blood*, Flynn decided to live life on a grander scale. He bought a ketch, took up tennis (at which he became very good), and allowed himself to fall into fierce drinking habits (at which he was even better than he was at athletics). His life with tempestuous, career-despairing Lili was hellish to say the least. Most of the time in public and for the press they pretended a form of marital bliss, but behind the scenes were spats, even brawls, of the calibre that would make the Humphrey Bogart-Mayo Methot union so "memorable."

Early in 1937 Flynn's close friend Koets reappeared in his life. The two adventurous souls headed East followed by an angered Lili. Along the way Errol contracted "a minor species of gonorrhea" which Koets, a doctor, was "sure he could cure . . . swiftly." The duo planned to take a first hand look at the Spanish Civil War and Errol wangled a foreign correspondent's pass for the occasion. Still a British subject, he had little difficulty in leaving America and being admitted on the Continent. Before Spain, however, he was reunited with Lili Damita in Paris and he later recounted how he was beaten up by several lesbians in a Paris bordello.

In his autobiography, Flynn spends some time recounting his exciting adventures in the Spanish Civil War, where he sided with the Loyalists. Apparently, his only provable statements were the ones about his making headlines when it was thought he had been killed in the conflict. In her book, *The Garden of Allah* (Crown, 1970), columnist Sheilah Graham claims Ernest Hemingway gave little currency to Errol's colorful interviews about his involvement in the war. "But when it came time to collect the money [for the Loyalists' cause], Errol disappeared. He had pressing business in the toilet," she wrote. "Actually, Hemingway said, Errol had traveled only a few yards over the

---

[11]Frequent comparisons would be made between this India "desert" film and such other more out-and-out studies of British imperialism as *The Lives of a Bengal Lancer* (Paramount, 1935) *Gunga Din* (RKO, 1939), and the second of three versions of *Beau Geste* (Paramount, 1939).

Spanish border, then prudently turned back. He found it safer to limit his fighting to his films."

Upon his return from Spain, Errol was reunited with his wife and then he rewarded himself by purchasing a sailboat and sailing down the Atlantic Coast to the West Indies. In Nassau he took up skin diving, and *Life* Magazine photographers snapped pictures which appeared in the May 23, 1938 issue with the heading, "Errol Flynn: Glamour Boy."

Back in Hollywood, the brothers Warner rushed their new star through a series of movies aimed at taking advantage of his marquee lustre. Whether big or little films, they served to keep the new face in the limelight, and made Errol one of the biggest names at that studio.

Errol had been urging his employers to give him a chance at a more dramatic role, and consequently, he was thrust into *Green Light* (First National, 1937), based on the novel by Lloyd C. Douglas.[12] As directed by Frank Borzage, who was best known for turning out such romantic creations as *Seventh Heaven* (Fox, 1927) or *A Farewell to Arms* (Paramount, 1932), *Green Light* was a maudlin confection. It "showcased" Errol as a noble young doctor in love with a lovely young woman (Anita Louise). In the course of the celluloid soap opera she temporarily rejects him when she believes he was responsible for her mother's death (it was actually the fault of colleague Henry O'Neill). However, when Errol contracts a near fatal case of spotted fever in an experiment to prove the success of his new vaccine, Louise returns to the self-sacrificing physician. Any similarities between this unsubtle hogwash and such refined predecessors as *Arrowsmith* (United Artists, 1931)—or even the less pretentious remake of *Arrowsmith, I Married a Doctor* (First National, 1936)—were intentional. Although Errol seemed on occasion about to burst out in a smirk at the grand bits of nobility in *Green Light,* audiences of the day were perfectly willing to accept the filmfare on its given level. Flynn would go through his paces as idealist Dr. Newell Paige once again when, on January 21, 1938, he was heard on "Lux Radio Theatre" in an adaptation of *Green Light.*[13] Olivia de Havilland was his co-star on that occasion.

Jack L. Warner certainly had had too much experience dealing with temperamental stars not to be aware that self-indulgent Flynn might not only become his own worst enemy, but also a risky investment for the studio. Thus, before launching Errol as the lead of *The Prince and*

[12]The studio would turn out a more efficient adaptation of a Douglas novel with *White Banners* (1938), starring Fay Bainter, Claude Rains, and Jackie Cooper.

[13]Errol's other guest stints on "Lux Radio Theatre" included: *Captain Blood* (February 22, 1937) with Olivia de Havilland; *British Agent* (July 7, 1937) with Frances Farmer; *These Three* (December 6, 1937) with Barbara Stanwyck and Mary Astor; *The Perfect Specimen* (February 2, 1937) with Joan Blondell; *The Lives of a Bengal Lancer* (April 10, 1939) with Brian Aherne, C. Aubrey Smith and Jackie Cooper, *Trade Winds* (March 4, 1940) with Joan Bennett, Mary Astor and Ralph Bellamy, and *Virginia City* (March 26, 1941) with Martha Scott.

the Pauper (First National, 1937), the studio made extensive tests with Patric Knowles in the part of Miles Hendon. This adaptation of the Mark Twain novel would have been a suitable occasion to try out someone like Knowles in such a swashbuckling venture, because the hero's part was actually secondary to two other facets of the film: First was the gimmick of having the Mauch twins portray Prince Edward (Bobby) of England and his look-alike Tom Canty (Billy), the pauper son of a sadistic ruffian (Barton MacLane) who exchanges places with the prince; second was a lavish coronation scene to cap this costumed piece.[14] The elaboration was planned by the studio to take advantage of the publicity surrounding the coronation of England's King George VI.

However, the Warner hierarchy decided that Knowles was no Errol Flynn, nor even on a par with Twentieth Century-Fox's Tyrone Power, who had made such a good showing in the swashbuckling genre with *Lloyds of London* (1937).[15]

It hardly could be denied that *The Prince and the Pauper* was a resolute if overlong costume piece filled with pomp and circumstance and blessed with a rousing Erich Wolfgang Korngold score. Moreover, there was Claude Rains as the devious Earl of Hertford, as well as Montagu Love in a courtly performance as King Henry VIII and Barton MacLane as the vile John Ganty. Even the Mauch twins, who would enjoy a short vogue at Warner Bros. and with the moviegoing public, met with critical approval from hard-to-please Frank S. Nugent (*New York Times*). "Bobby and Billy justify their twinship completely, not merely by investing the Twain legend of mistaken royal identity with a pleasing degree of credibility, but by playing their roles with such straightforwardness and naturalness that the picture becomes one of the most likable entertainments of the year." However, Errol's performance smacked of an indifference on his part and that of the scripter (who gave him relatively little to do). Worst of all fates, romantic Errol had no lovely heroine with whom to romance within the two-hour film, making his oncamera presence somewhat superfluous. However, on the plus side, he did have a sword-fight scene with Alan Hale, the portly character actor who became his good friend and who appeared, usually as his staunch pal, in another eleven features with Flynn. Hale, a notorious scene stealer, rarely attempted any acting tricks with his buddy, a courtesy he showed to few other performers.

In June, 1937, *Another Dawn* (Warner Bros.) was issued, in which Errol took second billing to Kay Francis. Revamping the set from *The*

---

[14]David O. Selznick's *The Prisoner of Zenda* (United Artists, 1937), starring Ronald Colman and Madeleine Carroll, would also include a well-mounted coronation scene. Anglophilia was still the cultural thing in America of the 1930s.

[15]Knowles would later admit, "Errol knew he had no worries about my taking over from him, and the whole thing became a gag between us."

With Bobby Mauch, Barton MacLane, and Tom Wilson in *The Prince and the Pauper* (1937)

With Ian Hunter and Kay Francis in *Another Dawn* (1937)

Charge of the Light Brigade director William Dieterle did his best with this talky melodrama which had Errol in the role of Captain Denny Roark, a moral British army officer in a Sahara desert outpost. Roark falls in love with the wife (Francis) of his commanding officer, Colonel Wister (Ian Hunter). The dashing young man reminds her of her lover, who was killed in the First World War, and she accepts the Captain's love. Colonel Wister surprisingly understands the situation, and the trio, joined on occasion by Roark's sister Grace (a finely etched performance by Frieda Inescort), try to talk out the situation, which, as one would expect, is useless. In a gallant move, the Colonel embarks on a suicide mission, trying to undo a mistake he made in a previous battle with the Arabs. His imminent death provides the lovers with "another dawn" to find their happiness.

Called a "right and conventional and stagey little conversation piece" by B. R. Crisler (*New York Times*), the feature was one more of Warners' Anglophile films with Kay Francis again as a sophisticated woman of the world (which means she is beautiful, chic, and terribly unhappy), similar to the stereotype she had developed for *Transgression* (RKO, 1931) and *Mandalay* (Warner Bros., 1934). For Errol, *Another Dawn* was good boxoffice, because any well-mounted soap opera was exceedingly popular with thirties' audiences. But the film proved again, as in *Green Light,* that he was much more comfortable with a rapier in hand than sporting a tuxedo in a love triangle. Ironically, this was the exact opposite of his real-life proclivities.

If *Another Dawn* lacked the requisite excitement expected of a Flynn picture (twenty minutes of adventure sequences had been snipped from the film), his already steady group of fans were ill-prepared for *The Perfect Specimen* (First National, 1937). It was the actor's first comedy, and he played a role better suited for an unknown, instead of someone with Errol's already established image at the boxoffice.

Based on a Samuel Hopkins Adams' story, Flynn, as Gerald Beresford Wicks, is supposed to be the "perfect specimen" of a man as raised by his aunt (May Robson). The heir to a sizeable fortune, he is confined to his estate, where he constantly trains for mental and physical perfection. His strict discipline, however, is interrupted when the car of newspaper woman Mona Carter (played by brassy Joan Blondell) crashes into his front gate. Subsequently, he learns about the outside world from this level-headed gal. The flimsy film, directed by Michael Curtiz of all people, did show off the actor's seemingly natural bent for light-weight comedy. It also displayed, in one scene, his boxing prowess. He had learned the pugilistic art in his school days, and the studio, ever ready to fabricate new background for their already colorful celebrity, circulated the story that Errol had actually represented Australia in the 1928 Olympics at Amsterdam!

Rounding out 1937 was the publication of Errol's first book, *Beam*

Ends (Longmans), which detailed the seven-month voyage he and three friends made aboard the *Sirocco* from Sydney, Australia to Port Moresby in New Guinea, in 1930. He later said that writing that book had been far more enjoyable than making motion pictures. The preface to *Beam Ends* insists "no ghost writer's slick hand is evident here." The reviewers were split in their reaction to the tome. The august *Saturday Review of Literature* insisted, "It is a pity that the real adventure material of Flynn's past must appear suspect and emasculated through its presentation. But the Flynn fans may like it; they can take it." On the other hand the Boston *Transcript* offered, "It is a fine, virile, red-blooded, he-man's tale of adventure, quite decently and wittily written. It is the story of a man's adventures. He learned to love his ship and his shipmates as any good sailor should."

Book-writing aside, Errol returned to filmmaking. Undoubtedly, the epitome of all Errol Flynn features was *The Adventures of Robin Hood,* which Warner Bros. distributed in April, 1938. More than any other film, this Technicolor feature is considered *the* Errol Flynn picture. The actor portrays the devil-may-care Robin Hood out to right the array of evils which the heir-apparent to the British throne, Prince John (played by Claude Rains), wrought on twelfth-century England. Filmed in the three strip color process, the motion picture has been exceedingly popular ever since its initial release, giving Warners the excuse to reissue it in 1948 and again in the mid-1950s before selling it to television, where it is constantly re-run and enjoyed by each new generation of Flynn devotees.

The character of Robin Hood, taken from old English ballads and De Koven-Smith's 1890 light opera, was a part ideally suited for Flynn. Having played similar roles in *Captain Blood* and, to a lesser extent, in *The Prince and the Pauper,* the robust actor who was so good at archery, fencing, fighting, and courting, was an ideal portrayer of the costume character. It is interesting to note that Flynn was always proud of the fact that he did all his stunts himself in this film.

Initially directed by William Keighley, who was replaced by Michael Curtiz after his work showed a lack of action, *The Adventures of Robin Hood* bore little similarity to the earlier Douglas Fairbanks classic, because Fairbanks had copyrighted the material on which his version was based. James Cagney had originally been set for the Robin Hood part, but after he left Warners for a temporary stay at Grand National, the project was revamped for Errol with the studio alloting over two million dollars for the budget. Once again, executive producer Hal B. Wallis was in charge of the production, and the supporting cast was selected to repeat the approved formula of past Flynn screen adventures. Olivia de Havilland was set as Maid Marian Fitzwalter, Claude Rains as Prince John, Basil Rathbone as Sir Guy of Gisbourne, and Alan Hale as Little John.

Although taking place in the not-so-dark Middle Ages and dealing with the oppression of the Saxons by Norman knights, the motion picture was intended as a severe warning to contemporary dictators—Rains' Prince John had several counterparts in the world during the 1930s. As Robin of Locksley, Flynn is a soldier who has returned from the Third Crusade (a campaign to "drive the infidels from the Holy Lands") after England's King Richard the Lion-Hearted (Ian Hunter) is held captive by the great Islamic leader, Saladin. Once back in his homeland, Robin becomes incensed at the evils of Richard's conniving brother, Prince John. The patriotic nobleman soon finds himself forced off his lands and into a life as the leader of a band of outlaws in Sherwood Forest, which, as any school child can tell us, is located near the city of Nottingham, which is ruled by the wicked Sir Guy of Gisbourne (played here by Basil Rathbone).

The film contains many of the Robin Hood legends, including his meeting with bulbous Friar Tuck (Eugene Pallette) and Little John (Alan Hale) and, taking from the 1890 opera, Robin's love affair with a Norman ward of the king, Maid Marian (de Havilland), who is also being courted by the serpentine Sir Guy. After Marian saves Robin from being hanged, she is imprisoned, and Prince John sets out to be crowned king, only to have his plan thwarted by Richard's timely return. Richard and his men join with Robin and his bandits and, after a sword battle, including an incredibly well-staged duel scene between Robin and Sir Guy, John is defeated and exiled. Richard retakes the throne and Robin and Marian embark on a life of bliss.

One of the most admirable aspects of the better Flynn spectacles, and *Robin Hood* in particular, is the jocular tone of the proceedings. There is always tongue-in-cheek bantering to amuse viewers in between the vivid action scenes or the lush pageantry of the epic. For example, at the banquet hall urbane Rains says to de Havilland, "Take Sir Guy." The seemingly demure, innocent Miss Olivia responds, "Must I take him?", her wide-opened eyes and cute smile in intriguing contrast to the biting edge in her voice.

Later, in the forest, when Robin and Maid Marian are conversing, and she is pouting that the seeming renegade has the upper hand, he confides to her, "What a pity your manners don't match your looks." Surely a most unusual way for a gentleman to court a lady, but such dialogue was and would be standard practice for the Flynn-de Havilland love team. Then, of course, to point up the comic tone of the adventure, there is Una O'Connor's cackling, crackling Bess the Maid who, in her courtship with Much the Miller's Son (Herbert Mundin), gives the picture its own bawdy tone.

In passing, it is worth repeating that, while Flynn would soon be carping about feeling like an imposter "taking all that money for reciting ten or twelve lines of nonsense a day," there were few other actors in Hollywood who, in doublet and hose, could convincingly shout out such lines as, "Men! If you are willing to fight for our people, I want you." As Douglas Fairbanks had proved before him, it required an athletic gallant (or rake) with the requisite *savoir-faire* offscreen to play the charming scamp of a vital hero oncamera. Errol Flynn was such a man.

It goes almost without saying that the spectacular moments of the script stand out in this feature: Robin's splitting of an opponent's arrow[16] in the archery tournament, and the climactic duel between Rathbone and Flynn. The final encounter between Sir Guy and Robin is perhaps the best such athletic tussle ever recorded on film.

In the *New York Times,* Frank C. Nugent wrote of the spectacle, "[It is] a richly produced, bravely bedecked, romantic and colorful show, it leaps boldly to the forefront of this year's best and can be calculated to rejoice the eights, rejuvenate the eighties, and delight those in between." *Film Daily* voted it the best picture of the year, and it appeared in the *New York Times'* Ten Best Films list. It garnered Academy Awards for Cary Weyl's art direction, Ralph Dawson's editing, and Erich Wolfgang Korngold's original music score. The Academy also nominated it as one of the nine best pictures of the year (but the Oscar went to Columbia's *You Can't Take It with You*).

Never again would an Errol Flynn feature receive such accolades and never again would the actor, despite a number of fine upcoming roles, have such a perfect part on celluloid or in any other entertainment medium. For once he played a role that came extremely close to his real-life escapades. However, at Warner Bros. Robin Hood had a happy ending with the youthful lord finding love with Maid Marian. In real life, Errol found no such rewarding finale.

During the making of the film[17] Olivia de Havilland's offcamera affections for Errol were rekindled. She later recounted, "It was hard because Lili [Damita] was there on the set and on location. But by then I had little emotion invested in the situation. So it all turned out to be a romantic fantasy." Many of those close to Errol, and some who were not, such as Bette Davis, claim the only woman he ever really loved was Olivia de Havilland.

Fresh from the pinnacle of *The Adventures of Robin Hood,* Flynn

---

[16]Archery champion Howard Hill provided this stunning special effect.

[17]During the location filming for *Robin Hood* in Chico, California, it would be co-player Patric Knowles (Will Scarlett) who gave Errol his first flying lessons. Despite threatening messages from the studio, the two players continued their aerial pursuits, until one day a man from the Civil Aeronautics Authority showed up at the scene of their stunting. When Knowles landed his craft, his pilot's license was taken away (temporarily) and the studio manager insisted his employers were going to file a complaint with the Screen Actors Guild (he was fined one hundred dollars). Where had equal "villain" Errol been during all this skirmishing with the law? Asleep in a nearby car, having dozed off while learning his lines for the next day's filming.

In *The Adventures of Robin Hood* (1938)

With Olivia de Havilland in *Four's a Crowd* (1938)

next appeared in *Four's a Crowd* (Warner Bros., 1938). Directed by Michael Curtiz from Casey Robinson and Sig Herzig's screenplay, the film, like *The Perfect Specimen,* gave more than a hint of the actor's ability with comedy. The script had him as a public relations man who sets out to humanize a nasty millionaire (Walter Connolly) and in order to do so, he takes a job on his old newspaper for former boss Patric Knowles. He meets two girls, a reporter (Rosalind Russell) and the millionaire's daughter (Olivia de Havilland), and he romances both, but ends up at the altar with the reporter while the other girl marries his boss.

Four's a Crowd gave Flynn a few good lines and he was allowed to perform some semi-madcap slapstick. For romantically inclined film-goers there was the surprise twist of Errol not ending up with de Havilland.

Flynn remained in the celluloid guise of a newsman for his next Warners' project, the filming of Myron Brinig's novel *The Sisters* (1938). Originally, the leading female roles were to have been played by Kay Francis and Miriam Hopkins. But it proved to be Bette Davis and Anita Louise, who, along with Jane Bryan, assumed the parts of daughters of pharmacist Ned Elliott and his wife, Rose, played by Henry Travers and Beulah Bondi, in 1904 Silver Bow, Montana. At a ball celebrating the inauguration of President Theodore Roosevelt,

Louise (Davis), the eldest sister, meets Frank Medlin (Errol), a very attractive reporter who unfortunately has a few weaknesses of character, namely wanderlust and a fondness for liquor. Despite her better judgment, Davis falls in love with Errol and the two elope. Later, in San Francisco, pregnant Bette is deserted by her spouse, and she suffers a miscarriage during the ordeal of the city's big earthquake. Four years pass, and at a party back in Silver Bow celebrating the inauguration of President William Taft, Errol, who has been in the Orient for three years, appears on the scene. Davis forgives him.[18]

As a richly produced, turgid soap opera, *The Sisters* cannot be faulted, especially when the viewer is treated to a brief glimpse of the famed San Francisco earthquake (not on the same scale as MGM's *San Francisco* of 1936, but still a breathtaking, if brief, sequence). Because Anatole Litvak was essentially a woman's director and this picture literally cried out for feminine heroics, Errol's characterization tended to be lost in the shuffle. Also, it did not help matters that the dashing actor had too winning a personality to convincingly portray such an emotional child.

As for the Flynn-Davis relationship on the set, there could be no accord between the performers after Errol, the bigger boxoffice draw, insisted that despite his secondary role he be given top billing. Some sources believe that reckless Flynn was quite drawn to the self-sufficient Bette, but that she would have as little to do with him as working conditions permitted.

Two projects planned for Errol at Warners' did not materialize. Each of them seemed potential money winners at that, which made their abortive status all the more intriguing. One was a sequel to *The Adventures of Robin Hood,* to be entitled *Sir Robin of Locksley;* the other production was *The Gamblers,* to star Errol, Edward G. Robinson, Bette Davis, and Basil Rathbone.

But Errol did make *The Dawn Patrol* (Warner Bros., 1938), his fourth and final release of the year. It was a remake of the fine 1930 war film of the same name, and Errol portrayed Captain Courtney, the role originally played by Richard Barthelmess. Spiritedly directed by Edmund Goulding, who also helped rework the dialog from the early talkie version, the film is one of Errol's best. He gave a good, hard-hitting performance as a young flyer who perceives the futility of war but, upon promotion, can do nothing about it but send other young men to their deaths.

Basil Rathbone was cast as Major Brand, the part originally played by Neil Hamilton, and a young David Niven appeared as Lieutenant Scott, the role which Douglas Fairbanks, Jr. had performed in the 1930 edition. This new trio worked well together and made their parts in

[18]A discarded ending for the film had Flynn leaving Davis' life for good, and her finding happiness with her new employer, Ian Hunter.

this sturdy remake quite believable. Since America was still technically at peace (despite the war in Europe), the filmmakers tried to have their production remain "neutral" as to the virtues of peace or war. However, the film included a good many scenes of aerial combat. This allowed for inclusion of all of the flying footage from the first film into the remake, with new material shot at the studio's Calabasas Ranch.

Again a part of Warners' Anglophile tradition, *The Dawn Patrol* exemplified the stiff upper lip characteristics of the British fighting men of World War I. The film centered on the 59th Squadron of the English Royal Flying Corps, which has its headquarters in France. Fighting a superior German foe with outdated airplanes, the corps is constantly losing men in battle, much to the regret of its very human commander (Rathbone). His top flyer, Captain Courtney (Flynn), refers to the officer as a "butcher" for sending men to die in battle, but when Rathbone is promoted, it is he (Courtney) who must take the commander's place in the same position. He is forced to send his pal's (Niven) younger brother to his death. Later, the conscience-stricken Errol assumes a suicide mission for which Niven had previously volunteered. While trying to bomb a weapons storage area behind enemy lines, Flynn has an air duel with German ace von Richter, and both men are killed. Following Errol's death, it is Niven who takes over as commander— and so continues *la ronde de* war.

Perhaps two reasons why the performances in *Dawn Patrol* jelled so well were that cast members Flynn and Rathbone had worked together in the past, while Errol and co-player Niven were great offcamera buddies. Since his return from Spain, Errol had been sharing an apartment with Niven. (Errol and Lili were then undergoing one of their many split-ups.)[19] Later Flynn and Niven would share a beach house at Malibu which they and their friends would call "Cirrhosis-by-the-Sea." "Errol was an enchanting creature," Niven later said. "It was never-ending fun."

Over the years there have been unproven rumors that at one time Warner Bros. considered buying the options for *Gone with the Wind* and casting Bette Davis and Errol in the leads. Needless to say, that never came about.

If Errol would have seemed somewhat out of place as the rough-and-tumble Rhett Butler in *Gone with the Wind,* he was no less unlikely as Wade Hatton, who brings law and order to *Dodge City* (Warner Bros., 1939). It was the year of the big Western film revival, and, if Tyrone

[19]It was during this period of their on-again-off-again marriage that Errol and Lili jointly attended a party at Marion Davies' beach house. Flynn became entranced with a lovely guest there and took her for a stroll about the expansive premises. Once they reached what they assumed to be a safe retreat, they began making love. Suddenly the place was aglow with flood lights, and the vituperative screeching of an enraged Lili filled the air. It seemed that detectives patroling the grounds had spotted Errol at play and one of them had alerted Mrs. Flynn.

Power could be *Jesse James* (Twentieth Century-Fox), James Stewart cavort as *Destry Rides Again* (Universal), and John Wayne shine in *Stagecoach* (United Artists), then Flynn could ply his craft in the old West as well.

The Michael Curtiz-directed feature carefully establishes that Errol is an "Irish" soldier of fortune who has fought in India, Cuba, and with Jeb Stuart in the Civil War before coming westward. He arrives in Dodge City, Kansas, at a time when it is the northern-most shipping point to St. Louis and Chicago for longhorn cattle brought up the Chisholm Trail from Texas. The barroom brawl scene in the film has become a classic sequence and a piece of stock footage which has been used on many occasions for theatrical and television films.

Called by the *New York Times* "merely an exciting thriller for the kiddies, or for grown folk with an appetite for the wild and woolly," the Technicolor film boasted two leading ladies: Olivia de Havilland as Errol's love interest, Abbie Irving, and Ann Sheridan as Ruby Gilman, an attractive saloon girl. Along with Flynn, Alan Hale, Bruce Cabot, and Guinn "Big Boy" Williams were on hand to provide the action. The big, beefy, brawling film proved to be good boxoffice and became Errol's launching pad into the Western genre. Although the sagebrush image was never to eclipse his work as a swashbuckler, he was certainly equally at home on a horse as behind a sword.

With Bruce Cabot and Victor Jory in *Dodge City* (1939)

289

With Bette Davis in *The Private Lives of Elizabeth and Essex* (1939)

Reversing the billing from *The Sisters,* Bette Davis took top spot in *The Private Lives of Elizabeth and Essex* (Warner Bros., 1939) with Errol in the subordinate role of the dashing Earl of Essex. The film went through a number of title and script changes before going into production. First called *Elizabeth the Queen,* the title of the Maxwell Anderson Broadway play from which it was taken, then *The Knight and the Lady,* a title tag which upset Miss Davis, it was then switched to *Elizabeth and Essex.* That title, however, was copyrighted by Lytton Strachey for his book, so the ultimate release title was settled upon, which also pacified Errol who had demanded that his character's name appear in the title in deference to his taking second billing.

As much as Miss Davis loved playing Queen Elizabeth (as she would again in 1955 in Twentieth Century-Fox's *The Virgin Queen*), Errol disliked the role of Essex and, more importantly, of being reunited with the queen of the Fox lot. Obviously, he was ill at ease with her strong drive and facade of superiority and his physical fascination for her had long since vanished. His perennial co-star, Olivia de Havilland, had a small part as Elizabeth's lady-in-waiting, although she had some love scenes with Flynn's Essex, with whom—according to the script—she is in love. To add to Flynn's discomfort, Miss Davis made it continually clear that Errol was hardly a match for Laurence Olivier, whom she had wanted for the co-starring role.

Ironically, the part of Essex (1566-1601) proved to be ideal for Errol, since it provided him with an opportunity to emote as a dashing, but ambitious lord, who has the chance to fight England's enemies and romance her Queen. Basically, the plot has Elizabeth (1533-1603) torn between her love for power-hungry Essex and a peaceful policy for her country. The latter eventually wins out and the Queen reluctantly sends her lover to the chopping block.[20]

The historical romance, which concluded Flynn's first decade in the cinema, was not a great customer pleaser, despite the presence of two of Warners' weightiest stars. Thus, the screen teaming of Errol Flynn and Bette Davis ended with their second film, although they would each appear in segments of the all-celebrity variety show *Thank Your Lucky Stars* (Warner Bros., 1943).

While Errol's domestic life seemed a little more stable in 1940 with the birth of a son, Sean, on May 31, very few on the Hollywood scene were willing to place odds that the Flynn-Damita marriage would last much longer. In fact, it would be a thing of the past by 1941.

Now on an annual salary of some $250,000, Errol began the new decade in another Western, *Virginia City* (Warner Bros., 1940). The casting of the leads was a bit strange, what with Errol playing Kerry Bradford, a Union soldier, Miriam Hopkins as a rather mature saloon singer, Randolph Scott as a Confederate, and Humphrey Bogart (who had been in the studio's *The Oklahoma Kid,* 1939) as a leering Mexican bandit. To complicate matters, Bogart actively disliked both Flynn and Scott, which added unnecessary tension on the set. But, with the presence of demanding director Michael Curtiz and a supporting cast which included Alan Hale and Guinn "Big Boy" Williams, the film did get completed.

In *A Pictorial History of the Western Film* (Citadel Press, 1969) William K. Everson notes that this black-and-white feature "was slow in getting itself started but more than made up for this in its second half." By not using Technicolor and by employing revamped sets from *Dodge City,* the studio saved a good deal of money on the production. Popular in its day, *Virginia City,* along with *Dodge City,* would be reissued as a double-feature package in 1951.

Again with Michael Curtiz, Flynn returned to the swashbuckling field with *The Sea Hawk* (Warner Bros.), which was released in July, 1940. Today the film is best remembered for Sol Polito's photography and Erich Wolfgang Korngold's magnificent score. The feature, which cost $1.7 million, may very well be the best example of Flynn's work in a swashbuckler film.

The history of this motion picture is complicated, in that it used the title of Rafael Sabatini's novel, which had been made into a film in

---

[20]Deleted after the initial showing was the climactic sequence in which Flynn is marched down to the courtyard and mounts the platform to face the executioner.

With Miriam Hopkins in _Virginia City_ (1940)

In _The Sea Hawk_ (1940)

1924 with Milton Sills, but the plotline derived from Seton I. Miller's original screenplay, *Beggars of the Sea.* This synthesis was accomplished by Howard Koch and Seton I. Miller, and the result was a film which used sets and prop material from both *The Private Lives of Elizabeth and Essex* and *The Adventures of Robin Hood.*

The elaborate film opens on a spectacular note with a sea battle between a British ship commanded by Captain Geoffrey Thorpe (Errol) and a Spanish galleon mastered by Captain Lopez (Gilbert Roland). The Spanish are defeated. However, Errol receives a halfhearted reprimand from Queen Elizabeth (a much subdued monarch as interpreted by Flora Robson) and is sent to Panama to loot the Spanish treasure there. A spy in the queen's court (Henry Daniell) warns the Spanish of the upcoming adventure, and Geoffrey Thorpe and his men are captured and made galley slaves. When they escape, they bring word to the Queen about the Spanish Armada's planned attack on England. The invaders are defeated and the balance of world power shifts from Spain to England.

For the dueling scenes, which were supervised by Fred Cavens, Don Turner doubled for Flynn. Since Olivia de Havilland was rebelling against further sorties as the cardboard heroine of Errol Flynn screen capers, Brenda Marshall, a relative newcomer at the studio, was cast as Donna Maria, the niece of the Spanish ambassador (none other than Claude Rains, unrefutably villainous in his black goatee). Miss de Havilland's absence from the film proved how valuable she was to the Flynn outings, and whenever possible in the future she would appear in Errol's features.

For those viewers thriving on action—and director Curtiz[21] always insured that his adventure films had an overdose of that commodity—*The Sea Hawk* has a wide selection of choice episodes. There is the initial sea battle between the British and Spaniards, the ambush of Flynn and his men in a Panamanian swamp, Flynn and crew escaping their bondage as galley slaves, and, of course, the final physical encounter between Errol and Machiavellian Daniell.

Ironically, this would be Errol's last film in the real sword-and-smile mold until *The Adventures of Don Juan* (Warner Bros., 1948). By that time he would have lost much of the fortitude that had made him a top swashbuckler ranking at the top of the medium with Douglas Fairbanks.

---

[21]Hungarian Curtiz, whose difficulties with the English language almost rivaled that of Samuel Goldwyn, was famous for his malapropisms on the set. During the filming of *The Charge of the Light Brigade*, it is he who supposedly gave the command, "Bring on the empty horses." In the making of *The Sea Hawk*, the director had set the stage for a complicated encounter between the British and Spanish, with the extras poised to swing on ropes from one mock ship to another. Curtiz yelled for quiet, then barked out, "Everee-bodee lun-ge." The extras, assuming he has ordered a lunch break, hastily departed from the set.

For his last 1940 release, Warners threw historical fact to the wind (as they had done in *Sea Hawk,* which drew its own parallels to the World War II situation). *Santa Fe Trail* had nothing to do with the cattle drive trail of the same name. Instead, the feature centered on a pre-Civil War Jeb Stuart (Errol) who is in opposition to the violent abolitionist tactics of John Brown (Raymond Massey). The story opens with Flynn's 1854 graduation from West Point and his work as a frontier patrol man before he leads the band which puts an end to John Brown's raid on Harper's Ferry.

Moviegoers did not worry about the historical inaccuracies of *Santa Fe Trail,* for they found it to be an entertaining and larger-than-life action Western (even though the villains were not rustlers or rampaging Indians, but a religious-oriented abolitionist). Interwoven into the film's plot was a love rivalry between classmates Flynn and George Armstrong Custer (Ronald Reagan) over Kit Carson Halliday (Olivia de Havilland). The seasoned filmgoer did not require much foresight to guess that Olivia would choose Errol as her husband.[22] To counterbal-

[22]Kingsley Canham, in his chapter on Curtiz in *Hollywood Professionals* (Tantivy Press, 1973), points up that the director finishes "the film with yet another of [his] downbeat endings." As he explains, "The pitch of the film is immediately altered with the hanging of Brown, foretelling his vision of blood spilt to purge the sins of a guilty land; as Flynn and de Havilland wed on a train speeding away from the scene, the camera pulls back to follow the motion of the wheels as they revolve to the faint, rumbling rhythm of 'John Brown's Body' on the soundtrack. . . ."

With William Marshall, Van Heflin, Ronald Reagan, William Lundigan, and David Bruce in *Santa Fe Trail* (1940)

ance the ferocity of Massey's crusader and Van Heflin's money-hungry opportunist Rader, there were the comedy antics of Alan Hale and Guinn "Big Boy" Williams as two seasoned cowpokes who join up with Errol and Reagan. As Ted Sennett observes in *Warner Brothers Presents,* "Preposterous as history, this was still a lavish and spirited film with the thin (even emaciated) characterizations in its Robert Buckner screenplay overpowered by lots of action well staged by director Michael Curtiz."

Whatever his shenanigans offscreen, or whatever the judgment of Flynn's acting range may be, he was not entirely without justification when he begged the front office to give him a break and allow him a reprieve from his historical capers. The studio responded by casting him in *Footsteps in the Dark* (Warner Bros., 1941). Based on Ladislaus Fodor's play, *Blondie White,* Errol had the complicated yet lighthearted role of Francis Warren, an investment counselor who doubles as an amateur sleuth, resulting in his writing of a successful murder mystery. He keeps his writing a secret from his wife (played by Brenda Marshall), and goes out at night looking for plot material. Along the way, he gets mixed up in the murder of a jewel smuggler, and meets a burlesque dancer (Lee Patrick), the "Blondie White" of Fodor's work. These events cause Marshall and her mother (Lucile Watson) to doubt Errol, especially after he is accused of the smuggler's murder. After a series of deft maneuvers, however, director Lloyd Bacon brings the ninety-six minute feature to a close, with Ralph Bellamy, the perennial heroine-loser, being revealed as the real murderer.

During this loud, boisterous comedy, Flynn handled his part as well as could be expected, considering the story's hard-to-believe premise. However, again as in his past screen comedies, he was given less than satisfactory material with which to work and a role that was better suited to the likes of Warren William. Fortunately for Errol, he would not be stuck with a similarly bad entry until after World War II.

At this time, many from the Hollywood colony were enlisting in the Armed Services, but Errol was forced to remain on the home front because of ill health (which included recurrent malaria, tuberculosis, and an "athletic heart"). His pal David Niven, who had returned to England to join the British war effort, provided an insight into the Errol Flynn of the early 1940s: "I think Errol suffered because he didn't go off to war with the rest of us. It bothered him but he didn't show it, in fact he rarely betrayed his seriousness, he hardly ever unburdened himself. It would have been better for him if he could have instead of living behind a façade. Errol was a many-sided creature."

Although he could not fight on the real battle fronts, Warner Bros. saw no reason why Errol could not participate in their soundstage skirmishes. The *New York Times* called *Dive Bomber,* released in August, 1941, "the best of the new 'service films' to date," but the feature now seems quite dated and far too long (133 minutes). Directed by Michael Curtiz, from Frank Wead's original story, this Technicolor service film dealt with military physicians who attempt to find cures for the obstacles facing pilots involved in stratospheric flying. Flynn plays flight surgeon Douglas Lee who works with Commander Joe Blake (Fred MacMurray, on loan from Paramount). Blake is developing a high-altitude pressure suit, which would cost him his life. Thrown in for very good measure was Alexis Smith as the radiant love interest.

Much of *Dive Bomber* was shot at the Naval Air Station in San Diego, the Pensacola Naval Air Station, and on board the aircraft carrier *Enterprise.* This feature was the first of Errol's so-called single-handed attempts to win the war for democracy.

With Tyrone Power shining in *The Mark of Zorro* (1940) and *Blood and Sand* (1941) at Twentieth Century-Fox and Douglas Fairbanks, Jr. gaining recognition in *The Corsican Brothers* (United Artists, 1941), it is little wonder that Warners felt it was advisable to get Errol back into an historical costumer, this time for *They Died with Their Boots On* (1941). Unlike *Sante Fe Trail,* in which Errol's character had said, regarding the slave issue, "It's not our job to say who's right or wrong," there is no doubt in any viewer's mind that in *They Died with Their Boots On* Flynn's George Armstrong Custer[23] means business when he sets out to maintain the honor of the Seventh Cavalry. It is this honor which climaxes in the infamous battle of the Little Big Horn. Like *Santa Fe Trail, They Died with Their Boots On* was historically inaccurate. The feature reunited Errol and Olivia de Havilland for yet another screen match. This time around, the actress was given a much fuller character to play than the "Kit Carson" Halliday of *Sante Fe Trail.* As Elizabeth, the wife of the general (Errol) who dies in action, she champions her husband's death in Congress with a rousing speech that proves the actress was well ready for more dramatic assignments.

Although it was a long film (140 minutes), the picture is generally well-paced and not tiring and boasts of a fine musical score by Max Steiner. It follows Custer from his West Point years through his marriage to Elizabeth, his Civil War activity, and his final command. It is the latter that takes him and his men (over two hundred) to their death in a vicious encounter with Chief Crazy Horse (Anthony Quinn) and his Indians on June 25, 1876, at the fateful encounter in the Dakota

[23]Among those who have portrayed Custer on the screen are: Dustin Farnum in *Flaming Frontier* (Universal, 1926), Frank McGlynn in the serial, *Custer's Last Stand* (Stage and Screen, 1936), Ronald Reagan in *Santa Fe Trail,* James Millican in *Warpath* (Paramount, 1951), Sheb Wooley in *Bugles in the Afternoon* (Warner Bros., 1952), Britt Lomond in *Tonka* (Buena Vista, 1958), Phil Carey in *The Great Sioux Massacre* (Twentieth Century-Fox, 1965), Robert Shaw in *Custer of the West* (Cinerama, 1967), and Richard Mulligan in *Little Big Man* (National General, 1970). Wayne Maunder was the star of the television series, "The Legend of Custer" (ABC-TV, 1967-68).

Territory's Black Hills. Arthur Kennedy's portrayal of Ned Sharp, Jr.—the villainous character who sells guns to the Indians—added much to the picture, as did Sydney Greenstreet's cameo as General Winfield Scott.

They Died with Their Boots On was the first of seven features to be directed by Raoul Walsh. (Flynn had insisted that he could no longer work with Michael Curtiz, and the studio, mindful of keeping Errol in good humor, heeded his request.) Made at a cost of over two million dollars, the adventure story was a rewarding boxoffice success and proved to the studio, and to Flynn, that Walsh was indeed the director to guide Errol's further cinema course.[24] In his recent autobiography, *Each Man in His Time* (Farrar, Straus and Giroux, 1974), Walsh attests to his friendship with the star, which existed on and off the set.

By this time, Errol, a naturalized American citizen, had divorced Lili Damita.[25] He was now a free-wheeling spirit again about Hollywood, and when he wasn't carousing with his latest flame he was most likely settling a score with vituperative gossip columnist Hedda Hopper, (on one occasion he is said to have booted her in the backside at the fashionable Mocambo Club), or playing pranks on his friends. Once, however, Flynn was Walsh's victim in a bizarre gag. It was one that the director has delighted in recalling, and occurred when Errol's past mentor and drinking pal, John Barrymore, died (May 29, 1942). With the aid of Flynn's butler, Walsh placed the corpse of the Great Profile in Flynn's house. Errol came home quite inebriated from grief over Barrymore's demise, only to find him stone cold in his living room! Walsh claims that Flynn ran out of the house like a man who had just seen a ghost, which may be an understatement of how the actor reacted to the bizarre set-up.

Because Errol had collapsed during the filming of *They Died with Their Boots On* (his ailment was termed "nervous exhaustion"), he was given an extended holiday when the filming was completed. It was nearly ten months later before his next picture was ready for release. It was another war adventure, *Desperate Journey* (Warner Bros., 1942), in which he played Flight Lieutenant Terence Forbes of the R.A.F. bombers. With four other comrades (Ronald Reagan, Arthur Kennedy, Alan Hale and Hugh Sinclair), all of different Allied nationalities, he is

---

[24]In his autobiography, Walsh describes the problems in filming the great Indians-versus-cavalry battle scenes, detailing how the Screen Extras Guild insisted upon choosing the men to ride the horses, and that the group of non-equestrians who showed up on the outdoor set were almost immediately felled in action (they could not mount their steeds, or, if they did, they almost immediately slid off when the horses took a step). The first day's work saw sixty casualties.

[25]The terms of the divorce, which became final on March 31, 1942, required that Errol pay his ex-spouse $1,500 a month, tax free. As added inducement for the divorce, Flynn foolishly agreed to pay this sum as long as she never remarried. (She did not, until after his death.) As part of the community property law, she naturally received half of all his other properties.

shot down over Nazi Germany. In their wild attempt to escape to the Allied lines, the group blows up a chemical plant. They are pursued by the Nazis, who are led by Major Baumeister (Raymond Massey), but three of the quintet manage to escape. The finale finds the survivors hijacking a German bomber that had been designated to destroy London water works). As they head for the British Isles, these World War II Rover Boys are looking forward to adventures against the Japanese.

Easily described as pap for war audiences, this adventure feature was directed by Raoul Walsh and produced by Hal B. Wallis, the producer's last picture with Errol.

While *Desperate Journey* was in release, Errol was arrested and charged with statutory rape against two underage girls. He pleaded innocent but was forced to stand trial. The daily events in the Los Angeles courtroom fascinated Americans and, contrary to the studio's initial fears, made Errol even a bigger boxoffice sensation. A result of the trial was the national catchphrase, "in like Flynn."

The twenty-day trial cost Flynn some $50,000, most of which went to his attorney, the famous criminal lawyer Jerry Giesler. Three charges of statutory rape were brought against the actor. One charge alleged he had seduced waitress Betty Hansen at the home of his playboy friend Freddie McEvoy, to which the girl "didn't have no objections." Giesler was able to have that charge dismissed for lack of

With lawyers Jerry Giesler and Robert E. Ford and accuser Peggy Satterlee at the Los Angeles trial (November 4, 1942)

sufficient evidence. The second and third charges contended that Errol twice seduced pretty Peggy LaRue Satterle, a seventeen-year-old night-club entertainer. The incidents allegedly had occurred aboard Flynn's yacht some two years earlier. In the course of the trial, Giesler brought out the fact that the girl had previously lied about her age in order to obtain a driver's license, that she had an abortion from another affair, and that she had necrophiliac tendencies. After deliberating for some twenty-four hours, the jury of nine women and three men found Flynn not guilty.

During the much-headlined trial, two jurors, Elaine Forbes and Lor-ene Boehm, were accused by the state of fraud and deceit and were excused from duty. Miss Forbes was accused of pre-bias toward the defendant, while Mrs. Boehm was said to be "for Errol Flynn in a big way."

The publicity that surrounded the trial, and the intimate testimony, delighted a war weary country, but not Flynn.[26] He later admitted he had had a plane waiting at the local airport, ready to get him out of the country, in case he was found guilty. After the trial was over he antici-pated suicide—at least for a brief period. An apparent result of the trial was that his drinking increased and he evidently renewed his dabbling in narcotics.[27]

However, the statutory rape trial had one benefit, for during its course Errol met Nora Eddington. The eighteen-year-old, petite Miss Eddington was the daughter of Jack Eddington, then secretary to the sheriff of Los Angeles County. She was employed at the City Hall cigar counter, and after the trial he arranged a meeting with her. In her frank autobiography, *Errol and Me* (Signet Books, 1960) she "revealed" how the great lover eventually raped her, then professed his love. When his divorce from Lili Damita was final, he married Miss Eddington but kept the union a secret at first, by setting up a separate residence for her. On January 10, 1945, she would give birth to Flynn's second child, a daughter, Deirdre. Later, a second daughter, Rory, would be born, on March 12, 1947.

With the surprisingly good boxoffice receipts from *Desperate Jour-ney* during the statutory rape proceedings, Warner Bros. rushed his next film, *Gentleman Jim,* into theatres in October, 1942. It is probably the best of the films he made with director Raoul Walsh, in which both

[26]In his autobiography Flynn expressed the theory that the rape allegations had been a set-up, a way for Los Angeles authorities to get even with Jack L. Warner, whom Flynn felt had probably not paid off during a recent changeover in office. As it was, Errol was forced to borrow some $20,000 from his studio employer (at six percent interest!) to pay off some of his legal fees.

[27]During the course of the protracted courtroom case, Errol wondered how his father, still living in Ireland, was taking the news. Flynn could just imagine the adverse publici-ty circulating in the Shamrock Isle. Finally, a telegram arrived from the senior Flynn which read, "How was it, anyway?"

talents were in their prime. It is the story of the second world's heavy-weight champion, James J. Corbett (1866-1933), who won the title by knocking out the "unbeatable" John L. Sullivan (played by Ward Bond). This was Flynn's first starring vehicle without producer Hal B. Wallis, and Robert Buckner handled the production duties.

Based on Corbett's autobiography, *The Roar of the Crowd,* the motion picture was largely fictional due to legal entanglements regarding the late pugilist's estate. As a result, the names used in the film were fictitious, and a romance with Victoria Ware (Alexis Smith) was added to give the black-and-white feature love interest. Flynn's boxing experience in school stood him in good stead, making his scenes in the ring authentic. (Distaff filmgoers appreciated the occasion to study Errol's physique in such relatively scant clothing.) Corbett was the first of the modern "dancing" fighters, a precursor, in many respects, of Mohammed Ali. His knockout of Sullivan was one of the greatest upsets in boxing history, and the fight scene in the film was well staged and exceptionally exciting.

Perhaps the most endearing quality of *Gentleman Jim* was its success in capturing the spirit of the rowdy-but-gentle 1890s. It was a lively film with many of the fight scenes staged with obvious relish by director Walsh. Ward Bond gave one of his finest performances as John L. Sullivan and his presentation of the championship belt to Corbett at a victory party after the decisive ring battle is poignant for even the most seasoned moviegoer.

Periodically, Errol still would try to get himself into some branch of the military service, but his uncertain health (he collapsed again from exhaustion during the staging of the Sullivan-Corbett match) insured that no branch of the armed forces would accept him. It was a fact of life that rankled within him deeply, especially when an unknowing public and press would occasionally make snide remarks about virile Flynn being a coward by remaining on the home front. Occasionally, Errol worked in touring U.S.O. shows for the service men. At first he was reluctant to do so, but he later developed a blasé attitude toward such performances and usually spent his stage time kidding his own image, much to the delight of his audience. He also worked at putting on tennis matches for the war effort. He and Rudy Vallee often joined together in this endeavor, both being among the top Hollywood players on the court.

At age thirty-three, Errol's golden years of stardom were rapidly coming to a close, accelerated by his hard-hitting private life and by the irrevocable changes in lifestyles and entertainment standards which would eventually make his swashbuckling image an anachronism in the post-World War II movie industry. Although there still were to be a few good pictures left in his Warner Bros. work, his best screen appearances were already behind him. Since the trial, he was at the apex of his popularity, but the acclaim was not now so much for Flynn the actor and star, as it was for Flynn the personality. Never again, until the end of his life, would the moviegoing public take Flynn seriously as a craftsman. Such lack of recognition further embittered the not so cavalier performer who was always sensitive toward his fellow workers and felt that they never took him as seriously as he wished.

The beginning of his visible dissipation was also at hand. Those who knew him closely said that it was in these years that he truly became addicted to narcotics, and, when under the influence, he could become physically dangerous. In his autobiography, Flynn makes no mention of using drugs at this time, but he did admit that vodka was a "drug" to which he was addicted. Whatever the cause, with his physical deterioration would come the fragmentation of his career until it, too, passed from the scene a decade later.

Given Errol's obvious self-destructive tendencies, it was unfortunate that none of his acquaintances, friends, or employers was strong enough to take him in hand and salvage the still great potential. But Errol lived apart from people, even from himself, and protected his very vulnerable nature from nearly everyone. As director Lewis Milestone has aptly stated, "His faults harmed no one but himself." Errol was a little more precise than usual about his continual posturing when he admitted, "I allow myself to be understood as a colorful fragment in a drab world." On another occasion he confided, "The public has always expected me to a playboy, and a decent chap never lets his public down."

Edge of Darkness (Warner Bros., 1943), directed by Lewis Milestone, was not released until the statutory rape trial was over and Errol had been acquitted. Boxoffice response to the film was good, although his performance here was somewhat restrained, perhaps due to the fact he had been indicted during the filming.

The film, with Robert Rossen's screenplay of the William Woods' novel, *Edge of Darkness,* was blatant American war propaganda, with the Nazis as the usual dark villains. Errol was cast as Gunnar Brogge, a Norwegian fisherman, who leads a small village's activities against the Third Reich's forces. Other characters involved included Gunnar's fiancée, Karen (Ann Sheridan),[28] a doctor (Walter Huston), his wife (Ruth Gordon), another doctor (Morris Carnovsky), and a farmer (Monte Blue). While Flynn's role in the production was not overwhelming, his portrayal of the fisherman was solid and perhaps one of the most realistic he offered in any of his Warners' war pictures.

While involved in the statutory rape trial, Errol also contributed a guest bit to Warners' all-star war extravaganza, *Thank Your Lucky*

[28]Miss Sheridan, who was Errol's leading lady in three Warners pictures, would later say, "He was one of the wild characters of the world."

With Walt LaRue (kneeling) and Ann Sheridan in *Edge of Darkness* **(1943)**

Stars (1943). Nearly every big star and character player on the studio's roster was included in a series of blackout sketches. Most of the celebrities portrayed themselves. In his major scene, Errol, sporting a handlebar moustache out of the *Gentlemen Jim* era, did a song and dance saloon number, "That's What You Jolly Well Get," written by Frank Loesser and Arthur Schwartz. The actor was spritely in a takeoff on his hero character who "won the war and I won the one before." Featured in the sketch was 1920s' Warner Bros. star Monte Blue, who often worked in Errol's films. Although Errol did not share a real scene with Olivia de Havilland (she had a jive number with Ida Lupino and George Tobias), this was technically their final film together, concluding an eight-year professional relationship. In the finale to *Thank Your Lucky Stars,* Errol is on hand to do a final flip to his vocalizing talents, as he mouths an operatic number, then midway stops, while the singing (offcamera) continues.[29]

From the point of view of production values, there are obviously a great many differences between *Edge of Darkness* and *Northern Pursuit* (Warner Bros., 1943). Warners had pulled in its belt financially on this film, causing the *New York Times* to comment that it was "an outdoor picture which seems to have been written and played in an

---

[29]Looking full face at the camera, Errol blurts out in a chipper manner, "Oh that voice is so divine, I wish it were mine."

overheated room." Too long in its final ninety-four minutes, the feature was not well paced,[30] and the combination of Errol and Julie Bishop (fiancée of Northwest Canadian Mountie Flynn) was negligible to say the least. In fact, Gene Lockhart as Ernst, the Nazi spy out to help party leader (Helmut Dantine) plot sabotage activities from an outpost near Hudson Bay, nearly stole the show. Obviously, the studio thought they could get away with an inexpensive Flynn production, knowing that his offcamera publicity would carry the film at the ticket wickets. It did!

With so many of Hollywood's top stars away at war, Warner Bros. considered itself indeed fortunate to still have the services of the very useful Errol Flynn. The company negotiated a new contract with the actor which provided him with $200,000 per film, a percentage of the profits, and a direct hand in the selection of properties, directors, and cast. The studio also allowed him to form Thomson Productions, which was to co-produce his features with Warners.

Despite the seemingly munificent salary Flynn was earning in the mid-1940s, he was not indeed a rich man, particularly after paying ex-wife Lili Damita her monthly stipend, supporting his new wife and family, paying taxes, and covering the costs of his professional overhead and his profligate ways. During these years he worked largely because he needed the funds. As he later admitted, he was quite unhappy, and "mostly I walked through my pictures." It was during this period of stress that he began to drink vodka heavily, which he would conclude was "one of the slowest though most certain forms of suicide."

Errol's sole 1944 release, and the first under his new contract, was the mediocre *Uncertain Glory* (Warner Bros.), which Raoul Walsh directed. In a plot which had too many similarities to *Northern Pursuit,* Flynn played Jean Picard, a French thief who escapes execution during an air raid and is hunted down and captured by a policeman (Paul Lukas). Returning to Paris, the train they are riding is halted when a railroad bridge is bombed, and in a French village Errol meets Marianne (Jean Sullivan), a young French girl with whom he falls in love. In a rather gratuitously patriotic finale, Flynn's character allows him-

---

[30]In *The Hollywood Professionals, supra,* Kingsley Canham observes of *Northern Pursuit*: "The performances are routine, the musical score [by Adolph Deutsch] as banal as that of a serial, but the film is enhanced by excellent atmospheric photography, especially the highlighting of plotting faces and suspicious eyes, and the reasonable staging of the action sequences such as the ski chase in which camera placement again substitutes for material that today would be shot with the use of sophisticated paraphernalia such as hand-held cameras and helicopters." Canham also notes. "It bore some resemblances to Michael Powell's *49th Parallel,* released in America as *The Invaders* [Columbia, 1942], in that it represented a situation of Nazis landing in Canada on a mission of sabotage.... Walsh concentrates on the mounting of the action scenes [in contrast to Powell's focus on characterization] such as an avalanche caused by the German agents shooting their Indian guides, which spectacularly engulfs the Nazi killers leaving only one survivor."

self to be arrested as the alleged saboteur who has blown up a bridge. "Artificial in structure, mood and atmosphere," is how the *New York Times* labeled the 106-minute melodrama that lacked the sparkle of early Flynn adventures.

There were many filmgoers in the European Allied countries who had been angered when Errol's character in *Desperate Journey* had blithely said, "So much for the Germans . . . now on to Australia and the Japanese." In *Objective, Burma!* (Warner Bros., 1945), Errol was cast as Major Nelson, who, along with some three dozen American paratroopers, is dropped in the Burmese jungle to ferret out and destroy a Japanese radar station. The task is accomplished, but the rescue plan goes afoul and the men must march through 150 miles of jungle filled with Nipponese snipers. At the end of the 142-minute adventure, only a few survivors are rescued, but the mission has paved the way for the Allied aerial invasion of Burma.

When the British Lord Chancellor saw *Objective, Burma!* he agreed with his aroused fellow countrymen that the motion picture was at the very least overzealous in claiming that America had almost won the campaign singlehandly. The English were also aghast at the callousness of Flynn's character who, at one point in the film, after discovering the mangled bodies of some comrades, says of the Japanese, "Kill them all . . . every last one of them!" After playing in a British movie house for one week, *Objective Burma!* was withdrawn from English release. Not until 1952 was the motion picture allowed to be shown in England again, and then only with the addition of a diplomatic prologue.

The uproar over *Objective, Burma!* tended to obscure the fact that in this Raoul Walsh-directed[31] feature, Errol offered a very human, sincere performance. "There are no phony heroics by Errol Flynn," insisted the usually restrained *New York Times.* The picture was always one of Errol's favorites.

San Antonio (Warner Bros., 1945) was Errol's first Western since 1941. It was a comedown from his previous work in the genre, despite its Technicolor trimmings. David Butler's lacklustre direction and a mediocre script did little to help this expensively-mounted production which could not even equal the action of a B production from such studios as Republic, Monogram, or PRC.

---

[31]In his autobiography, director Walsh recalls the making of *Objective, Burma!*: "Errol was on his good behavior because he was writing a book when I was not using him. Between being gung-ho with his men and typing his life story, he had no time for anything more than half a dozen drinks, which to him was almost total abstention." Walsh also describes the lavishness with which Errol spent Warner Bros.' money while the star and director were in New York publicizing the war film. Explained Errol to Walsh, "They owed me that, Uncle, for working my ass off in those bloody swamps [actually, some marshy areas in Orange County, California]. I thought we'd never find the Japs."

With Mary Servoss, Erskine Sanford, and Jean Sullivan in *Uncertain Glory* (1944)

With William Prince (second from left), Henry Hull, Frank Tang, and Rodd Redwing in *Objective, Burma!* (1945)

From the dull *San Antonio,* Errol then drifted into a clinker called *Never Say Goodbye* (Warner Bros., 1946), his only film with director James V. Kern. Why Errol allowed himself to be a part of such sentimental fluff is hard to understand, unless one presumes that he no longer cared about his roles, only the money that he was making. The film was a series of tired situations revolving around the worn-out concept of a divorced couple (Errol and Eleanor Parker) who are brought back together by their little daughter (Patti Brady). The film did give Flynn a chance to perform some wheezy gags and do an imitation of Humphrey Bogart (complete with Bogie's dubbed voice).

More consequential for Flynn than *Never Say Goodbye* was the publication in 1946 of his book *Showdown.* The prose took a licking from the critics, but it had respectable sales due mainly to its author's reputation. Errol claimed that writing "helped me get rid of sense of futility." In analyzing this book, *The Saturday Review of Literature* reported, "though it contains absurdities, [it] is not all absurd. As an adventure tale it moves along at a good pace. The action scenes are well imagined and presented. . . . Like many another novel, *Showdown* is most successful where it is straight-forward story, weakest where it is most pretentious."

Both of the star's 1947 starring vehicles were directed by Peter Godfrey, but the first, *Cry Wolf* (Warner Bros.), was the best of the two.

With Patti Brady and Eleanor Parker in *Never Say Goodbye* (1946)

306

Novelist Errol Flynn and his book *Showdown* **(1946)**

Aboard his yacht *The Zaca* **(1946)**

Here Flynn was given his first opportunity to play a character who appeared to be decidedly villainous and possibly homicidal. His teaming with Barbara Stanwyck worked well and might have resulted in a fine acting duo had better projects been offered them. On the other hand, *Escape Me Never* (Warner Bros), the remake of a 1935 British film,[32] had been completed in early 1946 but had been shelved. Notoriously dull and unbelievable, *Escape Me Never* had Errol as a musical genius who fathers a child by a young woman (Ida Lupino) and later marries her when the fiancée (Eleanor Parker) of his brother (Gig Young) thinks her loved one was the father. Rounding out 1947, Errol did a guest bit in a modest Warners' feature *Always Together,* another entry starring that bland but likeable team of Robert Hutton and Joyce Reynolds. In a film-within-a-film sequence, Errol appeared along with Humphrey Bogart, Jack Carson, Dennis Morgan, Alexis Smith, and Eleanor Parker.

Silver River (Warner Bros., 1948) was Errol's last film with Raoul Walsh.[33] By this time, however, liquor had begun to take its toll. He was hard to handle on the set and obviously had decided he disliked working with such a tough helmsman as Walsh.

Outside of a visually exciting Civil War battle sequence which opens *Silver River,* the film was a pedestrian affair. Both Errol and co-star Ann Sheridan had seen better times, and neither seemed capable of instilling the proceedings with much sparkle.[34] Then too, Errol was cast as a rather disreputable soul, Captain Mike McComb, a cashiered Union officer who becomes a freebooter. He finds himself in Silver City, where he sends his buddy (Bruce Bennett) to his death and then marries his friend's worldly widow (Sheridan). She later leaves him and he eventually changes his ways, somewhat, for the better. As *Variety* analyzed of this vehicle, "[It's] long and there's too much footage devoted to talk." Action, not talk, had always been Errol's medium and his fans were tiring of not seeing action in his pictures.

In an effort to remedy the situation, Warner Bros. cast Errol in *Adventures of Don Juan,* which was released in December, 1948. In this last of Flynn's decent swashbuckling films, some of the sparkle of his former performances returned to the delight of his fans. Originally scheduled to be made in 1945 under Raoul Walsh's direction, the pic-

---

[32]The 1935 United Artists release had starred Elizabeth Bergner and Hugh Sinclair. It was based on a play by Margery Sharp, who had also written *The Constant Nymph.* Warners had filmed *The Constant Nymph* in 1943, at first planning to use Flynn, then casting Charles Boyer in the pivotal male role. *Escape Me Never* was a sort of "sequel" to that 1943 film.

[33]In his autobiography, Walsh does not even allude to *Silver River.*

[34]In a rainstorm sequence, Sheridan seeks shelters in Errol's wagon. He jibes at her, "Mrs. Moore . . . please! You could at least knock on the wheels before entering my wagon." The look in Sheridan's eyes at this point reminded viewers that the "Oomph" Girl still had great potential to offer oncamera.

**With Eleanor Parker
in *Escape Me Never* (1947)**

**With Ann Sheridan
in *Silver River* (1948)**

With Viveca Lindfors in *Adventures of Don Juan* (1948)

ture did not go into production until 1947, and then it was supervised by Vincent Sherman, a man more at ease with the more delicate type screen fare.[35] Viveca Lindfors, whom the studio hoped might be the new Ingrid Bergman, was Errol's co-star.

Errol played Don Juan de Marana, a seventeenth century Spanish adventurer who saves Queen Margaret (Lindfors) and King Philip III (Romney Brent) from the evil state minister, de Lorca (Robert Douglas). The film had more than its share of dueling, balcony climbing, and romancing, as well as a good satire on the historical main character.[36]

Errol performed yet another guest bit for Warner Bros., this time in *It's a Great Feeling* (1949), a Doris Day-Dennis Morgan-Jack Carson comedy about a fickle young girl from a small town who becomes the star of a movie musical. Flynn provided the plotline's big joke for the film, turning up as her hometown boyfriend, Jeffrey Brushdinkel—for everyone had assumed she was going to marry a small town yokel.

Flynn's contract with Warner Bros. had been modified in 1947 to permit him to make one film a year outside the studio, although it was not until 1949 that he did just that, making *That Forsyte Woman* at MGM (in exchange for William Powell doing *Life with Father* [1947] at the Burbank lot). Based on the first book (*A Man of Property*) of John Galsworthy's stately *The Forsyte Saga*, the film had Errol in the strong role of Soames Forsyte,[37] a stuffy, conventional man married to strong-willed independent Irene, played by Greer Garson.[38] The clash of characters leads to unhappiness and the wife falls for unconventional architect Robert Young, who dies. After Young's demise, she leaves her husband to marry his freespirited cousin (Walter Pidgeon), leaving Flynn's Soames with his wealth but a life without meaningful love. Rather a conventional and vapid love story, *That Forsyte Woman,* interestingly, remained one of Errol's favorite roles, perhaps because he worked so hard to make the part believable (at which he was rather successful).

By 1950 not only were the Hollywood studios having great financial

---

[35]Max Steiner replaced Erich Wolfgang Korngold as film composer, and the villainous de Lorca was played by Robert Douglas instead of the originally-cast George Coulouris.

[36]There was some similarity to the jocular tone of Douglas Fairbanks' spoof of the part in *The Private Life of Don Juan* (United Artists, 1934).

[37]Errol had rejected the more easily typed roles which were eventually played by Pidgeon and Young in the picture. In the 1970, twenty-six-part British teleseries based on *The Forsyte Saga*, Eric Porter appeared as Soames.

[38]In the foreword to *The Films of Errol Flynn (supra)*, Greer Garson relates: "I found Errol much more objective and modest than many performers. . . . In our picture he tackled a new type of role and revealed an unsuspected and admirable talent for characterization. 'Thank Heaven—at last an escape from cloak and dagger stuff!' he remarked. If he had lived longer—and more temperately—he would probably have emerged as the serious actor he longed to be, although I think eventually he would have preferred to earn a reputation as a writer."

With Greer Garson and Walter Pidgeon in *That Forsyte Woman* (1949)

With Alexis Smith in *Montana* (1950)

and artistic problems combatting the emergence of commercial television, new government anti-trust regulations, and restyled public tastes, but they also were faced with the delicate problem of coping with their aging male stars, most of them holdovers from the 1930s and early 1940s. Fox had its Tyrone Power, MGM its Clark Gable, Spencer Tracy, and Robert Taylor, Paramount its Alan Ladd, and Warner Bros., in particular, its Errol Flynn. Not quite sure what to do with their fast-maturing "bad boy," they shoved him into two Westerns, each as dull as the other.

Since *Adventures of Don Juan* had failed to generate sufficient box-office to please the company treasurer, the budgets for both Westerns were restricted.[39] Reteamed with Alexis Smith in *Montana* (1950), a no-longer vital Errol played an Australian sheepherder determined to bring his flocks to the cattle country of Montana, which eventually sets off a range feud. The one unique aspect to this mundane outing was the "dueting" of "Reckon I'm in Love" by Errol and Smith, with Flynn strumming on a guitar.

Next came *Rocky Mountain* (1950), which, unlike *Montana,* was not done in Technicolor but did have a better script. Its slim plot had Errol leading a group of Confederates (could he never escape the Civil War era?) to California, to stimulate a rebellion among outlaws for control of the West Coast. But the horsemen never reach their destination; they are killed along the way by Indians while they save Flynn's new-found love (Patrice Wymore).

Errol's marriage to Nora Eddington[40] came to an end in June, 1949, although they were to remain close friends until his death. She later wrote that drugs had almost taken over his life by this time, and she feared for her safety as he often became violent under the effects of narcotics. While he was in Europe on holiday, Errol had become embroiled in a torrid romance with Rumanian Princess Irene Ghica. With his Nora Eddington domestic chapter coming to a close, it seemed likely—so the rumors went—that Errol and the royal lady would wed. However, by the time the princess came to America to visit Errol, he was already engaged in a passionate liaison with Patrice Wymore, the young blonde Warner contract player who had been with him in *Rocky Mountain.*

On October 23, 1950, while Errol was in France on location for a film, he wed Patrice; he was then forty-one, she was twenty-three.

---

[39]Director Vincent Sherman (*Adventures of Don Juan*) has confirmed that at the outset of their film together, Errol promised him to be on good behavior and that he was for the first ten days or so of production. Then, reviews for *Never Say Goodbye* came to the star's attention, and he was so upset by their adverse tone, that he again took to drink and to other undisciplined behavior, which added a good many days and much additional time to the production schedule.

[40]She also appeared oncamera with Errol. She was seen as a lady in a coach in *Adventures of Don Juan* and in the short subject, *Cruise of the Zaca.*

There were two ceremonies, both performed in French; the civil ceremony took place at Monaco City Hall, and the religious one was held at the French Lutheran Church of the Transfiguration in Nice. Both times a nervous Patrice managed to mumble "oui" at the appropriate moments. (The bride's mother is said to have remarked to her daughter, "Oh, honey, I'm so glad you're getting married and settling down.")

But settling down was not part of Errol's lifestyle. Less than a month later, on November 22, he was involved in another statutory rape case. This time charges were pressed by a fifteen-year-old French girl named Denise Duvuvier. He refused to appear at the trial, the charge came to naught, and the case was dismissed. However, the constant barrage of adverse publicity deeply affected him. He seemed to be almost perpetually ill at ease, except when he was sailing the seas in his boat, *Zaca*.

Errol's final 1950 release was his second and last loanout to MGM. This film production of Rudyard Kipling's *Kim* was a Technicolor epic, empty of content, but a delight for the eyes. Errol and co-star Paul Lukas filmed some footage in India, and Flynn seemed to have a good time making the picture, although his part as the spy Mahbub Ali the Red Beard was actually only a supporting one to Dean Stockwell in the title role. Most of the movie was lensed in California and it was not overly popular with moviegoers, especially due to its lack of any love interest.

Ironically, Errol was originally scheduled to play the white hunter in *King Solomon's Mines* (MGM, 1950), a part which could have been memorable and given a boost to his sliding career. Instead, Britisher Stewart Granger got the role. The film was a huge boxoffice success, vastly eclipsing *Kim* and launching Granger onto a successful round as Metro's new swashbuckling hero.

Tired of working at Warners, where for years he had been feuding with Jack L. Warner mostly over money, Errol made the independent *Hello, God* (1951), in Italy as an obvious attempt to break his studio contract. It was also the first of two films with director William Marshall, and it led to nearly as many legal hassles as did his later independent project, *William Tell*. After completing his India-filmed scenes for *Kim*, Errol had stopped over in Italy and joined Marshall to make *Hello, God*, an allegorical story about four soldiers killed at Anzio Beach who ask God to take them into heaven, although they have died before their specified times. Errol later changed his mind about the project, probably realizing what its release would do to his Warners' contract and the yearly salary he badly needed to continue his lifestyle and to pay off his ex-wives. Legal entanglements would keep the picture out of theatres in the U.S. until 1958, when Cavalcade Pictures distributed the seventy-four-minute mishmash.

Errol's sole 1951 release, *The Adventures of Captain Fabian*, was issued by Republic and was produced-directed by William Marshall.

With Laurette Luez in a pose
for *Kim* (1950)

With son Sean on Lake Mead, Nevada
(July, 1951)

Flynn took sole screen credit for the adaptation of Robert Shannon's novel, *Fabulous Ann Madlock*, on which the film was based. Sadly dull, the adventure film essentially gave Errol only a supporting role, while Micheline Presle (Marshall's wife) and Vincent Price had the bulk of footage and the more interesting parts. The entire film was lensed in France.

Offscreen, 1951, was not a good year for Flynn. By this time he and his new wife Patrice were already showing signs of incompatability. (Patrice would later complain that Errol expected her to be everything to him, and that the pressure was just too much for her.) It was also in this year that Errol, while taking an evening on the town at New York's El Morocco, was slugged by Canadian millionaire Duncan McDonald. At that time the club was run by Errol's pal, John Perona, so the star refrained from getting into a slug fest with McDonald. It was not too much later that Flynn would decide that the only way to repay columnist Jimmy Fidler for some unflattering remarks in his column, would be to punch the news chronicler. Then there was the fight with Errol's stand-in, Jack Easton—and no one was quite certain just why the two men had come to blows.

Back at Warner Bros., the studio casually threw Errol into a very poor B film, *Mara Maru* (1952). Apparently, this film was made as cheaply as possible. It paired Errol with Ruth Roman. Frustrated on the home lot, Errol went over to Universal-International, the prime maker of cutlass-and-romance yarns in the early 1950s. He had a percentage deal on *Against All Flags* (1952),[41] a Technicolor feature which matched him with redhead Maureen O'Hara. The George Sherman-directed programmer is one of the few examples of spying in the swashbuckling genre, but it had little to offer with its eighteenth-century yarn about the infiltration of a Barbary pirate's stronghold on Madagascar.

His two short subjects, which were released by Warners in 1952, were far more interesting than his two features, perhaps because he made them both. The twenty-minute *Cruise of the Zaca* was turned out in 1946 but was held up from release due to Flynn's divorce from Nora Eddington. Involved in the production were several of Flynn's friends, his father, and the California Scripps Institute of Oceanography. The other two-reeler was *Deep Sea Fishing,* and it detailed the exploits of Errol and archer Howard Hill using rod and reel and bow and arrows to hunt marlin and sail fish. The ten-minute featurette, shot in Kodachrome near Acapulco, was narrated by Bob Edge.

Even before his marriage to Patrice Wymore, Flynn had fallen in love with the island of Jamaica. It was there that he shot much of *Cruise of the Zaca.* (The boat had been leased to Columbia for scenes

[41]Remade as *The King's Pirate* (Universal, 1967), with Doug McClure.

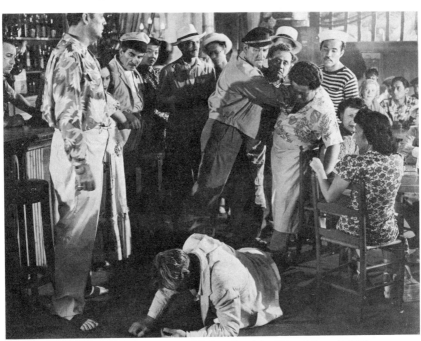

With Michael Ross and Richard Webb (on floor) in *Mara Maru* (1952)

315

in *The Lady from Shanghai* [1948].) Later, the actor set up "Errol Flynn Estates" on Jamaica and tied up several hundred thousand dollars in living quarters and a plantation. He moved there with Patrice after their marriage, due partly to his love of the island and partly because of a desire to remove himself from the pressures of alimony payments to Lili Damita and Nora Eddington.

By 1952, Errol's eighteen-year-old association with Warner Bros. was at an end. The studio accused him of "a breach of contract, holding up the company and general bad behavior." The company hoped he would pay them $100,000 to break his contract, but he refused. Finally, Jack L. Warner informed him they would put him in any parts that they wished, implying that they would be supporting roles or, even, heaven help him, bit parts. Errol still would not cough up the required money. Warner's bluff had been called. The contractual arrangement was terminated, with no money exchanging hands.

The Master of Ballantrae (Warner Bros., 1953), from Robert Louis Stevenson's novel, was the actor's last Warners' contract film. Filmed with frozen studios funds in England, Scotland, and Italy, this eighteenth-century costume romance was one of Errol's more substantial post-World War II efforts. It did better than most of his recent features in America, and it did very well in Europe.

Now freelancing, Errol was faced with the practical problem of pay-

As *The Master of Ballantrae* (1953)

In the uncompleted *William Tell* **(1954)**

ing for his expensive life. He decided to leave the United States and to live on the *Zaca*. Then, he flew to Rome to begin work on *Crossed Swords* (a.k.a., *Il Maestro Di Don Giovanni*) (United Artists, 1954). Milton Krims directed from his original screenplay. The picture was an attempt to revitalize the swashbuckler Flynn of old, but it emerged more as a dull parody of the actor's former vital self and his past glorious screen roles. The one pleasing distraction in the project was shapely Gina Lollobrigida. (While in Rome making this feature, Flynn's wife Patrice gave birth to Arnella Roma on December 25, 1953.)

Creative artists are notoriously bad businessmen, and Errol proved no different when he decided to join with producer Barry Mahon (who had made *Crossed Swords*) to create *William Tell*. Jack Cardiff, who had lensed previous Flynn films, was hired to direct and photograph the motion picture, and Errol was scheduled for the title role, with his old pal Bruce Cabot in support. Flynn hoped to use Hedy Lamarr for his leading lady, but he had to settle for Antonella Luldi. He supplied $430,000 for this CinemaScope production, which represented about half of the budget. The rest of the funds were to come from Italian backers. After a few weeks of filming, one of the Italian investors withdrew from the project. Errol tried in vain to obtain backing from Columbia Pictures, United Artists, and producer-director Herbert Wil-

317

cox. To cinch the debacle, Bruce Cabot, angered because he had not received his salary, attached Flynn's cars (his only assets) and then boasted about his legal maneuver.

William Tell was abandoned, and Flynn found himself broke and heavily in debt. "Following an early policy," he explained in his autobiography "when broke, put on your best clothes, if you have any and if you haven't—borrow them, make the tie neater, and go around hoping you never looked more prosperous." This business failure, nevertheless, was a tremendous blow to his ego, and he spent most of the next four years aboard the *Zaca*. A bitter man, rarely working, he wondered what had happened to himself and to his once lucrative career.

Although Britisher Wilcox would not finance the completion of *William Tell*, he did hire Errol to take second billing to his wife, Anna Neagle, in *Let's Make Up* (a.k.a., *Lilacs in the Spring*, United Artists, 1955). This rather mixed-up backstage romance was filmed in both black and white and color, and centered on Miss Neagle's performance of several roles, including Queen Victoria. The creaky plot gave Errol a chance to sing and dance with Anna to the song, "Lily of Laguna."

Twenty years after *Captain Blood,* Errol's last swashbuckler, *The Warriors* (a.k.a, *The Dark Avengers,* Allied Artists, 1955) opened in America. Made in England, it gave him a chance to appear as yet another historical character, this time as Prince Edward of England, known as the "Black Prince." After the Hundred Years War, Edward remains in France to watch over the conquered land of King Edward III (Michael Hordern), his father. The climactic attack on the castle was lensed on the leftover set from MGM's *Ivanhoe* (1952). Sadly, *The Warriors* met with little audience interest in the U.S. It is possible that some of Flynn's fans (the ranks had diminished greatly over the years) thought this was merely a reissue of one of his old Warners' pictures.

Let's Make Up had enjoyed a modest reception in England and it prompted Herbert Wilcox to again team Errol (once more billed second) with Anna Neagle. Wilcox based the film on an Ivor Novello musical, *King's Rhapsody* (United Artists, 1955). Patrice Wymore, looking exceptionally beautiful, was billed third in this would be operetta, which was released without any musical numbers. The film was slow and stodgy and a boxoffice dud on both sides of the Atlantic. Errol did not work again for nearly two years.

During these trying times he wandered aimlessly aboard the *Zaca*, occasionally going to England, Rome, or Paris, but mostly just drifting. "I had plenty of time to contemplate," he mused in *My Wicked, Wicked Ways.* From this contemplation he came to the conclusion that he was merely a public "phallic symbol" and "out like Flynn."

Although he considered himself finished in pictures and in show business in general, he received an offer from Universal, while in Paris, to portray the Turkish dictator Kemal Ataturk for $160,000. The picture

In *The Warriors* (1955)

With Finlay Currie
in *King's Rhapsody* (1955)

With Patrice Wymore Flynn
and their daughter Arnelia
in Hollywood (February, 1956)

was to be called *Istanbul* (1956), but he soon discovered the picture
had nothing to do with Ataturk. Instead, it was an adventure potboiler
to be shot in Hollywood, the last place he wanted to be. Still "even
though contracts may not be signed, you can't back out," said Errol in
his autobiography and he returned to the film capital to do the movie
which turned out to be a remake of the Fred MacMurray-Ava Gardner
Singapore (Universal, 1947), with locale shots in Turkey. Except for
Nat King Cole's oncamera singing and Flynn's satisfactory appearance
as the tired man of the world, the movie was tedious going for everyone
concerned.

Early in 1957, United Artists issued another B Flynn picture, called
The Big Boodle. This black-and-white feature was as much a travelogue of pre-Castro Havana as it was a mystery about a gambler (Errol)
involved with two beautiful women (Rosanna Rory and Gia Scala).
The kindest of critics admitted that the much-aged Errol, with his
ravaged looks, now had a "new credibility" at portraying *roués.*

Another form of employment came Errol's way when he entered the
television field. In England he starred in the syndicated "Errol Flynn
Theatre," which contained thirty-nine half-hour episodes and was
shown on American television in 1957. He hosted all the shows and
acted in six of them, some of these with Patrice Wymore. He made his

320

With Carlos Rivas in *The Big Boodle* (1957)

With Sheb Wooley (standing, dark hat) in the "Playhouse 90" episode *Without Incident* (CBS-TV, June 6, 1957)

actual U.S. video debut on April 4, 1956, on NBC-TV's "Screen Directors Playhouse" in *The Sword of Villon,* in which he played the French poet, Francois Villon.[42] It was technically his last swashbuckler role, one that would have been ideal for him a decade or more before. On June 6, 1957, he played on "Playhouse 90" in *Without Incident.* During this period he entered the recording arena, making a dramatic LP record of *The Three Musketeers* in the role of D'Artangan.[43]

A part which was ideal for the declining star, and one which brought back his professional prominence, was that of Mike Campbell in Ernest Hemingway's *The Sun Also Rises* (Twentieth Century-Fox, 1957). For some unexplained reason, producer Darryl F. Zanuck, who hardly knew Errol, chose him for the part. After some prodding from his wife, Flynn accepted the assignment with its fourth billing in this film based on Hemingway's 1926 novel. Errol received heady reviews, and talk of an Academy Award nomination. When compared to his less resilient co-stars, Errol's performance as the harddrinking, lonely, bitter, and wasted man in love with Brett (Ava Gardner), who, in turn, adores an impotent writer (Tyrone Power), had a strength to it that compensated for his being too old for the part. Errol's characterization of Mike Campbell, the only performance hailed by critics, may well be his finest acting work. Unfortunately, the movie typed him, and his last two major screen roles were in the same mold as *The Sun Also Rises:* both philosophic drunks, a part Errol knew inside and out.

Just about the time *The Sun Also Rises* was released in August, 1957, Errol launched a million-dollar law suit against *Confidential* Magazine, claiming the publication's lurid story of his being the host to wild sex parties was libelous. "It's so nice to be the one who's doing the suing for a change," he volunteered to the press. Like Maureen O'-Hara, he was one of the few performers who ever took legal action against the seemingly scurrilous stories printed of their supposed exploits. Errol won his point, but any financial returns he saw from the action were slight.

Not so strangely, with the rise in his popularity again and his return to steady work, Errol's once "happy" marriage to Patrice Wymore came to an end and they separated. Said Flynn, "It is hard for me to stay interested in any one woman in the world for very long. . . . Patrice was and is fine, but I got bored." Miss Wymore's comments varied. On one occasion she said, "Oh, I'm in touch with him all the time, through the newspapers. That's why I filed suit for separate maintenance. If it's

[42]Among the notable onscreen Francois Villons were Ronald Colman in *If I Were King* (Paramount, 1938) and Oreste in the operetta *The Vagabond King* (Paramount, 1956).
[43]The disc was originally issued with Basil Rathbone's rendering of *Oliver Twist* on Columbia Records. Errol's side was reissued in the mid-1960s on a Columbia cheaper subsidiary label, Harmony Records. This time, Flynn was paired with another Basil Rathbone record, ironically, *The Adventures of Robin Hood.* Recently, Command Performance Records issued Errol in a radio rendition of *The Three Musketeers.*

going to be a long-distance marriage, it might as well be recognized by law as such." At another time she offered, "I wish I could hate him but I can't. He could charm the birds out of the trees."

Actually, there was more to the Flynns' separation than met the public eye at the time, for Errol had found a new interest. Her name was Beverly Aadland, and he met her when she was on the Warner Bros. lot doing a bit in *Marjorie Morningstar* (1958). Errol had returned to his alma mater to play the part of his old friend John Barrymore in *Too Much, Too Soon* (1958), which featured Academy Award winner Dorothy Malone as the Great Profile's profligate daughter, Diana. The exploitive feature focused on the sensational and treaded heavily over reality as it unraveled the relationship of the faltering Barrymore in his declining Hollywood years with his self-willed daughter Diana, fresh on the movie scene to try to establish herself as a great star of the new generation.

Of playing John Barrymore, Flynn wrote in *My Wicked Wicked Ways,* "For once in my long career I worked hard at the characterization that I thought should be presented. I tried hard to remember him, to underplay, to underemphasize and in this way to get nearest to the recesses of the mind and heart of a great human being." Again, the critics approved of Flynn, but of nothing else about *Too Much, Too Soon.* Errol's old boss and one-time business enemy, Jack L. Warner, could never get over how the once handsome Flynn had deteriorated into no more than a burnt-out candle.

The facts of the Beverly Aadland chapter of Errol's life are not very

With Beverly Aadland at a Hollywood party (September 15, 1959)

323

clear. Her age at the time of their initial meetings is even debatable. She and her mother, as well as most sources, claim she was fifteen, but some other sources, including some psychologists, say she was emotionally closer to twelve or thirteen. Whatever her age, she was soon living with Errol, becoming his "small companion" to whom his autobiography was dedicated.

"My Beverly was only 15 and still a virgin when she met Errol Flynn. A few hours later she was still 15 . . . but she wasn't a virgin anymore." This is how Florence Aadland, Beverly's mother, began her 1965 book, *The Beautiful Pervert* (originally called *The Big Love*), which graphically detailed her daughter's two years as Errol's mistress.

The story of Errol's relationship with Beverly was not widely known outside the film colony, but after his death it was the cause of quite a public stir. For at that time, Beverly sued his estate seeking to win some money. Whatever the sleazy headlines did to the memory of that relationship after Errol died, it may well have been this young girl who brought Flynn whatever emotional comfort he received from life during his last two years. At this point in his life, doctors actually wondered how he was staying alive. Years of alcohol and drugs had more than taken their toll of this one-time swashbuckler. His public reaction to criticism of his life style was: "I'll live this half of my life, I don't care about the other half."

For his last major film role Errol again worked for producer Darryl F. Zanuck, who was releasing his independent productions through Twentieth Century-Fox. Errol received top star billing in the screen version of Romain Gary's book, *The Roots of Heaven* (1958). William Holden was originally scheduled to star in the role of Morel, the leader of a group of people dedicated to save the African elephants from exploitation and extinction. Holden withdrew from the project and Trevor Howard replaced him. Flynn was cast as Major Forsythe, a drunk (what else?) who had betrayed his men to the Nazis in World War II and now found solace in the bottle. Others in the cast were Juliette Greco, Zanuck's latest protegée, Eddie Albert, Orson Welles, and Errol's old colleague, Paul Lukas.

With a bottle as a constant companion, Errol had little difficulty in combatting the hundred-forty-degree temperatures in French Equatorial Africa during the location filming. He also had another companion to take his mind off the situation; his young love, Beverly, had made the trip to the "Dark Continent" with the former swashbuckler. How the star managed to whisk an underaged girl out of the U.S. and into Africa has yet to be explained.

The Roots of Heaven was a boxoffice turkey, and received scarce praise from reviewers for its artistic pretentions. The film ended the possibility of any forthcoming movie roles for Flynn, but he did not remain idle for long. Before his foray into Africa, Errol had appeared on national television on the quiz show "The $64,000 Question," one of the most popular programs of its day. He made $32,000 on the show, but declined to reach for the jackpot sum. Columnist Sheilah Graham later quoted him as saying, "It was all fixed," but that he "knew all the answers."

In an odd decision made out of desperation, boredom, or rising to a challenge, Errol decided to return to the stage in the Broadway-bound *The Master of Thornfield,* an adaptation of Charlotte Bronte's *Jane Eyre.* His wealthy friend, Huntington Hartford, had adapted the play. However, after advance openings in Detroit and Cincinnati, Errol left the production. "I wasn't happy in the play," he writes in his autobiography, much as I wanted to do something in the legitimate theatre. I thought the play in its present form was too archaic." Others claim Flynn had trouble remembering his lines in the role of Rochester.[44]

Next, Errol got involved in what would be the last real adventure of his already amazing life. He traveled to Cuba, where he supposedly fought in the hills with Fidel Castro and his guerrilla forces. How much Errol really had to do with Castro is hard to tell; the junket was as vague as his activities in the Spanish Civil War. At any rate, he did have the poor taste to appear on the NBC-TV "Tonight Show" draped in a Cuban flag, although at the time Castro had not yet officially become *persona non grata* with the American Government.

Out of the Cuban escapade came Errol's final screen appearance, *Cuban Rebel Girls* (Joseph Brenner Associates, 1959). It was a cheap exploitation film, which was shown only on the grind-house circuit. Produced and directed by friend Barry Mahon, with script and narration by Errol, the film had minimal entertainment or educational values. Filmed as cheaply as possible, the picture claimed to be a semi-documentary about the Cuban Revolution, but it was released at a time when Castro was hardly popular with the U.S. (By the time the film was unspooled, Errol's written accounts of the Cuban campaign had already been syndicated in American newspapers under the title, "I Fought with Castro.")

Looking for yet another source of income to put his finances in some order, Errol next embarked on his third book, this time an autobiography. To writer Earl Conrad he dictated over 200,000 words which Conrad transformed into the bestselling *My Wicked, Wicked Ways,* which G. P. Putnam & Sons issued in 1960 after Errol's death. The next year it was issued in paperback by Dell Books (and reissued in 1974). To date, it has sold over one million copies.

It was in 1959 that New York doctors informed Errol he had only a few more months to live. His drinking, drugs, and wild life were given

---

[44]John Emery took over for Flynn during the play's remaining brief fling.

as the causes for his physical breakdown. He took the news calmly, almost proudly. He would tell Nora Eddington, "Don't be unhappy; you know I've lived twice and I've had a marvelous life."

Somehow he managed to keep going, however, despite his declining health. He even managed to give two more performances before he died. He starred as a guest in *The Golden Shanty* episode on NBC-TV's "Goodyear Theatre." The filmed segment was telecast on November 9, 1959, three weeks after his death. Shot on a three-day schedule, its director, Arthur Hiller, said Errol was "in poor health," and "it was painful to watch this once graceful athlete barely able to climb out of a [prop] wagon." Early in October, 1959, Errol appeared on "The Red Skelton Show" in a hobo sketch in which he traded comic banter with the comedian.

Fading health was not Errol's only problem at this time, for Patrice Wymore had sued him for divorce, stating he no longer supported her or their daughter. At that time, Errol was living with Beverly at Hollywood's Garden of Allah Hotel. When Woodsey, as Flynn referred to Beverly, heard the news of the divorce proceedings, she supposedly did a war dance around the pool, wearing nothing but a brief towel.

According to Beverly's mother, Florence, Errol had planned to wed the girl and they were even contemplating having a family, although the actor had previously undergone a vasectomy. Beverly told her mother, "He says there's a 50-50 chance that another operation will fix him up again . . . his doctor seems to be confident."

Sadly, the end came for Errol when he was trying to make money, probably to pay off his debts and to support his young love. He and Beverly had traveled to Vancouver, British Columbia, to sell the *Zaca* for $100,000. When they had arrived, he said he felt badly and was taken to the home of one Dr. Garant Gould, who administered a pain killer. For a while, Errol told amusing stories about John Barrymore and W.C. Fields to the doctor before the sedation took effect. He was then taken to the physician's bedroom and was advised to lie down on the floor to relieve his aching back condition. He fell asleep, and when Beverly looked in on him sometime later, he was dead, apparently from heart failure.

On October 20, 1959, he was buried in Forest Lawn Cemetery, instead of in his beloved Jamaica, as he had requested. Although the funeral was attended by over a thousand persons, it retained appropriate dignity. Errol's old pals, Guinn Williams, Raoul Walsh, and Michael Romanoff, were among his pallbearers. Jack L. Warner, of all people, delivered the eulogy and Dennis Morgan sang "Home Is the Sailor."

Although he certainly had not been in decent health, Errol never really seemed to realize he was so close to death's door in the last years of his life. His autobiography, at the conclusion, finds him in Jamaica

Pallbearers Michael Romanoff, Mickey Rooney, Jack Oakie, Raoul Walsh, and Guinn "Big Boy" Williams at Errol Flynn's funeral (October 20, 1959)

and seemingly at peace with the world. "The second half-century looms up, but I don't feel the night coming on." That is how he and Earl Conrad ended his life story.

Errol may well have foreseen the debacle that his estate would cause in the years following his death. His three wives and Beverly Aadland, along with his creditors and the Internal Revenue Service, fought over his estate, which amounted to over $2,670,000, including properties in Hollywood and Jamaica, the *Zaca*, two films (*William Tell, Cuban Rebel Girls*), and various other assets.

The government acquired most of Flynn's property for back taxes and, as recently as 1968, the estate was appraised at two million dollars by the Internal Revenue Service, with liabilities at $1.7 million. The IRS still contends it is owed $125,000 in back taxes. According to Flynn's will, daughters Deirdre and Rory each were to receive $10,000, money which is long since gone. Deirdre, a pretty girl in her late twenties, has tried several careers, including that of a stuntgirl (at Warner Bros.) and actress, and she recently made news by dating actor Earl Holliman. Rory Flynn, two years Deirdre's junior, is a model in Paris. The two girls are presently estranged.

On November 26, 1971, Flynn's California estate was declared insolvent and probate proceedings were ordered terminated. The only asset

327

left was a lot on Sunset Plaza Drive, and it was sold for ten thousand dollars. The IRS had a $49,235 lien on the lot, the California State Tax Board had another lien of $10,484 on Flynn's estate, and the Los Angeles County Tax Board, an additional lien of $2,295.

Lili Damita, who received about a million dollars from Errol during his lifetime, married Alan Loomis, after Flynn's death, and today she resides in Fort Dodge, Iowa and Palm Beach, Florida. Their son, Sean Flynn, has been listed as missing in action in Cambodia since April 5, 1970 (he was a magazine war photographer), along with CBS newsman Dana Stone. He was working for the CBS network as a cameraman, and had already been injured on that job. During the 1960s he had tried a brief film career, even appearing in *The Son of Captain Blood* (Paramount, 1964), and a few spy and adventure quickies in Europe. However, the handsome son was not successful in films and he turned to a more profitable career as a photographer.

After twelve years of constant litigation, the bulk of the remaining assets from Errol's estates, namely his Jamaican "Errol Flynn Estates," went to his third wife, Patrice. Today, she operates the two-thousand-acre estate at Port Antonio, raising Hereford cattle and growing coconuts. Their daughter, Arnella, is still in school.

The greatest furor after Flynn's death came when Beverly Aadland sued his estate, claiming she was entitled to a portion of the money since she was "taught . . . a lewd, wanton and wayward way of life" by the late star. Patrice Wymore, in her defense plea, suggested to the court that Beverly's suit (for five million dollars in damages) was "predicated upon the assumption that Miss Aadland had moral character which was subject to being impaired." Not only did Beverly lose her case, but she was taken from her mother's custody and placed in a foster home. After two subsequent unsuccessful marriages, she returned to the public eye as a nightclub singer. Today she still continues in that capacity in Springfield, Massachusetts.

Now some fifteen years after his death, Errol's screen career and exhausting life style are far from forgotten.[45] His features are shown constantly on television and his better films still play in theaters, revival houses, and on the college campus circuit. His autobiography is still in print and his other two books are collectors' items which claim a large price in used book stores and at auctions. And now Universal Pictures has hired Bob Merrill to script *The Errol Flynn Story* for 1976

---

[45]Contrary to popular belief, the lack of a marker on Flynn's Forest Lawn grave site does not indicate the actor has been overlooked in death. According to one associate of the late performer, "The family wanted to avoid the publicity seekers, as has been the case with Rudolph Valentino. His friends know where he is buried, and it is easier this way." (A tannish brick wall and a modestly-sized bronze statue of a sad woman with downcast eyes provide landmarks for Errol's grave.) On the other hand, in early 1975 Deirdre Flynn told *Andy Warhol's Interview*, "Ronny Sehdlo, a guy who used to be my father's secretary, and I went to Forest Lawn one night with our Mark-a-Lots and composed

filming. Perhaps the one aspect of Errol Flynn that most people, especially his adventure-loving fans, did not or do not realize was that he was a human being capable of great and deep feeling. In his autobiography he described an incident which happened to him in Cincinnati when he was appearing in the Huntington Hartford play. He was depressed by the play and the course of his life. As he was leaving the theatre, an elderly lady in a wheelchair approached him and thanked him "for all the wonderful hours of happiness" he had given her in his performances.

"I walked off thinking," wrote Flynn, "maybe I haven't been such a loss after all. Anybody who can bring a few moments of happiness to another human life certainly can't be wasting his time in an otherwise fear-ridden and very often drab world. Maybe it hasn't all been so futile. Maybe it wasn't all a waste.

"Maybe all that I am in this world and all that I have been and done comes down to nothing more than being a touch of color in a prosaic world. Even that is something."

---

what we thought was a brilliant epitaph—something like: 'Here lies the end of an era.' we sneaked in and out of there—we were really careful—because his grave is in like a private area where there's only three or four graves. We wrote out this whole thing on the blank headstone with the angel over it. We didn't tell anybody and the next day in the paper it said, 'VANDALS MARK UP ERROL FLYNN'S GRAVE!" Now the fact that he was buried in Forest Lawn to begin with is unbelievable. My father hated Hollywood. He hated Jack Warner. He didn't want to be in Forest Lawn where he thought he might end up next to Jack Warner. The very idea repulsed him. He didn't dig this town or a lot of the people in it."

Feature Film Appearances

IN THE WAKE OF THE BOUNTY (Expeditionary Films, 1933), 70 min.
Producer-director-screenplay, Charles Chauvel; music director, Lionel Hart; sound, Arthur Smith, Clive Cross; camera, Tasman Higgins; editor, William Sheperd.

Mayne Lynton (Captain Bligh); Errol Flynn (Fletcher Christian); Victor Gourier (The Blind Fiddler); John Warwick (Young); Patricia Penman (Isabella); Arthur Greenaway (Narrator).

MURDER AT MONTE CARLO (First National—British, 1935), 70 min.
Director, Ralph Ince; based on the story by Tom Van Dycke; screenplay, Michael Barringer; art director, G. H. Ward; camera, Basil Emmott.

Eve Gray (Gilian); Errol Flynn (Dyter); Paul Graetz (Dr. Heinrich Becker); Lawrence Hanray (Collum); Ellis Irving (Marc Orton); Henry Victor (Major); Brian Buchel (Yates); Peter Gawthorne (Duprez); Molly Lamont (Margaret Becker); Gabriel Toyne (Wesley); James Dale (Gustav); Henry Longhurst (Editor); Ernest Sefton (Sankey).

THE CASE OF THE CURIOUS BRIDE (First National, 1935), 80 min.
Associate producer, Harry Joe Brown; director, Michael Curtiz; based on the novel by Erle Stanley Gardner; screenplay, Tom Reed; music, Bernhard Kaun; art directors, Carl Jules Weyl and Anton Grot; assistant director, Jack Sullivan; gowns, Orry-Kelly; sound, Dolph Thomas; special effects, Fred Jackman and Fred Jackman, Jr.; camera, David Abel; editor, Terry Morse.

Warren William (Perry Mason); Margaret Lindsay (Rhoda Montaine); Donald Woods (Carl Montaine); Claire Dodd (Della Street); Allen Jenkins (Spudsy); Barton MacLane (John Lucas); Phillip Reed (Dr. Millsap); Winifred Shaw (Doris Pender); Thomas Jackson (Toots Howard); Olin Howland (Wilbur Strong); Warren Hymer (Pender); Charles Richman (C. Phillip Montaine); Errol Flynn (Gregory Moxley); Mayo Methot (Florabelle); Robert Gleckler (Byrd the Detective); James Donlan (Fritz the Detective); George Humbert (Luigi); Henry Kolker (Stacey); Hector Sarno (Greek Proprietor); Antonio Filauri (Pierre); Mary Green (Girl); Bruce Mitchell and Frank G. Fanning (Detectives); Paul Hurst (Fibo); Milton Kibbee (Reporter); Tom Wilson (Cab Starter); Nick Copeland (Cab Driver); Olive Jones (Telephone Operator); Ky Robinson (Cop); Frank Bull (Broadcaster); George Guhl (Typist).

DON'T BET ON BLONDES (Warner Bros., 1935), 60 min.
Associate producer, Samuel Bischoff; director, Robert Florey; screenplay, Isabel Dawn and Boyce DeGaw; assistant director, Eric Stacey; dialog director, Arthur Greville Collins; art director, Esdras Hartley; music director, Leo F. Forbstein; camera, William Rees; editor, Thomas Richards.

Warren William ("Odds" Owen); Guy Kibbee (Colonel Jefferson Davis Youngblood); Claire Dodd (Marilyn Young); William Gargan ("Numbers"); Errol Flynn (David Van Dusen); Hobert Cavanaugh (Philbert O'Slemp); Vince

Barnett (Brains); Spencer Charters (Doc); Clay Clement (T. Everett Markham); Walter Byron (Dwight Boardman); Eddie Shubert (Steve); Jack Norton (J. Mortimer Slade); Maude Eburne (Ellen Purdy); Mary Treen (Switchboard Operator); Herman Bing (Professor Friedrich Wilhelm Gruber); Joseph Crehan (Doctor); Selmer Jackson and Cyril Ring (Men); Paul Fix (Youth); Ferdinand Schumann-Heink (Laboratory Assistant); Marc Lawrence, Jack Pennick, Ben F. Hendricks, Constantine Romanoff, Frank Moran, and Jack Low (Gangsters); Milton Kibbee (Cashier); Pat Somerset (Usher); Buddy Williams (Black Man).

CAPTAIN BLOOD (First National, 1935), 119 min.

Executive producer, Hal B. Wallis; associate producers, Harry Joe Brown and Gordon Hollingshead; director, Michael Curtiz; based on the novel by Rafael Sabatini; screenplay, Casey Robinson; music, Erich Wolfgang Korngold; orchestrators, Hugo Friedhofer and Ray Heindorf; assistant director, Sherry Shourds; fencing master, Fred Cavens; dialog director, Stanley Logan; art director, Anton Grot; gowns, Milo Anderson; sound, C. A. Riggs; special effects, Fred Jackman; camera, Hal Mohr; additional camera, Ernest Haller; editor, George Amy.

Errol Flynn (Dr. Peter Blood); Olivia de Havilland (Arabella Bishop); Lionel Atwill (Colonel Bishop); Basil Rathbone (Captain Levasseur); Ross Alexander (Jeremy Pitt); Guy Kibbee (Hagthorpe); Henry Stephenson (Lord Willoughby); George Hassell (Governor Steed); Forrester Harvey (Honesty Nuttall); Frank McGlynn, Sr. (Reverend Ogle); Robert Barrat (Wolverstone); Hobart Cavanaugh (Dr. Bronson); Donald Meek (Dr. Wacker); David Torrence (Andrew Baynes); J. Carrol Naish (Cahusac); Pedro de Cordoba (Don Diego); Leonard Mudie (Lord Jeffries); Jessie Ralph (Mrs. Barlowe); Stuart Casey (Captain Hobart); Halliwell Hobbes (Lord Sunderland); Colin Kenny (Lord Dyke); E. E. Clive (Court Clerk); Holmes Herbert (Captain Gardiner); Mary Forbes (Mrs. Steed); Reginald Barlow (Dixon); Ivan F. Simpson (Prosecutor); Denis d'Auburn (Lord Gildoy); Vernon Steele (King James); Georges Renavent (French Captain); Murray Kinnell (Clerk in Governor Steed's Court); Harry Cording (Kent); Maude Leslie (Baynes' Wife); Chris-Pin Martin (Sentry); Tom Wilson and Henry Otho (Pirates); David Thursby (Lookout); Yola D'Avril, Renee Terres, Lucille Porcett, and Tina Minard (Girls in Tavern); Alphonse Martell, Andre Cheron and Frank Puglia (French Officers).

THE CHARGE OF THE LIGHT BRIGADE (Warner Bros., 1936), 116 min.

Executive producer, Hal B. Wallis; associate producer, Samuel Bischoff; director, Michael Curtiz; story, Michel Jacoby; screenplay, Jacoby and Rowland Leigh; art director, John Hughes; assistant director, Jack Sullivan; dialog director, Stanley Logan; technical adviser, Captain E. Rochfort-John; technical adviser of military drills-tactics, Major Sam Harris; music, Max Steiner; orchestrator, Hugo Friedhofer; director of horse action, B. Reeves Eason; gowns, Milo Anderson; sound, C. A. Riggs; special effects, Fred Jackman and H. F. Koenekamp; camera, Sol Polito; editor, George Amy.

Errol Flynn (Major Geoffrey Vickers); Olivia de Havilland (Elsa Campbell); Patric Knowles (Captain Perry Vickers); Donald Crisp (Colonel Campbell); Henry Stephenson (Sir Charles Macefield); Nigel Bruce (Sir Benjamin Warrenton); David Niven (Captain James Randall); G. P. Huntley, Jr. (Major Jowett);

Spring Byington (Lady Octavia Warrenton); C. Henry Gordon (Surat Khan); E. E. Clive (Sir Humphrey Harcourt); Lumsden Hare (Colonel Woodward); Robert Barrat (Count Igor Zvolonoff); Walter Holbrook (Cornet Barclay); Charles Sedgwick (Cornet Pearson); J. Carrol Naish (Subahdar Major Puran Singh); Scotty Beckett (Prema Singh); Princess Beigum (Prema's Mother); George Regas (Wazir); Helen Sanborn (Mrs. Jowett); Dick Botiller (Native); Jon Kristen and Frank Lackteen (Panjaris); Michael Visaroff (Russian General); Arthur Thalasso (Sepoy); Carlyle Moore, Jr. (Junior Officer); Reginald Sheffield (Bentham); Georges Renavent (General Canrobart); Denis d'Auburn (Orderly); Craufurd Kent (Captain Brown); Holmes Herbert (General O'Neill); Yakima Canutt (Double for Errol Flynn).

GREEN LIGHT (First National, 1937), 85 min.

Executive producer, Hal B. Wallis; associate producer, Henry Blanke; director, Frank Borzage; based on the novel by Lloyd C. Douglas; screenplay, Milton Krims; art director, Max Parker; assistant director, Lew Borzage; music, Max Steiner; orchestrator, Hugo Friedhofer; gowns, Orry-Kelly; sound, Robert B. Lee; special effects, Fred Jackman, Jr., H. F. Koenekamp, and Willard Van Enger; camera, Byron Haskin; editor, James Gibbon.

Errol Flynn (Dr. Newell Paige); Anita Louise (Phyllis Dexter); Margaret Lindsay (Frances Ogilvie); Sir Cedric Hardwicke (Dean Harcourt); Walter Abel (Dr. John Stafford); Henry O'Neill (Dr. Endicott); Spring Byington (Mrs. Dexter); Erin O'Brien-Moore (Pat Arlen); Henry Kolker (Dr. Lane); Pierre Watkin (Dr. Booth); Granville Bates· (Sheriff); Russell Simpson (Sheepman); Myrtle Stedman and Shirley Lloyd (Nurses); Wade Boteler (Traffic Cop); Jim Pierce (Harcourt's Chauffeur); Jim Thorpe (Indian); Milton Kibbee (Other Man).

THE PRINCE AND THE PAUPER (First National, 1937), 120 min.

Executive producer, Hal B. Wallis; associate producer, Robert Lord; director, William Keighley; based on the novel by Mark Twain and the play by Catherine Chishold Cushing; screenplay, Laird Doyle; art director, Robert Haas; assistant director, Chuck Hansen; music, Erich Wolfgang Korngold; orchestrators, Hugo Friedhofer and Milan Roder; gowns, Milo Anderson; sound, Oliver S. Garretson; special effects, Willard Van Enger and James Gibbons; camera, Sol Polito; editor, Ralph Dawson.

Errol Flynn (Miles Hendon); Claude Rains (Earl of Hertford); Henry Stephenson (Duke of Norfolk); Barton MacLane (John Canty); Billy Mauch (Tom Canty); Bobby Mauch (Prince Edward); Alan Hale (Captain of the Guard); Eric Portman (First Lord); Montagu Love (Henry VIII); Robert Warwick (Lord Warwick); Halliwell Hobbes (Archbishop); Lionel Pape and Leonard Willey (Lords); Elspeth Dudgeon (Grandmother Canty); Fritz Leiber (Father Andrews); Murray Kinnell (Hugo); Ivan F. Simpson (Clemens); Lionel Braham (Ruffler); Helen Valkis (Jane Seymour); Phyllis Barry (Barmaid); Rex Evans (Rich Man); Lester Matthews (St. John); Robert Adair and Harry Cording (Guards); Mary Field (Tom Canty's Mother); Noel Kennedy, Billy Maguire, and Clifford Severn (Urchins); Gwendolyn Jones (Lady Elizabeth); Leyland Hodgson (Watchman); Holmes Herbert and Ian MacLaren (Doctors); Forrester Harvey (Meaty Man); Sidney Bracy (Man in Window); Ernie Stanton (Guard); Tom Wilson (One-Eyed Beggar).

ANOTHER DAWN (Warner Bros., 1937), 73 min.

Executive producer, Hal B. Wallis; associate producer, Harry Joe Brown; director, William Dieterle; screenplay, Laird Doyle; assistant director, Frank Heath; dialog director, Stanley Logan; music, Erich Wolfgang Korngold; orchestrators, Hugo Friedhofer and Milan Roder; art director, Robert Haas; gowns, Orry-Kelly; sound, Robert B. Lee; special effects, Willard Van Enger and James Gibbons; camera, Tony Gaudio; editor, Ralph Dawson.

Kay Francis (Julia Ashton); Errol Flynn (Captain Denny Roark); Ian Hunter (Colonial John Wister); Frieda Inescort (Grace Roark); Herbert Mundin (Wilkins); Billy Bevan (Hawkins); Kenneth Hunter (Sir Charles Benton); G. P. Huntley, Jr. (Lord Alden); Clyde Cook (Sergeant Murphy); Richard Powell (Henderson); Charles Irwin (Kelly); David Clyde (Campbell); Spencer Teakle (Fromby); Ben Welden (Victor Romkoff); Mary Forbes (Mrs. Benton); Eily Malyon (Mrs. Farnold); Reginald Sheffield (Wireless Operator); Charles Austin (Yeoman); Tyrone Brereton (Soldier); Yorke Sherwood (Station Master); Will Stanton (John's Caddy); Neal Kennedy (Julia's Caddy); J. R. Tozer (Butler); Martin Garralaga (Ali, the Servant); Major Sam Harris (Guest); Leonard Mudie (Doctor); Jack Richardson (Lang); Stefan Moritz (Arab Horseman); Clare Vedera (Innkeeper).

THE PERFECT SPECIMEN (First National, 1937), 97 min.

Executive producer, Hal B. Wallis; associate producer, Harry Joe Brown; director, Michael Curtiz; based on the story by Samuel Hopkins Adams; screenplay, Norman Reilly Raine, Lawrence Riley, Brewster Morse, and Fritz Falkenstein; art director, Robert Haas; assistant director, Frank Heath; music, Heinz Roemheld; dialog director, Gene Lewis; gowns, Howard Shoup; sound, Everett A. Brown; special effects, Byron Haskin, Edwin DuPar, and Rex Wimpy; camera, Charles Rosher; editor, Terry Morse.

Errol Flynn (Gerald Beresford Wicks); Joan Blondell (Mona Carter); Hugh Herbert (Killigrew Shaw); Edward Everett Horton (Mr. Gratton); Dick Foran (Jinks Carter); May Robson (Mrs. Leona Wicks); Beverly Roberts (Alicia); Allen Jenkins (Pink); Dennie Moore (Clarabelle); Hugh O'Connell (Hotel Clerk); James Burke (Snodgrass); Granville Bates (Hooker); Harry Davenport (Carl Carter); Tim Henning (Briggs); Lee Phelps (Head of State Patrol); John Hiestand (Commentator); Eddy Chandler (State Police Captain); Wilfred Lucas (Deputy Sheriff); Spencer Charters (Station Master); Harry Hollingsworth and Frank Mayo (Detectives); Evelyn Mulhall (Sarah); Charlie Sullivan (Timekeeper); Pat West (Fight Announcer).

THE ADVENTURES OF ROBIN HOOD (Warner Bros., 1938), C-102 min.

Executive producer, Hal B. Wallis; associate producer, Henry Blanke; directors, Michael Curtiz and William Keighley; based upon Robin Hood legends; screenplay, Norman Reilly Raine and Seton I. Miller; assistant directors, Lee Katz and Jack Sullivan; dialog director, Irving Rapper; music, Erich Wolfgang Korngold; orchestrators, Hugo Friedhofer and Milan Roder; archery supervisor, Howard Hill; fencing master, Fred Cavens; Technicolor director, Natalie Kalmus; Technicolor consultant, Moran Padelford; art director, Carl Jules Weyl; makeup, Perc Westmore; costumes, Milo Anderson; sound, C. A. Riggs; technical adviser, Louis Van Den Ecker; joust scenes director, B. Reeves Eason; camera, Sol Polito and Tony Gaudio; associate Technicolor camera, W. Howard Greene; editor, Ralph Dawson.

Errol Flynn (Sir Robin of Locksley [Robin Hood]); Olivia de Havilland (Maid Marian); Claude Rains (Prince John); Basil Rathbone (Sir Guy of Gisbourne); Ian Hunter (King Richard); Eugene Pallette (Friar Tuck); Alan Hale (Little John); Melville Cooper (High Sheriff of Nottingham); Patric Knowles (Will Scarlett); Herbert Mundin (Much the Miller's Son); Una O'Connor (Bess the Maid); Montagu Love (Bishop of Black Canon); Harry Cording (Dickon Malbott); Robert Warwick (Sir Geoffrey); Robert Noble (Sir Ralfe); Kenneth Hunter (Sir Mortimer); Leonard Willey (Sir Essex); Colin Kenny (Sir Baldwin); Lester Matthews (Sir Ivor); Howard Hill (Captain of Archers); Ivan F. Simpson (Proprietor of Kent Road Tavern); Charles McNaughton (Crippen); Lionel Belmore (Humility Prin, the Tavern Keeper); Janet Shaw (Humility's Daughter); Craufurd Kent (Sir Norbett); Ernie Stanton, Olaf Hytten, Peter Hobbes, and Sidney Baron (Robin's Outlaws); Hal Brazeale (High Sheriff's Squire); Leonard Mudie (Town Crier); Phillis Coghlan (Saxon Woman); Leyland Hodgson (Norman Officer); Reginald Sheffield (Herald); Holmes Herbert (Referee); Wilson Benge (Monk); Nick de Ruiz (Executioner); Dick Rich (Soldier).

FOUR'S A CROWD (Warner Bros., 1938), 91 min.

Executive producer, Hal B. Wallis; associate producer, David Lewis; director, Michael Curtiz; story, Wallace Sullivan; screenplay, Casey Robinson and Sig Herzig; music, Heinz Roemheld, Ray Heindorf; assistant director, Sherry Shourds; art director, Max Parker; dialog director, Irving Rapper; gowns, Orry-Kelly; sound, Robert B. Lee; camera, Ernest Haller; editor, Clarence Kolster.

Errol Flynn (Robert Kensington Lansford); Olivia de Havilland (Lorri Dillingwell); Rosalind Russell (Jean Christy); Patric Knowles (Patterson Buckley); Walter Connolly (John P. Dillingwell); Hugh Herbert (Silas Jenkins); Melville Cooper (Bingham); Franklin Pangborn (Preston); Herman Bing (Herman the Barber); Margaret Hamilton (Amy); Joseph Crehan (Butler Pierce); Joe Cunningham (Young); Dennie Moore (Buckley's Secretary); Gloria Blondell (Lansford's First Secretary); Carole Landis (Lansford's Second Secretary); Renie Riano (Mrs. Jenkins) Charles Trowbridge (Dr. Ives); Spencer Charters (Charlie).

THE SISTERS (Warner Bros., 1938), 99 min.

Executive producer, Hal B. Wallis; associate producer, David Lewis; director, Anatole Litvak; based on the novel by Myron Brinig; screenplay, Milton Krims; dialog director, Irving Rapper; assistant director, Jack Sullivan; art director, Carl Jules Weyl; music, Max Steiner; orchestrator, Hugo Friedhofer; gowns, Orry-Kelly; sound, C. A. Riggs; camera, Tony Gaudio; editor, Warren Low.

Bette Davis (Louise Elliott); Errol Flynn (Frank Medlin); Anita Louise (Helen Elliott); Jane Bryan (Grace Elliott); Ian Hunter (William Benson); Henry Travers (Ned Elliott); Beulah Bondi (Rose Elliott); Donald Crisp (Tim Hazleton); Dick Foran (Tom Knivel); Patric Knowles (Norman French); Alan Hale (Sam Johnson); Janet Shaw (Stella Johnson); Lee Patrick (Flora Gibbon); Laura Hope Crews (Flora's Mother); Harry Davenport (Doc Moore); Irving Bacon (Norman Forbes); Mayo Methot (Blonde); Paul Harvey (Caleb Ammon);

Arthur Hoyt (Tom Selig); John Warburton (Lord Anthony Bittick); Stanley Fields (Ship's Captain); Ruth Garland (Lora Bennett); Larry Williams (Young Man); Vera lewis, Lottie Williams, and Mira McKinney (Women); Lee Phelps (Announcer); Robert Homans (Editor); Stuart Holmes (Bartender); Constantine Romanoff (Spectator); Susan Hayward, Rosella Towne, Paulette Evans, and Frances Morris (Telephone Operators); Richard Bond (Boy).

THE DAWN PATROL (Warner Bros., 1938), 103 min.
Executive producer, Hal B. Wallis; associate producer, Robert Lord; director, Edmund Goulding; based on the story *The Flight Commander* by John Monk Saunders, Howard Hawks; screenplay, Seton I. Miller and Dan Totheroh; assistant director, Frank Heath; technical adviser, Captain L. G. S. Scott; music, Max Steiner; orchestrator, Hugo Friedhofer; art director, John Hughes; sound, C. A. Riggs; special effects, Edwin A. DuPar; camera, Tony Gaudio; editor, Ralph Dawson.

Errol Flynn (Captain Courtney); David Niven (Lieutenant Scott); Basil Rathbone (Major Brand); Donald Crisp (Phills); Melville Cooper (Watkins); Barry Fitzgerald (Bott); Carl Esmond (Von Mueller); Peter Willes (Hollister); Morton Lowater (Ronny Scott); Michael Brooke (Squires); James Burke (Flaherty, the Motorcyle Driver); Stuart Hall (Bentham, the Singer); Herbert Evans (Scott's Mechanic); Sidney Bracy (Ransom, Brand's Orderly); John Sutton (Adjutant); George Kirby (Kirby, the Orderly); John Rodion (Russell, the Replacement); Wally Reardon (Cleaver); Gordon Thorpe (Smythe); Gilbert Wilson (Moorehead); Anthony Marsh (Rutherford); Norman Willis (German Aviator); Hal Brazeale (Gregory); Tom Seidel (Jones).

DODGE CITY (Warner Bros., 1939), C-105 min.
Executive producer, Hal B. Wallis; associate producer, Robert Lord; director, Michael Curtiz; screenplay, Robert Buckner; assistant director, Sherry Shourds; dialog director, Jo Graham; music, Max Steiner; orchestrator, Hugo Friedhofer; art director, Ted Smith; costumes, Milo Anderson; makeup, Perc Westmore; technicolor consultant, Morgan Padelford; sound, Oliver S. Garretson; special effects, Byron Haskin and Rex Wimpy; camera, Sol Polito; associat Technicolor camera, Ray Rennahan; editor, George Amy.

Errol Flynn (Wade Hatton); Olivia de Havilland (Abbie Irving); Ann Sheridan (Ruby Gilman); Bruce Cabot (Jeff Surrett); Frank McHugh (Joe Clemens); Alan Hale (Rusty Hart); John Litel (Matt Cole); Victor Jory (Yancy); Henry Travers (Dr. Irving); Henry O'Neill (Colonel Dodge); Guinn "Big Boy" Williams (Tex Baird); Gloria Holden (Mrs. Cole); Douglas Fowley (Munger); William Lundigan (Lee Irving); Georgia Caine (Mrs. Irving); Charles Halton (Surrett's Lawyer); Ward Bond (Bud Taylor); Bobs Watson (Harry Cole); Nat Carr (Crocker); Russell Simpson (Orth); Clem Bevans (Charlie the Barber); Cora Witherspoon (Mrs. McCoy); Joe Crehan (Hammond); Thurston Hall (Twitchell); Chester Clute (Coggins); Monte Blue (Barlow, the Indian Agent); James Burke (Cattle Auctioneer); Robert Homans (Mail Clerk); George Guhl (Jason the Marshal); Spencer Charters (Clergyman); Bud Osborne (Stagecoach Driver/Waiter); Wilfred Lucas (Bartender); Milton Kibbee (Printer); Vera Lewis (Woman); Ralph Sanford (Brawler); William Merrill McCormick (Man); Fred Graham (Al); Pat O'Malley and Henry Otho (Conductors).

THE PRIVATE LIVES OF ELIZABETH AND ESSEX (Warner Bros., 1939), C-106 min.

Executive producer, Hal B. Wallis; associate producer, Robert Lord; director, Michael Curtiz; based on the play *Elizabeth the Queen* by Maxwell Anderson; screenplay, Norman Reilly Raine and Aeneas MacKenzie; assistant director, Sherry Shourds; technical adviser, Ali Hubert; music, Erich Wolfgang Korngold; orchestrators, Hugo Friedhofer and Milan Roder; art director, Anton Grot; costumes, Orry-Kelly; makeup, Perc Westmore; dialog director, Stanley Logan; color consultant, Morgan Padelford; sound, C. A. Riggs; special effects, Byron Haskin and H. F. Koenekamp; camera, Sol Polito; associate Technicolor camera, W. Howard Greene; editor, Owen Marks.

Bette Davis (Queen Elizabeth); Errol Flynn (Earl of Essex); Olivia de Havilland (Lady Penelope Gray); Donald Crisp (Francis Bacon); Alan Hale (Earl of Tyrone); Vincent Price (Sir Walter Raleigh); Henry Stephenson (Lord Burghley); Henry Daniell (Sir Robert Cecil); James Stephenson (Sir Thomas Egerton); Nanette Fabray (Mistress Margaret Radcliffe); Ralph Forbes (Lord Knollys); Robert Warwick (Lord Mountjoy); Leo G. Carroll (Sir Edward Coke).

VIRGINIA CITY (Warner Bros., 1940), 121 min.

Executive producer, Hal B. Wallis; associate producer, Robert Fellows; director, Michael Curtiz; screenplay, Robert Buckner (uncredited, Norman Reilly Raine and Howard Koch); assistant director, Sherry Shourds; dialog director, Jo Graham; music, Max Steiner; orchestrator, Hugo Friedhofer; art director, Ted Smith; makeup, Perc Westmore; sound, Oliver S. Garretson and Francis J. Scheid; special effects, Byron Haskin and H. F. Koenekamp; camera, Sol Polito; editor, George Amy.

Errol Flynn (Kerry Bradford); Miriam Hopkins (Julia Haynes); Randolph Scott (Vance Irby); Humphrey Bogart (John Murrell); Frank McHugh (Mr. Upjohn); Alan Hale (Olaf "Moose" Swenson); Guinn "Big Boy" Williams (Marblehead); John Litel (Marshal); Moroni Olsen (Cameron); Russell Hicks (Armistead); Douglass Dumbrille (Major Drewry); Dickie Jones (Cobby); Monte Montague (Stage Driver); Frank Wilcox (Officer); George Regas (Half-breed); Russell Simpson (Gaylord); Thurston Hall (General Meade); Victor Kilian (Abraham Lincoln); Charles Middleton (Jefferson Davis); Brandon Tynan (Trenholm); Charles Trowbridge (Seddon); Howard Hickman (General Page); Charles Halton (Ralston); Roy Gordon (Major General Taylor); Ward Bond (Sergeant); Sam McDaniel (Sam); Bud Osborne (Stage Driver); Lane Chandler (Soldier Clerk); Tom Dugan (Spieler); Walter Miller, Reed Howes (Sergeants); Paul Fix (Murrell's Henchman); Ed Keane (Officer); Wilfred Lucas (Southerner)

THE SEA HAWK (Warner Bros., 1940), 126 min.

Executive producer, Hal B. Wallis; associate producer, Henry Blanke; director, Michael Curtiz; screenplay, Howard Koch, Seton I. Miller; assistant director, Jack Sullivan; dialog director, Jo Graham; art director, Anton Grot; costumes, Orry-Kelly; makeup, Perc Westmore; music, Erich Wolfgang Korngold; orchestrators, Hugo Friedhofer, Milan Roder, Ray Heindorf, and Simon Bucharoff; technical advisers, Ali Hubert, Thomas Manners, and William Kiel; fencing master, Fred Cavens; sound, Francis J. Scheid; special effects, Byron Haskin and H. F. Koenekamp; camera, Sol Polito; editor, George Amy.

Errol Flynn (Captain Geoffrey Thorpe); Brenda Marshall (Donna Maria Alvarez de Cordoba); Claude Rains (Don Jose Alvarez de Cordoba); Flora Robson (Queen Elizabeth); Donald Crisp (Sir John Burleson); Henry Daniell (Lord Wolfingham); Alan Hale (Carl Pitt); Una O'Connor (Martha, Miss Latham); William Lundigan (Danny Logan); James Stephenson (Abbott); J. M. Kerrigan (Eli Matson); Gilbert Roland (Captain Lopez); Julien Mitchell (Oliver Scott); David Bruce (Martin Burke); Frank Wilcox (Martin Barrett, a Galley Slave); Herbert Anderson (Eph Winters); Clifford Brooke (William Tuttle); Charles Irvin (Arnold Cross); Clyde Cook (Walter Boggs); Edgar Buchanan (Ben Rollins); Ellis Irving (Monty Preston); Montagu Love (King Phillip II); Francis McDonald (Samuel Kroner); Pedro de Cordoba (Captain Mendoza); Ian Keith (Peralta); Jack La Rue (Lieutenant Ortega); Fritz Leiber (Inquisitor); Halliwell Hobbes (Astronomer); Alec Craig (Chartmaker); Frank Lackteen (Captain Ortiz); Victor Varconi (General Aguerra); Lester Matthews (Lieutenant—Palace Officer); Leonard Mudie (Officer); Robert Warwick (Captain Frobisher); Harry Cording and Nestor Paiva (Slavemasters); Frederic Worlock (Darnell); David Thursby (Driver); Michael Harvey (Sea Hawk); Gerald Mohr (Spanish Officer); Leyland Hodgson and Colin Kenny (Officers); Craufurd Kent (Lieutenant); Elizabeth Sifton and Mary Anderson (Maids of Honor).

SANTA FE TRAIL (Warner Bros., 1940), 110 min.

Executive producer, Hal B. Wallis; associate producer, Robert Fellows; director, Michael Curtiz; screenplay, Robert Buckner; dialog director, Jo Graham; assistant director, Jack Sullivan; art director, John Hughes; music, Max Steiner; orchestrator, Hugo Friedhofer; costumes, Milo Anderson; makeup, Perc Westmore; sound, Robert B. Lee; special effects, Byron Haskin and H. F. Koenekamp; camera, Sol Polito; editor, George Amy.

Errol Flynn (Jeb Stuart); Olivia de Havilland ("Kit Carson" Halliday); Raymond Massey (John Brown); Ronald Reagan (George Armstrong Custer); Alan Hale (Barefoot Brody); Guinn "Big Boy" Williams (Tex Bell); Van Heflin (Rader); Henry O'Neill (Cyrus Halliday); William Lundigan (Bob Halliday); John Litel (Harlan); Gene Reynolds (Jason Brown); Alan Baxter (Oliver Brown); Moroni Olsen (Robert E. Lee); Erville Alderson (Jefferson Davis); Susan Peters (Charlotte Davis); Frank Wilcox (James Longstreet); David Bruce (Phil Sheridan); Charles D. Brown (Major Sumner); William Marshall (George Pickett); Russell Simpson (Shoubel Morgan); George Haywood (John Hood); Joseph Sawyer (Kitzmiller); Hobart Cavanaugh (Barber Doyle); Spencer Charters (Conductor); Ward Bond (Townley); Wilfred Lucas (Weiner); Charles Middleton (Sentry); Russell Hicks (J. Boyce Russell); Napoleon Simpson (Sampson); Roy Barcroft (Engineer); Lane Chandler (Adjutant); Richard Kipling (Army Doctor); Nestor Paiva and Trevor Bardette (Agitators); Eddy Waller (Man); Libby Taylor (Negress); Ed Cobb (Guard); Creighton Hale (Telegraph Operator); William Hopper (Officer); Reverend Neal Dodd (Preacher); Addison Richards (Sheriff).

FOOTSTEPS IN THE DARK (Warner Bros., 1941), 96 min.

Executive producer, Hal B. Wallis; associate producer, Robert Lord; director, Lloyd Bacon; based on the play *Blondie White* by Ladislaus Fodor, English version, Bernard Merivale and Jeffrey Dell; screenplay, Lester Cole and John Wexley; assistant director, Frank Heath; dialog director, Hugh MacMullan; art director, Max Parker; gowns, Howard Shoup; makeup, Perc Westmore; music, Frederick Hollander; choreography, Robert Vreeland; sound, Francis J. Scheid; special effects, Rex Wimpy; camera, Ernest Haller; editor, Owen Marks.

Errol Flynn (Francis Warren); Brenda Marshall (Rita Warren); Ralph Bellamy (Dr. Davis); Alan Hale (Inspector Mason); Lee Patrick (Blondie White); Allen Jenkins (Wilfred); Lucile Watson (Mrs. Archer); William Frawley (Hopkins); Roscoe Karns (Monahan); Grant Mitchell (Carruthers); Maris Wrixon (June Brewster); Noel Madison (Fissue); Jack LaRue (Ace Vernon); Turhan Bey (Ahmed); Frank Faylen (Gus); Garry Owen (Jackson); Sarah Edwards (Mrs. Belarde); Frank Wilcox (Harrow); Olaf Hytten (Horace); Harry Hayden (Willis); John Dilson (Coroner); Creighton Hale (Harlan); Winifred Harris (Miss Perry); David Newell (June Brewster's Escort); William Hopper (Police Secretary); Sonny Boy Williams (Tommy); Betty Farrington (Mrs. Jenkins).

DIVE BOMBER (Warner Bros., 1941), C-133 min.
Executive producer, Hal B. Wallis; associate producer, Robert Lord; director, Michael Curtiz; story, Frank Wead; screenplay, Wead and Robert Buckner; assistant director, Sherry Shourds; dialog director, Hugh MacMullan; music, Max Steiner; orchestrator, Hugo Friedhofer; art director, Robert Haas; makeup, Perc Westmore; chief pilot, Paul Mantz; aeronautical technical adviser, S. H. Warner, Commander, U.S.N.; technical adviser, J. R. Poppe, Captain (MC)U.S.N.; technicolor color director, Natalie Kalmus; sound, Francis J. Scheid; special effects, Byron Haskin and Rex Wimpy; aerial camera, Elmer Dyer and Charles Marshall; camera, Bert Glennon and Winton C. Hoch; editor, George Amy.

Errol Flynn (Lieutenant Douglas Lee); Fred MacMurray (Commander Joe Blake); Ralph Bellamy (Dr. Lance Rogers); Alexis Smith (Linda Fisher); Regis Toomey (Tim Griffin); Robert Armstrong (Art Lyons); Allen Jenkins (Lucky Dice); Craig Stevens (John Thomas Anthony); Herbert Anderson (Chubby); Moroni Olsen (Senior Flight Surgeon); Louis Jean Heydt (Swede); Dennie Moore (Mrs. James); Cliff Nazarro (Corps Man); Ann Doran (Helen); Addison Richards (Senior Flight Surgeon); Russell Hicks and Howard Hickman (Admirals); William Hopper, Charles Drake, Gig Young, Larry Williams, Alan Hale, Jr., Sol Gorss, Don Turner, James Anderson, David Newell, and Stanley Smith (Pilots); Richard Travis (Commanding Officer); Dick Wessel (Mechanic); Creighton Hale (Hospital Attendant); Tom Dugan (Corpsman); Charlotte Wynters (Hostess); Alice Talton (Girl at Newsstand); Tod Andrews (Telephone Man).

THEY DIED WITH THEIR BOOTS ON (Warner Bros., 1941), 140 min.

Executive producer, Hal B. Wallis; associate producer, Robert Fellows; director, Raoul Walsh; screenplay, Wally Kline and Aeneas MacKenzie; music, Max Steiner; dialog director, Edward A. Blatt; assistant director, Russell Saunders; technical adviser, Lieutenant Colonel J. G. Taylor, U.S. Army, Retired; art director, John Hughes; gowns, Milo Anderson; makeup Perc Westmore; sound, Dolph Thomas; camera, Bert Glennon; editor, William Holmes.

Errol Flynn (George Armstrong Custer); Olivia de Havilland (Elizabeth

338

Bacon Custer); Arthur Kennedy (Ned Sharp, Jr.); Charles Grapewin (California Joe); Gene Lockhart (Samuel Bacon); Anthony Quinn (Crazy Horse); Stanley Ridges (Romolus Taipe); John Litel (General Phil Sheridan); Walter Hampden (Senator Sharp); Sydney Greenstreet (General Winfield Scott); Regis Toomey (Fitzhugh Lee); Hattie McDaniel (Callie); G. P. Huntley, Jr. (Lieutenant Butler); Frank Wilcox (Captain Webb); Joseph Sawyer (Sergeant Doolittle); Minor Watson (Senator Smith); Gig Young (Lieutenant Roberts); John Ridgely (Second Lieutenant Davis); Joseph Crehan (President Grant); Aileen Pringle (Mrs. Sharp); Anna Q. Nilsson (Mrs. Taipe); Harry Lewis (Youth); Tod Andrews (Cadet Brown); William Hopper (Frazier); Selmer Jackson (Captain McCook); Pat McVey (Jones); Renie Riano, Minerva Urecal, Virginia Sale (Nurses); Vera Lewis (Head Nurse); Frank Orth (Station Master); Hobart Bosworth (Clergyman); Irving Bacon (Salesman); Roy Barcroft (Officer); Lane Chandler (Sentry); Ed Keane (Congressman); Francis Ford (Veteran); Frank Ferguson (Grant's Secretary); Herbert Heywood (Newsman).

DESPERATE JOURNEY (Warner Bros., 1942), 107 min.
    Executive producer, Hal B. Wallis; associate producer, Jack Saper; director, Raoul Walsh; screenplay, Arthur T. Horman; assistant director, Russell Saunders; dialog director, Hugh MacMullan; music, Max Steiner; orchestrator, Hugo Friedhofer; art director, Carl Jules Weyl; makeup, Perc Westmore; gowns, Milo Anderson; technical adviser for F.A.F. sequences, S/L O. Cathcart-Jones R.C.A.F.; sound, C. A. Riggs; special effects, Edwin DuPar; camera, Bert Glennon; editor, Rudi Fehr.

    Errol Flynn (Lieutenant Terrence Forbes); Ronald Reagan (Flying Officer Johnny Hammond); Nancy Coleman (Kaethe Brahms); Raymond Massey (Major Otto Baumeister); Alan Hale (Flight Sergeant Kirk Edwards); Arthur Kennedy (Flying Officer Jed Forrest); Ronald Sinclair (Flight Sergeant Lloyd Hollis); Albert Basserman (Dr. Mather); Sig Rumann (Preuss); Patrick O'Moore (Squadron Leader Lane Ferris); Felix Basch (Dr. Herman Brahms); Ilka Gruning (Frau Brahms); Elsa Basserman (Frau Raeder); Charles Irwin (Captain Coswick); Robert O. Davis (Kruse); Henry Victor (Henrich Schwartzmuller); Hans Schumm and Robert Stephenson (Gestapo Men); Walter Brooke (Warwick); William Hopper (Aircraftsman); Rolf Lindau (Sergeant); Otto Reichow (Private Koenig); Sigfried Tor (Private Rasek); Philip Van Zandt (Soldier); Roland Varno (Unteroffizier); Sven Hugo Borg (Mechanic); Helmut Dantine (Co-Pilot); Bruce Lester (Assistant Plotting Officer); Kurt Katch (Hesse); Victor Zimmerman (Captain Eggerstedt).

GENTLEMAN JIM (Warner Bros., 1942), 104 min.
    Producer, Robert Buckner; director, Raoul Walsh; based on the life of James J. Corbett and the Corbett autobiography, *The Roar of the Crowd;* screenplay, Vincent Lawrence and Horace McCoy; assistant director, Russell Saunders; dialog director, Hugh Cummings; technical adviser, Ed Cochrane; music, Heinz Roemheld; orchestrator, Ray Heindorf; art director, Ted Smith; gowns, Milo Anderson; makeup, Perc Westmore; montages, Don Siegel and James Leicester; sound, C. A. Riggs; camera, Sid Hickox; editor, Jack Killifer.

    Errol Flynn (James J. Corbett); Alexis Smith (Victoria Ware); Jack Carson (Walter Louwrie); Alan Hale (Pat Corbett); John Loder (Clinton DeWitt); William Frawley (Billy Delaney); Minor Watson (Buck Ware); Ward Bond (John

L. Sullivan); Madeleine Le Beau (Anna Held); Rhys Williams (Harry Watson); Arthur Shields (Father Burke); Dorothy Vaughan (Ma Corbett); James Flavin (George Corbett); Pat Flaherty (Harry Corbett); Wallis Clark (Judge Geary); Marilynn Phillips (Mary Corbett); Art Foster (Jack Burke); Charles Wilson (Gurney); Frank Mayo (Governor Stanford); Harry Crocker (Charles Crocker); Henry O'Hara (Huntington); Fred Kelsey (Sutro); Jean Del Val (Renaud); William Davidson (Donovan); Carl Harbaugh (Smith); Mike Mazurki (Kilrain); Joe King (Colonel McLane); Frank Hagney (Mug); Wee Willie Davis (Flannagan); Wade Crosby (Manager); Lon McCallister (Page Boy); Georgia Caine (Mrs. Geary); Wade Boteler (Policeman); Mary Gordon (Irish Woman); Emmet Vogan (Stage Manager); Monte Blue, William Hopper, Milton Kibbee, and Hooper Atchley (Men); Lester Dorr (Reporter); Lee Phelps and Pat O'Malley (Detectives).

EDGE OF DARKNESS (Warner Bros., 1943), 120 min.

Producer, Henry Blanke; director, Lewis Milestone; based on the novel by William Woods; screenplay, Robert Rossen; assistant directors, Sherry Shourds and James McMahon; technical advisers, Frank U. Peter Pohlenz, E. Wessel Klausen, and Gerald Lambert; dialog director, Herschel Daugherty; art director, Robert Haas; set decorator, Julia Heron; gowns, Orry-Kelly; makeup, Perc Westmore; montages, Don Siegel and James Leicester; music, Franz Waxman; orchestrator, Leonid Raab; sound, Everett A. Brown; special effects, Lawrence Butler and Willard Van Enger; camera, Sid Hickox; editor, David Weisbart.

Errol Flynn (Gunnar Brogge); Ann Sheridan (Karen Stensgard); Walter Huston (Dr. Martin Stensgard); Nancy Coleman (Katja); Helmut Dantine (Captain Koenig); Judith Anderson (Gerd Bjarnessen); Ruth Gordon (Anna Stensgard); John Beal (Johann Stensgard); Morris Carnovsky (Sixtus Andresen); Charles Dingle (Kaspar Torgersen); Roman Bohnon (Lars Malken); Richard Fraser (Pastor Aalesen); Art Smith (Knut Osterholm); Tom Fadden (Hammer); Henry Brandon (Major Ruck); Tonio Selwart (Paul); Helene Thimig (Frida); Frank Wilcox (Jensen); Francis Pierlot (Mortensen); Lottie Williams (Mrs. Mortensen); Monte Blue (Petersen); Henry Rowland (Helmut); Virginia Christine (Hulda); Torben Meyer (Clerk); Kurt Kreuger (Blond Soldier); Kurt Katch (Captain); Vera Lewis (Woman); Peter Van Eyck (German Soldier).

THANK YOUR LUCKY STARS (Warner Bros., 1943), 127 min.

Producer, Mark Hellinger; director, David Butler; story, Everett Freeman and Arthur Schwartz; screenplay, Norman Panama, Melvin Frank, and James V. Kern; songs, Arthur Schwartz and Frank Loesser; orchestral arranger, Ray Heindorf; music adaptor, Heinz Roemheld; orchestrator, Maurice de Packh; vocal arranger, Dudley Chambers; assistant director, Phil Quinn; choreography, LeRoy Prinz; art directors, Anton Grot and Leo K. Kuter; set decorator, Walter F. Tilford; gowns, Milo Anderson; makeup, Perc Westmore; sound, Francis J. Scheid and Charles David Forrest; special effects, H. F. Koenekamp; camera, Arthur Edeson; editor, Irene Morra.

Eddie Cantor (Himself and Joe Simpson); Joan Leslie (Pat Dixon); Dennis Morgan (Tommy Randolph); Humphrey Bogart, Bette Davis, Olivia de Havilland, Errol Flynn, John Garfield, Ida Lupino, Ann Sheridan, Dinah Shore, Alexis Smith, Spike Jones & His City Slickers, Jack Carson, Alan Hale, and

George Tobias (Themselves); S. Z. Sakall (Dr. Schlenna); Hattie McDaniel (Gossip); Ruth Donnelly (Nurse Hamilton); Edward Everett Horton (Farnsworth); Joyce Reynolds (Girl with Book); Richard Lane (Barney Jackson); Don Wilson (Announcer); Henry Armetta (Angelo); Willie Best (Soldier); Jack Mower and Creighton Hale (Engineers); Frank Faylen (Sailor); Mike Mazurki (Olaf); Noble Johnson (Charlie, the Indian); Marjorie Hoshelle and Anne O'Neal (Maids); Mary Treen (Fan); James Burke (Interne Guard); Boyd Irwin (Man); *Errol Flynn Number:* Monte Blue, Art Foster, Fred Kelsey, Elmer Ballard, Buster Wiles, Howard Davies, Tudor Williams, Alan Cook, Fred McEvoy, Bobby Hale, Will Stanton, Charles Irwin, David Thursby, Henry Iblings, Earl Hunsaker, Hubert Head, Dudley Kuzelle and Ted Billings (Pub characters).

NORTHERN PURSUIT (Warner Bros., 1943), 94 min.

Producer, Jack Chertok; director, Raoul Walsh; based on the story *Five Thousand Trojan Horses* by Leslie T. White; screenplay, Frank Gruber and Alvah Bessie; assistant director, James McMahon; technical adviser, Bruce Carruthers; dialog director, Hugh Cummings; art director, Leo K. Kuter; set decorator, Casey Roberts; gowns, Leah Rhodes; makeup, Perc Westmore; music, Adolph Deutsch; orchestrator, Jerome Morass; sound, Stanley Jones; montages, Don Siegel and James Leicester; special effects, E. Roy Davidson; camera, Sid Hickox; editor, Jack Killifer.

Errol Flynn (Steve Wagner); Julie Bishop (Laura McBain); Helmut Dantine (Colonel Hugo von Keller); John Ridgely (Jim Austin); Gene Lockhart (Ernst); Tom Tully (Inspector Barnett); Bernard Nedell (Dagor); Warren Douglas (Sergeant); Monte Blue (Jean); Alec Craig (Angus McBain); Tom Fadden (Hobby); Carl Harbaugh (Radio Operator); Fred Kelsey (Conductor); Herbert Heywood (Farmer); Arno Frey (Submarine Captain); Robert Hutton (Guard); Robert Kent and John Forsythe (Soldiers); Jay Silverheels, George Urchel, and Joe Herrera (Indians); Russell Hicks (Chief Inspector); Milton Kibbee (Hotel Clerk); Lester Matthews (Colonel).

UNCERTAIN GLORY (Warner Bros., 1944), 102 min.

Producer, Robert Buckner; director, Raoul Walsh; story, Joe May and Laszlo Vadnay; screenplay, Vadnay, Max Brand; dialog director, James Vincent; assistant director, James McMahon; technical adviser, Paul Coze; art director, Robert Haas; set decorator, Walter F. Tilford; makeup, Perc Westmore; music. Adolph Deutsch; orchestrator, Jerome Moross; sound, Oliver S. Garretson; special effects, E. Roy Davidson; camera, Sid Hickox; editor, George Amy.

Errol Flynn (Jean Picard); Paul Lukas (Marcel Bonet); Jean Sullivan (Marianne) Lucile Watson (Mme. Maret); Faye Emerson (Louise); James Flavin (Captain of Mobile Guard); Douglas Dumbrille (Police Commissioner); Dennis Hoey (Father La Clerc); Sheldon Leonard (Henry Duval); Odette Myrtil (Mme. Bonet); Francis Pierlot (Prison Priest); Wallis Clark (Razeau); Victor Kilian (Latour); Albert Van Antwerp (Vitrac); Carl Harbaugh (Innkeeper); Joel Friedkin (Veterinary); Ivan Triesault (Saboteur); Creighton Hale (Prison Secretary); Joyce Tucker (Michele Bonet); Paul Panzer (Train Guard); Hans Schumm (Gestapo Agent); Zina Torchina (Peasant Girl); Mary Servoss (Drover's Wife); Erskine Sanford (Drover); Sarah Padden (Peasant Woman on Bus); Trevor Bardette and Michael Mark (Passengers on Train).

OBJECTIVE, BURMA! (Warner Bros., 1945), 142 min.

Producer, Jerry Wald; director, Raoul Walsh; story, Alvah Bessie; screenplay, Ranald MacDougall and Lester Cole; assistant director, Elmer Decker; art director, Ted Smith; set decorator, Jack McConaghy; music, Franz Waxman; orchestrator, Leonid Raab; technical adviser, Major Charles S. Galbraith, U.S. Army Parachute Troops; makeup, Perc Westmore; dialog director, John Maxwell; sound, C. A. Riggs; special effects, Edwin DuPar; camera, James Wong Howe; editor, George Amy.

Errol Flynn (Major Nelson); James Brown (Sergeant Treacy); William Prince (Lieutenant Jacobs); George Tobias (Gabby Gordon); Henry Hull (Mark Williams); Warner Anderson (Colonel Carter); John Alvin (Hogan); Mark Stevens (Lieutenant Barker); Richard Erdman (Nebraska Hooper); Anthony Caruso (Miggleori); Hugh Beaumont (Captain Hennessey); John Whitney (Negulesco); Joel Allen (Brophy); George Tyne (Soapy); Rodric Redwing (Sergeant Chattu); William Hudson (Hollis); Asit Koomar (Ghurka); Lester Matthews (Major Fitzpatrick); John Sheridan (Co-pilot); Caryle Blackwell, Jr. (Pilot); Kit Carson, Neil Carter, Helmert Ellingwood, Shephard Houghton, Peter Kooy, and Harlan Miller (Paratroopers); Erville Anderson (General Stilwell).

SAN ANTONIO (Warner Bros., 1945), C-111 min.

Producer, Robert Buckner; director, David Butler; screenplay, Alan LeMay and W. R. Burnett; assistant director, William Kissel; dialog director, Frederick De Cordova; art director, Ted Smith; set decorator, Jack McConaghy; wardrobe, Milo Anderson; makeup, Perc Westmore; music, Max Steiner; orchestrator, Hugo Friedhofer; songs, Ted Koehler, M. K. Jerome, and Ray Heindorf; Jack Scholl and Charles Kisco; and Larry Spier; choreography, LeRoy Prinz; color consultant, Leonard Doss; sound, Everett A. Brown; special effects, Willard Van Enger; camera, Bert Glennon; editor, Irene Morra.

Errol Flynn (Clay Hardin); Alexis Smith (Jeanne Starr); S. Z. Sakall (Sacha Bozic); Victor Francen (Legare); Florence Bates (Henrietta); John Litel (Charlie Bell); Paul Kelly (Roy Stuart); John Alvin (Pony Smith); Monte Blue (Cleve Andrews); Robert Shayne (Captain Morgan); Robert Barrat (Colonel Johnson); Pedro de Cordoba (Ricardo Torreon); Tom Tyler (Lafe McWilliams); Chris-Pin Martin (Hymie Rosas); Charles Stevens (Sojar Harris); Poodles Hanneford (San Antonio Stage Driver); Doodles Weaver (Square Dance Caller); Dan White (Joey Sims); Ray Spiker (Rebel White); Al Hill (Hap Winters); Wallis Clark (Tip Brice); Harry Cording (Hawker); Chalky Williams (Poker Player); Bill Steele (Roper); Howard Hill (Clay's Henchman); Arnold Kent (Dancer); Don McGuire and John Compton (Cowboys); Eddie Acuff (Gawking Cowboy); Si Jenks (Station Boss); Denver Dixon (Barfly); Snub Pollard (Dance Extra); Cliff Lyons (Errol Flynn's Double); Harry Semels (Mexican); Francis Ford (Old Cowboy Greeting Coach); William Gould and Jack Mower (Wild Cowmen); Brandon Hurst (Gambler).

NEVER SAY GOODBYE (Warner Bros., 1946), 97 min.

Producer, William Jacobs; director, James V. Kern; story, Ben and Norma Barzman; adaptor, Lewis R. Foster; screenplay, Kern and I.A.L. Diamond; assistant director, Phil Quinn; dialog director, Robert Stevens; art director, Anton Grot; set decorator, Budd Friend; makeup, Perc Westmore; wardrobe,

Leah Rhodes; music, Frederick Hollander; orchestrator, Leonid Raab; paintings-sketches, Zoe Mozert; sound, Stanley Jones; special effects, William McGann and Willard Van Enger; camera, Arthur Edeson; editor, Folmar Blangsted.

Errol Flynn (Phil Gayley); Eleanor Parker (Ellen Gayley); Lucile Watson (Mrs. Hamilton); S. Z. Sakall (Luigi); Forrest Tucker (Corporal Fenwick Lonkowski); Donald Woods (Rex DeVallon); Peggy Knudsen (Nancy Graham); Tom D'Andrea (Jack Gordon); Hattie McDaniel (Cozy); Patti Brady (Phillippa "Flip" Gayley); Helen Pender (Louise); William Benedict (Messenger Boy); Charles Coleman (Withers); Arthur Shields (McCarthy); Doris Fulton (Hat Check Girl); Tom Tyler and Monte Blue (Policemen); Sam McDaniel (Porter); Roy Gordon (Detective).

CRY WOLF (Warner Bros., 1947), 83 min.

Producer, Henry Blanke; director, Peter Godfrey; based on the novel by Marjorie Carleton; screenplay, Catherine Turney; assistant director, Claude Archer; dialog director, Felix Jacoves; art director, Carl Jules Weyl; set decorator, Jack McConeghy; wardrobe, Travilla; Miss Stanwyck's wardrobe, Edith Head; makeup, Perc Westmore; music, Franz Waxman; orchestrator, Leonid Raab; sound, Charles Lang; special effects, William McGann and Robert Burks; camera, Carl Guthrie; editor, Folmar Blangsted.

Errol Flynn (Mark Caldwell); Barbara Stanwyck (Sandra Marshall); Richard Basehart (James Demarest); Geraldine Brooks (Julie Demarest); Jerome Cowan (Senator Caldwell); John Ridgely (Jackson Laidell); Patricia Barry (Angela); Rory Mallison (Becket); Helene Thimig (Marta); Paul Stanton (Davenport); Barry Bernard (Roberts the Groom); John Elliott (Clergyman); Lisa Golm (Mrs. Laidell); Jack Mower (Watkins); Paul Panzer (Gatekeeper); Creighton Hale (Dr. Reynolds).

ESCAPE ME NEVER (Warner Bros., 1947), 104 min.

Producer, Henry Blanke; director, Peter Godfrey; based on the novel *The Fool of the Family* and the play *Escape Me Never* by Margaret Kennedy; screenplay, Thomas Williamson; assistant director, Claude Archer; dialog director, Robert Stevens; music, Erich Wolfgang Korngold; orchestrators, Hugo Friedhofer and Ray Heindorf; ballet sequences, LeRoy Prinz; art director, Carl Jules Weyl; set decorator, Fred M. MacLean; ballet costumes, Travilla; wardrobe, Bernard Newman; makeup, Perc Westmore; sound, Dolph Thomas; special effects, Harry Barndollar and Willard Van Enger; camera, Sol Polito; editor, Clarence Kolster.

Errol Flynn (Sebastian Dubrok); Ida Lupino (Gemma Smith); Eleanor Parker (Fernella MacLean); Gig Young (Caryl Dubrok); Reginald Denny (Ivor MacLean); Isobel Elsom (Mrs. MacLean); Albert Basserman (Professor Heinrich); Ludwig Stossel (Steinach); Milada Mladova, George Zoritch, and the Corps de Ballet (Ballet Sequence); Frank Puglia (Guide); Hector Sarno (Waiter); Alfredo Sabato and Mario Siletti (Gondoliers); Helene Thimig (Landlady in Tyrolean Sequence); Ivan Triesault (Choreographer); Doris Lloyd (Mrs. Cooper); Jack Ford (Double for Albert Basserman).

ALWAYS TOGETHER (Warner Bros., 1947), 78 min.

343

Producer, Alex Gottlieb; director, Frederick De Cordova; screenplay, Phoebe and Henry Ephron and I. A. L. Diamond; art director, Leo K. Kuter; set decorator, Jack McConaghy; assistant director, James McMahon; music, Werner Heymann; orchestrator, Leonid Rabb; music director, Leo F. Forbstein; sound, C. A. Rigg; montages, James Leicester; special effects, William McGann and Edwin DuPar; camera, Carl Guthrie; editor, Folmar Blangsted.

Robert Hutton (Donn Masters); Joyce Reynolds (Jane Barker); Cecil Kellaway (Jonathan Turner); Ernest Truex (Mr. Bull); Don McGuire (McIntyre); Ransom Sherman (Judge); Douglas Kennedy (Doberman); Humphrey Bogart, Jack Carson, Errol Flynn, Dennis Morgan, Janis Paige, Eleanor Parker, and Alexis Smith (Unbilled Guest Stars); Clifton Young, Harry Lewis (Reporters); Creighton Hale (Eric); Grady Sutton (Jack, the Soda Jerk); Chester Clute (Furrier); Philo McCullough (Moving Man); Wheaton Chambers (Court Clerk); Dewey Robinson (Street Cleaner).

SILVER RIVER (Warner Bros., 1948), 110 min.
Producer, Owen Crump; director, Raoul Walsh; based on the unpublished novel by Stephen Longstreet; screenplay, Longstreet, Harriet Frank, Jr.; assistant director, Russell Saunders; technical adviser for Civil War sequences, Colonel J. G. Taylor, U.S. Army, Rtd.; music, Max Steiner; orchestrator, Murray Cutter; dialog director, Maurice Murphy; art director, Ted Smith; set decorator, William G. Wallace; Miss Sheridan's wardrobe, Travilla; men's wardrobe, Marjorie Best; makeup, Perc Westmore; sound, Francis J. Scheid; montages, James Leicester; special effects, William McGann and Edwin DuPar; camera, Sid Hickox; editor, Alan Crosland, Jr.

Errol Flynn (Captain Mike McComb); Ann Sheridan (Georgia Moore); Thomas Mitchell (John Plato Beck); Bruce Bennett (Stanley Moore); Tom D'Andrea (Pistol Porter); Barton MacLane (Banjo Sweeney); Monte Blue (Buck Chevigee); Jonathan Hale (Major Spencer); Alan Bridge (Sam Slade); Arthur Space (Major Ross); Art Baker (Major Wilson); Joe Crehan (President Grant); Norman Jolley (Scout); Jack Davis (Judge Advocate); Harry Strang (Soldier); Norman Willis (Honest Harry); Ian Wolfe (Deputy); Jim Ames (Barker); Lois Austin and Gladys Turney (Ladies); Marjorie Bennett (Large Woman); Dorothy Christy and Grayce Hampton (Women); Joe Bernard (River Boat Captain); Harry Hayden (Schaefer, the Teller); Lester Dorr (Taylor); Russell Hicks (Edwards, the Architect); Fred Kelsey (Townsman); Ben Corbett (Henchman); Leo White (Barber); Franklyn Farnum (Officer); Bud Osborne (Posseman).

ADVENTURES OF DON JUAN (Warner Bros., 1948), C-110 min.
Producer, Jerry Wald; director, Vincent Sherman; story, Herbert Dalmas; screenplay, George Oppenheimer and Harry Kurnitz; assistant director, Richard Mayberry; dialog director, Maurice Murphy; art director, Edward Carere; set decorator, Lyle B. Reifsnider; costumes, Leah Rhodes, Travilla, and Marjorie Best; makeup, Perc Westmore; music, Max Steiner; orchestrator, Murray Cutter; fencing master, Fred Cavens; color consultant, Mitchell Kovaleski; sound, Everett A. Brown; special effects, William McGann and John Crouse; camera, Elwood Bredell; editor, Alan Crosland, Jr.

344

Errol Flynn (Don Juan de Marana); Viveca Lindfors (Queen Margaret); Robert Douglas (Duke de Lorca); Alan Hale (Leporello); Romney Brent (King Philip III); Ann Rutherford (Donna Elena); Robert Warwick (Count de Polan); Jerry Austin (Don Sebastian); Douglas Kennedy (Don Rodrigo); Jeanne Shepherd (Donna Carlotta); Mary Stuart (Catherine); Helen Westcott (Lady Diana); Fortunio Bonanova (Don Serafino); Aubrey Mather (Lord Chalmers); Una O'Connor (Duenna); Raymond Burr (Captain Alvarez); Tim Huntley (Catherine's Husband); David Leonard (Inn Keeper); James Craven (Captain of Horsemen); Leon Belasco (Don De Cordoba); Penny Edwards and Joan Winfield (Girls in Street); Barbara Bates (Innkeeper's Daughter); Pedro De Cordoba (Pachecho); David Bruce (Count D'Orsini); Monte Blue (Turnkey); Harry Woods (Guard); Nora Eddington (Lady in Coach).

IT'S A GREAT FEELING (Warner Bros., 1949), C-85 min.

Producer, Alex Gottlieb; director, David Butler; story, I. A. L. Diamond; screenplay, Jack Rose and Melville Shavelson; assistant director, Phil Quinn; music director-incidental music, Ray Heindorf; songs, Jule Styne and Sammy Cahn; choreography, LeRoy Prinz; orchestrators, Leo Shuken and Sidney Cutner; dialog director, Herschel Daugherty; art director, Stanley Fleischer; set decorator, Lyle B. Reifsnider; wardrobe, Milo Anderson; makeup, Perc Westmore; color consultant, Mitchell Kovaleski; sound, Dolph Thomas, Charles David Forrest; special effects, William McGann and H. F. Koenekamp; camera, Wilfrid M. Cline; editor, Irene Morra.

Dennis Morgan and Jack Carson (Themselves); Doris Day (Judy Adams); Bill Goodwin (Arthur Trent); Irving Bacon (Information Clerk); Claire Carleton (Grace); Harlan Warde (Publicity Man); Jacqueline de Wit (Trent's Secretary); David Butler, Michael Curtiz, King Vidor, Raoul Walsh, Gary Cooper, Joan Crawford, Sydney Greenstreet, Danny Kaye, Patricia Neal, Eleanor Parker, Ronald Reagan, Edward G. Robinson, Jane Wyman, and the Mazzone-Abbott Dancers (Themselves); Errol Flynn (Jeffrey Bushdinkel); Pat Flaherty (Charlie the Gate Guard); Wilfred Lucas (Mr. Adams); Joan Vohs (Model); Frank Cady (Oculist); Forbes Murray (Distinguished Man); Tom Dugan (Barfly—Wrestling Fan); Shirley Ballard (Beautiful Girl on Bike).

THAT FORSYTE WOMAN (MGM, 1949), C-114 min.

Producer, Leon Gordon; director, Compton Bennett; based on the novel *The Man of Property* by John Galsworthy; screenplay, Jan Lustig, Ivan Tors, and James B. Williams; additional dialog, Arthur Wimperis; assistant director, Robert Barnes; color consultants, Henri Jaffa and James Gooch; music, Bronislau Kaper; art directors, Cedric Gibbons and Daniel B. Cathcart; set decorators, Edwin B. Willis and Jack D. Moore; women's costumes, Walter Plunkett; men's costumes, Valles; makeup, Jack Dawn; sound, Douglas Shearer and Ralph Pender; camera, Joseph Ruttenberg; editor, Frederick Y. Smith.

Errol Flynn (Soames Forsyte); Greer Garson (Irene Forsyte); Walter Pidgeon (Young Jolyon Forsyte); Robert Young (Philip Bosinney); Janet Leigh (June Forsyte); Harry Davenport (Old Jolyon Forsyte); Lumsden Hare (Roger Forsyte); Halliwell Hobbes (Nicholas Forsyte); Aubrey Mather (James Forsyte); Matt Moore (Timothy Forsyte); Florence Auer (Ann Forsyte Hayman);

Phyllis Morris (Julia Forsyte Small); Marjorie Eaton (Hestor Forsyte); Evelyn Beresford (Mrs. Taylor); Gerald Oliver Smith (Beveridge); Richard Lupino (Chester Forsyte); Wilson Wood (Eric Forsyte); Gabrille Windsor (Jennie); Renee Mercer (Martha); Nina Ross (Louise); Constance Cavendish (Alice Forsyte); Charles McNaughton (Attendant); Tim Hawkins (Freddie); Reginald Sheffield (Mr. McLean); John Sheffield (Footman); Herbert Evans (M.C.'s Voice); Leyland Hodgson (Detective); Rolfe Sedan (Official); Billy Bevan (Porter); Lilian Bond (Maid); Norman Rainey (Footman).

MONTANA (Warner Bros., 1950), C-76 min.

Producer, William Jacobs; director, Ray Enright; story, Ernest Haycox; screenplay, James R. Webb, Borden Chase, and Charles O'Neal; assistant director, Oren Haglund; dialog director, Gene Lewis; art director, Charles H. Clarke; set decorator, G. W. Bernsten; wardrobe, Milo Anderson; Mr. Flynn's wardrobe, Marjorie Best; makeup, Perc Westmore; color consultant, William Fritzche; music, David Buttolph; orchestrators, Leo Shuken and Sidney Cutner; song, Mack David, Al Hoffman, and Jerry Livingston; sound, Francis J. Scheid; camera, Karl Freund; editor, Frederick Richards.

Errol Flynn (Morgan Lane); Alexis Smith (Maria Singleton); S. Z. Sakall (Poppa Schultz); Douglas Kennedy (Rodney Ackroyd); James Brown (Tex Coyne); Ian MacDonald (Slim Reeves); Charles Irwin (MacKenzie); Paul E. Burns (Tecumseh Burke); Tudor Owen (Jock); Lester Matthews (George Forsythe); Nacho Galindo (Pedro); Lane Chandler (Jake Overby); Monte Blue (Charlie Penrose); Billy Vincent (Baker); Warren Jackson (Curley Bennett); Forrest Taylor (Clark); Almira Sessions (Gaunt Woman); Gertrude Astor and Nita Talbot (Women); Philo McCullough (Bystander); Dorothy Adams (Mrs. Maynard); Jack Mower and Creighton Hale (Ranchers); Maude Prickett and Jessie Adams (Ranchers' Wives).

ROCKY MOUNTAIN (Warner Bros., 1950), 83 min.

Producer, William Jacobs; director, William Keighley; based on the story "Ghost Mountain" by Alan LeMay; screenplay, LeMay and Winston Miller; art director, Stanley Fleischer; set decorator, L. S. Edwards; music, Max Steiner; orchestrator, Murray Cutter; assistant director, Frank Mattison; wardrobe, Marjorie Best; sound, Stanley Jones; camera, Ted McCord; editor, Rudi Fehr.

Errol Flynn (Lafe Barstow); Patrice Wymore (Johanna Carter); Scott Forbes (Lieutenant Rickey); Guinn "Big Boy" Williams (Pap Dennison); Dick Jones (Jim Wheat); Howard Petrie (Cole Smith); Slim Pickens (Plank); Chubby Johnson (Gil Craigie); Buzz Henry (Kip Waterson); Sheb Wooley (Kay Rawlins); Peter Coe (Pierre Duchesne); Rush Williams (Jonas Weatherby); Steve Dunhill (Ash); Alex Sharp (Barnes); Yakima Canutt (Ryan); Nakai Snez (Man Dog).

KIM (MGM, 1950), C-113 min.

Producer, Leon Gordon; director, Victor Saville; based on the novel by Rudyard Kipling; screenplay, Gordon, Helen Deutsch, and Richard Schayer; assistant director, George Rhein; technical adviser, I. A. Hafsjee; color consultants, Henri Jaffa and James Gooch; art directors, Cedric Gibbons and Hans Peters; set decorators, Edwin B. Willis, Arthur Krams, and Hugh Hunt; makeup, William Tuttle and Ben Lane; costumes, Valles; sound, Douglas Shearer and Standish Lambert; montages, Peter Ballbusch; special effects, A. Arnold Gillespie; camera, William V. Skall; editor, George Boemler.

Errol Flynn (Mahbub Ali, the Red Beard); Dean Stockwell (Kim); Paul Lukas (Lama); Robert Douglas (Colonel Creighton); Thomas Gomez (Emissary); Cecil Kellaway (Hurree Chunder); Arnold Moss (Lurgan Sahib); Reginald Owen (Father Victor); Laurette Luez (Laluli); Richard Hale (Hassan Bey); Roman Toporow and Ivan Triesault (Russians); Hayden Rorke (Major Ainsley); Walter Kingsford (Dr. Bronson); Henry Mirelez (Wanna); Frank Lackteen (Shadow); Frank Richards (Abul); Henry Corden and Peter Mamakos (Conspirators); Donna Martell (Haikun); Jeanette Nolan (Foster Mother); Rod Redwing (Servant); Michael Ansara (Guard); Stanley Price (Water Carrier); Movita Castenada (Woman with Baby); Edgar Lansbury (Young Officer); Francis McDonald (Letter Writer); Adeline DeWalt Reynolds (Old Maharanee); Mike Tellegan (Policeman); Richard Lupino (Sentry); Olaf Hytten (Mr. Fairlee); George Khoury (Little Man).

HELLO GOD (1951), 64 min.
Producer-director screenplay, William Marshall; sound, Victor Appel; camera, Paul Ivano, Henry Freulich, and Leo Barboni.

Errol Flynn (The Man on Anzio Beach); Sherry Jackson (Little Indian Girl); William Marshall (Narrator); and: Joe Muzzuca and Armando Formica.

ADVENTURES OF CAPTAIN FABIAN (Republic, 1951),100 min.
Producer, William Marshall; associate producer, Robert Dorfmann; director, Marshall; based on the novel *Fabulous Ann Madlock* by Robert Shannon; screenplay, Errol Flynn; assistant director-technical adviser, Marc Maurette; music, René Clorec; technical collaborator, Guy Seitz; sets, Eugene Lourie and Max Douy; costumes, Arlington Valles; sound, Roger Cosson; camera, Marcel Grignon; editor, Henri Taverna.

Errol Flynn (Captain Michael Fabian); Micheline Presle (Lea Marriotte); Vincent Price (George Brissac); Agnes Moorehead (Aunt Jesebel); Victor Francen (Henri Brissac); Jim Gerlad (Constable Gilpin); Helena Manson (Madam Pirott); Howard Vernon (Emil); Roger Blin (Phillipe); Valentine Camax (Housekeeper); Georges Flateau (Judge Jean Brissac); Zanie Campan (Cynthia Winthrop); Reggie Nalder (Constant); Charles Fawcett (Defense Attorney); Aubrey Bower (Mate).

MARA MARU (Warner Bros., 1952), 98 min.
Producer, David Weisbart; director, Gordon Douglas; story, Philip Yordan, Sidney Harmon, and Hollister Noble; screenplay, N. Richard Nash; assistant director, William Kissel; music, Max Steiner; orchestrator, Murray Cutter; art director, Stanley Fleischer; set decorator, Lyle B. Reifsnider; Miss Roman's wardrobe, Milo Anderson; makeup, Gordon Bau; sound, C.A. Riggs; special effects, H. F. Koenekamp; camera, Robert Burks; editor, Robert Swanson.

Errol Flynn (Gregory Mason); Ruth Roman (Stella Callahan); Raymond Burr (Brock Benedict); Paul Picerni (Steven Ranier); Richard Webb (Andy

Callahan); Dan Seymour (Lieutenant Zuenon); Georges Renavent (Ortega); Robert Cabal (Manuelo); Henry Marco (Perol); Nestor Paiva (Captain Van Hoten); Howard Chuman (Fortuno); Michael Ross (Big China); Paul McGuire (First Mate); Ben Chavez, Leon Lontoc, and Alfredo Santos (Policemen); Don Harvey (Larry); Ralph Sancuyo (Harbor Policeman); Leo Richmond and Ted Laurence (Motor Cops).

AGAINST ALL FLAGS (Universal, 1952), C-83 min.

Producer, Howard Christie; director, George Sherman; story, Aeneas Mac-Kenzie; screenplay, MacKenzie and Joseph Hoffman; assistant directors, John Sherwood, Phil Bowles, and James Welch; color consultant, William Fritzche; art directors, Bernard Herzbrun and Alexander Golitzen; set decorators, Russell A. Gausman and Oliver Emert; costumes, Edward Stevenson; makeup, Bud Westmore; music, Hans J. Salter; dialog director, Irwin Berwick; sound, Leslie I. Carey and Joe Lapis; special camera, David S. Horsley; camera, Russell Metty; editor, Frank Gross.

Errol Flynn (Brian Hawke); Maureen O'Hara (Spitfire Stevens); Anthony Quinn (Roc Brasiliano); Alice Kelley (Princess Patma); Mildred Natwick (Molvina MacGregor); Robert Warwick (Captain Kidd); Harry Cording (Gow); John Alderson (Harris); Phil Tully (Jones); Michael Ross (Swaine); Bill Radovich (Hassan); Paul Newlan (Crop Ear Collins); Lewis Russell (Oxford); Arthur Gould-Porter (Lord Portland); Olaf Hytten (King William); Lester Mathews (Sir Cloudsley); Tudor Owen (William); Maurice Marsac (Captain Moisson); James Craven (Captain Hornsby); Keith McConnell (Quartermaster); Charles Fitzsimons (Flag Lieutenant); Michael Ferris (Quartermaster); Chuck Hamilton and Carl Saxe (Pirates); Ethan Laidlaw (Townsman); Dave Kashner (Flogger).

THE MASTER OF BALLANTRAE (Warner Bros., 1953), C-89 min.

Director, William Keighley; based on the novel by Robert Louis Stevenson; screenplay, Herb Meadow; additional dialog, Harold Medford; music, William Alwyn; music conductor, Muir Mathieson; assistant director, Frank Mattison; fencing master, Patrick Crean; color consultant, Joan Bridge; art director, Ralph Brinton; costumes, Margaret Furse; makeup, George Frost; sound, Harold King; camera, Jack Cardiff; editor, Jack Harris.

Errol Flynn (Jamie Durrisdeer); Roger Livesey (Colonel Francis Burke); Anthony Steel (Henry Durrisdeer); Beatrice Campbell (Lady Alison); Yvonne Furneaux (Jessie Brown); Felix Aylmer (Lord Durrisdeer); Mervyn Johns (MacKellar); Charles Goldner (Mendoza); Ralph Truman (Major Clarendon); Francis de Wolff (Bull); Jack Berthier (Arnaud); Gillian Lynn (Marianne); Moultrie Kelsall (MacCauley).

CROSSED SWORDS (United Artists, 1954), C-86 min.

Producers, J. Barrett Mahon and Vittorio Vassarotti; associate producers, Nato de Angelis, Arthur Villiesid; director-screenplay, Milton Krims; art director, Arrigo Equini; costumes, Nino Novarese; makeup, C. Gambarelli; camera, Jack Cardiff.

Errol Flynn (Renazo); Gina Lollobrigida (Francesca); Cesare Danova (Raniero); Nadia Gray (Fulvia); Paola Mori (Tomasina); Roldano Lupi (Pavoncello); Alberto Rabagliati (Gennarelli); Silvio Bagolini (Buio); Renata Chiantioni (Spiga); Mimo Billi (Miele); Pietro Tordi (The Duke); Ricardo Rioli (Lenzi).

LET'S MAKE UP (United Artists, 1954), C-94 min. (a.k.a., LILACS IN THE SPRING.)

Producer-director, Herbert Wilcox; based on the play *The Glorious Days* by Robert Nesbitt; screenplay, Harold Purcell; music, Harry Parr Davies; incidental score-arranger, Robert Farnon; production numbers orchestrator-conductor, Harry Acres; choreography, Philip and Betty Buchel; assistant director, Frank Hollands; art directors, William C. Andrews, Leonard Townsend, Albert Witherick, and A. Van Montagu; Miss Neale's dresses, Anthony Holland; wardrobe supervisor, Maude Churchill; makeup, Harold Fletcher; sound, Peter Handford and Len Shilton; camera, Max Green; editor, Reginald Beck.

Anna Neagle (Carole Beaumont/Lilian Grey/Queen Victoria/Nell Gwyn); Errol Flynn (John Beaumont); David Farrar (Charles King/King Charles); Kathleen Harrison (Kate); Peter Graves (Albert Gutman/Prince Albert); Helen Haye (Lady Drayton); Scott Sanders (Old George); Alma Taylor, Hetty King (Women in Dress Circle); Alan Gifford (Hollywood Director); Jennifer Mitchell (Young Carole); Gilliam Harrison (Very Young Carole); George Margo (Hollywood Reporter).

THE WARRIORS (Allied Artists, 1955), C-85 min. (a.k.a., THE DARK AVENGER.)

Producer, Walter Mirsch; director, Henry Levin; screenplay, Daniel B. Ullman; music, Cedric Thorpe Davie; song, Davie and Christopher Hassall; music conductor, Louis Levy; art director, Terence Verity; set decorator, Harry White; costumes, Elizabeth Haffenden; makeup, L. V. Clark; assistant director, Terence Hunter; technical adviser, Charles R. Beard; sound, Leslie Hammon and Len Shilton; camera, Guy Green; editor, E. B. Jarvis.

Errol Flynn (Prince Edward); Joanne Dru (Lady Joan Holland); Peter Finch (Count de Ville); Yvonne Furneaux (Marie); Patrick Holt (Sir Ellys); Michael Horden (King Edward III); Moultrie Kelsall (Sir Bruce); Robert Urquhart (Sir Philip); Vincent Winter (John Holland); Noel Willman (Du Guesclin); Frances Rowe (Genevieve); Alastair Hunter (Libean); Rupert Davies (Sir John); Ewan Solon (D'Estell); Richard O'Sullivan (Thomas Holland); Jack Lambert (Dubois); John Welsh (Gurd); Harold Kasket (Aranud); Leslie Linder (Francois Le Clerc); Robert Brown and John Phillips (French Knights).

KING'S RHAPSODY (United Artists, 1955), 93 min.

Producer-director, Herbert Wilcox; based on the musical play by Ivor Novello and Christopher Hassall; screenplay, Pamela Bower, Christopher Hassall; additional dialog, A. P. Herbert; music arranger-conductor, Robert Farnon; art director, William A. Andrews; costumes, Anthony Holland; choreography, Jon Gregory; sound, Peter Handford, Len Shilton, and Red Law; camera, Max Greene; editor, Reginald Beck.

Anna Neagle (Marta Karillos); Errol Flynn (King Richard); Patrice Wymore (Princess Cristiane); Martita Hunt (Queen Mother); Finlay Currie (King Paul); Francis de Wolff (The Prime Minister); Joan Benham (Countess Astrid); Reginald Tate (King Peter); Miles Malleson (Jules); Edmund Hockridge (Singer's Voice).

ISTANBUL (Universal, 1957), C-84 min.

Producer, Albert J. Cohen; director, Joseph Pevney; story, Seton I. Miller; screenplay, Miller, Barbara Gray, and Richard Alan Simmons; assistant directors, Joseph E. Kenny and Ray de Camp; color consultant, William Frizche; art directors, Alexander Golitzen and Eric Orbom; set decorators, Russell A. Gausman and Julia Heron; costumes, William Thomas; makeup, Bud Westmore; dialog director, Leon Charles; music supervisor, Joseph Gershenson; songs, Jay Livingston and Ray Evans; Victor Young and Edward Heyman; special camera, Clifford Stine; camera, William Daniels; editor, Sherman Todd.

Errol Flynn (Jim Brennan); Cornell Borchers (Stephanie Bauer [Karen Fielding]); John Bentley (Inspector Nural); Leif Erickson (Charlie Boyle); Torin Thatcher (Douglas Fielding); Martin Benson (Mr. Darius); Nat "King" Cole (Danny Rice); Peggy Knudsen (Marge Boule); Werner Klemperer (Paul Renkov); Vladimir Sokoloff (Aziz); Frederic Melchior (Said); Jan Arvan (Kazim); Nico Minardos (Ali); Didi Ramati (Sabiya); Otto Reichow and Michael Dale (Thugs); Peri Hatman (Turkish Travel Agent); Hillevi Rombin (Air Hostess); Michael Raffetto (Priest); Ted Hecht (Lieutenant Sarac); David Bond (Dr. Sarica); Roland Varno (Mr. Florian); Albert Carrier (Mauret); Edward Colmans (Hotel Clerk); Paul Thierry (Middle-Aged Man); Franco Corsaro (Butler); Peter Norman (Clerk); Bobker Ben Ali (Customs Man); Manuel Paris (Waiter); George Calliga (Headwaiter).

THE BIG BOODLE (United Artists, 1957), 83 min.

Producer, Lewis F. Blumberg; director, Richard Wilson; based on the novel by Robert Sylvester; screenplay, Jo Eisinger; music, Raul Lavista; assistant director, Henry Hartman; makeup, Anita Guerrero; camera, Lee Garmes; editor, Charles L. Kimball.

Errol Flynn (Ned Sherwood); Pedro Armendariz (Colonel Mastegui); Rossana Rory (Fina Ferrer); Gia Scala (Anita Ferrer); Sandro Giglio (Armando Ferrer); Jacques Aubuchon (Miguel Collada); Carlos Rivas (Carlos Rubin); Charles Todd (Griswold); Guillermo Alvarez Guedes (Casino Manager); Carlos Mas (Chuchu); Rogelio Hernandez (Salcito); Velia Martinez (Secretary); Aurora Pita (Sales Girl).

THE SUN ALSO RISES (Twentieth Century-Fox, 1957), C-129 min.

Producer, Darryl F. Zanuck; director, Henry King; based on the novel by Ernest Hemingway; screenplay, Peter Viertel; music, Hugo Friedhofer; music conductor, Lionel Newman; orchestrator, Maurice de Packh; Spanish music, Alexander Courage; orchestrators, Bernard Mayers and Arthur Morton; guitar music, Vicente Gomez; art directors, Lyle R. Wheeler and Mark-Lee Kirk; set decorators, Walter M. Scott, Paul S. Fox, and Jack Stubbs; executive wardrobe designer, Charles LeMaire; Miss Gardner's wardrobe, Fontana Sisters; make-up, Jack Obringer; assistant director, Stanley Hough; bullfight sequences staged by Miguel Delgado; brass bands director, Ramon Hernandez; sound, Bernard Freericks and Frank Moran; camera, Leo Tover; editor, William Mace.

Tyrone Power (Jake Barnes); Ava Gardner (Lady Brett Ashley); Mel Ferrer (Robert Cohn); Errol Flynn (Mike Campbell); Eddie Albert (Bill Gorton); Gregory Ratoff (Count Mippipopolous); Juliette Greco (Georgette); Marcel Dalio (Zizi); Henry Daniell (Doctor); Bob Cunningham (Harris); Danik Patisson (The Girl); Robert Evans (Pedro Romero); Eduardo Noriega (Mr. Braddock); Jacqueline Evans (Mrs. Braddock); Carlos Muzquiz (Montoya); Rebecca Iturbi (Frances); Carlos David Ortigos (Romero's Manager).

TOO MUCH, TOO SOON (Warner Bros., 1958), 121 min.
Producer, Henry Blanke; director, Art Napoleon; based on the book by Diana Barrymore, Gerold Frank; screenplay, Art and Jo Napoleon; music, Ernest Gold; assistant director, George Vieira; art director, John Beckman; set decorator, George James Hopkins; costumes, Orry-Kelly; makeup, Gordon Bau; dialog supervisor, Eugene Busch; sound, Francis E. Stahl; camera, Nick Musuraca and Carl Guthrie; editor, Owen Marks.

Dorothy Malone (Diana Barrymore); Errol Flynn (John Barrymore); Efrem Zimbalist, Jr. (Vincent Bryant); Ray Danton (John Howard); Neva Patterson (Michael Strange); Murray Hamilton (Charlie Snow); Martin Milner (Lincoln Forrester); John Dennis (Walter Gerhardt); Edward Kemmer (Robert Wilcox); Robert Ellenstein (Gerold Frank); Kathleen Freeman (Miss Magruder); John Doucette (Crowley); Michael Mark (Patterson); Francis DeSales, Jay Jostyn (Imperial Pictures Executives); Herb Ellis and Louis Quinn (Assistants); Robert S. Carson (Associate); Paul Bryar (Bill); Sid Tomack (Harry; Dick Harrison (Swimming Companion); Jack Lomas and Larry Blake (Reporters); Don Hayden (Theatre Manager); James Elsegood (Diana's Tango Partner); Bess Flowers and Charles Evans (Guests); Lyn Osborn (Man); Nesdon Booth (Spectator); Jack Rice (Druggist); Gail Bonney (Nurse).

THE ROOTS OF HEAVEN (Twentieth Century-Fox, 1958), C-131 min.
Producer, Darryl F. Zanuck; associate producer, Robert Jacks; director, John Huston; based on the novel by Romain Gary; screenplay, Gary and Patrick Leigh-Fermor; art directors, Stephen Grimes and Raymond Gabutti; set decorator, Bruno Avesani; costumes, Rosine Delamare; makeup, George Frost; music, Malcolm Arnold; "Minna's Theme," Henri Patterson; assistant director, Carlo Lastricati; technical adviser, Claude Hettier de Boislambert; sound, Basil Fenton Smith; special effects, Fred Etcheverry; special camera effects, L. B. Abbott; camera, Oswald Morris; second unit camera, Skeets Kelly, Henri Persin, and Gilles Bonneau; editor, Russell Loyd.

Errol Flynn (Major Forsythe); Juliette Greco (Minna); Trevor Howard (Morel); Eddie Albert (Abe Fields); Orson Welles (Cy Sedgewick); Paul Lukas (Saint Denis); Herbert Lom (Orsini); Gregoire Aslan (Habib); Andre Luguet (Governor); Friedrich Ledebur (Peer Qvist); Edric Connor (Waitari); Olivier

Hussenot (The Baron); Pierre Dudan (Major Scholscher); Marc Delnitz (De Vries); Dan Jackson (Madjumba); Maurice Cannon (Haas); Jacques Marin (Cerisot); Habib Benglia (Korotoro); Bachir Toure (Yussef); Alain Saury (A.D.C.); Roscoe Stallworth (N'Dolo); Assane Fall (Inguele); Francis de Wolff (Father Fargue).

CUBAN REBEL GIRLS (Joseph Brenner Associates, 1959), 68 min.
   Producer-director, Barry Mahon; screenplay, Errol Flynn.

   Errol Flynn (Himself/narrator); Beverly Aadland (Beverly); John MacKay (Johnny); Jackie Jackler (Jacqueline); Marie Edmund (Maria); Ben Ostrovsky (Raoul); and: Regnier Sanchez, Esther Oliva, Todd Brody, Al Brown, and Clelle Mahon.

6′ 2″
196 pounds
Black hair
Brown eyes
Taurus

Stewart Granger

Being a leading man on stage and screen has many obvious rewards, including fame, hefty salaries, and the pick of properties. On the other hand, there are definite liabilities in being termed "a leading man" rather than an actor. Reviewers and the public tend to take the performer for granted, assuming that his good looks and congenial public personality is the sole basis for his success. Producers, ever anxious to insure the success of their properties, are afraid to let such leading men break their molds, for fear of disappointing audiences or incurring the displeasure of the critics. Thus a vicious circle begins, with soon the typed leading man beginning to question his own professional adequacy. Such was the lot of British-born Stewart Granger, once known as the "glamour boy" and forever labeled by American moviegoers in the Fifties as the dimpled he-man of swashbuckling features.

He was born James Lablache Stewart in London on Tuesday, May 6, 1913. From the beginning he was called Jimmy, a nickname that would follow him through his lifetime. At the time of his birth, his father, Major James Stewart, a retired army officer, was fifty years old. Many years later, the son would tell Ruth Waterbury of *Photoplay* Magazine, "We were always two generations apart in views and habits.

We never had any intimacy at all. My first real memory of my father is when I was nine and he died."

Jimmy's mother, Frederica (Lablache) Stewart, came from a distinguished theatrical family. Her grandfather, Luigi Lablache, was the foremost bass of his era. Her father, Frederick, also a singer, had headed his own touring company. Frederica's mother had been leading lady on the English stage to luminaries such as Sir Henry Irving. Jimmy's mother planned a career in grand opera for her son.

In the years before the death of the senior Stewart, the family spent their summers and their holidays at their house on the Cornish Coast. There, Jimmy passed most of his time with the Cornish fishermen from whom he learned the art of catching and gutting fish. These outdoorsmen also taught their earthy slang to the youthful disciple who then shocked, not only his parents, but also their friends, by his prolific, though innocent cussing.

When Jimmy reached adolescence, his voice was tested for possible singing talents. Later, he would say that a certain maestro shook his head and said, "You have a fine voice—for two notes. After that you're a frog." With the shattering of the dream that her son should become a singer, Mrs. Stewart decided that he might do well in the field of medicine, perhaps as a nerve specialist. However, she neglected to consider the cost of sending him through years of schooling for this specialty, and finally settled on his following the less strenuous course of becoming a general practitioner. He was enrolled at Epsom College as a pre-med student, but after two years he was convinced that it was a waste of time and money. He once said, "To be a G.P. you have to be three-quarters saint, and there was no saint in my make-up whatsoever."

He had always been a devoted movie fan. "As an urchin, I popped goose pimples over the Gish sisters in a reissue of *The Birth of a Nation* [sic] and in my twenties when I discovered what Hollywood could do with decolletage, my veins went boing-boing." Therefore, when his friend, Michael Wilding, a neophyte actor, suggested that he try working in films as an extra, Jimmy thought this idea was a very good one.

Wilding informed him that the pay was not much—a guinea a day—but the fringe benefits to be derived from meeting "some very exciting fluff" were not to be frowned upon. "I was stony broke at the time," Jimmy has said, "but it was the latter inducement which won me over to grease paint." He did extra work in a Wardour film comedy, *A Southern Maid* (1933), starring Bebe Daniels, and then was Ben Lyon's stand-in for *I Spy* (Wardour, 1933). The following year he did a bit in *Give Her a Ring* (Pathe), featuring Wendy Barrie, but further screen activities had to be delayed because he had injured his thumb.

According to the story relayed by Jimmy to Pete Martin of the *Saturday Evening Post* in 1951, he visited a doctor's office for treatment of his thumb where a woman "studied" him and popped the question, "How'd you like to be a stage actor?" She said that she could arrange an audition with the Webber-Douglas Theatre School and "they might give you a scholarship." He claims to have read Shakespeare—badly— at the audition but, nonetheless, he was given a scholarship. He admitted to Pete Martin, "By coincidence, the coach had been a young actress in my grandfather's theatrical troupe, and I think that she must have had a lech for the old boy, which made her lenient with me."

After completing the training at Webber-Douglas, which included boxing and fencing, he went into repertory at Hull. His first professional stage appearance was at the Little Theatre on August 19, 1935, where he played the role of Andrea Strozzi in *The Cardinal*. Eventually, he played lead parts with the Hull group and changed his name from Jimmy Stewart to Stewart Granger. He blithely reasoned that there could not be two "stars" with the same name.

Next, he did a stint with the Birmingham Repertory company, then with the Malvern Festival group[1] in 1936 and 1937. The young actor moved up to London's West End as an understudy in Flora Robson's *Autumn*, which Basil Dean opened at the St. Martin's Theatre on October 15, 1937. The fledgling performer made his London stage debut at the Drury Lane Theatre (June 9, 1938) as Captain Hamilton in *The Sun Never Sets*, and among his other credits that year was Lord Ivor Cream to Vivien Leigh's *Serena Blandish* (Gate Theatre, September 13, 1938).

Three days before *Serena Blandish* opened, Stewart married Elspeth March,[2] a sensitive, much-admired actress who selflessly campaigned to better her husband's career by introducing him to highly placed people in the cinema world.

After that, Stewart found himself even busier on the stage. He had parts in *I Am the King* (1939) and *Jerusalem* (1939), and then was invited to join the Old Vic company. He appeared with them at the Buxton Festival in August, 1939, and, during October, was part of the group at the Streatham Hill Theatre productions.[3] He was back in the West End swim in 1940 with two plays, *Tony Draws a Horse* and *A House in the Square*. Then, that June, he toured in *Titian Red* in the role of Michael Davidson.

[1]His roles included Warwick in *Saint Joan*, Sir Broadfoot Basham in *On the Rocks*, Sir John Melvil in *The Clandestine Marriage*, St. John Rivers in *Jane Eyre*, General Su in *Lady Precious Stream*, Alastair in *The Millionairess*, King Magnus in *The Apple Cart*, Charles Surface in *The School for Scandal*, and Glundalca in *Tom Thumb the Great*.

[2]Born Jean Elspeth Mackenzie in 1912, she studied for the stage at the Central School of Speech Training and Dramatic Art. Her first stage appearance was in 1932 in *Jonah and The Whale*. From 1934 to 1937, she was engaged at the Birmingham Repertory Theater and at the Malvern Festivals, and on both occasions she worked with Stewart. She, too, was in *Autumn* at St. Martin's Theatre (1937). Thereafter, she was in repertory, until 1940, when she left the stage for four years of service as a driver for the American Red Cross.

[3]His roles included Tybalt in *Romeo and Juliet*, Leontine in *The Good-Natured Man*, Dunois in *Saint Joan*, and Anthony Anderson in *The Devil's Disciple*.

It was only to be expected that a good-looking, young actor would come to the attention of moviemakers. A scout from Twentieth Century-Fox's British division saw Granger on the stage and offered him a featured part in the Anglo-American comedy, *So This Is London* (Twentieth Century-Fox, 1939), which dealt with an attempted union of British and American bakery firms.[4] Among the cast of this George M. Cohan farce was George Sanders.

In the autumn of 1939, the declaration of war between England and Germany ended the Old Vic's national tour of *St. Joan,* and Stewart returned to London. At the Ealing Studios, he enacted the supporting role of a British naval officer in one of the better propaganda films, *Convoy* (Associated British Film Distributors, 1940). Under Captain Armitage (Clive Brook), *H.M.S Cruiser Apollo* saves the convoy of merchant ships from an attacking German battleship. Britain's *Monthly Film Bulletin* rated the picture as "the most exciting, lifelike and restrained account of the Navy's work in wartime yet seen on the screen."[5]

In the spring of 1940, twenty-seven-year-old Stewart enlisted in the Gordon Highlanders and was later transferred to the Black Watch Regiment. In 1941 he received an invalid's discharge due to severe stomach ulcers. With the shortage of actors for stage and screen work, he found several jobs. On stage, he toured in *To Dream Again* (June, 1942), and in September, 1942, he succeeded Owen Nares as Maxim de Winter in *Rebecca,* then playing at the Lyric Theatre.

More important to his career, he returned to moviemaking. In *Secret Mission* (General Film, 1942),[6] he portrayed a German officer in occupied France who is outwitted by a British Intelligence force sent to discover the strength of the Nazi defense. Also in the cast were Stewart's old friend, Michael Wilding, and another relative newcomer to the screen, James Mason.

Granger's screen progress would have been heightened by *Thursday's Child* (Pathe, 1943), had the film not been limited by its distributors to remote sections of London where few top newspaper critics saw it.[7] Modestly budgeted and directed by Rodney Ackland, the film is a "shrewd and gentle study of the effect on an ordinary suburban family of their daughter [Sally Ann Howes] becoming a child film star" (*London Daily Mail*). Stewart, in sixth billing, portrayed a handsome film star whom the thirteen-year-old girl meets when she enters the film profession at the Marathon Studios.

---

[4]In Fox's earlier edition of *So This Is London* (1930), Will Rogers and Irene Rich had the leads, while Bramwell Fletcher played the role Granger inherited.

[5]The film's director, Pen Tennyson, while later serving in the British Navy, was killed in action.

[6]Released in the U.S. on August 28, 1944.

[7]Having been re-edited in 1946, the film was reissued in mid-April of that year when it was "discovered" by the London critics.

With Carla Lehmann in *So This Is London* (1939)

He had second billing in *The Lamp Still Burns* (General Film, 1943), a feature dealing with the social scene in wartime Britain.[8] Adapted from the novel *One Pair of Feet* by Monica Dickens, the film portrays the lives of nurses in a London hospital, specifically student Nurse Clark (Rosamund John). Stewart is a patient referred to as "Punctured Lung," whose love life is aided and abetted by the ubiquitous student nurse who seems to have a finger in many pies. Critic C. A. Lejeune of the *London Observer* found Stewart to be "everything a probationer might dream of." *Variety* was less enthused about Granger, passing his appearance off with, "He gives an adequate performance."

Then Gainsborough Films discovered Stewart when James Mason decided to switch roles for *The Man in Grey* (General Film, 1943). Scheduled to play the romantic cavalier, Mason decided to alter his screen image by playing the villain instead. By agreeing to fill the vacancy left by Mason, Stewart laid the foundation for the film career that would be his. He signed a contract with Gainsborough that would later be assumed by J. Arthur Rank when the studio was incorporated into Rank's empire.

The Man in Grey derives from Lady Eleanor Smith's novel of roman-

[8]The film was produced by Leslie Howard, who was lost on an official British government goodwill flight to Portugal on June 1, 1943.

With Phyllis Calvert in _The Man in Grey_ (1943)

tic swappings in the upper classes of Britain's Regency period. Clarissa Rohan, played by Phyllis Calvert, is the wife of the arrogant, cold Marquis of Rohan (Mason). She is in love with the dashing Cavalier named Peter Rokeby (Stewart), while her husband takes her best friend, Hesther (Margaret Lockwood), as his mistress.[9] Eventually, Hesther murders the evil Marquis, which leaves the way open for Granger's Peter Rokeby to woo Calvert's Clarissa Rohan.

In fourth billing, Stewart's _The Man in Grey_ performance attracted the attention of London critic C. A. Lejeune, who wrote: "His screen technique is entirely undisciplined. He threw away, with a prodigal nonchalance, the sort of moments veterans have taken years to achieve. As a star performer, he is still quite brilliantly bad. I don't know any British actor I would sooner sign as a prospect." With the film's release on the other side of the Atlantic in 1945 (by Universal), Bosley Crowther of the _New York Times_ commented happily, "We have never known an actor with such a ravishing dental smile." The Leslie Arliss-directed film became a boxoffice hit in England and led many to believe that perhaps the British Isles had discovered their own Errol Flynn.

To help remind the British that there really was a time without German bombs, Gainsborough made a film of the Michael Sadleir

---

[9]To avoid possible audience confusion between Mason and Granger in this film, Stewart's hair was dyed a blond tone. He was furious about this matter, but there was little he could do about it.

novel *Fanny by Gaslight* (General Film, 1944) about the manners and morals of a more genteel era.[10] The Victorian period, unfortunately, was inhabited by people who were as avaricious and scheming as those of the 1940s. Lord Manderstoke (James Mason) is scheming to tighten his aristocratic paws on the ill-gotten Hopwood money by killing the patriarch (played by John Laurie) and making a concerted play for the wife (played by Nora Swinburne). When the Hopwood daughter, Fanny (Phyllis Calvert), finds love with a young man, Harry (Stewart), the evil Manderstoke considers Harry a rival for the legacy and forces him into a duel. Although the lover is almost killed, righteousness prevails as Fanny and her heart-throb survive to see another day. The critic of the *London Sunday Times* liked "the agreeable insouciance of Stewart Granger." For many, Stewart possessed all the dashing swagger of Robert Donat and Michael Redgrave at their best. If Granger's acting acumen was far below these two esteemed performers, his virile presence had a similar energy as that of England's favorite acting son, Laurence Olivier.

A mawkish *Love Story* (Eagle Lion, 1944) was the motion picture through which Stewart achieved wide popularity in Britain.[11] The

[10]Released in the U.S. through United Artists in February, 1948, as *Man of Evil.*

[11]Released in the U.S. by Universal in June, 1947, as *A Lady Surrenders.* The American critics were not very kind to the feature. "A foreign label does not increase the value of a long, dull, wordy tear-jerker." (*New York Herald-Tribune*) "[The British demonstrate]

With James Mason in *Fanny by Gaslight* (1944)

London Observer's C. A. Lejeune enthused, "Mr. Stewart Granger doesn't need to bother about being a bit out of practice in acting, he looks so scrumptious." In this film, Margaret Lockwood—the English answer to Joan Crawford—is a robust concert pianist dying of a heart disease. While taking a holiday at Cornwall and creating her composition, "The Cornish Rhapsody,[12] the "weakened" woman meets a physically sound young man (Stewart), out of uniform. After what seemed to be hours of histrionics, she learns that he is an ex-R.A.F. mining engineer on the verge of blindness due to war wounds. (It was sort of a combination of *Dark Victory, One Way Passage, This Above All,* and *The Other Love*.) They skirt romance while neither confesses his or her ailments until another girl (Patricia Roc) unwittingly forces a showdown. The R.A.F. fellow has a successful operation and gathers the pianist to his powerful chest after she faints at a performance of her composition at Albert Hall. The last we see of them, he is skyborne in a squadron of bombers while she (dressed in a swimsuit, yet) bravely waves to him from a cliff top. All this high-powered schmaltz and overacting were exactly what the entertainment-starved British desired.

Concerning Stewart's next film, William Whitebait in the *New Statesman* wrote, "It is notably bad." The film, *Madonna of the Seven Moons* (Eagle Lion, 1944) had stern-faced Phyllis Calvert as a woman with a split personality. Directed by Arthur Crabtree—who was more often employed as a cinematographer than a director for the Gainsborough stock company film productions—the feature tells the bizarre story of the respectable wife (Calvert) of an Italian wine merchant (Peter Glenville). In her second personality, she frequently gallivants to Florence, where she carries on with a half-gypsy bandit (Stewart). The film broke boxoffice records in the British Isles, but when it was released in America, the *New York Herald-Tribune* felt obliged to alert its readers about this "tangled tale of rape, amnesia, and amorality," which the paper insisted "is as cluttered in execution as it is in subject matter." Other reviewing sources were more appreciative of Stewart's good looks, if not his brand of acting.

It was on July 22, 1944, that "matinee idol" Stewart became a father, when Elspeth gave birth to a boy christened Jamie.

By 1945, the long-standing British film industry was reaching a new peak of influence, with J. Arthur Rank, the flour magnate, responsible for a good deal of the new importance gained by the English motion picture business. By winning financial control over a number of British studios (including Denham, Gainsborough, Gaumont, and Pine-

that they can dish out a drama of tragic love with all the dreary nobleness of their Hollywood cousins." (*New York Times*)

[12]A piano concerto specially written for the film by Hubert Bath and played by Harriet Cohen, backed by The National Symphony Orchestra.

With Phyllis Calvert, Jean Kent, Nancy Price, and Peter Glenville in *Madonna of the Seven Moons* **(1944)**

wood) it was his contention that, after the war, only an enormous empire such as his had the power to compete with American movie producers in the struggle for world markets. Along with Stewart Granger, a few of those magical figures who leaped into British (and subsequently global) film prominence were James Mason, Deborah Kerr, John Mills, Rex Harrison, Glynis Johns, Michael Redgrave, Wendy Hiller, Michael Wilding, Dulcie Gray, Patricia Medina, and Stanley Holloway. (Such other established British names as Margaret Lockwood, Phyllis Calvert, and Ann Todd would journey back and forth across the Atlantic, but would never gain much professional standing in Hollywood.)

Granger ushered in the year that would see world peace with a wartime romance picture, *Waterloo Road* (General Film, 1945).[13] Written and directed by Sidney Gilliat, Stewart is seen in his first really unsympathetic role as a draft-dodging racketeer/bully who attempts to seduce the wife (Joy Shelton) of a private soldier (John Mills). The soldier goes A.W.O.L. to track down the would-be seducer, and, on finding him, engages in a bloody fight. Of course, Stewart is dispatched and

---

[13]Released in the U.S. in January, 1949, by Eagle Lion.

With Joy Shelton in *Waterloo Road* **(1945)**

the soldier is reunited with his wife. *Variety* appropriately noted that the film boasted "skillful direction and admirable casting." Particularly outstanding in this flashback-prone story were Alastair Sim as the neighborhood doctor and George Carney as a pigeon fancier. For those following Stewart's film rise—and there were many such people in England—*Waterloo Road* was an upswing from the over-wrought nature of *Madonna of the Seven Moons,* but it was not exactly the type of role that could or would endear him to the public.

On July 16, 1944, C. A. Lejeune had written for the *New York Times,* "This Mr. Granger, by the way, is a young man who will bear watching. The customers on this side like his dark looks and his dash; he puts them in mind, they say, of Cary Grant, an actor whose work Mr. Granger admires and studies closely." Lejeune went on to report that Stewart, a close friend of Laurence Olivier and Vivien Leigh, rode horseback with them every Sunday. It was through the introduction by Miss Leigh to producer-director Gabriel Pascal that Stewart was cast in "the dashing role" of Apollodorus in his filmization (backed by J. Arthur Rank) of George Bernard Shaw's 1898 play *Caesar and Cleopatra* (Eagle Lion, 1946).[14] James Mason, the first choice for the Apollodorus role, had turned it down in favor of making *The Wicked Lady* (Eagle Lion, 1945).

[14]Other Shaw plays put to film by Pascal were *Pygmalion* (General Film, 1938) and *Major Barbara* (General Film, 1941).

The production, with its opulent sets by John Bryan and its costumes by Oliver Messel, took over a year to complete and inspired a good deal of wrath among English folk who thought the enormous budget (well over six million dollars) could have been better used for defense or welfare projects. Heralded for its use of Technicolor, the feature was described by Peter Burnup in the English edition of *Motion Picture Herald* to be "of immensity and beauty unsurpassed hitherto on this side of the Atlantic." In spite of the lavish production values and Shaw's personal selection of the two leads, Claude Rains and Vivien Leigh, the wordy 138-minute feature was neither a critical nor a commercial success. Critics such as those of the *London Daily Sketch* felt that "the direction is so completely uninspired, so heavy-handed (to the point of 'ham') that the film falls, flat as a pancake." The world of motion pictures in 1946 was not yet ready to grasp to its bosom Shaw's acidic interpretation of the aging emperor and the child queen of the Nile.

As Apollodorus,[15] Stewart was costumed with earbobs, skintint, and decorative armor as a dandy in Cleopatra's life prior to Mark Anthony. The role gave him his first on screen chance to display his agility at flexing his muscles and his prowess at swordplay. (Bosley Crowther of the *New York Times* found him "handsome and suave" in his interpre-

---

[15]In the Claudette Colbert-Warren William *Cleopatra* (Paramount, 1934), Irving Pichel was Apollodorus, while in the Elizabeth Taylor-Richard Burton-Rex Harrison *Cleopatra* (Twentieth Century-Fox, 1963), Cesare Danova had the part.

With Cecil Parker and Claude Rains in *Caesar and Cleopatra* (1946)

tation of the hale and hardy soul.) Also in the large cast was a teenaged girl named Jean Simmons, who played the part of a harpist at Cleopatra's court.[16] "She was a funny little thing," Stewart would recall years later. "She giggled when I looked at her."

As one of the pillars of Gainsborough Films, Stewart was next put to work in *Caravan* (General Film, 1946). Reviewer P. L. Mannock of the *London Daily Herald* was convinced that this offering might better "be called *Love from a Granger*." Two women (Anne Crawford and Jean Kent) of totally different social backgrounds love him. As Richard, a novelist in Spain during 1830, searching for local color, he courts the beautiful Oriana Camperdene (Crawford) of English-Spanish descent. His competition for her affections is Sir Francis Castleton (Dennis Price), who arranges for his murder through the henchman Wycroft (Robert Helpmann). Stewart's Richard is shot in the head, but he miraculously recovers under the care of the lovely gypsy maiden, Rosal (Jean Kent). Now a victim of amnesia he adjusts to his situation by marrying the fiery Rosal in a rousing gypsy ceremony. When the name Oriana pops up in a conversation, however, his memory suddenly returns and he is determined to seek retribution from the villainous Castleton and Wycroft. The April 14, 1946 issue of *The People* predicted, "Stewart Granger will draw you to the box-office for this artificial, novelettish Anglo-Saxon romantic drama."[17]

Again, Stewart inherited a role rejected by enormously popular James Mason, that of Nicolo Paganini, the Genoa-born composer and violin virtuoso (1782-1849). The Gainsborough story came to the screen as *The Magic Bow* (General Film, 1946), and the *London Daily Graphic* branded it as "a luxuriously dressed period piece, totally incredible and of a banality so complete it is almost impressive." While the real Paganini was a sexually-starved, unkempt skirt chaser who engaged in heavy gambling, the screen biography cleaned him up. In portraying the man, Stewart approached the women (Phyllis Calvert and Jean Kent)[18] in his tidied life with gentlemanly awe. Stewart's

[16]She was born Jean Merilyn Simmons in London on January 31, 1929, the youngest of four children of Charles and Winifred Ada (Loveland) Simmons. Her father taught physical education-swimming. In 1943, after four years of living in Somerset (to avoid the London blitz), she returned to the city with her family and was enrolled in the Aida Foster School of Dancing. Her first film role was in *Give Us the Moon* (General Film, 1944), starring Margaret Lockwood. Her work in *The Way to the Stars* (United Artists-British, 1944) led to a contract with J. Arthur Rank.

[17]*Caravan* was filmed entirely in England. When the film reached the U.S. in April, 1949, it was palmed off in limited release. The *New York Times,* appraising the situation, reported: "Whatever it is about gypsies, romantic period adventures and Stewart Granger that attracts the British film makers, it must be something awfully powerful. Granger, a tall, dark-haired, muscled gent . . . is again caught up with gitanos (Granada gitanos, that is). . . . Granger and the rest of the cast alternate between grappling with stilted lines and an embarrassingly archaic situation with neither the players nor plot making much entertainment, while *Caravan* moves with the speed of an oxcart."

[18]Margaret Lockwood had refused to be in the picture and was replaced by Kent.

With Jean Kent and Robert Helpmann in *Caravan* (1946)

With Phyllis Calvert in *The Magic Bow* (1946)

fiddling[19] was dubbed by Yehudi Menuhin, eliciting the *Daily Graphic*'s comment, "[Stewart] appears to be sawing wood with one hand and milking a cow with the other." The *London Daily Herald* agreed that his fingering of the bow left much to be desired, but also stated, "In any case, to many thousands of impressionable young women he will, more than ever, be their idealised Magic Beau."

Early in 1947, Stewart, who had become a father for the second time the previous year (Lindsay had been born on January 24, 1946), toured Europe with an ENSA unit, the British equivalent of the U.S.O. He performed scenes from *Gaslight* with Deborah Kerr. On his return to London he met Jean Simmons again, and found that she was no longer a little girl. "Everything had grown up." The beautiful Miss Simmons, who has been likened to both Vivien Leigh and Elizabeth Taylor, was now a star in her own right, having clicked onscreen with *Great Expectations* (J. Arthur Rank, 1945). Stewart became her advisor.

Stewart's next picture is perhaps the one that clinched his popularity with American audiences. The story was as good as was his performance in the role of a dashing, energetic Irish rebel leader in *Captain Boycott* (General Film, 1947).[20] Filmed at County Mayo, Ireland, this

[19]Among the Paganini compositions utilized were "Caprice Number Twenty," "Vidin Concerto #1 in D Major," "Moto Perpetuo," as well as Beethoven's "Violin Concerto in D Major" and Bazzini's "La Ronde des Lutins." Regarding the surfeit of music in the film, the *New York Herald-Tribune* carped, "The screen, however, is not a concert hall; and this wrapping-up of good music in a moth-eaten shadow play is no more beguiling than it has been on past cinematic occasions."

[20]At his own request, Robert Donat appeared onscreen for two minutes as Charles Stewart Parnell, for a fee of 1,000 pounds, establishing the "cameo" before it was called cameo.

With Kathleen Ryan in *Captain Boycott* (1947)

With Valerie Hobson in *Blanche Fury* (1948)

J. Arthur Rank production narrates the story of an English landowner, Captain Charles Boycott (Cecil Parker), in 1880 who is not doing right by his Irish farmers. Since the land tillers lack the ability to rebel openly, they walk out on him, and even the local tradespeople refuse to sell him goods or to humor him in any way. Hence, the use of the word "boycott" in the English language to designate any similar actions. The *News of One World* critic credited Stewart with giving "the best performance of his career."[21]

With his elevation in the hearts of filmgoers, Stewart's weekly salary also escalated. In 1938 he had been earning about three pounds weekly, but by 1947 he was getting 15,000 pounds a film. The Rank publicity department was pleased to tell the intrigued public that the Grangers had "a large comfortable house in the heart of Surrey, a fleet of cars, two children and fame." There were many on the British film front who insisted that popularity and affluence[22] had gone to Stewart's head, that he was difficult to work with, and that his arrogance was no rumor. On the other hand, a defender of Granger's "temperament" at the time insisted he was the "kind of chap who'll swear at you as a form of endearment."

A country estate named Clare Hall serves as the nineteenth-century focal point of the Technicolor vehicle, *Blanche Fury* (General Film, 1948). The $1.5-million feature was yet another movie based on the popular novels by Joseph Shearing.[23]

In the Marc Allegret-directed picture, set in a mysterious English countryside, Laurence Fury (Michael Gough) and his father (Walter Fitzgerald) wrongfully take possession of the Clare Hall estate when the legal heir is absent. The declared owner's steward, Philip Thorn (Stewart), on the other hand, claims that, as the illegitimate son of the prior titleholder, he is the proper owner of Clare Hall. While trying to prove his rights of ownership, he stalks about the place in a dark, towering rage that simmers down only towards the end of the picture. Into this troubled climate steps Blanche (Valerie Hobson) to act as governess to the owner's child (Suzanne Gibbs). Blanche later weds Laurence, but on their nuptial day, she begins an affair with the open-shirted Philip Thorn. (Elspeth Grant in the *London Daily Graphic* noted about the Granger-Hobson love scenes that the couple's "passionate embraces will have Mr. Granger's fans swooning dead away all over the cinema.") With Blanche's blessing, Thorn murders the male

---

[21]On the other hand, Alan Wood in *Mr. Rank* (1952) believes, "In *Captain Boycott*, a good script by Launder and Wolfgang Wilhelm was spoilt by a decision to play Stewart Granger in the leading role, upsetting the balance of the story."

[22]Granger's custom-made green and black Bentley car was rumored to have cost over 8,000 pounds.

[23]Other films based on the works of Joseph Shearing (the nom de plume of a woman writer) were *Moss Ross* (Twentieth Century-Fox, 1947), *The Mark of Cain* (General Film, 1948), and *So Evil My Love* (Paramount, 1948).

Furys and plots the murder of the child, but fate intervenes and the child is accidentally killed. While Thorn goes to the gallows, Blanche carries his child, who will one day be the rightful heir to Clare Hall.

Concerning this picture, which was based on the famous Rush murder case, the *London Daily Express* summed up: "There is so much emotion . . . everyone looks ready to go off pop at any minute." *Variety* saw this morose tale as "a curious mixture of degenerate nobility with melodramatic staples." Regarding Granger's appearance, *Variety* was quick to point out, "His best moments are those of passion, but the camera and the script are occasionally less kind to him than it has been to his co-star."

J. Arthur Rank and Stewart went even further back in history—the seventeenth century—for *Saraband for Dead Lovers* (General Film, 1948).[24] In this large-scale production, directed by Michael Relph and Basil Dearden, Granger is the Swedish Count Philip Konigsmark (1665-1694), dallying at the court of Hanover and, in particular, with the Princess Sophia Dorothea (Joan Greenwood). She is married to the drunken, fat Prince George Louis (Peter Bull), who ultimately became King George I of England. When the romantic liaison is revealed by the jealous Countess Platen (Flora Robson), the princess is summarily tossed into a dungeon and the Count killed. Once again, Stewart displayed his deftness with a sword in this film. The *London Daily Herald* noted the picture was "photographed in subdued, gloomy colour," that Granger is "little more than a solemn, passionless bore, whose violent end left me completely calm."

While Stewart strongly advised Jean Simmons *not* to play the complex role of Ophelia in Rank's *Hamlet* (1948),[25] starring Laurence Olivier, he campaigned against typecasting for himself and let it be known that he wanted to try his hand at comedy. "I object to being constantly typed," he told the press. "Some of the pictures in which I have appeared have made me feel ashamed of myself." Rank studio executives were not too happy with his public statement, but since he represented a boxoffice goldmine, he was permitted to have his way.

In his next film, *Woman Hater* (General Film, 1948), directed by Terence Young, he is a lord who claims he is fed up with women (he even quotes Diogenes to prove his point). However, he invites a French movie actress (Edwige Feuillere, in her British debut) to his home to demonstrate that her boredom with men is phony. He masquerades as his own employee and prepares to sweep her off her feet. In doing so, they fall madly in love with one another. To get laughs

---

[24]Released in the U.S. by Eagle Lion in 1949, with the title abbreviated to *Saraband* (a Spanish Court dance of the period).

[25]Her interpretation of the role gained favorable critical comments, and she garnered an Academy Award nomination as Best Supporting Actress (she lost to Claire Trevor of Warner Bros.' *Key Largo*).

With Anthony Quayle (left) in *Saraband for Dead Lovers* (1948)

With Edwige Feuillere in *Woman Hater* (1948)

within the lengthy 105-minute feature, Stewart resorts to falling off a horse, diving into a foot of water, falling down stairs, getting drunk, being ducked in a lake, buried in mud, and receiving innumerable cracks on the skull. *The People's* Ross Shepherd answered his own question, "Does Mr. Granger make me roar with laughter? . . . He does not."

Stewart, realizing his love for Jean Simmons, agreed to divorce proceedings from his wife in 1948. On April 13, in an undefended case, Elspeth was granted a *decree nisi* and awarded custody of the two children. It was all very civil and pleasant between the ex-spouses.

At twenty, Miss Simmons was still considered a minor, and Stewart promised her parents that they would not marry until she was legally an adult. In 1949, they appeared together in a comedy-drama for Rank entitled *Adam and Evelyne* (General Film).[26] As gambler Adam Black, Stewart "inherits" the orphaned daughter, Evelyne (Simmons), of a friend. After two years, when the girl returns from a finishing school, would-be daddy falls in love with her.

Then Stewart and Jean appeared together in a London stage revival of Leo Tolstoy's *The Power of Darkness* (Lyric Theatre: April 28, 1949). However, it failed after a few performances. By this time, Stewart's Rank contract had expired and he chose not to renew it. Allegedly,

[26]Released through Universal in the U.S. in 1949 as *Adam and Evalyn.*

With Jean Simmons in *Adam and Evelyne* (1949)

he had never forgiven the studio for not promoting his name sufficiently in the advertisements for *Saraband for Dead Lovers*. (On the other
side of the coin, the film company executives had decided that the
braggadocio nature of Granger on and off the set was no longer worth
the trouble.) Since he was then England's number one actor (Glynis
Johns was the top actress in the same *Kinematograph Weekly* survey),
there was no doubt that other producers would rush in where Rank
now feared to tread. Alexander Korda approached Granger with the
proposition of enacting *The King's General*, another James Mason reject, but Stewart's eyes were focused on what lay on the other side of
the Atlantic. MGM of Hollywood had made attractive come-hither
signs and he was ready to respond to a seven-year contract reputedly
worth one and one half million dollars.

On signing the Metro pact in 1949, Stewart jubilantly informed the
press: "It's not everybody who has a chance to get a fresh start in a
career at thirty-six. I made all those pictures for Rank at a time when
we were trying to make too many, and there aren't many of them that I
am proud of. Except in a few localities like New York, nobody knows
me in America, and actually, I can start all over again."

Always favorably inclined toward the British, Hollywood was ready
for the latest import from the Isles, but its columnists were a bit dazed
by Granger's unwillingness to talk about his private life. On that subject, he was tight-lipped. Stewart, the movie fan, spent his first few
days looking over the town. Sidney Skolsky reported, "I'm amused
when Stewart Granger, movie star, turns and gawks like a tourist at
movie star Clark Gable." Deborah Kerr, also imported to Hollywood
by MGM (at a slightly earlier date) explained the feeling to actor Richard Carlson, the author of an article in *Colliers* Magazine: "Going to
Hollywood is like having your first baby. You don't know quite what's
happening to you, but you do know it's something wonderful. You
don't quite believe it all. And afterward no thrill in your life will ever
be as great."

Whether or not brawny and single Stewart (Jean Simmons was still
back in England) knew what was happening, he was heard over "Lux
Radio Theatre" the evening of December 11, 1949, in an hour's dramatization of *B. F.'s Daughter* (MGM, 1948). Barbara Stanwyck repeated
her role as the heroine of the title, an heiress who believes she can buy
her husband's success. Stewart played the supposedly malleable spouse
(created on film by Van Heflin).

For his first Hollywood-produced feature, Stewart was sent to Africa
for a remake of the 1937 Gaumont-British film, *King Solomon's Mines*
(MGM, 1950), adapted from H. Rider Haggard's 1885 novel. Stewart
played Allan Quartermain[27] (played in 1937 by Cedric Hardwicke), a

---

[27]At one point, Warner Bros.-borrowed Errol Flynn was to do *King Solomon's Mines*, but
he was shifted to the less prestigious *Kim* (MGM, 1950).

With Richard Carlson and Deborah Kerr in *King Solomon's Mines* **(1950)**

tough great white hunter hired by Elizabeth Curtis (Deborah Kerr) to lead a safari in quest of her husband, who has been missing for some two years. In the man's last letter was a map leading to the King Solomon diamond mines. With the lady's brother (Richard Carlson), they set out on a trip that is both exciting and dangerous. For this film, Stewart's hair was silvered at the temples to give him an air of maturity which proved overpowering, not only to Kerr's plucky Mrs. Curtis, who never really loved her husband anyway, but to American women who saw the finished film, as well. The group locates the mines, along with the remains of the lady's spouse. They barely escape with their lives (and no diamonds) from a hostile Watusi tribe, and the film concludes with Granger embracing Kerr and saying, "It seems we're going to live." He pats the top of her red hair and the three adventurers face the long trek back to civilization.

During the five-month location shooting in Africa,[28] Stewart is reported to have said, "The place has a hold on me. I seem to have been here in a previous incarnation. Something tells me that I'm destined to die here." To counter the charges that Stewart was a difficult actor with whom to work (according to co-director Compton Bennett), co-director Andrew Marton told Pete Martin of *The Saturday Evening Post*, "The way I see it, I'm lucky to have an actor working for me who's willing to

[28]The excess on-location footage was incorporated into *Watusi* (MGM, 1959).

drive himself harder than any director would drive him. In my opinion, he's got guts in proportion to his ego." Co-star Deborah Kerr said, "Women sense that there's a bit of the brute in him. A woman's intuition tells her that being a gentleman hasn't watered down his virility, and that he would as soon thwack her on the rear as not." Richard Carlson's comments added, "Everything about him is on a huge scale —his physique, his voice, his laugh, his enthusiasm, his frustrations, his temperament and his generosity. I often had the feeling he would have been happier as an Elizabethan." Another co-worker likened him to John Barrymore—without the booze. The comparison, on being printed in California newspapers with due dispatch, was better than any bit of publicity that a public relations person could have invented.

On reviewing the results of his first photo-posing session for studio portraits, Stewart let loose with a tirade at the man in charge of the gallery. "I heard stuff I've never listened to before," the man said, "and I've been around here since I was tall enough to squint into the back end of a camera." The more printable of Stewart's lament included, "You've ruined me. You've taken the bags from under my eyes and the lines out of my face. You've left me no gray hair, and it took me years and a lot of hard work to get those things."

MGM, whose star roster included some big names (Clark Gable, Spencer Tracy, Van Johnson, Robert Walker, William Powell, Gene Kelly, Fred Astaire, Howard Keel, Robert Taylor, Mario Lanza, Dick Powell, and Red Skelton) was very happy with their new adventure star and hurriedly announced that his production schedule would include Kipling's Soldiers Three, Daniel Defoe's Robinson Crusoe,[29] Rafael Sabatini's Scaramouche, and Sir Walter Scott's Ivanhoe.[30]

Jean Simmons arrived in Hollywood in 1950 on a loan basis from J. Arthur Rank to RKO for the role of Lavinia in Androcles and the Lion. On December 20, 1950, with Michael Wilding (who flew in from New York) as the only guest and standing as best man, Stewart and Jean were married in Tucson, Arizona, in a private home ceremony conducted by a Methodist minister. He was thirty-seven, she was twenty-one. After a brief honeymoon in Arizona, the couple returned to Hollywood, where Stewart went into the production of Soldiers Three (MGM, 1951).

Miss Simmons, however, discovered that the remaining six months of her Rank contract had been bought by Howard Hughes of RKO. While work was delayed on Androcles and the Lion, Jean sat at home because Hughes claimed that their oral agreement forbade her being loaned to other studios. In the ensuing law case, Hughes' battery of attorneys claimed that Granger, as Jean's advisor, was demanding that

[29]United Artists would eventually film Robinson Crusoe in 1954 with Dan O'Herlihy.
[30]MGM's Ivanhoe (1952) would headline Robert Taylor as the bold knight.

RKO pay $500,000 to Jean, as well as $100,000 to him for the new home they had bought in Brentwood, and that they take an option on a story he owned. In turn, Stewart accused Hughes of slander and libel. The case was eventually settled with RKO paying the Grangers $250,000 plus $35,000 in lawyer's fees. In addition, Jean agreed to loanouts at $200,000 per film. Stewart has admitted that his legal coup against the great Hughes is one of the proudest achievements in his life.

Soldiers Three, called "silly, unimaginative and flavorless" by Bosley Crowther of the *New York Times,* has Stewart in a slapstick role as one of three British Tommies (the other two were played by Robert Newton and Cyril Cusack) in India.[31] After this let-down, Metro placed their hot property in a contemporary vehicle, *The Light Touch* (MGM, 1951), filmed in Tunis, Sicily, and Italy, and written and directed by Richard Brooks. The film has Stewart as a thief who steals a Renaissance painting. He plans to reproduce the masterpiece with the help of a girl (Pier Angeli) and to cut his partners (George Sanders, Norman Lloyd, Mike Mazurki) out of the take. Instead he tumbles for the young girl, marries her, and is converted to more honest ways. *The Light Touch* was hardly what the title indicated, and the film did little for Granger's screen reputation as the boisterous gallant of the 1950s.

---

[31]At one point, years before, *Soldiers Three* had been announced as a project for Clark Gable, Spencer Tracy, and Wallace Beery.

With Robert Newton and Cyril Cusack in *Soldiers Three* (1951)

With George Sanders and Pier Angeli in a publicity pose for *The Light Touch* (1951)

Dorothy Kilgallen cooed in a *New York Journal-American* column in 1951: "I lived through the Clark Gable vogue, the Robert Taylor excitement, the Van Johnson hysteria and I did some fluttering over Gregory Peck. But, so help me, I have never seen anything like the way ladies with high boiling points and high intelligence are falling to pieces over Mr. Granger." At that same time, in Hollywood, Stewart publicly referred to Michael Wilding as "rather a gorgeous boy," which raised the eyebrows of certain columnists who apparently didn't understand the different nuance that expression has for a British speaker. Soon after the gossip had begun, Granger was at a party given by Van Johnson, and he stood up before the guests and began, "I hear there's a rumor I'm not interested in women." In frankly earthy terms, he then proceeded to inform the surprised group *exactly* why he liked women.[32]

His next film in release was *The Wild North*, also known as *The Big*

---

[32]Twelve years later, in 1963, in Hedda Hopper's book *The Whole Truth and Nothing But*, she told how she had tried to talk Elizabeth Taylor out of marrying Michael Wilding, because, "In the first place, he's too old for you. And the rumor around town is that Michael Wilding and Stewart Granger are very, very close." When the book was published, Wilding sued for three million dollars. Settling out of court, Hopper and her publisher, Doubleday & Co., shared in a $100,000 payment to Wilding, and the insinuation was omitted from all future printings.

North, (MGM, 1952). With the mountains and snows of Idaho substituting for that of the Canadian great northwoods, it was an "adventure" story shot in the new Ansco color process. Granger appeared as Jules Vincent, a simple fur trapper accused of murder. He battles wolves, blizzards, and Indians, and falls in love with Cyd Charisse (in a very small, non-dancing role) before he proves his innocence to the Mountie (Wendell Corey) who has been trying to capture him. The story is not much at all, but the scenery is breathtaking.

Thanks to the compilation feature *That's Entertainment* (United Artists, 1974), MGM will probably be best remembered in the 1950s for its rash of screen musicals. While this may be a fair appraisal of the output of the Dore Schary-run studio, Metro also did much to stimulate the waning swashbuckling film cycle with its Stewart Granger features, each more lavishly packaged than the one before it. As *Life* Magazine, which featured Stewart on its May 26, 1952 cover, sized it up, "For years Hollywood has been looking for a glib and handsome actor who can fence with swords or words, wear fancy costumes and quicken the hearts of females without sickening the males." Stewart Granger filled the bill.

Next on the Granger lineup was *Scaramouche* (MGM, 1952).[33] Ra-

[33]The word Scaramouche is Italian for "little skirmisher," the comic who appeared in eighteenth-century *commedia dell' arte*.

With Wendell Corey and Cyd Charisse in *The Wild North* **(1952)**

376

With Mel Ferrer in *Scaramouche* (1952)

fael Sabatini wrote the novel in 1921 and Ramon Novarro played the lead in the 1923 silent version by Metro Films. It was first announced that Stewart would play both the lead and the role of the hero's cousin. Then it was decided that Fernando Lamas and Ricardo Montalban would assume the respective parts instead. Finally, it was agreed that Granger should be the lead, but that another actor, Mel Ferrer, should portray the villain. Elizabeth Taylor originally was to have been the heroine, with Ava Gardner as the beauteous Lenore, roles eventually assumed by Janet Leigh and Eleanor Parker respectively. When it was finally firm that Stewart would enact the lighthearted actor-adventurer, Andre Moreau, in the Metro remake, he arranged for private showings of the Novarro version. Then he trained for eight weeks with a fencing master.

In *Scaramouche*, Andre Moreau, a man of questionable birth, is a happy fellow who dallies with the ladies and evades duel-at-dawn threats of irate husbands by hiding behind his theatrical mask as Scaramouche. He loves Lenore (red-headed Miss Parker), an actress with the theatrical caravan, "Binet Presents Les Comediens Celebres" (Robert Coote is Binet). Andre plans to marry Lenore, but his best friend (Richard Anderson) fails to show up with the ring. It develops that this Philippe has been writing and distributing pamphlets that proclaim "Liberté, egalité, and fraternité," which upsets Queen Marie Anto-

377

inette (Nina Foch). The queen's dastardly cousin, Noel, Marquis de Maynes (Mel Ferrer) ends Philippe's writing days by thrusting a sword into him.

Andre's marriage is further delayed as he swears vengeance against Noel, France's most brilliant swordsman. Meanwhile, he meets Aline de Gavrillac (Leigh), the queen's protegé, with whom he sincerely falls in love (Noel loves her too). One night, in a brightly lighted theatre, Andre spots Noel seated in a box. He rips off his mask and leaps from the stage, scales a column, until he is face to face with Noel, and both brandish their swords. They fence—with intermittent spurts of Technicolored blood—from box to box, between rows of seats, into the gilded lobby, down the center aisle, and back onto the stage.

The well-publicized dueling scene runs eight minutes, the longest fencing sequence in cinematic history. (The previous record-holder had been in MGM's *The Three Musketeers,* [1948] with a three-and-a-half-minute sequence.) According to studio publicists, Stewart and Ferrer had to memorize eighty-seven separate sword counts which incorporated twenty-eight stunts and situations. To complete the action scene, they used eighteen swords and each wore out two pairs of shoes. "Casualties" included several potted plants, numerous props, and four slashed canvas backdrops.

As the film draws to a close, the oncamera theatre audience cries "Scaramouche," and Andre sends Noel's sword spinning out of his hand. He raises his sword to run Noel through, but cannot do it. It is then explained that Noel and Andre are really brothers and he could not kill his own sibling. For a moment, Andre is dumbfounded at the news, but then roars with laughter, "My loving brother, tender, gentle Noel, Marquis de Maynes." The defeated Noel is forced to retreat and Andre is now free to love Aline. The tempestuous Lenore gives the couple her blessings and walks off holding the arm of a gentleman looking suspiciously like Napoleon.

Variety might point out that *Scaramouche* "never seems to be quite certain whether it is a costume adventure drama or a satire on costume adventure dramas," but *Cue* Magazine was more on target when it proclaimed that the film "shapes up as a roaring romantic spectacle." As for Stewart's onscreen scampering, the *New York Times'* Bosley Crowther wrote, "He's got the teeth for laughing and the manner for confronting a mad world. He also appears to sense completely that he is not playing history." *The Saturday Review,* in spite of the eight-minute dueling scene, concluded that Granger "seems strangely earth-bound, more buckle than swash." However, the magazine did admit, "And if neither he nor the girls are any more eighteenth century than the atom bomb, the general tongue-in-cheek approach makes all of it quite easy to take." Certainly, the $3.5 million production proved its point, that audiences would flock to a well-proportioned period adventure yarn, especially one with such an engaging hero. Was Granger as athletic as Douglas Fairbanks, as swaggering and dashing as Errol Flynn, or as classic and sensitive as Tyrone Power? Filmgoers were still not quite sure, but they recognized Stewart Granger as the swash-buckling star of the year, if not of the decade or of a lifetime.

On September 29, 1952, Stewart and Jean Simmons were heard but not seen when they repeated their *Adam and Evelyne* roles in an abridged version for "Lux Radio Theatre."

On the January 8, 1953 release in London of Stewart's next film, the *Daily Sketch* warned, "Watch out, Errol Flynn—someone is rivalling you as a swashbuckling film adventurer. It's Stewart Granger!" And swashbuckle he did in the dual role of the king and his cousin in the new remake of *The Prisoner of Zenda* (MGM, 1952).[34] This rendition of the Anthony Hope novel of 1893, directed by Richard Thorpe, used much of the same script as the 1937 production, although one must admit that the later version lacked the classically euphonious voices of the former (Ronald Colman, Madeleine Carroll, Raymond Massey, Mary Astor).

Again, it is English sportsman Rudolph Rassendyll (Stewart) who treks to Ruritania on a hunting trip as his drunken look-alike cousin is

[34]First presented in 1922 by Metro-Goldwyn with Lewis Stone, while a second version, in 1937, came from United Artists, and starred Ronald Colman.

With Deborah Kerr and Robert Douglas in *The Prisoner of Zenda* (1952)

379

about to be crowned king. A group of plotters against the throne, led by the silky Rupert of Hentzau (James Mason) drug the king designate and abduct him to the castle at Zenda. The monarch's true friends, Robert Coote and Louis Calhern, persuade the Englishman to pose as the new ruler for the coronation so that the people will not know that the actual king has been taken prisoner. Rassendyll is well trained in the royal graces by his two cohorts, but they failed to inform him of the beauty and kindness of the king's betrothed, Flavia (Deborah Kerr). They soon fall in love, although she knows he is not the true king. After the elaborate coronation festivities[35] Rassendyll takes sword in hand and besieges the castle, where he almost singlehandedly rescues the king and sends Rupert to his maker. The throne is saved. As Rassendyll prepares to return home to England, he beseeches Flavia to join him, but she insists on seeing through her obligations as queen of Ruritania and he leaves alone.

As if it needed to be done, Otis T. Guernsey, Jr. (*New York Herald-Tribune*) proclaimed *The Prisoner of Zenda* a "transparent" hit. He explained, "It maintains the happy insolence of a romantic daydream, it has a villain worthy of the hero's steel in the person of James Mason, and it comes to a climax with a roaring saber duel."

Granger's next film was *Salome.* The Beckworth Corporation, which was partially owned by Rita Hayworth, borrowed him for the role of

[35]Just as the Colman version of *The Prisoner* tied in its coronation scenes with the crowning of King George VI in 1937, so the 1953 edition of the ceremonies was timed to coincide with the spring festivities surrounding the crowning of England's new queen, Elizabeth II.

With Rita Hayworth in a publicity shot for *Salome* (1953)

Claudius, a Roman captain turned Christian in this 1953 Columbia release. The beautiful Miss Hayworth had top billing as the temptress of biblical yore, and Stewart received second billing in a role that actually could have been played by any number of handsome actors in Hollywood. But his name, it was hoped, would guarantee good boxoffice receipts. Although advertised as "The Screen Achievement of 1953," and including an impressive supporting cast (Charles Laughton, Judith Anderson, Sir Cedric Hardwicke, and Basil Sydney), Harry Kleiner's screenplay and William Dieterle's direction made a wet dishrag of the outing.

From their home high in the Los Angeles hills, Stewart and Jean looked down upon the expansive colony that was the source of their livelihood. The house, itself, was small with only two bedrooms, but was walled generously with glass. Having become a hunter, Stewart's trophies of his African trips occupied space in every room, along with skin rugs, mounted animal heads, paintings of various wild animals, and collected drawings and paintings of his wife. There was a swimming pool, of course, and Sundays were generally spent barbecuing steaks for their friends: the James Masons, the Michael Wildings (Michael Wilding and Elizabeth Taylor), producer Sam Zimbalist and his wife, Deborah Kerr, and Tony Bartley, the Richard Burtons, and Jean's newest friend from *The Actress* (MGM, 1953), Spencer Tracy.

To many members of the press, Stewart was considered a snob, possibly because he still refused to talk about his private life. He reasoned: "I don't think I'm a snob. My friends don't think I'm a snob. I think that for the good of the movie industry a star must be different; he shouldn't trot about having dinner with strangers, be seen sitting on the curb at parades, hang about corner drug stores or have his picture taken washing his own socks. It happens that Jean and I would like to do these things, but we avoid them. So we are snobs." An English newspaperman had written that Stewart's manner was making him the "most unpopular Englishman in Hollywood," but Stewart was indifferent to such opinions registered by members of the Fourth Estate. In truth, he was a perfectionist, a hard worker, an outspoken individual, and, because of his opinions, was called a rebel. He could not have cared less, or so it seemed.

MGM teamed the Grangers in *Young Bess* (1953), with Jean winning top billing. Called by *Newsweek* Magazine "an exceedingly free improvisation on Elizabethan themes and a handsome, Technicolored show window," the film, based on a Margaret Irwin novel, tells of the years in the life of Elizabeth I (1533-1603) before she became the imperious monarch. She wins admiration from her father, Henry VIII (once again played by Charles Laughton), and, after his death, persuades her half-brother, young king Edward (Rex Thompson), to order First Lord Admiral of the Navy Thomas Seymour (Granger) to marry

381

her father's widow, Catherine Parr (Deborah Kerr). But Seymour finds that he loves two women, Elizabeth and Catherine and, after the death of Catherine, he confesses his feelings for the young princess. She admits that her love for him is also strong. But nothing tangible comes of their affair (beyond 112 minutes of screen entertainment), for Seymour's brother, who is also the King's Lord Protector (Guy Rolfe), arranges that he be executed in the Tower of London.

As MGM had anticipated, a good deal of publicity was generated by

On the set of *Young Bess* (1953) with director George Sidney and Jean Simmons

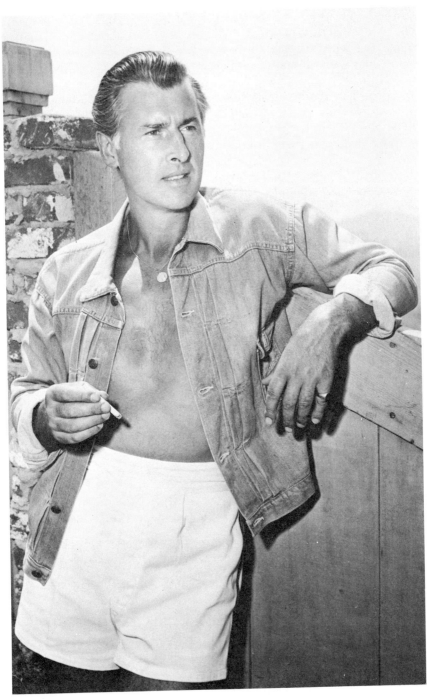

In 1953

Jean and Stewart joining the ranks of real-life husband-and-wife teams who acted together onscreen.[36] Jean was asked about her oncamera romancing with Stewart. "I feel more self-conscious about playing love scenes with him now, with everybody on the set watching, than I did before we were man and wife."

Granger had another death scene as the bad brother of Robert Taylor in *All the Brothers Were Valiant* (MGM, 1953).[37] It was inevitable that MGM should pair their two adventure stars in the same picture, but it is unfortunate that it could not have been in a better vehicle ("Regulation romance-adventure spectacle," said *Variety*). The film takes place in the 1850s, with Taylor as the master of a whaling ship and Stewart on board attempting to influence the crew into forgetting about whales and concentrating on finding a cache of sunken pearls. Bosley Crowther called the shots on this Richard Thorpe-directed semi-misfire when he wrote in the *New York Times*, "[It is] a lot of pseudo-salty South Seas whoop-de-do, put together with little distinction and without going off the studio lot."

Late in 1953, Stewart, a man who never minced words, let loose at a

---

[36]Among such recent teams were Tony Curtis-Janet Leigh in *Houdini* (Paramount, 1953), Rex Harrison-Lilli Palmer rematched in *The Fourposter* (Columbia, 1952) and *Main Street to Broadway* (MGM, 1953).

[37]A remake of the 1923 Metro silent. Lon Chaney had played Mark, the bad brother, a part reinterpreted by Stewart.

With Betta St. John in *All the Brothers Were Valiant* (1953)

ubiquitous columnist in the MGM commissary, when he was asked by that person about rumors that all was not well with the Granger marriage. "I merely suggested that he remove himself to a warmer climate," Stewart later remembered of the incident, "and offered to help him on his way. And I believe I suggested he change his name and offered a few rather uncomplimentory suggestions." He added, "It's odd that even the people who live in Hollywood cleave to the stupid belief that the only way a man can prove he loves his wife is to gaze into her eyes like a spring-struck boy every moment they are together. My love for my wife is genuine, but if it takes my fancy I might chase her down Hollywood Boulevard pelting her with marshmallows." Of his pretty wife whose career was a jumble of inconsequential films with only an occasional good one such as *The Actress,* he also said, "I have the perfect wife. She cannot cook. She does Gene Kelly routines around the pool while I prepare supper. She cannot make a bed. She will not pick up things. She simply lives in her work."

Since the 6'2" actor was so often compared to the late John Barrymore, MGM perhaps felt compelled to dust off an old property that formerly belonged to Warner Bros. and which had starred the Great Profile in 1924. *Beau Brummell* (MGM, 1954)[38] was producer Sam Zimbalist's way of tossing this comparison at the world. Stewart is, of course, Captain George Brummell (1778-1840) of the King's Guard, who quarrels with the fat Prince of Wales (Peter Ustinov)[39] over the latter's design of wide epaulettes for the guardsmen's uniform. As he is kicked out of the regiment, he says, "Society is very imperfect. There is a great deal I would like to change." Luckily for him, since he has squandered his small inheritance and since his good education has equipped him to do absolutely nothing, the obese prince later takes a liking to him and accepts him as a friend and fashion advisor. "When you are a nobody you must be very careful of your dignity," he admits. But later he argues again with his royal chum, who has now become England's George IV. This time he is exiled, and although, "I do not propose to accept obscurity," he dies, tubercular and poor, with his name to be forever associated with men's high fashions.[40]

Although made handsome with sets, costumes, color, and a miscast

[38]Originally a play in four acts by Clyde Fitch, staged in 1889 with Richard Mansfield (who had commissioned the drama), and revived in 1916, starring Arnold Daly.

[39]In *Ustinov in Focus* (Tantivy Press, 1971), by Tony Thomas, the actor talks about the film: "It was fun to do, and I like that period of British history. The script made the Prince out to be a rather touching figure, a man who was a fool and a frump and suffered because of it. He was not much more than a rather charming misfit in history.... He was a man who was risible, and yet if he suddenly looked at you I imagine you would feel terribly sorry for him."

[40]Even Granger's onscreen death scene is stolen (!) by Ustinov, with the latter coming to see his long-time friend, opening the musical snuff box (which plays "For He's a Jolly Good Fellow"), which Brummell had given him, and then departing, not daring to look back at his dying comrade.

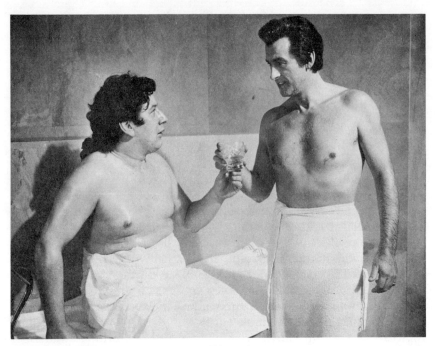

With Peter Ustinov in *Beau Brummell* (1954)

Elizabeth Taylor as Beau's sometimes love interest, the film flopped badly at the nation's boxoffices. Part of the picture's problem was that, although the 113 minutes was to be based on the foppish Beau Brummell ("This was a man. Beau Brummell. Reckless, romantic, rogue. Lover, gambler, adventurer"), Granger's character was not clearly defined by the script. It left open the question in the viewer's mind whether he was merely a social climber or a man of sterling principles. Moreover, since the movie became a study of set pieces and conversational moods, it required a good deal of Granger beyond his usual flashing smile and agile physical actions. He had to do more than posture and strut about, and either he was not up to it or could not cope with the role.[41]

Thus, what should have been a film centered on Granger's portrayal of the fashion plate turned into something quite different. It became a vehicle for Ustinov's Prince of Wales and his rather dotty father, King George III (Robert Morley). Only occasionally does Granger's Beau

[41]Granger would later say to Louella O. Parsons: "I'll admit we were all on edge while making that [*Beau Brummell*]—and no wonder. It was an extremely difficult film to make. The costumes couldn't have been more handsome, but they were skin tight, uncomfortable and after a long day under hot lights we were all exhausted. . . . I tell you, Louella, there were times when I despaired of ever finishing, what with the occasional adverse weather conditions and the demands of a script that required staying in character every minute on the set. But, sincerely, I do think we brought it off. I believe it is quite a superior film."

come alive, as, at a party near the anti-climax, he snidely remarks to Lord Byron (Noel William) about his former royal pal, "Who is your fat friend?" This scene proved that, when provoked, Granger the actor could be as vituperative with a word as with a rapier.

It would be Ustinov who would best articulate the time-locked nature of a costume picture like *Beau Brummell,* which would (or could) not be made on such a grand scale in the 1970s. "Things have changed in the film industry, he told writer Tony Thomas, for *Ustinov In Focus, infra,* "The kind of romanticized story telling about historical figures in which the producers took liberties is no longer acceptable. People have begun to wonder what the exact historical position of these characters was, and perhaps this is a good thing. History as told by most film-makers has been largely nonsense, like a curious and colourful dream that has never been really lived. This is is fine for children but doubts creep into the adult mind about the desirability of having lived long ago. Primitive medicine, thumbscrews and witch hunting tend to convince me I am well off where I am."

After playing in six period films, Stewart emerged in December, 1954, in a contemporary CinemaScope romantic drama called *Green Fire* (MGM). With partner Paul Douglas, he is in search of diamonds in Columbia, where they are diverted when they meet an anguished proprietress of a coffee plantation (Grace Kelly). It was truly amazing how, while eluding bandits and overcoming floods, landslides, and

With Grace Kelly in *Green Fire* (1954)

With George Sanders, Liliane Montevecchi, and Oliver Blake in *Moonfleet* (1955)

mine cave-ins, Miss Kelly remains well-coiffured with hardly as much as a particle of dust showing on her many costume changes. The two freebooters ultimately give up the diamond quest in favor of helping her grow coffee.

For *Moonfleet* (MGM, 1955), Stewart was back in eighteenth-century costumes as "a man of bad character and evil reputation." He is cynical and ruthless as Jeremy Fox, supreme smuggler. But, suddenly, he finds himself the protector of an orphaned boy (Jon Whiteley), for whom he ultimately gives up his life. Filmed at the Culver City Studio, with exterior sea scenes lensed at Oceanside, director Fritz Lang gave the adventure story a romantic overtone.[42] For many critics, Stewart's performance here is the most disciplined of his Hollywood career. America regarded *Moonfleet* as just another widescreen color tale, but the French press, always devoted to Fritz Lang's professionalism, named the picture the best foreign film of 1955.

[42]Of the film's plot finale, director Lang told Peter Bogdonovich in *Fritz Lang in America* (Praeger, 1969): "It was something else: the little boy loves and admires the hero, Stewart Granger, who says when he leaves, 'I will come back to you.' He is dying and I wanted to show that 'I will come back to you' is the last thing this man can do for the boy. He sails away and the boy stands at the shore, and we see that Granger dies in the boat, but that it goes on anyway because his dead hand still holds the sail. That was my ending. But the producer chose an ending that had been shot before, and that he had promised me 'word of honour' would never be used: the boy comes back with the little girl and says, 'This is my estate.' Which I think is horrible; and this was put in."

Stewart declined to star as a colonial spy in MGM's *The Scarlet Coat* (1955)[43] in order to go to England to make a film with his wife.[44] The result was *Footsteps in the Fog* (Columbia, 1955), which wound up on the bottom half of double bills. Regardless of its unfavorable reviews, the Arthur Lubin-directed feature is excellent fodder for devotees of the Victorian era. The plush settings and costumes make it very easy on the eyes. In the context of the drama, Stewart, who has poisoned his wife, is found out and blackmailed by his sweet-faced maid (Simmons), who eventually assumes command of the household. This was to be Granger's fourth and final screen appearance with Miss Simmons.

While Jean went to work, against Stewart's advice, in an offbeat bit of casting as the Salvation Army girl in *Guys and Dolls* (Samuel Goldwyn/MGM, 1955), he entertained his two children in Hollywood and its environs. Elspeth March's ill health prevented her from caring for the children (aged eleven and nine) on a full-time basis. "They are enchanted with America," Granger told Ruth Waterbury of *Photoplay,* "and, of course, they are enchanted with Jean."

In contrast to the soggy *All the Brothers Were Valiant,* Stewart and Robert Taylor swapped characterizations for *The Last Hunt* (MGM, 1956). Stewart portrays the good buffalo hunter who likes Indians, especially a young Indian girl (Debra Paget). Taylor, on the other hand, is a hunter obsessed with killing buffalo *and* Indians. Written and directed by Richard Brooks, the picture was shot largely in Custer State Park in South Dakota, which houses the protected U.S. herd of buffalo.

While Jean was working on *Guys and Dolls* and while Stewart was in Pakistan filming *Bhowani Junction* (MGM, 1956), persistent rumors of marital discontent circulated around Hollywood, but both principals flatly denied the existence of a rift in their domestic relationship.

Bhowani Junction was not released until May, 1956, thirteen months after the production had begun, because of editing necessitated by complaints from the government of India regarding the film's approach to the country's caste system and other customs. Filmed largely in that country, some of the interiors were, nonetheless, shot in England with an all-British cast save one, Ava Gardner of North Carolina. Director George Cukor would have preferred Trevor Howard in the lead role, but Stewart—described by Cukor to Gavin Lambert in *On Cukor* (G. P. Putnam's 1972) as "just a movie star"—got the part of the British Colonel Rodney Savage. The character narrates the film and is the man whom a promiscuous Eurasian girl (Ava) selects as the man to

---

[43]Cornel Wilde did the part instead.

[44]There was talk of Granger and Simmons starring in De Laurenttis' *War and Peace* (Paramount, 1956), but it was another husband-and-wife team, Mel Ferrer and Audrey Hepburn, who got the roles.

Posing with Ava Gardner for *Bhowani Junction* (1956)

love. The resultant feature was very much a tempest in an Indian teapot.

Following a period of uncertainty, when Jean thought she might like to return to England to live, the Grangers became American citizens on June 8, 1956. They were naturalized in a ceremony at a Los Angeles court by federal judge Perison M. Hall. On September tenth of that year, a seven-pound, three-ounce daughter was born, named Tracy in honor of the Granger's friend, Spencer. The baby's mother was twenty-seven; the father was forty-three.

Stewart was cinematically reunited with Ava Gardner in *The Little Hut* (MGM, 1957), a witless attempt at comedy about three people on a deserted (soundstage) island. The trio, a wife (Ava), a husband (Stewart), and her almost-lover (David Niven) generated little heat let alone any lascivious thoughts in any of the film's viewers. Later in 1957, Stewart went Western as a cowboy who kills a bad man in full view of the township citizens in *Gun Glory* (MGM). Oddly enough, the town then attempts to ostracize him. His debut in a sagebrush affair was not in the same league with swashbuckler Errol Flynn's premier performance out West (*Dodge City,* Warners Bros., 1939), but Granger did all right with the Western dialog. "Congratulations to Stewart Granger!" cheered the *New York Daily News.* "The handsome-profiled British actor gives us Western twang with a vengeance in *Gun Glory.* He never forgets he's being an American. Not even a trace of a broad A. A right realistic job."

Domestic news played a big part in Granger's life in 1957. The March issue of *Confidential* Magazine devoted several pages to exploring "The ants in Stewart Granger's pantry," relating an alleged weekend tryst at Number 12 Charles St. in London, where Stewart was supposedly entertaining in a very bachelor fashion. It was also in 1957 that Stewart and Jean purchased an 8,000-acre ranch in Nogales, Arizona, near the Mexican border, and set up legal residency. There, Stewart concentrated on raising cattle and importing a white French beef-on-the-hoof called The Charolais.

When Jean was asked (yet again) about her marriage to the seemingly incorrigible Granger, she explained, "I knew what Jimmy was like when I married him so why would I or any woman want to change a man—just because you become his wife. I've always believed if you want something to work you make it work. In other words, you don't fight it. People change automatically in marriage, if they are supposed to change. The whole truth is, I wouldn't want to change Jimmy—if I could! A 'perfect' husband, whatever that means, would be a pretty dull bloke, don't you think?"

Rather than negotiate a contract renewal with MGM—he wanted more money than hard-pressed Metro could afford—he went to England to film a murder mystery. The picture was *The Whole Truth*

(Columbia, 1958) and he played opposite Donna Reed. With Stewart, Miss Reed, and George Sanders capering about the Riviera like so many pawns, the only mystery to the picture was why anyone of the caliber of the stars involved would have participated in the first place.

While in London, Granger confided to a reporter from the *Sunday Express*, "Acting now bores the hell out of me. I know I haven't a nutshell of talent compared to my wife." However, he hung around England long enough to star in *Harry Black and the Tiger* (Twentieth Century-Fox, 1958) which also took him to India for location shooting. As a character with a wooden leg, he was not expected to play his usual active role, but it would seem that scenarist Sydney Boehm and/or director Hugo Fregonese could have squeezed more life into Granger's portrayal. He spends a good part of his celluloid time imbibing and bemoaning his fear of a certain tiger. After completing this production, Granger half-kiddingly told a newsman, "If you don't like me, personally, the scenery is beautiful and you can't go wrong on the tiger—a wonderful, awesome animal."

For the first time since 1944, Stewart was away from the silver screen for a year. Again, the columnists insisted that the marriage was a rocky one, and again the "Gilbraltar" Grangers denied it. Then, in 1960, while Stewart was working in California and Washington on *North to Alaska* (Twentieth Century-Fox, 1960), Jean went to England for *The Grass Is Greener* (Universal, 1960).

With Donna Reed and Gianna Maria Canale in *The Whole Truth* (1958)

With Anthony Steel in _Harry Black and the Tiger_ (1958)

From London she announced her intentions of seeking a divorce, and three weeks later (July 7) in Nogales, which was her legal residence, she filed for the action on grounds of "outrageous cruelty." Louella O. Parsons asked, "Why all the shenanigans? In the beginning, I think the British Stewart was determined that his lovely English bride of over nine years would not get a divorce with his approval. He seemed on the verge of a nervous breakdown every time I called to check him over persistent rumors that he and Jean were through."

Jean's divorce was granted on August 12, 1960, when she received custody of Tracy (Granger would have his daughter for three weeks a year), but disclaimed ownership of the Arizona ranch.[45] On November 1, 1960, she married Richard Brooks, the Hollywood director. Stewart's remarks to the press included: "I don't mind Jean leaving me. It's like a child breaking away from an over-protective parent. But it's the guy she chose—that's what got me. Can you imagine anyone wanting to marry Richard Brooks? The trouble with me is that I did everything for Jean in our marriage. I taught her how to read, how to talk, how to walk, how to carry herself. I taught her art, literature, current events. She was such a child. Our entire relationship was like Pygmalion. She would hear my conversation at the dinner table, my point of view on various subjects, and then when we had guests, she would spout my point of view as her own. I must say she had the decency to leave the Mercedes 190 I had given her."[46]

[45]Granger would say to the press, "I've been 25 years in the movie business but the greatest thrill of my life was as a Britisher running an American ranch, winning blue ribbons for my French cattle. . . . Jean and I have been knocking our brains out making movies all over the world to pay for the cattle. In about three years we had both planned to settle down in Arizona for good—and never make another picture. I guess now I'll die an actor instead of a cattleman."

[46]He also stated publicly, "I still love Jean. She says she will be happier free. Time will tell. My main worry is for Tracy, whom we both love. We hope the divorce won't be catastrophic for our daughter."

With Fabian, John Wayne, and Capucine in *North to Alaska* (1960)

In *North to Alaska,* in CinemaScope and color, Stewart plays miner George Pratt, in second billing to John Wayne. Within the film, they have hit it big in the Alaskan gold rush of 1900, and Sam (Wayne) sails to Seattle to buy additional mining equipment and to bring back George Pratt's fiancée, while George remains behind to construct a honeymoon cabin. But Sam finds that his friend's fiance has wed another man. He then encounters Michele (Capucine) in a pick-up joint called "The Hen House" and persuades her to return with him to Nome. George is extremely unhappy with the news that his girl has not waited for him and resents having Angel in his cabin. "What the hell's going on here?" he shouts angrily. "Who is this dame?" Sam tries to introduce Angel, but George interrupts, "Jennie couldn't make it, but this tramp could, huh?" Left alone, she accidentally calls him "mon chou" ("my little cabbage"), a name which Jennie used to call him, and they become friends. Later, a con man (Ernie Kovacs) jumps their claim, and once again without gold, the partners decide to begin anew, with Angel winding up in Sam's arms.

Stewart sold his ranch in 1961 for more than $2.5 million at an enormous capital gain. He was to admit to the press later, "I had a devil of a time selling the place. The new owners have subdivided the ranch and converted it into a small town called Keno Springs. I'm sorry about that." By 1961 his hair was sprinkled generously with white, which enhanced his onscreen image of virility, but his career was definitely on the wane (he had seemed awkward, along with Fabian Forte, playing second fiddle to John Wayne in *North to Alaska*). He picked up and moved, first to England where it was rumored that he would re-marry Elspeth March. His comment was an emphatic: "She is my very best friend."

Stewart was seen in 1961 in a film made in Britain, *The Secret Partner*, released through MGM. It turned out to be a routine melodrama in which he tries to prove his innocence of an embezzlement charge. Negotiations for him to co-star with Susan Hayward in *I Thank a Fool* (MGM, 1962) fell through (Peter Finch took over for Granger), as did hopes that he would go to Africa for *Dark Memory*, based on a Jonathan Latimer suspense story. But he did go to Italy as the *Swordsman of Siena* (MGM, 1962), a swashbuckling film throwback to an earlier time. As an English adventurer in sixteenth-century Italy, he dashes and fences his way into and out of the guard of the tyrannical governor (Riccardo Garrone). He likewise dashes his way into the heart of Sylva Koscina (who replaced the more boxoffice-worthy Gina Lollobrigida). Said *Variety* of this B quality affair, "Granger looks good and plays his role with pleasant dash. He is no Errol Flynn or Fairbanks, but he does have a certain amount of charm."

**With Sylva Koscina
in *Lo Spadaccino Di Siena*
(*Swordman of Siena*) (1961)**

Stewart remained on th Continent for the Italian-French *Sodom and Gomorrah* (Twentieth Century-Fox, 1963).[47] This was filmed in English and Italian with directors Robert Aldrich and Sergio Leone guiding Stewart in the pivotal role. He is the Biblical man Lot who leads a band of Hebrews to the cities of Sodom and Gomorah, whose ruler is the power-mad Queen Bera (Anouk Aimee).[48] When the cities are destroyed, it is Pier Angeli as Lot's wife who is turned into a pillar of salt. Compared to most of the European-produced costume entries, this one was excessively heavily-mounted and boasted a sterling cast, but was hardly worth all the effort.

On June 12, 1964, Granger married Caroline Lecerf, the blonde Miss Belgium for 1962. David Niven was their best man. The third Mrs. Granger was twenty-two; Stewart was fifty-one.

His voice was dubbed again in the Italian-made *Commando* (released in the U.S. in 1964 by American International) as the leader of a mission to capture an Algerian resistance leader. He did a cameo, along with David Niven, Walter Pidgeon, Jean Paul Belmondo, and scores of others in a Rome-filmed satire of *The Longest Day* (Twentieth Century-Fox, 1963) called *The Shortest Day* (Titanus, 1963). *The Secret Invasion* (United Artists, 1964) took Granger to Yugoslavia, where he played a British intelligence officer who offers five convicted criminals their freedom for rescuing an Italian general from a Nazi prison. It was sort of a poor man's forerunner to *The Dirty Dozen* (MGM, 1967). In *The Crooked Road* (released in the U.S. in 1965 by Seven Arts), he is the Duke of Orgagna, the not very pleasant dictator of a small country in the Balkans who is the subject of an exposé by newsman Robert Ryan. When the Duke is murdered, the exposé becomes superfluous and the reporter departs with the duke's widow (Nadia Gray).

In 1964, Stewart, who obviously had no inclination toward retirement, entered the German-Yugoslavian series of films based on the Karl May stories of frontier Arizona, with the Yugoslavian landscapes substituting for the American southwest. The adventures centered on the characters of Old Surehand (also called Shatterhand) the self-appointed lawman, and the young Apache Chief Winnetou (always played by Pierre Brice). Old Surehand was alternately portrayed by Lex Barker, Guy Madison, and Granger. Stewart's three entries in the sure-fire series were—under their U.S. release titles—*Frontier Hellcat* (Columbia, 1966), *Rampage at Apache Wells* (Columbia, 1966), and *Flaming Frontier* (Warner Bros.-Seven Arts; 1968). *Variety,* in criticizing the first film, summed up all three films with: "Stewart Granger contributes a colorful portrayal. It won't make the critics rave but one can imagine youngsters will take a fancy to this well-built crack shot and his mannerisms. With his nonchalance paired with tongue-in-

---

[47]Italian-French production with voices, including Granger's, dubbed into English.
[48]Miss Aimee had that classic camp line, "Welcome, Sodomites."

With Scilla Gabel in *Sodome E Gomorra* (1961)

With Raf Vallone
in *The Secret Invasion* (1964)

With Nadia Gray
in *The Crooked Road* (1964)

With Pierre Brice in *Unter Geiern (Frontier Hellcat)* **(1964)**

cheek, his impressive white hair and beautiful teeth, he makes a hero the femmes will go for."

Stewart then starred as an FBI agent involved with tracking down a smuggling racket in Hong Kong in *Red Dragon* (Woolner, 1967), as well as participating in such other German-Italian spy action films as *Das Geheimnis der Gelben Monche* (a.k.a. *How to Kill a Lady,* 1966), and *Gern Hab Ich Die Frauen Gekilit* (a.k.a., *Requiem for a Secret Agent,* 1966). For Paramount he made a Hollywood-conceived film in Kenya, which was released in the U.S. in 1967 as *The Last Safari.* In the role of a white-maned senior safari guide, Stewart sets off on a one-man search for a killer elephant. He is joined by Kaz Garas[49] (in top billing), who portrays an American playboy millionaire. When they do locate the elephant, after several near-fatal clashes with natives, animals, and police, the hunter is unable to kill the big object of his search. The musical score by Johnny Dankworth, plus a convincing performance by still robust Stewart, make *The Last Safari* a surprisingly worthwhile adventure outing.

On March 11, 1968, a daughter was born to the Grangers in Switzerland, where they then made their home.* The child, Stewart's fourth, was named Samantha.

---

[49]A Hal B. Wallis find whose career was short and skimpy.

*Stewart had given up his American citizenship to reside in Switzerland.

In *The Last Safari* (1967)

With Susan Hampshire in *The Trygon Factor* (1967)

In 1969, Americans saw Stewart in a British-made film (Rialto), which had passed through England two years earlier. As Cooper-Smith of Scotland Yard in *The Trygon Factor* (Warner Bros.-Seven Arts, 1967), he attempts to unravel the mystery of a little old lady (Cathleen Nesbitt) who, in order to save her country estate from going under, sets up a phony convent as a front for her gold-smuggling enterprise. The story never does explain the meaning of its title.

Caroline Lecerf Granger divorced her husband in 1969, and he returned to Hollywood to make the Universal telefeature *Any Second Now* (NBC-TV, 1969). It was the story of an aging Lothario who panics when his wife (Lois Nettleton) catches him in a tryst. He rigs an accident to kill her for her money before she can divorce him. As *Daily Variety* would report, it was not a happy venture for Granger: "There is, however, one jarring note in the otherwise faultless thriller, and that's the casting of Stewart Granger as the husband-roue of a much younger heiress. While Granger, in his video debut, performs well, he is much older than the girl to whom he is wed, in fact looks old enough to be her father. It makes for a distracting factor in an otherwise excellent meller. Physical appearance of actor does not jibe with the script lines which seem tailored to a younger dame chaser." How time had passed!

It was in 1970 that Stewart made his teleseries debut. After eight seasons on the air, NBC-TV's "The Virginian" was in need of new faces and a title change for its ninety-minute installments. Gone were such lead role players as Lee J. Cobb, Charles Bickford, and John McIntire, and in their place came Stewart as Colonel Alan Mackenzie, new owner of Shiloh. At the end of a long British army career, Mackenzie comes to Wyoming to seek a new beginning after the death of his wife. "Men from Shiloh" debuted on September 16, 1970, with James Drury, Doug McClure, and Lee Majors continuing as the show's co-stars. Granger proved rather stuffy in the opening episodes as the newcomer to Medicine Bow, but he soon demonstrated that he had a flair for outdoorsmanship and for gentlemanly behavior. The program, as such, lasted twenty-four episodes, or one more season.

In press interviews in 1970, he said, "Anyway, I'm retired from pictures after 20 [plus six] years. James Mason made it from leading man to character actor, but I didn't. At 57, I'm just an old leading man. And everytime I get dignified, someone calls me Farley Granger." The star, who spent a good deal of his time in the guest room of Elspeth March's home (behind London's Dorchester Hotel), also admitted, "I'm independently wealthy. I'm not working for the money. But I support two wives and all my children, including the twenty-five-year-old [son Jamie]. Well, why not? He's a darling chap."

He returned to England, but came out of retirement to join the long roster of actors who have portrayed Sherlock Holmes. His try at the

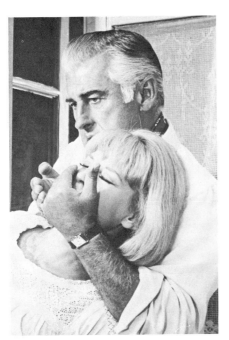

**With Lois Nettleton
in *Any Second Now* (NBC-TV 1969)**

**With Bernard Fox in *Sherlock
Holmes: The Hound of the
Baskervilles* (ABC-TV, 1972)**

Arthur Conan Doyle creation was for an ABC-TV "Movie of the Week," *The Hound of the Baskervilles*.[50] The ninety-minute color movie, which premiered on Saturday, February 12, 1972, served as a series pilot that did not find a sponsor. Said *Daily Variety* for the record, "Granger, running danger of stepping into footsteps of his most prominent predecessor, Basil Rathbone, avoids it by providing warmer, less cerebral and authoritative characterization which Baker Street Irregulars may deplore but serves to carry the story."

Two years later, from his three-hundred-acre villa at Marbella, Spain, Stewart said to the press, "They say in America that once you've been in the major league, you don't like going into the minor league. Doing television for me is minor league." He lashed out at movie fans with, "They disgust me. It's no wonder you never saw actors walking on the streets of Hollywood. They had good reasons for wanting to be alone. Fans make you antisocial." (In mid-1975 Stewart began building a house in the Costa del Sol's Estepona region of Spain.)

He admitted his preference for the hermit-like life he had adopted.

[50]The Holmes part was played by Robert Rendel in the 1931 First Division edition, and by Basil Rathbone in Twentieth Century-Fox's 1939 offering. There have been at least three English picturizations of the story: in 1921 with Ellie Norwood, in 1931 with John Stuart, in 1959 with Peter Cushing. (NBC-TV has mapped out a new two-hour telefeature for the 1975-1976 video season on Sherlock Holmes, to be lensed in London.)

"People call me moody. That's because I don't like them and they don't like me." He was banned from the "in" place at Marbella because "I had a stand-up argument with Mel Ferrer, whom I dislike intensely, over a petty parking problem there."

Regarding love, Granger said recently, "The one great thing is to fall in love. But I haven't given much love because I'm a very selfish man. My marriages have gone wrong, and eventually you dry up. I doubt that I'll ever fall in love because I have a heart like a walnut."

Regarding his film career: "I've made some seventy films, and not one of them I'm really proud of. I never had a part that tested me as an actor. . . . You know, if I'd done just one film like *Inherit the Wind*, I could have retired and said I did that. I would have been proud."

Feature Film Appearances

A SOUTHERN MAID (Wardour, 1933), 85 min.
Director, Harry Hughes; based on the play by Harry Graham and Dion Clayton Calthrop; screenplay, Austin Melford, Arthur Woods, Frank Miller, and Frank Launder.

Bebe Daniels (Dolores/Juanita); Clifford Mollison (Jack Rawden/ Willoughby); Harry Welchman (Francisco del Fuego); Lupino Lane (Antonio Lopez); Hal Gordon (Pedro); Morris Harvey (Vasco); Amy Veness (Donna Rosa); Nancy Brown (Carola); Basil Radford (Tom); Stewart Granger (Bit).

GIVE HER A RING (Pathe, 1934), 79 min.
Producer, Walter C. Myrcoft; director, Arthur Woods; based on the play *Fraulein Falsch Verbunden* by H. Rosenfeld; screenplay, Clifford Grey, Ernst Wolff, Marjorie Deans, and Wolfgang Wilhelm.

Clifford Mollison (Paul Hendrick) Wendy Barrie (Karen Swenson); Zelma O'Neal (Trude Olsen); Erik Rhodes (Otto Brune); Bertha Belmore (Miss Hoffman); Olive Blakeney (Mrs. Brune); Diamond Brothers (Repair Men); Nadine March (Karen's Friend); Jimmy Godden (Uncle Rifkin); Syd Crossley (Gustav); Richard Hearne (Drunk); Stewart Granger (Diner); Maurice Winnick's Ciro's Club Band (Themselves).

SO THIS IS LONDON (20th Century-Fox-British, 1939), 80 min. (U.S. release: 20th Century-Fox, 1940, 75 min.).
Director, Thornton Freeland; based on the play by George M. Cohan; adaptation, Arthur Goodrich; screenplay, William Conselman; camera, Otto Kanturek; editor, James B. Clark.

Alfred Drayton (Lord Worthing); Robertson Hare (Henry Honeycutt); Ethel Revnell (Dodie); Gracie West (Liz); Berton Churchill (Hiram Draper); Lily Cahill (Mrs. Draper); Carla Lehmann (Elinor Draper); Fay Compton (Lady Worthing); Stewart Granger (Lawrence); George Sanders (Dr. Dereski); Mavis Clair (Mrs. Honeycutt); Aubrey Mallalieu (Butler); David Burns (Drunk).

CONVOY (Associated British Film Distributors, 1940), 90 min.
Associate producer, Sergei Nolbandov; director, Pen Tennyson; screenplay, Tennyson, Patrick Kirwan; camera, Roy Kellino and Gunther Krampf.

Clive Brook (Captain Tom Armitage); John Clements (Lieutenant David Cranford); Edward Chapman (Captain Eckersley); Judy Campbell (Lucy Armitage); Penelope Dudley Ward (Mabel); Edward Rigby (Mr. Matthews); Charles Williams (Shorty Howard); Allan Jeayes (Commander Blount); Albert Lieven (Commander of U-37); Michael Wilding (Dot); Harold Warrender (Lieutenant-Commander Martin); David Hutcheson (Captain Sandeman); George Carney (Bates); Al Millan (Knowles); Charles Farrell (Walker); John Laurie (Gates); Hay Petrie (Skipper); John Glyn Jones and Mervyn Johns (Mates); Edward Lexy (Skipper); Stewart Granger (Sutton).

SECRET MISSION (General Film Distributors, 1942), 94 min.

Producer, Marcel Hellman; director, Harold French; story, Shaun Terence Young; screenplay, Anatole de Grunwald and Basil Bartlett; camera, Bernard Knowles, Cyril Knowles.

Hugh Williams (Peter Garnett); James Mason (Raoul de Carnet); Michael Wilding (Nobby Clark); Carla Lehmann (Michele de Carnet); Nancy Price (Violette); Roland Culver (Red Gowan); Betty Warren (Mrs. Clark); Karel Stepanek (Major Lang); Percy Walsh (Fayolle); Beatrice Varley (Mrs. Donkin); Brefni O'Rourke (Father Jouvet); F. R. Wendhausen (General von Reichmann); John Salew (Captain Grune); Herbert Lom (M.O.); Stewart Granger (Lieutenant Jackson).

THURSDAY'S CHILD (Pathe, 1943), 81 min.

Producer, John Argyle; director, Rodney Ackland; based on the novel by Donald Macardle; screenplay, Donald Macardle and Rodney Ackland

Sally Ann Howes (Fennis Wilson); Wilfrid Lawson (Frank Wilson); Kathleen O'Regan (Ellen Wilson); Eileen Bennett (Phoebe Wilson); Stewart Granger (David Penley); Marianne Davis (Gloria Dewey); Gerhardt Kempinski (Rudi Kaufmann); Felix Aylmer (Mr. Keith); Margaret Yarde (Mrs. Chard); Vera Bogetti (Mme. Felicia); Percy Walsh (Charles Lennox); Ronald Shiner (Joe); Pat Aherne (Lance Sheridan).

THE LAMP STILL BURNS (General Film Distributors, 1943), 90 min.

Producer, Leslie Howard; director, Maurice Elvey; based on the novel *One Pair of Feet* by Monica Dickens; screenplay, Elizabeth Baron, Roland Pertwee, and Major Neilson; camera, Jack Hildyard.

Rosamund John (Hilary Clarke); Stewart Granger (Larry Rains); Godfrey Tearle (Sir Marshall Frayne); Sophie Stewart (Christine Morris); John Laurie (Mr. Hervey); Margaret Vyner (Pamela Siddell); Cathleen Nesbitt (Matron); Eric Micklewood (Dr. Trevor); Joyce Grenfell (Dr. Barrat); Joan Maude (Sister Catley); Grace Arnold (Sister Sprock); Jenny Laird (Ginger Watkins); Megs Jenkins (Nurse); Wylie Watson (Diabetic); Ernest Thesiger (Chairman); Brefni O'Rourke (Lorimer).

THE MAN IN GREY (General Film Distributors, 1943), 116 min. (U.S. release: Universal, 1945).

Producer, Edward Black; director, Leslie Arliss; based on the novel by Lady Eleanor Smith; screenplay, Margaret Kennedy, Leslie Arliss, Doreen Montgomery; camera, Arthur Crabtree.

Margaret Lockwood (Hesther Shaw); Phyllis Calvert (Clarissa Rohan); James Mason (Marquis of Rohan); Stewart Granger (Peter Rokeby); Raymond Lovell (Prince Regent); Nora Swinburne (Mrs. Fitzherbert); Helen Haye (Lady Rohan); Martita Hunt (Miss Patchett); Amy Veness (Mrs. Armstrong); Diana King (Jane Seymour); Beatrice Varley (Gypsy); Roy Emerton (Gamekeeper); A. E. Matthews (Auctioneer).

FANNY BY GASLIGHT (General Film Distributors, 1944), 108 min. (U.S. release: **MAN OF EVIL,** United Artists, 1948, 90 min.).

Producer, Edward Black; director, Anthony Asquith; based on the novel by Michael Sadleir; screenplay, Doreen Montgomery and Aimee Stuart; camera, Arthur Crabtree.

Phyllis Calvert (Fanny Hopwood); James Mason (Lord Manderstoke); Wilfrid Lawson (Chunks); Stewart Granger (Harry Somerford); Margaretta Scott (Alicia); Jean Kent (Lucy Beckett); John Laurie (Mr. Hopwood); Stuart Lindsell (Clive Seymour); Nora Swinburne (Mrs. Hopwood); Amy Veness (Mrs. Heaviside); Ann Wilton (Carver); Helen Haye (Mrs. Somerford); Cathleen Nesbitt (Kate Somerford).

LOVE STORY (Eagle Lion, 1944), 108 min. (U.S. release: **A LADY SURRENDERS,** Universal, 1947).

Producer, Harold Huth; director, Leslie Arliss; based on the novel by J. W. Drewbell; screenplay, Arliss and Doreen Montgomery; music directors, Louis Levy and Sydney Beer; music, Hubert Bath; camera, Bernard Knowles.

Margaret Lockwood (Lissa Cambell); Stewart Granger (Kit Firth); Patricia Roc (Judy Martin); Tom Walls (Tom Tanner); Reginald Purdell (Albert); Moira Lister (Carol); Dorothy Bramhall (Susie); Vincent Holman (Prospero); Joan Rees (Ariel); Walter Hudd (Ray); A. E. Matthews (Colonel Pitt Smith); Beatrice Varley (Mrs. Rossiter); Harriet Cohen (Pianist).

MADONNA OF THE SEVEN MOONS (Eagle Lion, 1944), 110 min.

Producer, R. J. Minney; director, Arthur Crabtree; based on the novel by Margery Lawrence; screenplay, Roland Pertwee and Brock Williams; camera, Jack Cox.

Phyllis Calvert (Maddalena [Rosanna]); Stewart Granger (Nino Barucci); Patricia Roc (Angela); Peter Glenville (Sandro Barucci); John Stuart (Guiseppi); Jean Kent (Vittoria); Nancy Price (Mme. Barucci); Peter Murray Hill (Logan); Reginald Tate (Ackroyd); Dulcie Gray (Nesta); Amy Veness (Tessa); Hilda Bayley (Mrs. Fiske).

WATERLOO ROAD (General Film Distributors, 1945), 76 min. (U. S. release: Eagle Lion, 1949).

Producer, Edward Black; director-story, Sidney Gilliat; screenplay, Val Valentine; camera, Arthur Crabtree.

John Mills (Jim Colter); Stewart Granger (Ted Purvis); Aliastair Sim (Dr. Montgomery); Joy Shelton (Tillie Colter); Beatrice Varley (Mrs. Colter); Alison Leggatt (Ruby); Leslie Bradley (Mike Duggan); Jean Kent (Toni); George Carney (Tom Mason); Wylie Watson (Tattooist); Arthur Denton (Fred); Vera Frances (Vera); Ben Williams (Corporal Lewis); Anna Konstam (May); Wallace Lupino (Uncle).

405

CAESAR AND CLEOPATRA (Eagle Lion, 1946) C-138 min. (U.S. release: United Artists, 1946, C-126 min.).
Director, Gabriel Pascal; based on the play by George Bernard Shaw; screenplay, Shaw, Marjorie Deans, and W. P. Lipscomb.

Vivien Leigh (Cleopatra); Claude Rains (Julius Caesar); Stewart Granger (Apollodorus); Flora Robson (Ftatateeta); Francis L. Sullivan (Pothinus); Renee Asherson (Iras); Basil Sydney (Rufio); Cecil Parker (Britannus); Olga Edwardes (Charmian); Ernest Thesiger (Theodotus); Raymond Lovell (Lucius Septimus); Stanley Holloway (Belzanor); Antony Eustrel (Achillas); Leo Genn (Bel Affris); Alan Wheatley (The Persian); Esme Percy (Major Domo); Gibb McLaughlin (High Priest); James McKechnie and Michael Rennie (Centurions); Jean Simmons (Girl).

CARAVAN (General Film Distributors, 1946), 122 min. (U.S. release: Eagle Lion, 1947, 84 min.).
Producer, Harold Huth; director, Arthur Crabtree; based on the novel by Lady Eleanor Smith; screenplay, Roland Pertwee; art director, John Bryan; music, Walford Hyden; music director, Louis Levy; camera, Stephen Dade; editor, Charles Knott.

Stewart Granger (Richard Darrell); Jean Kent (Rosal); Anne Crawford (Oriana Camperdene); Dennis Price (Sir Francis Castleton); Robert Helpmann (Wycroft); Gerard Heinz (Don Carlos); Enid Stamp Taylor (Bertha); David Horne (Charles Camperdene); John Salew (Diego); Arthur Goullet (Suiza); Julian Somers (Manoel); Peter Murray (Juan); Sylvie St. Clair (Marie); Mabel Constanduros (Woman); Jusef Ramart (Jose); Gypsy Petulengro (Paco).

THE MAGIC BOW (General Film Distributors, 1946), 106 min. (U.S. release: Universal, 1947, 105 min.).
Producer, R. J. Minney; director, Bernard Knowles; based on the novel by Manuel Komroff; screenplay, Roland Pertwee; music director, Basil Cameron; art director, A. Mezzei; camera, Jack Cox; editor, Alfred Roome.

Stewart Granger (Paganini); Phyllis Calvert (Jeanne); Jean Kent (Blanchi); Dennis Price (Paul de la Roche); Cecil Parker (Germi); Felix Aylmer (Pasini); Frank Cellier (Antonio); Marie Lohr (Countess de Vermand); Henry Edwards (Count de Vermand); Mary Jerrold (Teresa); Betty Warren (Landlady); Antony Holles (Manager); David Horne (Rizzi); Charles Victor (Peasant); Eliot Makeham (Giuseppe); Yehudi Menuhin (Soloist).

CAPTAIN BOYCOTT (General Film Distributors, 1947), 93 min. (U.S. release: Universal, 1947, 88 min.).
Producers, Frank Launder and Sidney Gilliat; director, Launder; based on the novel by Philip Rooney; screenplay, Launder, Wolfgang Wilhelm, Paul Vincent Carroll, and Patrick Campbell; art director, Edward Carrick; music, William Alwyn; music director, Muir Mathieson; camera, Wilkie Cooper; editor, Thelma Myers.

Stewart Granger (Hugh Davin); Kathleen Ryan (Anne Killain); Cecil Parker (Captain Charles Boycott); Robert Donat (Charles Parnell); Alastair Sim (Father McKeogh); Mervyn Johns (Watty Connell); Noel Purcell (Daniel McGinty); Niall McGinnis (Mark Killain); Maureen Delaney (Mrs. Davin); Eddie Byrne (Sean Kerrin); Liam Gaffney (Michael Fagan); Liam Redmond (Martin Egan); Edward Lexy (Sergeant Demsey); Maurice Denham (Colonel Strickland); Joe Linane (Auctioneer); Bernadette O'Farrell (Mrs. Fagan); Ian Fleming and Reginald Purdell (Reporters).

BLANCHE FURY (General Film Distributors, 1948), C-95 min. (U.S. release: Universal, 1948, C-93 min.).
Producer, Anthony Havelock-Allan; director, Marc Allegret; based on the novel by Joseph Shearing; screenplay, Audrey Erskine Lindop, Hugh Mills, and Cecil McGivern; music, Clifton Parker; camera, Guy Green and Geoffrey Unsworth; editor, Jack Harris.

Stewart Granger (Hugh Davin); Kathleen Ryan (Anne Killain); Cecil Parker Fitzgerald (Simon Fury); Michael Gough (Lawrence Fury); Maurice Denham (Major Frazer); Sybilla Binder (Louisa); Edward Lexy (Colonel Jenkins); Allan Jeayes (Wetherby); Suzanne Gibbs (Lavinia Fury); Ernest Jay (Calamy); George Woodbridge (Aimes); Arthur Wontner (Lord Rudford); Amy Veness (Mrs. Winterbourne); M. E. Clifton-James (Prison Governor).

SARABAND FOR DEAD LOVERS (General Film Distributors, 1948), C-96 min. (U.S. release: **SARABAND,** Eagle Lion, 1949, C-95 min.).
Associate producer, Michael Relph; directors, Relph and Basil Dearden; based on the novel by Helen Simpson; screenplay, John Dighton and Alexander Mackendrick; music, Alan Rawsthorne; music director, Ernest Irving; art directors, Jim Morahan and William Kellner; sound, Stephen Dalby; camera, Douglas Slocombe; editor, Michael Truman.

Stewart Granger (Count Philip Koenigsmark); Joan Greenwood (Sophia Dorothea); Francoise Rosay (Electress Sophie); Flora Robson (Countess Platen); Frederick Valk (Ernest Augustus); Peter Bull (Prince George-Louis); Anthony Quayle (Durer); Megs Jenkins (Frau Busche); Michael Gough (Prince Charles); Jill Balcon (Knesbeck); Cecil Trouncer (Major Eck); David Horne (Duke George William); Mercia Swinburne (Countess Eleanore); Miles Malleson (Lord of Misrule); Allan Jeayes (Governor); Guy Rolfe (Envoy).

WOMAN HATER (General Film Distributors, 1948), 105 min. (U.S. release: Universal, 1949, 69½ min.).
Producer, William Sistrom; director, Terence Young; story, Alec Coppel; screenplay, Robert Westerby and Nicholas Phipps; art director, Carmen Dillon; music director, Muir Mathieson; camera, Andre Thomas; editor, Vera Campbell.

Stewart Granger (Lord Terence Detchett); Edwige Feuillere (Colette Marly); Ronald Squire (Jameson); Jeanne de Casalis (Claire); Mary Jerrold (Lady

Datchett); David Hutcheson (Robert) W. A. Kelly (Patrick); Georgina Cookson (Julia); Henry Edwards (Major); Stewart Rome (Colonel Weston); Valentine Dyall (George Spencer); Richard Hearne and Cyril Ritchard (Revellers); Graham Moffatt (Fat Boy); Miles Malleson (Vicar).

ADAM AND EVELYNE (General Film Distributors, 1949), 92 min. (U. S. release: ADAM AND EVALYN, Universal, 1949).

Producer-director, Harold French; story, Noel Langley; screenplay, Langley, Lesley Storm, George Barraud, and Nicholas Phipps; art director, Paul Allan; music, Mischa Spoliansky; music director, Muir Mathieson; sound, W. Lindop, Desmond Dew; camera, Guy Green.

Stewart Granger (Adam Black); Jean Simmons (Evelyne Wallace); Helen Cherry (Moira Hannen); Joan Swinstead (Molly); Edwin Styles (Bill Murray); Raymond Young (Roddy Black); Beatrice Varley (Mrs. Parker); Wilfrid Hyde White (Colonel Bradley); Fred Johnson (Chris Kirby); Geoffrey Denton (Inspector Collins); Peter Reynolds (David); Irene Handl (Manageress).

KING SOLOMON'S MINES (MGM, 1950), C-102 min.

Producer, Sam Zimbalist; directors, Compton Bennett and Andrew Marton; based on the novel by H. Rider Haggard; screenplay, Helen Deutsch; art directors, Cedric Gibbons and Conrad A. Nervig; set decorators, Edwin B. Willis and Keogh Gleason; costumes, Walter Plunkett; Technicolor consultants, Henri Jaff and James Gooch; sound, Douglas Shearer; camera, Robert Surtees; editor, Nervig and Ralph E. Winters.

Deborah Kerr (Elizabeth Curtis); Stewart Granger (Allan Quartermain); Richard Carlson (John Goode); Hugo Haas (Smith); Lowell Gilmore (Eric Masters); Kimural (Khiva); Siriaque (Umbopa); Sekaryongo (Chief Gagool); Baziga (King Twain); Ivargwema (Blue Star); Benempinga (Black Circle); John Banner (Austin); Henry Rowland (Traum); Gutare (Double for Umbopa).

SOLDIERS THREE (MGM, 1951), 87 min.

Producer, Pandro S. Berman; director, Tay Garnett; based on the novel by Rudyard Kipling; screenplay, Marguerite Roberts, Tom Reed, and Malcolm Stuart Boylan; music, Adolph Deutsch; art directors, Cedric Gibbons and Malcolm Brown; camera, William Mellor; editor, Robert J. Kern.

Stewart Granger (Private Archibald Ackroyd); Walter Pidgeon (Colonel Brunswick); David Niven (Captain Pindenny); Robert Newton (Private Jock Sykes); Cyril Cusack (Private Dennis Malloy); Greta Gynt (Crenshaw); Frank Allenby (Colonel Groat); Robert Coote (Major Mercer); Dan O'Herlihy (Sergeant Murphy); Michael Ansara (Manik Rao); Richard Hale (Govind-Lal); Walter Kingsford (Fairfax); Charles Cane (Boggs); Patrick Whyte (Major Harrow); Movita Castenada (Proprietress); Charles Lang (Merchant); Cyril McLaglen (Scot); Harry Martin, Pat O'Moore, and Dave Dunbar (Cavalrymen); Stuart Hall (Lieutenant); John Sheehan (Drunk); Clive Morgan and Pat Aherne (Soldiers).

THE LIGHT TOUCH (MGM, 1951), 110 min.

Producer, Pandro S. Berman; director, Richard Brooks; story, Jed Harris and Tom Reed; screenplay, Brooks; music director, Miklos Rozsa; art directors, Cedric Gibbons and Gabriel Scognamillo; camera, Robert Surtees; editor, George Boemler.

Stewart Granger (Sam Conride); Pier Angeli (Anna Vasarri); George Sanders (Felix Guignol); Kurt Kasznar (Mr. Aramescu); Joseph Calleia (Lieutenant Masairo); Larry Keating (Mr. Hawkley); Rhys Williams (MacWade); Norman Lloyd (Anton); Mike Mazurki (Charles); Hans Conried (Leopold); Renzo Cesana (Father Dolzi); Robert Jefferson (Bellboy); Aram Katcher (Butler); Andre Charisse (Guest); Gladys Holland and Louise Colombet (French Women); George Dee (French Man); Paul de Corday (French Telephone Clerk); Robert Conte (Waiter); Louis Velarde (Arab Boy Juggler); Albert Ben Astar (Hamadi Mahmoud).

THE WILD NORTH (MGM, 1952) (a.k.a., THE BIG NORTH), C-97 min.

Producer, Stephen Ames; director, Andrew Marton; story-screenplay, Frank Fenton; art directors, Cedric Gibbons and Preston Ames; music, Bronislau Kaper; camera, Robert Surtees; editor, John Dunning.

Stewart Granger (Jules Vincent); Wendell Corey (Constable Pedley); Cyd Charisse (Indian Girl); Morgan Farley (Father Simon); Howard Petrie (Brody); Houseley Stevenson (Old Man); Lewis Martin (Sergeant); John War Eagle (Indian Chief); Ray Teal (Ruger); Clancy Cooper (Sloan); J. M. Kerrigan (Calahan); Henry Corden (Clerk); Robert Stephenson (Drunk); G. Pat Collins (Bartender); Russ Conklin (Indian); Brad Morrow (Boy); Emile Meyer (Jake); Henri Letondal (John Mudd); Holmes Herbert (Magistrate); Cliff Taylor and Rex Lease (Members of Quartette).

SCARAMOUCHE (MGM, 1952), C-118 min.

Producer, Carey Wilson; director, George Sidney; based on the novel by Rafael Sabatini; screenplay, Ronald Miller and George Froeschel; art directors, Cedric Gibbons and Hans Peters, set decorators, Edwin P. Willis and Richard Pefferie; costumes, Gile Steele; makeup, William Tuttle; Technicolor consultants, Henri Jaffa and James Gooch; montages, Peter Ballbusch; music, Victor Young; sound, Douglas Shearer; special effects, A. Arnold Gillespie, Warren Newcombe, and Irving G. Ries; camera, Charles Rosher; editor, James E. Newcom.

Stewart Granger (Andre Moreau); Eleanor Parker (Lenore); Janet Leigh (Aline de Gavrillac); Mel Ferrer (Noel, Marquis de Maynes); Henry Wilcoxon (Chevalier de Chabrillaine); Nina Foch (Marie Antoinette); Richard Anderson (Philippe de Valmorin); Robert Coote (Gaston Binet); Lewis Stone (Georges de Valmorin); Elisabeth Risdon (Isabelle de Valmorin); Howard Freeman (Michael Vanneau); Curtis Cooksey (Fabian); John Dehner (Doutreval); John Litel (Dr. Dubuque); Jonathan Cott (Sergeant); Dan Foster (Pierrot); Owen McGiveney (Punchinello); Hope Landin (Mme. Frying Pan); Frank Mitchell (Harlequin); Carol Hughes (Pierrette); Richard Hale (Perigore); Henry Corden

(Scaramouche the Drinker); John Eldredge (Clerk); Mitchell Lewis (Major Domo); Ottola Nesmith (Lady in Waiting); Dorothy Patrick (Dorie); John Sheffield (Flunkey); Douglas Dumbrille (President); Frank Wilcox (DeCrillion); Anthony Marsh (Capelier); John Crawford (Vignon); Bert LeBaron (Fencing Opponent).

THE PRISONER OF ZENDA (MGM, 1952), C-101 min.

Producer, Pandro S. Berman; director, Richard Thorpe; based on the novel by Anthony Hope; screenplay, John Balderstone and Noel Langley; music, Alfred Newman; orchestrator, Conrad Salinger; art directors, Cedric Gibbons and Hans Peters; set decorators, Edwin B. Willis and Richard Pefferle; make-up, William Tuttle; assistant director, Sid Sidman; Technicolor consultants, Henri Jaffa and Robert Brower; sound, Douglas Shearer; special effects, Warren Newcombe; camera, Joseph Ruttenberg; editor, George Roemler.

Stewart Granger (Rudolf Rassendyll/King Rudolf V); Deborah Kerr (Princess Flavia); James Mason (Rupert of Hentzau); Louis Calhern (Colonel Zapt); Jane Greer (Antoinette de Mauban); Lewis Stone (The Cardinal); Robert Douglas (Michael, Duke of Strelsau); Robert Coote (Fritz von Tarlenheim); Peter Brocco (Johann); Francis Pierlot (Josef); Tom Browne Henry (Detchard); Eric Alden (Krafstein); Stephen Roberts (Lauengram); Bud Wolfe (Bersonin); Peter Mamakos (De Gautet); Joe Mell (R. R. Guard); Elizabeth Slifer (Woman); Michael Vallon (Assistant Passport Official); Kathleen Freeman (Gertrude); Bruce Payne (Court Chamberlain); John Goldsworthy (Archbishop); Doris Lloyd (Ambassador's Wife); Stanley Logan (British Ambassador); George Lewis, Hugh Prosser (Uhlan Guards); Forbes Murray (Nobleman with Cardinal); Frank Elliott (Dignitary); Mary Carroll (German Wife); Alex Pope (Husband); Jay Adler (Passport Official); Peter Votrian (Newsboy).

SALOME (Columbia, 1953), C-103 min.

Producer, Buddy Adler; director, William Dieterle; story, Jesse L. Lasky, Jr., Harry Kleiner; screenplay, Kleiner; choreography, Valerie Bettis; music, George Duning; music for dances, Daniele Amfitheatrof; art director, John Meehan; camera, Charles Lang; editor, Viola Lawrence.

Rita Hayworth (Princess Salome); Stewart Granger (Commander Claudius); Charles Laughton (King Herod); Judith Anderson (Queen Herodias); Sir Cedric Hardwicke (Caesar Tiberius); Alan Badel (John the Baptist); Basil Sydney (Pontius Pilate); Maùrice Schwartz (Ezra); Rex Reason (Marcellus Fabius); Arnold Moss (Micha); Sujata and Asoka (Oriental Dance Team); Robert Warwick (Courier); Carmen D'Antonio (Salome's Servant); Michael Granger (Captain Quintus); Karl "Killer" Davis (Slave Master); Joe Shilling, David Wold, Ray Beltran, Joe Sawaya, Anton Northpole, and Carlo Tricoli (Advisors); Mickey Simpson (Herod's Captain of the Guards); Franz Roehn and William McCormick (Advisors); Eduardo Cansino (Roman Guard); Lou Nova (Executioner); Fred Letuli and John Wood (Sword Dancers); William Spaeth (Fire Eater); Duke Johnson (Juggling Specialty); Earl Brown (Galilean Soldier); George Khoury and Leonard George (Assassins); Tris Coffin (Guard); Rick Vallin (Sailor); John Parrish and Sam Scar (Politicians).

YOUNG BESS (MGM, 1953), C-112 min.

Producer, Sidney Franklin; director, George Sidney; based on the novel by Margaret Irwin; screenplay, Jan Lustig and Arthur Wimperis; art directors, Cedric Gibbons and Urie McCleary; music, Miklos Rozsa; camera, Charles Rosher; editor, Arthur E. Winters.

Jean Simmons (Young Bess); Stewart Granger (Thomas Seymour); Deborah Kerr (Catherine Parr); Charles Laughton (King Henry VIII); Kay Walsh (Mrs. Ashley); Guy Rolfe (Ned Seymour); Kathleen Byron (Anne Seymour); Cecil Kellaway (Mr. Parry); Rex Thompson (Edward); Robert Arthur (Barnaby); Leo G. Carroll (Mr. Mums); Norma Varden (Lady Tyrwhitt); Alan Napier (Robert Tyrwhitt); Noreen Corcoran (Young Bess at Age Six); Ivan Triesault (Danish Envoy); Elaine Stewart (Anne Boleyn); Dawn Addams (Kate Howard); Doris Lloyd (Mother Jack); Lumsden Hare (Archbishop Cranmer); Lester Matthews (Sir William Paget); Fay Wall (Woman); Patrick Whyte (Officer); Frank Eldridge and John Sheffield (English Officers); Carl Saxe (Executioner); Ann Tyrrell (Mary); Major Sam Harris, Raymond Lawrence, and David Cavendish (Council Men); Clive Morgan and Charles Keane (Halbadiers); Ian Wolfe (Stranger); Reginald Sheffield (Court Recorder); John Trueman (Yeoman).

ALL THE BROTHERS WERE VALIANT (MGM, 1953), C-101 min.

Producer, Pandro S. Berman; director, Richard Thorpe; based on the story by Ben Ames Williams; screenplay, Harry Brown; art directors, Cedric Gibbons and Randall Duell; set decorators, Edwin B. Willis and Hugh Hunt; costumes, Walter Plunkett; makeup, William Tuttle; assistant director, Al Jennings; music, Miklos Rozsa; sound, Douglas Shearer; special effects, A. Arnold Gillespie and Warren Newcombe; camera, George Folsey; editor, Ferris Webster.

Robert Taylor (Joel Shore); Stewart Granger (Mark Shore); Ann Blyth (Priscilla Holt); Betta St. John (Native Girl); Keenan Wynn (Silva); James Whitmore (Fetcher); Kurt Kasznar (Quint); Lewis Stone (Captain Holt); Robert Burton (Asa Worthen); Peter Whitney (James Finch); John Lupton (Dick Morrell); Jonathan Cott (Carter); Mitchell Lewis (Cook); James Bell (Aaron Burnham); Leo Gordon (Peter How); Michael Pate (Varde); Clancy Cooper (Smith); Frank de Kova (Stevenson); Henry Rowland (Jones); John Damler (Second Mate); Glenn Strange (Chanty Man); Alexander Pope (Fat Man); Frankie Crane and James Davis (Native Crewmen); Tyler McVey (John Shore); John Doucette (George); Morgan Roberts (Black Sailor).

BEAU BRUMMELL (MGM, 1954), C-113 min.

Producer, Sam Zimbalist; director, Curtis Bernhardt; based on the play by Clyde Fitch; screenplay, Karl Tunberg; art director, Alfred Junge; costumes, Elizabeth Haffenden; makeup, Charles Parker; music, Richard Addinsell; music director, Muir Mathieson; sound, A. W. Watkins; special camera effects, Tom Howard; camera, Oswald Morris; editor, Frank Clarke.

Stewart Granger (Beau Brummell); Elizabeth Taylor (Lady Patricia); Peter Ustinov (Prince of Wales); Robert Morley (King George III); James Donald

(Lord Edwin Mercer); James Hayter (Mortimer); Rosemary Harris (Mrs. Fitzherbert); Paul Rogers (William Pitt); Noel Willman (Lord Byron); Peter Dyneley (Midger); Charles Carson (Sir Geoffrey Baker); Ernest Clark (Dr. Warren); Peter Bull (Mr. Fox); Mark Dignam (Mr. Burke); Desmond Roberts (Colonel); David Horne (Thurlow); Ralph Truman (Sir Ralph Sidley); Elwyn Brook-Jones (Mr. Tupp); George De Warfaz (Dr. Dubois); Henry Oscar (Dr. Willis); Harold Kasket (Mayor); Maurice Kaufman (Lord Alvanley); D. A. Clarke-Smith (Sir John Wyatt); Gordon Phillott (Roper Sr.); Francis Drake (Roper, Jr.); Thomas Gallagher (Bruiser); Dennis Shaw (Dog Man); Bessie Love (Maid); Yvonne Andre (Madame Binard); Gordon Whiting (Squerry); Kenneth Hyde, Clement McCallin (Footmen); Margaret Withers (Countess); Len Talbot (Weight Lifter).

GREEN FIRE (MGM, 1954), C-100 min.

Producer, Armand Deutsch; director, Andrew Marton; screenplay, Ivan Goff and Ben Roberts; art directors, Cedric Gibbons and Malcolm Browne; set decorators, Edwin B. Willis and Ralph Hurst; color consultant, Alvord Eiseman; assistant director, Joel Freeman; makeup, William Tuttle; costumes, Helen Rose; music, Miklos Rozsa; song, Rozsa and Jack Brooks; sound, Wesley C. Miller; special effects, A. Arnold Gillespie and Warren Newcombe; camera, Paul Vogel; editor, Harold F. Kress.

Stewart Granger (Rian X. Mitchell); Grace Kelly (Catherine Knowland); Paul Douglas (Vic Leonard); John Ericson (Donald Knowland); Murvyn Vye (El Moro); Jose Torvay (Manuel); Robert Tafur (Father Ripero); Joe Dominguez (Jose); Nacho Galindo (Officer Perez); Charlita (Dolores); Natividad Vacio (Hernandez); Rico Alaniz (Antonio); Paul Marion (Roberto); Bobby Dominguez (Juan); Charles Stevens and Joe Herrera (Bandits); David Garcia (Target Boy); Martin Garralaga (Gonzales); Rudolfo Hoyos, Jr. (Pedro the Bartender); Yvonne Doughty (Mexican Girl).

MOONFLEET (MGM, 1955), C-89 min.

Producer, John Houseman; associate producer, Jud Kinberg; director, Fritz Lang; based on the novel by J. Meade Falkner; screenplay, Jan Lustig and Margaret Fitts; music, Miklos Rozsa; costumes, Walter Plunkett; Flamenco music, Vicente Gomez; assistant director, Sid Sidman; art directors, Cedric Gibbons and Hans Peters; camera, Robert Planck; editor, Albert Akst.

Stewart Granger (Jeremy Fox); George Sanders (Lord Ashwood); Joan Greenwood (Lady Ashwood); Viveca Linfors (Mrs. Minton); Jon Whiteley (John Mohune); Liliane Montevecchi (Gypsy); Melville Cooper (Felix Ratsey); Sean McClory (Elzevir Block); Alan Napier (Parson Glennie); John Hoyt (Magistrate Maskew); Donna Corcoran (Grace); Jack Elam (Damen); Dan Seymour (Hull); Ian Wolfe (Tewkesbury); Lester Matthews (Major Hennishaw); Skelton Knaggs (Jacob); Richard Hale (Starkill); John Alderson (Greening); Ashley Cowan (Tomson); Booth Colman (Captain Stanhope); Frank Ferguson (Coachman); Lillian Kemble Cooper (Mary Hicks); Guy Kingsford (Captain Hawkins); Ben Wright (Officer); Wilson Wood (Soldier); John O'Malley (Lieutenant Upjohn).

FOOTSTEPS IN THE FOG (Columbia, 1955), C-90 min.

Producers, Mike Frankovich and Maxwell Setton; director, Arthur Lubin; based on the novel *The Interruption* by W. W. Jacobs; screenplay, Dorothy Reid and Lenore Coffee; art director, Wilfred Shingleton; music director, Benjamin Frankel; costumes, Beatrice Dawson and Elizabeth Haffenden; assistant director, Ronald Spencer; camera, Chirstopher Challis; editor, Alan Osbiston.

Stewart Granger (Stephen Lowry); Jean Simmons (Lily Watkins); Bill Travers (David MacDonald); Finlay Currie (Inspector Peters); Ronald Squire (Alfred Travers); Belinda Lee (Elizabeth Travers); William Hartnell (Herbert Moresby); Frederick Leister (Dr. Simpson); Percy Marmont (Magistrate); Margery Rhodes (Mrs. Park); Peter Bull (Brasher); Sheila Manahan (Rose Moresby); Norman Macowan (Grimes); Cameron Hall (Corcoran); Victor Maddern (Jones); Arthur Howard (Vicar); Barry Keegan (Constable Burke); Peter Williams (Constable Farrow).

THE LAST HUNT (MGM, 1956), C-108 min.

Producer, Dore Schary; director, Richard Brooks; based on the novel by Milton Lott; screenplay, Brooks; music, Daniele Amfitheatrof; assistant director, Robert Sanders; art directors, Cedric Gibbons and Merrill Pye; camera, Russell Harlan; editor, Ron Lewis.

Robert Taylor (Charles Gilson); Stewart Granger (Sandy McKenzie); Lloyd Nolan (Woodfoot); Debra Paget (Indian Girl); Russ Tamblyn (Jimmy); Constance Ford (Peg); Joe DeSantis (Ed Black); Ainslie Pryor and Terry Wilson (Buffalo Hunters); Ralph Moody (Indian Agent); Fred Graham (Bartender); Ed Lonehill (Spotted Hand); Dan White (Deputy); William "Bill" Phillips (Man); Jerry Martin (Barber); Roy Barcroft (Barfly); Rosemary Johnston (Woman).

BHOWANI JUNCTION (MGM, 1956), C-110 min.

Producer, Pandro S. Berman; director, George Cukor; based on the novel by John Masters; screenplay, Sonya Levien and Ivan Moffat; art directors, Gene Allen and John Howell; music, Miklos Rozsa; costumes, Elizabeth Haffenden; camera, Freddie Young; editors, Frank Clarke and George Boemler.

Ava Gardner (Victoria Jones); Stewart Granger (Colonel Rodney Savage); Bill Travers (Patrick Taylor); Abraham Sofaer (Surabhai); Francis Matthews (Ranjit Kasel); Marne Maitland (Govindaswami); Peter Illing (Ghanshyam); Edward Chapman (Thomas Jones); Freda Jackson (The Sadani); Lionel Jeffries (Lieutenant Graham McDaniel); Alan Tilvern (Ted Dunphy).

THE LITTLE HUT (MGM, 1957), C-78 min.

Producers, F. Hugh Herbert and Mark Robson; director, Robson; based on the play by Andre Roussin and the English stage adaptation by Nancy Mitford; screenplay, Herbert; music, Robert Farnon; song, Eric Maschwitz, Marcel Stellman, and Peggy Cochrane; costumes, Christian Dior; assistant director, David Middlemas; art director, Elliot Scott; camera, Freddie Young; editor, Ernest Walter.

Ava Gardner (Lady Susan Ashlow); Stewart Granger (Sir Philip Ashlow); David Niven (Henry Brittingham-Brett); Walter Chiari (Mario); Finlay Currie (Reverend Brittingham-Brett); Jean Cadell (Mrs. Brittingham-Brett); Jack

Lambert (Captain MacWade); Henry Oscar (Mr. Trollope); Viola Lyel (Miss Edwards); Jaron Yaltan (Indian Gentleman).

GUN GLORY (MGM, 1957), C-89 min.

Producer, Nicholas Nayfack; director, Roy Rowland; based on the novel *Man of the West* by Philip Yordan; screenplay, William Ludwig; art directors, William A. Horning and Merrill Pye; music, Jeff Alexander; costumes, Walter Plunkett; assistant director, George Rhein; camera, Harold J. Marzorati; editor, Frank Santillo.

Stewart Granger (Tom Early); Rhonda Fleming (Jo); Chill Wills (Preacher); Steve Rowland (Young Tom Early); James Gregory (Grimsell); Jacques Aubuchon (Sam Winscott); Arch Johnson (Gunn); William Fawcett (Martin); Carl Pitti (Joel); Lane Bradford (Ugly); Rayford Barnes (Blondie); Ed Mundy (Ancient); Gene Coogan, Michael Dugan, and Jack Montgomery (Farmers); Bud Osborne (Clem); May McAvoy (Woman); Steve Widders and Charles Hebert (Boys).

THE WHOLE TRUTH (Columbia, 1958), 84 min.

Producer, Jack Clayton; director, John Guillermin; based on the stage and television play by Philip Mackie; screenplay, Jonathan Latimer; assistant director, Ronald Spencer; art director, Tony Masters; music, Mischa Spoliansky; music director, Lambert Williamson; makeup, Roy Ashton; wardrobe, Bridget Sellers; sound, F. Ryan, Bob Jones, and John Aldred; camera, Wilkie Cooper; editor, Gerry Hambling.

Stewart Granger (Max Paulton); Donna Reed (Carol Paulton); George Sanders (Carliss); Gianna Maria Canale (Gina Bertini); Michael Shillo (Inspector Simon); Richard Molinas (Gilbert); Peter Dyneley (Willy Reichel); John Van Eyssen (Archer); Philip Vickers (Jack Leslie); Jimmy Thompson (Assistant); Hy Hazell (American Woman); Carlo Justini (Leading Man); Agnes Lauchlan (Englishwoman); Jacques Cey (Barman); Hugo De Varnier (Hotel Receptionist); Yves Chanteau (Rouget); Jean Driant (Male Servant); Joan Benham, Mignon O'Doherty, Jan Holden, and Laurie Main (Party Guests).

HARRY BLACK AND THE TIGER (20th Century-Fox, 1958), C-117 min.

Producer, John Brabourne; director, Hugo Fregonese; based on the novel *Harry Black* by David Walker; screenplay, Sydney Boehm; music, Clifton Parker; music director, Muir Mathieson; art director, Arthur Lawson; makeup, T. Sforzini; assistant director, Jack Causey; second unit director, Don Sharp; special tiger camera, Charles Trigg; camera, John Wilcox; editor, Reginald Beck.

Stewart Granger (Harry Black); Barbara Rush (Christian Tanner); Anthony Steel (Desmond Tanner); I. S. Johar (Bapu); Martin Stephens (Michael Tanner); Frank Olegario (Dr. Chowdhury); Kamala Devi (Nurse Somola); John Helier (German Sergeant); Jan Conrad (Tower Guard); Gladys Boot (Mrs. Tanner); George Curzon (Mr. Philip Tanner); Carl Conway (Mannfred); Archie Duncan (Woolsey); John Rae (Fisherman); Michael Seaver and Andre Maranne (Frenchmen); Tom Bowman, Harold Siddons, Allan McLelland, and Norman Johns (British Officers).

NORTH TO ALASKA (20th Century-Fox, 1960), C-122 min.

Producer-director, Henry Hathaway; based on both the unproduced play *Birthday Gift* by Laszlo Fodor and the idea by John Kafka; screenplay, John Lee Mahin, Martin Rackin, and Claude Binyon; music, Lionel Newman; orchestrators, Urban Thielmann and Bernard Mayers, choreography, Josephine Earl; song, Robert P. Marcucci, Peter De Angelis, and Russell Faith; art directors, Jack Martin Smith and Duncan Cramer; set decorators, Walter M. Scott and Stuart A. Reiss; costumes, Bill Thomas; makeup, Ben Nye; assistant director, Stanley Hough; second unit director, Richard Talmadge; sound, Alfred Bruzlin and Warren B. Delaplain; special camera effects, L. B. Abbott and Emil Kosa, Jr.; camera, Leon Shamroy; editor, Dorothy Spencer.

John Wayne (Sam McCord); Stewart Granger (George Pratt); Capucine (Michelle); Ernie Kovacs (Frankie Canon); Fabian (Billy Pratt); Mickey Shaughnessy (Boggs); Karl Swenson (Lars); Joe Sawyer (Commissioner); Kathleen Freeman (Lena); John Qualen (Lumberjack); Stanley Adams (Breezy); Stephen Courtleigh (Duggan); Douglas Dick (Lieutenant); Jerry O'Sullivan (Sergeant); Fred Graham (Ole); Frank Faylen (Arnie); Alan Carney (Bartender); Fortune Gordien (Lumberjack); Esther Dale (Picknicker); Hobo (Clancy the Dog); Kermit Maynard (Townsman).

THE SECRET PARTNER (MGM, 1961), 92 min.

Producer, Michael Relph; director, Basil Dearden; screenplay, David Pursall and Jack Seddon; music-music director, Philip Green; production designer, Elliot Scott; art director, Alan Withy; assistant director, George Pollock; wardrobe, Felix Evans; makeup, Bob Lawrence; sound, A. W. Watkins, Gerry Turner, and J. B. Smith; camera effects, Tom Howard; camera, Harry Waxman; editor, Raymond Poulton.

Stewart Granger (John Brent); Haya Harareet (Nicole Brent); Bernard Lee (Detective Superintendent Hanbury); Hugh Burden (Charles Standish); Lee Montague (Detective Inspector Henderson); Melissa Stribling (Helen Standish); Conrad Phillips (Alan Richford); John Lee (Clive Lang); Norman Bird (Ralph Beldon); Peter Illing (Strakarios); Basil Dignam (Lyle); William (James) Fox (Brinton); George Tovey (Vickers); Sydney Vivian (Dock Foreman); Paul Stassino (Man in Soho Street); Colette Wilde (Girl in Car); Peter Welch (McLaren).

LO SPADACCINO DI SIENA (French-Italian, 1961), C-96 min. (U.S. release: **SWORDSMAN OF SIENA**, MGM, 1962).

Producer, Jacques Bar; director, Etienne Perier; story, Anthony Marshall; screenplay (English version) Michael and Fay Kanin and Alec Coppel; art director, Alberto Boccianti; assistant director, Gus Agosti; music, Mario Nascimbene; sound, Kury Doubrowsky; camera, Tonino Delli Colli; editors, Robert and Monique Isnardon.

Stewart Granger (Thomas Stanwood); Sylva Koscina (Orietta Arconti); Christine Kaufmann (Serenella Arconti); Riccardo Garrone (Don Carlos); Tullio Carminati (Father Giacomo); Alberto Lupo (Paresi); Fausto Tozzi (Hugo); Tom Felleghi (Spanish Captain); Carlo Rizzo (Gino); Claudio Gora (Leoni); Marina Berti (Countess of Osta).

SODOMA E GOMORRA (Italian-French, 1961), C-154 min. (U.S. release: **SODOM AND GOMORRAH,** 20th Century-Fox, 1963).

Producer, Goffredo Lombardo; directors, Robert Aldrich and Sergio Leone; screeenplay, Hugo Butler and Giorgio Prosperi; second unit director, Oscar Rudolph; art director, Ken Adam; set decorators, Gino Brosio and Emilio D'Andria; costumes, Giancarlo Bartolini Salimbeni; makeup, Euclide Santoll; prolog-main titles, Maurice Binder; assistant director, Gus Agosti; music, Miklos Rozsa; choreography, Archie Savage; sound, Kurt Dubrowsky; special effects, Lee Zavits, Serse Urbisaglia, and Wally Veevers; camera, Silvano Ippoliti, Mario Montouri, and Cyril Knowles; editor, Peter Tanner.

Stewart Granger (Lot); Pier Angeli (Ildith); Stanley Baker (Astaroth); Rossana Podesta (Shuah); Anouk Aimee (Queen Bera); Claudio Mori (Maleb); Rik Battaglia (Melchir); Giacomo Rossi Stuart (Ishmael); Feodor Chaliapin (Alabias); Aldo Silvani (Nacor); Enzo Fiermonte (Eber); Scilla Gabel (Tamar); Antonio De Teffe (Captain); Massimo Pietrobon (Isaac); Andrea Tagliabue (Eber's Son); Francesco Tensi (Old Man); Mitzuko Takara (Orpha); Liana Del Balzo (Hebrew Woman); Alice and Ellen Kessler (Dancers); Mimmo Palmara (Mimmo).

MARCIA O CREPA *(March or Die)* (Italian-Spanish-German, 1962) 95 min. (U.S. release: **COMMANDO,** American International, 1964).

Director, Frank Wisbar; story, Arturo Tofanelli, screenplay, Wisbar, Guiseppe Mangione, Nino Guerrini, William Demby, and Enrico Bercovic; music, Angelo Francesco Lavagnino; art director, Enrique Alarcon; assistant directors, Antonio Linares and Wieland Liebske; sound, Luigi Puri; camera, Cecilio Paniagua; editor, Mario Serandrei.

Stewart Granger (Captain Le Blanc); Dorian Gray (Nora); Maurizio Arena (Dolce Vita); Ivo Garrani (Colonel Dionne); Fausto Tozzi (Brescia); Riccardo Garrone (Paolo); Carlos Casaravilla (Ben Bled); Peter Carsten (Barbarossa); Hans Von Borsody (Fritz); Rafael Luis Calvo (Kappa-kappa); Dietmar Schoenher (Petit Prince); Leo Anchoriz (Garcia).

IL GIORNO PIU CORTO COMMEDIA UMARISTICA *(The Shortest Day)* (Titanus, 1963), 95 min.

Director, Sergio Corbucca.

With: Annie Giradot, Walter Pidgeon, Gino Cervi, Virna Lisi, Folco Lulli, Simone Signoret, Jacques Sernas, Daniel Mele, Francisco Franchi, Ciccio Ingrassia, Toto, Sylva Koscina, Steve Reeves, Yvonbe Sanson, Walter Chiari, Umberto Orsini, Eleanora Rossi Drago, Stewart Granger, Thomas Milian, Giacomo Rossi Stuart, Renato Rascel, Jean-Paul Belmondo, Susan Strasberg, Philipe Leroy, Ettore Manni, Massimo Serato, Paulo de Filippo, Scilia Gabel, F. Citti, Aldo Fabrizi, Eduardo de Filippo, Giulliano Gemma, Marcello Mastroiani, Sergio Fantoni, Nino Castelnuovo, Ugo Tognazzi, Peter Baldwin, Vittorio Gassman, Alberto Lupo, Gino Ferzetti, Alberto Lupo, Sandra Milo, Renato Salvatori, A. Nazzari, David Niven, Gordon Scott, R. Risso, L. Salce, Francisco Mule, Massimo Girotti.

THE SECRET INVASION (United Artists, 1964), C-95 min.

416

Producer, Gene Corman; director, Roger Corman; screenplay, R. Wright Campbell; assistant director, Charles Griffiths; art director, John Murray; set decorator, Ian Love; music, Hugo Friedhofer; sound, Gene Corso; special effects, George Brackmell; camera, Arthur E. Arling; editor, Ronald Sinclair.

Stewart Granger (Major Richard Mace); Raf Vallone (Roberto Rocca); Henry Silva (John Durrell); Mickey Rooney (Terrence Scanlon); Edd Byrnes (Simon Fell); William Campbell (Jean Saval); Mia Massini (Mila); Helmo Kindermann (German Fortress Commandant); Enzo Fiermonte (General Quadri); Peter Coe (Marko); Nan Morris (Stephana); Helmut Schneider (German Captain); Giulio Marchetti (Italian Officer); Nicholas Rend (Captain of Fishing Boat); Kurt Bricker (German Naval Lieutenant); Katrina Rozan (Peasant Woman); Craig March (Peter).

THE CROOKED ROAD (Gala, 1964), 92 min. (U.S. release: Seven Arts, 1965, 90 min.).
Executive producer, Jack O Lamont; producer, David Henley; director, Don Chaffey; based on the novel *The Big Story* by Morris L. West; screenplay, Chaffey and J. Garrison; music, Bojan Adamic.

Robert Ryan (Richard Ashley); Stewart Granger (Duke of Orgagna); Nadia Gray (Cosima); Marius Goring (Harlequin); George Coulouris (Carlo); Robert Rietty (Police Chief); Catherine Woodville (Elena).

UNTER GEIRN (*Among Vultures*) (German-French-Yugoslavian, 1964) C-102 min. (U.S. release: **FRONTIER HELLCAT,** Columbia, 1966, C-98 min.).
Producer, Horst Wendlandt; director, Alfred Vohrer; based on the novel by Karl May; screenplay, Eberhard Keindorff and Johanna Sibelius; music, Martin Boettcher; costumes, Irms Pauli; art director, Vladimir Tadej; assistant director, Charles Wakefield; camera, Karl Loeb; editor, Hermann Haller.

Stewart Granger (Old Surehand); Pierre Brice (Winnetou); Elke Sommer (Annie); Goetz Goerge (Martin Baumann); Walter Barnes (Old Baumann); Sieghardt Rupp (Preston); Mila Blach (Weller); Renato Baldini (Leader); Mario Girotti (Baker, Jr.); Louis Velle (Gordon); Taddy Fox (Old Wabbles); Voja Miric (Steward); Stole Arandjelovic (Milton); Dusan Bulajic (Bloomfield); Dunia Rajter (Betsy); George Mitic (Wakedeh).

DER OLPRINZ (Rialto-Jadran, 1965) C-91 min. (U.S. release: **RAMPAGE AT APACHE WELLS,** Columbia, 1966, C-91 min.).
Producer, Horst Wendlandt; director, Harold Philipps; screenplay, Philipps and Fred Denger; set designer, Dusko Jericeirc; music, Martin Boettcher; special effects, Erwin Lange; camera, Heinz Holscher; editor, Hermann Haller.

Stewart Granger (Old Surehand); Pierre Brice (Winnetou); Mache Maril (Lizzy); Harold Leipnitz (The Oil Prince); Mario Girotti (Richard Forsythe); Antze Weisgerber (Mrs. Ebersbach); Walter Barnes (Cambell); Gerhard Frickhoffer (Kovacz); Vladimir Leib (Knife); Slobodan Dimetryevic (Butler); Davor Antolic (Paddy); Veljko Maricic (Bergmann); Ilya Ivezec (Webster); Zvonimir Cronko (Billy Forner); Peter Poetrovic (Jimmy); Branko Supek (Jack); Marinco Cosic (Tobby).

OLD SUREHAND 1, TEIL (German-Yugoslavian, 1965), C-93 min. (U.S. release: **FLAMING FRONTIER,** Warner Bros.-Seven Arts, 1968).

Executive producer, Horst Wendlandt; producer, Wolfgang Kuhnlandt; director, Alfred Vohrer; based on a novel by Karl May; screenplay, Eberhard Keindorff, Johanna Sibelius, and Fred Denger; music, Martin Boettcher; art director, Vladimir Tadej; assistant director, Eva Ebner; costumes, Irms Pauli; sound, Matija Barbalic; special effects, Erwin Lange; camera, Karl Loeb; editor, Hermann Haller.

Stewart Granger (Old Surehand); Pierre Brice (Winnetou); Letitia Roman (Judith); Larry Pennell (The General); Mario Girotti (Toby); Wolfgang Lukschy (Judge Edwards); Erik Schumann (Captain Miller); Paddy Fox (Jeremy Wabble); and: Aleksandar Gavric, Valdimir Hedar, Dusco Janicijevic, Hermina Pipinic, and Jelena Jovanovic.

DAS GEHEIMNIS DER DREI DSCHUNKEN (German-Italian, 1965), C-90 min. (U.S. release: **RED DRAGON,** Woolner Bros., 1967).

Producer, Gero Wecker; director, Ernst Hofbauer; based on the novel *River of the Three Junks* by Georges Godefrot; screenplay, Hans-Karl Kubiak and W. P. Zibaso; additional dialog, George Higgins; art director, Max Mellini; music-music director, Riz Ortolani; assistant director, Eberhard Schroeder; sound, Gunther Kortwich; camera, Werner M. Lenz; editors, Hella Faust and Eugenio Alabasio.

Stewart Granger (Michael Scott); Rosanna Schiaffino (Carol); Harald Juhnke (Smoky); Paul Klinger (Norman); Margit Saad (Blanche); Sieghardt Rupp (Pierre Milot); Paul Dahlke (Harris); and: Helga Sommerfeld, Franco Fantasia, Horst Frank, Chitra Ratana, and Suzanne Roquette.

DAS GEHEIMNIS DER GELBEN MONCHE (Intercontinental-Pea, 1966), C-102 min. (U.S. release: **TARGET FOR KILLING** [a.k.a., **HOW TO KILL A LADY**]).

Executive producer, Karl Spiehs; producer, Paul Waldherr; director, Manfred R. Köhler; screenplay, Anstol Bratt; assistant director, Otto Stenzel; art director, Nino Borghi; costumes, Inge Lüttich; music, Marcello Giombini; camera, Siegfried Hold; editor, Manfred R. Köhler.

Stewart Granger (Jim Vine); Karin Dor (Sandra Perkins); Curt Jurgens (Giant); Rupert Davies (Saadi); Adolfo Celi (Henry Perkins); Klaus Kinski (Caporetti); and: Mollie Peters, Scilla Gabel, Allen Pinson, Demeter Bitenc, Erika Remberg, Luis Induni, Wilbert Gurley, and Jose Marco Rosello.

GERN HAB' ICH DIE FRAUEN GEKILLT (Intercontinental-Metheus, 1966), C-94 min. (U.S. release: **REQUIEM FOR A SECRET AGENT**).

Producer, Günter Eulau; directors, Sheldon Reynolds, Louis Soulones, Alberto Cardone, and Robert Lynn; screenplay, Rolf Olsen, Ernesto Gastaldi, and Vittorio Salerno; music, Claudius Alzner; art director, Nino Borghi; camera, Siegfried Hold.

Stewart Granger (David Porter); Lex Barker (Glenn Cassidy); Pierre Brice (Brice); Karin Dor (Denise); Margaret Lee (Linda); Pascale Petit (Lotty); Agnes Spaak (Nelly); Johanna Matz (Monique); and: Walter Giller, Klaus Kinski, Alan Pinson, Tita Barker, Richard Münch, and Peter Vogel.

THE LAST SAFARI (Paramount, 1967), C-110 min.
Producer-director, Henry Hathaway; based on the novel *Gilligan's Last Elephant* by Gerald Hanley; screenplay, John Gay; music-music director, John Dankworth; art director, Maurice Fowler; makeup, Neville Smallwood; wardrobe, Brian Owen-Smith; assistant director, Ron Carr; sound, Norman Bolland, Gordon K. McCallum; camera, Ted Moore; second unit camera, John Coquillon; editor, John Bloom.

Kaz Garas (Casey); Stewart Granger (Miles Gilchrist); Gabriella Licudi (Grant); Johnny Sekka (Jama); Liam Redmond (Alec Beaumont); Eugene Deckers (Refugee); David Munyua (Chongu); John De Villiers (Rich); Wilfred Moore (Game Warden); Jean Parnell (Mrs. Beaumont); Bill Grant (Commissioner); John Sutton (Harry); Kipkoske (Gavai); Labina (Chief of Village); and: The Masai Tribe Wakamba Tribal Dancers.

THE TRYGON FACTOR (Warner Bros.-Seven Arts, 1967), C-87 min.
Executive producer, Ian Warren; producer, Brian Taylor; director, Cyril Frankel; story, Derry Quinn; screenplay, Quinn and Stanley Munro; art director, Roy Stannard; set decorator, Hazel Peisel; color and costume coordinator, Stephen Andrews; production consultant, Wolfgang Kuhnlenz; assistant director, Stuart Freeman; music, Peter Thomas; sound, David Bowman; special effects, Ted Samuels; camera, Harry Waxman; editor, Oswald Hafenrichter.

Stewart Granger (Superintendent Cooper-Smith); Susan Hampshire (Trudy Emberday); Robert Morley (Hubert Hamlyn); Cathleen Nesbitt (Livia Emberday; Brigitte Horney [Sister General (Mrs. Hamlyn)]); Sophia Hardy (Sophie); James Robertson Justice (Sir John); Eddi Arent (Clossen); Diane Clare (Sister Clare); James Culliford (Luke Emberday); Allan Cuthbertson (Detective Thompson); Colin Gordon (Dice); Borienko (Nailer); Conrad Monk (Pasco); Russell Waters (Sergeant Chivers); Richardina Jackson (Black Nun); John Barrett (Guide); Jeremy Hawk (Bank Manager); Hilary Wonter (Man at Hotel); Inigo Jackson (Ballistics Expert).

ANY SECOND NOW (NBC-TV, 1969),.C-120 min.
Producer, Gene Levitt; associate producer, Paul Freeman; director, Levitt; based on the story by Levitt, Robert Mitchell, and Harold Jack Elcom; teleplay, Levitt; camera, Jack Marta; editor, David Eric Rawlins.

Stewart Granger (Paul Dennison); Lois Nettleton (Nancy Dennison); Joseph Campanella (Dr. Raul Valdez); Dana Wynter (Jane Petersen); Katy Jurado (Senora Vorhis); Tom Tully (Howard Lanihan); Marion Ross (Mrs. Hoyt); Eileen Wesson (American Girl).

SHERLOCK HOLMES: THE HOUND OF THE BASKERVILLES (ABC-TV, 1972), C-90 min.

Executive producer, Richard Irving; producer, Stanley Kallis; director, Barry Crane; based on the novel by Sir Arthur Conan Doyle; teleplay, Robert E. Thompson; camera, Harry Woolf; editor, Bill Mosher.

Stewart Granger (Sherlock Holmes); Bernard Fox (Dr. Watson); William Shatner (George Stapleton); Anthony Zerbe (Dr. John Mortimer); Sally Ann Howes (Laura Frankland); John Williams (Arthur Frankland); Ian Ireland (Sir Henry Baskerville); Jane Marrow (Beryl Stapleton); Alan Calliou (Inspector Lestrade); Brendan Dillon (Barrymore); Arline Anderson (Mrs. Barrymore); Billy Bowles (Cartwright); Chuck Hicks (Seldon); Karen Kondan (Mrs. Mortimer).

6' 2½"
198 pounds
Brown hair
Brown eyes
Aquarius

Victor Mature

When one is constantly publicized as "The Hunk" and is the beefcake idol of office girls everywhere, it is difficult to be taken seriously as a performer. It certainly did not help Victor Mature's case that he refused—at least publicly—to take his acting in earnest.

Oncamera he would often stride through a Herculean film role apparently oblivious to the actors or sets about him. Yet on other occasions, as in Twentieth Century-Fox's *My Darling Clementine* (1946) or their *The Robe* (1953), he displayed a vital sincerity that was remarkable. If only his home studio, Fox, had allowed him to expand his acting talent rather than flexing his muscles on film. The outcome of his many years in pictures would have been far more productive for the star.

Victor John Mature was born in Louisville, Kentucky, on Saturday, January 29, 1916. He was the only of the three Mature children (two boys, one girl) to survive infancy. His father, Marcellius G. Mature, an Italian born in Innsbruck, Austria, immigrated to the United States in 1890 when he was thirteen and had eventually settled in Louisville. He took up the trade of a scissors grinder and knife sharpener, and married a French-Swiss girl, Clara, the daughter of a doctor.

Victor was a large-boned, healthy child with curly black hair. As he grew up, he fostered an inner rebellion against his father's strict old-country manner and life. Years later, he was to say, to the press, "I always understood my mom, but my dad. . . . We weren't close!" Victor attended the George H. Tingley Public School in Louisville for a time, but he was soon expelled for his errant ways. He was also asked to leave St. Paul's and St. Xavier's parochial schools because of his undisciplined manner. St. Joseph's Academy in Bardstown, Kentucky, tolerated Victor's presence for only a short while, as did the Kentucky Military Institute at Linden, where it was hoped the youth might learn to settle down.

At the age of fourteen, Victor staged such a fuss against further formal education that the authorities relented and allowed him to quit school. He worked with his father at door-to-door grinding and sharpening, but when Marcellius bettered himself by investing in and becoming an executive of a commercial refrigeration plant, Victor turned to the wholesale jobbing of candy. His customers described him as a "born salesman," and he often earned as much as $150 a week, which was a healthy salary in the early 1930s.

Although he was only fifteen years old, his rugged appearance and muscular frame made him look older. He was especially popular with his feminine customers. A year later he went into the wholesale candy business for himself, which proved to be a rather successful venture. Nine months after that he bought a part ownership in a restaurant.

According to most sources, Victor's decision to leave Louisville came on the heels of a social rebuff by one of the city's belles at the 1935 debutante ball. When he asked the girl to dance, she reportedly called him a "dirty son of a common knife grinder," then slapped his face. "I told myself I'd never return," he informed Robert Coughlan of *Life* Magazine in 1941, "until the name Mature was so big that those society people would eat dirt."

A short time later, he lost six hundred dollars when he sold out his interest in the restaurant, but packed his Chevrolet coupe with candy and canned goods, and, with forty-one dollars in his pocket, proclaimed that he was driving to Hollywood, "where a guy with brains can make more than the President of the United States." Marcellius Mature, although unhappy with his son's plans to become an actor, had learned long ago the futility of arguing with him. His advice to the California-bound youth was, "As long as people think you're dumber than you are, you'll make money."

According to the established Mature legend, he arrived in Hollywood with a bankroll of eleven cents. After selling the supply of candy he had lugged across country, he rented a partially burned-out garage and registered with all the casting agencies. One registrar suggested that he gain a little acting experience and advised Victor to contact the Pasadena Playhouse. There, at a Sunday night open audition he was offered a small part by Gilmor Brown, the playhouse's director. On November 16, 1936, twenty-year-old Victor's acting career began on the well-worn stage of the Pasadena Playhouse in *Paths of Glory.*

Along with his dramatic debut, he became a full-fledged, tuition-paying acting student. To lower his overhead, he moved from his garage abode to an almost forgotten empty piano crate which had been stashed in a corner of a building on the Pasadena campus. He shared the makeshift accommodations with Duke, a Samoyed dog he had acquired to keep him company, until the duo was discovered by the playhouse authorities. They were asked to vacate. From the boards of the piano crate, Victor fashioned the frame of a tent and covered it with an expanse of theatre-owned canvas. Gilmor Brown gave young Victor permission to pitch the tent in his backyard. To pay his tuition, Victor took on assorted odd jobs: floor scrubbing, dish washing, car greasing and polishing, baby sitting, and dog walking, to name a few. The future movie star once estimated that he survived on an average budget of forty-six cents a day while he was learning to act.

In the spring of 1937, he convinced Gilmore Brown that he ought to be awarded a playhouse scholarship in exchange for the work he did backstage. Gilmor accepted the proposal; Victor stopped paying his tuition in cash. After playing a succession of small parts, he was given his first lead role in 1938 in *Autumn Crocus.* Among those to see this production was motion picture producer Charles R. Rogers, who was then planning a film on the life of Gus Edwards. Rogers thought that Victor might be suitable for a role in the production. The producer went so far as to inform the trade press that Victor "is a rival to Clark Gable, Robert Taylor and Errol Flynn." Rogers' movie, *The Star Maker* (Paramount, 1939), starring Bing Crosby, was made, but without Victor. Nor did Mature's hoped-for acting contract with Rogers ever materialize.

If Victor's movie acting ambitions were still just dreams, his romantic life was becoming more concrete. On January 30, 1938, he married another Pasadena Playhouse student, Frances Evans, who went by the professional name of Frances Charles. The couple decided to keep their union a secret, so Victor continued to live in his tent and she remained in the girls' dormitory. The marriage proved a mistake and it was annulled the following year.

Although the Hollywood casting offices never did get around to calling him, Victor acted in more than sixty plays[1] in the Pasadena Theatre, including *To Quito and Back,* in which he had the starring role. Carl Schroeder, editor of *Screen Guide,* did a magazine story on Victor during the run of this play, and the article came to the attention of film producer-director Hal Roach. Roach took more than a casual

---

[1]Some accounts detail that Victor even acted in one of his own dramas, *The Incorrigible One,* written when he was fifteen.

notice of the virile young man and gave him the featured role of Lefty (tenth billing) in *The Housekeeper's Daughter* (United Artists, 1939) at one hundred dollars a week. As a lovesick gangster on screen for no more than five minutes, he spoke about twenty-five words of dialog and was required to slap the picture's star, glamorous Joan Bennett. He told J. Marks of *Interview* Magazine in 1972, "Well, I wasn't too good at it in those days, so I actually hit her pretty hard and knocked her wig off.[2] Bennett was livid. Hal Roach came over with a serious expression on his face and whispered to me: 'Next time hit her a little harder.' "

Soon after the film's release in September, 1939, the Hal Roach Studio received some twenty thousand letters from fans inquiring about the obviously well-built novice. Such a response to a new screen personality in a small role was almost unprecedented. (Some Hollywood authorities recalled that back in 1931 Clark Gable had made a similar boxoffice impact by smacking oncamera Barbara Stanwyck in *Night Nurse* and Norma Shearer in *A Free Soul.*)

Roach immediately signed Victor to a term contract at $250 a week and set four writers (Mickell Novak, George Baker, Joseph Frickert, and Grover Jones) to work concocting a screenplay that would give Victor Mature much more screen time. Meanwhile, Roach, whose contract stable had lost Stan Laurel and Oliver Hardy but still included John Hubbard, Marjorie Woodworth, ZaSu Pitts, Carole Landis, and Patsy Kelly, found the task of taming Mature's image for commercial purposes a formidable task. The actor refused to change his name. However, he did agree to give up his tent life in favor of a furnished house, which he shared with Jules Seltzer, a Roach press agent, and two fan magazine editors, Carl Schroeder and Walt Ramsay. What better way to achieve a fast press build-up than by residing with men whose professional livelihood depended on the revelations of suddenly popular movie actors! Victor's sex appeal and rugged, masculine face were exploited to the hilt, preparing the public for his next screen appearance.

In April, 1940, in *One Million B.C.* (United Artists),[3] moviegoers saw their new hero wearing animal skins and loin cloths in the focal role of Tumak, the leader of earth's prehistoric "rock people." There could be no doubt but that the 204-pound giant (6' 2½") had muscles from his calves to his neck. A mammoth tosses him from a mountain cliff and he descends safely to the land of the "shell people," where he finds the fairhaired Loana (Carole Landis), looking as if she had just concluded an expensive session in a 1940 beauty parlor. Nevertheless, they fall in love and he escorts her upstairs to his mountaintop lair. The table manners she teaches his bemused tribe are interrupted when a neigh-

---

[2]Miss Bennett, in her early brunette days, wore wigs to cover her naturally blonde locks.

[3]Remade in 1966 by Twentieth Century-Fox, starring John Richardson and Raquel Welch.

With Joan Bennett in *The Housekeeper's Daughter* (1939)

With Carole Landis in *One Million B.C.* (1940)

boring volcano erupts, stampeding a variety of dangerous animals bearing fourteen-letter names. Throughout his adventures, Tumak is clean-shaven, although all the other cavemen are bearded. Apparently, that is comedy-maker Roach's method of identifying him as the good guy, for surely Tumak's many talents did not include the art of electrolysis. Victor and Miss Landis made a handsome couple, despite their manner of communicating almost exclusively by grunts or groans (speech was not yet realized in *One Million B.C.*).

The critics poked fun at the Roach-directed film (helmed by both Hal Sr. and Hal Jr.).[4] The *New York Times* labeled the fantasy outing "a bargain-counter excursion into paleontology," while *P.M.* described the unique feature as "romance in the early Pleistocene days or what happened to the Capulets and Montagues when men lived in caves and hunted with sharpened sticks." The highlight of the film was supposed to be the special effects[5] of Roy Seabright and Elmer Raguse, but John Baxter, in *Science Fiction in the Cinema* (Tantury Press, 1970), echoed the most critical opinion of today when he declared, "The ineptly organized battles between lizards are less impressive than Mature's shambling ardour." As for the actor's contribution, the *New York Times* reasoned that Victor is "perhaps lucky that his first [sic] assignment is in a very immature picture." Archer Winsten of the *New York Post* assessed that Mature "is good in a brunette primitive way."

For those who questioned the artistic merits of *One Million B.C.,* they had only to wait until October, 1940, to view Roach's next outing, *Captain Caution* (United Artists). It made the previous "camp" film look much better by comparison. MGM had had great success with its adaptation of Kenneth Roberts' novel, *Northwest Passage* (1940), but Roach's version of Roberts' *Captain Caution* was "a singularly unexciting and dawdling screen offering" (William Boehnel, *New York World-Telegram*); or, as Theodore Strauss *(New York Times)* noted, "Pistols and dirks do not a drama make."

Victor was again in the lead role. As Dan Marvin, better known as Captain Caution, he is commander of the American merchant vessel *Olive Branch* during the War of 1812. Aboard the craft are a crew of stalwarts plus Corunna Dorman (Louise Platt), the curly-haired daughter of the late commander (Robert Barrat). She is soon coveted by scheming pirate Slade (Bruce Cabot). The film provided many jobs for the extras registered at Central Casting, most of whom probably not knowing if they were on the good ship or the bad ship. Unfortunately, the audience was also unable to distinguish heroes from villains. How-

---

[4]D. W. Griffith directed the tests for the leads, but disappeared from the production when the actual filming began.
[5]The team was Oscar-nominated but lost to Lawrence Butler and Jack Whitney for their work on *The Thief of Bagdad* (Korda-United Artists).

With Leo Carrillo and Louise Platt in *Captain Caution* **(1940)**

ever, few viewers really seemed to care, as long as the bare-chested Mature defeated the scoundrel Cabot.

Certainly, at this early point in his career, few critics judged Victor as a celluloid threat to such swashbuckling favorites as Errol Flynn and Douglas Fairbanks, Jr., but the reviewers felt obligated to report to the readers the status of Mature's ability. "His work is, bluntly, amateurish," said Boehnel of the *World-Telegram,* while Wanda Hale (*New York Daily News*), in her two-and-a-half-star review of *Captain Caution,* complained, "As to acting, Mature is the antithesis of his name." Archer Winsten (*New York Post*) hit upon the most obvious aspect of the player's qualification for stardom: "[He] is equipped for the role only in physical aspects."

However, Victor was recognized for his 1940 screen "achievements" in the *Harvard Lampoon* when they announced their annual awards on January 26, 1941: Mature, along with former Boston debutante Leila Ernst, was selected as the least likely to succeed in Hollywood.

At this point, Victor's personal life seemingly consisted of nothing but escorting one new girl after another on the Los Angeles nightclub circuit. At different times he was seen and photographed at Hollywood club spots with Carole Landis, Phyllis Brooks, Wendy Barrie, Alice Faye, and Lana Turner. With the publication of such photographs

427

(many of them staged for obvious publicity purposes), he became the undisputed champion of male glamour. He admitted to the press that he preferred petite blondes and that he avoided exercise in any form except for an occasional swim. His favorite foods were reported to be ice cream, lamb chops, and Coca Cola, with only an infrequent use of either tobacco or alcohol. By mid-1940, his favorite companion was Betty Grable, newly divorced from Jackie Coogan and not yet involved with either George Raft or Harry James. His reason for preferring the Twentieth Century-Fox film favorite was: "She makes me laugh."

By 1940, Hal Roach was in a financial pinch and agreed to let RKO share Victor's contract. A six-picture pact was arranged, whereby Roach would receive most of the salary that would accrue to Victor for his screen services. RKO placed him in their 1940 version of the 1925 stage musical *No, No, Nanette*.[6] In Ken Englund's screen adaptation, the supporting role of William was written especially for Victor. As a Broadway producer of musicals, he is one of Nanette's (Anna Neagle) suitors, but he loses her to Tom (Richard Carlson). The memorable Vincent Youmans songs were relegated to background music. Directed in the role of Nanette by her producer-husband Herbert Wilcox, Britain's Miss Neagle never looked prettier.

---

[6]The property had been filmed ten years earlier by First National and would be remade by Warner Bros. in 1950 as *Tea for Two*.

With Anna Neagle in *No, No, Nanette* (1940)

It was then that Victor and his associates reckoned that his acting career wouldn't get anywhere unless he had some legitimate professional exposure. Feelers were sent out on Broadway, and when interest was shown by New York's Group Theatre, he went East to investigate. As he would later explain to reporters: "One of the reasons I was anxious to get away from Hollywood was to slay, while it was still in the process of growing, the legend that I was just a glamour boy with a lucky streak. Nobody seems to care very much that I'm an actor only because I like acting and have wanted to make it my life's work ever since I left home in Louisville when I was seventeen."

Victor's companion for the trip to Manhattan was Betty Grable. They spent their first evening in New York at a dinner party hosted by Miss Grable's agent, Louis Shurr, whose sharp eyes picked out Victor as a possibility for a role in Moss Hart's new play, *Lady in the Dark*. Arrangements were negotiated, and Victor gave up the Group Theatre in favor of romancing Gertrude Lawrence as the *Lady*. In the part of movie hero, Randy Curtis, Victor was on stage for forty minutes of the nearly three-hour show. He had 133 lines of dialog and was required to sing one verse of a Kurt Weill song.

After the play's Boston showing, which had begun on January 5, 1941, the show opened at New York's Alvin Theatre on January 24. Produced by Sam H. Harris at a cost of $130,000, the musical was presented on four revolving stages and brought recognition to newcomers Danny Kaye and Macdonald Carey. *Time* Magazine referred to Victor as the "latest in Hollywood's series of almost outrageously beautiful young men." *Life* proclaimed him the "new matinee idol," and stated that he "combines the most striking qualities of Robert Taylor, Nils Asther and Gargantua."

The Moss Hart dialog provided a description of Victor's stage character that was to stick with the actor throughout most of his screen career. Just before his entrance on stage, the character Randy Curtis is called a "beautiful hunk of man." The label was immediately picked up by columnists and was to become synonymous with the name Victor Mature. Few people seemed to recall, at that time or later, that Victor had received commendable press notices for his Broadway debut: "He plays with an engaging manner, simply, directly and effectively" (Sidney B. Whipple, *New York World Telegram*); "[he] managed to be both simple and fatuous with little effort" (George Greedley, *New York Morning Telegraph*); "[he] is unobjectionably handsome and affable" (Brooks Atkinson, New York *Times*).

While souvenir seekers hounded the stage door of the Alvin Theatre for Victor's autograph or an article of his attire (buttons or a piece of cloth), he devoted his offstage hours to escorting various beauties to Manhattan's night spots. After Miss Grable's return to California where she would soon supersede Alice Faye as Fox's leading musical comedy star, he was paired with Gene Tierney, Vera Zorina, Mrs. Liz Whitney, and musical revue celebrity Bernice Parks. At the Stork Club he was voted by three hundred New York models as the man with whom they would most like to be cast upon a desert island; at Hunter College for Women he was chosen as the first king of the senior hop; he crowned the queen of the annual Stenographers' Ball where he kissed all ten of the fluttery candidates; he endorsed a popular hair tonic for men; and he was photographed with Sara Delano Roosevelt, the President's mother, in an appearance on behalf of British and Greek war relief.

When it was revealed that Victor's bicep measured fifteen inches around when he flexed his arm, Don Blackman, the light heavy-weight black wrestling champion of the world whose bicep measured sixteen inches, wrote him, "You are my favorite male star and muscle man in the white race." But Victor declined an invitation from Blackman to spend two weeks working out in the ring with him. The actor went on record, stating, "I can act, but what I've got that the others don't have is this," meaning his body. *Life* pointed out that he "came by this through no fault of his own" and took particular note of the fact that Victor did not do any body building exercises and of his penchant for nocturnal club hopping until four or five in the morning. Nevertheless, Victor indicated that he expected to remain in good physical shape until his late fifties, the age at which the male members of his family usually died.

Mature had an appendectomy on April 10, 1941, and after nearly a month's recuperation, he returned to *Lady in the Dark* on May 7, 1941 (Edward Trevor substituted for him on stage). Later in May he auctioned off an article of feminine underwear at a Manhattan benefit. The item was purchased by socialite Martha Stephenson Kemp, the widow of bandleader Hal Kemp who had been killed in an automobile crash in December, 1940. Victor then courted Mrs. Kemp in a fast affair that was supposed to end in marriage at St. Patrick's Cathedral on June 15, 1941. Or so the press and public thought. However, those who showed up at the Fifth Avenue Church that Sunday were disappointed.

Mrs. Paul Forester, Martha's mother, served as spokeswoman to explain to the annoyed fourth estate and fans just why the celebrated couple did not show up at the appointed place: "The mistake started when they went to the Municipal Building for the license last Wednesday. The man asked them to fill in the space as to the wedding date, and they said they didn't know. . . . He insisted on an approximate date and told them it was just routine, and they said, 'Oh, well, put down the fifteenth.' Then he asked them where, and they didn't know, but they said St. Patrick's because Mr. Mature goes there."

The nuptials did occur three days later at Martha's home at 957 Park Avenue. Justice Ferdinand Pecora of the New York State Supreme

Court performed the ceremony. Sherman Billingsley of the Stork Club was the best man, with Mrs. Leonard Lyons as matron of honor. The other guests included Martha's parents, banker Spencer Martin, Leonard Lyons, and Victor's chauffeur, Dan S. Wordsman. For the record—and this was Victor's proudest moment in society—the actor wore a light gray suit with a white pencil stripe and a white carnation in his lapel, and the bride wore a white silk dress with black scroll print, a chartreuse and black belt, and a white rose at the belt. Victor announced that the civil ceremony would be solemnized at the Church of St. Paul in Louisville, Kentucky, at the end of June. Victor was then twenty-six, his bride was twenty-two.

On June 15, 1941, at the start of a summer break, Mature left the cast of *Lady in the Dark* (his successor was Willard Parker when the show resumed on Labor Day, 1941)[7] and returned to Hollywood alone. It was stated publicly that Martha was remaining in New York to care for her one-year-old child Helen (from her marriage to Kemp) and to take care of a bad wisdom tooth. Martha joined him later in California, but did not remain for long. Rumors of a rift were persistent, and Victor finally stated, "Mrs. Mature finds me revolting. I'm a peasant, an earthy type. Mrs. Mature is a very lovely, sophisticated lady. She probably doesn't understand my kind of person. It makes me sort of confused."

Never shy about boosting his own stock (which would earn him the enmity of gossip columnists Louella Parsons, Hedda Hopper, and others) Victor took occasion now to rationalize the continuing campaign to make him the cinema's Mr. Irresistible: "I know that glamour stuff makes me look like a drip. But what did it do for me? I'll tell you, don't guess, it made me the hottest thing in pictures. . . . It made me somebody. Supposing nobody had paid any attention to me, hadn't written or said a thing about me? Where would I be now? Back in a tent perhaps, living on fifty cents a day. . . . I'd rather be where I am today, and be regarded as a jerk, than to have been ignored."

Hollywood producers did anything but ignore the availability of Victor for film work. His first post-Broadway feature film was on loan to veteran producer Arnold Pressburger for the screen adaptation of the 1926 play by John Colton, *The Shanghai Gesture* (United Artists, 1941). Because the drama had been set in a Chinese brothel with its study of vice versus virtue, no less than thirty-two previous script adaptations of the *The Shanghai Gesture* had been rejected as morally unsuitable by the motion picture production code office. It was Pressburger who goaded his old friend von Sternberg into working with three other scripters' versions to create a scenario that would pass muster with the Hays office. By switching the story's locale to a gambling house and changing the exotic Mother Goddam into the more

---

[7]In the 1944 Paramount film version, starring Ginger Rogers and Ray Milland, the role of Randy Curtis would be played by Jon Hall.

With Gene Tierney in *The Shanghai Gesture* (1941)

Hollywood-type Mother Gin Sling, von Sternberg made the script into a viable commercial property.

The casting of *The Shanghai Gesture,* considering von Sternberg had already "licked" the scripting problem, was an oddball assortment of choices, part fancy, part shrewdness, and part nostalgia. Ona Munson was transformed into a "Chinese Dietrich" to play Mother Gin Sling; Gene Tierney was assigned to play the alluring, destructive Poppy; Walter Huston played her staid father who was once the consort of the Medusa-tainted Munson; von Sternberg's pal Albert Basserman was hired to interpret the aging commissioner; and the equally well-known veteran Maria Ouspenskaya was on hand for a cameo as the non-speaking Amah. And for the role of the "Levantine sensualist," Victor was cast as Dr. Omar.[8] (In the original play the role had been the Japanese Prince Oshima. The Hays Office's rules on miscegenation required the character change.)

---

[8]One newspaper columnist, who thought his readers might appreciate the opportunity to decide for themselves which came first, Victor's persona as the corrupt Dr. Omar, or the scriptors' image of the character, printed the supposed scenario description of the figure: "DOCTOR OMAR—His last name is too difficult to pronounce and is never mentioned. His title of doctor is self-assumed. He is a swarthy young Apollo, dressed in fez and monocle, and wears a burnoose or is impeccably dressed in evening regalia. He originally came from Smyrna in the Levant. His father dealt in tobacco and came from Armenian stock, while the less stated about his mother the better. He is a mongrel with a great

Viewers of the day took *The Shanghai Gesture* in stride, almost allowing it to pass as just another offbeat film. But genre-dissecting critics, then and now, were to give heady accolades to this production. *Cahiers du Cinema* would rank the film as von Sternberg's "strangest and most fascinating work." In *The Cinema of Josef von Sternberg* (Tantivy Press, 1971) John Baxter would evaluate this release as "the last classic Sternberg film, an intricate ivory sculpture, with concentric globes of carefully wrought meaning." Herman G. Weinberg, in his critical study, *Josef von Sternberg* (Dutton, 1966), would insist that "the master of *chinoiserie* has done it again."

In such a film intent on emphasizing the exotic decoration to the detriment of the characters, it is difficult to assess the performers' work as anything more than extensions of the director's overall plan. Taking this into consideration, it is interesting to note that with Poppy, Tierney created her second most memorable 1940s screen role. (*Laura* at 1944 Twentieth Century-Fox was her most penetrating part of the decade.) In addition, Huston was more than usually restrained, and Victor, for the first time, used his potentially expressive face to exhibit complexity of character beneath his cold exterior.

In his third-billed role in *The Shanghai Gesture,* Victor plays the fez-topped Egyptian flesh merchant who is, in his own words, a "thoroughbred mongrel." He coldly receives Gene Tierney's Poppy as his property and puts her at the top of his list of "availables" within the walls of a "gambling hell" that is presided over by the girl's mother, Ona Munson's Mother Gin Sling. Two Oriental themes are suggested in the story: that all sins are paid for on New Year's Eve, and that the sins of a person are inherited by his children. These ideas come out when Tierney's Poppy goads her emotion-drained mother into action on the holiday eve. She tells Mother Gin Sling, "You are no more my mother than a toad." The mother shoots her with a pistol, leaving Poppy's father, Sir Guy Charteris (Walter Huston), wandering out into the holiday crowds, a crushed man.

Mature went from this drama to a loanout assignment at Twentieth Century-Fox in the non-musical version of *I Wake up Screaming* (1941)[9] with two former girlfriends, Betty Grable and Carole Landis. Directed by H. Bruce Humberstone, the film is an intriguing murder mystery, Bosley Crowther's statement in the *New York Times* that "the plot is nothing of any consequence" notwithstanding. When Vicky Lynn (Landis), a prospect for Hollywood stardom, is murdered, her sister (Grable) wants the culprit brought to justice. Victor, as publicist

---

fascination for women, who confuse his disdain for them with poise. He would sell anything he has for a price, and give away everything he has not got. He is the chief assistant of Mother Gin Sling who is probably the only creature on earth he respects."

[9]Also called *Hot Spot,* the film would be remade by Fox in 1953 as *Vicki,* with Jeanne Crain, Jean Peters, and Elliott Reid.

With Betty Grable in _I Wake Up Screaming_ (1941)

Frankie Christopher, the man credited with having discovered Landis' talent, becomes the prime suspect and is relentlessly pursued by the psychopathic cop (Laird Cregar) assigned to the case.

There seemed no end to the job opportunities for Victor at this point. Von Sternberg mentioned he wanted the actor for _Lady Paname,_ to be produced at United Artists (it never was); RKO requested his services for _Passage to Bordeaux;_ and Twentieth Century-Fox wanted him on the soundstages for _Highway to Hell._ But before Victor would agree to any offers, he demanded that his status with Roach be clarified. The producer-director was paying Mature a flat weekly salary of $450, but _The Shanghai Gesture_ producer Pressburger paid Roach $3,750 weekly. Victor felt that Roach's $3,300 weekly gravy was a bit too much. When Roach next offered to loan his much-in-demand player to Twentieth Century-Fox for _Song of the Islands_ (1942), at $22,000 for nine weeks' work, Victor rebelled. He demanded that Roach give him a share of the prosperity and refused to perform for less than $1250 a week, guaranteed for forty weeks a year.

In November, 1941, Fox bought Victor's contract from Roach for a reputed $80,000. With a special loanout provision to RKO, the agreement stipulated that Mature's salary would be $1200 a week. On the Fox lot, he quickly made friends with the publicity department staff,

434

who saw that his name got into the Los Angeles area newspapers as often as possible.

In his own inimitable way, Victor confided to one reporter at the time that because of the company's heavy investment in buying his contract, "the studio will have to make a success of me." He seemed blithely unconcerned, at least in public, about his competition on the new home lot, which included such actors as Don Ameche, Dana Andrews (on a contract shared with Samuel Goldwyn), Laird Cregar, Henry Fonda, Richard Greene, John Loder, George Montgomery, Lloyd Nolan, John Payne, Tyrone Power, Cesar Romero, John Sutton, and Shepperd Strudwick.

Both George Raft and Cesar Romero had wanted Victor's part in *I Wake up Screaming*, but there was no dispute over the role of Jefferson Harper in *Song of the Islands*; it was tailor-made for Mature. It teamed him for the second time with Betty Grable in a Technicolor concoction that one critic dubbed a "hula-Western." The *New York Times* proclaimed, "As a movie *Song of the Islands* is a great bathing suit advertisement." The plot was simplistic at best: Victor, as the son of an American cattle baron (George Barbier), arrives on a Pacific Island where he meets, loves, hates, and then loves again Eileen O'Brien

With Betty Grable, Thomas Mitchell, and Jack Oakie in *Song of the Islands* (1942)

435

(Grable), the vivacious daughter of a beachcomber played by Thomas Mitchell. O'Brien owns a stretch of beach land that Victor's Jefferson and his father want, to launch their joint cattle spread. Since Mitchell's pugnacious O'Brien is initially against selling the area to the cattle baron and his son, a convenient Romeo and Juliet situation is quickly established. But the seventy-five-minute fest ends on a happy note, with everyone dancing hulas, shaking hands, kissing, and being awfully friendly.

While the obvious assets of *Song of the Islands* were shapely Grable strutting, singing, and posing in an array of Dorothy Lamour-inspired costumes, and the hard-hitting humor of double-take king Jack Oakie, Victor added a special something to the proceedings, namely, beefcake appeal. The film's story required him to wear short-sleeved, tight-fitting net sweaters and flowered lava-lavas, both of which displayed his abundant muscle. Otis L. Guernsey, Jr. (*New York Herald-Tribune*) observed that Victor "must henceforth be known as the sweater-boy [a companion to sweater girl Lana Turner?]. He models a succession of gorgeous—the technicolor effect—knitted creations with undeniable grandeur and his brunette waves nicely complement Miss Grable's beautifully coiffured blonde locks." As in subsequent Fox films, Ben Gage performed Victor's soundtrack singing.

On October 19, 1941, Marcellius Mature died in Louisville of a heart attack. He was then sixty-four years old. His widow chose to continue living in the family home, but announced she planned to visit frequently with her famous son in California.

Meanwhile, producer Edward Small announced he wished to film the life story of Rudolph Valentino and that he wanted to borrow Victor from Fox. That project came to naught at the time,[10] but Fox had better plans for Victor. The studio was experiencing great success with its series of Tin Pan Alley nostalgia movies, and decided to fashion a feature around the life of composer Paul Dresser (1857-1911), loosely based on the story *My Brother Paul* by Theodore Dreiser. Harry Cohn of Columbia loaned his top gold mine, Rita Hayworth, to Twentieth for *My Gal Sal* (1942). Recently separated from husband Edward Judson, Rita was ripe for a heated love affair, and Victor filled the bill to perfection. During the shooting of one of his love scenes with titian-haired Miss Hayworth, Victor collapsed and was rushed to a hospital where his malady was diagnosed as "primrose poisoning." From his sick bed he revealed that his marital rift was irreparable and that Mrs. Mature would most likely obtain a divorce.

My Gal Sal proved to be slick fiction geared to the Twentieth Century-Fox mold. Victor hardly resembled the real-life, three-hundred-

[10]Columbia would film the "life" story of the cinema sheik in 1951, with Anthony Dexter in the title role. Franco Nero played the Italian-born movie star in a 1975 ABC-TV telefeature. Rudolf Nureyev was announced as the lead in Ken Russell's film biography.

With Rita Hayworth in *My Gal Sal* (1942)

pound Paul Dresser, but no matter. The actor gamely played banjo-plucking Dresser who leaves his Indiana home to join a tank town medicine show and eventually ends up in New York. In the city, he writes such songs as "On the Banks of the Wabash," "Blue and Gray," and the title song of the film, after falling in love with magical musical stage star Sally Elliott (Hayworth). Directed by Irving Cummings, the film features Rita "singing" eight melodies.[11] Since the true test of a picture of this sort is really the quality of music, Fox was in good shape; in addition to the Dresser tunes, Leo Robin and Ralph Rainger dreamed up such songs as "Me and My Fella and a Big Umbrella," "Midnight at the Masquerade," "Here You Are," and several others, all to bolster the rather tinny plot.

To Mature's credit, he handled his cardboard role in *My Gal Sal* with gusto. The critics, who would never be Victor's fans, were actually cordial to his performance. "Victor Mature, of all people, plays the central role of Dresser. Believe me or not, he plays it with remarkable assurance and manages to get away with instrumental playing and singing with a minimum of awkwardness." (*New York Herald-Tribune*). Said *Time* Magazine, "Although one of Hollywood's almost unbearably beautiful young males, Victor Mature plays the Dresser role, he is generally bearable."

Hedda Hopper once wrote, "In a town fraught with people who think they have I.Q.'s of 275 plus, Vic frankly admitted that he was a genius. That coy declaration got him reams of publicity from people irritated by the very thought of a 'ham' actor's having such an opinion of himself!" Victor also bought a Boxer dog, named him Genius, and acquired coveralls for the crew of his next picture with "Assistant Genius" stitched on their backs. Miss Hopper referred to Victor's antics as a "burlesque of pomposity." At another time, because he had not been asked to record for posterity his foot and hand prints in a block of cement in front of Grauman's Chinese Theatre on Hollywood Boulevard, Victor poked further fun at filmland's traditions by having concrete poured into a square in front of his dressing room. With reporters and photographers at the scene, he took down his trousers and gingerly imprinted the fresh cement with the outline of his behind. Studio heads, however, prevented the story or photographs from reaching the newspapers.

When Mature spread word to the press that he was considering the purchase of Valentino's home, "The Falcon's Lair," a good friend of the dead idol made several acid comments regarding the proposed real estate transaction. Those comments were headlined in the press with, "Pola Negri Says Mature Not the Type to Play Valentino Role." None

---

[11]Nan Wynn actually performed the offcamera vocals for Rita, managing to make the dubbing a close approximation of the star's talking voice. (One can only speculate how Alice Faye, Fox's original choice for the part, would have handled the assignment.)

of this, however, seemed to bother Vic. As Hedda Hopper explained, "That's what he wanted. He didn't care how loudly people screamed, just so as they screamed Mature—first name, Vic." One of those to yelp the loudest in print was W. H. Mooring, the Hollywood correspondent for the British *Picturegoer* Magazine. He informed his readers that Mature was not a favorite in the tinsel town, and that indeed the man had deliberately set out "to become Hollywood's self-avowed disciple of conceit and vulgarity."

In his next film, *Footlight Serenade* (Twentieth Century-Fox, 1942), Victor is Tommy Lundy, the world's heavy weight boxing champion, large on muscle, conceit, and boast, but small on brains. He is bare-torsoed throughout much of the picture, as is top-billed over co-star John Payne, his sparring partner in a Broadway musical in which the Champ finds himself. When Victor makes passes at the show's star (Betty Grable), he is angrily confronted in the onstage ring by his sparring mate, who also happens to be secretly wed to spunky Betty. The black-and-white film is not memorable for either its flimsy plot (even *The Prizefighter and the Lady*, MGM, 1933, with Myrna Loy and Max Baer was more fun) or its dull songs ("I'm Still Crazy for You," "I Heard the Birdies Sing," etc.). According to *Newsweek* Magazine, the picture's high spot is "probably Mature's confident interpretation of the brash, immature lady killer. While there are those who will dis-

With Phil Silvers and Betty Grable (right) in *Footlight Serenade* (1942)

439

With Lucille Ball in *Seven Days' Leave* (1942)

count this performance as a triumph of type casting, Mature manages
the role with the saving grace of humor and self-kidding."

Victor's obligatory loanout to RKO came in the form of a not-very-
funny comedy with music called *Seven Days' Leave* (1942), in which
he is an Army corporal (with hair cropped to Army brevity) on furlough
who must marry the high-brow daughter (Lucille Ball) of a wealthy
family before he can collect a hundred-thousand-dollar inheritance.
The film was judged as having "a B picture atmosphere which it never
quite shakes off" (*New York Sun*). The procedures were laced with
specialty acts performed by Ginny Simms, Harold Peary, Marcy Mc-
Guire, Arnold Stang, the orchestras of Freddy Martin and Les Brown,
and the "Truth or Consequence" show of Ralph Edwards and his
company. Few people were impressed by this hodgepodge show, and
in this stint away from the Fox home lot Victor was panned by the
critics. "Mature is still knocking the dames dead (that's what the script
sez), and he's over-acting (which the script doesn't say) with his utter-
ances of the inane dialog" (*Variety*).

Poor notices for *Seven Days' Leave* hardly bothered Victor, for he
had other items on his mind. For one thing, he confessed to newsmen,
"I haven't arrived yet. You know how I know this? It's because other
players in this studio [Twentieth Century-Fox] don't invite me to their
parties.

"To be invited to parties in Hollywood, you have to amount to something. You have to be important. I will know when I am important when I am invited to parties."

On the same subject, Victor added that when success did hit, he intended to be a regular guy. "I don't want to get that front, that attitude which demands front tables in clubs, which causes one to forget one's early friends. I know I can keep on being regular."

No sooner was *Seven Days' Leave* in the can, than Victor joined the United States Coast Guard, on July 2, 1942, as a Seaman Second Class. Although he was under subpoena to appear at a court hearing in which his wife sought a temporary alimony of $510 monthly pending trial of a divorce suit,[12] he reported for duty at San Pedro California. His wife's attorney charged that he had enlisted as "a convenient out." Later in the year, Victor's request for a transfer to Connecticut was granted, and Rita Hayworth, against her employers' orders, rendezvoused with him there. He gave her a diamond and ruby ring before setting sail for active convoy duty in the North Atlantic.

On February 10, 1943, Martha Stephenson Kemp Mature ended her marriage with a divorce in Las Vegas, Nevada. (On April 28, 1946, she would wed screen writer St. Clair McKelway.)

Meanwhile, Columbia's sex goddess Hayworth met Orson Welles, who was in Hollywood with his magic act. Rita toured servicemen's camps with him as part of the act in which he sawed her in half. On September 7, 1943, they were married. At a port off the frigid North Atlantic waters, Victor heard the news by radio. Although he was hard hit by the announcement, he quipped, "Now, I know that the way to a woman's heart is by sawing her in half." The words were repeated around the world and he became a figure of noble character to his shipmates who had earlier tagged him "The Beautiful Hunk of Junk."

After fourteen months of sea duty, Victor was returned to the States in June, 1943, where at Brighton Marine Hospital (near Boston, Massachusetts) he underwent dental surgery to extract two rear molars. It was also reported that while at sea he had sustained a slight injury to his right leg. That autumn he personally sold $270,000 worth of war bonds while on tour. He said, "They come from people who hear you tell stories about their sons and they buy bonds like crazy!"

Now a Chief Boatswain's Mate, Victor was awarded a commendation from Russell R. Waesche, Commandant of the U.S. Coast Guard, for outstanding work on the bondfront and battlefront, and was given a twenty-five-day leave, much of which was spent in Hollywood. Besides dating blonde actresses Betty Hutton, K. T. Stevens, and Veronica Lake, he was heard over NBC radio on the "Ginny Simms Show,"

---

[12]On February 7, 1942, when it was made public that the Matures were on the verge of a divorce, Martha announced, "This is the first time I've heard about it. If you hear anymore, let me know."

when he introduced Coast Guardsmen Melvin Baldwin and Roy O'Malley, the lone survivors of *the Escanaba,* a cutter that was sunk by German torpedoes. He also appeared on "Lux Radio Theatre" on October 25, 1943, with Lana Turner and Gene Lockhart in an hour version of *Slightly Dangerous,* originally a MGM film of the same year that had starred Miss Turner with Robert Walker and Walter Brennan. Victor donated the salary he received from both shows to the Coast Guard Relief Fund. For this generosity, his leave was extended an additional five days, and during this period he met Anne Shirley, the actress ex-wife of John Payne. They saw each other every day and Miss Shirley told a reporter, "We'd like to get married before his leave's up, but we don't know where or when."[13] Victor was then placed on shore duty and was assigned to play in the all-Coast Guard musical revue, *Tars and Spars* which opened in Miami, Florida in April, 1944.

Designed as a Spars recruitment device, the show played film-vaude-ville theatres across the nation. After the tour, he was re-assigned to duty in the Philippine Islands. As a recipient of the Good Conduct Ribbon, Victor performed sea duty for a total of thirty months and, finally, was discharged on November 26, 1945.

He had no place to live on his return to Hollywood, so he moved into his fifteen-foot-square dressing room (#116), where he slept on a couch and cooked meals on an electric grill. He told reporters that his accommodations agreed with him in that they provided rapid access to the Mocambo. Twentieth Century-Fox signed the twenty-nine-year-old actor to a new contract, which gave him a weekly salary of three thousand dollars.

He barely had returned to the California social scene when he began dating nineteen-year-old Buffy Cobb Chapman, recently divorced from attorney Greg Bautzer. However, Victor insisted to the press, "I don't want to marry yet. I've been married twice already. . . . You just can't keep on making mistakes. Next time I want to be sure it will last.'" The romance with Miss Chapman did not last, and he was thereafter linked, largely for publicity purposes, with Fox star June Haver.

While Mature had been occupied in the armed services, the complexion of the male star roster at Fox had redefined itself. While other studio leads (such as Tyrone Power, John Payne, George Montgomery, Henry Fonda, and the often-at-Fox Lon McCallister) had also joined the military forces, there had remained still active on the Fox sound-stages such male lead stars as Dana Andrews, Cornel Wilde, Dick Haymes, William Eythe, Richard Conte, and other draft exempt souls who filled the breach in the acting roles and (temporarily at least) won the public's favor. During these very war years Fox would switch from its Latin American good neighbor policy to its apple pie wholesome

---

[13]They were not destined for marriage to each other. In 1945, Miss Shirley married producer-writer Adrian Scott.

filmmaking period, favoring such products as *Wilson* (1944), *Home in Indiana* (1944), *State Fair* (1945), and *Centennial Summer* (1946). (These were just the sort of films in which Victor's virile screen persona would have been out of keeping.) It would not be until *Gentleman's Agreement* (1947), *The Snake Pit* (1948), and *Pinky* (1949) that Twentieth would swing into its post-World War II "relevance" period, balancing its rash of Betty Grable-June Haver-Jeanne Crain-Clifton Webb attractions with films such as these topical studies.

With the major exception of Tyrone Power, who was showcased in the lush adaptation of Somerset Maugham's *The Razor's Edge* (1946), Fox's Darryl F. Zanuck took little care in properly handling his returning male stars so that their post-war films would quickly reestablish them with their filmgoing public. Victor was no exception. In December, 1945, he started work on *Three Little Girls in Blue* (1946), a color musical designed to display the talents of June Haver, Vivian Blaine, Celeste Holm, and Vera-Ellen. Fortuitously for Mature, director John Brahm's footage was scrapped a short way into production, and, when H. Bruce Humberstone took over the directing, Victor and Cesar Romero were replaced by George Montgomery and Frank Latimore respectively.

Victor was then thrust into John Ford's *My Darling Clementine* (1946),[14] a "horse opera for the carriage trade" (*Time* Magazine). More than just another sagebrush tale, it attempted to develop a philosophical insight into the right-over-wrong moral issue in the cleansing of the town of Tombstone in 1881. The Earp Brothers, Virgil (Tim Holt) and Morgan (Ward Bond), led by Wyatt (Henry Fonda), enter Tombstone after their herd is stolen and their brother James (Don Garner) is killed by crusty old man Clanton (Walter Brennan) and his gang. The town is run by consumptive Doc Holliday (Victor), whose medical practice long ago has given way to questionable practices. He takes an immediate liking to the Earps; Wyatt becomes the marshal and falls in love with Doc's discarded fiancée, Clementine Carter (Cathy Downs). Doc prefers to maintain his earthy mistress Chihuahua (Linda Darnell), who is later killed. In the famous shootout at the O.K. Corral, Doc joins the Earps against the Clantons, where he, too, is killed. However, it is Doc who, in forfeiting his life, has made it possible for Tombstone's rejuvenation. Photographed by Joseph MacDonald in Monument Valley, California, the outdoor scenes are especially gratifying in this man's picture.

In his first Western, Victor gave a solid performance as the Boston aristocrat turned gambler and killer. In his most complex screen char-

---

[14] *My Darling Clementine* is a revamping of Allan Dwan's *Frontier Marshal* (Twentieth Century-Fox, 1939); much of the subject matter would later reappear in John Sturges' *Gunfight at the O.K. Corral* (Paramount, 1957) and Sturges' *Hour of the Gun* (United Artists, 1967).

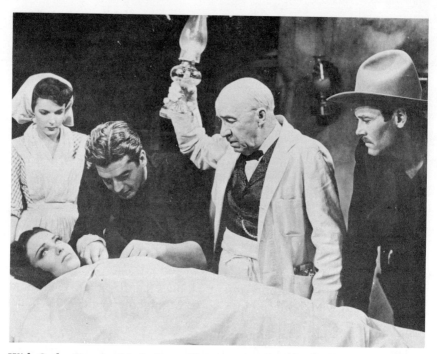

With Cathy Downs, Linda Darnell, J. Farrell MacDonald, and Henry Fonda in *My Darling Clementine* (1946)

acterization to date, Mature appeared as a blackguard who winds up on the side of the law. He is a sexually ambiguous man who, despite his two lady loves, has a strong affinity for "Law and Order" Wyatt Earp, giving the film many understated tones of diverse sexuality. Unlike the comparatively simple Wyatt, Doc is a complex man, his intellectuality held at bay in the old West. The depth of his soul is seen clearly in the sequence in which a drunken actor (Alan Mowbray) falters through the "To be or not to be" speech from Hamlet, and the erudite Doc concludes the bard's stanzas, foreshadowing the fate that Holliday will soon meet in the big showdown.

For his performance in *My Darling Clementine,* Victor received some very decent reviews.[15] *Variety* observed, "Improvement in Mature's thesping is marked by a degree of emotional expression and facial animation not seen in his former roles." *Time* Magazine was less subtle, stating that he "actually does some acting as the dipsomaniac doctor-turned-renegade." *Cosmopolitan* Magazine gave accolades to Mature when it cited him as having given the best supporting performance of the month.

---

[15]Darryl F. Zanuck would later say of the film and Mature, "[It] was an *homage,* a valentine. It was a compendium of all western cliches. But it was expertly made and had an unforgettable performance by Henry Fonda, and even a strong one by Victor Mature, not a great Western, but a pure Western."

The combination of Victor's serious performance in *Clementine* and his abstinence from much nightclubbing since returning home, led many to believe that the actor was a changed man. He even bought a house, which added a sense of respectability to his reputation. However, after Mary Morris interviewed him late in 1946 for *P.M.,* she claimed in her write-up (entitled "Mr. Beautiful") that "he's still bawdy, reckless, free and breezy."

The house, at a modest cost of $13,000, was located at 11261 Brookhaven Avenue in West Los Angeles, with neighbors close at hand who were not in the least awed at having him in their midst. "It's really the first Hollywood home I've ever had," he told Hedda Hopper. "I've been living in tents, dressing rooms and garages so long that I just decided to get me a house." He added: "The main reason I quit going to nightclubs is that I hardly know anybody at them any more. I've done a lot of clowning and had a heck of a lot of fun. But I've come to know that fame and money mean nothing to a man unless he has the respect of people for what he can do. If I'm going to be an actor, I figure I must do my best at my job."

In 1947, Fox's Tyrone Power was going dramatic in *Nightmare Alley* and swashbuckling through *Captain from Castile;* the same studio's Cornel Wilde was being romantic in *The Homestretch* and cavalier in *Forever Amber;* Victor, who would have given an interesting account of himself in any of these roles, appeared in *Moss Rose* (Twentieth Century-Fox, 1947). He played an aristocratic soul who is suspected of killing a Cockney chorine in Victorian England. He is blackmailed by the dead girl's friend (Peggy Cummins), hounded by a dapper Scotland Yard detective (Vincent Price), but protected by his distinguished mother (Ethel Barrymore). The killer's trademarks, a moss rose and a Bible, are left at the scene of the killing. The Gregory Ratoff-directed feature reaches a high level of suspense, but it cannot compare with *Kiss of Death* (Twentieth Century-Fox, 1947) which followed.[16]

Within this latter screenplay by Ben Hecht and Charles Lederer, and under Henry Hathaway's direction, Victor turned in the best acting job of his career. As Nick Bianco, a petty thief, he joins a small gang to rob a jewelry store on Christmas Eve so that his family may have Christmas presents. He is caught and sent to prison with the promise from the assistant District Attorney (Brian Donlevy) of a lighter sentence if he will reveal the names of his accomplices. When Nettie (Coleen Gray), a friend, visits him with the news that his wife has killed herself and that his kids are in an orphanage, he rats on the men and is set free.[17] One of the suspects (Richard Widmark) escapes conviction,

---

[16]Fox would remake *Kiss of Death* as a Western, *The Fiend Who Walked the West* (1958), with Hugh O'Brian and Robert Evans respectively in the Mature and Widmark roles.

[17]The footage with Patricia Morison as Nick's wife was cut before the film's release.

With Coleen Gray in *Kiss of Death* (1947)

whereupon he terrorizes Nick, Nettie, and the two children. Nick pleads with him to leave the innocent alone, and sets himself up as bait. He is wounded, but sneering, psychopathic Widmark is caught and convicted.

Widmark, in his screen debut, stole most of the scenes in which he appeared,[18] but as Thomas M. Pryor observed in his *New York Times* review, "Victor Mature has, if you'll pardon the pun, really matured as an actor. . . . There is a depth and a mobility to his present role not heretofore noticeable." *Time* Magazine thought that he "apparently needed nothing all this time but the right kind of role—for once, he has it." If there was any fault to find with Mature's performance as the sensual, animalistic Nick Bianco, it was director Hathaway's persistence in trying to glorify the character's "true" nature, such as when Donlevy's assistant D.A. Di Angelo says of Mature's Nick, "No guy could have kids like that and be a crook."

Victor was cited by the Building and Safety Department of Los Angeles in November, 1947, regarding the zoning requirements of his home. The department charged him with converting his garage into living quarters and building a stairway to a sundeck, both of which were contrary to zoning laws. He claimed that structural alterations

---

[18]For many years, Widmark's screen career would revolve around this type of role.

were done to provide living space for a buddy from the Coast Guard, Bud Evans and his wife, Ella. The department agreed not to seek a complaint against Victor when he confirmed he would obtain a building permit for a second garage.

Although Victor did not go over to RKO as planned for Dore Schary's *Crossfire* (1947), with Robert Ryan and Robert Mitchum, he did remain at Fox for a Western called *Fury at Furnace Creek* (1948). This unengaging tale required him to twirl six-shooters and look excessively arrogant while avenging the Apache massacre at Furnace Creek, arranged by three ne'er-do-wells (Albert Dekker, Fred Clark, and Roy Roberts). Coleen Gray was on hand to provide a mild romantic interlude between raids, brawls, and shootings.

While Victor was nearing the completion of his next film, *The Law and Martin Rome,* he was injured when a piece of heavy machinery that was being transported on the "New York" street set toppled to the ground at his feet. A doctor quickly determined that the toes of one foot were broken. Mature performed his remaining scenes with the cameras focused above his ankles.

In a title change, the film hit the screen as *Cry of the City* (Twentieth Century-Fox, 1948), with Victor as a New York policeman in pursuit of Martin Rome (Richard Conte), a childhood friend who has murdered a cop. Directed by Robert Siodmak, it is a realistic cops-and-robbers

With Ken Christy and Fred Clark in *Cry of the City* (1948)

447

hunt set against the starkness of New York City. Filmed in black and white, it is a page from the theme of *Manhattan Melodrama* (MGM, 1934). A. Weiler wrote in the *New York Times* that Victor, "an actor once suspected of limited talents, turns in a thoroughly satisfying job as the sincere and kindly cop." [There were plans to team Victor with his *Cry of the City* co-star Coleen Gray in yet another remake of *Seventh Heaven,* but nothing came of this 1948 project.]

In Yuma, Arizona, on Saturday, February 28, 1948, five days after completing work on *Cry of the City,* Victor married a non-professional, the blonde and pretty Dorothy Stanford Berry. They had met the previous summer at Laguna Beach, and Dorothy later recalled, "I thought he was wonderful. Right from the first! It may not have been love at first sight, but he was so alive and exciting! And, we seemed to enjoy all the same things." The marriage was performed by a justice of the peace and witnessed by Bud and Ella Evans; Dorothy wore a white gabardine dress which Victor had given her. He wore a blue sport shirt, a blue sport coat with tan slacks and over-sized white tennis shoes that afforded comfort for his healing toes. After a two-day honeymoon at the Del Mar Hotel in Yuma, they returned to West Los Angeles, where they were joined by Dorothy's son of her previous marriage, five-year-old Mike. Dorothy remarked a few days after the wedding, "All I can think is that my life before Vic must have been a very empty existence."

In July, 1948, Mature was named by Lucia Carroll Schroeder in the case of her divorce from Carl Schroeder, Victor's former roommate. Mrs. Schroeder stated, "Victor Mature had the habit of calling him day or night. He'd go right over. On Christmas day, 1946, Victor Mature called in the middle of the day and he [Carl] left and was gone all afternoon and evening."

A few months later in October, 1948, Victor was selected by the International Artists Committee as one of the five most virile men in America. (His weight that year reached an all-time high for him—232 pounds.) On December 2, 1948, his voice was heard on CBS radio in "The Hallmark Playhouse" presentation of *Old Man Minick,* narrated by host and author James Hilton.

For his overdue loanout to RKO, Victor showed up in 1949's *Easy Living* (originally entitled *Interference)* as an aging professional gridiron hero whose selfish, overambitious wife (Lizabeth Scott) prevents him from accepting a secure job as a college coach.[19] Ordered, due to a heart condition, to quit throwing the pigskin, he slugs his pretty wife and tells her that she will play ball his way and accompany him to a small town, or else! She goes, but no one in the audience really cared who did what to whom by the end of the dull seventy-seven-

[19]For an interesting comparison of performances, the reader is referred to Charlton Heston's enactment of an aging football star in *Number One* (United Artists, 1969).

minute feature. Seen in supporting roles were Lucille Ball as the faithful sports club secretary and Sonny Tufts as the halfback's best pal.

Right after *Easy Living* came *Red, Hot and Blue* (1949),[20] which Victor made on loanout to Paramount. He appeared in a role that had been rejected by Ray Milland. First entitled *The Broadway Story,* then *Restless Angel,* the script has Victor as an arty stage director struggling to make a name for himself and to overcome the notoriety of having dizzy showgirl Eleanor Collier (Betty Hutton) as his girlfriend. Mature's serious-minded Danny James is aghast when Hutton's Eleanor gets involved in a (comedy) gangland murder and must fight her way through mobster complications with the help of bemused Mature. The rambunctious blonde bombshell had four Frank Loesser tunes to belt out (including "Hamlet" and "I Wake up in the Morning Feeling Fine"), which allowed Mature plenty of time to relax between numbers. Although the Damon Runyon-like film was of little consequence, Mature offered a more than adequate interpretation in his straight-guy characterization, supplying "some substance to support the fuss-'n-feathers script" (*Variety*).

Mature's *Red, Hot and Blue* Paramount deal had come about because he was already on the Marathon Street lot for *Samson and Deli-*

[20]In no way related to the 1936 Broadway offering of the same title which had starred Ethel Merman and Jimmy Durante.

With June Havoc and Jane Nigh in *Red, Hot and Blue* **(1949)**

449

lah (1949), which had already been filmed, but was released after the Betty Hutton musical.

Screen epics had always been Cecil B. DeMille's forte. In the mid-1930s he had planned to film the story of Samson and Delilah with Henry Wilcoxon and Miriam Hopkins starred, but these plans were dropped, partially because he was unable to substantiate the meeting of the Old Testament muscle man and the delectable temptress. Then, he discovered Vladimir Jabotinsky's book, *Judge and Fool,* which described Delilah as the younger sister of the Philistine beauty Semadar, who had rejected Samson's marriage proposal. DeMille convinced Paramount to acquire the screen rights to the novel at a cost of $5,000, and set about composing a screenplay with Jesse L. Lasky, Jr. and Frederic M. Frank.

Burt Lancaster, the Hal B. Wallis-Paramount contractee, had been DeMille's tentative choice as Samson, but he was rejected after DeMille viewed *Kiss of Death* and took measure of Mature's acting as well as his girth. He borrowed him from Fox for the sum of $100,000 (half went to Victor), but was horrified, at an undressing of his newest star, to find that he had bought the services of an over-weight actor whose muscles had turned to flab. Immediately, Victor was dispatched to the Paramount gym where he underwent weeks of intensive training with a physical conditioner named Joe Davies, to whom DeMille paid $250 weekly. In November, 1948, soon after the filming began, Victor bared his torso for Hedda Hopper and said, "Get a load of Samson. Darryl Zanuck won't recognize me when I get back on the home lot. I've lost eighteen pounds [bringing his weight down to 214 pounds] and I've learned to throw those biceps."

From the start of production, DeMille referred to *Samson and Delilah* as "a story of the power of prayer," a tag line that became the feature's motto. However, whatever prayers DeMille uttered asking that courage be bestowed upon Victor in facing a real lion in controlled combat were not powerful enough to be heard. Mature flatly refused to grapple with a live lion and said, "Look, C.B., there's only one Mature and I would hate to see him go this way."[21] Against DeMille's better judgment ("I never use stuffed animals in my pictures if it can be helped"), the lion that Victor met in combat, indeed, came from a taxidermist. The scene, filmed on a closed set, with guards posted at all doors to prevent leakage of DeMille's embarrassing compromise, began with a live, snarling, "tame" lion's appearance on top of a rock. When Samson is handed a spear by Delilah (Hedy Lamarr), he says, "I don't need that. He's only a young lion." At the film's New York opening, the dialog line was met with gales of laughter. Against his wishes,

---

[21]Back in 1919 DeMille had similar problems with another star, Gloria Swanson, who, in *Male and Female* (Paramount), refused to allow a heavily sedated lion to lightly paw her, until the director bribed the actress with some expensive jewelry.

With Hedy Lamarr in *Samson and Delilah* (1949)

In *Samson and Delilah*

451

DeMille was forced to delete it from the final release print. Hedy Lamarr, in her 1966 Bartholomew House autobiography *Ecstasy and Me,* wrote: "Once, when I thought Victor was upstaging me—which, with his great size, was always a problem—I complained to Mr. DeMille. 'Victor always works it so that it's his face and my back to the camera, and you are not using reverse shots.' The director knew how to mollify me on that point : 'Do you think there are any men in America who would rather look at his face than your ass?' "

The film's release on October 21, 1949, was accompanied by a nationwide promotional fete that included the packaging by Kellogg Foods of cornflakes boxes bearing photographs of Victor in his revealing Samson costume.

Despite the criticism of such journals as the weekly *Variety* ("It's a fantastic picture for this era in its size, in its lavishness, in the corniness of its story telling and in its old-fashioned technique"), the public took to the film—to the tune of $11.5 million in distributors' domestic rentals. *Variety* further said of Victor's character, "For the kids, Samson is the greatest invention since Superman." For nightclub comedians, this Biblical epic provided the basis for many jokes, one of the more famous being, *"Samson and Delilah* proves one thing for certain: Victor Mature has a bigger chest than Hedy Lamarr." The colossal film and its comic-strip role may have given Victor's screen career new impetus, but it was a part that he has not yet been able to live down.

Offcamera, Victor went into the retail television business. From his dressing room (where he frequently lived whenever things got emotionally rough at home), he sold television sets at discount prices. In spite of his unconventional carryings-on throughout much of his Fox days, he confided to Aljean Harmetz in a 1971 interview in the *New York Times,* "I took acting five times as seriously as anyone else. I just couldn't show it. Some kind of complex, I guess. In the car, driving to a premiere, I used to be scared to death. Then the door opened and I would leap out, going like ape dung."

Of course, there were those writers and co-workers who considered Mature to be nothing more than a conceited ham. "I'm not really like that," he told J. Marks of *Interview* in 1972, and added: "It's my face, you see. I just have the kind of expression which makes me look as if I smelled something bad. When I used to walk into a room, unless I was wearing a great big smile, I always looked bored or self-impressed. But, to the contrary, I was generally scared. In fact, the trouble with my whole career was that I didn't stand up and say my piece like Bette Davis and other stars like that who really fought the studios and got what they wanted. Me, I was the very model of a modern major studio-owned star, doing what I was told to do and keeping my mouth shut."

To columnist Sheilah Graham, in 1949, he confessed, "I'd like to leave this picture business with $250,000. Half a million would be even better." Miss Graham named him as one of her ten favorite male stars because: "His gaiety is infectious. His energy is irresistible. He never makes plans. I love Victor because he's such a crazy, attractive, friendly son-of-a-gun."

By 1950, the bliss of the wedded Matures had degenerated into a relationship wrought with arguments and separations. One Hollywood fan magazine columnist gave an opinion: "Friends of the Vic Matures fear their near break-up may be the last."[22]

"You couldn't buy me a back scratcher if I had the seven-year itch," Betty Grable smartly informs Victor in *Wabash Avenue* (Twentieth Century-Fox, 1950) as she, a shimmy dancer in old Chicago, refuses the favors of the gambler he portrays. Later, when she lays a slap across his smug face, he says, "You enjoy doing that don't you?" This fast-paced musical remake of Grable's *Coney Island* (Twentieth Century-Fox, 1943), with Victor and Phil Harris in roles previously played by George Montgomery and Cesar Romero, has a plot that is played for fun and is not to be taken seriously. In the fourth Grable-Mature outing, Betty scampered through the ninety-two colorful minutes aided by

[22]Mrs. Mature sued for divorce in 1949, but there was a reconciliation, and she dismissed the action. After one of their quarrels in November, 1949, Victor admitted, "I've been in the doghouse all week, but that's par for us, you know. I didn't dream this was going to happen. She was home with me last night. . . . I'm certainly surprised."

With Betty Grable and Phil Harris in *Wabash Avenue* (1950)

453

such Mack Gordon-Josef Myrow tunes as "Down on Wabash Avenue" and the titillating "May I Tempt You with a Big Red Apple?" Ben Gage again performed Victor's soundtrack vocalizing.

After making a token guest star appearance in *I'll Get By* (Twentieth Century-Fox, 1950), an updated musical remake of the company's *Tin Pan Alley* (1940), Victor joined with Ann Sheridan in *Stella* (Twentieth Century-Fox, 1950). In this modest comedy, he is one of the few sane people involved in the dizzy scheme of a dizzy family to cash in on the double indemnity insurance policy of a boozed-up uncle. As the insurance investigator Victor falls in love with Ann, the daughter in the loony clan. The family's antics are orchestrated by brother-in-law Carl (David Wayne), who has buried the uncle in an old Indian cemetery, thus making the uncle's remains not so easily extractable. Carl then provides a "stand-in" for the dead man. Although Victor and Miss Sheridan shared top billing honors, their roles were actually supporting Wayne.

Back in 1947, RKO had decided to rehash the Cary Grant-Laraine Day feature, *Mr. Lucky* (1943), and to disguise the revamping, had acquired the rights to a gangster story. The amalgam was geared to be Victor's 1948 studio picture. However, career-conscious Victor was wary of the script as it stood, and made *Easy Living* instead. When RKO revived the project for the 1950 releasing season, Mature was still dissatisfied with the scenario and went on suspension in January of

With Ann Sheridan and Leif Erickson in *Stella* (1950)

In *Gambling House* (1950)

that year, rather than abide by Fox's ultimatum that he report to the RKO soundstages or else. RKO eventually agreed to rewrite the script to Mature's requirements, and the film, *Gambling House* (1950), was produced and released. In it he was foreign-born crook Marc Fury, who is acquitted of a murder rap, but is then threatened with deportation. Social worker Terry Moore enters his life and convinces him that being a law-abiding American is the nearest thing to heaven. He disavows his underworld connections and really becomes her all-American. The film was a long eighty minutes of melodramatic folderol.

Eleven months were to pass before he appeared in another film; during his screen absence he discovered the profitability of investing in real estate.

Back on the screen for Howard Hughes' RKO release, *The Las Vegas Story* (1952), he is a deputy sheriff involved with Jane Russell, Hughes' buxom darling of the crooked-mouth pout and the sometimes-whiney voice. Alone and together, they come into contact with murder, dice tables, Hoagy Carmichael, and Vincent Price. However, Russell's song, "My Resistance is Low," Carmichael's chirping of his own novelty tune, "The Monkey Song," and an extended helicopter-car chase did little to lighten this leaden screen offering.

It was more out of expediency than out of a desire on Victor's part that he appeared in *Androcles and the Lion* (RKO, 1952). George Bernard Shaw's one-hour play had been staged several times (in 1915, 1925, and 1946—it would be staged again in 1968). When it was an-

455

With Jean Simmons in *Androcles and the Lion* (1952)

nounced that the play would be filmed, Howard Hughes allowed producer Gabriel Pascal and director-co-adaptor Chester Erskine their
freedom in assembling the cast.[23] However, the casting would undergo
several changes from Pascal's and Erskine's original choices. At first,
Rex Harrison was chosen to play Caesar, Jean Simmons to play Lavinia, Dana Andrews for the Captain, Robert Newton to portray Ferrovius, and—in a bit of unique casting—Harpo Marx was the choice for
Androcles. But when the film was five weeks in production, the eccentric billionaire Hughes had a brainstorm; he had seen comedian Alan
Young on television and decided that he, instead of Marx, would be
ideal as Androcles. The filming was stopped to accommodate this casting change, and by the time production could resume, Rex Harrison
was no longer available. He was replaced by Maurice Evans, and when
filming finally got underway again, the new cast included Victor in the
role of the Captain[24] and Elsa Lanchester as Megaera, as well as Jean
Simmons, Robert Newton, Evans, and Young.

From almost any angle, *Androcles and the Lion* was unsatisfactory
screen fare. One of the chief faults was that by extending the story from
one hour to ninety-eighty minutes, the plodding scenarists allowed the

---

[23]In 1933, Samuel Goldwyn had announced that Eddie Cantor would star in a screen
version of the Shaw comedy.
[24]At one point, James Donald was cast as the Roman Captain.

script to become "vulgar and shallow" (*Saturday Review*). As a motion picture, the satirical account of the Christian tailor, Androcles (Young), who earns lasting devotion from a lion from whose paw he has removed a thorn, was protracted and overly-cute, as well as replete with technical flaws. Miss Simmons as the Christian girl Lavinia, whom Victor loves and wins, was the film's saving grace. As for Mature's performance, he "plays the handsome Roman captain as if he were captain of a college eleven, and on the losing side at that" (*Saturday Review*).

Because Zanuck's Twentieth Century-Fox had such an overabundance of home-grown and borrowed male leads the top executives were perfectly willing to continue lending out Mature's screen services to any studio that put in a decent bid. MGM borrowed Victor for what was to be Esther Williams' most lavish Technicolor swim-musical, *Million Dollar Mermaid* (1952). During the life story of Australian-born Annette Kellerman (Williams), Victor, as James Sullivan, an American carnival promoter, meets the former polio victim in London after she has become the amateur swim champion of New South Wales. As a publicity stunt, he persuades her to swim twenty-six miles down the Thames River. Then they go to New York, but fail to get the desired Hippodrome booking. She finds notoriety of a different sort in Boston

With Esther Williams and Thomas P. Dillon in *Million Dollar Mermaid* (1952)

457

when she is arrested for indecent exposure in a swimsuit that is far removed from the swim fashion of the period. The publicity proves to be a springboard to success and she achieves her goal of appearing at the mammoth Hippodrome. When she shows more than a passing interest in the theatre's manager (David Brian), Mature's jealous James Sullivan departs for Hollywood. She, too, winds up in Hollywood where she suffers a severe accident on a studio set. Sullivan, now the promoter of a canine movie star, persuades her to regain her career confidence as well as her affections for him. Busby Berkeley conceived and directed two of Miss Williams' above-water ballet numbers, the most spectacular and unforgettable of which was produced with colored smoke streams.[25]

Back at Twentieth, Victor received a leftover casting assignment as a bureaucratic Washington lobbyist in *Something for the Birds* (1952), a supposed comedy that struggled along on half a wing. He befriends Patricia Neal, badly miscast as a sort of early-day ecologist intent on saving the birds of California from extinction.

Victor began 1953 at Twentieth in the role of an American Army lieutenant of Greek parentage in *Glory Brigade,* doing battle on behalf of the United Nations forces in Korea. He is bitterly opposed to the leader (Alexander Scourby) of the infantrymen from Greece, whom he blames for the loss of a platoon. Lee Marvin, also in the cast, commented twenty years later to Ron Caylor of the *National Enquirer,* "I spent most of the filming with my hands over my eyes, hoping nobody would recognize me, it was so bad."

---

[25]Extracts from this sequence are a highlight of *That's Entertainment* (United Artists, 1974).

In *The Glory Brigade* (1953)

At RKO, for *Affair with a Stranger* (1953), Mature was required to play "comedy" with Jean Simmons. Neither of them did well in Richard Flournoy's trite screenplay. In this pallid tale, told mostly through flashback, Victor's Bill Blakeley is revealed as a playwright who would rather gamble than do anything else. He persuades his serious-minded wife-model Carolyn (Simmons), to support him until he makes the big times. His play opens the night their baby dies, and when they adopt a child later, Simmons' Carolyn devotes all her attention to it. To be polite as possible about the matter, Victor was not credible as the arched-brow dramatist. One of the film's few passable moments occurs when Monica Lewis, as the siren of the piece, sings "Kiss and Run."

After four screen roles that threatened to stagnate his acting career, Victor was chosen by producer Frank Ross to fill the number three star slot in Twentieth's super-colossal *The Robe* (1953). Adapted from the Lloyd C. Douglas best-selling novel[26] and directed by Henry Koster, it was the first feature to be filmed in CinemaScope, advertised as "the new dimensional photographic marvel you see without glasses!" This process was further heralded as the "greatest step forward in entertain-

[26]The 1942 novel would be in its sixtieth printing of the English edition by the time of the 1953 picturization; Ross had been planning the film since the mid-1940s, but wartime restrictions on production held up the then RKO project.

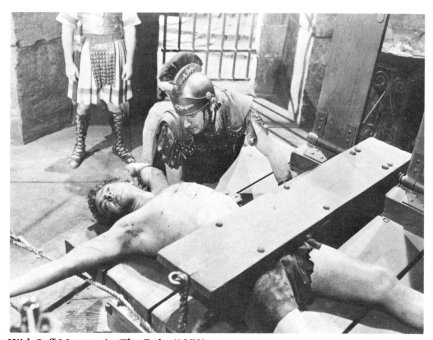

With Jeff Morrow in *The Robe* (1953)

459

ment history" because of its miracle mirror screen (usually sixty-eight by twenty-four feet), Stereophonic Sound, and Anamorphic Lens.

Victor, described by Bosley Crowther in the *New York Times* as "muscular and moody," is Demetrius, the Greek slave of Marcellus Gallio (Richard Burton) and a convert to the teachings of Jesus. A loyal and dedicated believer in Christ, Demetrius is later joined in his belief by his Roman tribune-master who was in charge of the crucifixion. Gallio later becomes obsessed with Christ's robe after placing it about his shoulders. Jean Simmons, in her third appearance with Mature, is the lovely Roman lady, Diana,[27] smitten with love for Burton's Gallio.

Nominated for Academy Awards in several categories, including Best Picture and Best Actor (Burton), the film garnered only a few in the final voting (art direction-set direction; costume design, and color). When asked by J. Marks of *Interview,* in 1972, if he resented never having won an Oscar, Victor replied, "Not really. I didn't deserve one to tell you the truth. . . . When I finally did something which a lot of people considered excellent—mean[ing] my role as Demetrius in *The Robe,* Zanuck repeatedly refused to put me up for the nomination as Best Supporting Actor because he insisted that there were no supporting actors in *The Robe*—only stars. That was the only thing I ever really liked seeing myself on the screen." Mike Connolly of the *Hollywood Reporter* also liked it and even had predicted in January, 1954, that both Victor and Jean Simmons would receive Oscar nominations.

Look Magazine predicted, "*The Robe* promises to be the picture that leads Hollywood out of the desert into the rich vineyards." It certainly proved a bonanza for Twentieth Century-Fox, eventually gaining[28] for the studio $17.5 million in U.S.-Canadian distributors' rentals alone. It certainly revitalized Mature's career, leading some Hollywood jokesters to quip that in the new era CinemaScope, he was the only actor big enough to fill the big screen.

Just prior to the release of *The Robe* (on September 16, 1953), Victor, a golf fanatic by then, applied for a membership to the Los Angeles Country Club; he was told by a board member that the club did not accept actors. Kiddingly, Victor replied, "Hell, I'm no actor and I've got twenty-eight pictures and a scrapbook of reviews to prove it." The release of *The Robe* and the excellent reviews the film garnered for him belied that ironic comment.

A month later, to capitalize on Victor's prominence in *The Robe,* Universal released *The Veils of Bagdad* (1953) for which he had been borrowed earlier. Across the sands of Palm Springs, he swashed into action as a muscular palace guard in sixteenth-century Bagdad. In

---

[27]At one point in the 1940s, Ingrid Bergman was the choice for this coveted assignment.

[28]It reportedly cost $4.5 million to make, and was later sold to television for a two-million-dollar fee, making its video debut on Easter Sunday, March 26, 1967, on NBC-TV.

In *The Veils of Bagdad* (1953)

colorful costumes, he turns the heads of Mari Blanchard and Virginia Field, but what was required to match his zest was a leading lady of the Maria Montez mold. That sort of screen combination, had it ever materialized, might have proved very interesting.

Dangerous Mission (1954), one of RKO's inexpensive offerings, came next. Filmed in 3-D on location at Montana's Glacier National Park, it is the account of a sensitive girl (Piper Laurie) who has witnessed a big city murder. She flees west, with the villain (Vincent Price) and a New York policeman (Victor) hot in pursuit. The scenery received the best notices in this celluloid offering, which concluded his RKO obligations.[29]

Although he was now the successful owner of a chain of television stores in southern California, Victor was glum over his artistically low-keyed acting career and rented a house for two months at Rancho Santa Fe, California, near San Diego, close to what is considered to be one of the best golf courses in the West. Golfing had developed into a major love of his life when he had been recuperating from a leg injury in which most of the ligaments had been torn. Mature had not been at the rented house for a week when fourteen telephone calls came from Twentieth asking that he return to Hollywood at once to re-assume the

---

[29]He had been scheduled to go to RKO for the Dick Powell-directed *Split Second* (1953), but work on *The Glory Brigade* prevented the loanout.

role of Demetrius in Frank Ross' sequel to *The Robe.* A writer for *Silver Screen* Magazine proclaimed, "Vic galloped back faster than you can say $5,000 a week."

Demetrius and the Gladiators (1954), also in CinemaScope, began with the final scene from *The Robe,* showing Burton and Miss Simmons (both unbilled) walking to their martyred deaths. As a prisoner of the Romans, Demetrius is drafted to serve at the school for gladiators, headed by the brutal Strabo (Ernest Borgnine). He is severely abused and kicked about, until he encounters ravishing, titian-haired Messalina (Susan Hayward), the wife of Emperor Claudius (Barry Jones). She takes the sensitive brute to her hide-away villa, where they engage in 1954-style tempestuous abandon. Eventually, Demetrius mends his errant ways, but apparently too soon, for this sequel grossed only $4.25 million in distributors' domestic rentals.

Zanuck was so impressed by the new boxoffice potential of the historical epic,[30] that he lavished a reported five-million-dollar budget[31] on the screen version of Mika Waltari's *The Egyptian* (1954). To play

---

[30]MGM had its *Valley of the Kings* (1954), Warner Bros. delivered *Land of the Pharoahs* (1955), Universal offered *Abbott and Costello Meet the Mummy* (1955), and Columbia toyed with *Joseph and His Brethren,* which was to have starred Rita Hayworth, and, via Paramount, Cecil B. DeMille produced and directed a remake of *The Ten Commandments* (1956).

[31]A good deal of the budget was expended on the 67 sets. The $605,000 devoted to the "environs" included a throne room ($85,000), the temple of Aton ($78,000), the Valley of the King set ($75,000), Thebes waterfront street ($60,000), Hefer's quarters ($60,000), women's quarters at the palace ($55,000), Sinuhe's dispensary ($20,000), the littlest Royal Princess' nursery ($15,000).

With Susan Hayward in *Demetrius and the Gladiators* (1954)

With Edmund Purdom and Michael Wilding in *The Egyptian* (1954)

the title role of Sinuhe, director Michael Curtiz brought in Britain's Edmund Purdom, a comparative newcomer to the screen. It is doubtful whether Marlon Brando, originally cast as Sinuhe (he walked out on the production), could have done much better than Purdom with the ill-conceived role; the Philip Dunne-Case Robinson screenplay told an uneven and drifting story.[32] Much public and private discussion revolved around Zanuck's "discovery," Bella Darvi, who was assigned the pivotal, demanding role of Nefer the Babylonian courtesan, and the fact that Gene Tierney, in a sort of miniature film comeback, was portraying the regal Baketamon. There was also talk that Victor, as Horemheb, lifelong friend of the ruler (Michael Wilding), has "a chance to show his knees again." (*New York Post*)

Set fourteen centuries before the birth of Christ, the film, despite its eye-catching and gaudy sets, costumes and hordes of extras, "has an almost unavoidable remoteness that prevents the viewer from identifying himself from the characters involved." (*New York Herald-Tribune*) At heart, the lead characters were not a very engaging lot: starry-eyed Wilding engulfed by his passion for a one-god religious system; spiteful Tierney eager to revenge Purdom's rejection of her by cavort-

---

[32]Told in flashback, the exiled Sinuhe writes his story, stating: "Soon the jackals and vultures will make a poor meal of me but nothing can silence the voice in my heart. For I, Sinuhe, am one with all humanity. I shall live in human tears and laughter, in justice and injustice, in weakness and strength. As a human being I shall live eternally in mankind."

ing with virile, opportunistic Mature; Simmons, a pure peasant girl, whose devotion to Purdom almost leads her astray from her religious pursuits (she ends up dying when her religious sect is suppressed); young doctor Purdom who trifles with courtesan Darvi and regal Tierney, but actually loves Simmons; aggrandizing Mature who aims to take the throne away from epileptic Pharoah Wilding; and Peter Ustinov as a scalawag and one-time slave, now a servant of Purdom.[33]

Mature appreciated his stepped-up salary at Fox, but he could hardly take *The Egyptian* seriously. He jokingly announced that the role of Horemheb was "the greatest switcheroo of my recent career," explaining that in both *The Robe* and *Demetrius and the Gladiators* he was a "man who put God above country," while in *The Egyptian* he puts "country above God." When not engaged in the film's action sequences—one of the highlights was the Mature-Purdom lion hunting expedition as they careened over the terrain in their chariot—Victor had Riviera golf pro Willie Hunter on the set for some extracurricular sports coaching. In fact, on one Sunday off during the filming of *The Egyptian,* Mature won the pro-amateur golf championship at the Long Beach municipal golf course.

When *The Egyptian* produced distributors' domestic rentals of only $4.25 million, Zanuck abandoned plans to film *Egypt by Three,* which would have continued the exploits of Mature and Tierney on the Egyptian throne.

On loan to MGM, Victor's next film was *Betrayed* (1954), much of which was filmed on location in Holland. In a rather absurd way, it relates the story of Dutch resistance fighters during the German occupation of 1943, whose leader is known as "The Scarf" (Victor). The London authorities assign a radio operator (brunette Lana Turner) to "The Scarf," to establish closer Allied coordination. "Tell London to go coordinate their cockroaches," he says defiantly. Disguised as a Nazi officer, he takes Lana, who happens to be a former German collaborator, to his headquarters, where he consistently calls her "dear." "If you don't trust anyone, they can never betray you," he informs her before dashing off to visit his mother (Nora Swinburne). He is angered at finding his mama with her head shaved, the price paid for alleged collaboration with the Nazis. When he discovers that she was unjustly charged and punished, he sends word to London, "Tell them I'll fight

---

[33]In *Ustinov in Focus (Tartivy Press, 1971)* Tony Thomas quotes Ustinov on his recollections of this picture. "I could barely keep a straight face. Michael Wilding was dressed in white robes and a huge conical hat, looking like a big salt shaker. If someone had said, 'Pass the salt,' a giant would have passed Michael Wilding. I told him this and from then on he couldn't play his part for laughing. I felt very guilty. Poor Victor Mature was always leaping into chariots and galloping off into Death Valley. He had to say absurd lines like, 'No lips of mine will ever touch this chalice.' I don't think anybody would ever say that. I would much rather hear, 'Take the filthy cup back.' It was all very silly."

like I've never fought before," and becomes a spy for the Third Reich. When Lana informs a Dutch intelligence officer (Clark Gable) of the switch in allegiance, he and a guard shoot "The Scarf." *Betrayed* was as outmoded in its entertainment values as the lack lustre pairing of the once sparkling Turner-Gable love team (which first surfaced in *Honky Tonk*, MGM, 1941.

Victor had definitely passed out of his Biblical film phase, but he was still to appear in costume pictures. He was loaned to Universal-International as *Chief Crazy Horse* (1955). On viewing the product, Bosley Crowther (*New York Times*) observed, "Mr. Mature stalks grimly and grandly, with his head up and nostrils flanged, looking less like a flesh-and-blood Indian than like one of a cigar-store tribe." A prediction within the Dakota-Sioux tribe was that one of their youths would grow up to become a great chief and win a stunning victory over the ever-expanding white man. Throughout the tale, Crazy Horse believes he is that person, and sure enough, he defeats Yellow Hair Custer at Little Big Horn. Later, he is done in by his own tribesman, Little Big Man (Ray Danton).

Back at Twentieth, Victor rejected a co-starring role in the Tyrone Power-Susan Hayward action feature, *Untamed* (1955),[34] but he did agree to star in the Richard Fleischer-directed *Violent Saturday* (1955),

---

[34]Richard Egan replaced him in the part.

With Keith Larsen in *Chief Crazy Horse* (1955)

about the carefully planned heist of a bank in an Arizona mining town. The robbery, engineered on a typically peaceful Saturday at noon by three cold-blooded crooks (portrayed by Lee Marvin, Stephen McNally, and J. Carrol Naish) irrevocably affects the lives of certain townspeople. Victor is the Arizonian family man who proves to be the hero. During the filming of *Violent Saturday,* he was incapacitated for a few days with severe "lumbo-sacro strain" suffered when he smashed into a door while dodging moving props on the set.

Violent Saturday also represented his final screen work for Twentieth Century-Fox. It ended a liaison of fifteen years and nineteen Fox features, of which only some five are really worth remembering. Like fellow actor Tyrone Power, who also would soon depart the lot, Victor and the studio had drained one another nearly dry of possible variations in casting. Particularly under the forthcoming Buddy Adler regime at Fox, the celluloid product would be geared to the younger filmgoer, and feature less mature players such as Robert Wagner, Jeffrey Hunter, Don Murray, Bradford Dillman, Tony Randall, Pat Boone, and Cameron Mitchell.

In 1955, Victor was again sued for divorce. On November 8, Dorothy Berry Mature, in a Santa Monica courtroom, was awarded a default divorce consisting of a $500,000 settlement.[35] Her attorney revealed

---

[35]The couple had separated, finally, on August 13, 1954. On December 3, 1954, she obtained a $1200 monthly temporary alimony pending trial of the divorce suit.

In *Violent Saturday* (1955)

466

that Mature's earnings included $2,750 a week, as well as an additional $25,000 a year from stocks and bonds. Dorothy informed the court, "Nine-tenths of my married life has been spent waiting for Mr. Mature to come home."

Although he was thirty-nine years old—a dangerous age for any screen leading man—Victor was still in excellent physical condition. If he could no longer command a leading spot at a major studio, there were the lesser film houses which welcomed his acting services. He rejected the obvious opportunities that television and a lucrative video series would provide (it would be too much work), and instead chose to negotiate a six-film pact with United Artists which extended over a five-year period and allowed Victor's production company to participate in the proceeds.

Interspersed with his United Artists ventures were several action entries for Harry Cohn's Columbia Pictures. He appeared as a trapper turned cavalry scout in *The Last Frontier* (1956), with Guy Madison and Robert Preston, each of whom was also trying to hold onto sagging movie careers, and Anne Bancroft who was still attempting to find her slot in the acting trade. Anthony Mann directed this soldier-versus-Indians feature with little distinction. *Safari* (Columbia, 1956), filmed in Africa by Warwick Productions of Britain, was a Western-type story set in the Kenya Bush country. Victor is a hunter whose family is done in by the Mau Mau's, but he overcomes their evil plot and wins the hand of stern Janet Leigh. In *The Sharkfighters* (United Artists, 1956), most of which was filmed off the coast of Cuba, Mature is a U.S. Naval lieutenant commander who has maintained a personal vendetta against sharks. His destroyer sank during World War II and his crew had been devoured by the hungry scavenger fish. "Sharks got lousy table manners," he tells us, and takes to the ocean waters with knife in hand in a futile attempt to exterminate them all.

Even though his celebrity heydays of the 1940s were long gone, Victor was still good news copy. He confided to the press on the subject of matrimony, "The trouble is that I can't get along without a wife, and when I have one, I can't live with her."

From the Cuba location sites of *The Sharkfighters*, Victor journeyed to England to join Warwick Productions for four films, all released in the United States by Columbia on double-bill programs. It was ironic that at this later stage in his career he finally would be playing a wide variety of action leads. In *Zarak* (1956), lensed in England, India, and Burma, he had the title role, a goatee, a turban, and buxom Anita Ekberg. He portrayed a bad man of India who plagues the British with his marauding sorties.

The Ken Hughes-directed *The Long Haul* (Columbia, 1957) was a far more sturdy film project than most of Mature's efforts at this time. Filmed in England and Scotland, it told of an American ex-G.I. (Vic-

With Anita Ekberg in *Zarak* (1957)

tor) whose British wife (Diana Dors) maneuvers him into settling down near her parents in Liverpool. Then, because of her ambitious dreams, she persuades him to pursue several lucrative and dishonest pastimes. One rather harrowing segment of the film details a frenzied truck drive along narrow stony street sides. Said *Variety* of Mature's performance, "[He] makes a convincing figure of the straight-forward guy who turns cheat on his wife and his work."

Pickup Alley (a.k.a., *Interpol,* Columbia, 1957) kept the actor in modern surroundings. Paired again with Anita Ekberg, Victor is the U.S. narcotics agent in search of a dope-smuggling ring, and especially eager to capture the crazed killer (Trevor Howard) of his sister. The locales switch from New York to London to Lisbon, on to Rome and then back to New York, all of which helped spark the action in this ninety-two minute programmer.

While Mature was in England plying his acting craft, he also managed to create a few (anti)social headlines of his own. *Confidential* Magazine, in its May, 1957 issue, took delight in detailing "Victor Mature's Lost Weekend with a Babe." The luridly-phrased article alleged that on the weekend of September 29, 1956, while in his apartment on Grosvenor Square in London, he "entertained"—nonstop—a young blonde woman named Maxine Lee. A further installment in *Confidential* suggested that on a later occasion, one of Mature's would-be playmates was not a curvaceous lovely, but a boy dressed in drag as a prank.

Mature returned to Hollywood in 1958 to work under the direction of Frank Borzage, the noted craftsman who had been professionally idle for nearly a decade. The project was *China Doll* (United Artists, 1958), a somewhat poignant and offbeat love story of World War II.[36] As an Air Force captain in China, he becomes drunk one evening and wakes up the next morning to discover he is the owner of a young Chinese housekeeper (Li Li Hua). When she later becomes pregnant, he weds her. After the birth of a daughter, the wife is killed in an air raid, and the hysterical Mature soon after is shot down in a Japanese raid. While Ward Bond, as Father Cairns, received the best critical notices, *Variety* recorded, "Mature displays his share of love, emotion and humor." Borzage reportedly paid Mature a salary of $125,000 for the picture. Plans for the two industry men to form a joint production company did not come about, nor did Victor's plans to produce a film entitled *Escape from Andersonville* ever reach the planning boards.

Warwick Productions provided Mature with further screen work with *Tank Force!* (a.k.a., *No Time to Die,* Columbia, 1958). Victor's third screen assignment with director Terence Young. It was another World War II tale ("An unsatisfying piece of work in which a great

---

[36]Some critics were particularly tough on this often touching drama: "This is a far-fetched, very sentimental, tear-jerking story that cannot stand critical scrutiny" (Archer Winsten, *New York Post*). Paul V. Beckley (*New York Herald Tribune*) made the interesting side comment in his review, "I have too much respect for him [Mature] to relish seeing him in such an ungainly piece.

With Luciana Paluzzi in *Tank Force* (1958)

deal of effort seems to have gone astray through unimaginative writing and direction. There have been too many first-class war films for there to be room for inferior stuff," *Variety*). This time, Victor is an American serving with a British tank crew and is one of five P.O.W.s who escapes into the Libyan desert where they are betrayed by the Arabs. He is tortured by the Germans, but the group escapes a second time. Only he and his fellow escapee (Anthony Newley) survive to be rescued later by the British.

In another Warwick production, Victor portrayed Kasim Khan, the tribal chieftain of India who becomes *The Bandit of Zhobe* (Columbia, 1959). He turns outlaw when his wife and child are murdered by Thuggee tribesmen disguised as British soldiers. The Thuggees then murder other British subjects in the name of Kasim. His innocence is revealed by the daughter (Anne Aubrey) of a British major (Norman Wooland), and he dies a hero in defense of the English claims. Even the less discriminating filmgoer could not help note that Victor was indeed too mature and too heavy to play such youthful roles now, especially when he laced his performance with a wooden stoicism that gave his characterization little of the necessary dash and spice.

United Artists' *Escort West* (1959) was shot in California's San Fernando Valley shortly after the completion of *China Doll*. With a semblance of a southern drawl, Victor is a Confederate soldier on his

In *The Bandit of Zhobe* (1959)

With Rhonda Fleming in *The Big Circus* (1959)

way West after the war, accompanied by his daughter (Reba Waters). They meet, among others, the Drury sisters (Elaine Stewart and the ex-Howard Hughes protegée, Faith Domergue) en route to Oregon. Faith dies at the hands of a Modoc Indian, but the others trek on to new horizons. Also in the cast of this "routine, hackneyed" (*Variety*) Western was John Hubbard, another ex-Hal Roach contract player.

Victor may have had hopes for the resurgence of his wobbly career in films with Allied Artists' *The Big Circus* (1959), but much of what he was required to do onscreen had previously been done, and on a far grander scale, by Charlton Heston in DeMille's *The Greatest Show on Earth* (Paramount, 1952) and by Burt Lancaster in *Trapeze* (United Artists, 1956). Nevertheless, *The Big Circus,* with its cast of "big names" (including Red Buttons, Rhonda Fleming, Kathryn Grant, Peter Lorre, David Nelson, and Vincent Price) provides the standard thrills of big top life, even though the story is at best routine. Mature is the owner of the traveling circus which is on the edge of bankruptcy. The problems brought about by his performers, both human and animal, a bank examiner (Buttons), and a press agent (Fleming) do not improve the tense situation. There is also a train wreck which is not as spectacular as DeMille's version, but it sets the stage for the "show must go on" plot. The more somber viewer could only wonder how a circus owner such as Mature could retain his sanity in the midst of such overwhelming odds.

471

If *The Big Circus* did not noticeably improve Victor's industry standing, *Timbuktu* (United Artists, 1959), released before *Circus,* was another setback. The film was released at a time when the vogue for desert films had just about dried up, even for the kiddie trade. About the most that can be said for it is that it's "camp," complete with stock villain (John Dehner), *femme fatale* (Yvonne De Carlo), and hero (Victor).

Nineteen hundred fifty-nine also saw two changes in Victor's personal life. On Feburary 3, in Louisville, Mature's mother, Clara, died after an illness of five years. Then, on September 27, the still matrimonially optimistic actor took a fourth stab at marriage. In Capri, he wed Adrienne Joy Urwick, whom he had met in Europe. Known professionally as Joy Urwick, the actress-daughter of a London physician was twenty-five; Mature was twenty years her senior. Because the Capri marriage vows were not recognized as legal in the United States, the couple were re-wed on December 12, 1959, in Tijuana, Mexico. The Matures took up residence at Rancho Santa Fe, from where Victor stated, "There are seventy-two golf courses in the area and I play golf at least twenty days a month. So, I'm very happy down here."

On December 23, 1959 the FBI arrested an unemployed Chicago factory worker calling herself Mrs. Violet Mature who claimed that Victor was her husband as well as the father of her ten-year-old child. She had written many letters to both Victor and Joy, in which she had

With Yvonne De Carlo in *Timbuktoo* (1959)

472

threatened to disfigure Joy with acid or to shoot her for taking away her "husband." The woman, whose real name was Violet Dembos, was sentenced to jail and to court-ordered psychotherapy.

Victor then sauntered off to Italy, where certain other Hollywood screen personalities had attained a degree of success in cloak-and-sandal quickie features. He enacted *Hannibal* (Warner Bros., 1960) with elephants and Rita Gam in an "epic" that *Variety* ranked "dramatically crude and ponderously paced." Edgar G. Ulmer, long-time low-budget director and something of a cultist favorite, was unable to coax a lifelike performance from Victor, particularly in the romantic sequences. Indeed, Mature might well have studied Howard Keel's manly performance as the famed Alps-crosser Hannibal in the underrated *Jupiter's Darling* (MGM, 1955).

Two years later Mature reappeared on the screen in the 1960 Italian-lensed *The Tartars* (MGM, 1962), in which he was the Viking chief to Orson Welles' chief of the Tartars. The general consensus was that the dubbed film was "trash" (*New York Times*). *Variety* offered a commentary on the two once-upon-a-time stars: "Watching Mature and Welles, one feels the same sense of regret as that inspired by the spectacle of viewing two ex-world-heavyweight champions battling it out on the comeback trail for the Eastern Yugoslavian title."

Following his Italian debacle, Victor announced his retirement with, "I loaf very gracefully. There's a lot to be said about loafing if you know how to do it gracefully."

On December 8, 1964, producer-director Sidney Pink filed a damage suit against Mature for the sum of $1,175,000, charging that the ex-Fox star had maneuvered himself a free trip to Europe by falsely promising to work in a feature to be shot in Spain beginning July, 1964. Pink further alleged that Victor had no intention of starring in the movie, but showed up on the set with a friend, Fred Carlson, whom he wanted to place on the payroll (at one hundred dollars a day) as his double. Victor was summarily replaced by Rory Calhoun in the film, *Finger on the Trigger* (Allied Artists, 1965), but the suit lingered on until December, 1969, when it was settled out of court for less than ten thousand dollars.

In 1966, Victor again traveled to Europe, specifically to Rome, where he worked as an aging, hammy screen idol named Tony Powell in *After the Fox (Caccia Alla Volpe,* United Artists, 1966). His brief return to filmmaking had three positives working for it: Vittorio de Sica as director, a screenplay by Neil Simon (his first), and Peter Sellers as the picture's star. The finished product, unfortunately, was only mildly amusing, with Victor's almost cameo performance the most realistic of the entire cast. Some viewers stated that he was merely playing himself—self-centered, pompous, phony—but whether true or not, his incisive characterization held the attention of the movie viewers.

As *Hannibal* **(1960)**

With Peter Sellers and Martin Balsam in *After the Fox* (1966)

Two years later, he accepted an even smaller role in *Head* (Columbia, 1968), with the little-talented singing quartet called The Monkees. Co-produced and co-scripted by Jack Nicholson, the feature deals with pot and its affects. In his brief film sequence, Victor appears as a giant named The Big Victor whose dandruff problem is caused by The Monkees inhabiting his scalp! His well-publicized appearance in this feckless film only further increased the growing "camp" status of Victor Mature. His acting reputation took another backward slide each time *Samson and Delilah* was reissued in movie theatres or shown on television.

Adrienne Joy Urwick Mature sued for a divorce on Feburary 6, 1969, on the standard ground of "extreme cruelty." Twentieth Century-Fox publicist Johnny Campbell, a friend of Victor's for thirty years, has said, "These gals marry him and think they're going to change his lifestyle, and they don't. He stays the same and they get disillusioned." In interviews, Mature has never made any specific comments about his marital experiences or about any of his ex-wives in particular.

Soon after Joy departed the Mature scene, Victor met former model, Yvonne Huston, a thirty-four-year-old brunette divorcee, the mother of three children. He has called her "the key to my happiness," although he has refused comment on the possibility of a fifth marriage. "Look," he told newsmen, "there are some personal things I don't like to discuss and this is one of them. But I do think every man should have a woman." Miss Huston's uncle, a Pasadena, California restaurateur, said, "I think it is very serious. He wants to get married, but she doesn't. I'm not sure why."

In 1971, Victor again came out of retirement for the comedy, *Every Little Crook and Nanny* (MGM, 1972). Yvonne accompanied him to location shooting in Los Angeles, London, and Naples. Of his acceptance of the role in the film, he told writer Aljean Harmetz, "It just so happened that they caught me when I felt like saying, 'Yeah.' If they'd only got me two weeks later, I'd have said, 'No.' " Of his preparation for the role of Carmine Ganucci, an underworld czar, he said, "I find myself prowling around the house at two, three A.M. thinking about the script and raiding the icebox."

Under the direction of Cy Howard, Ganucci in *Every Little Crook and Nanny* heads for a vacation in Italy, leaving a nanny (Lynn Redgrave[37]) to care for his precocious twelve-year-old son (Phillip Graves). The son is kidnapped on the order of the nanny, and a demand for his safety is made to the tune of $50,000. The nanny eventually takes off with the money, with further intentions of muscling in on the underworld's smuggling operations. Kevin Thomas (*Los Angeles Times*)

[37]In her first American-made film.

With Maggie Blye in *Every Little Crook and Nanny* (1972)

gave the best obituary for this film and perhaps for Mature's acting career: "With each occasional new picture, Victor Mature, who doesn't need the money, threatens permanent retirement, which would be a crying shame at a time when there are so few authentic movie stars in the grand manner still active. But nobody, neither Mature nor the many other proven actors involved in the hapless *Every Little Crook and Nanny,* needs a picture like this one."

"I doubt if I'll ever do another picture," Victor insisted when his *Nanny* chores were ended. "Nobody ever died from loafing." When asked if he would have ever considered playing a nude scene in any film, he replied, "There's not enough money in the world to get me to play a nude scene. I still have three cousins alive."

In July, 1973, it was announced by producer-director Dico Dimitrov that Victor had been cast as an American government official who helps Czar Nicholas II and his family to escape from 1918 Russia. The Dico Production film, to be called *The Escape of Nicholas and Alexandra,* was to be based on Dimitrov's theory that the Russian Imperial family was not executed by the Bolsheviks. It was to be a multi-million-dollar Panavision color epic to be filmed in Spain and Finland. Although Dimitrov later announced that Joan Fontaine and Rossano Brazzi would portray the Imperial couple, the plans did not materialize.

Hank Grant reported in the *Hollywood Reporter* in May, 1974, that Victor "may well be the next Hollywood film veteran to bounce on the Broadway boards. Understand he has a choice from two musicals and a new straight play." Nothing developed from this rumor.

Then to the Matures' great joy and to Hollywood's general amazement, Victor announced that his wife was pregnant. On Sunday, March 16, 1975, she gave birth to a girl whom they named Victoria. When asked if his belated parenthood had convinced him to want more offspring, Victor replied smiling to the press, "I don't want to overdo it."

Although it now seems likely that once dashing, reckless Victor Mature will remain permanently[38] retired from the entertainment field ("I haven't had an agent in years . . . I'll do something if it's good") his legend lives on. In fact, it continues to grow.

Many cinema historians have reclassified his former standing as a studio-manufactured movie star to that of a very competent actor who never received his proper due on the Hollywood soundstages or from the fourth estate.

---

[38]As a lark, Victor agreed to make a cameo appearance, along with many other veteran stars, in *Won Ton Ton the Dog Who Saved Hollywood* (Paramount, 1976).

Feature Film Appearances

THE HOUSEKEEPER'S DAUGHTER (United Artists, 1939), 76 min.
Producer-director, Hal Roach; story, Donald Henderson Clarke; screenplay, Rian James and Gordon Douglas; art director, Charles D. Hall; music director, Lud Gluskin; music, Amedeo de Filippi; camera, Norbert Brodine; editor, William Ziegler.

Joan Bennett (Hilda); Adolphe Menjou (Deakon Maxwell); John Hubbard (Robert Randall); William Gargan (Ed O'Malley); George E. Stone (Benny); Peggy Wood (Olga); Donald Meek (Editor Wilson); Marc Lawrence (Floyd); Lilian Bond (Gladys); Victor Mature (Lefty); John Hyams (Professor Randall); Leila McIntyre (Mrs. Randall); Luis Alberni (Veroni); Rosina Galli (Mrs. Veroni); Tom Dugan (Floyd's Boy); J. Farrell MacDonald (Captain); James Flavin (Detective).

ONE MILLION B.C. (United Artists, 1940), 80 min.
Producer Hal Roach directors, Hal Roach and Hal Roach, Jr., and (uncredited) (D. W. Griffith); story-screenplay, Mickell Novak, George Baker, and Joseph Frickert; art director, Charles D. Hall; music, Werner Heymann; narration written by Grover Jones; special effects, Roy Seawright; camera, Norbert Brodine.

Victor Mature (Tumak); Carole Landis (Loana); Lon Chaney, Jr. (Akhoba); Conrad Nagel (Archaelogist-Narrator); John Hubbard (Ohtao); Robert Kent (Mountain Guide); Mamo Clark (Nupondi); Mary Gale Fisher (Wandi); Nigel De Brulier (Peytow); Inez Palange (Tohana); Edgar Edwards (Skakana); Jacqueline Dalya (Ataf); Adda Gleason, Rosemary Theby, Audrey Manners, Patricia Pope, Ed Coxen, Creighton Hale, Ben Hall, Jimmy Boudwin, Chuck Stubbs, Boots Le Baron, Dick Simons, Jean Porter, Katherine Frye, and Ora May Carlson (Shell People); Ricca Allen, Harry Wilson, John Northpole, Harold Howard, Henry Sylvester, Norman Budd, Lorraine Rivero, Aida Hernandez, Betty Greco, Frank Tinajero, and James Coppedge (Klang People); Yakima Canutt (Stunts).

British release title: **MAN AND HIS MATE.**

CAPTAIN CAUTION (United Artists, 1940), 85 min.
Producers, Hal Roach, Richard Wallace, and Grover Jones; director, Wallace; based on the novel by Kenneth Roberts; screenplay, Jones; art directors, Nicolai Remisoff and Charles D. Hall; music, Phil Ohman; songs, Ohman and Foster Carling; special effects, Roy Seawright; camera, Norbert Brodine; editor, James Newcomb.

Victor Mature (Daniel Marvin); Louise Platt (Corunna Dorman); Leo Carrillo (Lucien Argandeau); Bruce Cabot (Slade); Robert Barrat (Captain Dorman); Vivienne Osborne (Victorine Argandeau); Miles Mander (Lieutenant Strope); El Brendel (Slushy); Roscoe Ates (Chips); Andrew Tombes (Sad Eyes); Aubrey Mather (Mr. Potter); Alan Ladd (Hugh Newton); Pat O'Malley (Fish Peddler); Lloyd Corrigan (Commander Stannage); Ted Osborne (Captain Stephen Decatur); Ann Codee (Landlady); Romaine Callender (English Officer); Pierre Watkin (American Consul); Clifford Severn, Jr. (Travers); Bud Jamison (Blinks); Olaf Hytten (Stannage's Aide); Stanley Blystone (Sailor); George Lloyd (Sailor

Taking Medicine); Frank Lackteen (Slade's Mate).

NO, NO NANETTE (RKO, 1940), 96 min.
Producer, Herbert Wilcox; associate producer, Merrill G. White; director, Wilcox; based on the musical comedy by Frank Mandel, Otto Harbach, Vincent Youmans, and Emil Nyitray; screenplay, Ken Englund; songs, Youmans, Irving Caesar, and Otto Harbach; camera, Russell Metty; editor, Elmo Williams.

Anna Neagle (Nanette); Richard Carlson (Tom); Victor Mature (William); Roland Young (Mr. Smith); Helen Broderick (Mrs. Smith); ZaSu Pitts (Pauline); Eve Arden (Winnie); Tamara (Sonya); Billy Gilbert (Styler); Stuart Robertson (Stillwater, Jr. and Stillwater, Sr.); Dorothea Kent (Betty); Aubrey Mather (Remington); Mary Gordon (Gertrude); Russell Hicks (Hutch); Benny Rubin (Max); Margaret Armstrong (Dowager); George Noisom (Messenger Boy); Lester Derr (Travel Agent); John Dilson, Cy Ring, and Joey Ray (Desk Clerks); Sally Payne (Maid); Torben Meyer (Furtlemertle); Victor Wong (Houseboy); Bud Geary (Taxi Driver); Chris Franke (Hansom Driver); Keye Luke (Man); Muriel Darr, Georgianna Young, and Marion Graham (Show Girls); Minerva Urecal (Woman in Airport); Julius Tannen (Ship Passenger).

THE SHANGHAI GESTURE (United Artists, 1941), 106 min.
Producer, Arnold Pressburger; director, Joseph von Sternberg; based on the play by John Colton; screenplay, von Sternberg, Karl Vollmoeller, Geza Herczeg, and Jules Furthman; art director, Boris Leven; set directors, Howard Bristol; murals, Keye Luke, Miss Munson's costumes, Royer; Miss Tierney's costumes, Oleg Cassini; wigs, Hazel Rogers; music, Richard Hageman; camera, Paul Ivano; editor, Sam Winston.

Gene Tierney (Poppy Charteris); Walter Huston (Sir Guy Charteris); Victor Mature (Dr. Omar); Ona Munson (Mother Gin Sling); Phyllis Brooks (Dixie Pomeroy); Albert Basserman (The Commissioner); Maria Ouspenskaya (The Amah); Eric Blore (The Bookkeeper); Ivan Lebedeff (The Gambler); Mike Mazurki (The Coolie); Clyde Fillmore (The Comprador); Grayce Hampton (The Social Leader); Rex Evans (Brooks, a Counselor); Mikhail Rasumny (The Appraiser); Michael Delmatoff (The Bertender); Marcel Dalio (The Croupier); John Abbott (The Escort).

I WAKE UP SCREAMING (a.k.a., HOT SPOT) (20th Century-Fox, 1941), 80 min.
Producer, Milton Sperling; director, H. Bruce Humberstone; based on the novel by Steve Fisher; screenplay, Dwight Taylor; music, Cyril J. Mockridge; song, Harold Barlow and Lewis Harris; camera, Edward Cronjager; editor, Robert Simpson.

Betty Grable (Jill Lynn); Victor Mature (Frankie Christopher [Botticelli]); Carole Landis (Vicky Lynn); Laird Cregar (Ed Cornell); William Gargan (Jerry McDonald); Alan Mowbray (Robin Ray); Allyn Joslyn (Larry Evans); Elisha Cook, Jr. (Harry Williams); Morris Ankrum (Assistant District Attorney); May Beatty (Mrs. Handel); Cyril Ring, Chick Chandler, Basil Walker, and Bob Cornell (Reporters); Stanley Clements (Newsboy); Tim Ryan, James Flavin, and Dick Rich (Detectives); Stanley Blystone (Cop); Cecil Weston (Police Matron); Brooks Benedict (Extra); Forbes Murray (Mr. Handel); Harry Seymour (Bartender); Edward McWade and Paul Weigel (Old Men).

SONG OF THE ISLANDS (20th Century-Fox, 1942), C-75 min.
Producer, William LeBaron; director, Walter Lang; screenplay, Joseph Schrank, Robert Pirosh, Robert Ellis, and Helen Logan; music director, Alfred Newman; songs, Mack Gordon and Harry Warren, Gordon and Harry Owen; choreography, Hermes Pan; camera, Ernest Palmer; editor, Robert Simpson.

Betty Grable (Eileen O'Brien); Victor Mature (Jefferson Harper); Jack Oakie (Rusty); Thomas Mitchell (O'Brien); George Barbier (Harper); Billy Gilbert (Palola's Father); Hilo Hattie (Palola); Lillian Porter (Palola's Cousin); Hal K. Dawson (John Rodney); Harry Owens and His Royal Canadians (Themselves); Amy Cordone (Specialty); Bruce Wong (House Boy); Bobby Stone and Rudy Robles (Native Boys); Alex Pollard (Valet); Harold Lishman (Old Native).

MY GAL SAL (20th Century-Fox, 1942), C-102 min.
Producer, Robert Bassler; director, Irving Cummings; suggested by the story "My Brother Paul" by Theodore Dreiser; screenplay, Seton I. Miller; Darrell Ware, and Karl Tunberg; art directors, Richard Day and Joseph C. Wright; set decorator, Thomas Little; costumes, Gwen Wakeling; makeup, Guy Pearce; music director, Alfred Newman; choreography, Hermes Pan, Val Raset; songs, Paul Dresser, Leo Robin and Ralph Rainger; Technicolor directors, Natalie Kalmus and Henri Jaffa; sound, Alfred Bruzlin and Roger Heman; camera, Ernest Palmer; editor, Robert Simpson.

Rita Hayworth (Sally Elliott); Victor Mature (Paul Dreiser); John Sutton (Fred Haviland); Carole Landis (Mae Collins); James Gleason (Pat Hawley); Phil Silvers (Wiley); Walter Catlett (Colonel Truckee); Mona Maris (Countess Rossini); Frank Orth (McGuinness); Stanley Andrews (Mr. Dreiser); Margaret Moffat (Mrs. Dreiser); Libby Taylor (Ida); John Kelly (John L. Sullivan); Curt Bois (De Rochement); Gregory Gaye (Garnier); Andrew Tombes (Corbin); Albert Conti (Henry); Charles Arnt (Tailor); Chief Thundercloud (Murphy); Hermes Pan (Specialty Dancer); Robert Lowery, Dorothy Dearing, and Michael "Ted" North (Sally's Friends); Harry Strang (Bartender); Milton Kibbee, Luke Cosgrave, Ernie Adams, John "Skins" Miller, and Joe Bernard (Men); Ed Dearing and Edward McNamara (Policemen); Rosina Galli (Maid); Eddy Waller (Buggy Driver); Terry Moore (Carrie); Clarence Badger, Kenneth Rundquist, Delos Jewkes, and Gene Ramey (Quartette); George Melford (Conductor); Billy Curtis (Midget Driver).

FOOTLIGHT SERENADE (20th, 1942), 80 min.
Producer, William LeBaron; director, Gregory Ratoff; based on the story "Dynamite" by Fidel LaBarba and Kenneth Earl; screenplay Robert Ellis, Helen Logan, and Lynn Starling; art director, Richard Day; music director, Charles Henderson; songs, Leo Robin and Ralph Rainger; choreography, Hermes Pan; camera, Lee Garmes; editor, Robert Simpson.

John Payne (Bill Smith); Betty Grable (Pat Lambert); Victor Mature (Tommy

Lundy); Jane Wyman (Flo LaVerne); James Gleason (Bruce McCay); Phil Silvers (Slap); Cobina Wright, Jr. (Estelle Evans); June Lang (June); Frank Orth (Doorman); Mantan Moreland (Dresser); Irving Bacon (Porter); Charles Tannen (Stage Director); George Dobbs (Dance Director); Sheila Ryan (Girl); Frank Coghlan, Jr. (Usher); Harry Barris (Composer); Trudy Marshall (Secretary); Don Wilson (Announcer); John Dilson (Clerk).

SEVEN DAYS' LEAVE (RKO, 1942), 87 min.

Producer, Tim Whelan; associate producer, George Arthur; director, Whelan; screenplay, William Bowers, Ralph Spence, Curtis Kenyon, and Kenneth Earl; music director, C. Bakaleinkoff; choreography, Charles Walters; songs, Frank Loesser and Jimmy McHugh; art directors, Albert S. D'Agostino and Carroll Clark; special effects, Vernon L. Walker; camera, Robert De Grasse; editor, Robert Wise.

Victor Mature (Johnny Grey); Lucille Ball (Terry); Harold Peary (The Great Gildersleeve); Mapy Cortes (Mapy); Ginny Simms (Ginny); Freddy Martin & His Orchestra, Les Brown & His Orchestra, and Lynn, Royce & Vanya (Themselves); Cast of *The Court of Missing Heirs* and Ralph Edwards & Company of *Truth or Consequences* (Themselves); Peter Lind Hayes (Jackson); Marcy McGuire (Mickey); Walter Reed (Ralph Bell); Wallace Ford (Sergeant Mead); Arnold Stang (Bitsy); Buddy Clark (Clarky); Charles Victor (Charles); King Kennedy (Gifford); Charles (Andre); Harry Holman (Justice of Peace); Addison Richards (Captain Collins); Sergio Orta (Himself); Jack Gardner (Announcer); Willie Fung (Houseboy); Ronnie Rondell (Miller, the Chauffeur); Richard Martin, Frank Martinelli, and Russell Hoyt (The Financial Trio); Henry DeSoto (Maitre d'Hotel); Charles Hall and Ed Thomas (Waiters); Max Wagner (Military Police); Ralph Dunn (Cop); Allen Wood (Groom); Charles Flynn (Guard).

MY DARLING CLEMENTINE (20th Century-Fox, 1946), 97 min.

Producer, Samuel G. Engle; director, John Ford; based on a book by Stuart N. Lake; story, Sam Hellman; screenplay, Engle and Winston Miller; art directors, James Basevi and Lyle Wheeler; set decorators, Thomas Little and Fred J. Rode; music, Cyril Mockridge; music arranger, Edward Powell; music director, Alfred Newman; assistant director, William Eckhardt; sound, Eugene Grossman and Roger Heman; special camera effects, Fred Sersen; camera, Joseph MacDonald; editor, Dorothy Spencer.

Henry Fonda (Wyatt Earp); Linda Darnell (Chihuahua); Victor Mature (Doc Holliday); Walter Brennan (Old Man Clanton); Tim Holt (Virgil Earp); Cathy Downs (Clementine); Ward Bond (Morgan Earp); Alan Mowbray (Granville Thorndyke); John Ireland (Billy Clanton); Roy Roberts (Mayor); Jane Darwell (Kate); Grant Withers (Ike Clanton); J. Farrell MacDonald (Bartender); Russell Simpson (John Simpson); Don Garner (James Earp); Francis Ford (Town Drunk); Ben Hall (Barber); Arthur Walsh (Hotel Clerk); Louis Mercier (Francois); Mickey Simpson (Sam Clanton); Fred Libby (Phin Clanton); William B. Davidson (Owner of Oriental Saloon); Mae Marsh (Woman); Earle Foxe (Gambler); Aleth "Speed" Hansen (Townsman and Guitar Player); Don Barclay (Opera House Owner); Harry Woods (Marshal); Charles Stevens (Indian Charlie); Frank Conlan (Piano Player).

MOSS ROSE (20th Century-Fox, 1947), 82 min.

Producer, Gene Markey; director, Gregory Ratoff; based on the novel by Joseph Shearing; adaptation, Niven Busch; screenplay, Jules Furthman and Tom Reed; art directors, Richard Day, Mark-Lee Kirk; set decorators, Edwin B. Willis and Paul S. Fox; music, David Buttolph; orchestrators, Edward Powell and Maurice de Packh; music director, Alfred Newman; assistant director, Ad Schaumer; sound, George Leverett and Roger Heman; special camera effects, Fred Sersen; camera, Joe MacDonald; editor, James B. Clark.

Peggy Cummins (Belle Adair); Victor Mature (Sir Alexander Sterling); Ethel Barrymore (Lady Sterling); Vincent Price (Inspector Clinner); Margo Woode (Daisy Arrow); George Zucco (Graxton); Patricia Medina (Audrey); Rhys Williams (Deputy Inspector Evans); Felippa Rock (Liza); Carol Savage (Harriett); Victor Wood (Wilson); Patrick O'Moore (George Gilby); Billy Bevan (White Horse Cabby); Michael Dyne (Assistant Hotel Manager); John Rogers (Fothergill); Charles McNaughton (Alf); Alex Frazer (Mr. Bulke); Gilbert Wilson, Stanley Mann (Footmen); John Goldsworthy (Minister); Alex Harford (Cassian); Sally Sheppard (Maid); Colin Campbell (Art Gallery Attendant); Leonard Carey (Coroner); Tom Moore (Foreman in Coroner's Court); Wallace Scott and Colin Kenny (Cab Drivers); Francis Pierlot (Train Conductor); Doreen Munroe (Woman Lodger).

KISS OF DEATH (20th Century-Fox, 1947), 98 min.

Producer, Fred Kohlmar; director, Henry Hathaway; based on a story by Eleazar Lipsky; screenplay, Ben Hecht and Charles Lederer; art directors, Lyle Wheeler and Leland Fuller; set decorator, Thomas Little; music, David Buttolph; orchestrator, Earle Hagen; assistant director, Abe Steinberg; sound, W. D. Flick and Roger Heman; camera, Norbert Brodine; editor, J. Watson Webb.

Victor Mature (Nick Bianco); Brian Donlevy (D'Angelo); Coleen Gray (Nettie); Richard Widmark (Tom Udo); Taylor Holmes (Earl Howser); Howard Smith (Warden); Karl Malden (Sergeant William Cullen); Anthony Ross (Williams); Mildred Dunnock (Ma Rizzo); Millard Mitchell (Max Schulte); Temple Texas (Blondie); J. Scott Smart (Skeets); Wendell Phillips (Pep Mangone); Lew Herbert and Harry Kadison (Policemen); John Kullers (Prisoner); Victor Thorley (Sing Sing Guard); Iris Mann (Congetta); Marilee Grassini (Rosaria); Norman McKay (Captain Dolan); Robert Karnes (Hoodlum); Harry Carter and Robert Adler (Detectives); Yvonne Rob (Customer); Gloria O'Connor and Consuela O'Connor (Giggling Girls); Harold Crane (Mr. Morgemann); Mel Ruick (Mr. Morgemann's Assistant); Jack Rutherford, Lawrence Tiernan, Bernard C. Sell, and Arthur Holland (Policemen); John Marley (Al); Gregg Martell (Turnkey); Lee Sanford (Chips Cooney); John Stearns (Harris); Eda Heinemann (Mrs. Keller); Arthur Kramer (Mr. Sulla); Jesse White (Taxi Driver); Tito Vuolo (Luigi)

FURY AT FURNACE CREEK (20th Century-Fox, 1948), 88 min.

Producer, Fred Kohlmar; director, H. Bruce Humberstone; story, David Garth; screenplay, Charles G. Booth; additional dialog, Winston Miller; art directors, Lyle Wheeler and Albert Hogsett; set decorator, Thomas Little; music, David Raksin; orchestrators, Herbert Spencer and Maurice De Packh;

482

music director, Alfred Newman; assistant director, William Eckhardt; makeup, Ben Nye and George Lane; costumes, Rene Hubert; sound, Eugene Grossman and Harry M. Leonard; special effects, Fred Sersen; camera, Harry Jackson; editor, Robert Simpson.

Victor Mature (Cash); Coleen Gray (Molly Baxter); Glenn Langan (Rufe); Reginald Gardiner (Captain Walsh); Albert Dekker (Leverett); Fred Clark (Bird);. Charles Kemper (Peaceful Jones); Robert Warwick (General Blackwell); George Cleveland (Judge); Roy Roberts (Al Shanks); Willard Robertson (General Leads); Griff Barnett (Appleby); Frank Orth (Evans); J. Farrell MacDonald (Pops); Charles Stevens (Artego); Jay Silverheels (Little Dog); Robert Adler (Leverett Henchman); Harry Carter (Clerk); Mauritz Hugo and Howard Negley (Defense Counsels); Harlan Briggs (Prosecutor); Si Jenks (Jury Foreman); Guy Wilkerson and Edmund Cobb (Court Clerks); Kermit Maynard (Scout); Paul Newlan (Bartender); Ted Mapes (Man); George Chesebro, Al Hill, and Jerry Miley (Card Players); Minerva Urecal (Mrs. Crum); Ray Teal (Sergeant); Alan Bridge (Lawyer); Oscar O'Shea (Jailer).

CRY OF THE CITY (20th Century-Fox, 1948), 95 min.
Producer, Sol C. Siegel; director, Robert Siodmak; based on the novel by Henry Edward Helseth; screenplay, Richard Murphy; art directors, Lyle Wheeler and and Albert Hogsett; set decorators, Thomas Little and Ernest Lansing; music, Alfred Newman; orchestrator, Herbert Spencer; music director, Lionel Newman; assistant director, Jasper Blystone; makeup, Ben Nye, Harry Maret, and Pat McNally; costumes, Bonnie Cashin; sound, Eugene Grossman and Roger Heman; special effects, Fred Sersen; camera, Lloyd Ahern; editor, Harmon Jones.

Victor Mature (Lieutenant Candella); Richard Conte (Martin Rome); Fred Clark (Lieutenant Collins); Shelley Winters (Brenda); Betty Garde (Mrs. Pruett); Berry Kroeger (Niles); Tommy Cook (Tony); Debra Paget (Teena Riconti); Hope Emerson (Rose Given); Roland Winters (Ledbetter); Walter Baldwin (Orvy); June Storey (Miss Boone); Tito Vuolo (Papa Roma); Mimi Aguglia (Mama Roma); Konstantin Shayne (Dr. Veroff); Howard Freeman (Sullivan); Dolores Castle (Rosa); Claudette Ross (Rosa's Daughter); Tiny Francone (Perdita); Elena Savonarola (Francesca); Thomas Ingersoll (Priest); Vito Scotti (Julio); Robert Karnes and Charles Tannen (Internes); Oliver Blake (Caputo); Antonio Filauri (Vaselli); Eddie Parks (Mike); Jane Nigh (Nurse); Martin Begley (Bartender); Michael Sheridan (Detective).

EASY LIVING (RKO, 1949), 77 min.
Producer, Robert Sparks; director, Jacques Tourneur; based on the story "Education of the Heart" by Irwin Shaw; screenplay, Charles Schnee; art directors, Albert S. D'Agostino and Alfred Herman; set decorators, Darrell Silvera and Harley Miller; music, Roy Webb; music director, C. Bakaleinikoff; assistant directors, James Lane, Joel Freeman, and Nate Slott; makeup, Robert M. Cowan and Lee Greenway; costumes, Edward Stevenson; sound, Earl Wolcott; camera, Harry J. Wild; editor, Frederic Knudtson.

Victor Mature (Pete Wilson); Lucille Ball (Anne); Lizabeth Scott (Liza Wilson); Sonny Tufts (Tim McCarr); Lloyd Nolan (Lenahan); Paul Stewart (Ar-

483

gus); Jack Paar (Scoop Spooner); Jeff Donnell (Penny McCarr); Art Baker (Howard Vollmer); Gordon Jones (Bill Holloran); Dick Erdman (Buddy Morgan); William "Bill" Phillips (Ozzie); Charles Lang (Whitey); Kenny Washington (Benny); Julia Dean (Mrs. Belle Ryan); Everett Glass (Virgil Ryan); James Backus (Dr. Franklin); Robert Ellis (Urchin); Steven Flagg (Gilbert Vollmer); Alex Sharp (Don); Russ Thorson (Hunk Edwards); June Bright (Billy Duane); Eddie Kotal (Curley); Audrey Young (Singer); The Los Angeles Rams (Themselves); Dick Ryan (Bartender); Steve Crandall (Reporter); Ray George (Referee); William Erwin and Carl Saxe (Men).

RED, HOT AND BLUE (Paramount, 1949), 84 min.

Producer, Robert Fellows; director, John Farrow; story, Charles Lederer; screenplay, Farrow and Hagar Wilde; art directors, Hans Dreier and Franz Bachelin; set decorators, Sam Comer and Ross Dowd; songs, Frank Loesser; music director, Joseph J. Lilley; orchestrators. Van Cleave and Troy Sanders; choreography, Billy Daniel; assistant director, William H. Coleman; makeup, Wally Westmore, Bill Bood, and Charles Boerner; costumes, Edith Head; sound, Hugo Grenzbach and Gene Garvin; camera, Daniel L. Fapp; editor, Eda Warren.

Betty Hutton (Eleanor Collier); Victor Mature (Danny James); William Demarest (Charlie Baxter); June Havoc (Sandra); Jane Nigh (No-No); Frank Loesser (Hair-Do Lempke); William Talman (Bunny Harris); Art Smith (Laddie Corwin); Raymond Walburn (Mr. Creek); Onslow Stevens (Captain Allen); Joseph Vitale (Garr); Jack Kruschen (Steve); Percy Helton (Stage Manager); Philip Van Zandt (Head Waiter); Dorothy Abbott (The Queen); Herschel Daugherty (Laertes); Don Shelton (Hamlet); Noel Neill, Paul Lees, James Cornell, Joey Ray, Douglas Spencer, and James Davies (Members of Theatre Group); Julie Adams (Starlet); Billy Daniel and Rita Lupino (Dance Team); James Burke (Doorman); Tim Ryan (Stranger); Arlene Jenkins (Newspaper Woman); Robert Kellard (Police Switchboard Operator); Marie Thomas, Jacqueline Park (Showgirls); Jimmy Dundee (Gangster); Frank Alten (Karl Mueller); Lester Dorr (Workman).

SAMSON AND DELILAH (Paramount, 1949), C-127 min.

Producer-director, Cecil B. DeMille; based upon the History of Samson and Delilah in the Holy Bible, Judges: 13-16, and *Judge and Fool* by Vladimir Jabotinsky; screen treatment, Jabotinsky and Harold Lamb; screenplay, Jesse L. Lasky, Jr., and Frederic M. Frank; art directors, Hans Dreier and Walter Tyler; set decorators, Sam Comer and Ray Moyer; music director, Victor Young; Technicolor directors, Natalie Kalmus and Robert Brower; assistant director, Edward Salven; makeup, Wally Westmore, Harold Lierly, and William Wood; costumes, Edith Head, Gus Peters, and Dorothy Jenkins, Gwen Wakeling, and Elois Jenssen; choreography, Theodore Kosloff; sound, Harry Lindgren and John Cope; special effects, Gordon Jennings, Paul Lerpae, and Devereaux Jennings; process camera, Farciot Edouart and Wallace Kelley; camera, George Barnes; Holy Land location camera, Dewey Wrigley; editor, Anne Bauchens.

Hedy Lamarr (Delilah); Victor Mature (Samson); George Sanders (Saranof Gaza); Angela Lansbury (Semadar); Henry Wilcoxon (Ahtur); Olive Deering (Miriam); Fay Holden (Hazel); Julia Faye (Hisham); Rusty Tamblyn (Saul);

William Farnum (Tubal); Lane Chandler (Teresh); Moroni Olsen (Targil); Francis J. McDonald (Story Teller); William "Wee Willie" Davis (Garmiskar); John Miljan (Lesh Lakish); Arthur Q. Bryan (Fat Philistine Merchant); Laura Elliot (Spectator); Victor Varconi (Lord of Ashdod); John Parrish (Lord of Gath); Frank Wilcox (Lord of Ekron); Russell Hicks (Lord of Ashkelon); Boyd Davis (Priest); Fritz Leiber (Lord Sharif); Mike Mazurki (Leader of Philistine Soldiers); Davison Clark (Merchant Prince); George Reeves (Wounded Messenger); Pedro de Cordoba (Bar Simon); Frank Reicher (Village Barber); Colin Tapley (Prince); Charles Evans (Manoah, Samson's Father); George Zoritch and Hamil Petroff (Sword Dancers); Frank Mayo (Master Architect); James Craven (Prince); Lloyd Whitlock (Chief Scribe); Craufurd Kent (Court Astrologer); Harry Woods (Gammad); Stephen Roberts (Bergam at Feast); Ed Hinton (Makon at Feast—Double for Victor Mature); Carl Saxe (Slave); Nils Asther and Harry Cording (Princes); Charles Meredith (High Priest); Pierre Watkin (Second Priest); John "Skins" Miller (Man with Burro); Lester Sharpe (Saddle Maker); Edgar Dearing and Hugh Prosser (Tax Collectors); John Merton (Assistant Tax Collector); Al Ferguson (Villager); Fred Kohler, Jr. (Soldier); Tom Tyler (Philistine Captain of Gristmill); Brahm van den Berg (Temple Dancer); Eric Alden (Courtier); Bob Kortman (Vendor); Philo McCullough (Merchant); Ted Mapes (Captain Killed by Jawbone); Bert Moorhouse (Spectator); Gertrude Messinger, Betty Boyd, Dorothy Adams, Betty Farrington, Claire DuBrey, and Greta Granstedt (Women); Byron Foulger, Stanley Blystone, Crane Whitley, and Kenneth Gibson (Men); Jeff York (Spectator); Charles Dayton (Midget at Arena); Henry Wills (Saran's Charioteer).

WABASH AVENUE (20th Century-Fox, 1950), C-92 min.

Producer, William Perlberg; director, Henry Koster; screenplay, Harry Tugend and Charles Lederer; music director, Lionel Newman; songs, Mack Gordon and Josef Myrow; art directors, Lyle Wheeler and Joseph C. Wright; camera, Arthur E. Arling; editor, Robert Simpson.

Betty Grable (Ruby Summers); Victor Mature (Andy Clark); Phil Harris (Uncle Mike); Reginald Gardiner (English Eddie); James Barton (Hogan); Barry Kelley (Bouncer); Margaret Hamilton (Tillie Hutch); Jacqueline Dalya (Cleo); Robin Raymond (Jennie); Hal K. Dawson (Healy); Colette Lyons (Beulah); Charles Arnt (Carter); Walter Long and Billy Daniel (Dancers); Marion Marshall (Chorus Girl); Percy Helton (Ship's Captain); Dorothy Neumann (Reformer); Alexander Pope (Charlie); Henry Kulky (Joe); Dick Crockett (Bartender); John "Skins" Miller (Drunk); Harold Cornsweet (Bartender); George Beranger (Wax Museum Attendant); David Clarke (Workman); Paul "Tiny" Newlan (Bouncer); Ruby Dale Hearn and Barbara A. Pellegrino (Tumbling Act); Michael Ross and Mickey Simpson (Policemen); Douglas Carter (Ferris Wheel Operator).

I'LL GET BY (20th Century-Fox, 1950), C-83 min.

Producer, William Perlberg; director, Richard Sale; based on the screen story by Robert Ellis, Helen Logan, and Pamela Harris; screenplay, Mary Loos and Richard Sale; art director, Lyle Wheeler; songs, John LaTouche, Ted Fetter, and Vernon Duke; Bud Green and Michael Edwards; Mack Gordon and Harry Warren; Ted Koehler and Harold Arlen; Gordon and Josef Myrow; B. G. DeSylva, Irving Caesar, and George Gershwin; Sammy Cahn and Jule Styne; Roy Turk and Fred Ahlert; and Shamus O'Connor and J. J. Stamford;

orchestrator, Herbert Spencer; Technicolor director, Leonard Doss; camera, Charles G. Clarke; editor, J. Watson Webb, Jr.

June Haver (Liza Martin); William Lundigan (William Spencer); Gloria De Haven (Terry Martin); Dennis Day (Freddy Lee); Harry James (Himself); Thelma Ritter (Miss Murphy); Steve Allen (Peter Pepper); Danny Davenport (Chester Dovley); Reginald Gardiner, Jeanne Crain, Dan Dailey, and Victor Mature (Guest Stars); Tom Hanlon (Announcer); Peggy O'Connor (U.S.O. Girl); Harry Semour (Stage Manager); Harry Lauter and Don Hicks (Assistant Directors); Charles Tannen (Director); Kathleen Hughes (Secretary); Vincent Renno (Head Waiter); Bob McCord (Commentator); John Butler (Man by Fireplace); Paul Picerni (Marine Sergeant); Dick Winslow (Cooky Myers).

STELLA (20th Century-Fox, 1950), 83 min.
Producer, Sol C. Siegel; director, Claude Binyon; based on the novel by Doris Miles Disney; screenplay, Binyon; music director, Lionel Newman; art directors, Lyle Wheeler and Mark-Lee Kirk; camera, Joe MacDonald; editor, Harmon Jones.

Ann Sheridan (Stella); Victor Mature (Jeff De Marco); David Wayne (Carl Granger); Randy Stuart (Claire); Marion Marshall (Mary); Frank Fontaine (Don); Leif Erickson (Fred); Evelyn Varden (Flora); Lea Penman (Mrs. Calhoun); Joyce MacKenzie (Peggy Denny); Hobart Cavanaugh (Tim Gross); Charles Halton (Mr. Beeker); Chill Wills (Officer); Lorelie Witek (Cigarette Girl); Paul Harvey (Ralph Denny); Mary Bear (Myra); Larry Keating (Gil Wright); Walter Baldwin (Farmer).

GAMBLING HOUSE (RKO, 1950), 80 min.
Producer, Warren Duff; director, Ted Tetzlaff; story, Erwin Gelsey; screenplay, Marvin Borofsky and Allen Rivkin; art directors, Albert S. D'Agostino, Alfred Herman; music director, C. Bakaleinikoff; camera, Harry J. Wild; editor, Roland Gross.

Victor Mature (Marc Fury); Terry Moore (Lynn Warren); William Bendix (Joe Farrow); Zachary A. Charles (Willie); Basil Ruysdael (Judge Ravinek); Donald Randolph (Lloyd Crane); Damian O'Flynn (Ralph Douglas); Cleo Moore (Sally); Ann Doran (Della); Eleanor Audley (Mrs. Livingston); Gloria Winters (B. J. Warren); Don Haggerty (Sharky); William E. Green (Doctor); Jack Kruschen (Burly Italian); Eddy Fields (Fat Man Pickpocket); Victor Paul, Joseph Rogato, Guy Zanette (Italian Immigrants); Kirk Alyn (F.B.I. Man); Jack Stoney (Detective); Sherry Hall (Robbins); Vera Stokes (Station Wagon Driver); Leonidas Ossetynski (Mr. Sobieski); Loda Halama (Mrs. Sobieski); Homer Dickinson (Doorman); Forrest Burns (Milkman); Carl Davis (Big); Chester Jones (Elevator Attendant); Bert Moorhouse (Burke); Art Dupuis (Porter); Stanley Price (Gorman).

THE LAS VEGAS STORY (RKO, 1952), 88 min.
Producer, Robert Sparks; director, Robert Stevenson; based on a story by Jay Dratler; screenplay, Earl Felton and Harry Essex; art directors, Albert S. D'Agostino and Feild Gray; music director, C. Bakaleinikoff; songs, Hoagy Carmichael; Orrin Tucker; Camera, Harry J. Wild; editor, George Shrader.

Jane Russell (Linda Rollins); Victor Mature (Dave Andrew); Vincent Price (Lloyd Rollins); Hoagy Carmichael (Happy); Brad Dexter (Thomas Hubler); Gordon Oliver (Drucker); Jay C. Flippen (Harris); Will Wright (Fogarty); Bill Welsh (Martin); Ray Montgomery (Desk Clerk); Colleen Miller (Mary); Robert Wilke (Clayton); Syd Saylor (Matty); George Hoagland, Roger Creed, Jimmy Long, Bert Stevens, Norman Stevans, Ben Harris, Ted Jordan, and Philip Ahlm (Men); Mary Bayless, Mary Darby, Barbara Freking, Jean Corbett, Hazel Shaw, and Evelyn Lovequist (Women); Clarence Muse (Pullman Porter); Dorothy Abbott, Joan Mallory, and Jane Easton (Waitresses); Mavis Russell (Blonde); Midge Ware (Chief Money Changer); John Merrick (Gus); Brooks Benedict (Stickman Dealer); Paul Frees (District Attorney); Carl Sklover (Dealer); Connie Castle (Guest); Milton Kibbee (Coroner); Al Murphy (Bartender); Howard Darbeen (Stickman).

ANDROCLES AND THE LION (RKO, 1952), 98 min.

Producer, Gabriel Pascal; director, Chester Erskine; based on the play by George Bernard Shaw; adaptation, Erskine and Ken Englund; music director, C. Bakaleinikoff; music, Frederick Hollander; art directors, Albert S. D'Agostino and Charles F. Pyke; set decorators, Darrell Silvera and Al Grenzbach; technical advisor, Aldo Tomasani-Barbarossa; makeup, Mel Bern; Miss Simmons' gowns, Emile Santiago; production designer, Harry Horner; special camera effects, Linwood Dunn; sound, John Cass and Clem Portman; camera, Harry Stradling; editor, Roland Gross.

Jean Simmons (Lavinia); Alan Young (Androcloes); Victor Mature (Captain); Robert Newton (Ferrovius); Maurice Evans (Caesar); Elsa Lanchester (Megaera); Reginald Gardiner (Lentulus); Gene Lockhart (Menagerie Keeper); Alan Mowbray (Editor); Noel Willman (Spintho); John Hoyt (Cato); Jim Backus (Centurian); Lowell Gillmore (Metellus); Millard Sherwood (Christian); Charles Hall (Town Crier); Larry McGrath (Vendro); Coint Dorrington (Officer in Forrest); John Merton, Alex Sharp, Don Garett, Jack Shea, Clark Howatt, and Harry Lauter (Officers); Lillina Clayes and Midge Ware (Christian Women); Harry Cording, John Packard, Bob Foulk, Gaylord "Steve" Pendleton, Strother Martin, and Jackson Halliday (Soldiers); Woody Strode (The Lion); Chet Marshall (Call Boy); Dick Elliott (Ox Cart Driver); Michael Road (Retiarius); Richard Reeves (Secutor).

MILLION DOLLAR MERMAID (MGM, 1952), C-115 min.

Producer, Arthur Hornblow, Jr; director, Mervyn LeRoy; screenplay, Everett Freeman; music director, Adolph Deutsch; orchestrator, Alexander Courage; production numbers staged by Busby Berkeley; choreography, Audrene Brier; art director, Cedric Gibbons; set decorators, Edwin R. Willois and Richard Pefferie; camera, George J. Folsey; editor, John McSweeney, Jr.

Esther Williams (Annette Kellerman); Victor Mature (James Sullivan); Walter Pidgeon (Frederick Kellerman); David Brian (Alfred Harper); Donna Corcoran (Annette at Age Ten); Jesse White (Doc Cronnel); Maria Tallchief (Pavlova); Howard Freeman (Aldrich); Charles Watts (Policeman); Wilton Graff (Garvey); Frank Ferguson (Prosecutor); James Bell (Judge); James Flavin (Conductor); Willis Bouchey (Director); Adrienne D'Ambricourt (Marie, the Housekeeper); Charles Heard (Official); Clive Morgan (Judge); Queenie Leonard (Mrs. Graves); Stuart Torres (Son); Leslie Denison (Purser); Wilson Benge

(Caretaker); James Aubrey (Pawnbroker); Patrick O'Moore (Master of Ceremonies); Elizabeth Slifer (Soprano); Mary Earle, Bobby Hale, T. Arthur Hughes, and Percy Lennon (Bits); Al Ferguson (London Bobby); Vernon Downing (Newspaper Man); Creighton Hale (Husband); Kay Wiley (Woman); George Wallace (Bud Williams); James L. "Tiny" Kelly (Policeman); Paul Frees (Band Leader); Paul Bradley (Defense Attorney).

British released title: **THE ONE-PIECE BATHING SUIT.**

SOMETHING FOR THE BIRDS (20th Century-Fox, 1952), 81 min.
Producer-director, George Stevens; based on stories by Alvin M. Josephy, Joseph Petracca, and Boris Ingster; screenplay, Ingstar and I. A. L. Diamond; music, Sol Kaplan; music director, Lionel Newman; art directors Lyle Wheeler and George Patrick; set decorators, Thomas Little and Bruce Macdonald; camera, Joseph La Shelle; editor, Hugh S. Fowler.

Victor Mature (Steve Bennett); Patricia Neal (Anne Richards); Edmund Gwenn (Johnnie Adams); Larry Keating (Patterson); Gladys Hurlbut (Mrs. Rice); Hugh Sanders (Grady); Christian Rub (Leo); Wilton Graff (Taylor); Archer MacDonald (Lemmer); Richard Garrick (Chandler); Ian Wolfe (Foster); Russell Gaige (Winthrop); John Brown (Mr. Lund); Camillo Guercio (Duncan); Joan Miller (Mac); Madge Blake (Mrs. Chadwick); Norman Field (Judge); Gordon Nelson (O'Malley); Emmett Vogan (Beecham); John Ayres (Congressman Walker); Charles Watts (Jessup); Rodney Bell (Announcer); Norma Varden (Congresswoman Bates); Elizabeth Flournoy (Receptionist); Herbert Lytton (Captain); Fred Datig, Jr. (Bellhop); Paul Power (Court Clerk); Robert Livingston (General); Edmund Cobb (Reporter); Joan Shawlee (Woman in Station).

THE GLORY BRIGADE (20th Century-Fox, 1953), 82 min.
Producer, William Bloom; director, Robert D. Webb; screenplay, Franklin Coen; art directors, Lyle Wheeler and Lewis Creber; choreography, Matt Mattox; camera, Lucien Ballard; editor, Mario Mora.

Victor Mature (Lieutenant Sam Prior); Alexander Scourby (Lieutenant Nikiss); Lee Marvin (Corporal Bowman); Richard Egan (Sergent Johnson); Nick Dennis (Corporal Marakis); Roy Roberts (Sergeant Chuck Anderson); Alvy Moore (Private Stone); Russell Evans (Private Taylor); Henry Kulky (Sergeant Smithowsky); Gregg Martell (Private Ryan); Lamont Johnson (Captain Adams); Carleton Young (Captain Davis); Frank Gerstle (Major Sauer); Stuart Nedd (Lieutenant Jorgenson); George Michaelides (Private Nemos); John Verros (Captain Charros); Alberto Morin (Sergeant Lykos); Archer MacDonald (Sergeant Kress); Peter Mamakos (Colonel Kallicles); Father Patrinakos (Chaplain); John Haretakis, Costas Morfis, David Gabbai, and Nico Minardos (Greek Soldiers).

AFFAIR WITH A STRANGER (RKO, 1953), 89 min.
Producer, Robert Sparks; director, Roy Rowland; story-screenplay, Richard Flournoy; art directors, Darrell Silvers and Clarence Steenson; song, Sam Coslow; camera, Harold J. Wild; editor, George Amy.

Jean Simmons (Carolyn Parker); Victor Mature (Bill Blakeley); Mary Jo Tarola (Dolly Murray); Monica Lewis (Janet Boothe); Jane Darwell (Ma Stanton); Dabbs Gree (Happy Murray); Wally Vernon (Joe); Nicholas Joy (George Craig); Olive Carey (Cynthia Craig); Victoria Horne (Mrs. Wallace); Lillian Bronson (Miss Crutcher); George Cleveland (Pop); Billy Chapin (The Older Timmy); Louise Torres (Timmy Wallace); Ted Von Eltz (Mr. Culpepper); Mary Jane Carey (Edith); Dan Bernaucci (Other Cab Driver); Frank Wilcox (Dr. Strong); Walter Woolf King (Harry Casino); Jack Lomas (Temple the Cop); Bob Jellison (Pudgy Man); Chester Jones and James Adamson (Porters); Paul Maxey (Jerry); Franklin Farnum (Man); Fred Graham (Mounted Cop); Alvy Moore (TV Announcer); Eileen Howe (Secretary).

THE ROBE 20th Century-Fox, 1953), C-135 min.
Producer, Frank Ross; director, Henry Koster; based on the novel by Lloyd C. Douglas; adaptation, Gina Kaus; screenplay, Philip Dunne; art directors, Lyle Wheeler and George W. Davis; music, Alfred Newman; camera, Leon Shamroy; editor, Barbara McLean.

Richard Burton (Marcellus Gallio); Jean Simmons (Diana); Victor Mature (Demetrius); Michael Rennie (Peter); Jay Robinson (Caligula); Dean Jagger (Justus); Torin Thatcher (Senator Gallio); Richard Boone (Pilate); Betta St. John (Miriam); Jeff Morrow (Paulus); Ernest Thesiger (Emperor Tiberius); Dawn Addams (Junia); Leon Askin (Abidor); Frank Pulaski (Quintus); David Leonard (Marcipor); Michael Ansara (Judas); Nicholas Koster (Jonathan); Francis Pierlot (Dodinius); Thomas Browne Henry (Marius); Anthony Eustrel (Sarpendon); Pamela Robinson (Lucia); Jay Novello (Tiro); Emmett Lynn (Nathan); Sally Corner (Cornelia); Rosalind Ivan (Julia); George E. Stone (Gracchus); Marc Snow (Auctioneer); Mae Marsh (Woman); George Keymas (Slave); John Doucette (Ship's Mate); Ford Rainey and Sam Gilman (Ships' Captains); Cameron Mitchell (Voice of Christ).

THE VEILS OF BAGDAD (Universal, 1953), C-82 min.
Producer, Albert J. Cohen; director, George Sherman; story-screenplay, William R. Cox; art directors, Alexander Golitzen and Emrich Nicholson; choreography, Eugene Loring; camera, Russell Metty; editor, Paul Weatherwax.

Victor Mature (Antar); Mari Blanchard (Selina); Guy Rolfe (Kasseim); Virginia Field (Rosanna); James Arness (Targut); Leon Askin (Pascha Hamman); Nick Cravat (Ahmed); Gregg Palmer (Oaman); Ludwig Donath (Kaffar); Howard Petrie (Karsh); Charles Arnt (Zapolya); Jackie Loughery (Handmaiden); David Sharpe (Ben Ali); Sammy Stein (Abdallah); Bobby Blake (Beggar Boy); Glenn Strange (Mik-Kel); Charles Wagenheim (Bedouis Spy); Tom Renesto (Wrestler); Bob St. Angelo (Soldier Guard); Stuart Whitman (Sergeant); Ben Welden (Stout Wrestler); George Lewis (Captain); Dale Van Sickel (Messenger).

DANGEROUS MISSION (RKO, 1954), C-75 min.
Producer, Irwin Allen; director, Louis King; story, Horace McCoy and James Edmiston; screenplay, McCoy, W. R. Burnett, and Charles Bennett;

assistant director, James W. Lane; music, Roy Webb; art directors, Albert S. D'Agostino and Walter Keller; camera, William Snyder; editor, Gene Palmer.

Victor Mature (Matt Hallett); Piper Laurie (Louise Graham); William Bendix (Joe Parker); Vincent Price (Paul Adams); Betta St. John (Mary Tiller); Steve Darrell (Katoonai); Marlo Dwyer (Mrs. Elster); Walter Reed (Dobson); Dennis Weaver (Pruitt); Harry Cheshire (Elster); George Sherwood (Mr. Jones); Maureen Stephenson (Mrs. Jones); Fritz Apking (Hawthorne); Kem Dibbs (Johnny Yonkers); John Carlyle (Bellhop); Frank Griffin (Tedd); Trevor Bardette (Kicking Bear); Roy Engel (Hume); Grace Hayle (Mrs. Alvord); Jim Potter (Cobb); Sam Shack, Craig Moreland, Ralph Volkie, and Mike Lally (Firefighters).

DEMETRIUS AND THE GLADIATORS (20th Century-Fox, 1954), C-101 min.

Producer, Frank Ross; director, Delmer Daves; based on characters from the novel *The Robe* by Lloyd C. Douglas; screenplay, Philip Dunne; art directors, Lyle Wheeler and George W. Davis; assistant director, William Eckhart; music, Franz Waxman and Alfred Newman; choreography, Stephen Papich; camera, Milton Krasner; editors, Dorothy Spencer and Robert Fritch.

Victor Mature (Demetrius); Susan Hayward (Messalina); Michael Rennie (Peter); Debra Paget (Lucia); Anne Bancroft (Paula); Jay Robinson (Caligula); Barry Jones (Claudius); William Marshall (Glydon); Richard Egan (Dardanius); Ernest Borgnine (Strabo); Charles Evans (Cassius Chaerea); Everett Glass (Kaeso); Karl Davis (Macro); Jeff York (Albus); Carmen de Lavallade (Slave Girl); John Cliff (Varus); Barbara James and Willetta Smith (Specialty Dancers); Selmer Jackson (Senator); Douglas Brooks (Cousin); Fred Graham (Decurion); Dayton Lummis (Magistrate); George Eldredge (Chamberlain); Paul Richards (Prisoner); Ray Spiker, Gilbert Perkins, Paul Stader, Jim Winkler, Lyle Fox, Dick Sands, and Woody Strode (Gladiators); Paul "Tiny" Newlan (Potter); Allan Kramer (Clerk); Paul Kruger (Courtier); Richard Burton and Jean Simmons (In film clip from *The Robe*).

THE EGYPTIAN (20th Century-Fox, 1954), C-140 min.

Producer, Darryl F. Zanuck; director, Michael Curtiz; based on the novel by Mika Waltari; screenplay, Philip Dunne and Casey Robinson; music, Alfred Newman and Bernard Herrmann; choreography, Stephen Papich; art directors, Lyle Wheeler, and George W. Davis; camera, Leon Shamroy; editor, Barbara McLean.

Jean Simmons (Merit); Victor Mature (Horemheb); Gene Tierney (Baketamon); Michael Wilding (Akhnaton); Bella Darvi (Nefer); Peter Ustinov (Kaptah); Edmund Purdom (Sinuhe); Judith Evelyn (Taia); Henry Daniell (Mikere); John Carradine (Grave Robber); Carl Benton Reid (Senmut); Tommy Rettig (Thoth); Anitra Stevens (Nefertiti); Donna Martell (Lady in Waiting); Mimi Gibson (Princess); Carmen De Lavallade (Dancer); Harry Thompson (Nubian); George Melford, Lawrence Ryle (Priests); Ian MacDonald (Ship's Captain); Michael Granger (Officer); Don Blackman (Nubian Prince); Mike Mazurki (Death House Foreman); Peter Reynolds (Sinuhe at Age Ten); Tyler McDuff (Cadet); Angela Clarke (Kipa); Edmund Cobb (Patient in Dispensary); George Chester (Nubian Guard); Michael Ansara (Hittite Commander); Harry

Corden (Hittite Officer); Geraldine Bogdonovich (Tavern Waitress); Eglfshe Harout (Syrian at Nefer's).

BETRAYED (MGM, 1954), C-108 min.
Director, Gottfried Reinhardt; screenplay, Ronald Millar and George Froeschel; music, Walter Goehr; camera, Freddie Young; editors, John Dunning and Raymond Poulton.

Clark Gable (Colonel Pieter Deventer); Lana Turner (Carla Van Oven); Victor Mature (The Scarf); Louis Calhern (General Ten Eyck); O. E. Hasse (Colonel Helmuth Dietrich); Wilfrid Hyde White (General Charles Larraby); Ian Carmichael (Captain Jackie Lawson); Niall MacGinnis (Blackie); Nora Swinburne (The Scarf's Mother); Roland Culver (General Warsleigh); Leslie Weston (Pop); Christopher Rhodes (Chris); Lilly Kann (Jan's Grandmother); Brian Smith (Jan); Anton Diffring (Captain Von Stranger).

CHIEF CRAZY HORSE (Universal, 1955), C-86 min.
Producer, William Alland; co-producer, Leonard Goldstein; director, George Sherman; story, Gerald Drayson Adams; screenplay. Adams and Franklin Coen; assistant directors, Marsh Green, Phil Bowles, and Dick Evans; music, Frank Skinner; music director, Joseph Gershenson; costumes, Rosemary Odell; art directors, Alexander Golitzen and Robert Boyle; camera, Harold Lipstein; editor, Al Clark.

Victor Mature (Chief Crazy Horse); Suzan Ball (Black Shawl); John Lund (Major Twist); Ray Danton (Little Big Man); Keith Larsen (Flying Hawk); Paul Guilfoyle (Worm); David Janssen (Lieutenant Colin Cartwright); Robert Warwick (Spotted Tail); James Millican (General Crook); Morris Ankrum (Red Cloud/Conquering Bear); Donald Randolph (Aaron Cartwright); Robert F. Simon (Caleb Mantz); Stuart Randall (Old Man Afraid); Pat Hogan (Dull Knife); Dennis Weaver (Major Carlisle); John Peters (Sergeant Guthrie); Henry Wills (He Dog); Willie Hunter, Jr. (Cavalryman); Charles Horvath (Hardy); Robert St. Angelo (Sergeant); David Miller (Lieutenant).

British release title: **VALLEY OF FURY.**

VIOLENT SATURDAY (20th Century-Fox, 1955), C-91 min.
Producer, Buddy Adler; director, Richard Fleischer; based on the novel by William L. Heath; screenplay, Sydney Boehm; assistant director, Joseph E. Rickards; costumes, Kay Nelson; music, Hugo Friedhofer; orchestrator, Edward B. Powell; music director, Lionel Newman; art directors, Lyle Wheeler and George W. Davis; camera, Charles G. Clarke; editor, Louis Loeffler.

Victor Mature (Shelley Martin); Richard Egan (Boyd Fairchild); Stephen McNally (Harper); Virginia Leith (Linda); Tommy Noonan (Harry Reeves); Lee Marvin (Dill); Margaret Hayes (Emily); J. Carroll Naish (Chapman); Sylvia Sidney (Elsie); Ernest Borgnine (Stadt); Dorothy Patrick (Helen); Billy Chapin (Steve Martin); Brad Dexter (Gil Clayton); Donald Gamble (Bobby); Raymond Greenleaf (Mr. Fairchild) Richard Murray (Georgie); Robert Adler (Stan); Ann Morrison (Mrs. Stadt); Kevin Corcoran (David Stadt); Donna Corcoran (Anna Stadt); Noreen Corcoran (Mary Stadt); Boyd "Red" Morgan (Slick); Harry Seymour (Conductor); Jeri Weil, Pat Weil, and Sammy Ogg

(Amish Children); John Alderson (Amish Farmer); Esther Somers (Amish Woman on Train).

LAST FRONTIER (Columbia, 1955); C-98 min.
  Producer, William Fadiman; director, Anthony Mann; based on the novel *The Gilded Rooster* by Richard Emery Roberts; screenplay, Philip Yordan and Russell S. Hughes; art director, Robert Peterson; music director, Morris Stoloff; music, Leigh Harline; orchestrator, Arthur Morton; song, Lester Lee and Ned Washington; assistant director, Sam Nelson; camera, William Mellor; editor, Al Clark.

  Victor Mature (Jed); Guy Madison (Captain Riordan); Robert Preston (Colonel Frank Marston); James Whitmore (Gus); Anne Bancroft (Corinna Marston); Russell Collins (Captain Clark); Peter Whitney (Sergeant Major Decker); Pat Hogan (Mungo); Manuel Donde (Red Cloud); Guy Williams (Lieutenant Benton); Mickey Kuhn (Luke); William Calles (Spotted Elk); Jack Pennick (Corporal); Robert St. Angelo (Sentry); William Traylor (Soldier).

SAFARI (Columbia, 1956), C-91 min.
  Executive producers, Irving Allen and Albert R. Broccoli; producer, Adrian D. Worker; director, Terence Young; story, Robert Buckner; screenplay, Anthony Veiller; art director, Elliot Scott; music director, Muir Mathieson; music, William Alwyn; song, Alwyn and Paddy Roberts; camera, John Wilcox; editor, Michael Gordon.

  Victor Mature (Ken); Janet Leigh (Linda); John Justin (Brain Sinden); Roland Culver (Sir Vincent Brampton); Liam Redmond (Ray Shaw); Earl Cameron (Jeroge); Orlando Martins (Jerusalem); Juma (Odongo); Lionel Ngakane (Kakora); Slim Harris (Renegade); Harry Quashie (O'Keefe); Cy Grant (Chief Massai); John Wynn (Charley); Arthur Lovegrove (Blake); May Estelle (Augy); Christopher Warbey (Kenny); John Cook (District Commissioner); Bob Isaacs (Henderson).

THE SHARKFIGHTERS (United Artists, 1956), C-73 min.
  Producer, Samuel Goldwyn, Jr.; director, Jerry Hopper; story, Jo and Art Napoleon; screenplay, Lawrence Roman and John Robinson; music, Jerome Moross; song, Mercy Ferrer and Cesar Portillo; music director, Emil Newman; camera, Lee Garmes; editor, Daniel Mandell.

  Victor Mature (Lieutenant Commander Ben Staves); Karen Steele (Martha Staves); James Olson (Ensign Harold Duncan); Philip Coolidge (Lieutenant Commander Leonard Evans); Claude Akins (Chief "Gordy" Gordon); Rafael Campos (Carlos); George Neise (Commander George Zimmer); Nathan Yates (Captain Ruiz); Jesus Hernandez (Vincente); Master Sergeant Lorin Johns and CPO David Westlein (Themselves); Charles Collingwood (Narrator).

ZARAK (Columbia, 1957), C-99 min.
  Producers, Irving Allen and Albert R. Broccoli; associate producer, Phil C. Samuel; director, Terence Young; based on the novel *Zarak Khan* by A. J. Bevan; screenplay, Richard Maibaum; associate directors, Yakima Canutt and

492

John Gilling; music, William Alwyn; song, Norman Gimbel and Alwyn; music director, Muir Mathieson; assistant directors, Jack Martin and Bluey Hill; camera, John Wilcox, Ted Moore, and Cyril Knowles; editors, Alan Osbiston and Bert Rule.

Victor Mature (Zarak Khan); Michael Wilding (Major Ingram); Anita Ekberg (Salma); Bonar Colleano (Biri); Finlay Currie (The Mullah); Bernard Miles (Hassu); Frederick Valk (Haji Khan); Eunice Gayson (Cathy); Peter Illing (Ahmad); Eddie Byrne (Kasim); Patrick McGoohan (Moor Larkin); Harold Goodwin (Sergeant Higgins); Alec Mango (Akbar); Oscar Quitak (Youssuff); George Margo (Chief Jailor); Conrad Phillips (Young Officer).

THE LONG HAUL (Columbia, 1957), 88 min.
Producer, Maxwell Setton; associate producer, Tom Morahan; director Ken Hughes; based on the novel by Mervyn Mills; screenplay, Hughes; art director, John Hoesli; music director, Richard Taylor; music director-arranger, Trevor Duncan; assistant directors, Fred Slark and Ronnie Spencer; camera, Basil Emmett; editor, Raymond Poulton.

Victor Mature (Henry Miller); Gene Anderson (Connie Miller); Patrick Allen (Joe Easy); Diana Dors (Lynn); Liam Redmond (Casey); Peter Reynolds (Frank); Michael Wade (Butch Miller); Dervis Ward (Mutt); Murray Kash (Jeff); Jameson Clark (MacNaughton); John·Harvey (Superintendent Macrea); Roland Brand (Army Sergeant); Stanley Rose (Foreman); Raymond Barry (Depot Manager).

PICKUP ALLEY (a.k.a., INTERPOL) (Columbia, 1957), 92 min.
Producers, Irving Allen, Albert R. Broccoli; associate producer, Phil C. Samuels; director, John Gilling; based on a story by A. J. Forrest; screenplay, John Paxton; art director, Paul Sheriff; makeup, Roy Ashton; music, Richard Bennett; music director, Muir Mathieson; wardrobe, Elsa Fennell; assistant director, Bluey Hill; camera, Ted Moore; editor, Richard Best.

Victor Mature (Charles Sturgis); Anita Ekberg (Gina Berger); Trevor Howard (Frank McNally); Bonar Colleano (Amalio); Alec Mango (Salko); Peter Illing (Baris); Martin Benson (Jarolli); Marne Maitland (Guido); Eric Pohlmann (Fayala); Betty McDowall (Drug Addict); Sidney Tafler (Curtis); Gaylord Cavallarc (Amalio's Brother); Lionel Murton (Murphy); Harold Kasket (Kalish); Peter Elliott (Badek); Alfredo Rizzo (Abbata); Umberto Fiz (Monello); Kevin Stoney (Policeman).

CHINA DOLL (United Artists, 1958), 88 min.)
Executive producer, Robert E. Morrison; producer-director, Frank Borzage; based on the story "Time Is a Memory" by Kitty Buhler, based on another story by James Benson Nablo and Thomas F. Kelly; screenplay, Buhler; assistant director, Lew Borzage; production designer, Howard Richmond; makeup, Layne Britton; music Henry Vars; sound, Paul M. Holly; camera effects, David Koehler; camera, William Clothier; editor, Jack Murray.

Victor Mature (Captain Cliff Brandon); Li Li Hua (Shu-Jen [Precious Jewel]); Ward Bond (Father Cairns); Bob Mathias (Lieutenant Phil Gates); Johnny

Desmond (Sergeant Steve Hill); Elaine Curtis (Alice Nichols); Stuart Whitman (Lieutenant Dan O'Neill); Ann McCrea (Mona Perkins); Danny Chang (Ellington); Ken Perry (Sergeant Ernie Fleming); Tige Andrews (Corporal Carlo Menotti); Steve Mitchell (Corporal Dave Reisner); Don Barry (Sergeant Hal Foster); Ann Paige (Sally); Denver Pyle (Colonel Wiley); Tita Aragon (Shiso-Mee).

TANK FORCE! (a.k.a., NO TIME TO DIE, Columbia, 1958), C-103 min.

Producers, Irving Allen, Albert R. Broccoli; associate producer, Phil C. Samuel; director, Terence Young; story, Richard Maibaum; screenplay, Maibaum and Young; assistant director, Bluey Hill; music, Kenneth V. Jones; music director, Muir Mathieson; art director, John Box; technical advisor, Major K. P. Harris; makeup, William Lodge and Tom Smith; wardrobe, John McCorry; sound, Bert Ross; special effects, Cliff Richardson and Roy Whybrow; camera, Ted Moore; second unit camera, Cyril Knowles; editor, Bert Rule.

Victor Mature (Thatcher); Leo Genn (Sergeant Kendall); Bonar Colleano (Pole); Luciana Paluzzi (Carola); George Coulouris (Commandant); Robert Rietty (Alberto); Martin Boddey (S. S. Colonel); Alfred Burke (Captain Ritter); David Lodge (Australian Sergeant Major); George Pravda (Volkswagen Sergeant); Alan Tilvern (Silvernio); Percy Herbert and Kenneth Cope (English Soldiers); Maxwell Shaw (Sheikh); Anne Aubrey (Girl in Lido); Andreas Malandrinos (Cook); Ernest Walder (German Corporal); Sean Kelly (Bartlett); Anthony Newley (Noakes); Kenneth Fortesque (Johnson).

THE BANDIT OF ZHOBE (Columbia, 1959), C-80 min.

Producers, Irving Allen and Albert R. Broccoli; associate producer, Harold Huth; director, John Gilling; story, Richard Mailbaum; screenplay, John Gilling; assistant director, Ted Sturgis; wardrobe, Elsa Fennell; makeup, Colin Garde; art director, Duncan Sutherland; music, Kenneth V. Jones; music director, Muir Mathieson; song, Jones and Len Praverman; sound, Bert Ross and Alan Pattillo; camera, Ted Moore; second unit camera, Cyril Knowles; editor , Bert Rule.

Victor Mature (Kasim Khan); Anne Aubrey (Zena Crowley); Anthony Newley (Corporal Stokes); Norman Wooland (Major Crowley); Dermot Walsh (Captain Saunders); Walter Gotell (Azhad); Sean Kelly (Lieutenant Wylie); Paul Stassino (Hatti); Laurence Taylor (Ahmed); Dennis Shaw (Hussu); Murray Kash (Zecco); Maya Koumani (Tamara).

ESCORT WEST (United Artists, 1959), 75 min.

Producers, Robert E. Morrison and Nate H. Edwards; director, Francis D. Lyon; based on a story by Steven Hayes; screenplay, Leo Gordon and Fred Hartsook; assistant director, William Beaudine, Jr.; art director, Alfred Ybarra; set decorator, Mowbray Berkeley; makeup, Layne Britton; costumes, Elmer Ellsworth and Neva Rames; sound, Earl Crain, Sr.; special effects, David Koehler; camera, William Clothier; editor, Otto Ludwig.

Victor Mature (Ben Lassiter); Elaine Stewart (Beth Drury); Faith Domergue (Martha Drury); Reba Waters (Abbey Lassiter); Noah Beery, Jr. (Jamison); Leo

Gordon (Vogel); Rex Ingram (Nelson); John Hubbard (Lieutenant Weeks); Harry Carey, Jr. (Travis); Slim Pickens (Wheeler); Roy Barcroft (Doyle); William Ching (Captain Poole); Ken Curtis (Burch); X Brands (Tago); Chuck Hayward and Charles Soldani (Indians); Claire Dubrey (Mrs. Fenniman).

TIMBUKTU (United Artists, 1959), 91 min.
Producer, Edward Small; director, Jacques Tourneur; screenplay, Anthony Veiller and Paul Dudley; art director, Bill Glasgow; set decorator, Darrell Silvera; makeup, Layne Britton; costumes, Elva Martien; technical advisor, Feridun; music, Gerald Fried; sound, John Kean and Roy Cropper; special effects, Joe Zomar and Alex Weldon; camera, Maury Gertsman; editor, Grant Whytock.

Victor Mature (Mike Conway); Yvonne De Carlo (Natalie Dufort); George Dolenz (Colonel Dufort); John Dehner (Emir); Marcia Henderson (Jeanne Marat); James Foxx (Lieutenant Marat); Leonard Mudie (Mohamet Adani); Paul Wexler (Suleiman); Robert Clarke (Captain Girard); Willard Sage (Major Leroux); Mark Dana (Captain Rimbaud); Larry Perron (Dagana); Steve Darrell (Nazir); Larry Chance (Ahmed); Allan Pinson (Sergeant Trooper).

THE BIG CIRCUS (Allied Artists, 1959), C-108 min.
Producer, Irwin Allen; director, Joseph M. Newman; story, Allen; screenplay, Allen, Charles Bennett, and Irving Wallace; assistant director, Bill McGarry; music directors, Paul Sawtell and Bert Shefter; song, Sammy Fain and Paul Francis Webster; art director, Albert S. D'Agostino; set decorator, Robert Priestly; choreography, Barbette; costumes, Paul Zastupnevich; makeup, William Tuttle; technical advisor, Jimmie Wood; sound, Franklin Milton and Conrad Kahn; sound effects, Finn Ulback and Bert Schoenfeld; optical effects, Robert R. Hoag; camera, Winton C. Hoch; editor, Adrienne Fazan.

Victor Mature (Henry Jasper Whirling); Red Buttons (Randy Sherman); Rhonda Fleming (Helen Harrison); Kathryn Grant (Jeannie Whirling); Gilbert Roland (Zach Colino); Vincent Price (Hans Hagenfeld); Peter Lorre (Skeeter); David Nelson (Tommy Gordon); Adele Mara (Mama Colino); Howard McNear (Mr. Lomax); Charles Watts (Jonathan Nelson); Steve Allen (Himself); Hugo Zacchini (Human Cannonball); Dick Walker (Lion Tamer); The Flying Alexanders (Aerialists); Gene Mendez (Wirewalker); The Ronnie Lewis Trio (High-Ladder Equilibrists); and: The Jungleland Elephants, Tex Carr and His Chimpanzees, and Dick Berg's Movieland Seals.

HANNIBAL (Warner Bros., 1960), C-103 min.
Producer, Ottavio Poggi; directors, Edgar G. Ulmer, (uncredited) Ludovico Bragaglia; story, Poggi; treatment, Allesandro Continenza; screenplay, Mortimer Braus; art director, E. Kromberg; set decorator, G. Gentill; music, Carlo Rustichelli; music director, Franco Ferrara; costumes, Bartolini and Salimbeni; assistant director, N. Zanchin; camera, R. Masciocchi; editor, R. Cinquini.

Victor Mature (Hannibal); Rita Gam (Sylvia); Gabriele Ferzetti (Fabius Massimus); Milly Vitale (Danila); Rik Battaglia (Hasdrubal); Franco Silva (Maharbal); Mario Girotti (Quintilius); Mirko Ellis (Mago); Andrea Aureli (Varro).

THE TARTARS (a.k.a., I TARTARI), MGM, 1962), C-83 min.
Producer, Riccardo Gualino; director, Richard Thorpe; director Italian dialog version, Ferdinando Baldi; screenplay, Sabatino Ciuffini, Ambrogio Molteni, Gaio Fratini, Oreste Palella, and Enimmo Salvi; additional English dialog, Julian Vroome de Kassel; music, Renzo Rossellini; art directors, Oscar D'Amico, and Pasquale D'Alpino; costumes, Giovanna Natili; camera, Amerigo Gengarelli and Elios Vercelloni; editor, Maurizio Lucidi.

Victor Mature (Oleg); Orson Welles (Burandai); Folco Lulli (Togrul); Liana Orfei (Helga); Bella Cortez (Samia); Luciano Marin (Eric); Arnoldo Foa (Chu-Lung); Furio Meniconi (Sigrun).

AFTER THE FOX (a.k.a., CACCIA ALLA VOLPE, United Artists, 1966), C-102 min.
Producer, John Bryan; director, Vittorio De Sica; screenplay, Neil Simon and Cesare Zavattini; second unit directors, Giogio Stegani and Richard Talmadge; music director, Burt Bacharach; song, Bacharach and Hal David; costumes, Piero Tosi; titles, Maurice Binder; art director, Mario Garbuglia; camera, Leonida Barboni; editor, Russell Lloyd.

Peter Sellers (Aldo Vanucci); Britt Ekland (Gina); Lidia Brazzi (Teresa Vanucci); Victor Mature (Tony Powell); Paolo Stoppa (Pollo); Tino Guazzelli (Siepi); Mac Romay (Carlo); Akim Tamiroff (Okra); Martin Balsam (Harry); Maria Grazia Buccelli (Okra's Sister); Lando Buzzanca (Captain of the Guardia); Tiberio Murgia (Policeman); Enzo Fiermonte (Raymond); Carlo Croccolo (Cafe Proprietor); Maurice Denham (Chief of Interpol); Pier Luigi Pizzi (Doctor).

HEAD (Columbia, 1968), C-86 min.
Executive producer, Bert Schneider; producers, Bob Rafelson and Jack Nicholson; director, Rafelson; screenplay, Rafelson and Nicholson; art director, Sydney Z. Litwack; set decorator, Ned Parsons; assistant director, Jon Andersen; music director, Ken Thorne; choreography, Toni Basil; songs, Gerry Goffin and Carole King; Peter Tork; King and Toni Stern; and Nilsson; costumes, Gene Ashman; special effects, Chuck Gaspar; special color effects, Burton Gershfield and Bruce Lane; camera, Michel Hugo; editor, Mike Pozen.

Peter Tork, David Jones, Micky Dolenz and Michael Nesmith (The Monkees); Annette Funicello (Minnie); Victor Mature (The Big Victor); Timothy Carey (Lord High 'n Low); Logan Ramsey (Officer Faye Lapid); Abraham Sofaer (Swami); Vito Scotti (I, Vitteloni); Charles Macaulay (Inspector Shrink); T. C. Jones (Mr. and Mrs. Ace); Charles Irving (Mayor Feedback); William Bagdad (Black Sheik); Sonny Liston (Extra); Percy Helton (Heraldic Messenger); Ray Nitschke (Private One); Frank Zappa (The Critic); Carol Doda (Sally Silicone); Terry Garr (Testy True); June Fairchild (The Jumper); I. J. Jefferson (Lady Pleasure).

496

EVERY LITTLE CROOK AND NANNY (MGM, 1972), C-92 min.

Producer, Leonard J. Ackerman; associate producer, Nicky Blair; director, Cy Howard; based on the novel by Evan Hunter; screenplay, Howard, Jonathan Axelrod, and Robert Klane; music, Fred Karlin; song, Karlin and Tylwyth Kymry; production designer, Philip Jefferies; set decorator, James I. Berkey; wardrobe, Margo Baxley and Buckey Rous; assistant director, Ted Schilz; sound, Bruce Wright and Harry W. Tetrick; camera, Philip Lathrop; editor, Henry Berman.

Lynn Redgrave (Nanny [Miss Poole]); Victor Mature (Carmine Ganucci); Paul Sand (Benny Napkins); Maggie Blye (Stella Ganucci); Austin Pendleton (Luther); John Astin (Garbugli); Dom DeLuise (Azzecca); Louise Sorel (Marie); Phillip Graves (Lewis Ganucci); Lou Cutell (Landruncola); Leopoldo Trieste (Truffatore); Pat Morita (Nonaka); Phil Foster (Lieutenant Bozzaris); Pat Harrington (Willie Shakespeare); Katharine Victory (Jeanette Kay); Mina Kolb (Ida); Bebe Louise (Sarah); Sally Marr (Ida's Mother); Lee Kafafian (Bobby).

6' 1"
174 pounds
Brown hair
Brown eyes
Libra

Cornel Wilde

In the Forties, charm was Cornel Wilde's most saleable screen commodity. With his dark, curly hair, gleaming smile, and solid physique, he was the frosting on the cake in such pictures as Twentieth Century-Fox's *Centennial Summer* (1946) and *Forever Amber* (1947). When he attempted to project the complexities of composer Frederic Chopin in *A Song to Remember* (Columbia, 1945) he fell flat on his face.

Yet, in the Fifties and Sixties, Cornel emerged as a more than competent director/producer/actor in a series of personal film projects, which usually told of man's struggle to survive against alien society, as in *The Naked Prey* (Paramount, 1965). These pictures require one to reassess the scope and depth of Cornel Wilde as both performer and private citizen. Obviously he was and is far more than just a refugee from costume film epics.

Cornelius Louis Wilde was born in New York City on Wednesday, October 13, 1915. He and his older sister, Edith, were the children of Louis and Renee Wilde, citizens of Hungary. In 1915, their father was stationed in New York as export manager of a Hungarian firm handling perfumes and cosmetics. The family was forced to return to Hungary at the outset of World War I when Louis was commissioned captain in a cavalry unit. In 1920, the Wildes returned to New York under the immigration quota, but due to a nervous disorder contracted in the war, Louis was not able to work on a full-time basis.

A quick-witted, intelligent, and aggressive youngster, Cornelius graduated from New York's prestigious Townsend Harris High School at the age of fourteen, but his hopes of going on to college were postponed; his father's health did not improve and he was in constant pain or under sedation. The family then deemed it wise to return to Hungary, where Louis could receive medical care at government expense. While they were there Mr. Wilde negotiated for a cavalry disability pension.

Cornelius traveled for six months through France and Czechoslovakia. He returned to Budapest and enrolled in an art school, where he also took up the Hungarian national sport of fencing. By his sixteenth birthday he could speak six languages fluently: Hungarian, French, German, Italian, Russian and English.

After a year, the Wilde family once again made the long ocean voyage to New York. Determined that he would obtain a college education, Cornelius worked at various odd jobs to save money toward this goal. Over a period of two years he sold toys in Macy's basement, worked as a commercial artist, sold advertising for a French-language newspaper, and served as a counselor for a boys' club.

In 1933, he enrolled in New York's City College for a four-year premedical course while working nights at the Bendiner and Schlesinger Pharmacy Company. He completed the course work in three years, and was offered a scholarship to the College of Physicians and Surgeons at Columbia University. As an avocation and to keep in shape, he continued fencing and won several medals while representing the Joseph Vince Salles d'Armes in intercollegiate competitions. He was chosen for the U.S. fencing team in the 1936 Olympics, but fate intervened in the form of the Theodore Irvine Studio of the Theatre. As a result, he was to put aside his pursuit of a medical career as well as the opportunity to fence in the Berlin Olympic arena. After he became active in the Theodore Irvine group, he decided that his future lay in the theatre.

In 1935, he joined a stock company in Saugerties, New York, a venture which proved to be ill-fated. The company folded after a week, and Cornelius fell back on his past experience as a boys' club counselor. In this position, he staged a youngsters' production of Eugene O'Neill's *The Emperor Jones,* and was then recalled to Manhattan for a lead role, along with Gladys Shelley, in *Moon over Mulberry Street* (Lyceum Theatre: September 4, 1935, 303 performances). It was for this play that he shortened his name to Cornel. Of this comedy by Nicholas Cosentino, *Women's Wear Daily* said, "[It is] a mild, inoffensive and uninteresting little play." The same publication went on to note, "The boy of Mulberry Street, played by Cornel Wilde, is projected very stiffly but this youth, who, under able direction, would likely show promise." Cornel left this show—which had already incurred the wrath of various Italian-American groups for its ethnic slurs—and was replaced in the production by Norman Stuart.

Cornel elected to sign with the Theatre Guild for their presentation of Ladislas Fodor's *Love Is Not Simple,* starring Ina Claire and Dennis King. The Philip Moeller-staged comedy opened on November 4, 1935, at the Chestnut Street Opera House in Philadelphia and closed on November 16. Billed as "Cornell Wydle," Cornel played the part of a student in this production, which never made it to New York.

In the summer of 1936, he joined the Ivoryton Stock Company in Connecticut, and in the fall of that year, he won a featured part in the costume drama, *Daughters of Atreus* (44th Street Theatre: October 14, 1936, 13 performances). The play by Robert Turney was based on the Greek tragedies of Aeschylus and Sophocles and detailed the sacrifice of Iphegenia and the murder of Klytaimnestra by Orestes. Mme. Maria Ouspenskaya, of the Moscow Art Theatre, was featured as Polymnia. Cornel had a supporting role as Phaon. Among others in the supporting cast were such aspiring actors as Tom Neal (Hippolytos), Edmond O'Brien (Pylades), and Gale Gordon (Agamemnon).

Just as Hollywood was enjoying its golden age, so Broadway was experiencing its richest theatrical decade, and in the productive stage season, Cornel was never long without work. For *Having Wonderful Time* (Lyceum Theatre: February 20, 1937, 310 performances), Jules (later John) Garfield and Katherine Locke had the leads, and Cornel had the bit part as Doc. His tiny role required him to announce from an offstage speaker, "Luncheon is served," and not much else. Thus, to earn extra money, Cornel gladly accepted the post of assistant stage manager. To fill in his time backstage while the cast was going through its paces of detailing life and love at the Catskills' resort of Camp Kare-Free (as envisioned by playwright Arthur Kober), Cornel wrote a play, a fencing comedy which he called *Touché*. He became so absorbed in this creative endeavor that he forgot his loudspeaker line on three separate performances and was fired. He had finished writing his play, using the pseudonym of Clark Wales, but now he needed a paying job.

His career was on rather tenuous grounds when, on September 21, 1937, Wilde eloped to Elkton, Maryland, with a young actress known as Patricia Knight.[1] They had met at a booking office in New York ten months earlier, and, although she had refused his many requests for a date, "I had to make a test and so I asked her if she would make the test with me. Much as she disliked me, she couldn't resist that, because she was looking for work." Her dislike obviously turned to love. At the time of their marriage Cornel was twenty-two and she was seventeen.

---

[1]She was born Marjory Heinzen in Boston, the daughter of a leather broker. Cornel later recalled, "When we married I had exactly $35 and we couldn't spare any of that for a ring, so Pat used one she'd had since childhood."

The couple spent their honeymoon performing in an unsuccessful off-Broadway revival of *Moon over Mulberry Street,* which was later presented in Brooklyn, Jersey City, and other lesser booking spots. Cornel did some translating of German and Hungarian plays into English for the not very generous sum of eighty-six dollars a play. Because he was fluent in several languages, he frequently found employment doing character roles that called for different foreign dialects on radio shows, especially "The March of Time." In the spring of 1938, he and Patricia participated in a drama festival at Ann Arbor, Michigan. They then spent the summer in stock at Gloucester, Massachusetts.

Back in New York when he wasn't taking assignments *on* radio shows, Cornel was attempting to peddle his scripts *for* radio programs, and he did sell a few, including one for Kate Smith's show. He continued making the rounds of casting agents, and later was approached to join the cast of *The White Plume.* It was an operetta version of *Cyrano de Bergerac,* adapted by Charles O. Locke, with a score by Samuel Pokrass and additional songs by Vernon Duke. George Houston (the co-stager) was Cyrano, with Ruby Mercer as Roxanne and Eric Mattson as Christian. Other hopefuls in the cast included Hope Emerson and Hal Forde. Rather than his stage presence, it was Cornel's fencing ability which earned him a role in the show as performer and unofficial coach to the other fencers. The ambitious production played a two-week pre-Broadway engagement at the Forrest Theatre in Philadelphia in early 1939, but the venture collapsed soon after that.

Next came *Jeremiah* (Guild Theatre:February 3, 1939, 35 performances), a stern anti-war play written by Stefan Zweig in 1917 and translated by John Gassner. Kent Smith was in the title role, in a cast that included Alfred Ryder, Effie Shannon, Arthur Byron, and Cornel as Nehemiah. The production did not meet with the anticipated favorable audience response. As the *New York Daily News* saw it, "The drama of lamentations has a hard row to hoe in a time of general lamentations." Regarding the cast, *Variety* reported, "Doubtful if any performances could enliven such a musty script."

In the summer of 1939, Cornel was back at the Bass Rocks Theatre in Gloucester, Massachusetts, appearing with Mary Brian in *French without Tears.* That fall, back in New York, Cornel was cast in Victor Wolfson's *Pastoral* (Henry Miller Theatre: November 1, 1939, 14 performances). Cornel appeared as Reef Tabanian. Set in a Catskill farmhouse, the short-lived show was faulted by the *New York Times* for its "too mildly piquant" comedy flavor and was soon forgotten by almost everyone.

Cornel had a bit of good luck in 1939 when he was hired by Laurence Olivier and Vivien Leigh as a technical advisor on the fencing sequences for their $120,000 revival of *Romeo and Juliet,* to be staged in New York the following year. He was also signed to assume the role

501

of Tybalt while Patricia was contracted for a smaller part. Since Olivier was commissioned by MGM to co-star in *Pride and Prejudice* (1940), to be filmed in Hollywood, rehearsals for the play took place there. While he was in Hollywood, Warner Bros. proposed a contract to Cornel after he had tested with them for several months. It seemed a lucrative venture for him from several angles, but at that time he was unable to do more than just talk about it. (Meanwhile, Patricia had lost their baby in a miscarriage.)

Romeo and Juliet tried out in San Francisco and Chicago, where it enjoyed a reasonable amount of success. In New York, however, it met with resistance upon its debut at the 55th Street Theatre (May 9, 1940). Despite a cast that included Olivier, Leigh, Edmond O'Brien (as Mercutio), Dame May Whitty (as the Nurse), Alexander Knox (as Friar Laurence), Halliwell Hobbes (Capulet), and Cornel, the show closed after only thirty-six performances. During the rehearsal period and in the brief run of the drama, Cornel received a total of eighteen scars from dueling with Olivier, who according to Wilde, "sometimes forgot certain aspects" of the art of fencing.

With the closing of *Romeo and Juliet,* Cornel's next professional step was an obvious one when Warners renewed their offer. There was money to be made in Hollywood, and he had become discouraged with the tribulations of trying to make a success of himself on the New York stage. He wanted to provide a home for his wife other than hotel living, and he was fed up with the deprivation that "real" acting involved. There was every reason for him to take advantage of a film contract and to "go Hollywood." He was convinced this path would lead to fame and fortune, as it eventually did.

His first screen appearance was in a bit part in *The Lady with Red Hair* (Warner Bros., 1940), which starred Miriam Hopkins as the great stage actress, Mrs. Leslie Carter, and Claude Rains as impresario David Belasco. In a recent letter, Wilde termed his debut cinema role as "nothing much."

Next, he was tested for a feature part in Raoul Walsh's *High Sierra* (Warner Bros., 1941), a film originally planned as a starring vehicle for Paul Muni. Muni balked at playing another gangster and tore up his studio contract. Warners' George Raft did not want to assume a role in which the character died at the end of the film, so it was resident baddie Humphrey Bogart who got the role, paving another step toward his emerging stardom. Wilde got the thirteenth-billed role in the film because, as he told Gordon Gow of *Films and Filming,* years later "The camerawork in most tests is very slapdash. I looked sombre and dark and, I suppose, vicious." He appears in the well-regarded feature as Louis Mendoza,[2] a Mexican hotel desk clerk employed at a swank

[2]Played by Perry Lopez in the 1955 Warners' remake, *I Died a Thousand Times,* starring Jack Palance, Shelley Winters and Lee Marvin.

southern California resort hotel, the Tropico Inn. He is the inside man for a carefully planned robbery engineered by the last of the Dillinger mob, Mad Dog Roy Earle (Bogart). The holdup is carried out on schedule, but two of the crooks (Arthur Kennedy and Alan Curtis) are killed while trying to escape the police, and the loot is burned. Mendoza then is captured and fingers Earle and his girl friend (Ida Lupino). Aside from Bogart's magnificent performance, most critical attention went to Lupino's moll, the freshness of Joan Leslie's Velma, and the sturdiness of Kennedy and Curtis.

A low-budget B film followed. In *Knockout* (Warner Bros., 1941), also known as *Right to the Heart,* a prizefight drama, Cornel is a boxer dispatched by the rising young champ (Arthur Kennedy). While Cornel describes his part as a "nice guy; blah," there are many who regard this tight-knit little feature as a solid entry, and especially laud Kennedy's performance. Others in the cast included two ex-Paramount players, Olympa Bradna and Anthony Quinn.[3]

Because of his disgust with most of his Warner Bros. stay, Cornel tends to ignore (or forget) much of his work at the studio. In fact, he insists that he was not in *Kisses for Breakfast* (Warner Bros., 1941). Cornel's role as Chet Oakley was not much, but neither was the feature, which starred Dennis Morgan and Jane Wyatt. "[It] turns out as a curious admixture of slapstick and farce comedy" (*Variety*). Much in the vein of *I Love You Again* (MGM, 1940), but without the felicity of that William Powell-Myrna Loy encounter, the Warners' attempt is too filled with silly hokum as amnesiac Morgan remarries (this time to Wyatt), forgetting that up north he already has a spouse (Shirley Ross).

By August, 1941, since he had not yet been given a chance at "real" acting, Cornel knew that if he remained with Warners he would have no opportunity to climb out of the "young character heavy" mold in which the studio had carelessly placed him. His agent arranged a screen test with Twentieth Century-Fox, but on Cornel's conditions. The conditions were that he would select his own material for the test, which was to be filmed in two segments. He wrote a comedy bit for himself, similar to a monologue that might have been done by Bob Hope, in which he stated all the things he had wanted to say on his first date with Patricia Knight but had not. For the other portion of the test he performed a dramatic scene from *The White Steed* for which he affected an Irish brogue.[4]

Hollywood's and the Hearst newspaper chain's powerful lady of the

---

[3]In *"B" Movies* (Curtis, 1973), author Don Miller stated, "The best Warner 'B' of 1941 was *Knockout.* The threadbare tale of a boxer who acquires a big head and subsequently gets his comeuppance seemed fresh and original because of M. Coates Webster's screenplay and its handling by director William Clemens."

[4]In the 1939 Broadway presentation of *The White Steed,* Barry Fitzgerald had played the character that Wilde chose for the test.

columns, Louella O. Parsons, saw Cornel's screen test and wrote about him in her next piece, saying that she had seen nothing better since Paul Muni had come to Hollywood. "I was insecure enough to carry that newspaper clipping in my wallet for two years," Cornel told Gordon Gow.

Darryl F. Zanuck of Twentieth Century-Fox liked what he saw, too, and offered a contract. Cornel was able to obtain a release from Warners and accepted Zanuck's bid.

His new employers put him to work at once in an inexpensive comedy, *The Perfect Snob* (Twentieth Century-Fox, 1941). He had the part of Mike Lord, the alleged poor boy who actually owns a Hawaiian sugar plantation and vies with pal Anthony Quinn for the hand of a millionaire's daughter (Lynn Bari). Neither the Honolulu locales (courtesy of the Fox backlot) or the storyline was great shakes, but the game cast (especially Bari as the daughter and Charlotte Greenwood and Charlie Ruggles as her harassed parents) made the double-bill fodder very enjoyable.

As often happens in moviemaking, the casting of Cornel in this film was almost accidental. The part had originally been announced for John Sutton, a Fox contractee who had been paired with Miss Bari, the Queen of the B's, in *Moon over Her Shoulder* (Twentieth Century-Fox,

With Anthony Quinn and Lynn Bari in a publicity shot for *The Perfect Snob* (1941)

1940). But the India-born actor had developed a case of influenza. Regarding Cornel's appearance in this film, *Variety* decided that "screen newcomer Wilde carries his role with ease, displaying a personality that indicates he can stay around Hollywood beyond the first option date."

"As an action film of the more rudimentary kind, *Manila Calling* [Twentieth Century-Fox, 1942] is continuously noisy." So reported the *New York Times* of this action feature whose plot involved the Japanese invasion of the Philippines. The versatile cast included Lloyd Nolan as hero Lucky Matthews, Carole "the Ping Girl" Landis as the heroine, and a supporting cast that boasted James Gleason, Ralph "Dick Tracy" Byrd, Elisha Cook, Jr., and Martin Kosleck. Cornel had an opportunity to wax dramatic as a civilian caught in the Axis thrust. He, along with most of the cast, is killed by the enemy's bombs. The well-paced film was Mr. Zanuck's way of selling patriotism, and the sounds of guns and aircraft were appropriately loud. Cornel's reaction to *Manila Calling* is: "I hated the film and remember as little as possible about it."

With such on-the-lot competition as Dana Andrews, Alan Curtis, Richard Derr, John Loder, George Montgomery, Ted North, John Sutton, and Shepperd Strudwick—not to mention the front ranks of male players (Don Ameche, Henry Fonda, Richard Greene, Victor Mature, John Payne, Tyrone Power, Cesar Romero)—it was little wonder that Cornel struggled one step forward and half a step backward in his efforts to gain recognition from his employers, as well as from the public.

Wilde's biggest role to that date came with *Life Begins at Eight-Thirty* (Twentieth Century-Fox, 1942), directed by Irving Pichel from the Emlyn Williams' play, *Yesterday's Magic*.[5] Nunnally Johnson produced and wrote the screenplay about an aging actor (Monty Woolley), a reprobate who remains drunk most of the time hoping to keep his crippled daughter (Ida Lupino) by his side. His insecurity is aggravated with the introduction of a new beau (Cornel), who wants to marry her. Bosley Crowther, in the *New York Times* singled Cornel out by writing, "Cornel Wilde, a newcomer, betrays a trace of juvenility as the oddly impulsive young suitor."

On February 22, 1943, Patricia Knight Wilde gave birth to a daughter. Born in a Los Angeles hospital, the infant was christened Wendy.

Due to an old back injury, Cornel was exempt from serving with the Armed Forces during World War II, but he gave freely of his time at the Hollywood Canteen, on USO tours, and participated in many hospital tours.

Considering the fact that so many of the eligible Hollywood actors

[5]In the 1942 Broadway play, Alfred Drake played the role of Robert, which Cornel would play in the film version.

With Monty Woolley and Ida Lupino in *Life Begins at Eight-Thirty* (1942)

With Sonja Henie and Jack Oakie in *Wintertime* (1943)

were away on military duty, it was rather strange that Cornel did not gain more film roles than he did during this period. He next showed up sixth billed as Sonja Henie's bland romantic interest in her final skating whirl[6] in Twentieth Century-Fox's *Wintertime* (1943). With dimpled Sonja skating and dancing, and Jack Oakie and Cesar Romero providing questionable laughs in a weak plot, Cornel had little to do but stand by and watch the proceedings with a fixed, toothy smile.

For several years, Columbia Pictures had had an idea for a film on Frederic Chopin's life (1810-1849) but did nothing about it until early 1944, when it was felt that the time was right for a story of a composer of classical music.[7] When rumors started circulated about Columbia's big plans, Cornel pleaded with his agent for three months to set up a screen test for him to play the role of the musician.

No luck! Here he had found finally a screen story idea that he believed in and that would provide the chance to show his peers that he could act. His frustration was compounded by the general opinion among studio heads that he was not the type; he was too healthy looking.[8] Then, at the Hollywood YMCA where he fenced regularly, he met Charles Vidor, who was to direct the Chopin film. Vidor enjoyed fencing with Cornel, and, as Wilde once said to the press: "He suddenly got the idea that I would be right for Chopin." Vidor gave him the chance to make a test. "I asked the wardrobe people to make the shoulders narrower and, of course, the make-up was paler than I'd had in previous films. And I didn't use robust movements," he was to say in 1970. "One of the things I felt vehemently then and always have, is that acting should be what the word literally means. You should be portraying something other than yourself, not merely playing facets of yourself in different situations." It took four tests before the Columbia top brass, including Harry Cohn, were convinced that he was their man, after which a trade deal was arranged with Twentieth. Cornel was loaned to Columbia in exchange for Alexander Knox for the title role in Darryl F. Zanuck's *Wilson.*

Although José Iturbi (unbilled) was to supply the piano playing of the screen Chopin, director Vidor wanted several camera shots of Cornel's hands on the keyboard in synchronization with the music. Cornel

[6]Her Fox leading men had included: Don Ameche for *One in a Million* (1936), Tyrone Power for *Thin Ice* (1937), Don Ameche and Cesar Romero for *Happy Landing* (1938), Richard Greene and Cesar Romero for *My Lucky Star* (1938), Tyrone Power and Rudy Vallee in *Second Fiddle* (1939), Ray Milland and Robert Cummings in *Everything Happens at Night* (1939), John Payne in *Sun Valley Serenade* (1941), and *Iceland* (1942).

[7]Warner Bros. had its Cole Porter story *Night and Day* (1946) and George Gershwin biography *Rhapsody in Blue* (1945) in the works, MGM would counter with their Jerome Kern's tale, *Till the Clouds Roll By* (1946) and the Schumann account, *Song of Love* (1947), Universal had its *Song of Scheherazade* (1947) the alleged chronicle of Rimsky-Korsakov, and Twentieth Century-Fox had its own rash of screen biographies of Tin Pan Alley composers.

[8]Chopin was short, slight, effeminate, aristocratic, and consumptive.

With Merle Oberon in *A Song to Remember* (1945)

practiced with a concert pianist for some four hundred hours, learning
to play a dozen intricate passages. Teacher and pupil used two pianos,
one silent and one audible. The professional pianist played a few bars
on the audible piano, and Cornel would repeat those bars on the silent
piano until he could synchronize his fingers with his instructor's.

Much of Sidney Buchman's screenplay for the Technicolor film was
fictional (and that is being charitable), but it afforded a more workable
story by exaggerating the composer's relationship with George Sand
(Merle Oberon), the woman novelist who took a man's name and wore
men's trousers.[9]

A Song to Remember (Columbia, 1945) begins in a village near Warsaw when Chopin is the ten-year-old prodigy of his teacher, Joseph
Elsner (badly overplayed by Paul Muni). Later, as a young man, he
goes to Paris with Elsner, where he meets and conducts a passionate
love affair with the possessive, mercurial Aurore—George Sand. She

---

[9]The 113-minute feature is filled with awkward moments: Lady George Sand advises
Chopin, "You could make miracles of music in Majorca," but later warns him, "Dis-
continue that so-called Polonaise jumble you've been playing for days." Reflecting how
cowed and awed some of Hollywood's "creative" set was by classical music, there is the
moment in *A Song to Remember* when the camera pans in on a piano recital. Outside, a
group of enraptured workers stand at attention, whispering to one another, "Sh-hh-hh!
Liszt!" Evidentally, the scripter felt moviegoers were in need of a reminder that classical
music was to be treated with reverence.

introduces him to the continental musical set of Paris, but he ends their affair ten years later when he disobeys her wishes and embarks on a concert tour to raise money for beleaguered Poland. (One soul warns him "to make this tour is literally and actually suicide.") On the road, his lifelong affliction, tuberculosis, gets the better of him, he begins to cough blood, and soon collapses. On his deathbed, he asks to see Sand, but she replies by messenger that she is too busy (she is having her portrait painted). He dies in Paris at the age of thirty-nine.

On the film's release in January, 1945—it had a splashy debut at Radio City Music Hall on the twenty-fifth—*Newsweek* Magazine stated, "The film's best performance is that of a comparative newcomer, Cornel Wilde, as the troubled, inspired Pole." *Life* Magazine found that "the story does such grave injustice to historical fact that *A Song to Remember* becomes a romanticized travesty on Chopin's life." The *New York Times* voiced, "José Iturbi . . . is the real star of the picture, for it is the score which sings most brilliantly. Mr. Wilde is not called upon to demonstrate much acting ability."

On working with Muni, an actor he had admired, Cornel has said, "He was very difficult to work with. Far from generous with a new, young actor—me. He wouldn't even read the lines with me when we first started. He said he didn't want to hear how I did it, he had no interest in how I portrayed it; he had his own conception of Chopin and he told me that he had worked on his role in relation to that conception."[10]

Despite all the difficulties that Cornel experienced in performing in *A Song to Remember*, a sufficient number of the members of the Academy of Motion Picture Arts and Sciences thought he gave a decent enough job to honor him with an Academy Award nomination as Best Actor of 1945. However, the Oscar was given to Ray Milland for *Lost Weekend* (Paramount) at the first kleig-lighted, black-tie gala since the war started. But the "comparative newcomer," who had been typed by Warners as a heavy and by Twentieth as the all-American hero, proved to Hollywood that he could act. More importantly, the moviegoers had found him very appealing.

In its July, 1946 issue, *Photoplay* Magazine printed a letter from two Albuquerque, N.M., fans, Anne Medic and Betty Bates. The two young ladies wrote: "How the Hollywood masterminds could have passed up Cornel Wilde's performance as Chopin . . . and instead given the coveted award to Ray Milland . . . is a little beyond our comprehen-

---

[10]In *Paul Muni: His Life and His Films* (A.S. Barnes, 1974), Michael B. Druxman points out that it was Glenn Ford who was Muni's choice to play Chopin, but that actor was in the Marines at the time. Then, too, Harry Cohn had barred Muni's wife-mentor-coach Bella from the set and the star could not be properly handled. Muni's words to Wilde on the first day of shooting were: "Dear boy, I have done considerable research on Chopin and have my own interpretation as to how he should be portrayed. I will play to my conception . . . not yours."

sive powers. . . . The role of Chopin was no easy task; and Mr. Wilde did not just portray Chopin, he was the famous composer."

With his newly gained fame, all the fan magazines pitched in to publicize the newest sexy screen heart-throb. It was revealed that the six-foot, one-inch hero weighed 170 pounds and had brown eyes, brown hair, and had to shave twice a day. His pet nickname for himself was said to be "Hormel" Wilde and he considered his wife prettier than any of his leading ladies.

It was further told that Cornel liked to cook and to eat. His favorite food was fish covered with French sauces and he loved to chew persimmons for an afternoon snack. Although he was of Hungarian descent, it was learned that he disliked Hungarian foods because of the spices. The Wilde home, an English-style Beverly Hills canyon house, was neatly furnished inside and tailored outside, because he enjoyed mowing lawns, pruning trees, and setting rock gardens. Reading in bed was a joy of his, but it was reported that he always fell asleep too quickly. While in that reclining position, he wore pajamas, kept the windows open, and did not use a pillow. Columnist Sidney Skolsky reported in the *Hollywood Citizen-News,* "He will tell you that his wife is an obliging person and that anything he does anywhere is okay with her."

By special arrangement (and before the release of *A Song to Remember)* Cornel's contract was revised in early 1945 to include a proviso for a loanout to Columbia for one picture a year through 1948. Under the new deal, and to capitalize on his fencing talents (which Fox would not do since they had Tyrone Power for those swashbuckling assignments), Columbia put him into an original story by Wilfrid Pettitt entitled *A Thousand and One Nights* (1945) as a singing Aladdin.[11] He "sang" one song only. In vivid Technicolor and directed by Alfred E. Green, it is not clear whether or not the film was intended as a spoof of the Maria Montez genre of harem movies. With Phil Silvers as his comedic sidekick, Aladdin rubs his lamp to produce a red-haired genie (Evelyn Keyes) who shoos away the very blonde, very bold princess (Adele Jergens) who has had her eyes on the lamp's owner. "I was prime material for all that crap," Cornel has confessed to reporters. "I looked too right for it. My face wasn't rough-hewn. It took a bit of age for me to look tougher and hard-bitten. I had it in the acting, but at that time I didn't look it—except for being physically strong." When one compares Cornel's Alladin to that of Donald O'Connor in *The Wonders of Aladdin* (Embassy, 1961), a very childish film at best, Wilde's performance is all the more gratifying.

---

[11]Mario Lanza, a tenor, was originally chosen to sing for Cornel, but he was dropped when it was felt that a baritone's voice was more befitting Cornel's physical appearance. Wilde's voice was dubbed by Tom Clark.

With Ethan Laidlaw (foreground, with whip), Phil Silvers, Gus Schilling, and Nestor Paiva in *A Thousand and One Nights* (1945)

Back at Twentieth, he was cast as Gene Tierney's writer-husband in *Leave Her to Heaven* (1945), described by Bosley Crowther in the *New York Times* as a "piece of cheap fiction done up in Technicolor and expensive sets." Ben Ames Williams wrote the one-million-copy bestseller, and Jo Swerling adapted it for the screen, leaving the lead figure (Tierney) as viperous as possible under existing production rules. As Richard, a man who has written a couple of novels with psychologically loaded titles such as *Time Without End* and *The Deep Well*, Cornel is unable to understand his beautiful, pouting, jealous wife, Ellen (Tierney).

This innocence which permeates Wilde's performance throughout much of *Leave Her to Heaven* would be his (near) surface stock-in-trade throughout the 1940s, giving his well-muscled appearance a vulnerable, appealing tone. Within this John M. Stahl-directed feature, Cornel's Richard Harland is so absorbed with his quest for personal recognition through writing, that he does not seem to care whether his wife wanders the countryside alone while he pounds away at his typewriter. In wanting him to herself, Ellen gets rid of potential intruders, beginning with his crippled young brother (Darryl Hickman), who drowns in Back-of-the-Moon Lake, Maine, while she watches. Next,

With Jeanne Crain in *Leave Her to Heaven* (1945)

she tosses herself down a flight of stairs to induce a miscarriage, and finally, she poisons her own coffee when she realizes that her husband is in love with her cousin (Jeanne Crain). Better he should have chosen the lovely cousin in the first place, but then there would have been no morose, maudlin tale.

James Agee in *Time* Magazine stated, "It is hard to work up any sustained sympathy for the upright characters," and the general criticism of Tierney's performance was expressed as "wooden." Nevertheless, she was put into the running for an Oscar as Best Actress of 1945, but rightfully lost to Joan Crawford of *Mildred Pierce* (Warner Bros.) However, Leon Shamroy managed to garner an Award for Best Color Cinematography for the film. In Cornel's opinion, *Leave Her to Heaven* "was a sumptously-made example of what Hollywood could do in that era of the 1940s. Beautiful, good cutting, off-beat characters. That was one I really liked."

In January, 1946, Cornel was placed on suspension for a brief time because he refused to undertake the role of a French teacher who is amused by, and in love with, a high school girl named *Margie* (Twentieth Century-Fox, 1946). His refusal was based on his belief that it was a secondary role, designed as back-up for Jeanne Crain in her first starring picture. He was replaced by Glenn Langan in the film that went on to gross 4.1 million dollars.

Instead, Cornel was seen next in Columbia's *The Bandit of Sherwood Forest* (1946) as Robert of Nottingham, the son of Robin Hood.

With Anita Louise in *The Bandit of Sherwood Forest* (1946)

In Technicolor, England's queen-mother (Jill Esmond) and her lady-in-waiting, Lady Catherine Maitland (Anita Louise), escape the palace ruled by the evil, ambitious regent (Henry Daniell). To Sherwood Forest they flee, in search of Robin Hood (Russell Hicks), presumably the only man alive who can rescue young King Henry III (Maurice R. Tauzin) from the regent who plans the death of the boy-king. In the forest the ladies meet a handsome, brash, curly-haired forester (Cornel) who offers to guide them to Robin. After the elderly Mr. Hood assembles his team of bowmen, he introduces the young forester as his son, who, he says, will lead the attack on the castle. With whizzing arrow and flashing sword, the son of Robin rescues the king and kills the wicked regent. He then lays down his weapons to marry Lady Catherine, while his followers, along with the royal household, express their approval.

For those moviegoers who remembered Douglas Fairbanks' turn (1920) or that of Errol Flynn (1938) as Robin Hood, it required a bit of a readjustment to accept wholesome, guileless Cornel in this imitation of the adventures of Robin Hood (*pere* or *fils*). However, once comparisons to swaggering Fairbanks or dashingly gallant Errol were forgotten, Cornel's performance had its own charm. He handled the athletics with ease and conviction, demonstrating that his fencing experience was not wasted. He may have been a bit too boyish in his courtship of the too coquettish Anita Louise, but there was a pleasing robustness to Wilde's capering that was endearing on its own terms. Evidentally, the public approved of Cornel and *The Bandit of Sherwood Forest* package, for the film grossed over three million dollars in distributors' domestic rentals.

Cornel was given the opportunity to again use a French accent in Twentieth Century-Fox's *Centennial Summer* (1946), that studio's answer to MGM's *Meet Me in St. Louis* (1944), featuring Judy Garland. The MGM bid for nostalgia won hands down, for the Otto Preminger production is a bit too lazy.[12] As John Kobal would write in *Gotta Sing Gotta Dance* (1971), "The score was Jerome Kern's last, and though the film is not without pleasure, the final result suffers from coyness, ornate self-indulgence and a sluggish pace, lacking that most vital ingredient, imagination."

In this 102-minute color excursion, Cornel is Philippe Lascalles, visiting Philadelphia in 1876 during the Exposition in honor of the birth of the United States. A pair of pretty sisters (Jeanne Crain and Linda Darnell) vie for his attentions and sing the rather pedestrian

---

[12]In *The Cinema of Otto Preminger* (Tantivy Press, 1971), the director told Gerald Pratley: "Today, I would not be capable of spending three or four months on *Centennial Summer*—neither the story or the characters would interest me. That is really a film I wouldn't do today. It was successful and it worked, and at that time it probably served some purpose in my life, and in my career. It's hard to say why, I can't tell you why I did it."

With Jeanne Crain, Dorothy Gish, Constance Bennett, Buddy Swan, and Barbara Whiting in *Centennial Summer* (1946)

score with voices dubbed. Wilde's oncamera competition in this period exercise was William Eythe, whose Fox days would soon end, driving the handsome actor onto the skids. The gambit of Cornel's character having linguistic problems dealing with the Yankees soon lost its glitter, and if it were not for Wilde's natural charm, the characterization would have become an unmitigated bore. Female moviegoers were particularly struck by Cornel's outfit in the extended costume ball sequence—he is dressed in doublet, mutton-sleeved shirt vest, topped by a ruffled collar.

At the start of 1947, Twentieth Century-Fox revealed that Cornel's salary had reached three thousand dollars per week, and that he had received more fan mail in the last quarter of 1946 than any other star on Zanuck's roster. It was a heady status, but it did not guarantee Cornel everything his professional heart might wish. For example, he and Robert Turney (who had written the play *Daughters of Atreus,* 1936) prepared a screen treatment of the life of Lord Byron that Cornel wanted to do, but the studio rejected the project.

On the other hand, Cornel's emergence as a star saw a supposedly long-buried feature come to light. Back in 1940, when Cornel had first come to Hollywood, he had been involved in an abortive film project dealing with a struggling young actor who becomes a press agent, helps out a down-and-out director (Dennis Brent), and renews a romance with a past girlfriend (Helen Beverly). Producer Jack Krieger took this footage, inserted some unrelated specialty acts (ranging from the DeCastro Sisters to the Terry Twins and the Slim Gaillard Trio) and released it on state-to-state distribution deals, as *Stairway for a Star*. Undiscerning filmgoers who were drawn into theatres showing this potpourri feature might well have wondered why or how Cornel had regressed, both histrionically and in years.

More up to date was Cornel's appearance in *The Homestretch* (Twentieth Century-Fox, 1947). From the title, one can surmise that the film deals with the racetrack; it was released just a few days ahead of the annual Kentucky Derby run. While Wanda Tuchock's original screenplay provided no earth-shattering dialog, Arthur Arling's color camera work gave excellent shots of various tracks and races. The "plot" involved Cornel as Jock Wallace of Maryland, a happy thoroughbred owner/trainer married to puritanical New Englander Maureen O'Hara. They quarrel when Helen Walker comes into the scene in pursuit of him, but they reconcile on Derby Day when their two horses take the top honors. The *New York Times'* critic declared that Cornel "is handsome and manly, both in dinner jacket and swimming trunks." While Victor Mature, Glenn Langan, or even Dick Haymes (if they had

With Glenn Langan and Maureen O'Hara in *The Homestretch* (1947)

added some songs for him to croon) could have handled the undemanding characterization assigned to Cornel in *The Homestretch,* he and Maureen O'Hara[13] made a very handsome oncamera couple, two performers who should have been teamed more often than they were, for with her fiery nature and his calm demeanor, they balanced each other's celluloid temperaments.

As a novel, *Forever Amber* was the hottest item to invade the bookstores since *Gone with the Wind.* The war-weary public of 1944 and 1945 virtually gobbled it up, lending fame and fortune to the hitherto unknown writer, Kathleen Winsor. The voluminous tale of seventeenth-century Amber St. Claire of London, whose bed-hopping including some twenty young healthy males, was banned in Boston, making it a "must read" on nearly everyone's list. Twentieth Century-Fox, always prone to purchasing bestsellers for filmization, quickly bought the screen rights for $200,000 and assigned Ring Lardner, Jr., Philip Dunne, and Jerome Cady to adapting the 956-page, 300,000-word book.

On his way home from the war, Zanuck discovered in London a blonde Welsh-Irish actress, Peggy Cummins, who was then on stage in the London run of *Junior Miss.* He sent for the nineteen-year-old Peggy and cast her as Amber. To director John M. Stahl, she was "like a little girl dressed up in her mother's clothes." Nevertheless, Zanuck envisioned her as a blonde Vivien Leigh, and the character of Amber as equal, or better, to Scarlett O'Hara or to Paulette Goddard's *Kitty,* then in production at Paramount.

In March, 1946, the estimated $4.5 million production began rolling at California's Monterey Peninsula. In lavish costumes designed by Rene Hubert, Miss Cummins was surrounded by a cast of handsome men (Cornel, Glenn Langan, George Sanders, and Vincent Price) in their Clinton Sandeen-created costumes of brocades that ran as high as thirty-five dollars a yard. After several production stoppages, the film was halted in May, 1946. One of the major difficulties, it developed, was Miss Cummins, who did not measure up physically to the fictional Amber. Topping the scale at one hundred pounds, the five-foot, one-inch-tall girl was not woman enough. The studio claimed a loss of $500,000, but implied that the money was retrievable when production could be resumed.

In October, 1946, the project was revived under the direction of Otto Preminger.[14] Buxom Linda Darnell took over as Amber and Richard

---

[13]In *The Great Movie Stars: The International Years* (St. Martin's Press, 1972) David Shipman reflects: "For years he was a sort of male Maureen O'Hara, confined to medium-budget swashbucklers and action melos. Like her, his acting career was at its peak in the 40s, but unlike her, his charm was limited. Ditto his acting ability."

[14]When Zanuck informed Preminger that he would have to direct *Forever Amber,* the

With Peggy Cummins (later replaced)
on the first day of shooting for
Forever Amber (1947)

Greene replaced Vincent Price, who had gone on to another studio project. Cornel then demanded more money for his sizeable role. His request was met with a suspension, but this problem was surmounted with an amicable readjustment in his pay scale.

Within the 138-minute *Forever Amber,* the village wench Amber meets army officer Bruce Carlton (Cornel) and his friend Lord Almsbury (Greene) as they pass through her town. Without encouragement, she follows them to London, where she becomes pregnant by Carlton before he goes off to sea. She is then tossed into debtor's prison, but is released in time to have her baby in more pleasant surroundings.

Later on within the epic, she is kept by Captain Morgan (Langan) until she embarks on a London stage career. When Morgan is killed in a duel, she hastily marries an eighty-year-old duke (Richard Haydn), from whom she expects a sizeable inheritance. She defies the duke when she rushes to a deserted house to nurse her true love, Carlton, back to health during the Black Plague of 1665, only to learn that he intends to marry another (Jane Dall). The duke is burned to death in

director, as he recalls in *The Cinema of Otto Preminger, supra* replied, "Darryl, when this book was submitted to the producers I couldn't even finish reading it . . . it was a horrible book. I couldn't make this film. . . . If I start it you will fire me." Although Zanuck promised Preminger anything he wanted, to salvage the project, the studio mogul insisted MGM's Lana Turner could not be borrowed and that contractee Linda Darnell would have to suffice. Years later, Preminger recalled, "I think it took seventeen weeks. I made the picture and I was unhappy with it. But, oddly enough, I was in Paris and the Cinematheque Francaise loved that film! They told me to look at it again, and I will maybe."

the Great Fire of London (1666), and Amber becomes the mistress of King Charles II (Sanders), a wise man who understands her perfectly. Carlton and his lady prepare to leave England for a new life in Virginia, when Amber gives up their son to him.

The "burning" of London took place at the Twentieth lot at three o'clock one autumn morning, and resulted in hundreds of telephone calls to the Beverly Hills fire department from worried neighbors. On top of that, to produce the proper effect, the fire had to be filmed a total of five times. Then began the enormous task of editing the 229,000 feet of film down to a length between 13,000 and 18,000.

The six-million-dollar film was released in October, 1947, and was promptly relegated to the Condemned List by the National Legion of Decency, whose members considered it a "glorification of immorality and licentiousness." This was followed by an edict from Francis Cardinal Spellman, Archbishop of New York, which was to be read at all masses in the archdiocese advising that Catholics "may not see *Forever Amber* with safe conscience." All of this, of course, was boxoffice music to the ears of Zanuck and the film's producer, William Perlman.

Virginia Wilson of *Motion Picture* Magazine wrote, "I consider Cornel definitely miscast," while James Agee in *Time* Magazine said that Cornel "uses both his facial expressions frequently." Understandably, even though this was one of the biggest films in which Cornel would appear, it is not by far his best-remembered screen performance.

Between the completion of *Amber* and its release, Cornel was shuttled to Columbia for his annual outing there. In *It Had to Be You* (1947) he pursues an heiress (Ginger Rogers), but he is really a figment

With Ginger Rogers and Percy Waram in *It Had To Be You* (1947)

519

of her imagination. Anyway, he appears on screen as an American Indian (tribe unknown) whose favorite word is "How!" or "How?" Meant to be a comedy, the film is pure corn, but Cornel confessed to Louella O. Parsons that Columbia was his favorite studio. "I make my best pictures at Columbia," he told her. (But at this point, contractee Larry Parks, who had scored in *The Jolson Story*, 1946, was the studio's favorite male player and in 1947 he would appear with Rita Hayworth in *Down to Earth*, a rather feckless musical comedy-fantasy, and in the swashbuckling entry, *The Swordsman*.)

On the homefront, things were hectic. As of October, 1947, the Wildes had separated three times. At the third separation, Cornel announced to the Los Angeles press: "There is only one cause. I have been so absorbed in work, because of a constant succession of pictures that I have not been able to bring to my wife the share of happiness she deserves. She merits a far happier life than the one she has experienced in the last year and we do not see any way of remedying the situation."

A week later they reconciled—again. Patricia, on the other hand, made no secret of her passion for a screen career of her own. For that purpose, she dated various influential professionals which, on the surface, did not appear to bother Cornel. Miss Parsons observed for her readers' benefit, "I'll bet if Pat committed a murder, he'd whitewash her. I've seen a lot of men in love in my day, but I've never seen one as adoring and blind to all faults as Cornel." After one of the reconciliations, Patricia wrote a letter to Hedda Hopper, stating "Cornel is absolutely everything to me. True, I want to work. All of us have creative tendencies, and mine seem to lean in one direction of the arts. But, if work interferes with my marriage, I'll settle for no career." In late 1947, Patricia appeared in two films, but created no large sensation in either: *Roses Are Red* (Twentieth Century-Fox) and *The Fabulous Texan* (Republic).

Meanwhile, Cornel was once again suspended by his home studio for refusing two roles. Douglas Fairbanks, Jr. replaced him in *That Lady in Ermine* (Twentieth Century-Fox, 1948), with Betty Grable, but Cornel was forced to relent and take the lead role in *The Walls of Jericho* (Twentieth Century-Fox, 1948). The suspension prompted Louella O. Parsons to write that Cornel was "hard to handle, temperamental, and possessed of an inflated ego." A feud between the actor and the columnist erupted, one that would last for two years.

The Walls of Jericho was written for the screen by Lamar Trotti, who adapted his scenario from the 1947 novel by Paul Wellman. The setting is Jericho, Kansas, a small town in many ways. Cornel is an attorney wed to a dipsomaniac (Ann Dvorak). Linda Darnell, the wife of the town newspaper publisher (Kirk Douglas), makes a pass at him, which he ignores. She then begins a gossip campaign against the lawyer. This is made easy by his apparent interest in a recent attractive law school

With Ann Dvorak, Marjorie Rambeau, and Linda Darnell in *The Walls of Jericho* (1948)

graduate (Anne Baxter). Egged on by Darnell, Dvorak shoots him and as he lies in the hospital between life and death, Baxter informs him that she has publicly confessed her love for him, and that the town is rid of the evil Darnell.

Performing under John M. Stahl's direction, Cornel appeared at a disadvantage in this tale of the midwest in the 1900s. As the *New York Times* would confirm, "[Although he] makes a fairly convincing counsel, [he is] one who often is peculiarly placid under stress."

Cornel was described by one critic as "muscularly attractive" for his part in *Road House* (Twentieth Century-Fox, 1948). Well directed by Jean Negulesco, from the screenplay by Edward Chodorov, the film relates the story of a psychotic roadhouse owner (Richard Widmark) who arranges for the prison parole of his friend (Cornel) after framing him on a fake robbery charge in the first place. He wants to further torture the poor guy for being in love with his girlfriend-singer (Ida Lupino). Miss Lupino, doing her own singing, introduced the song "Again," which went on to become a popular standard. As manager of the roadhouse, Cornel was required to protect the patrons as well as the employees. In a brutal fight scene, he whips a troublemaker for tossing Ida on top of the bar. The snarling, burly troublemaker was played by a three-hundred-pound ex-wrestler named Louis Bacigalupi, once known as the meanest wrestler in Los Angeles County.

With Ida Lupino in *Road House* **(1948)**

With Patricia Knight in *Shockproof* **(1949)**

Cornel's seven-year term contract with Twentieth Century-Fox ended with *Road House,* and he decided to freelance. The studio did not argue with his career decision, since he had proved to be a casting problem to them, not only with his repeated refusals to accept certain assignments, but because of his insistence that his wife be given star status.

Columbia gave in to his requests by starring them together in a low budget film called *Shockproof* (1949), which was sneaked into second-rate theatres as part of a double bill. Today, because of director Douglas Sirk's higher esteem, the film is regarded more favorably.[15]

In this Samuel Fuller-Helen Deutsch scripted project, Cornel is parole officer Griff Marat assigned to parolee Jenny Marsh (Patricia). He breaks up an affair she has with a gambler (John Baragrey), who was originally responsible for her going to jail. She shoots and kills the man, accidentally, and, together she and Cornel go to the police. Columnist Cal York wrote in *Photoplay:* "Pretty and comely Pat certainly has every right to a career of her own, no one denies that fact. But the town wonders why Cornel insisted it be at the expense of his own career after he fought and struggled to achieve a place of his own."

In March, 1949, Cornel and Patricia went to Switzerland, where he labored in Lazar Wechsler's production, *Four Days Leave* (Film Classics, 1950). Before leaving, he referred to his joint career with his wife by saying, "From now on we will lead our professional lives separately. And never the twain shall meet."[16] In this black-and-white feature made with English soundtrack dialog, Cornel is an American sailor on leave in the Alps who finds romance with a sales clerk (Josette Day). Others involved in this European co-production were Simone Signoret, John Baragrey, and Alan Hale, Jr. In this piece of fluff, more notice went to the champion skiers than to the cast or to the story.

Returning to the States, Cornel (or at least Patricia) must have had a change of mind about their announced commitment to separate careers. The couple, along with John Baragrey, tried their skills in a new

---

[15]In *Sirk on Sirk* (Viking Press 1972), the director told Jon Halliday: "As you may know, the original title [for *Shockproof*] was *The Lovers,* and there was something great in Fuller's ending, which was then changed by Helen Deutsch and Columbia, which I think was a shame. There was something gutty in Fuller's original script. The character of the copy was interesting. He fell in love. He left his job. He hid. And then it ended with shooting it out with the other policeman. Cop against cop. It was very melodramatic, of course, but in between the battle sequences there were situations of love. Love that cannot be fulfilled. Love in extreme circumstances, love socially conditioned . . . and impossible. In Fuller's ending the guy had changed. Something had started blooming in that goddam cop's soul. Of Miss Knight, Sirk recollects: "[Her] rather angular handsomeness, the pale lipstick face, with eyes trying to hide something, and an attitude of sameness about her against the changing backgrounds and melodramatic action. She was not enormously talented as an actress, but I decided to use this very lack of experience— and she was most flexible and willing and kind of understood what I was after—the sparse freedom of human existence."

[16]In 1950 Patricia would have the third female lead in Eagle Lion's *The Second Face.*

With Josette Day in *Four Days Leave* **(1950)**

comedy, *Western Winds,* by Charlotte Francis. During the month of August, 1950, the trio performed in the pre-Broadway outing at the summer theatres in Dennis, Cape Cod, Massachusetts, Westport, Connecticut (where, with a $11,800 weekly gross, they broke the house record), and at Marblehead, Massachusetts. However, it was later decided that the show would not do well in New York.

Back in Hollywood, the Wildes paid $77,000 for a mansion formerly owned by Norma Talmadge, set atop a hill in exclusive Bel Air.

In 1950, Cornel announced the formation of his own independent production company and acquired the screen rights to Leslie T. White's novel, *Lord Johnnie.* He was to play the title role, a highwayman and duelist, with Yvonne De Carlo pencilled in as his leading lady. Although his plans included filming in England, with Irving Rapper directing, the project did not materialize.

There were many who said that thirty-five-year-old Cornel was passe in the Hollywood of the 1950s, and to prove their point, they had only to refer to *Two Flags West* (Twentieth Century-Fox, 1950). Cornel returned to his old studio in fourth billing as a Union Army officer, Captain Mark Bradford, who wears a patch over his sightless right eye. In this film ("a gallant picture which may not have the brilliance or the dash of one supervised by veteran John Ford but will fully pass muster, nonetheless"—*New York Times*) Cornel's contributions, while substantial to the plot, were artistically negligible.

524

Cornel is the officer in the Rock Island, Illinois prison camp, who offers full pardon to the Confederate prisoners, headed by Colonel Clay Tucker (Joseph Cotten) if they will join the Union cavalry to fight Kiowa Indians in New Mexico. His pitch includes: "I don't mind saying that I'd be proud to have you with me as a unit, officers and men. Why don't you come along? The war's over for you, that's a fact and my offer is a way out of this stinking pest hole." He further tells them, "It's no charity picnic you're invited to. It's a soldier's life at forty cents a day."

The Confederates join up and the unit is sent to Fort Thorn, which is run by a tough Northern colonel (Jeff Chandler), who hates all rebels. His sultry, unhappy widowed sister-in-law is Elena Kenninston (Linda Darnell), about whom Cornel's character says, "The first time I ever saw her I fell head over heels and the first time I saw her she was being married to another man." Leon Shamroy's camera work, Alfred Newman's scoring, and Robert Wise's direction helped to make this film entertaining and fast-moving. Quite naturally, the highlight of the feature was the climactic Indian attack on the fort, with both sides giving their all (at least so it seemed on the big screen).

Very obviously, Cornel did not have his heart in such film work as *Two Flags West,* particularly when he was thrust into such a humiliatingly small assignment. Much more to his liking would be to reactivate his pet project of portraying Lord Byron on screen. Hedda Hopper wrote on this matter: "The casting would be quite apt. Cornel has a great deal of the temperament, as well as the dash and looks, of the moody, handsome poet." It was an ambition, however, that would never see fruition.

Just when it seemed that Cornel's career was taking a nose dive, Cecil B. DeMille, that perennial rescuer of fading film stars, came to the rescue. DeMille selected Wilde for the important role of "the outstanding aerial daredevil, the debonair king of the air, the great Sebastian" for *The Greatest Show on Earth* (Paramount, 1952). Because the character of Sebastian was to speak with a French accent, DeMille had earlier hired a French actor for the role, but let him go when it was discovered that he could not climb a rope hand over hand properly. Gymnastic Cornel displayed no such problem in that area, but he soon found that he had acrophobia—fear of heights. This was eased by lowering the trapeze and placing burlap bags in the net so he was not able to see the floor through the holes. He trained with a circus trapeze man at Paramount for several weeks before the company went on location, in February, 1951, to the winter headquarters of Ringling Brothers and Barnum and Bailey in Sarasota, Florida. Paramount paid $250,000 for the use of the circus motto and its equipment.

Within the spectacular production, Sebastian and Holly (Betty Hutton) are the star aerialists of the circus managed by Brad (Charlton

Heston). Sebastian has a yen for Holly and in a moonlit haystack scene, he says seductively, "You are beautiful, exciting, like wine. You know, women are like wine. Some are like sweet sauterne, some are warm like burgundy." He insists she is like "champagne—sparkling, tantalizing. You make a man's head spin. Oh. I have wandered a little—but how else could I appreciate what I have found now?"

After all that, she still prefers Brad, and Sebastian later tells her, "I think you have stardust mixed up with sawdust." Holly is jealous of Sebastian's position in the important center ring and goads him into performing daring acts without a net. He cuts his net away before attempting a double somersault over the bar and through a hoop, and falls. "Walk me off," he begs Brad and Buttons the clown (James Stewart), who run to his assistance. "Do not rob me of my exit." As he is placed into an ambulance he informs Holly, "When I come back, cheri, you will fall for me."

He does return from the hospital, but it is with a paralyzed, deformed right hand. Holly blames herself and promises to wed him. Sensation later returns to his hand, but in the melee of the circus train wreck, he discovers that Holly really does love Brad. He donates some of his blood to the injured Brad with the words, "Take all of it you want. It will make him a better man—give him fire." Sebastian is always the showman. Eventually, he winds up with Angel (Gloria Grahame) the elephant girl.

With Charlton Heston and Betty Hutton in *The Greatest Show on Earth* (1952)

Newsweek Magazine declared, "Wilde plays what could have been a garden variety of rake with considerable charm and muscular plausibility."

DeMille was angered with the "B" rating that the Legion of Decency gave his circus epic film due to a suggestive costume worn by Miss Grahame and because shreds of dialog were considered offensively suggestive. His anger was assuaged on the night of March 19, 1953, when *The Greatest Show on Earth* was named the Best Picture of 1952 by the Motion Picture Academy of Arts and Sciences. It also received the Best Screenplay Award and DeMille was handed the Thalberg Award for eminence in the profession.

The Greatest Show on Earth, through its initial and subsequent releases, would eventually gross over fourteen million dollars in U.S. and Canadian distributors' rentals. Over the years, critical reaction to the rather unsubtle scenario and the very basic acting by most of the cast would grow more intense, robbing the film of much of the prestige it once enjoyed with the public. In the early 1950s, a favorite joke among nightclub comedians was to impersonate Cornel's Great Sebastian, pantomiming his oncamera attempts to keep his deadened arm hidden under a folded trenchcoat, and exaggerating the mock Gallic dialog patter he had to utter in the picture. On December 1, 1963 for NBC-TV's tribute to the Cecil B. DeMille, Wilde and Hutton were reunited (on video tape) to recreate some of their high-wire acrobatics for the television audience.

Five months before the official release of the DeMille feature, Patricia Knight obtained a divorce in Reno, Nevada, on August 30, 1951. She obtained custody of daughter Wendy, with Cornel ordered to pay $200 weekly alimony and child support.

A few days later, on September 4, 1951, Cornel married former nightclub songstress-turned-actress Jean Wallace, in Santa Monica, California.[17] The ex-wife of Franchot Tone, Miss Wallace was the

---

[17]Born October 12, 1923, in Chicago, Jean was the daughter of Mary and John T. Wallasek, an insurance salesman. (Her aunt, Veronica Seward, had been in silent films.) In 1939, after graduating from high school, Jean had met producer Earl Carroll at a club dance. He told her to look him up in Hollywood; she did. She met actor Franchot Tone in July, 1941, and on October 18, they were wed. They had two children, Pascal Franchot Tone (born July 29, 1943) and Thomas Jefferson Tone (born September 16, 1945). The Tones' marriage blew up in August, 1948. During and following the divorce, there were headlined reports of the vicious custody battle between the former spouses for the two children. Tone initially won the foray, claiming that Jean was an unfit mother and that she associated with Johnny Stompanato, the alleged henchman of gangster Mickey Cohen. (Stompanato was to gain further and final notoriety when he was stabbed to death in 1957 by Lana Turner's daughter Cheryl Crane.) Tone had also reminded the court that in November, 1949, his ex-wife had stabbed herself with a butcher knife, saying at the time, "I did it just for laughs." On January 28, 1950, Jean wed thirty-three-year-old former Army sergeant Jim Lloyd Randall in Tijuana. On June 13th of that year, she sued for a decree of annulment or divorce, claiming that he had not complied with the laws of Mexico when they were wed.

mother of two sons. She also was responsible for her nine-year-old sister, Karol. At the time of their marriage, officiated over by Judge Arthur Crum, Cornel was thirty-five and Jean was twenty-seven. Beautiful and blonde, the second Mrs. Wilde (who resembled Patricia Knight in many ways) had been under contract to Paramount since 1941 and had appeared in several movies. She had, among other roles, a bit in Bob Hope's *Louisiana Purchase* (1941). Later in the decade she would be under contract to Cornel's studio, and, while at Twentieth Century-Fox, would appear in such films as *It Shouldn't Happen to a Dog* (1946) and *When My Baby Smiles at Me* (1948). In 1949 Jean was seen oncamera in two features with her then ex-spouse, Franchot Tone, *The Man on the Eiffel Tower* (RKO) and *Jigsaw* (United Artists). In 1950 she joined with Jack Carson and Lola Albright in *The Good Humor Man* (Columbia), and the following year she had the co-lead with Richard Wright in *Native Son* (Classic).

In April, 1952, one month after *The Greatest Show on Earth* was introduced to movie audiences, RKO decided it would be a good time to release its Wilde swashbuckler film that had been shot almost two and a half years previously.[18] It had originally been called *Sons of the Musketeers,* but now hit the screen with its title changed to *At Sword's Point.* Within this reworking of Alexander Dumas' *Twenty Years After,* the aging queen of France (Gladys Cooper) calls for the help of her three musketeers to put down the tyranny of a scheming nobleman (Robert Douglas). The original trio, plus one, are either too old or dead, and the bid for help is answered by their healthy sons (Cornel, Alan Hale, Jr., and Dan O'Herlihy). The descendant of Athos, however, is his beautiful daughter (Maureen O'Hara) whose mastery of fencing all but surpasses that of her male counterparts.

In the lacy but empty storyline, the son of D'Artagnan (Cornel) finds a place in his heart for the plucky lass. In rallying the support of the descendants of all those who aided their fathers, Cornel addresses them: "The honor and the glory of saving the king and thereby saving France have been bestowed upon us. To achieve this we have pledged our lives. I know you will not fail your fathers or your kind. You know what is to be done—do it, and God be with you." From then on, it is all for one and one for all. Unfortunately, while both Cornel and Maureen

[18] *At Sword's Point* had been conceived in 1949 to take advantage of the flurry of interest in swashbuckling films occasioned by MGM's 1948 edition of *The Three Musketeers.* However, when Howard Hughes took over the controls of RKO he was determined to revamp the entire studio, including the reassessment of any films already prepared for release. Having two of his own protegées (Jane Russell and Faith Domergue) to promote, he had no interest in furthering Maureen O'Hara's career (she soon left RKO) and saw no reason to release the film at that time.

It was while *At Sword's Point* was being lensed in 1949 that columnist Sidney Skolsky revealed to his *Photoplay* Magazine readers, "Cornel Wilde makes no secret of it, so I guess it's okay to tell that for certain scenes in a picture he keeps that curl in place with a bobby pin."

With Alan Hale, Jr., Dan O'Herlihy, George Magrill, and Maureen O'Hara in *At Sword's Point* (1952)

were game subjects, director Lewis Allen failed to fortify the stars' maneuvering with enough grandness of ambiance, plot, or inspiration, to give their energetic swordplay any validity in the cardboard child's tale.

A person who remained anonymous and who had worked with Cornel on this film confided to Hedda Hopper. "I've never seen a more cooperative man on a sound stage. Between scenes he rehearsed his swordplay, or helped with publicity. I never heard him complain. In one sequence, he worked for six hours with his arms suspended by chains."

As the new husband of Jean Wallace, Cornel received a good deal of extra publicity. It was in 1952 that she obtained custody of her two children, reminding the court that in September, 1951, Franchot Tone and fellow actor Tom Neal had been involved in a slugfest over the affections of sometimes actress Barbara Payton. After the fracas, Tone required plastic surgery on his face. Later that year, he and Miss Payton had wed but were soon divorced.

It was also in 1952 that Cornel signed a two-picture pact with Columbia, guaranteeing him a salary of $100,000 per film plus fifty percent of the net profits earned in the western hemisphere and the right to select his own screen stories. The first project chosen was not a particu-

With Teresa Wright in *California Conquest* **(1952)**

larly lively affair, nor was it produced on a very confidence-inspiring budget. In *California Conquest* (Columbia, 1952), Cornel affected a Spanish accent as Don Arturo Bordega, who is in favor of California's annexation by the United States. Teresa Wright is the girl in this dull Lew Landers-directed feature. During the location shooting in northern California, in June, 1951, Cornel was leading a chase on horseback across rocky terrain when the cinch on his saddle broke and he was hurtled from his mount. He landed head-first against a boulder and barely missed being trampled by the pursuing horses. He was flown to Hollywood for X-rays, which proved negative, although he suffered from double vision and severe head and back pains for several days after the accident.

That same year at Warner Bros., he was a U.S. Army officer involved with the French underground during World War II. Everything about *Operation Secret* seemed flat, and he returned to costumes and swords at Twentieth Century-Fox for a very studied remake of Tyrone Power's *Son of Fury* (1942). In the celluloid replay, *Treasure of the Golden Condor* (1953), which used almost identical camera set-ups for each scene, Cornel was Frenchman Jean-Paul, who flees the persecution of his uncle (George Macready) by escaping to Guatemala to seek his fortune. He also finds Constance Smith there. He returns to France to reclaim the birthright that was denied him by the unscrupulous uncle

530

With Karl Malden in *Operation Secret* (1952)

With Leo G. Carroll in *Treasure of the Golden Condor* (1953)

and a bad cousin (Anne Bancroft). The *New York Times* approved of Cornel's agility (not in the Tyrone Power theatrical manner, but still impressive by 1950s standards), and noted he "adds surprising incisiveness" to the part.

Cornel happened to be a part of *Main Street to Broadway* (MGM, 1953) because he was passing through New York at production time. It is difficult to believe that he had nothing better to do, but he is seen briefly as himself attending a Broadway opening. Of the entire project (profits were to go to the American Theatre Wing), the film's director, Tay Garnett, has gone on record as saying simply, "What a waste."

In 1953, Patricia Knight, who was no longer appearing in films, took Cornel to court in an effort to raise his alimony payments to her to $750. The judge ordered the payments raised to four hundred dollars a week, but when Patricia went to Europe later that year, Cornel obtained custody of their daughter when it became apparent that the child's mother had no intention of returning. She had decided to marry Niels Larson, a Danish businessman and former newspaperman, which she did on October 24, 1954.

On August 18, 1953, Jean Wallace's mother, Mrs. Mary Ingham, age sixty, was killed in a hit-and-run accident in Los Angeles. Jean later sued the city for $50,000.

That same year, Cornell appeared in *Saadia* (MGM). French Morocco

With Mary Murphy in *Main Street to Broadway* (1953)

was the locale for this Albert Lewin production, which had been budgeted at $1,250,000. Cornel's salary for ten weeks of acting the part of a sheik was $75,000. In spite of its lofty cost figure, the film is a spiritless affair, blunted by pretentiousness. The only notable aspects of this very talky drama were the beauty of Rita Gam as the girl, Saadia, who loves the shiek, and Christopher Challis' stunning camera work.

Like MGM's *Executive Suite* (May, 1954), Twentieth Century-Fox's *Woman's World* (September, 1954) offered a frequently sharp look at the underhanded tactics employed by executives in wrangling a corporate promotion. With MGM, it was a furniture-manufacturing firm in black and white, with Fox, it is a multi-million-dollar motor company in DeLuxe color, CinemaScope, and Stereophonic sound. *Suite* boasted seven top-ranking stars, so did *World*. In the latter, President Gifford (Clifton Webb) needs a new general manager for his New York-based headquarters. Since he is acquainted with the three most likely candidates for the job (Cornel, Van Heflin, and Fred MacMurray), he decides to inspect their wives, too (respectively, June Allyson, Arlene Dahl, and Lauren Bacall). The three couples are invited to spend a weekend at his swank home where he can really look them over. It is a sleazy way of making a selection and the girls know it full well. Allyson is cute and nervous, Dahl wants the job for her husband and is willing to do anything for it, Bacall could not care less. It is soon made

With June Allyson in *Woman's World* (1954)

533

clear that Cornel would rather return to his midwest office and he is not saddened when Mr. President makes the logical choice (Heflin), but only on the condition that he get rid of his conniving, back-biting wife.

In the *World* cast, most of the celebrity players had enjoyed their peak cinema fame in the 1940s, and by the mid-1950s their images were becoming ragged about the edges. Cornel was no exception, and, as he had revealed in *It Had to Be You,* comedy—broad or narrow— was not his forte. His manner alternating between ingenuousness and intensity was not suited to the pummeling banter (and the usual accompanying slapstick) of the discipline.

Despite its many faults, the 1954 RKO Western, *Passion* found Cornel much more at ease. In this slow-moving feature set in California of old, Cornel is a virulent, vengeful man in pursuit of the Mexican ruffians who have massacred his wife (Yvonne De Carlo) and her relatives. He catches up with them, one by one, and also "gets" his sister-in-law who amazingly resembles his dead wife. (Both roles are played with fine brio by the vital, if unsubtle, Miss De Carlo.)

In February, 1954, the Wildes had formed Theodora Productions with Cornel as president and Jean as vice president and secretary. They announced that their firm would produce pictures for both theatrical and television release, with two properties, *Byron* and *The Assassins,* scheduled as cinema features. Their immediate plan for television was a half-hour film for "G.E. Theatre," *The Blond Dog.*[19]

---

[19]Aired on CBS-TV on March 6, 1955, with Cornel in his video acting debut.

With Yvonne De Carlo in *Passion* (1954)

With Helen Walker in *The Big Combo* (1955)

At the start of 1955, the U.S. Treasury Department revealed Cornel's 1954 earnings to have been $275,000, and in February, 1955, Theodora Productions unveiled its first major film work, *The Big Combo* (Allied Artists). Starring Cornel, Jean Wallace, and Richard Conte, it deals with a cop (Cornel) and a gangster (Conte) and the girl (Jean) they both desire. Cornel, as was to be expected, wins out, but only after eighty-five minutes of violence, brutality, and killing.[20] Of this saga of an honest cop who is the self-appointed smasher of the crime syndicate, the *New York Times'* critic used the words "shrill, clumsy and rather old-fashioned," and summed it up as "a sputtering, misguided antique."

With the collapse of Cornel's plan for a Broadway revival of *Seventh Heaven*,[21] he jaunted over to MGM for *The Scarlet Coat* (1955). His fencing was put to good use as a Colonial spy[22] who infiltrates the

[20]One near nauseous torture scene found Cornel in the capture of Conte. The latter has a hearing aid plugged into the former's ear with the attached radio going full force. Later Conte has a bottle of hair tonic forced down Cornel's throat.

[21]Originally staged in 1922 with George Gaul and Helen Menken. Charles Farrell, co-star of the 1927 Fox film version, appeared on Broadway in the late 1930s in a revival of the Austin Strong romantic drama. In 1937 Twentieth Century-Fox remade the vehicle with Simone Simon and James Stewart starred. The unsuccessful 1955 Broadway musical (lyrics by Stella Unger, music by Victor Young) starred Gloria De Haven.

[22]Stewart Granger, who had become MGM's and Hollywood's leading exponent of the swashbuckling genre in the 1950s, had rejected the role.

With Anne Francis in *The Scarlet Coat* **(1955)**

British inner circle where he uncovers the plot to turn West Point over to the Tories. Although Benedict Arnold (Robert Douglas) escapes, the traitor's associates (Michael Wilding and George Sanders) are sent where all scheming, loyal Britons are sent. Filmed in Tarrytown, New York, the locale provided many a beautiful background for the widescreen color cameras.

Storm Fear (United Artists, 1955) represents Cornel's debut as a director. Produced by his Theodora Company, Wilde also starred. The end result ("There's material enough for two or three movies," decided the *New York Daily News)* is uneven, but it manages to have several highly professional moments. Cornel is Charlie, a wounded heel of a bank robber who, with accomplices Benjie and Edna (Steven Hill and Lee Grant), camps on the Idaho mountain doorstep of his older brother, Fred (Dan Duryea).

Since childhood, *Storm Fear*'s Charlie has felt inadequate compared to his brother and stammers whenever he meets him. Fred and his wife (Jean Wallace) are none too pleased to have Charlie, Benjie, and Edna as uninvited guests—as a result of a snow storm—and the robbers are soon forced out into the blizzard. Duryea, as the man of many frustrations, gives the more biting performance in this middling dramatic exercise.

Cornel's next film, *Hot Blood* (Columbia, 1956), is a Technicolor tale

With Jane Russell in *Hot Blood* (1956)

of love, hate, and greed among a tribe of Los Angeles gypsies. As Stephan, a sort of renegade gypsy who has worked in a carnival, Cornel agrees to wed Annie (Jane Russell), a wandering tribeslady. His reason for marrying her, a girl he heartily dislikes, is to acquire a two-thousand-dollar dowry settled upon them by the group's king, Luther Adler, who is also Stephan's older brother. After the couple's left hands are joined, Adler marries them by pricking their hands with a knife and saying, "Let the blood flow as one for now and forever and let the sun and the moon be our witness."

After the ceremony, she whispers to her groom, "Don't look like you've been sentenced to death." He replies huskily, "Ya, I only got life." But, he does not plan to stay married to her. When they are alone, he tells her, "A gypsy wife, even a bad one, has got to be faithful to only one man, that's our law. There's no law that says a husband has got to be a husband to the wife." In due time, however, he realizes that fate has reversed his feelings, and he finds that he has fallen in love with his statuesque spouse. By then, she has changed her mind about him and leaves. He sets out to find her and hopes to re-change her mind. As in all films about gypsies, there is a great deal of dancing.[23]

---

[23]Among the more asinine aspects of this verveless drama (it would have made a wonderful Maria Montez vehicle a decade prior) was the dancing by Cornel and Russell. Rarely has the cinema witnessed more obvious examples of doubling for the stars. For example,

537

In *Storm Fear* (1955)   In 1956

After the unsuccessful *Hot Blood,* Cornel would have been well-advised to have accepted Cecil B. DeMille's offer for him to work in the remake of *The Ten Commandments* (Paramount, 1956). However, says Wilde, "I didn't think it was a good role, so I pulled out." He was replaced in this boxoffice bonanza by John Derek.

In September, 1956, Jean Wallace talked her husband into participating in a full marriage ceremony in a Catholic church. "I convinced him that that was the only way I would ever feel really married," she told the press.

Star of India (United Artists, 1956) boasted some fetching "location" filming in the Aosta region of northern Italy. It was the most appealing aspect of this inexpensive endeavor produced by the British. Once again, Cornel is a Frenchman—a soldier in the service of King Louis XIV (Basil Sydney), who returns from the wars in India to find that his fortunes have been confiscated by the villainous Narbonne (Herbert Lom). Jean, as a young widow and a Dutch agent, joins him in his search for a gem known as the Star of India. "Wilde makes a determined cavalier," was the best that Frank Quinn *(New York Daily Mirror)* could say of Cornel's performance.

Wilde would strike a semi-Greco-like pose in a medium shot, then director Nicholas Ray (of *Johnny Guitar,* Republic, 1954, fame) would pull the cameras back—very far, indeed —while co-choreographer Matt Mattox performed the actual foot-stomping gyrations. Similarly, co-choreographer Sylvia Lewis performed the high kicking and sprinting for equally clumsy Russell.

With Herbert Lom in *Star of India* (1956)

"Cornel Wilde is being adventuresome again," proclaimed the *New York Herald-Tribune* of his outing in England and Africa for *Beyond Mombasa* (Columbia, 1956). Wilde has said "Ouch!" when reminded of the film that has him searching for an African witchcraft cult suspected of killing the discoverer (his brother) of a gold mine. It proves to be the seemingly kind uncle (Leo Genn) of heroine Donna Reed (she dresses up to the nines in the heart of the jungle) who did the dastardly deed. Most critical approval for this just-one-more East African safari yarn went to trumpeter Eddie Calvert who shone in his nightclub scene bit.

The rise and fall of harem dramas in the history of the cinema is a long procedure, but *Omar Khayyam* (Paramount, 1957) did its best to bury the cycle. In eleventh-century Persia, the Shah (Raymond Massey) is about to lose his throne through the scheming of court intriguer Hasani (Michael Rennie). But the Shah can rest easy because the persian poet Omar (Cornel) rides into view, falls in love with Sharain (Debra Paget), a member of the potentate's harem, and sticks around to spout verse, cavort through the court, the marketplace, and the hills, and ends up saving the day. Cornel's *The Ten Commandments'* replacement, John Derek, was on tap as the Shah's son and heir apparent. As the *New York Times'* critic would confirm for the more serious-minded, "Mr. Wilde composes the oft-quoted lines of the *Rubaiyat*

With Donna Reed in *Beyond Mombasa* (1957)

under circumstances better suited to the restless ingestion of popcorn than the formulation of serious verse." (It is veiled beauty Paget who observes to her beloved, "Oh Omar—the best verses always come suddenly to you.")

Having reconfirmed his status in the diminishing swashbuckling field, Cornel turned to more serious, if less successful, filmfare. As producer-director of *The Devil's Hairpin* (Paramount, 1957), he gave himself the unsympathetic role of a racing-car champ, Nick Jargin, who is responsible for an accident that cripples his brother Johnny (Larry Pennell). Nick then "steals" the brother's girlfriend, Kelly (Jean Wallace). Sitting in his car on the track grid, Cornel's Nick thinks back on all these events which have made him so unpopular with so many people. In the course of this big race (a mightly long time coming in the story's VistaVision-color unraveling), the race driver learns the meaning of ethics.

At the finale, champion Nick decides, "No more races for me. I was lucky today. Next time Botari [Jack Kosslyn] would take me. He's a better driver."

Newsman: "What then?"

Nick: "Marriage, a home, and kids—if the lady will cooperate."

Kelly: "Will we be married tomorrow?"

Nick: "Today."

With Debra Paget in *Omar Khayyam* (1957)

With Mary Astor and Jean Wallace in *The Devil's Hairpin* (1957)

Dorothy Masters, in her three-star *New York Daily News* review said of *The Devil's Hairpin,* "Although previous Theodora Films have aimed for—and frequently hit—targets on a tangent the shooting never has been as persistently successful." On the other hand, *Variety* was more realistic when it said that the picture was "not one of his best." In fact, Cornel received better notices for his guest-starring appearance on television's "Father Knows Best" video series.

In July, 1957, Louella O. Parsons revealed in her column that Italian producer Ponti Gerosi had offfered Cornel the lead opposite Gina Lollobrigida in the projected film *Anne of Brooklyn.* The film, which Miss Parsons said was to be directed by co-star Vittorio De Sica, did not come to pass. Nor did *One Wife Is Enough* see the light of movie theatres. Cornel was considering starring in this Albert Zugsmith property about an Albanian Moslem, a robust mountaineer with two wives. Another project which intrigued Cornel in the following months was *The Eagle Flies Alone,* detailing the life of Frank Jarecki, an airman who escapes from Poland to Denmark. Norman Retchin and Delbert Mann were to be involved with Cornel in this semi-documentary film study for Paramount release.

Cornel and Jean did trek to Caracas, Venezuela, for their production *Maracaibo* (Paramount, 1958). He is a fire-fighting ace ("I'm strictly a hit and run man," he insists) vacationing at Caracas with his lady love

542

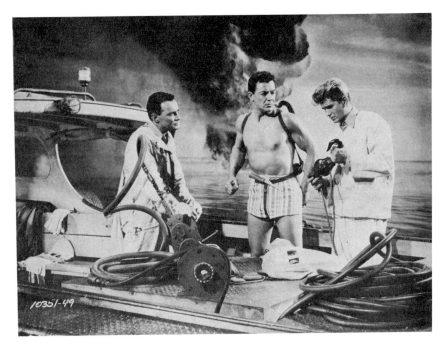

With Jack Kosslyn and Michael Landon in *Maracaibo* **(1958)**

novelist (Jean), when an offshore oil well catches fire at Maracaibo. He is called to the holocaust to help put out the gigantic blaze. Cornel also directed the film, which demonstrated that he had become far more at ease behind the cameras than in front of them.

A heart attack took the life of Cornel's father on July 23, 1958, in New York City. Louis Wilde was then seventy-two and living at the Hotel Ansonia on West 74th Street with his wife Renee. It was also in 1958 that Cornel gallantly accompanied his wife to court when she again came to legal loggerheads with ex-husband Franchot Tone. He insisted that their son Pascal be allowed to attend the private Hill School in the East, as several generations of Tones had done. The court ruled in Franchot's favor.

Cornel laid down his director's megaphone once again when he went to Columbia for *Edge of Eternity* (1959), with Don Siegel directing.[24] Released to neighborhood theatres as part of a double bill, the film has Cornel as a stubborn deputy sheriff in pursuit of the man who

---

[24]In *Don Siegel; Director* (Curtis) 1974), actor Jack Elam tells author Stuart M. Kaminsky: *"Edge of Eternity* was originally called *The Dancing Lady.* I was offered the picture by a friend of mine, Ken Sweet, a film editor, who had written it with me in mind for the lead. Well, I had the script at home and one night when Don was over playing cards he read it and said it was a damn good script. He said, 'I think I can go over to Columbia and get this made.' And he did with Ken Sweet as producer and co-writer. But Columbia said they had to have a star in the lead and I was no star.

has killed three people in the area surrounding a gold mine not far from the Grand Canyon. He eventually learns that it is Scotty O'Brien (Mickey Shaughnessy) the local bartender who is the culprit. In a cable car, some nine thousand feet above the Canyon's floor, he slugs it out with the pursued (Shaughnessy) while the heroine (Victoria Shaw) gasps appropriately.[25] In this durable, rather modest melodrama, Cornel was far more resolute than under his own direction, although admittedly still not a remarkably decisive hero. Even at this pre-cultist point in his career, director Siegel was able to extract almost as much from his performers as from the scenario's action and the locales' potentials.

After the succession of generally unmemorable films, Cornel spent much of the next three years in television production, and at an unsuccessful attempt to revive his long-standing Lord Byron plans. He was seen on Ed Sullivan's "Toast of the Town" CBS-TV show in January,

---

"We were originally thinking of making the picture for about $80,000 and we could have bypassed Columbia. . . . But it probably never would have been made. Columbia gave Ken and Don a budget of something like $700,000."

[25]The cable car gambit had been used to remarkable affect by Carol Reed in *Night Train to Munich* (Twentieth Century-Fox, 1940), and cropped up in such later films as *Second Chance* (RKO, 1953), *Night Passage* (Universal, 1957), and *Where Eagles Dare* (MGM, 1969).

With Victoria Shaw in *Edge of Eternity* (1959)

1960, when he performed a scene—live—from Frank and Doris Hursley's script of Byron's life. That same month, on January third, Cornel co-starred with Janet Blair on the NBC-TV special *Around the World with Nellie Blye,* a sixty-minute musical dealing with rival reporters in the 1890s global jaunt. Neither the Jack Brooks songs, the show, or its leads received impressive press notices.

In the fall of 1960, the Wildes were in Italy preparing for a new project, *Constantine Il Grande,* which would be released in the United States as *Constantine and the Cross* in 1962 through Embassy Pictures. One September evening, the actor and his wife were nightclubbing near the Via Veneto, when a patron insisted on dancing with Jean. Cornel asked the Italian to step outside to settle the matter, but the latter declined.

If Cornel had displayed such hot-tempered chivalry in *Constantine and the Cross,* the film might have emerged a more rousing adventure. As was reported in the *New York Times,* "Cornel Wilde as the great emperor who established Christianity in Rome walks through this key role as if he were an earnest fellow who had just been inspired in Sunday School." In this Lionello De Felice-directed costume farce, Christine Kaufmann had the female lead.

Under the banner of Emblem Productions, Cornel co-produced

With Christine Kaufmann in *Constantine and the Cross* (1962)

With Michael Meacham (third from left), Mark Dignam, Brian Aherne, Archie Duncan, and Reginald Beckwith in *Sword of Lancelot* (1963)

(with Bernard Luber), directed, and starred with his wife in *Sword of Lancelot* (Universal, 1963).[26] Also known as *Lancelot and Guinevere,* the film's exteriors were photographed in Yugoslavia[27] with interiors done at the Pinewood Studios in London. This film proved to be Cornel's best in almost a decade, and reminded audiences that he was still filmdom's most proficient sword wielder. It also indicated that, as a director, he was able to set up authentic-looking battle scenes, such as the one used when the Normans burn the barbarious Vikings out of a forest. At this point Cornel, as the French-accented Lancelot, says, "You can bet your baptism I have killed enough today to last a lifetime."

The triangle love story of Lancelot-Guinevere-King Arthur is well known by historians and movie fans alike,[28] but never was Lancelot more muscular, nor Guinevere (Jean Wallace) more fair of hair or love-

---

[26]Cornel invested some $300,000 of his own money into the venture.

[27]A castle and moat set were constructed at Divcibare, a mountain town some 4,250 feet above sea level.

[28]Among the films dealing with King Arthur, et al. are *A Connecticut Yankee at King Arthur's Court* (Fox, 1921), *Connecticut Yankee in King Arthur's Court* (Paramount, 1949), *Adventures of Sir Galahad* (Columbia serial, 1949) *Knights of the Round Table* (MGM, 1953), the animated feature, *The Sword in the Stone* (Buena Vista, 1963), *Camelot* (Warner Bros.-7 Arts, 1967), and Robert Bresson's *Lancelot du Lac* (1974).

lier. Too, Brian Aherne's Arthur is the epitome of benevolence until he learns the truth about his prospective bride and his favorite knight. Then he behaves like a fool for believing that the girl might actually prefer him to her younger, more handsome lover. For the most part, the feature is colorful, action-filled entertainment and was the hypodermic needed to bolster Cornel's sagging career.

The star made a few television guest appearances in 1964 (ABC's "Greatest Show on Earth," NBC's "Kraft Suspense Theatre"), but his interests were primarily elsewhere. He had found a story that originated as a radio show about fur trappers pursued by Indians in Wyoming. He has said, "I bought it, changed the site to Africa and read Stanley's diary and some material by Livingstone. The main idea was using man as a beast and hunting him."

With Jean, he went to the African bush in the winter of 1964-1965 to film *The Naked Prey* (Paramount, 1966). Co-produced with Sven Parsson, Cornel also directed and starred in the unique story. On the second day of shooting, the company was inaugurated into the hazards of bush living when the unit manager was bitten by a cobra. In February, 1954, an iguana took a liking to one of Cornel's shins and had to be killed before it would release its hold. Cornel was flown to a London hospital for tetanus shots. After undergoing plastic surgery for repair of his torn skin, Cornel quipped from his hospital bed, "I'm probably

In *The Naked Prey* (1966)

the only actor in town who has had a shin lift." Back in the Transvaal, he was offered a fifteen-year-old wife by a powerful tribal chieftain named Shwasa. "But I have a wife," Cornel protested. "I have a wife; she's here with me." The chief, with six spouses, was astounded that any man could be happy with just one.

On March 4, 1965, Jean Wallace Wilde was called from London to Los Angeles when the Wilde home in the exclusive Trousdale Estates area was reported to have been looted. Furs, gowns, jewelry, and twenty guns had been stolen by thieves who made their way through the darkened house with the use of wooden matches. Jean told reporters, "There must be 10,000 matches in the house. It's lucky it didn't burn down."

The Naked Prey was previewed at the San Sebastian Film Festival in Spain on June 3, 1965, when Cornel stated that its cost was under a million dollars and said that his next three films had already been selected: *The Gang Lords, Beach Red,* and *The Nowhere City.*

The hero of *The Naked Prey* is "Man" (Cornel), the leader of a safari in the 1860s who is prevented from giving trinkets to a group of tribesmen. Deprived of their gifts, the natives attack the safari and murder the white men by various ghastly means, but the leader (Cornel) is stripped of clothing and shoes and is forced to make a run for his life. Given a brief headstart, "Man" is viciously pursued by the ferocious tribesmen. To survive, he resorts to eating raw animal meat and manages to kill two of his pursuers with a crude spear he has fashioned himself. He makes friends for a while with a young native boy who is on his way to his village. The two travel together for a time. Later, as the angry tribesmen are about to close in on him, "Man" spots a white building across a field. He makes a wild dash for the bastion, reaching the haven just in time.

Nominated for an Oscar for Best Story and Screenplay written directly for the screen, *The Naked Prey* lost out to the French-conceived *A Man and a Woman* (Allied Artists). But the motion picture received sufficient praise from the critics to compensate for the loss. "*The Naked Prey* spills more beauty, blood and savagery upon the screen than any African adventure drama since *Trader Horn.* . . . *Prey* gathers fierce momentum as a classic, single-minded epic of survival with no time out for fainthearted blondes or false heroics" (*Time* Magazine). "Raw yet touching story of a struggle for survival. ... Film is an artistic achievement of which producer-director-star Cornel Wilde and associates can be justifiably proud. . . . The film assaults the senses with appropriate audio-visual depictions of exhaustion, intense heat, repelling (but logical) brutality and starvation" (*Variety*). "*The Naked Prey* is one of the most exciting chase movies to come our way" (Judith Crist, "NBC Today Show").

The *New York Times* ran one of the few reviews that found major faults with the film. "A poor and tasteless motion-picture entertainment. . . . A fundamental weakness stems from the fact that its protagonist is barely introduced to the audience. [Regarding the slaughter of the white men by the natives], it is disgusting stuff and the wise viewer will get out of the theater before the chase has begun. . . . Interspersed with this coarse action are shots of lion eating antelope, frogs eating other frogs, vultures eating anything that is dead. It is called symbolism."

On the whole, however, *The Naked Prey* remains the landmark in Cornel's acting-directing career and demonstrates that at this crucial point in his life (he was now fifty years old) he had found a directorial style perfectly suited to hard-hitting action filming. That the almost-Olympic performer was in such a good physical state astounded many viewers.[29] Others were more interested in pondering the apparent fact that Wilde's performance appeared to benefit by his paucity of dialog within the course of the ninety-six-minute chase.

On March 28, 1967, Cornel's mother died of a heart attack in Greenville, South Carolina at the home of her daughter and son-in-law, Dr. J. H. Crooks.

In August of that same year, Cornel parted company with Screen Gems over a dispute about the proposed video series, "Pieces of Eight," an underwater adventure yarn. The amicable disagreement was over the approach to the story.

Also in 1967, Theodora Productions came up with what Howard Thompson of the *New York Times* called Cornel's "best picture to date," *Beach Red* (United Artists). Taken from Peter Bowman's novel, a Book-of-the-Month Club selection, it was filmed in the Philippines and details the story of a U.S. Marine infiltration of a Japanese-held island during World War II. Cornel directed and starred as the invaders' commander, Captain MacDonald, with Jean Wallace appearing in the flashback sequences that established the captain's relationship with his wife.

Regarding this rather basic, if over-ambitious study of the futility of war, *Variety's* Lee Beaupre decided. "Sincere anti-war pic defeated by vague screenplay and lethargic pace. . . . Notably absent are the usual stereotypes. The trouble with the screenplay is that little is substituted for these wisely-avoided clichés. The central characters are spokesmen for different points of view, not real, full-bodied people. The acting suffers as a result." The reviewer goes on to point out: "In marked contrast to the script's trite theatricalism and skimpy development, Wilde has directed the battle scenes with unrelenting realism. The

---

[29]Because he was required to run between eight and ten miles a day during the filming of *The Naked Prey,* Cornel gave up smoking cigarettes. "And that was it. I honestly didn't like the taste of smoking nor the smell, and within a short time after quitting I couldn't stand the smell when someone in the room was smoking."

On the set of *Beach Red* (1967) with Dale Ishimoto

irony of *Beach Red,* however, is that Wilde's unyielding verisimilitude only reinforces the tedium of the script. . . . There also seems little reason for Wilde's totally inflectionless readings in the flashbacks recalling his wife." Others, such as the reviewer for *Time Magazine,* emphasized that "in the end blood and treacle flow at an equal rate."

While Wilde protested that *Beach Red* was an out-and-out anti-war film, the releasing company promoted the film on both its gore (arms being blown off, severed limbs floating in the water), and nudity (in the flashback sequence for the Japanese officer's remembrances of domestic life back home). After the initial spurt of public interest in the feature, the daily boxoffice take waned noticeably below expectation. In retrospect, *Beach Red* is not a milestone but a stepping stone in Wilde's directorial career.[30]

In 1969, after a two-year absence from the screen, (a film project, *The Raging Sea,* never developed), Cornel appeared in a cameo assignment

[30]In his *The American Cinema* (E. P. Dutton & Co., 1968), author Andrew Sarris reflects: "Cornell [sic] Wilde's first film, *Storm Fear,* was notable for its half-baked intensity and the actor-director's bizarre imitation of Marlon Brando after years of having other directors exploit Wilde's expressionless good looks. Wilde's turnabout was comparable to Dick Powell's at that moment when the sappiest tenor of the thirties became one of the toughest private eyes of the forties. Wilde's most recent efforts—*The Naked Prey* and *Beach Red*—are nothing if not ambitious. Wilde is still too bland as both actor and director to be given major consideration, but he does reveal a modestly likable personality in over its head with themes oversized for the talent and skill available."

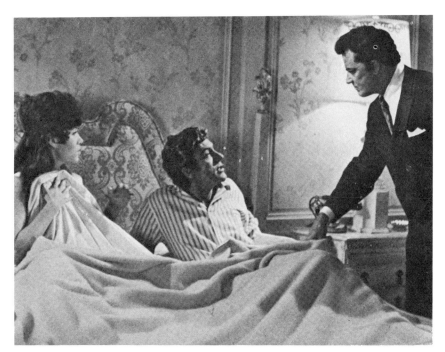

With Michele Lee and Dick Van Dyke in *The Comic* **(1969)**

in the much-underrated feature *The Comic* (Columbia). In this biting backyard look at Hollywood, starting in the 1920s, with Dick Van Dyke as comedy star Billy Bright and Mickey Rooney as his sidekick Cockeye, Wilde was oncamera briefly as Frank Powers, a big-time movie director who has his problems with silent actors.

No Blade of Grass (MGM), Cornel's seventh directorial job, was released in 1970. A futuristic story from the novel by John Christopher, it was filmed rather cheaply in England and Cornel functioned only as its director. Starring Nigel Davenport and Jean Wallace, it depicts the effects of pollution on the human will to exist through drought and starvation. In November, 1970, Cornel was issued a certificate of recognition by the Southern Chapter of the California Environmental Health Association in connection with this film. The statement accompanying the certificate read: "Because the ecological disasters depicted in *No Blade of Grass* are occurring in various areas of the world today, our association wished to recognize Wilde's efforts to bring these problems to the attention of the public."

Whatever personal satisfaction Cornel felt for receiving the above tribute, it could not disguise the fact that *No Blade of Grass* met with relatively little critical or public interest, most likely because fast-failing MGM was hardly in a position to promote a film of this specialized nature. When the picture had its delayed release in England in 1972, it

551

was lambasted by such generally level-headed publications sources as the British *Monthly Film Bulletin.* "The prophetic warning of *No Blade of Grass* is completely vitiated by the crudity of its social stereotypes . . . while the moral disintegration of the individual characters lack any psychological strength or consistency." As for Wilde's participation in the venture, the same reviewer noted. "A new champion of Good Causes in popular entertainment, Cornel Wilde—his indignation rapidly degenerating into a kind of journalistic sensationalism—poses little challenge to Stanley Kramer. . . . The violence here lacks the intensity of *Beach Red* or *The Naked Prey* and leaves Wilde's naive social and psychological formulas firmly holding the floor."

In May, 1971, Cornel journeyed to Alaska for research on Jack Curtis' novel, *The Kloochman,* but his plans to put the story onto film were later shelved.

In February, 1972, he was seen on television in a Jeff Corey-directed episode of Rod Serling's "Night Gallery." In the episode, entitled *Deliveries in the Rear,* he is a teacher in "the art of surgery" who uses cadavers that are freshly killed by a couple of unsavory cronies for a small fee. Although the teacher is openly condemned for his use of human bodies for his dissecting classes, he is not aware that the bodies provided are killed on the spot. He thinks they are obtained legally from undertakers who cannot identify them. He tells his trusting students, "No individual life is of any consequence if it means the saving of many lives." The next body that is wheeled into his classroom is unveiled, and it is that of his fiancée (Rosemary Forsyth), whereupon he emits a long, gruesome scream. Finis.

On November 21, 1972, Cornel was seen in his first movie made for television, CBS-TV's *The Gargoyles.* The horror story casts him as an anthropology professor who, along with his daughter (Jennifer Salt), finds bizarre skeletons in a desert shed. They are warned of evil doings in the crags, but they persist in uncovering the "mystery." The reviews for this undistinguished effort were cruel but honest. "Director B. W. L. Norton apparently was busy elsewhere while the actors scrambled through the action. Wilde perseveres but he is defeated by the illogical steps. . . . When the gargoyles lay an egg, it's really a big one." (*Daily Variety*)

In 1974 Cornel was awarded the James K. Hackett award for his contribution to the arts as an actor-director-producer-writer. The annual trophy is administered by the Speech and Theatre Department of the City College of New York.

The many-faceted Cornel added screenplay writing to his list of accomplishments with an original story, *The Treasure,* which went before the cameras on March 14, 1974 on Bonaire Island in the Netherland West Indies. He produced the film for his Symbol Productions, and also directed, starred and did stunt work in this semi-documentary which is about a search for underwater treasure. It was not unlike the projected "Pieces of Eight" scheme that had gone awry with Screen Gems back in 1967.

Re-titled *Shark's Treasure,* United Artists released Wilde's venture in mid-July, 1975, hoping to cash in on the excitement caused by Universal's shark film, *Jaws.* "Unhappily," reported an unusually severe *Variety,* "the film offers little cinema treasure for anyone. The acting is broad to the point of childish, the direction by Wilde is stale, the script by Wilde doesn't quite work." Yet the picture garnered some $2,000,345 in distributors' rentals during its first seven weeks of release. Explaining the picture's appeal, the Hollywood *Reporter* detailed, "Some of the finest sequences ever filmed. Yaphet Kotto [as part of Wilde's salvage team] lives up to his reputation as the 'black Brando.' The photography by Jack Atcheler and Al Giddings (underwater) is often breathtaking." Or as the Los Angeles *Free Press* reasoned, "Wilde likes to make survival films and does them very well indeed. It all works. The homosexual relationship between [Cliff] Osmond and [David] Gilliam couldn't have been acted or directed better."

On the basis of the success of *Shark's Treasure,* United Artists, who now releases MGM product, has decided to reissue Wilde's *No Blade of Grass,* and the star-director is currently trying to package a project entitled *Four Foot Six,* about a performing midget. And he reactivated

With Jennifer Salt   In *Shark's Treasure* (1975)
in *Gargoyles* (CBS-TV, 1972)

a long-planned project about Alaska, now entitled *Nomi,* with the Alaskan pipeline as backdrop. Partly based on a Jack Curtis novel, with a screen treatment by Wilde and a scenario by Louis Nelius, Wilde's agent Paul Kohner insists production will begin in mid-1976, allowing Cornel to be the first to deal with Alaska on a very contemporary basis.

Currently, when they are not traveling around the globe, Cornel and Jean make their home in Beverly Hills, California. His unmarried daughter, Wendy, apparently has had no acting aspirations.[31]

Cornel Wilde today remains an actor who will fight for his belief in screen roles. Although he preferred to suffer suspensions and salary halts at Twentieth Century-Fox, rather than subject himself to roles which he felt were inferior, he did an about-face in later films when he appeared in many that were out-and-out failures. It is suspected that he knowingly sacrificed his acting career by taking the money earned on bad projects and investing that cash where he thought it would do the most good for his own peace of mind—in his own offbeat screen productions. It has gained him a good deal of respect in the industry.

[31]Jean's younger son by Tone, Thomas, was married on July 9, 1972 to Miss Mallory Hathaway of Owings Mills, Maryland. He was a graduate of Washington University and has been employed in recent years by Drexel-Firestone, Inc., New York investment bankers, in their syndicate department.

Feature Film Appearances

THE LADY WITH RED HAIR (Warner Bros., 1940), 80 min.

Associate producer, Edmund Grainger; director, Curtis Bernhardt; based upon the memoirs of Mrs. Leslie Carter; story, H. Brewster Morne and Norbert Faulkner; screenplay, Charles Kenyon and Milton Krims; art director, Max Parker; music, Heinz Roemheld; music director, Leo F. Forbstein; gowns, Milo Anderson; makeup, Perc Westmore; technical advisor, Lou Payne; dialog director, Hugh Cummings; sound, Oliver S. Garretson; camera, Arthur Edeson; editor, James Gibbon.

Miriam Hopkins (Mrs. Leslie Carter [Caroline Dudley]); Claude Rains (David Belasco); Richard Ainley (Lou Payne); John Litel (Charles Bryant); Laura Hope Crews (Mrs. Dudley); Helen Westley (Mrs. Frazier); Mona Barrie (Mrs. Brooks); Victor Jory (George Clifton); Fritz Leiber (Mr. Foster); Cecil Kellaway (Mr. Chapman); Florence Shirley (Daisy Dawn); Johnny Russell (Dudley Carter); Maris Wrixon (Miss Annie Ellis); Cornel Wilde (Mr. Williams); Helene Millard (Mrs. Ballard); Paul Stanton (Mr. Winter); Halliwell Hobbes (Judge); John Hamilton (Mr. Graham); Frank Wilcox (Mr. Lynn); Selmer Jackson (Henry De Mille); Thomas Jackson (Frank Harer); William Davidson (Stock Company Manager); Virginia Brissac (Mrs. Humbert); Doris Lloyd (Teacher); Alexis Smith (Extra at Wedding); Creighton Hale (Eddie the Reporter); William Hopper (Theatre Attendant); Maurice Cass (Artist); John Ridgely (Paul, in *The Lady from France* scene); Russell Hicks (Host); Cyril Ring (Playwright); Huntley Gordon (John, in *Mrs. Hadley*).

HIGH SIERRA (Warner Bros., 1941), 100 min.

Executive producer, Hal B. Wallis; associate producer, Mark Hellinger; director, Raoul Walsh; based on the novel by W. R. Burnett; screenplay, Burnett and John Huston; art director, Ted Smith; dialog director, Irving Rapper; gowns, Milo Anderson; makeup, Perc Westmore; music, Adolph Deutsch; orchestrator, Arthur Lange; sound, Dolph Thomas; camera, Tony Gaudio; editor, Jack Killifer.

Humphrey Bogart (Roy Earle); Ida Lupino (Marie Garson); Alan Curtis (Babe Kozak); Arthur Kennedy (Red Hattery); Joan Leslie (Velma); Henry Hull ("Doc" Banton); Barton MacLane (Jake Kranmer); Henry Travers (Pa Goodhue); Elisabeth Risdon (Ma Goodhue); Cornel Wilde (Louis Mendoza); Minna Gombell (Mrs. Baugham); Paul Harvey (Mr. Baugham); Donald MacBride (Big Mac); Jerome Cowan (Healy); John Eldredge (Lon Preiser); Isabel Jewell (Blonde); Willie Best (Algernon); Arthur Aylesworth (Auto Court Owner); Robert Strange (Art); Wade Boteler (Sheriff); Sam Hayes (Radio Commentator); George Lloyd (Gangster); Erville Alderson (Farmer); Gerald Mackey (Boy); Cliff Saum (Shaw); William Hopper and Louis Jean Heydt (Men); William Gould (Watchman); Maris Wrixon (Blonde); Eddie Acuff (Bus Driver); Frank Moran and Lee Phelps (Officers); Harry Hayden (Druggist); Ralph Sanford (Fat Man).

KNOCKOUT (a.k.a., RIGHT TO THE HEART, Warner Bros., 1941), 73 min.

Associate producer, Edmund Grainger; director, William Clemens; story, Michael Fessier; screenplay, M. Coates Webster; camera, Ted McCord; editor, Doug Gould.

Arthur Kennedy (Johnny Rocket); Olympe Bradna (Angela Grinnelli); Virginia Field (Gloria Van Ness); Anthony Quinn (Trego); Cliff Edwards (Pinky); Cornel Wilde (Tom Rossi); William Edmunds (Louis Grinnelli); Richard Ainley (Allison); John Ridgely (Pat Martin); Frank Wilcox (Denning); Ben Welden (Pelky); Vera Lewis (Mrs. Turner); Charles Wilson (Monigan); Edwin Stanley (Doctor); William Hopper, Herbert Anderson, and Creighton Hale (Reporters); Steve (Gaylord) Pendleton (Stanley); Grace Hayle (Mrs. Smithers); Frank Faylen, Paul Phillips, and Jack Merrick (Fighters); Frank Mayo (Doctor); Frank Moran, Elliott Sullivan, David Kerwin, and Jimmy O'Gatty (Pugs); Frank Riggi (Hanson; Pat O'Malley (Announcer).

KISSES FOR BREAKFAST (Warner Bros., 1941), 82 min.
Producer, Harlan Thompson; director, Lewis Seiler; based upon a play by Yves Mirande and Andre Mouezy-Eon and the play by Seymour Hicks; screenplay, Kenneth Gamet; camera, Arthur Edeson; editor, James Gibbon.

Dennis Morgan (Rodney Trask); Jane Wyatt (Laura Anders); Shirley Ross (Juliet Marsden); Lee Patrick (Betty Trent); Jerome Cowan (Lucius Lorimer); Una O'Connor (Ellie); Romaine Callender (Dr. Burroughs); Barnett Parker (Phillips); Lucia Carroll (Clara Raymond); Cornel Wilde (Chet Oakley); Willie Best (Arnold); Louise Beavers (Clotilda); Clarence Muse (Old Jeff); Leon Belasco (Accompanist); Frank Orth (T. C. Barett the Hobo); John Sheehan (Police Captain); Edgar Dearing (Motorcycle Cop); Fred Graham (Double for Cornel Wilde).

THE PERFECT SNOB (20th Century-Fox, 1942), 62 min.
Producer, Walter Morosco; director, Ray McCarey; screenplay, Lee Loeb and Harold Buchman; music director, Emil Newman; camera, Charles Clarke; editor, J. Watson Webb.

Charlie Ruggles (Dr. Mason); Charlotte Greenwood (Martha Mason); Lynn Bari (Chris Mason); Cornel Wilde (Mike Lord); Anthony Quinn (Alex Moreno); Alan Mowbray (Freddie Browning); Chester Clute (Nibsie Nicholson); LeRoy Mason (Witch Doctor); Jack Chefe (Waiter); Biddle Dorsay (Boat Driver); Matt McHugh (Baggage Man); Charles Tannen (Chauffeur); Frances Gladwin and Marilyn Kinsley (Girls); David Hopi and Salvadore Barroga (Natives).

MANILA CALLING (20th Century-Fox, 1942), 81 min.
Producer, Sol M. Wurtzel; director, Herbert I. Leeds; screenplay, John Larkin; art directors, Richard Day and Lewis Creber; music directors, Emil Newman and Cyril J. Mockridge; camera, Lucien Andriot; editor, Alfred Day.

Lloyd Nolan (Lucky Matthews); Carole Landis (Edna Fraser); Cornel Wilde (Jeff Bailey); James Gleason (Tom O'Rourke); Martin Kosleck (Heller); Ralph Byrd (Corbett); Charles Tannen (Fillmore); Ted (Michael) North (Jamison); Elisha Cook, Jr. (Gillman); Harold Huber (Santoro); Lester Matthews (Wayne Ralston); Louis Jean Heydt (Watson); Victor Sen Yung (Amando); Rudy Robles, Angel Cruz, and Carlos Carrido (Moro Soldiers); Ken Christy (Logan); Leonard Strong (Japanese Officer); Richard Loo and Charles Stevens (Filipinos); Ted Hecht (Japanese Announcer).

LIFE BEGINS AT 8:30 (20th Century-Fox, 1942), 85 min.

Producer, Nunnally Johnson; director, Irving Pichel; based on the play *Light of Heart* by Emlyn Williams; screenplay, Johnson; music, Alfred Newman; art directors, Richard Day and Boris Leven; camera, Edward Cronjager; editor, Fred Allen.

Monty Woolley (Madden Thomas); Ida Lupino (Kathi Thomas); Cornel Wilde (Robert); Sara Allgood (Mrs. Lothian); Melville Cooper (Barty); J. Edward Bromberg (Gordon); William Demarest (Officer); Hal K. Dawson (Producer); Milton Parsons (Announcer); William Halligan (Sergeant McNamara); Inez Palange (Mrs. Spano); Charles La Torre (Mr. Spano); James Flavin (Policeman); Colin Campbell (Dresser); Fay Helm (Ruthie); George Holmes (Jerry); Wheaton Chambers (Floorwalker); Bud Geary (Cab Driver); Netta Packer (Maid); Alec Craig (Santa Claus); Cyril Ring (Box Office Man).

WINTERTIME (20th Century-Fox, 1943), 82 min.

Producer, William Le Baron; director, John Brahm; story, Arthur Kober; screenplay, E. Edwin Moran, Jack Jevne, and Lynn Starling; songs, Leo Robin and Nacio Herb Brown; music directors, Alfred Newman and Charles Henderson; choreography, James Gonzales and Carlos Romero; musical sequences supervised by Fanchon; art directors, James Basevi and Maurice Ransford; set decorator, Thomas Little; assistant director, Saul Wurtzel; costumes, Rene Hubert; special effects, Fred Sersen; sound, Roger Heman; camera, Joe MacDonald and Glen MacWilliams; editor, Louis Loeffler.

Sonja Henie (Nora); Jack Oakie (Skip Hutton); Cesar Romero (Brad Barton); Carole Landis (Flossie Fouchere); S. Z. Sakall (Hjalmar Ostgaard); Cornel Wilde (Freddy Austin); Woody Herman and Band (Themselves); Helene Reynolds (Mrs. Laly); Don Douglas (Jay Rogers); Geary Steffen (Jimmy, the Skating Partner); Matt Briggs (Russell Carter); Georges Renavent (Bodreau); Jean Del Val (Constable); Arthur Loft (Advertising Man); Charles Irwin (Drunk); Eugene Borden and Muni Seroff (Working Men); Kay Linaker (Wife); Dick Elliott (Husband); Charles Trowbridge (Mr. Prentice); Nella Walker (Mrs. Prentice); Claire Whitney, Betty Roadman, Leila McIntyre, and Kate Harrington (Bridge Players).

A SONG TO REMEMBER (Columbia, 1945), C-113 min.

Producer, Lou Edelman; director, Charles Vidor; based on the story by Ernst Marischka; screenplay, Sidney Buchman; art directors, Lionel Banks and Van Nest Polglase; set decorator, Frank Tuttle; assistant director, Abby Berlin; music director, Morris Stoloff; music supervisor, Mario Silva; music recordings, William Randall; Technicolor director, Natalie Kalmus; sound, Lodge Cunningham; editor, Charles Randall.

Paul Muni (Professor Joseph Elaner); Merle Oberon (George Sand); Cornel Wilde (Frederick Chopin); Stephen Bekassy (Franz Liszt); Nina Foch (Constantia); George Coulouris (Louis Pleyel); Sig Arno (Henri Dupont); Howard Freeman (Kalbrenner); George Macready (Alfred DeMusset); Claire Dubrey (Madame Mercier); Frank Puglia (Monsieur Jollet); Fern Emmett (Madame Lambert); Sybil Merritt (Isabelle Chopin); Ivan Triesault (Monsieur Chopin); Fay Helm (Madame Chopin); Dawn Bender (Isabelle Chopin at Age Nine);

Maurice Tauzin (Chopin at Age Ten); Roxy Roth (Paganini); Peter Cusanelli (Balzac); William Challee (Titus); William Richardson (Jan); Gregory Gaye (Young Russian); Henry Sharp (Russian Count); Ian Wolfe (Pleyel's Clerk); Eugene Bordon (Duc of Orleans); Al Luttringer (De La Croux).

A THOUSAND AND ONE NIGHTS (Columbia, 1945), C-93 min.

Producer, Samuel Bischoff; director, Alfred E. Green; story, Wilfrid H. Pettitt; screenplay, Pettitt, Richard English, and Jack Henley; art directors, Stephen Goosson and Rudolph Sternad; set decorator, Frank Tuttle; assistant director, Rex Bailey; music, Marlin Skiles; music director, Morris Stoloff; Technicolor director, Natalie Kalmus; process camera, Ray Cory; sound, Lambert Day; camera, Ray Rennahan; editor, Gene Havlick

Cornel Wilde (Aladdin); Evelyn Keyes (The Genie); Phil Silvers (Abdullah); Adele Jergens (Princess Armina); Dusty Anderson (Novira); Dennis Hoey (Sultan Kamar Al-Kir/Prince Hadji); Philip Van Zandt (Grand Wazir Abu-Hassan); Gus Schilling (Jafar); Nestor Paiva (Kahim); Rex Ingram (Giant); Richard Hale (Kofir the Sorcerer); Carole Mathews, Pat Parrish, and Shelley Winters (Hand Maidens); Vivian Mason (Exotic Girl); Trevor Bardette (Hasson); Dick Botiller (Ramud); Cy Kendall (Auctioneer); Charles LaTorre (Innkeeper); Frank Lackteen (Camel Driver); Mari Jinishian (Dancer); Frank Scannell, Patric Desmond (Retainers).

LEAVE HER TO HEAVEN (20th Century-Fox, 1945), C-111 min.

Producer, William A. Bacher; director, John M. Stahl; based on the novel by Ben Ames Williams; screeenplay, Jo Swerling; assistant director, Joseph Behm; Technicolor director, Natalie Kalmus; music, Alfred Newman; orchestrator, Edward B. Powell; art directors, Lyle Wheeler and Maurice Ransford; set decorators, Thomas Little and Ernest Lansing; special camera effects, Fred Sersen; sound, E. Clayton Ward; camera, Leon Shamroy; editor, James B. Clark.

Gene Tierney (Ellen Berent); Cornel Wilde (Richard Harland); Jeanne Crain (Ruth Berent); Vincent Price (Russell Quinton); Mary Phillips (Mrs. Berent); Ray Collins (Glen Robie); Gene Lockhart (Dr. Saunders); Reed Hadley (Dr. Mason); Darryl Hickman (Danny Harland); Chill Wills (Leick Thorne); Paul Everton (Judge); Olive Blakeney (Mrs. Robie); Addison Richards (Bedford); Harry Depp (Catterson); Grant Mitchell (Carlson, the Bank Vice-President); Milton Parsons (Medcraft, the Mortician); Earl Schenck (Norton); Hugh Maguire (Lin Robie); Betty Hannon (Tess Robie); Kay Riley (Nurse); Mae Marsh (Fisherwoman); Audrey Betz (Cook at Robie's Rancy); Guy Beach (Sheriff); Jim Farley (Conductor).

THE BANDIT OF SHERWOOD FOREST (Columbia, 1946). C-85 min.

Producers, Leonard S. Picker and Clifford Sanforth; directors, George Sherman and Henry Levin; based on the novel *Son of Robin Hood* by Paul A. Castleton; story, Castleton and Wilfred H. Pettitt; screenplay, Pettitt and Melvin Levy; Technicolor directors, Natalie Kalmus and Francis C. Cugat; assistant director, Wilbur McGaugh; art directors, Stephen Goosson and Rudolph Sternad; set decorator, Frank Kramer; music, Hugo Friedhofer; music director, Morris Stoloff; sound, Lambert Day; camera, Tony Gaudio, William Snyder, and George B. Meehan, Jr.; editor, Richard Fantl.

Cornel Wilde (Robert of Nottingham); Anita Louise (Lady Catherine Maitland); Jill Esmond (Queen Mother); Edgar Buchanan (Friar Tuck); Henry Daniell (The Regent); George Macready (Fitz-Herbert); Russell Hicks (Robin Hood); John Abbott (Will Scarlet); Lloyd Corrigan (Sheriff of Nottingham); Eva Moore (Mother Meg); Ray Teal (Little John); Leslie Denison (Allan-A-Dale); Ian Wolfe (Lord Mortimer); Maurice R. Tauzin (The King); Mauritz Hugo, Philip Van Zandt, Robert Williams, Harry Cording, Ralph Dunn, and Dick Curtis (Men-at-Arms); Nelson Leigh, George Eldredge, Robert Scott, and Ross Hunter (Robin Hood's Men); Ferdinand Munier (Innkeeper); Dan Stowell and Lane Chandler (Outlaws); Ted Allan (Captain of the Watch); Gene Stutenroth (Jailer); Jimmy Lloyd (Crossbowman); Holmes Herbert (Baron).

CENTENNIAL SUMMER (20th Century-Fox, 1946), C-102 min.
Producer-director, Otto Preminger; based on the novel by Albert E. Idell; screenplay, Michael Kanin; Technicolor directors, Natalie Kalmus and Richard Mueller; assistant director, Arthur Jacobson; art directors, Lyle Wheeler and Lee Fuller; set decorator, Thomas Little; music director, Alfred Newman; vocal arranger, Charles Henderson; orchestrators, Maurice de Packh, Herbert Spencer, and Conrad Salinger; songs, Jerome Kern and Oscar Hammerstein II; Leo Robin and E. Y. Harburg; choreography, Dorothy Fox; sound, W. D. Flick and Roger Heman; special camera effects, Fred Sersen; camera, Ernest Palmer; editor, Harry Reynolds.

Jeanne Crain (Julia Rogers); Cornel Wilde (Philippe Lascalles); Linda Darnell (Edith Rogers); William Eythe (Benjamin Franklin Phelps); Walter Brennan (Jessie Rogers); Constance Bennett (Zenia Lascalles); Dorothy Gish (Harriet Rogers); Barbara Whiting (Susanna Rogers); Larry Stevens (Richard Lewis. Esq.); Kathleen Howard (Deborah); Buddy Swan (Budley Rogers); Charles Dingle (Snodgrass); Avon Long (Specialty); Florida Sanders (Dance Specialty); Gavin Gordon (Trowbridge); Eddie Dunn (Mr. Phelps); Lois Austin (Mrs. Phelps) Harry Strang (Mr. Dorgan); Frances Morris (Mrs. Dorgan); Reginald Sheffield (President Grant); William Frambes (Messenger Boy); Paul Everton (Senator); Billy Wayne (Attendant); Winifred Harris (Governor's Wife); Ferris Taylor (Governor); Sam McDaniel, Fred "Snowflake" Toones, Napoleon Whiting, and Nicodemus Stewart (Red Caps); Hans Moebus (Subject in Still Life); Joe Whitehead (Railroad Clerk).

STAIRWAY FOR A STAR (Stairway for a Star Corp., 1947), 74 min.
Producer, Jack Krieger.

Cornel Wilde (Jimmy Banks); Helen Beverly (Jane Adams); Dennis Brent (George Blanck); and: Linda Lee Hill, Robert Pitkin, Eileen Pollack, Sam Wolfe, Donald Whalen, Gregory Knox and Linda Lombard, Janine Frestova and Felix Sadovsky, The Slim Gaillard Trio, The Terry Twins, Searles and Gallian, and The Three DeCastro Sisters.

THE HOMESTRETCH (20th Century-Fox, 1947), C-96 min.
Producer, Robert Bassler; director, H. Bruce Humberstone; screenplay, Wanda Tuchock; Technicolor directors, Natalie Kalmus and Richard Mueller;

assistant director, Henry Weinberger; art directors, James Basevi and Leland Fuller; set decorators, Thomas Little and Walter M. Scott; music, David Raksin; music director, Alfred Newman; orchestrator, Edward Powell; sound, E. Clayton Ward and Harry M. Leonard; special camera effects, Fred Sersen; camera, Arthur Arling; editor, Robert Simpson.

Cornel Wilde (Jock Wallace); Maureen O'Hara (Leslie Hale); Glenn Langan (Bill Van Dyke); Helen Walker (Kitty Brant); James Gleason (Doc Ellborne); Henry Stephenson (Balcares); Margaret Bannerman (Ellamae Scott); Ethel Griffies (Aunt Martha); Tommy Cook (Pablo); Nancy Evans (Sarah); John Vosper (Cliff); Michael Dyne (Julian Scott); Edward Earle (Mac); Charles Stevens (Mexican Father); Nina Campana (Mexican Mother); Rose Mary Lopez (Mexican Girl); Claire Du Brey (Carl); Anne O'Neal (Maid); Harry Cheshire (Colonel Albright); George Reed (Dee Dee); Juan Torena (Hernandez); Inez Palange (Gypsy Woman); Edmund Cobb (Mac's Helper); Buddy Roosevelt (Brakeman); Clinton Rosemond (Black Man); Keith Hitchcock (Bobbie).

FOREVER AMBER (20th Century-Fox, 1947), C-138 min.
Producer, William Perlberg; director, Otto Preminger; based on the novel by Kathleen Winsor; adaptation, Jerome Cady; screenplay, Ring Lardner, Jr. and Philip Dunne; Technicolor directors, Natalie Kalmus and Richard Mueller; art director, Lyle Wheeler; set decorators, Thomas Little and Walter M. Scott; music, David Raksin; orchestrators, Maurice de Packh and Herbert Spencer; music director, Alfred Newman; assistant director, Saul Wurtzel; sound, Alfred Bruzlin and Harry M. Leonard; special camera effects, Fred Sersen; camera, Leon Shamroy; editor, Louis Loeffler.

Linda Darnell (Amber St. Clair); Cornel Wilde (Bruce Carlton); Richard Greene (Lord Almsbury); George Sanders (King Charles II); Richard Haydn (Earl of Radcliffe); Jessica Tandy (Nan Britton); Anne Revere (Mother Red Cap); John Russell (Black Jack Mallard); Jane Ball (Corinne Carlton); Robert Coote (Sir Thomas Dudley); Leo G. Carroll (Matt Goodgroome); Natalie Draper (Countess of Castelmaine); Margaret Wycherly (Mrs. Song); Alma Kruger (Lady Redmond); Edmond Breon (Lord Redmond); Alan Napier (Landale); Perry "Bill" Ward (Little Bruce); Richard Bailey (Bob Starling); Houseley Stevenson (Mr. Starling); Bob Adler, Gilchrist Stuart, David Murray, and Arthur Elliott (Cavaliers); Skelton Knaggs (Blueskin); Peter Shaw (Deacon); Jimmy Ames (Galeazzo); Vernon Downing (Fop); Lillian Molieri (Queen Catherine); Ian Keith (Tybalt); Frederic Worlock (Actor); Norma Varden (Mrs. Abbott); Edith Evanson (Sarah); Ellen Corby (Marge); James Craven (Messenger); Tempe Pigott (Mid Wife); Cyril Delevanti (Cobbler); Cecil Weston (Woman); Ottola Nesmith (Mrs. Chiverton); Pati Behrs (Makeup Artist); Eric Noonan (First Mate); Robert Greig (Magistrate).

IT HAD TO BE YOU (Columbia, 1947), 98 min.
Producer, Don Hartman; assistant producer, Norman Deming: directors, Don Hartman and Rudolph Mate; story, Hartman and Allen Boretz; screenplay, Norman Panama and Melvin Frank; art directors, Stephen Goosson and Rudolph Sternad; set decorators, Wilbur Menefee and William Kiernan; music director, Morris Stoloff; assistant director, Sam Nelson; sound, Jack Haynes; camera, Mate and Vincent Farrar; editor, Gene Havlick.

Ginger Rogers (Victoria Stafford); Cornel Wilde ("George"/Johnny Blaine); Percy Waram (Mr. Stafford); Spring Byington (Mrs. Stafford); Ron Randell (Oliver H. P. Harrington); Thurston Hall (Mr. Harrington); Charles Evans (Dr. Parkinson); William Bevan (Evans); Frank Orth (Conductor Brown); Harry Hays Morgan (George Benson); Douglas Wood (Mr. Kimberly); Mary Forbes (Mrs. Kimberly); Nancy Saunders (Model); Douglas D. Coppin (Boy Friend); Virginia Hunter (Maid of Honor); Michael Towne (Fireman); Fred Sears (Tillerman, the Fireman); Jerry Hunt (Indian Boy); Carol Nugent (Victoria at the Age of Six); Judy Nugent (Victoria at the Age of Five); Mary Patterson (Victoria at the Age of Three); Paul Campbell (Radio Announcer); Ralph Peters and Gary Owen (Cab Drivers); Harlan Warde (Atherton); Myron Healey (Standish); Jack Rice (Floorwalker); Anna Q. Nilsson (Saleslady); George Chandler (Man); Vernon Dent (Man in Drug Store); Vera Lewis (Mrs. Brown); Oscar O'Shea (Irish Neighborhood Watchman); Maurice Prince and Joe Gray (Prize Fighters).

THE WALLS OF JERICHO (20th Century-Fox, 1948), 106 min.

Producer, Lamar Trotti; director, John M. Stahl; based on the novel by Paul Wellman; screenplay, Trotti; assistant director, Arthur Jacobson; music, Cyril Mockridge; orchestrators, Herbert Spencer and Maurice De Packh; music director, Lionel Newman; art directors, Lyle Wheeler and Maurice Ransford; set decorators, Thomas Little and Paul S. Fox; makeup, Ben Nye, Henry Vilardo, and Allan Snyder; costumes, Kay Nelson; sound, Alfred Bruzlin and Roger Heman; special effects, Fred Sersen; camera, Arthur Miller; editor, James B. Clark.

Cornel Wilde (Dave Connors); Linda Darnell (Algeria Wedge); Anne Baxter (Julia Norman); Kirk Douglas (Tucker Wedge); Ann Dvorak (Belle Connors); Colleen Townsend (Marjorie Ransome); Henry Hull (Jefferson Norman); Barton MacLane (Gotch McCurdy); Griff Barnett (Judge Hutto); William Tracy (Cully Caxton); Art Baker (Peddigrew); Frank Ferguson (Tom Ransome); Ann Morrison (Nellie); Hope Landin (Mrs. Hutto); Helen Brown (Mrs. Ransome); Norman Leavitt (Adam McAdam); Whitford Kane (Judge Foster); J. Farrell MacDonald (Bailiff); Dick Rich (Mulliken); Will Wright (Dr. Patterson); Daniel White (Loafer); Gene Nelson (Assistant Prosecutor); Tom Moore (Man); Milton Parsons (Joe); Patricia Morison (Mrs. Landon); Dorothy Granger and Ann Doran (Gossips); Cecil Weston (Head Nurse); William H. Gould (Politician).

ROAD HOUSE (20th Century-Fox, 1948), 95 min.

Producer, Edward Chodorov; director, Jean Negulesco; story, Margaret Gruen and Oscar Saul; screenplay, Chodorov; art directors, Lyle Wheeler and Maurice Ransford; set decorator, Thomas Little; music, Cyril Mockridge; orchestrators, Herbert Spencer and Earle Hagen; music director, Lionel Newman; assistant director, Tom Dudley; costumes, Kay Nelson; makeup, Ben Nye, Tom Tuttle, and Bill Riddle; sound, Alfred Bruzlin and Harry M. Leonard; special effects, Fred Sersen; camera, Joseph La Shelle; editor, James B. Clark.

Ida Lupino (Lily Stevens); Cornel Wilde (Pete Morgan); Celeste Holm (Susie Smith); Richard Widmark (Jefty Robbins); O. Z. Whitehead (Arthur); Robert Karnes (Mike); George Beranger (Lefty); Ian MacDonald (Police Captain); Grandon Rhodes (Judge); Jack G. Lee (Sam); Marion Marshall (Millie); Jack Edwards, Jr. and Don Kohler (Men); Kathleen O'Malley and Blanche Taylor (Girls); Charles Flynn and Ray Teal (Cops); Clancy Cooper (Policeman at Club); Robert Foulk (Policeman); Harry Seymour (Desk Clerk); Heinie Conklin (Court Clerk); Cecil Weston (Woman).

SHOCKPROOF (Columbia, 1949), 79 min.

Producer, S. Sylvan Simon; associate producer, Earl McEvoy; director, Douglas Sirk; screenplay, Helen Deutsch and Samuel Fuller; assistant director, Earl Bellamy; costumes, Jean Louis; makeup, Clay Campbell; art director, Carl Anderson; set decorator, Louis Diage; music, George Duning; music director, Morris Stoloff; sound, Lodge Cunningham; camera, Charles Lawton, Jr.; editor, Gene Havlick.

Cornel Wilde (Griff Marat); Patricia Knight (Jenny Marsh); John Baragrey (Harry Wesson); Esther Minciotti (Mrs. Marat); Howard St. John (Sam Brooks); Russell Collins (Frederick Bauer); Charles Bates (Tommy Marat); Gilbert Barnett (Barry); Frank Jaquet (Monte); Ann Shoemaker (Dr. Daniels); King Donovan (Joe Wilson); Claire Carleton (Florie Kobiski); Al Eben (Joe Kobiski); Fred Sears and Jimmy Lloyd (Clerks); Isabel Withers (Switchboard Operator); Virginia Farmer (Mrs. Terrence); Charles Jordan (Hot Dog Man); Buddy Swan (Teenage Boy); Crane Whitley (Foreman); Robert R. Stephenson (Drunk); Richard Benedict ("Kid"); Cliff Clark (Police Lieutenant); Arthur Space (Police Inspector); Charles Marsh (Manager).

FOUR DAYS LEAVE (Film Classics, 1950), 98 min.

Producer, Praesans L. Wechsler; director, Leopold Lindtberg; story, Richard Schweitzer; screenplay, Richard Lindtberg and Curt Siodmak; dialog, Ring Lardner, Jr; music, Robert Blum; camera, Emil Berna.

Cornel Wilde (Stanley Robin); Josette Day (Suzanne); Simone Signoret (Yvonne); John Baragrey (Jack); Richard Erdman (Eddy); Alan Hale, Jr. (Joe); George Petrie (Sidney); Leopold Biberti (Walter Hochull); Robert Bichler (Fred); Christiane Martin (Madeleine).

TWO FLAGS WEST (20th Century-Fox, 1950), 92 min.

Producer, Casey Robinson; director, Robert Wise; story, Frank S. Nugent; screenplay, Nugent and Casey Robinson; music director, Alfred Newman; art directors, Lyle Wheeler and Chester Gore; camera, Leon Shamroy; editor, Louis Loeffler.

Joseph Cotten (Colonel Clay Tucker); Linda Darnell (Elena Kenniston); Jeff Chandler (Kenniston); Cornel Wilde (Captain Mark Bradford); Dale Robertson (Lem); Jay C. Flippen (Sergeant Terrance Duffy); Noah Berry, Jr. (Cy Davis); Harry Von Zell (Ephriam Strong); John Sands (Lieutenant Adams); Arthur Hunnicutt (Sergeant Pickens); Jack Lee (Courier); Robert Adler (Hank); Harry Carter (Lieutenant Reynolds); Ferris Taylor (Dr. Magowan); Sally Corner (Mrs. Magowan); Everett Glass (Reverend Simpkins); Marjorie Bennett (Mrs. Simpkins); Lee Macgregor (Cal); Roy Gordon (Captain Stanley); Aurora Castillo (Maria); Stanley Andrews (Colonel Hoffman); Don Garner (Ash Cooper).

THE GREATEST SHOW ON EARTH (Paramount, 1952), C-153 min.

Producer, Cecil B. DeMille; associate producer, Henry Wilcoxon; director, Cecil B. DeMille; story, Frederic M. Frank, Theodore St. John, and Frank Cavett; screenplay, Frank, St. John, and Barre Lyndon; assistant director, Edward Salven; music, Victor Young; songs, Young and Ned Washington; John Ringling North and E. Ray Goetz; and Henry Sullivan and John Murray Anderson; art directors, Hal Periera and Walter Tyler; set decorators, Sam Comer and Ray Moyer; technical advisor, John Ringling North; dialog director, James Vincent; makeup, Wally Westmore; costumes, Edith Head and Dorothy Jenkins; sound, Harry Lindgren and John Cope; special camera effects, Gordon Jennings, Paul Lerpae, and Devereaux Jennings; camera, George Barnes; additional camera, J. Peverell Marley, Wallace Kelley; editor, Anne Bauchens.

Betty Hutton (Holly); Cornel Wilde (Sebastian); Charlton Heston (Brad); Dorothy Lamour (Phyllis); Gloria Grahame (Angel); James Stewart (Buttons); Emmett Kelly (Himself); Henry Wilcoxon (Detective); Lyle Bettger (Klaus); Lawrence Tierney (Henderson); John Kellogg (Harry); John Ridgely (Jack Steelman); Frank Wilcox (Circus Doctor); Bob Carson (Ringmaster); Lillian Albertson (Button's Mother); Julia Faye (Birdie); John Ringling North (Himself); Noel Neill (Noel); John Crawford (Jack); Gertrude Messinger (Gertrude); Adele Cook Johnson (Mable); Robert W. Rushing and William J. Riley (Policemen); Lane Chandler (Dave); Howard Negley (Truck Boss); Jimmie Dundee (Utility Man); Ken Christy (Spectator); Beverly Washburn (Girl); Syd Saylor and Lestor Dorr (Circus Barkers); Fred Kohler, Jr. (Fireman); Stanley Andrews (Man); Bess Flowers and Kathleen Freeman (Women); Edmond O'Brien (Midway Barker); Tuffy Genders (Tuffy); Ethan Laidlaw (Hank); Dale Van Sickel (Man in Train Wreck); William Boyd (Himself); Bing Crosby, Bob Hope, and Mona Freeman (As Themselves-Spectators in Grandstands).

AT SWORD'S POINT (RKO, 1952), C-81 min.

Producer, Harold T. Brandt; director, Lewis Allen; based on *Twenty Years After* by Alexander Dumas; screenplay, Aubrey Wisberg and Jack Pollexfen; art directors, Jack Okey, and Albert D'Agostino; music director, C. Bakaleinikoff; camera, Ray Rennahan; editors, Samuel E. Beetle and Robert Golden.

Cornel Wilde (d'Artagnan); Maureen O'Hara (Claire); Robert Douglas (Lavelle); Gladys Cooper (Queen); June Clayworth (Claudine); Dan O'Herlihy (Aramis); Alan Hale, Jr. (Porthos); Blanche Yurka (Madam Michon); Nancy Gates (Princess Henriette); Edmond Breon (Queen's Chamberlain); Peter Miles (Louis); George Petrie (Chalais); Moroni Olsen (Old Porthos); Boyd Davis (Dr. Fernand); Holmes Herbert (Mallard); Lucien Littlefield (Corporal Gautier); Claude Dunkin (Pierre); Pat O'Moore (Monk); Tristram Coffin (Regent Guard); Reginald Sheffield (Cardinal); Julia Dean (Mme. d'Artagnan); Philip Van Zandt (Jacques); Gregory Marshall (Henrique).

British release title: **SONS OF THE MUSKETEERS.**

CALIFORNIA CONQUEST (Columbia, 1952), C-79 min.

Producer, Sam Katzman; director, Lew Landers; story-screenplay, Robert E. Kent; art director, Paul Palmentola; music director, Mischa Bakaleinikoff; camera, Ellis W. Carter; editor, Richard Fantl.

Cornel Wilde (Don Arturo Bordega); Teresa Wright (Julia Lawrence); Alfonso Bedoya (Jose Martinez); Lisa Ferraday (Helena de Gagarine); Eugene Iglesias (Ernesto Brios); John Dehner (Fredo Brios); Ivan Lebedeff (Alexander Rotcheff); Tito Renaldo (Don Bernardo Mirana); Renzo Cesana (Fray Lindos); Baynes Barron (Igancio); and: Rico Alaniz, William P. Wilkerson, Edward Colmans, Alex Montoya, Hank Patterson, and George Eldredge.

OPERATION SECRET (Warner Bros. 1952), 108 min.

Producer, Henry Blanke; director, Lewis Seiler; story, Alvin Josephy and John Twist; screenplay, Harold Medford and James Webb; music, Roy Webb; orchestrators, Leo Shuken, and Sid Cutner; music director, Ray Heindorf; sets, William T. Kuehl; camera, Ted McCord; editor, Clarence Kolster.

Cornel Wilde (Peter Forrester); Steve Cochran (Marcel Brevoort); Phyllis Thaxter (Maria); Karl Malden (Major Latrec); Paul Picerni (Armand); Lester Matthews (Robbins); Jay Novello (Herr Bauer); Dan O'Herlihy (Duncan); Ed Foster (Claude); Claude Dunkin (Rene); Wilton Graff (French Official); Baynes Barron (Henri); Philip Rush (Zabreski); Robert Shaw (Jacques); Henry Rowland (German M.P.); Dan Riss (Sergeant); Gayle Kellogg (Corporal); John Beattie (Radio Operator); George Dee, Rudy Rama, Monte Pittman, Anthony Eisley, Joe Espitallier, and Harry Arnie (Marquises); Harlan Warde (Major Dawson); Charles Flynn (German Civil Officer); Wayne Taylor (Etienne).

TREASURE OF THE GOLDEN CONDOR (20th Century-Fox, 1953), C-93 min.

Producer, Jules Buck; director, Delmer Daves; based on the novel *Benjamin Blake* by Edison Marshall; screenplay, Daves; music, Sol Kaplan; art directors, Lyle Wheeler and Albert Hogsett; camera, Edward Cronjager; editor, Robert Simpson.

Cornel Wilde (Jean-Paul); Constance Smith (Clara); Finlay Currie (McDougal); Walter Hampden (Pierre); Anne Bancroft (Marie); George Macready (Marquis); Fay Wray (Marquise); Leo G. Carroll (Dondel); Konstantin Shayne (Curate); Louis Heminger (Indian Chief); Tudor Owen (Fontaine); Gil Donaldson (Count De Bayoux); Ken Herman (Francois); Bobby Blake (Stable Boy); Jerry Hunter (Jean Paul at the Age of Ten); Wende Weil (Marie at the Age of Eight-and-One-Half); Ray Beltram (Medicine Man); Alphonse Martell (Artist); House Peters, Sr. (Magistrate) May Wynn (Maid); Paul Bryar (Guard); Camillo Guercio (Prosecutor).

MAIN STREET TO BROADWAY (MGM, 1953), 97 min.

Producer, Lester Cowan; director, Tay Garnett; story, Robert E. Sherwood; screenplay, Samson Raphaelson; art director, Perry Ferguson; assistant director, James Anderson; music, Ann Ronell; song, Richard Rodgers and Oscar Hammerstein II; camera, James Wong Howe; editor, Gene Fowler, Jr.

Tom Morton (Tony Monaco); Mary Murphy (Mary Craig); Agnes Moorehead (Mildred Waterbury); Herb Shriner (Frank Johnson); Rosemary De Camp (Mrs. Craig); Clinton Sundberg (Mr. Craig); Florence Bates, Madge Kennedy, Carl Benton Reid, Frank Ferguson, and Robert Bray (Fantasy Sequence); Tal-

564

lulah Bankhead, Ethel Barrymore, Lionel Barrymore, Gertrude Berg, Shirley Booth, Louis Calhern, Leo Durocher, Faye Emerson, Oscar Hammerstein II, Rex Harrison, Helen Hayes, Joshua Logan, Mary Martin, Lilli Palmer, Richard Rogers, John Van Druten, Cornel Wilde, Bill Rigney, Chris Durocher, and Arthur Shields (Themselves).

SAADIA (MGM, 1953), C-82 min.

Producer-director, Albert Lewin; story, Francis D'Autheville; screenplay, Lewin; art director, John Hawkesworth; camera, Christopher Challis; editor, Harold F. Kress.

Cornel Wilde (Si Lahssen); Mel Ferrer (Henrik); Rita Gam (Saadia); Michael Simon (Bou Rezza); Cyril Cusack (Khadir); Wanda Rotha (Fatima); Marcel Poncin (Moha); Anthony Marlowe (Captain Sabert); Helen Vallier (Zoubida); Mahjoub Ben Brahim (Almed); Jacques Dufilho (Bandit Leader); Bernard Farrel (Lieutenant Camuzac); Richard Johnson (Lieutenant Girard); Alec Mango (Brahim); Edward Leslie (Villager).

WOMAN'S WORLD (20th Century-Fox, 1954), C-94 min.

Producer, Charles Brackett; director, Jean Negulesco; story, Mona Williams; screenplay, Claude Binyon, Mary Loos, and Richard Sale; additional dialog, Howard Lindsay and Russell Crouse; assistant director, Henry Weinberger; music, Cyril J. Mockridge; art director, Lyle Wheeler; camera, Joe MacDonald; editor, Louis Loeffler.

Clifton Webb (Gifford); June Allyson (Katie); Van Heflin (Jerry); Lauren Bacall (Elizabeth); Fred MacMurray (Sid); Arlene Dahl (Carol); Cornel Wilde (Bill Baxter); Elliott Reid (Tony); Margalo Gillmore (Evelyn); Alan Reed (Tomaso); David Hoffman (Jerecki); George Melford (Worker at Auto Assembly Plant); George E. Stone, George Eldredge, Paul Power, Jonathan Hole, Rodney Bell, Carleton Young, and William Tannen (Executives); George Spaulding (Ship's Captain); Maude; Prickett (Mother); Melinda Markey (Daughter); Beverly Thompson, Eileen Maxwell, and Virginia Maples (Models); Kathryn Card, Billie Bird, Louise Robinson, and Jean Walters (Women in Bargain Basement).

PASSION (RKO, 1954) C-84 min.

Producer, Benedict Bogeaus; director, Allan Dwan; story-screenplay, Josef Leytes, Miguel Padilla, and Beatrice A. Dresher; adaptor, Howard Estabrook; art director, Van Nest Polglase; set decorator, John Sturtevant; costumes, Gwen Wakeling; music, David Raksin; music director, Louis Forbes; camera, John Alton; supervising editor, James Leicester; editor, Carl Lodato.

Cornel Wilde (Juan Obregon); Yvonne De Carlo (Rosa Melo/Tonya Melo); Rodolfo Acosta (Salvador Sandro); Raymond Burr (Captain Rodriguez); Lon Chaney, Jr. (Castro); John Qualen (Gasper Melo); Anthony Caruso (Sergeant Munoz); Frank De Kova (Martinez); Peter Coe (Colfre); John Dierkes (Escobar); Richard Hale (Don Domingo); Rozene Kemper (Señora Melo); Rosa Turich (Maracuita); Stuart Whitman (Vaguero Bernal); James Kirkwood (Don

Rosendo); Robert Warwick (Money Lender); Bella Mitchell (Senora Carrisa); Alex Montoya (Manuel Felipe); Zon Murray (Barca).

THE BIG COMBO (Allied Artists, 1955), 89 min.

Producer, Sidney Harmon; director, Joseph Lewis; screenplay, Philip Yordan; assistant directors, Mack Wright and Robert Justman; music, David Raksin; piano soloist, Jacob Gimpel; Miss Wallace's wardrobe by Don Loper; makeup, Larry Butterworth; special camera effects, Jack Rabin and Louis DeWitt; camera, John Alton; editor, Robert Eisen.

Cornel Wilde (Diamond); Richard Conte (Brown); Brian Donlevy (McClure); Jean Wallace (Susan Cabot); Robert Middleton (Captain Peterson); Lee Van Cleef (Fante); Earl Holliman (Mingo); Helen Walker (Alicia Brown); Jay Adler (Sam Hill); John Hoyt (Nils Dreyer); Ted De Corsia (Bettini); Helen Stanton (Rita); Roy Gordon (Audubon); Whit Bissell (Doctor); Philip Van Zandt (Mr. Jones); Steve Mitchell (Bennie Smith); Brian O'Hara (Malloy); Rita Gould (Nurse); Michael Mark (Hotel Clerk); Donna Drew (Miss Hartleby); Baynes Barron (Young Detective).

THE SCARLET COAT (MGM, 1955), C-101 min.

Producer, Nicholas Nayfack; director, John Sturges; screenplay, Karl Tunberg; assistant director, Fred Frank; costumes, Walter Plunkett; music, Conrad Salinger; art directors, Cedric Gibbons and Merrill Pye; camera, Paul C. Vogel; editor, Ben Lewis.

Cornel Wilde (Major John Bolton); Michael Wilding (Major John Andre); George Sanders (Dr. Jonathan Odell); Anne Francis (Sally Cameron); Robert Douglas (Benedict Arnold); John McIntire (General Robert Howe); Rhys Williams (Peter); John Dehner (Nathanael Greene); James Westerfield (Colonel Jameson); Ashley Cowan (Mr. Brown); Paul Cavanagh (Sir Henry Clinton); John Alderson (Mr. Durkin); John O'Malley (Colonel Winfield); Bobby Driscoll (Ben Petter); Robin Hughes (Colonel Tarleton); Anthony Dearden (Captain De Lancey); Vernon Rich (Colonel); Dabbs Greer (Captain Brewster); Olaf Hytten (Butler); Gordon Richards (Mr. Cameron); Leslie Denison (Captain Sutherland); Harlan Warde (Captain); Tristram Coffin (Colonel Varick); Byron Foulger (Man); Wilson Benge (Servant); Dennis King, Jr. (Boatswain's Mate); Robert Dix (Lieutenant Evans).

STORM FEAR (United Artists, 1955), 88 min.

Producer-director, Cornel Wilde; based on the novel by Clinton Seeley; screenplay, Horton Foote; music, Elmer Bernstein; assistant director, Horace Hough; camera, Joseph La Shelle; editor, Otto Ludwig.

Cornel Wilde (Charlie); Jean Wallace (Elizabeth); Dan Duryea (Fred); Lee Grant (Edna); David Stollery (David); Dennis Weaver (Hank); Steven Hill (Benjie); Keith Britton (Doctor).

HOT BLOOD (Columbia, 1956), C-85 min.

Producers, Howard Welsch, Harry Tatelman; director, Nicholas Ray; story, Jean Evans; screenplay, Jesse Lasky, Jr; music, Les Baxter; choreography,

Matt Mattox and Sylvia Lewis; assistant director, Milton Feldman; songs, Baxter and Ross Bagdasarian; camera, Ray June; editor, Otto Ludwig.

Jane Russell (Annie Caldash); Cornel Wilde (Stephen Torino); Luther Adler (Marco Torino); Joseph Calleia (Papa Theodore); Mikhail Rasumny (Old Johnny); Nina Koshetz (Nita Johnny); Helen Westcott (Velma); Jamie Russell (Xano); Wally Russell (Bimbo); Nick Dennis (Korka); Richard Deacon (Mr. Swift); Robert Foulk (Sergeant McGrossin); John Raven (Joe Randy); Joe Merritt (Skinny Gypsy); Faye Nuell (Gypsy Woman); Joan Reynolds (Girl); Ethan Laidlaw (Bit); Peter Brocco (Doctor); Les Baxter and Ross Bagdasarian (Gas Station Attendants); Manuel Paris (Elder).

STAR OF INDIA (United Artists, 1856), C-92 min.

Producer, Raymond Stross; director, Arthur Lubin; screenplay, Herbert Dalmas; additional dialog, Denis Freeman; art director, Cedric Dawe; music director, Muir Mathieson; music, Nino Rota; camera, C. Pennington-Richards; editor, Russell Lloyd.

Cornel Wilde (Pierre St. Laurent); Jean Wallace (Katrina); Herbert Lom (Narbonne); Yvonne Sanson (Madame de Montespan); John Slater (Emile); Walter Rilla (Van Horst); Basil Sydney (King Louis XIV); Arnold Bell (Captain).

BEYOND MOMBASA (Columbia, 1957), C-90 min.

Producer, Tony Owen; director, George Marshall; based on the story "The Mark of the Leopard" by James Eastwood; screenplay, Richard English and Gene Levitt; art director, Elliot Scott; music, Humphrey Searle; assistant director, Basil Keys; camera, Frederick A. Young; editor, Ernest Walter.

Cornel Wilde (Matt Campbell); Donna Reed (Ann Wilson); Leo Genn (Ralph Hoyt); Ron Randell (Elliott Hastings); Christopher Lee (Gil Rossi); Eddie Calvert (Trumpet Player); Dan Jackson (Ketimi).

OMAR KHAYYAM (Paramount, 1957), C-101 min.

Producer, Frank Freeman, Jr.; director, William Dieterle; screenplay, Barre Lyndon; art directors, Hal Pereiera and Joseph MacMillan Johnson; music, Victor Young; assistant director, Francisco Day; costumes, Ralph Jester; songs, Jay Livingston and Ray Evans; Mack David and Young; and Moises Vivanco; process camera, Farciot Edouart; special camera effects, John P. Fulton; camera, Ernest Laszlo; editor, Everett Douglas.

Cornel Wilde (Omar); Michael Rennie (Hasani); Debra Paget (Sharain); Raymond Massey (The Shah); John Derek (Malik, the Young Prince); Yma Sumac (Karina); Margaret Hayes (Zarada); Joan Taylor (Yaffa); Sebastian Cabot (Nizam); Perry Lopez (Prince Ahmud); Morris Ankrum (Imam Mowaffak); Abraham Sofaer (Tutush); Edward Platt (Jayhan); James Griffith (Buzorg); Peter Adams (Master Herald); Henry Brandon and Paul Picerni (Commanders); Kem Dibbs (Tutush Bodyguard); Valeria Allen (Harem Wife); Charles La Torre (Army Physician); Dale Van Sickel (Officer); John Abbott (Yusuf); Len Hendry (Courier); Joyce Meadows (Harem Girl); Abdel Salam Moussa (Shah's Soldier).

THE DEVIL'S HAIRPIN (Paramount, 1957), C-82 min.

Producer-director, Cornel Wilde; based on the novel *The Fastest Man on Earth* by James Edmiston; screenplay, Edmiston and Wilde; art directors, Hal Pereira and Hilyard Brown; assistant director, Bernard McEveety, Jr.; costumes, Edith Head; songs, Ross Bagdasarian; Van Cleave; set decorators, Sam Comer, and Grace Gregory; technical advisor, Joseph J. Weissman; makeup, Wally Westmore; sound, Gene Merritt and Winston Leverett; special camera effects, John P. Fulton; process camera, Farciot Edouart; camera, Daniel I. Fapp; editor, Floyd Knudston.

Cornel Wilde (Nick Jargin); Jean Wallace (Kelly James); Arthur Franz (Danny Rhinegold); Mary Astor (Mrs. Polly Jargin); Paul Fix (Doc); Larry Pennell (Johnny Jargin); Gerald Milton (Mike Houston); Ross Bagdasarian (Tani); Morgan Jones (Chico Martinez); Jack Kosslyn (Tony Botari); Louis Wilde (The Parrot); Jack Latham (Race Announcer); Mabel Lillian Rea (Redhead); Dorene Porter (Blonde); Sue England (Brunette); John Indrisano (Gate Guard); Mike Mahoney (Starter); Les Clark (Bill, the Bartender); Henry Blair (Newsboy).

MARACAIBO (Paramount, 1958), C-88 min.

Producer-director, Cornel Wilde; based on the novel by Stirling Silliphant; screenplay, Ted Sherdeman; art directors, Hal Pereira and Joseph MacMillan Johnson; set decorators, Sam Comer and Grace Gregory; assistant director, James Rosenberger; costumes, Edith Head; men's wardrobe, Sydney LaVine; song, Jefferson Pascal and Almeida; sound, Hugo Grenzbach and Winston Leverett; process camera, Farciot Edouart; special camera effects, John P. Fulton; camera, Ellsworth Fredericks; editor, Everett Douglas.

Cornel Wilde (Bic Scott); Jean Wallace (Laura Kingsley); Abbe Lane (Elena Holbrook); Francis Lederer (Miguel Orlando); Michael Landon (Lago Orlando); Joe E. Ross (Milt Karger); Jack Kosslyn (Raoul Palma); Lillian Buyeff (Mrs. Montera); George Ramsey (Mr. Montera); Martin Vargas, Lydia Goya, and Carmen D'Antonio (Dancers); Ampola del Vando (Amelia); Manuel Lopez (Boatman); George Navarro (Waiter); Frank Leyva (Bartender); Gregory Irvin (Boy Tourist).

EDGE OF ETERNITY (Columbia, 1959), C-80 min.

Producer, Kendrick Sweet; associate producer, Donald Siegel; director, Siegel; story, Ben Markson; screenplay, Marian Hargrove and Richard Collins; assistant director, Carter De Haven; music, Daniele Amfitheatrof; makeup, Ben Lane; flying sequences, Skymasters International; art director, Robert Peterson; set decorator, Frank A. Tuttle; camera, Burnett Guffey; editor, Jerome Thoms.

Cornel Wilde (Les Martin); Victoria Shaw (Janice Kendon); Mickey Shaughnessy (Scotty O'Brien); Edgar Buchanan (Sheriff Edwards); Rian Garrick (Bob Kendon); Jack Elam (Bill Ward); Alexander Lockwood (Jim Kendon); Dabbs Greer (Gas Station Attendant); Tom Fadden (Eli); Wendell Holmes (Sam Houghton); George Cisar (The Dealer); Buzz Westcott (Pilot); Ted Jacques (Suds Reese); Paul Bailey (Amphibian Pilot); John Roy (Whitmore); George "Smoky" Ross (Undersheriff); Hope Summers (Motel Lady); John Ayres (Coroner); Don Siegel (Pipe Smoker at Motel Wearing a Neck Scarf).

CONSTANTINE AND THE CROSS (Embassy, 1962), C-120 min.

Producer, Ferdinando Felicioni; director, Lionello De Felice; screenplay, Ennio De Concini, De Felice, Ernesto Guida, Franco Rossetti, Guglielmo Santangelo, Diego Fabbri, and Fulvio Palmieri; music, Mario Nascimbene; art director, Franco Lolli; costumes, Giancarlo Bartolini-Salimbene; camera, Massimo Dallamano; editors, Mario Serandrei and Gabriele Varriale.

Cornel Wilde (Constantine); Christine Kaufman (Livia); Belinda Lee (Fausta); Elisa Cegani (Helena); Massimo Serato (Maxientius); Fausto Tozzi (Hadrian); Tino Carraro (Maximianus); Carol Ninche (Constantius Cloro); Vittorio Sanipoli (Apuleius).

SWORD OF LANCELOT (Universal, 1963), C-116 min.

Executive producer, Cornel Wilde; producer, Bernard Luber; associate producer, George Pitcher; director, Wilde; based on the book *Morte D'Arthur* by Sir Thomas Mallory; music, Ron Goodwin; art directors, Maurice Carter and Jack Maxsted; assistant director, Rene Dupont; costumes, Terence Morgan; makeup, George Blackler; sound, Don Sharpe, Kevin Connor, and William Daniels; background camera, Karsh; camera, Harry Waxman; additional camera, Robert Thomson; editor, Frederick Wilson.

Cornel Wilde (Sir Lancelot); Jean Wallace (Queen Guinevere); Brian Aherne (King Arthur); George Baker (Sir Gawaine); Archie Duncan (Sir Lamorak); Adrienne Corri (Lady Vivian); Michael Meacham (Sir Modred); Iain Gregory (Sir Tors); Mark Dignam (Merlin); Reginald Beckwith (Sir Dragonet); John Barrie (Sir Bedivere); Richard Thorpe (Sir Gareth); Joseph Tomelty (Sir Kaye); Graham Stark (Rian); Geoffrey Dunn (Edric); Walter Gotell (Sir Cedric); Peter Prowse (Brandagorus); Christopher Rhodes (Ulfus); John Longden (King Leodogran); Bob Bryan (Sir Dorjak); Violetta Farjeon (French Serving Maid).

British release title: **LANCELOT AND GUINEVERE.**

THE NAKED PREY (Paramount, 1966), C-96 min.

Producer Cornel Wilde; co-producer, Sven Persson; director, Wilde; screenplay, Clint Johnston and Don Peters; assistant director, Bert Batt; wardrobe, Freda Thompson; musical advisor, Andrew Tracey; title backgrounds, Andrew T. Motjuoadi; camera, H. A. R. Thomson; editor, Roger Cherrill.

Cornel Wilde (The Man); Gert Van Der Berg (The Second Man); Ken Gampu (Warrior Leader); Patrick Mynhardt (Safari Overseer); Bella Randels (Little Girl).

BEACH RED (United Artists, 1967), C-105 min.

Producer-director, Cornel Wilde; based on the novel by Peter Bowman; screenplay, Clint Johnston, Donald A. Peters, and Jefferson Pascal; art director, Francisco Balangue; assistant directors, Derek Cracknell, Francisco Maclang; makeup, Neville Smallwood; wardrobe, Vincente Cabrera; song, Elbey Vid; special arrangements, Marty Paich; music, Colonel Antonio Buenaventura; special effects, Paul Pollard; camera, Cecil R. Cooney; editor, Frank P. Keller.

Cornel Wilde (Captain MacDonald); Rip Torn (Sergeant Honeywell); Burr

De Benning (Egan); Patrick Wolfe (Cliff); Jean Wallace (Julia MacDonald); Jaime Sanchez (Colombo); Genki Koyama (Captain Sugiyama); Gene Blakeley (Goldberg); Norma Pak (Nakano); Dewey Stringer (Mouse); Fred Galang (Lieutenant Domingo); Hiroshi Kiyama (Michio); Michael Parsons (Sergeant Lindstrom); Dale Ishimoto (Captain Tanaka); Linda Albertano (Egan's Girl Friend); Jan Garrison (Susie); Michio Hazama (Captain Kondo); Masako Ohtsuki (Colonel's Wife); Kiyoma Takezawa (Japanese Soldier); and: Charles Weaver, Juan Bona, Bill Dunbar, Ed Finlan, Phil Beinke, Rod Meir, and Pat Whitlock.

THE COMIC (Columbia, 1969), C-95 min.

Producers-directors-screenplay, Carl Reiner, Aaron Ruben; production designer, Walter Simonds; assistant director, Rusty Meek; music, Jack Elliott; costumes, Guy Verhille; sound, Charles J. Rice, Les Fresholtz, Arthur Piantadosi; camera, W. Wallace Kelley; editor, Adrienne Fazan.

Dick Van Dyke (Billy Bright); Michele Lee (Mary Gibson); Mickey Rooney (Cockeye); Cornel Wilde (Frank Powers); Nina Wayne (Sybil); Pert Kelton (Mama); Steve Allen (Himself); Barbara Heller (Ginger); Ed Peck (Edwin C. Englehardt); Jeannine Riley (Lorraine); Gavin MacLeod (First Director); Jay Novello (Miguel); Craig Huebing (Doctor); Paulene Myers (Phoebe); Fritz Feld (Armand); Jerome Cowan (Lawrence); Isabell Sanford (Woman); Jeff Donnell (Nurse); Carl Reiner (Al Schilling).

GARGOYLES (CBS-TV, 1972), C-90 min.

Executive producer, Roger Gimbel; producers, Bob Christiansen and Rick Rosenberg; director, B. W. L. Norton; teleplay, Stephen and Elinor Knapf; music, Robert Prince; camera, Earl Rath.

Cornel Wilde (Professor Mercer Boley); Jennifer Salt (Diana Boley); Grayson Hall (Mrs. Parks); Bernie Casey (Head Gargoyle); Scott Glenn (James Reeger); William Stevens (Police Chief); John Gruber (Jesse) Woodrow Chambliss (Uncle Willie); Jim Connell (Buddy); Tim Burns (Ray).

SHARK'S TREASURE (United Artists, 1975), C-95 min.

Producer-director-script, Cornel Wilde; music, Robert O. Ragland; marine coordinator, Clint Deen; assistant director, John Stoneman; sound, William Daniels; sound editor, Harold E. Wooley; camera, Jack Atcheler; underwater camera, Al Giddings; editor, Bryon "Buzz" Brandt.

Cornel Wilde (Jim); Yaphet Kotto (Ben); John Neilson (Ron); Cliff Osmond (Lobo); David Canary (Larry); David Gilliam (Johnny); Caesar Cordova (Pablo); Gene Borkan (Kook); Dale Ishimoto (Ishy); and: Mary Fisher, Clint Denn, Carmen Argenziano.

NO BLADE OF GRASS (MGM, 1970), C-96 min.

Producer-director, Cornel Wilde; based on the novel *Death of Grass* by John Christopher; screenplay, Sean Forestal and Jefferson Pascal; art director, Elliott Scott; music director, Burnell Whibley; songs, Louis Nelius and Charles Carroll; sound, Cyril Swern; special effects, Terry Witherington; camera, H. A. R. Thompson; editors, Frank Clarke and Eric Boyd-Perkins.

Nigel Davenport (John Custance); Jean Wallace (Ann Custance); Patrick Holt (David Custance); Ruth Kettlewell (Fat Woman); M. J. Matthews (George); Michael Percival (Police Constable); Tex Fuller (Mr. Beaseley); Simon Merrick (TV Interviewer); Anthony Sharp (Sir Charles Brenner); George Coulouris (Sturdevant); Anthony May (Pirrie); Wendy Richard (Clara); Max Hartnell (Lieutenant); John Lewis (Corporal); Norman Atkyns (Dr. Cassop); Nigel Rathborne (Davey); Christopher Lofthouse (Spooks); John Avison (Yorkshire Sergeant); Jimmy Winston, Richard Penny, and R. C. Driscoll (Huns); Christopher Wilson (Farmer); Brian Crabtree (Joe Harris); Bruce Myers (Bill Riggs); Derek Keller (Scott); Surgit Sood (Surgit); Malcolm Toes (Sergeant Major).

5′ 11½″
160 pounds
Black hair
Blue eyes
Gemini

Tony Curtis

Tony Curtis has long acknowledged that Cary Grant has always been his idol and model. "I would be happy if I could equal his career and his lasting power," says the former Bernard Schwartz of New York City. Today, nearly three decades after he entered films, Tony seems likely to prove his wish.

In the post-World War II era, Hollywood was eagerly seeking new faces to compete with the onslaught of commercial television. Tony was one of those groomed by Universal-International, along with Rock Hudson and others, to supplant the aging established stars. Curtis had the enthusiasm and raw energy, if not the natural talent, to succeed. With his boyish charm he was the ideal candidate to be the new hero for the studio's array of costumed entries. In *The Prince Who Was a Thief* (1950) and *The Black Shield of Falsworth* (1954), among others, he lived up to the faith that Universal had in him.

But Curtis aspired for far more than to rule a soundstage desert; he wanted to be accepted as an actor. If in the Fifties he and his actress wife Janet Leigh had been the love team of the decade, brash Tony made it known he was capable of much more. In *The Defiant Ones* (United Artists, 1958) he showed that he could handle dramatics, and in *Some Like It Hot* (United Artists, 1959) he displayed a gift for comedy (he also had a chance to do an oncamera imitation of Grant).

Stars come and go in the film business, but Tony has displayed remarkable staying ability. His status has see-sawed in the Sixties and Seventies as the results of a rash of bad features, a scorned teleseries, "The Persuaders," and an arrogance that press agents cannot always conceal. But "I'm Still Here" might well be his theme song in the mid-Seventies as the mature star continues onward, Bronx accent, dimpled smile, and all.

On Wednesday, June 3, 1925, at Flower and Fifth Avenue Hospitals on Manhattan's East 106th Street, a boy was born to Helen and Manuel Schwartz. Their first-born was named Bernard. The boy's parents, Jewish immigrants from Hungary, had met and were married the previous year in New York City. In Budapest Manuel had been an amateur stage actor, but he was prevented from following that profession in the United States because of his inability to speak acceptable English. Instead, he became a tailor. The family moved from the borough of Queens to the Bronx where Manny opened his own tailor shop, and, in 1927, a second son, Julius, was born. Times were hard, money was scarce, and the Schwartzes moved every six months or so, generally at the request of an irate, unpaid landlord. For one four-week period, Bernie and Julius were placed with a welfare home until Manny could find shelter and muster enough funds to support them.

Except for a rare visit to Central Park's "country," Bernie spent his childhood in the shadows of tenements, garbage cans, and rat-infested alleyways. One of the family's less fortunate moves was to Yorkville, which was then the center of the German-American Bund movements. Because the Schwartz boys were Jewish, the misled Fascist kids of the neighborhood heckled them mercilessly. No matter where they lived, though, they were teased and bullied because of their accents. The language spoken in the Schwartz home, wherever it may have been at the moment, was Hungarian with only an occasional English word tossed into the conservation. Consequently, the boys' method of communicating with non-Hungarians was ridiculed. For protection, Bernie had to be tough;[1] he fought, ran, lied, or cheated his way out of each situation. He was also responsible for his younger brother, a continuous task which he occasionally found burdensome.

Bernie got his spending money in many ways: by working for his father, by shining shoes, by selling newspapers, and by stealing. At the age of eleven he was accepted into a teenage gang called "The Black Hand," and, as he has recalled to the press, "I learned to fight with my hands, feet and anything else that was handy." He attended Public

---

[1]Because of his exceptionally good looks, Bernie recalls that as a youth he was subject to other kinds of taunts—propositions from older males.

School Eighty-Two infrequently. Instead, he acquired a different kind of education in the streets. When he was twelve, he was apprehended by the authorities and placed under the supervision of one Paul Schwartz—no relation—a neighborhood welfare worker. Paul Schwartz induced the "punk" youth to join the Boy Scouts, a move that was instrumental in transforming Bernie into a more honest, self-respecting kid. "If it hadn't been for him," the future star said years later, "I might have ended up like a lot of other kids in the neighborhood—doing a stretch up the river."

If the above all sounds like a snatch of scenario from a 1930s Warner Bros.-Dead End Kid movie, it is just a case of fiction imitating reality.

One afternoon during Bernie's thirteenth summer, when he was returning home from a park with Julius, the younger boy decided to take a shortcut. Bernie did not miss his brother until he had arrived home, and their concerned mother asked about him. A frantic search led to the police who had found Julius beneath the wheels of a truck driven by a drunken man. The boy died the next day. Bernie persisted in blaming himself for his brother's death, feeling that Julius would not have died had he, Bernie, kept a closer watch over him. As a reminder of his "neglect," he took a few items which had belonged to his brother and kept them as a sort of self-punishment.

At the age of fourteen, Bernie became a dedicated movie fan, much preferring the trips to the movie theatre to the hours spent with the streetcorner gangs or idling with the fellows about town. His favorite stars were Leslie Howard, Olivia de Havilland, James Cagney, Errol Flynn, and Cary Grant. He would imagine himself the hero of each picture he would see and would even memorize lines of dialog. After persistent tries, he managed a fair voice imitation of Cary Grant and also emulated the swashbuckling antics of Flynn. The rooftops of the tenements and their fire escapes provided ample, if not dangerous, props for leaping, scaling, and swinging.

He dreamed of becoming an actor—better yet, a movie star! Then, perhaps, the local kids would not make fun of him anymore. Every chance he got, he went to the movies. "For a dime, I'd sit all day." From the lobby of the RKO Fordham Theatre he appropriated a fifteen-inch-by-twenty-inch poster-portrait of Cary Grant, which he proudly hung above his cot at home. He even wrote a six-page letter to Hedda Hopper asking how he might get into movies. Her advice was to "Work hard, and if you've got what it takes, it'll happen."

In 1940, while another son, Bobby, was born to the poor tailor and his wife, Bernie entered Seward Park High School where his major interest was playing hookey. Whenever a movie star was scheduled to make a personal appearance in town, Bernie cut school, stole a ride on a trolley car and stood outside the theatre or hotel for a fleeting glimpse of the celebrity.

574

During this period, he had afternoon jobs, too, to supplement the meager Schwartz household income. "I guess I was too much of a dreamer to get really interested in most of the jobs." One of them was delivering ice at five dollars a week plus all the ice he could take home. At another time he worked in a broom factory, where his task was to cut off the excessive straw as the brooms came off the assembly line. He once admitted that his cutting was not always too even and "there are probably still housewives in New York sweeping their floors with odd-shaped brooms."

Although he did not have a very extensive wardrobe, he would dress up in his best some evenings, and join the intermission crowds at Broadway theatres. As the audiences filed in for the second act of a play, he would mingle with the theatre patrons and rush into the first empty seat available. Seldom, if ever, did he have the opportunity to see a Broadway play in its entirety. At the local YMCA, however, he took part in stage productions which he did see all the way through. In one play he had to enact the part of a girl.

In 1943, after seeing *Crash Dive* (Twentieth Century-Fox), starring Tyrone Power as a Naval submarine officer, the very impressionable Bernie would have it no other way but that he, too, should join the Navy. He quit high school a few weeks before he was due to graduate and, like Ty Power the movie hero, he chose submarine duty.

After completing boot camp, the U.S. Navy's new "skinhead" was assigned to the submarine *U.S.S. Dragonette* in the South Pacific.

In the Navy (1944)

While loading torpedoes aboard the *Dragonette* he was thrown into the ocean when a snapped winch chain struck him in the small of the back. For seven weeks he was confined to a hospital in Guam, suffering from a temporarily paralyzed leg and several broken fingers. During his convalescence a nurse read to him from Shakespeare. It renewed his interest in acting. Once recovered, he returned to submarine duty. He finished out the war and improved his impersonation of Cary Grant after repeated viewings of *Gunga Din* (RKO, 1939), one of the few films available on board the vessel. He was delighted whenever his shipmates suggested, "You oughta be an actor."

With the Japanese capitulation in 1945, Bernie returned to the squalor of what was commonly called "Hell's Kitchen," on Manhattan's West Side. After arriving home on a snowy December 19, 1945, the ex-sailor horsed around for a few months in local pool halls and even plotted a supermarket holdup. Then in 1946, he made the decision that would change his life and would lead to the fulfillment of his dreams.

Using his G.I. Bill benefits, he attended the Dramatic Workshop of the New School for Social Research. During his year of study there he also found time to act with the Yiddish Repertory Company, learning his lines phonetically. He accepted acting roles where he found them. He played the idiot son of the lighthouse keeper in *Thunder Rock,* which was presented at the Ninety-second Street YMCA. Another play in which he appeared while he was with the Workshop was *The Prince Who Learned Everything out of Books.*

At the end of the year, he joined the Stanley Wolf Stock Company, a catch-as-catch-can group. With them, he toured in what was known as the "Borscht Circuit" in New York's Catskill Mountains resort area. For his efforts, he was paid ten dollars a week. Late in 1947, he played stock with the Empire Players, a short-lived group that went broke, and learned to smoke for a role in *Waiting for Lefty.*

In 1948, he was cast in *Golden Boy* in Greenwich Village's Cherry Lane Theatre revival of the Clifford Odets play. When the actor who played the title role became ill, Bernie had the opportunity to play the Joe Bonaparte character for three consecutive nights. In the audience one of those evenings was a talent scout for Universal-International Studios. Although the scout found Bernie's speech similar to "an immigrant taxi driver with a mouthful of hot bagel," he liked the "pretty" face and saw him as a likely candidate for his studio's grooming program. "Wham, bam, thank you, ma'am," Bernie has said, "the next thing I knew I was in California with a seven-year contract.

While his proud but anxious parents remained in their tenement on Stebbins Avenue near Simpson Street in the Bronx, Bernie signed the Hollywood contract on his birthday, June 3, 1948. The contract was for seventy-five dollars a week, and provided for regular six-month options for salary increases of twenty-five dollars per interval. He was placed in Universal-International's earn-while-you-learn coterie of young hopefuls, which included Rock Hudson, Jeff Chandler, Richard Long, Rod McKuen, Piper Laurie, Lori Nelson, Meg Randall, and Mamie Van Doren. During these years, Universal would be staving off bankruptcy through the efforts of Donald O'Connor and Francis the Talking Mule, Abbott and Costello, and the teamwork of two contracted freelancers, Marjorie Main and Percy Kilbride, who turned out the Ma and Pa Kettle series. Other performers then under contract to the studio included pert Ann Blyth, shapely Shelley Winters, and exotic Yvonne De Carlo, as well as Marta Toren, Helena Carter, Peggie Castle, Peggy Dow, and Dorthy Hart. Charles Drake, Stephen McNally, and John Russell were also on the company's payroll at that time.

For twenty-three-year-old, blue-eyed, curly-haired Bernie, the chief problem of the moment was to select a new screen name for himself. He naively suggested Anthony Adverse (he had liked the novel), but this was vetoed by Bob Goldstein, a studio public relations man, who was in favor of James Curtis, a name Bernie considered fit only for "a schnook."

Although he was kept busy with a voice coach who hoped to rid him of his Bronx-Hungarian accent, and dramatic training classes, he once confessed: "That was the loneliest time of my life. I was in a strange city and in a new business. Just because I had a fast seventy-five-dollar-a-week contract didn't mean I would immediately meet all the top glamour girls and get palsy on the social circuit. They ribbed me about always being at the studio, always being the first to arrive at drama classes and the last to leave, always volunteering. I wanted to make good. I also didn't have any place to go."

On weekends, he went to movies, sometimes two a day. "It helped me learn more about acting and passed the time." About a month after his arrival in Hollywood, he arranged for his family to move West, which made his life less lonely. At the studio, however, he was soon the brunt of his co-workers' jokes because of his long, greasy hair and his wardrobe of heavily padded jackets and pegged trousers. It became regular fun for the other contract players to lock him in the steam room or to drop a sleeping tablet into his milk.

Nevertheless, on January 12, 1949, after the release of his first motion picture, *Criss Cross* (Universal), the fans' reactions were almost immediate. In the Robert Siodmak-directed cops 'n' robbers yarn starring Burt Lancaster, Yvonne De Carlo, and sneering Dan Duryea, Bernie (or James Curtis as he was billed) had the part of Miss De Carlo's dance floor partner in a bit that was captured on less than one foot of film. But young feminine moviegoers wrote to the studio asking for details on the exciting, pretty-faced fellow who slightly resembled John Derek.

Universal executives, including William Goetz, who was in charge

577

of production, felt that James (or Jimmy) was too weak a first name and changed it to the more masculine-sounding Anthony.[2] The publicity department then handed out biographical statistics (or a "driver") to the fan magazines, while the casting department kept him busy with small parts. In *City Across the River* (Universal, 1949), adapted by Irving Shulman from his novel *The Amboy Dukes,* Anthony appears as Mitch, a member of the Dukes gang of Brooklyn who becomes involved in the murder of a school teacher. Narrated by Drew Pearson, the unpretentious film tried, but failed, to provide an explicit reason for big-city delinquency. It starred Stephen McNally and featured Thelma Ritter and Luis Van Rooten as the distraught parents of an undisciplined teenager (Peter Fernandez). From Universal's training class came Al Ramsen and Mickey Knox, who were other members of the Dukes gang.

In *The Lady Gambles* (Universal, 1949), a rather forced study of compulsive betting that starred Barbara Stanwyck, Anthony was oncamera as a member of a racing gang. In *Johnny Stool Pigeon* (Universal, 1949), he again was a gangster—complete with black shirt and pin-striped suit—whose gang hoped to thwart the efforts of a Federal man (Howard Duff) to uncover its dope smuggling ring. In *Francis* (Universal, 1949), the first in a profitable series about a talking mule, Anthony played a U.S. Army captain.

His photographs frequently appeared in fan magazines and showed him having good, clean fun with starlets such as Joan Evans, Piper Laurie, Barbara Darrow, and Geraldine Brooks; and he continued to win a teenage following with brief, but apparently impressive, appearances; in *Winchester 73* (Universal, 1950), his first Western (starring James Stewart), and in *Sierra* (Universal, 1950), his second Western (starring Audie Murphy and his then estranged wife, Wanda Hendrix). The latter film premiered in San Francisco in June, 1950, when Murphy, Scott Brady (also in the film), Peggie Castle (not in the film, but along for studio publicity reasons since she was then Murphy's love interest), and Anthony were asked to walk onto the theatre stage following the screening.

They were introduced, one by one, and when Anthony's name was called, the audience let out a scream of joy. He had to be pushed onto the stage and then just stood there smiling until the shouting subsided. "I couldn't understand it," he later informed the press. "I knew I wasn't getting it because of my acting for I hadn't done any. Then I realized as never before that people can like you just because of your looks and personality. This was an odd experience for a guy who had

[2]A favorite Hollywood story concerns the time when Tony Curtis, an established film star, brought his father to the studio lot. One executive when introduced to Mr. Schwartz, queried, "But tell me, with a nice name like Curtis, why did you change it to Schwartz?"

With Patricia Medina, Loren Tindall, and Mikel Conrad in *Francis* (1949)

never been accepted in his own neighborhood back in the Bronx and who had to fight for survival."

Later in 1950, he played a less-than-honest fellow in *I Was a Shoplifter* (Universal), and then the studio abbreviated his name to the more intimate "Tony." As Tony Curtis, he was given fifth billing in *Kansas Raiders* as Kit Dalton, one of the infamous outlaws who joins with William Quantrill (Brian Donlevy) to wreak violent retaliation against the hated Yankees following the Civil War.

Universal-International was now ready to star their popular contract player and upped his salary from $225 a week to $275. His newly gained status earned him the right to move from a dressing room shared with several others to one shared with only Jeff Chandler.

Meanwhile, he had met MGM's Janet Leigh[3] at a party and had fallen in love. "I didn't think I had a chance," he told the inestimable Louella O. Parsons. "She came with Arthur Loew [the producer] and I was told she was his girl. But a little later when I heard that Arthur and

[3]She was born Jeanette Helen Morrison on July 26, 1927, in Merced, California. She attended school in Stockton, California and later matriculated at the College of the Pacific as a music major. At age fifteen she eloped with a nineteen-year-old boy named John Kenneth Carlyle, but the marriage was annulled four months later. While at college, she met a minor league bandleader, Stanley Reames, and wed him in 1946. It was also in 1946 that the girl's mother, employed at the Sugar Bowl Ski Lodge in Soda Springs, California, learned that resort guest Norma Shearer had spotted a picture of Jeanette on

579

Janet had split I moved right in and she was my girl from that time on." Neither studio was pleased with their romantic relationship, especially Universal. The prevalent opinion was that any serious romance would have a damaging effect on his career. It was felt that his host of fans preferred to think of him as unencumbered and available. While most fan magazine writers treated the young couple kindly, there were those who accused brash Tony of riding to success on Janet's calf-length skirts. She was an established star, with two marriages behind her, and was thought too mature for him. Nevertheless, they planned to be married in September, 1951. "If you dig someone," Tony said, "everything is right."

The summer before his wedding, on June 4, 1951, his first starring film was released. At a cost of one million dollars, *The Prince Who Was a Thief* presented him (in Technicolor) as a princely lad of the ancient East who is to be assassinated. His would-be assassin (Everett Sloane) turns soft and permits the boy to live. Thus, he grows up learning thievery from the best of thieves until it is revealed that he is the real prince and heir to the throne occupied by the Princess Yasmin (Peggie Castle). The handsome, muscular thief/prince leaps, swings, and fences his way to his rightful position, where he takes as his bride, the commoner Tina (Piper Laurie).

Because Universal, like other studios in post-World War II Hollywood, had been forced to new stringencies in budgeting productions, necessity had become the proverbial mother of invention. The company developed its own special formula for action films, turning them out with mindless precision. Since it had been proven that onscreen action, rather than substantial production and acting values, would carry this type of doublebill fodder at the boxoffice, the studio had little interest in exercising imagination in creating such products as *The Prince Who Was a Thief.* For example, it was a foregone conclusion that only the more credulous moviegoer would accept this slapdash backlot-filmed yarn as a full-bodied tale of old Tangier. It was, in fact, just another Western, dolled up with silks, chiffons, scimitars, sweating horses, and dastardly Arab villains. However, it was felt that few of the audiences for this type of film really minded such artificiality.

Purists might be offended that anyone would consider *The Prince* as a continuation of the 1920s-through-1940s cycle of swashbuckling film fare that had starred such heroes as Douglas Fairbanks (father or son), Errol Flynn, Tyrone Power, and Jon Hall. However, considering the economics of a television-frightened movie industry and the acting

Mrs. Morrison's desk. Miss Shearer forwarded the photo to MGM, and soon after, the girl was given a screen test. She was signed by Metro and given, almost immediately, a lead role opposite Van Johnson in *The Romance of Rosy Ridge* (MGM, 1947). Her MGM roles amounted to little more than pale imitations of June Allyson parts, but in 1949 she came to the attention of Howard Hughes, who induced Metro to loan her to RKO for *Holiday Affair* (1949) and other films.

With Piper Laurie in a pose for *The Prince Who Was a Thief* **(1951)**

capacity of Tony Curtis at that time, the film was all the actor deserved.

The *New York Times* was among those critical voices to suggest that Tony "somehow never manages to seem regal," and others complained that his elocution was sorely in need of improvement. (One just did not say "yonda" or refer to one's father as "fodder.") But on the plus side, Tony refused the use of a double: he did his own stunt work, and had learned his sword-handling from a Hollywood master, Ralph Faulkner, who would later say: "His sense of timing is remarkable and his muscular coordination perfect. His eagerness to learn was beyond restraint and on one or two occasions carried him beyond the point of safety."

A few weeks before the release of *The Prince Who Was a Thief*, handsome Tony was sent on a nationwide publicity tour, during which he was all but totally disrobed by screaming fans in each city he visited. In response to this situation, he was dressed in break-away suitcoats, which, when grabbed by anxious girls' hands, came apart easily and gave the grasper a sleeve or a lapel for her bedpost.

On June 3, 1951, his twenty-sixth birthday, he arrived in New York City. He raced to the Waldorf Towers Hotel where Janet Leigh was waiting. That evening, he appeared on live television with the comedy team of Dean Martin and Jerry Lewis (who were appearing at the Copacabana Club), and the following day, Tony and Janet were wed at 11:30 A.M. in Greenwich, Connecticut. Jerry Lewis was best man, with his wife, Patti, standing as matron of honor. The pretty blonde bride, two years Tony's junior, wore an aquamarine linen dress with a tiny plaid collar.

The couple honeymooned for a week at the Waldorf Towers, and Janet alerted the press, "There's only one thing we regretted about our elopement, and that is, it should have happened sooner." After Tony completed his hectic tour, the couple returned to California and rented a house near Malibu. By this time, Tony's personal wardrobe had improved greatly, thanks to the advice of suave Clifton Webb upon whom the young actor looked as the epitome of social grace. But he still wore his hair long in back with tiny curls flopping against his forehead. Whenever he visited the studio barbershop for a trim, the publicity department people were quick to pick up the cuttings to send to bobby-sox admirers whose letters contained requests for locks of his hair. (It was reported that each week ten thousand letters addressed to Tony Curtis were received at the studio.)

Since marriage gave the Curtis image an air of maturity, cynical writers no longer openly referred to him as a "male starlet" or "a male Yvonne De Carlo." Instead, thousands of words appeared in columns, fan magazines, women's magazines about Tony and Janet and their young love. They were photographed nearly everywhere doing just about everything. It must have seemed that their only privacy was in the bath and bedroom. Sheilah Graham, always free with her advice, advised the "dream couple" to "steer clear of the busybodies who tried to smooth-talk you out of marriage." She went on: "They said it would hurt your budding careers. Pure nonsense! Ask Crosby, Ladd, Grable or Crawford if wedding chimes sound box office doom. Marriage never hurt two who were suited for it—and you kids are right as rain for this husband-wife business. Don't let any studio executive, with an ice cube where his heart should be, tell you how to live your lives. Write the script yourselves."

"They [the studio] got embarrassed so they raised my salary to $700," Tony once recalled, to newsmen, and he was starred as a deaf mute pugilist in a modest film, *Flesh and Fury* (Universal, 1952). It was his first oncamera opportunity to really act and he did a respectable job, despite Bernard Gordon's cliché-ridden script. His fans were delighted with the many scenes in which he was clad only in boxing trunks. As Paul Callan, he becomes a ring champion under the tutelage of his honest trainer (Wallace Ford), while his girlfriend (Mona Freeman) works with him to help him regain his impaired hearing. An ambitious Jan Sterling almost leads him astray. The critic of the *New York Times* found that "muscular Mr. Curtis conveys his plight, for the most part, with a hesitant perplexity that seems natural enough." Tony now had a dressing room of his own. He had arrived, at least by Universal standards.

582

In *Flesh and Fury* (1952)

Tony had always been somewhat of a moody fellow, but this annoying trait worsened at this critical point in his life. Sam Israel, who was the director of publicity at Universal-International, said: "Some of us thought Tony was becoming aloof, that the initial successes he had might be affecting him adversely, that he was losing his sense of balance and value. We needn't have worried. Instead of getting a swelled head, Tony was brooding over what he considered his lack of experience." Some of that experience, Tony felt, could be gained with a Cary Grant type of role, so he asked for a comedy. Producer Ted Richmond came up with *No Room for the Groom* (Universal, 1952), a cute, but contrived and constantly tedious affair. He is a G.I., newly wed to Piper Laurie. Their problem is the consummation of their nuptials in a household overabundant with relatives. Tony tried hard, but he just was not ready for a comedy, especially one with such a belabored script and direction, which only a very seasoned sophisticate (such as Cary Grant) might have raised out of the doldrums.

If Jeff Chandler could make *The Battle at Apache Pass* (Universal, 1952) and Rock Hudson be featured in *Scarlet Angel* (Universal, 1952), then Tony could carouse through his own action adventure entry, *Son of Ali Baba* (Universal, 1952). Mr. Curtis was no chip off the studio block (e.g. Jon Hall of *Ali Baba and the Forty Thieves,* 1944), but added his own brand of vitality to the comic strip proceedings. It was

With Hugh O'Brian in *Son of Ali Baba* (1952)

his third cinematic go-'round with Piper Laurie. As Princess Azura, she is under the evil spell of the Caliph (Victor Jory at his most wicked) and is used to filch the golden treasure of the aging Ali (Morris Ankrum). The Caliph has not taken into account the presence of Ali's energetic son, Kasham (Tony), who wields a well-controlled scimitar in rescuing the fair princess. The Arabian Nights drama, heavy with sets, costumes, and Technicolor, never had prettier young people (Tony, Piper, Susan Cabot, and William Reynolds) inhabiting old Baghdad. Tony's major problem with his one-dimensional role was learning to walk in shoes with built-up heels, a feat he did not entirely master, as he often seemed to be limping.

After thirteen films for Universal, Tony's agent bargained anew with the studio, and his weekly salary was increased to $1,500. To recoup some of this investment, Universal loaned him to producer George Pal at Paramount for *Houdini* (1953).[4] With Janet Leigh, borrowed from MGM, Tony played the renowned magician (1874-1926) who falls in love with and marries the young lady Bess (Janet). After they are wed, the story rushes forward, and in the course of its unfolding, the audience is treated to a host of escape tricks—some based on the great Houdini's actual repertoire and some fictitious. Tony's Houdini es-

---

[4]In late 1974, both Columbia and Paramount announced that they were preparing new screen versions of the life of Harry Houdini.

In *Houdini* (1953)

capes from ropes, locks, chains, and trunks, while hanging from a
Manhattan skyscraper, getting dunked in the frozen Detroit River, or
after being secured inside London's most famous foolproof jail.

In 1953

Under George Marshall's direction, Tony was not required to be much more than his exuberant self. He made an attractive escape-artist, but the character of Houdini was permitted little depth. Wisely, the story relied on suspense and action for success. As was his style, Tony became absorbed learning the skills of the subject he would be portraying, in this case, stage magic. It was an enthusiasm that would gain him confidence in performing sleight-of-hand tricks proficiently for amazed friends, and, later, he extended his illusion acts for charity to the nightclub circuit.

Back at Universal, he was cast in *The All American,* the second of his three 1953 releases. It was a weak story designed as a showcase for several of the studio's trainees. Even though Tony was now above this sort of film, he had no alternative but to do as the bosses directed. With his hair cut back to a style closer to a crew cut, he plays a collegiate football star, Nick Bonelli, whose parents are killed in an automobile accident while they are on the way to see him play in a crucial game. The news of the accident is kept from him so that he will go on to win this big game. After the game, Nick learns of the accident and is enraged at the school officials. In retaliation, he quits the school and enrolls at another, where he gives up the gridiron and pursues his studies in architecture. Lori Nelson is on tap as a college employee who tries to convince him to play football, while Richard Long is in

With Gregg Palmer and Richard Long in *The All American* (1953)

587

the role of a rich snob who dislikes him. Mamie Van Doren appears a flippant waitress and Greg Palmer (a.k.a. Palmer Lee), as a classmate. According to undemanding *Photoplay* Magazine, Tony "looks his most attractive." The pigskin ball yarn was only one step above the shenanigans of similar vehicles such as *The Rose Bowl Story* (Monogram, 1952) or *Saturday's Hero* (Columbia, 1951).

In August, 1953, popular Tony Curtis received another pay hike, which raised his salary to $1,750 a week. He publicly admitted, "I never knew there was so much money." He defended the dying studio system with, "That's the nice thing about studios. They'll pay you what you're worth. If you go out and make a picture that brings in two million dollars, they'll give you a salary accordingly."

It is doubtful, however, that *Forbidden* (Universal, 1954), directed by Rudolph Mate (who also directed *Son of Ali Baba*), grossed two million dollars. The trade ads warned, "He's the kind of man who's out of bounds for any kind of woman!" In this 95-minute black-and-white feature, Tony plays Eddie Darrow, hired by gangland chief Lyle Bettger to locate the mobster's girlfriend Christine (Joanne Dru). She has departed for Macao and Eddie must follow in pursuit. Sure as shooting, they resume an old love affair. Eventually, Bettger turns up to muddy their lives and to rough up his hired man. The "Macao" of the piece was manufactured on the studio lot—and looked it.[5]

For *Beachhead* (Universal, 1954), however, the cast was treated to a location trip to Hawaii. In this drama about World War II Marines in action on a Japanese-held island in the Pacific, a reconnaissance team, headed by Sergeant Fletcher (Frank Lovejoy), is quickly cut down by enemy bullets. The action slows up considerably while Tony, as the young recruit, Burke, vies with Sgt. Fletcher for the affections of a French planter's daughter (Mary Murphy), whom they have rescued.

During his stay in Honolulu, Tony found he was just as popular there as he was on the mainland; he would stand for hours signing autographs and answering questions from his fans. He managed to wheedle respite from the 5 A.M. to 8 P.M. workday, and sailed to California. Almost immediately upon disembarking, he took possession of a new grey Cadillac convertible that he had ordered before leaving for Hawaii. The new car was added to his stable, which included a silver-grey Rolls Royce, and was called "real crazy" by its owner. His one complaint upon arriving home was that he could not see Janet until nightfall, because she was busy working all day in *Prince Valiant* (Twentieth Century-Fox, 1954).

In *Johnny Dark* (Universal, 1954), Tony had the title role, portraying an engineer at the Fielding Motor Company. He designs a racing model and then wins a Canada-to-Mexico race with the custom car. His fast

---

[5]At least for *Macao* (RKO, 1952), director Josef von Sternberg had actual location footage lensed at that Far Eastern port.

588

With Sunshine Akira Fukunaga, Frank Lovejoy, Eduard Franz, and Steamboat Mokuahi in *Beachhead* (1954)

driving also wins him the granddaughter (Piper Laurie) of his boss (Sidney Blackmer).

If Paramount could team Tony and Janet, then Universal reasoned it, too, could take advantage of the real-life husband-and-wife team. They were paired in *The Black Shield of Falsworth* (1954), the studio's first entry in CinemaScope. Based on the Howard Pyle novel about fourteenth-century England, *Men of Iron,* the plot had Tony in a role as the bad boy of the school of knights, similar to the role Robert Wagner had portrayed in the title part of *Prince Valiant.* Devoted fans often demand nothing more than Tony's onscreen presence to satisfy them, and as the errant knight, who eventually wins Lady Anne (Janet Leigh) while combatting the unconscionable Earl of Alban (David Farrar), Tony's appearance filled the bill. What did it matter that one film critic rightly claimed, "In a tin suit, he looks like a youngster in an oversized football uniform"?

Tony had always derived pleasure from giving gifts to his appreciative wife, ranging from flowers picked in their own yard to silk lounging pajamas and Cadillacs. But in 1954, nothing pleased him more than to prepare for the birth of their first child. The young couple, sadly, weren't to be parents that year. Janet suffered a miscarriage late in 1954.

With Janet Leigh in *The Black Shield of Falworth* (1954)

While his chief rivals on the Universal lot were Rock Hudson and Jeff Chandler, Tony continued to thrill his fans and to gain new ones with every added screen credit.

Always anxious to expand his professional horizons, the uncautious Tony next decided to try his skill in a screen musical. He threw himself into learning the trade of a song-and-dance man. For six weeks he was coached by expert dancer-actor Gene Nelson, who told reporters, "Tony started out by knowing absolutely zero about stage dancing, but before we were through he could perform with the best. He has an instinctive sense of rhythm and timing—two things that are gifts of God. Without them, no matter how hard you work, you're sunk. But Tony never took advantage of these talents, he worked twice as hard to develop them." The results of Nelson's tutoring were seen in *So This Is Paris* (Universal, 1954), filmed in Hollywood. In rather uninspired terms it dealt with three American sailors (Tony, Gene Nelson, and Paul Gilbert) who find fun and girls in France. Most of the singing was done by the girls (Gloria De Haven and Corinne Calvet), but Tony sang "The Two of Us" in duet with Miss De Haven. The soundtrack of the song was recorded by Mercury Records.

In *Six Bridges to Cross* (Universal, 1955), he is again an anti-establishment hero, a Massachusetts hood in on the famous 2.5 million-dollar Brinks armored car robbery. For this satisfactory thriller, Sal

In *Six Bridges to Cross* (1955)

Mineo portrayed Tony as a boy. Featured in the cast was George Nader, who would soon become a leading man at Universal.

If older Victor Mature and John Payne, two ex-Twentieth Century-Fox stars, could prance about in costume pictures for Columbia and United Artists, there was no stopping Universal from casting Tony in his own cutlass-and-kisses screen adventures. In *The Purple Mask* (Universal, 1955) he is a Scarlet Pimpernel type who rescues would-be victims from the French revolutionaries' guillotine. It must have pleased Tony to play a role similar to that enacted earlier (1934) by Leslie Howard, one of his idols, but neither he nor the screenplay, in this case, are remembered kindly. Angela Lansbury, cast in the supporting role of Madame Valentine, would also just as soon not be reminded of this hoary venture.

While Rock Hudson, who had hit the big time with Jane Wyman in *Magnificent Obsession* (Universal, 1954), was being reteamed with her in *All That Heaven Allows* (Universal, 1955) and while Warner Bros.' Tab Hunter was shining in *Battle Cry* (1955), Tony returned to the fight ring as a young man who was taught by his father (Jim Backus) that it is him against the world. In *The Square Jungle* (Universal, 1955), after nearly killing an adversary (John Day), he retreats into a shell, but learns that the world is not quite so bad as he imagines, for Day recovers and publicly forgives him. Of his performance in *The*

591

Square Jungle, the liberal Milton Luban of the *Hollywood Reporter* summed up the opinions of the more generous critics when he wrote, "The role is a perfect one for Curtis, demonstrating he is a fine dramatic actor indeed."

Throughout most of 1955, rumors were rampant in pre-Joyce Haber-Rona Barrett Hollywood and New York about discord in the Curtis household. Janet insisted to Hedda Hopper: "I wouldn't try to kid you, Hedda. Like all married couples, we've had our fights, but that doesn't mean we're not going to work things out." To Sheilah Graham, Janet said, "Who in the world can make definite statements about forever? But Tony and I love each other very much. We want our marriage to last." Columnist Dorothy Kilgallen revealed that Janet's secret hiding spot in New York during the marital quarrels was the East side apartment of friends, Jose Ferrer and his wife Rosemary Clooney.

Tony began weekly psychoanalysis, and, at the same time, was given the Annual Award of Merit by the George Washington Carver Memorial Institute "for the actor's assistance in the organization of Carver Youth Clubs to combat juvenile delinquency and for his active sponsorship of education libraries in Negro schools." On the homefront, his hobbies expanded to include collecting telescopes, microscopes, and miniature trains.

In the spring of 1956, Tony Curtis graduated to the "Actor" status, and many people finally began to regard him as a serious professional. The occasion was *Trapeze* (United Artists), a film appearance negotiated by his new agent, Lew Wasserman (head of Music Corporation of America), with the Hecht-Hill-Lancaster Company. Tony's salary was a reported $150,000. For weeks he trained arduously with Burt Lancaster in perfecting aerial stunts on a trapeze, before leaving for Paris where the film was lensed.

On this, his first visit to Paris, he checked in at the Hotel George V before seeing the sights with a French-English pocket dictionary provided him by producer-star Lancaster. During his Parisian visit, Janet, who was in London working on *Safari* (Columbia, 1956), journeyed across the channel to spend weekends with him. Tony publicly admitted a liking for the French: "They're all nice, once you get to know them. They really believe in 'live and let live,' and the right of the individual to be and do whatever he wants. If I feel tired and my feet hurt after standing around the set all day, I can sit down right on the Champs Elysees and take my shoes off and nobody will look twice."

Tony had second billing in *Trapeze;* his co-stars were Lancaster and Gina Lollobrigida; their director was Sir Carol Reed. About working with these two pros, Tony said, "In most of my U-I films I'd been teamed with players who were like me, fairly new, inexperienced. But here I was matched against top performers with a top director. It kept me right on my toes." Of Lancaster, he said, "What an actor! In my scenes with him, it was like being too near a turnace. I had to watch out, protect myself. I had to become a better actor."

Trapeze cost four million dollars to make, plus another two million for a pre-release advertising campaign. It was rather garishly bally-hooed as having the "global look" because of its "international array of world-renowned artists in a production of surpassing size and concept." As stars it claimed Americans Lancaster and Curtis, the Italian Gina, Mexico's Katy Jurado, plus the British director Reed.

The story, much of which is filmed in the authentic Parisian Cirque d'Hiver, concerns Mike, a crippled veteran aerialist (Lancaster), and his protege, Tino Orsini (Tony). It is Tino's ambition to perfect a triple somersault through the air. Lola (Gina) is also a flyer who, when spurned by the veteran, loosens her charms on Tino in order to make hot-tempered Mike jealous.

Tony's acting in *Trapeze* was acclaimed by William K. Zinsser in the *New York Herald-Tribune* as "particularly good at the end, when he feels a twinge of fear." Alton Cook of the *New York World-Telegram and Sun* noted, "The surprise is the depth and force of Tony Curtis. . . . The snarling frenzy with which he meets his misfortune is both pathetic and ruthless." (By January, 1975, the film had received over $7.5 million in rentals by distributors in the U.S. and Canada.) Tony, dubbed the "baron of beefcake" by *Picturegoer*'s Margaret Hinxman, may not have been the hottest young star[6] in Hollywood in 1956, but that was only because Warner Bros. had James Dean and MGM was promoting its handsome Marlon Brando type, Paul Newman.

In the spring of 1956, fan magazines announced the pregnancy of Janet Leigh Curtis with the same degree of expectation that might well have been accorded the re-birth of the Saviour or a happening in the Kennedy clan today. "If the baby is a boy," Tony told cooing Louella O. Parsons, "we plan to name him Joshua. It's a biblical name and it goes so well with Curtis." (Tony's legal name remained Bernard Schwartz.) Janet added, "We're hoping the baby will be born in June, because June is our lucky month. . . . Everything important has happened to us in the month of roses." (Such events included his birthday, her birthday, their wedding, and the signing of both their studio contracts.)

Thinking ahead to future freelancing days, the Curtises, in March of 1956, announced the formation of their own independent film company, known as Curtleigh Productions. They also purchased their first home, a rambling house in Beverly Hills. Meanwhile, Tony went to work on *The Rawhide Years* (Universal, 1956), a modestly budgeted

---

[6]The *Motion Picture Herald* and *Fame*, in their 1956 survey of the top ten boxoffice stars, listed William Holden, John Wayne, James Stewart, Burt Lancaster, Glenn Ford, Dean Martin & Jerry Lewis, Gary Cooper, Marilyn Monroe, Kim Novak, and Frank Sinatra as the hottest stars of the time.

Western, with Colleen Miller and Arthur Kennedy. For three weeks before production began, from nine until noon, he practiced trick riding on horseback. No one could fault Curtis for being lax about giving his physical best to any movie in which he appeared. The film's plot, which was not much, found him as Ben Matthews, a reformed riverboat gambler who returns home to discover that he is wanted for murder. Then the soundtrack noise begins as he confronts, shoots at, and fights with various members of a posse until his name is finally vindicated.

On June 17, 1956, daughter Kelly Lee Curtis was born in Hollywood. Janet announced she would not work until the baby was six months old. At this point in her career there were not that many demands for her celluloid services.

Mister Cory (1957), scripted and directed by Blake Edwards, is a slick Universal feature in Technicolor and CinemaScope. Tony plays a brash young fellow named Cory who quits the slums of Chicago to become a busboy in a swank Wisconsin resort hotel. There, among the wealthy, he meets a high-class tart (Martha Hyer) who says, "A lady can have her kicks with a guy like him but she never marries him." Under the tutelage of a pro (Charles Bickford), he becomes a smooth gambler and is ruthless in his quest for fortune. At the end, as he is shot by a drunken, jealous romantic rival (William Reynolds), he murmurs, "I got nothin." It was all reminiscent of a John Garfield chip-on-his-shoulder characterization from a Warner Bros. Depression film. The only problem was that Tony had yet to display the dramatic or emotional range that was so much a part of the explosive Garfield screen persona.

In August, 1956, during the filming of *Mister Cory,* Tony took time to appear in a short subject film for the Savings Bond division of the United States Treasury Department as a part of its fifteenth anniversary drive. Another accomplishment was his design (or so the studio claimed) of a new suit style which he modeled as *Mister Cory.* The garment, not for commercial marketing, featured a short coat, narrow lapels, rounded shoulders, split sleeve cuffs with buttons which could be unbuttoned and turn back. The trousers were high-waisted and tapered to a narrow leg line.

Tony hounded literally everyone involved with *Sweet Smell of Success* (United Artists, 1957) for the role of Sidney Falco, the slimy, small-time press agent in the Clifford Odets-Ernest Lehman scripted story. He admitted, "I felt like a kid who begs: 'Just give me *one* break, and I'll show 'em!' " Through his friendship with Burt Lancaster, who was to star in the film, he acquired five percent of the project on behalf of Curtleigh Productions from Hecht-Hill-Lancaster Productions, in addition to the role he so coveted. About his connection in producing the film, he voiced, "I love it. It's not because I can give orders. It's just

594

because of being consulted about things. . . . It's never like that in the major studios. They tell you what to do, and that's it."

English director Alexander Mackendrick was imported to helm the film which was to represent Tony's major breakthrough in top-line dramatics, in keeping with his wish to avoid the usual studio type-casting. In brief, the hard-hitting chronicle is about an amoral Broadway columnist named J. J. Hunsecker (Lancaster), a greedy, fearsome man (said to be patterned after Walter Winchell), who can make or break a career as he sees fit. Sidney Falco (Tony) is a press agent who plants notes about his clients in J. J.'s column. To pay for the special favors, he becomes the columnist's lackey. The final indignity occurs when he is told to plant a pack of marijuana cigarettes in the pocket of a jazz musician (Martin Milner), who has had the audacity to fall in love with Hunsecker's sister (Susan Harrison).

Also in the cast is Jeff Donnell, a Columbia Pictures' veteran, as Hunsecker's bovine secretary with a mad crush on Sidney. Jeff recently reminisced to us about working with Tony: "Up until that time, there had been all the publicity about Tony and Janet; all that terrible fan mag stuff about his leaning on her, etc. I really didn't look forward, particularly, to working with him, though at parties he was always very nice. But I learned to admire him so much; he was such a professional in that everything had to be perfect, and he was involved with bringing in the right kind of music. I was just elated to find someone who took such an interest in the making of a picture."

The *Washington, D.C. Star* critic, Harry MacArthur, rated Tony's performance with "first-rate acting." The jazz score by the Chico Hamilton Quintet and James Wong Howe's photography helped make the downbeat film more of a financial and critical winner.

The unheralded *The Midnight Story* (Universal, 1957) ranks as one of Tony's best films. An unpretentious "sleeper" shot on location in San Francisco's North Beach Italian section, it casts him as a motorcycle policeman, Joe Martini, who quits the force in order to devote all his time and energies to tracking down the killer of the priest who reared him. The top suspect (Gilbert Roland) takes him into his home, and there, Joe falls in love with the man's comely daughter (Marisa Pavan). Thanks to an ample number of red herrings, the audience is unaware of the killer's true identity until the proper climactic moment. A. H. Weiler (*New York Times*) stated that the producers "spin their tale in taut, professional style."

The Midnight Story marked the end of thirty-two-year-old Tony's contract with Universal-International, and agent Wasserman renegotiated a one-picture-a-year deal with the studio that had discovered his client.

On November 10, 1957, Tony made his television debut as a matador on CBS's "G.E. Theatre" in the episode *Cornada* (which means "thrust with a horn."). For two weeks, the actor trained with famed Mexican bullfighter Luis Briones to perfect his role of a sports figure making a comeback after a near-fatal injury. The night before his big return engagement, he dreams that he dies in the bull ring and, the next day, he is afraid to face the bull until he makes sure that the animal is different from the one in his nightmare.

Tony and Janet—he was now a bigger screen name than she was—both accepted parts in the Kirk Douglas-production company film for United Artists release, *The Vikings* (1958), adapted from Edison Marshall's bestselling novel of 1951. Tony's salary was $25,000 a week for the film, which, in turn, was budgeted initially at $3.7 million. The company journeyed to Norway in June, 1957, where Douglas arranged for the exclusive use of a fjord and the construction of a Viking village. He may have prayed for sunshine, but for his efforts he got continual dosages of rain. While waiting for the clouds to dissipate, Tony and his co-star-producer became good friends. Out of sixty days spent in Norway, the sun shone on just eleven. Consequently, much of the feature was shot in the rain. Douglas rationalized later, "The rain scenes have a black, brooding quality that go with the Viking character." From Norway, the troupe went to France for more location filming, and from there to West Germany for interior shots. The film's cost ultimately climbed to more than five million dollars.

The Richard Fleischer-directed story begins with Ragnar, the Viking Sea King (Ernest Borgnine), who kills the king of Northumbria and rapes the queen. Twenty-five years later the Norse's bastard son, Eric (Tony), is taken to Norway as a slave, although no one knows of his Royal origins. He hates Ragnar almost as much as he detests Einar (Douglas), his half-brother. The siblings fight when Eric unleashes his hawk which tears out Einar's left eye in blood-gushing Technicolor. Eric is then chained in a tidal pool to be eaten by crabs, but he calls upon the god Odin for help, and the tide fortuitously goes out.

When a captured Welsh princess, Morgana (Janet), is brought to the village, the combative brothers vie for her attentions, but it is Eric who wins her confidence and sails with her to England with the words, "Let's not question our flesh for wanting to remain flesh." Ragnar, Einar, and the entire Viking team follow in pursuit and confront Eric and an army of Englishmen at a seaside castle, where Eric loses his left hand and Ragnar is plunged into a pit alive with snarling, hungry wolves. In a climactic duel across the castle walls (not as grand as any of Errol Flynn's), Einar meets his death and Eric is left alone with Morgana and the English forces.

Tony, who grew a beard for his role, said, "I had to learn to use a two-handed broadsword with my left hand gone. D'you know what? I found I could do tricks with the stump, by knocking the sword, or using it as a lever." Lloyds of London refused to insure Tony for any potential accidents in this film because of the much-publicized visits to his analyst, and the Douglas company was lucky that the accidents which did happen during the hazardous production schedule did not result in major injury. Thanks to the gore onscreen and a costly, but effective, publicity campaign, the grotesquely structured and flavored film grossed a whopping $6.049 million in distributors' domestic rentals, certainly proving that North American filmgoers could indulge themselves with singularly bad taste in their choice of film entertainment.

Another novel (by Joe David Brown) provided the basis for Tony's next film, *Kings Go Forth* (United Artists, 1958), released a month after *The Vikings.* In the novel, it is 1944, and the Allied Armies are fighting what the author called "The Champagne Campaign" in the south of France. During the week the Allied soldiers killed Germans, while on weekends they killed bottles of booze on the Riviera. In the film, Tony plays Britt Harris, a rich boy who had dodged the draft for as long as was legally possible. He winds up a G.I. who proves himself brave in battle and charming with the ladies. He meets a girl (Natalie Wood), the daughter of a U.S. expatriate (Leora Dana), whose deceased husband was black. The soldier charms the girl into loving him, but then he learns from a lieutenant (Frank Sinatra) who loves the girl, that she is of mixed blood. The spoiled, reckless, snobbish soldier promises to

With Frank Sinatra in *Kings Go Forth* (1958)

597

marry her, but casually breaks the engagement at the last minute. Cruelly, he tells her mother, "I've been engaged to some girls, and not engaged to some girls, if you know what I mean. And some of them weren't the kind I'd've taken to the country club. But with the exception of your daughter, all of them were white." Distressed Natalie then tries to kill herself and Sinatra vows that he will kill the impudent soldier, but a German bullet does the job for him.

In its day, *Kings Go Forth* was considered very mature drama fare. In fact, a sequence showing one of the lead characters shooting up with dope was deleted from the release print as being of too strong a nature for 1958 filmgoers. *Variety* best judged Tony's characterization: "Curtis has had experience acting the heel and he does a repeat, though his is a tough character to swallow. He's best when acting the charm boy." On the other hand, the not-so-easy to please *Films in Review* noted, "Tony Curtis' part, however, is at least consistent and provides him with the kind of role in which he is always good—that of a stinker."

If the critics lambasted the makers of *Kings Go Forth* for bastardizing the book original, many moviegoers were willing to believe that any fan-popular leading man who plays a rough, unpleasant fellow oncamera (as Tony did here) must be a solid performer.

Offscreen, Tony and Sinatra became pals, and as a consequence the Curtises were qualified for membership in "The Clan" (a.k.a., "The Rat Pack"), the tight little group of jet-setters headed by free-wheeling Sinatra. "Frank Sinatra is one of the most exciting men I've ever met," boyish Tony once said. "He's had a tough fight out there. Maybe he's not the most tactful person, but the beautiful quality about Sinatra is you always know exactly where you stand with him."

In the summer of 1958, affluent Tony revealed to the press that Janet was again pregnant and that they had acquired a larger, eighteen-room house in Bel Air. To Hedda Hopper he allowed, "We had one and a half rooms in the house in New York City where I was born. I never realized I'd end up a country gentleman. People would have given odds I wouldn't even wind up a gentleman."

It was during this period that Tony met Cary Grant for the first time. They both attended a Screen Producers' Guild dinner at the Los Angeles Biltmore Hotel. "There he was, my idol," Tony remembered. "I was so shy and nervous about meeting him that I couldn't walk up to his table. So I watched him and followed when he went into the men's room." He introduced himself to Grant in the foyer of the men's lounge.

In his next film Tony tried, none too successfully, to affect a Southern accent for his role of Joker Jackson in Stanley Kramer's *The Defiant Ones* (United Artists, 1958). Bound in symbol and reality by a three-pound, twenty-nine-inch-long chain are a black convict, Noah Cullen

With Sidney Poitier in *The Defiant Ones* **(1958)**

(Sidney Poiter), and a white convict, John "Joker" Jackson (Tony). They hate each other and while conveyed in a prison van one wet night on a southern mountain road, they have a fist fight. Suddenly, a traffic accident enables them to escape.[7]

It is at this point that producer-director Kramer plugs the hole in the plot gimmick by having an oncamera reporter ask, "How come they chained a white man to a black?" The local sheriff replies, "The warden's got a sense of humor."

While running from a posse, Tony and Poitier continue to fight, verbally and physically, but are forced, because of the chain that binds them, to aid each other in moments of crisis, including an escape from a lynch mob. Eventually, they meet a farm boy who takes them to his mother (Cara Williams). She had been deserted by her man some eight months earlier. In her shed is the means by which the convicts break the chain, a feat that Jackson celebrates by climbing into bed with her as she tells him of the emptiness of life. "You fill it up with tears and you're a goner," he explains to her. "Fill it up with dreams." During the prologue to this scene of mutual seduction, he says, "It's been so

---

[7]While on the lam, the two men share the need to help one another, but at this point in the story there is no camaraderie: "Thanks for pulling me out," says Cullen when Jackson yanks him from the rapids. "Man" says Jackson, "I didn't pull you out . . . I stopped you from pulling me in."

long; I get the dreams mixed up with the real thing." She takes the pins from her bound-up hair (*a la* Martha Hyer in MGM's *Some Came Running,* 1958), and respounds, "It's real now." Huskily, he whispers, "Don't go 'way," and takes her.

Meanwhile, Noah has gone off by himself on a route directed by the woman, who confides to Jackson that he is headed toward death in the quicksand. Jackson chases after him to warn him of the danger. Now the two men are reunited in real friendship, bound by respect, liking, and a need to survive.

Of this very trend-setting film (far more than Kramer's later gossamer package for Columbia, *Guess Who's Coming to Dinner,* 1967), *Time* Magazine said, "Savory cinema, free of froth and sharply seasoned." Arthur Knight, in the *Saturday Review,* wrote: "The real revelation is Tony Curtis. He displays a hardness and toughness quite new to him. . . . The spiritual growth of this character, his gradual shedding of false pride and unreasoned resentments, provides the greatest single acting challenge in the film—and Curtis more than meets it." Bernie Schwartz of the Bronx had finally become a respected Hollywood actor.

Next, Tony took *The Perfect Furlough* (Universal, 1958) with wife Janet, Linda Cristal, and Elaine Stritch. He is a U.S. Army corporal who, after serving some seven months in all-male company in the Arctic, wins a furlough in Paris with a real-live movie star (Cristal). Of

With Linda Cristal (cutout) in *The Perfect Furlough* (1958)

course, they are righteously chaperoned by Liz Baker, the press agent (Elaine Stritch), Major Collins (King Donovan), and WAC Lieutenant Vicki Loren (Janet). Obviously, it is a Blake Edwards comedy and Tony's acting is so far superior to his 1952 attempts to provoke laughs *(No Room for the Groom)* that it is natural to wonder if, from the handshake with Cary Grant at the Biltmore Hotel, some of the old pro's style did not rub off. Even hard-nosed Bosley Crowther of the *New York Times* had to admit that he liked the film: "There's plenty to keep you giggling."

November, 1958, proved to be a sad as well as a happy time for Tony and Janet. The year first held tragedy when Tony's father died from a heart attack. Then, on November 21st, a second daughter was born to the idolized couple when Jamie Lee arrived at a Los Angeles hospital. And, just when Tony' screen career had reached an apex, he was seen in one of the classic comedies of the decade, *Some Like It Hot* (United Artists, 1959), of which he owned five percent.

It is doubtful that there is a soul in America over the age of nine who has not seen *Some Like It Hot,* if not in a movie theatre, then on the TV screen. The screenplay by Billy Wilder and I. A. L. Diamond, under the direction of Mr. Wilder, took four months to film, during which time Tony became very disenchanted with co-star Marilyn Monroe, who received top billing. Several years after her death, when most of

With Janet Leigh Curtis and their children Kelly Lee and Jamie in Hollywood (January, 1959)

With Marilyn Monroe in *Some Like It Hot* (1959)

the world was still bemoaning her loss, he told James Brady of *New York* Magazine, "I don't think Marilyn was gifted at all. She was a mean little seven-year-old girl, to quote Billy Wilder. Egotistical—she felt anyone else in a movie with her was a bit player. They're making a big *megillah* ["deal"] out of a very ordinary person."[8]

The plot of the tale: Two musicians, Joe (Tony) and Jerry (Jack Lemmon), are eye witnesses to the St. Valentine's Day massacre in 1929 Chicago. The atrocity was engineered by top racketeer Spats Colombo (George Raft). To escape gangland reprisals, they don women's clothes and join a Florida-bound all-girl band led by Sue (Joan Shawlee). Known as Josephine and Daphne respectively, Joe and Jerry have a tough time concealing their male identities from the girls, and Josephine/Joe falls for ukulele player/vocalist Sugar (Monroe), while Daphne/Jerry is pursued by an aging millionaire, Osgood Fielding (Joe E. Brown). Joe wants to know Sugar better and persuades Jerry to obtain Osgood's yacht for an evening when he, Joe, dressed again in men's wear, pretends to be an oil magnate.

For this highlight scene, actor Tony Curtis wears glasses and makes use of his Cary Grant voice in assuming the disguise within a disguise, and while the background music tinkles out "Stairway to the Skies," he makes love to his Sugar aboard the yacht. Their kisses steam his glasses as he asks her, "Where did you learn to kiss like that?" She replies, "I used to kiss for the milk fund." As her bosom heaves upward, he says, "Tomorrow, remind me to send a check for $100,000 to the milk fund."

Just as the boys are beginning to believe that they have evaded the gangsters successfully, Spats and his gang show up at their hotel for an underworld conference. When Spats is liquidated by a rival gang, headed by Little Bonaparte (Nehemiah Persoff), the cops arrive and Joe and Jerry (still in drag) run away with Sugar and Osgood in the latter's motor launch. Joe confesses to Sugar that he/she is not wealthy, while Jerry tells Osgood that he/she is a man, to which Osgood answers with two of the best-remembered words in movie history, "Nobody's perfect."

Turning *Some Like It Hot* into an 8.3-million-dollar boxoffice winner was no easy chore. As director Wilder would quip, "I have discussed this with my doctor and my psychiatrist and they tell me I'm too old and too rich to go through this again." Not only did Wilder have the usual problems with Marilyn's vain efforts to show up on the set on time, if at all, but he had to deal with her outrage when she learned that the comedy was to be shot in black-and-white. (Matters were further complicated because she was part-producer of the film.) While Wilder granted that she did look breathtaking in wide screen

---

[8]On one occasion, when asked what it was like to share romantic oncamera scenes with Miss Monroe, Tony responded, "It's like kissing Hitler."

and color, he was afraid that the multi-hued process would distort the values of the film. "In full color Jack Lemmon and Tony Curtis would be accused of transvestism if their make-up was light, and of impossible vulgarism if it was heavy." Marilyn finally conceded the point.

However, the months of shooting (August through November, 1958) were a strain on everyone and perhaps more so on Curtis than on any other of Marilyn's co-players. She was the type of performer who improved during retakes of a sequence, while he was just the opposite, losing freshness and spontaneity on each successive retake. This conflict of acting styles and habits nearly caused the film to be canceled on more than one occasion.

Another internal problem confronting Wilder on this project was the necessity to keep Tony's and Lemmon's drag act[9] from becoming too real a thing, something that would have offended 1959 filmgoers. Thus, throughout the film both female impersonators are constantly berating their fate for having to don uncomfortable female apparel. The ruse worked, particularly with both men-cum-women continually ogling Marilyn in a very manly way.

As *Variety* would point out of Tony's performance as Joe (Josephine), "It's obvious that Curtis enjoys the part of a comedian, and he makes the most of it." As for his teamwork with Lemmon, the *New York Times* concluded, "Both take to slapstick, double-takes and mugging as though they were charter members of the Keystone Kops. They give vigorous, top-flight performances that add greatly to the wacky goings-on."

In February, 1959, with the announcement of the 1958 Academy Award nominations, both Poitier and Tony were named among the competitors for Best Actor (for *The Defiant Ones*). But on the evening of April 6, 1959, at the Pantages Theatre, it was David Niven who received the Oscar for his performance in *Separate Tables* (United Artists). (The other two nominees were Spencer Tracy, for *The Old Man and the Sea*, Warner Bros., and Paul Newman, for *Cat on a Hot Tin Roof*, MGM.)

Also in 1959, Tony learned to play the flute and took up painting, photography, and gambling with the clan. ("How long could I go on playing cards and find that one week I was out $1,800? What in my background made me Nick-the-Greek all of a sudden?") He quit his psychiatric sessions which, in four years, had cost him $30,000. Since, with the help of astute ten percenter Lew Wasserman, he was now getting $700,000-plus per picture, he invested in California real estate and bought a part ownership in the professional basketball team known as the Phoenix (Arizona) Suns.

---

[9]Lemmon would repeat his Jerry (Daphne) bit in a cameo for *Pepe* (Columbia, 1960). In 1972, *Some Like It Hot* would be adapted for Broadway as a musical, with the title *Sugar*, with Robert Morse as Joe (Josephine).

If, back in 1949, anyone had forecast that some day Tony Curtis would be considered as not only an established film star but an old-guard player as well, the general consensus would have been "You're crazy!" But by 1959 the dying studio system had spawned a new generation of potential leading men, including George Hamilton, George Peppard, Fabian, James Darren, Frankie Avalon, Ray Danton, and John Saxon. In addition, there were the slightly older and more established Paul Newman, Steve McQueen, Rod Taylor, John Gavin, Don Murray, Jeffrey Hunter, and Robert Wagner, as well as a host of personalities gaining tremendous popularity from weekly video series (such as James Garner, Clint Eastwood, and James Arness).

Thus, it was not so strange when veteran Tony teamed up with even older veteran Cary Grant for a joint producing-acting venture, *Operation Petticoat* (Universal, 1959). As directed by Blake Edwards, it was an Establishment venture right down the line. Tony is an admiral's aide assigned to the *U.S.S. Sea Tiger*, a damaged World War II submarine, scheduled to be junked. The crew is determined that the craft will be repaired, and it is Tony who races about deftly stealing the necessities in order to keep the ship afloat. Grant, as the skipper, plays the facile straight man to Tony's rowdy character. According to *Daily Variety*, "Tony Curtis is a splendid foil, one of the two or three best young comedians around, and his own style meshes easily with Grant's."

With Cary Grant, Dick Crockett (rear), and Gavin McLeod in *Operation Petticoat* (1959)

On the set of this film, which grossed an astounding $9.5 million, Tony watched Cary's every movement and hung around his dressing room asking for professional advice. Tony openly admitted, "To this day, I feel like a name dropper whenever I say 'Cary.' I still get goose-pimples when I sit beside him."

In March, 1960, *Variety* reported that Tony was "one of the ten best-paid actors in Hollywood," and on March 29, he was seen on NBC-TV in the fifty-one-minute film, *The Young Juggler.* Produced by Curt-leigh, it was the story of St. Barnaby, the patron saint of variety acts. Tony said that television "gives me the chance to do roles I ordinarily wouldn't get in pictures." He added: "We made [it] for $200,000, but it has the look of an expensive picture. We shot it in color and used all the big standing sets at Universal. I knew where all the good sets are, having worked on them." He told of tentative plans to later release the film, with added footage, to theatres, but these plans did not materialize.

For *Who Was That Lady?* (1960), based on the Broadway comedy with Peter Lind Hayes and Mary Healy, Columbia reunited the mature young lovers, Tony and Janet, for the fourth time. In the cutesy domestic farce, spiced up by Dean Martin's presence, Leigh becomes a bit more than jealous when her college professor-hubby, egged on by television writer-pal Michael Haney (Martin), is found in the company of

With Dean Martin in *Who Was That Lady?* (1960)

In *The Rat Race* (1960)

two brainless but curvaceous show girls (Barbara Nichols and Joi Lansing). Thanks to the solid competence of the star trio, the George Sidney-directed comedy is mildly amusing.

Lady was followed by Paramount's *The Rat Race* (1960), adapted for the screen by Garson Kanin from his 1949 Broadway play that had starred Barry Nelson and Betty Field. As Pete Hammond, Jr., Tony is an eager, fresh saxophonist from Milwaukee who bounces into Manhattan hoping to make good. He boards in a rooming house where Peggy Brown (Debbie Reynolds) also lives. She is a jaded, disillusioned "taxi" dancer who cannot change her situation because of a sizeable debt that she owes her exploitative employer (Don Rickles). The story's unfolding reveals excellent character studies of those sour-faced, supposedly hard-hearted inhabitants of midtown Manhattan. In supporting roles, Jack Oakie and Kay Medford add warmth and comedy relief to this boy-meets-girl tale.

If *The Rat Race* was geared for popular consumption, Tony's next film was aimed at pleasing both finicky and easy-to-please moviegoers. It was *Spartacus* (Universal, 1960), a twelve million dollar costume epic shot in Super-Technirama and color. It was lensed, for the most part, on the Universal backlot under the direction of Stanley Kubrick,[10]

[10]A week after production began, the original director, Anthony Mann, had been fired and Kubrick hired to take his place.

In *Spartacus* (1960)

and written by Dalton Trumbo (the first Hollywood screenplay he wrote under his given name since the Red-hunting probes of 1947), from the novel by Howard Fast. Produced by Kirk Douglas for his Bryna Productions, exterior battle scenes were photographed in Spain. With a running time of 205 minutes, it was a mammoth undertaking. When released, Motion Picture *Herald* lauded, " . . . [it] emerges as a magnificent motion picture achievement of splendid stature."

By the standards of most movie epics, *Spartacus* was a very literate, thoughtful spectacle. Spartacus (Douglas) is the Tracian slave who, in the century before Christ, escapes from a gladiator training school at Capua, 130 miles south of Rome. He frees 90,000 Roman slaves, and during two years of revolt against oppression, his men defeat nine armies sent against them by the Roman Senate. Crassus (Laurence Olivier), the dictator of Rome, is the military strategist who finally defeats Spartacus and crucifies him and his remaining followers along the Appian Way. Tony has the supporting role of a handsome Roman poet, Antoninus, who is servant to Crassus, but who quits his comfortable surroundings, where he has favor, in order to join Spartacus' army. His reason for leaving Crassus is merely hinted at in the released film. The footage where Crassus attempts to seduce him was deleted on the assumption that 1960 audiences, not to mention the Production Code, would be shocked by a celluloid foray into homosexuality.

Time Magazine alluded to Tony's accent: "[It] suggests that the ancient Tiber was a tributary of the Bronx River." Nor were the other critics any kinder to him in this feature which eventually realized gross domestic receipts of over fourteen million dollars. Bosley Crowther (*New York Times*) chided, "Tony Curtis contrasts in theatricality with the easy, accomplished clowning of a Romanized Mr. [Peter] Ustinov." It was ironic that Tony, who had been reared in the Universal acting stable as a swashbuckling leading man, should fare better with the critics, if not always with the public, only in drama or comedy.

After their fifth and final joint onscreen appearance in cameos for *Pepe* (Columbia, 1960), Tony and Janet opened their home to women supporters of then presidential hopeful John F. Kennedy in October, 1960.[11] Although they had anticipated five hundred guests, two thousand women attended the fund-raising celebration, many of whom, it was assumed, just wanted to scan the inside of the Curtis home. Later, Tony and Janet attended the Kennedy-Lyndon Johnson inaugural ball, along with other Hollywood personalities such as Gene Kelly and Fredric March.

Tony had not enjoyed a good starring vehicle in some time, but *The Great Imposter* (Universal, 1960) remedied that situation. The film was based on the incredible but factual adventures of Ferdinand W. Demara, Jr. Curtis has the role of Demara, whose childhood dreams of the Walter Mitty variety remain with him into adulthood, when he makes

[11]At the time, Kennedy's sister Patricia was wed to Clan member Peter Lawford.

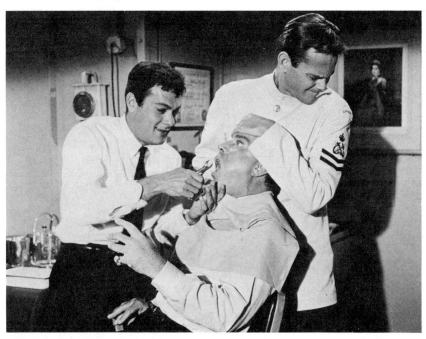

With Edmond O'Brien and Richard Sargent in *The Great Imposter* (1961)

many of them come true. Oncamera, Tony had the opportunity to portray Demara impersonating a clergyman, a monk, a deputy warden of a large prison, and a Canadian Naval surgeon. Tony carries off all of these professional guises in this believe-it-or-not account with the proper aplomb and twinkle of the eye.

On January 3, 1961, the cameras were set to roll on MGM's *Lady L*, based on Romain Gary's novel of a love affair between a titled Englishwoman and an anarchist. Tony and Gina Lollobrigida (both of *Trapeze* fame) were signed as the stars at $20,000 a week each. Robert Anderson submitted an initial draft of the script which was accepted by producer Julian Blaustein, but which director George Cukor disliked. A new script was prepared, but this time Blaustein vetoed it and then withdrew from the already risky project. Meanwhile, Tony and Gina were prevented by their contracts from working elsewhere, but they continued to receive their healthy MGM paychecks. The production was eventually shelved after eight months of delays.[12] Tony only too gladly went to work at Universal in *The Outsider* (1961).

In this Delbert Mann-directed feature, he is Ira Hayes, the Pima Indian of Arizona, one of the six Leathernecks to raise the American flag after the liberation of Iwo Jima in World War II. For this role, Tony rubbed his skin with stain, covered his curls with a straight-haired wig, and wore putty on his nose and chin. These physical changes did a great deal to give the actor the necessary confidence to carry through with consistency his portrayal of the shy youth from the Government reservation who joins the U.S. Marine Corps. There, he is befriended by Jim Sorenson (James Franciscus), a blonde, all-American, fun-loving guy. They become great pals, but Jim is killed soon after the world-famous flag raising at Iwo. Ira Hayes then broods and drinks while listening to recordings of the song "Where Are You?" ("Where can you be without me? I thought you cared about me"), smacking of a not altogether heterosexual relationship. On Ira's return to the U.S. he is unable to hold up under the acclaim he receives, and he hides away in his Arizona shanty home where he drinks continually. One night he wanders off into the desert and dies. A. H. Weiler (*New York Times*) understated the case when he evaluated Tony's performance as "genuinely restrained and surprisingly effective."

At this point, rumors of domestic unrest in the Curtis family were bandied about once again, seeming to confirm that the couple's spats on the soundstage had not been purely artistic differences of opinion. The scuttlebut gained further impetus when Janet left Tony at home while she joined Jeanne Martin (Mrs. Dean) and other prominent Sinatra Clan members on a trip to the Riviera. The sojourn was cut short

---

[12]*Lady L* finally saw the light of day in 1966 when MGM resurrected the idea, with Peter Ustinov directing Paul Newman and Sophia Loren in the lead roles. It was not a successful venture.

In *The Outsider* (1961)

when Janet's father committed suicide in California, leaving behind a note in which he allegedly stated his hatred for his wife. Tony took charge of family matters and consoled Janet to the extent of taking her with him (with their children) to Argentina in October, 1961.

In South America, he was set to star in the Harold Hecht production of *Taras Bulba* (United Artists, 1962), based on a novel by Nikolai Gogol. While waiting for shiploads of cameras, motor generators, and other filming paraphernalia to reach the company's locale in Salta (an Argentine northern province), Tony said to the press, "The thing that

With Yul Brynner in *Taras Bulba* (1962)

interested me most about *Taras Bulba* was the period in which the story takes place. It has never been done on the screen before; also it's the story of the Ukrainian Cossacks and their fight for freedom from the tyrannical Poles."

Then everything began going afoul for the Curtises. Janet contracted food poisoning, Tony developed a throat infection, and Jamie, their youngest, hurt herself in a bad fall. In frustration, Janet gathered her young ones and returned to California, leaving Tony alone with co-star Yul Brynner, the Argentine Army's men and horses (all members of the cast), and a seventeen-year-old German actress named Christine Kaufmann.

In December, 1961, on completion of *Taras Bulba*, Tony went to New York to fulfill personal appearance obligations for *The Outsider*. Miss Kaufmann also went to New York, where newspaper columnists indiscreetly chronicled the obvious romance burning between the two screen figures. On his return to Hollywood, Tony moved out of the Curtis mansion. When she was asked if Miss Kaufmann had broken up her marriage, Janet emphatically stated to newsmen, "That's perfectly ridiculous. Maybe Tony did take her out to dinner and see her in New York, but that certainly was not the reason for our breakup. Our differences had been growing for a long time."

Tony was considered the "heavy" by the news reporters, but when

Janet received her divorce on July 12, 1962, she was unable to wait the full year for it to become final, and on September 15, 1962, obtained a quickie dissolution to her eleven-year union in Juarez, Mexico. The same day, she was married in Las Vegas to Beverly Hills real estate broker, Robert Brandt. (Janet had received custody of Kelly and Jamie.)

Immediately following the divorce, Tony reportedly developed a strong affinity for hard liquor and became quite a party man. He said, "Divorce is such an emotional shock I don't think I ever want to go through it again. It's something I wouldn't wish on my worst enemy." Of his relationship with Miss Kaufman, he commented, "She's a lovely girl and very talented. Lots of stories have been written about our friendship. I have a great deal of respect for her." He also said, when asked about the possibility of marrying her, "I've got to take my time about marriage. I don't want to wind up twenty years from now with a string of five wives behind me."

Like his leading-man rival Rock Hudson, Tony was never away from the screen very long. Although a project to have him star in a biography of *Playboy* magazine tycoon Hugh Hefner fell flat, Curtis did plunge into *40 Pounds of Trouble* (1962) for Universal, which took him to Lake Tahoe, California and to Disneyland. The film is yet another variation of *Little Miss Marker* (Paramount, 1934), only not as felicitous as the Shirley Temple original or the Bob Hope-Lucille Ball remake, *Sorrowful Jones* (Paramount, 1949). Gambler Steve McCluskey (Tony) inherits a little girl (Claire Wilcox) and the problem of what to do with her. Suzanne Pleshette plays a Nevada casino singer in love with the gambler, and Phil Silvers portrays Bernie Friedman, along for the ride to provide some comedy flavor.

By the end of 1962, *Taras Bulba* was officially released. It was not a popular or critical success. To quote one critic, Bosley Crowther (*New York Times*), "It is one of those pictures in which masses of horses and men are the main attractions, and most of the action scenes have been slashed and shot to pieces." The story, set in the sixteenth century, centers around Andrei Bulba (Tony) and his father Taras (Brynner), Russian Cossacks who are hated by the Polish cavalry. Andrei nearly spoils the family name by loving a Polish girl (Kaufmann). As had been the case with *Spartacus* and, to a lesser extent, with *The Prince Who Was a Thief,* Tony's New York background had so permeated his inner and outer personality that it seemed impossible for him to shed or disguise it sufficiently to be credible in any costume venture, let alone as a Slavic horseman of a bygone century. It was the reverse of the problem Errol Flynn had encountered when playing in American Westerns (*Dodge City,* Warner Bros., 1939) or by Tyrone Power in medieval costume dramas (*Captain from Castile,* Twentieth Century-Fox, 1947). But unlike Tony, Flynn and Power had developed a swaggering, classy screen presence early in their film careers, which compensated for their frequent miscastings. As far as Tony was concerned, for better or worse, he was a very parochial performer, bound by the mid-twentieth century and by his very New York-like veneer.

Few people were surprised when, on February 8, 1963, Tony and Christine Kaufmann[13] were married at the Riviera Hotel in Las Vegas by Clark County District Judge George Marshall. Kirk Douglas was best man and Anne, Kirk's wife, was matron of honor. At eighteen it was Christine's first marriage. Tony was thirty-seven at the time of his second marriage. Following their nuptials, the newlyweds embarked on a honeymoon cruise on Lake Mead, and then took up housekeeping in a two-bedroom home in Los Angeles' Coldwater Canyon. After the wedding, Christine announced her plans to give up her acting career.

Despite the repeated proof in Tony's pictures that he was indeed capable of more than just the pretty-boy roles that had launched him in movies, many official and unofficial critics continued to single him out for scathing attacks. When a Dallas critic chose him to tie with Tab Hunter and Elvis Presley as the globe's worst actor, Tony wrote the man a letter saying, "You wouldn't know an actor if he sat down on your face." When television producer David Susskind blasted Tony for having "no talent and no taste," Tony fumed, "I've never met Mr. Susskind, and when I do I'm going to punch him right in the nose." Susskind's counter-reply was, "If I'm not the biggest admirer of Tony Curtis's talent, I've never questioned his virility or strength. He is, in my book, a passionate amoeba." Tony's overall reaction to critics was, "I can't stand critics. They're so damn chi-chi, smarty-pants."

"Here indeed is a mystery that is by turns fascinating, intriguing, exciting, and at all times wholly satisfying." This is the *Motion Picture Herald's* overstatement of *The List of Adrian Messenger* (Universal, 1963), directed in England and Ireland by John Huston, based on the mystery novel by Philip MacDonald. The property was owned by Kirk Douglas and the film starred George C. Scott as detective Anthony Gerthryn, who unmasks the killer of several murder victims. Huston had done much better with *The Maltese Falcon* (Warner Bros., 1941), and of the present film, he said, "I guess the real lure for moviegoers was the gimmick." The audience-grabbing trick was the use of guest stars—Tony, Frank Sinatra, Robert Mitchum, Douglas, and Burt Lancaster—each wearing artificial faces designed by makeup expert Bud Westmore. Each facial transformation required close to four hours with makeup artists, and when Tony, as an Italian organ grinder, shot his scenes at the entrance to Scotland Yard, no one recognized him. At

[13]Born in Lansdorf, Graz, Austria on January 11, 1945, the daughter of a former Luftwaffe pilot, she attended school in Munich, Germany. She made her movie debut in *Im Weissen Rössl* (1952) and then appeared as a dancer in the remake of *Salto Mortale* (1953). Among her other twenty-five films to date had been *Rosenrosli, Schweigende Engel, Maedchen in Uniform, Winter Vacation, The Last Days of Pompeii,* and Kirk Douglas' *Town without Pity* (United Artists, 1961).

the end of the lackadaiscal feature, a voice shouts, "Hold it! Stop! That's the end of the picture—but it's not the end of the mystery." One by one, the disguised guest celebrities appear front and center before the camera and peel off their clever rubber masks.

Some time before *Butch Cassidy and the Sundance Kid* (Twentieth Century-Fox, 1969), *The Sting* (Universal, 1973), or *California Split* (Columbia, 1974) played to the hilt the camaraderie of two males oncamera, Tony and Gregory Peck were co-starred in *Captain Newman, M.D.* (Universal, 1963). As Corporal Jackson Laibowitz, an orderly to Newman (Peck), the chief of the neuro-psychiatric section of an Army hospital in Arizona during World War II, Curtis provided some extraneous but well-received comedy relief. As the gleeful Jewish orderly, Tony's character says, "I feel like a civilian," and Peck's Newman suggests that he call him 'Sir' so he will feel more military. The stated age of the trouble-prone orderly is twenty-seven, a pose which Tony (at thirty-eight) had little trouble playing convincingly. The smoothness with which Tony and Peck performed their roles was eclipsed by the general excitement surrounding the intense performance by Bobby Darin as an emotionally unstable patient whom Newman cures, only to have the youth sent back to combat where he dies. (Darin was Oscar-nominated for his performance, but lost the Best Supporting Actor Award to Melvyn Douglas of *Hud*.)

Curtis was seen briefly as himself in *Paris When It Sizzles* (Paramount, 1964) in a scene at Orly Airport. Filmed two years earlier and shelved, the film was a fiasco despite the winning star combination of William Holden and Audrey Hepburn. A bad script and Holden's deficiency at comedy were its major faults. That same year, for *Wild and Wonderful* (Universal, 1964), Tony persuaded his wife to shirk her household chores to co-star with him. The film's original title, *Monsieur Cognac,* would have been more appropriate, since it is the artificially cute story of an alcoholic French Poodle that complicates its master's (Tony) romantic interests on his wedding night (to Kaufmann). The mediocre offering, which used the backlot Gallic sets for the Paris outdoor scenes, was released as the top of a double bill (with Allied Artists' *The Strangler*) at most neighborhood theatres.

On July 19, 1964, Tony became papa to a third daughter, the first-born child for Christine. The baby was christened Alexandra Theodora Dido Curtis.

Closely following the *Wild and Wonderful* dud was Tony's more pronounced fiasco, *Goodbye, Charlie* (Twentieth Century-Fox, 1964). It demonstrated just how inept a director Vincente Minnelli could be when he was called upon to supervise a too loosely constructed adult comedy that badly needed tight direction of all departments. It was based on the rather tasteless George Axelrod play about a murdered man who is reincarnated as a woman. It had been presented on Broad-

615

With Debbie Reynolds and Pat Boone in *Goodbye, Charlie* (1964)

way in 1959 with sophisticated Lauren Bacall as Charlie and suave Sydney Chaplin as her/his best pal, who is attracted by the new Charlie, yet confused by the entire change of sex situation. In the screen version, Debbie Reynolds was energetic but wrong for the part of Charlie, and Tony did his frantic best to hold up under the plodding Harry Kurnitz adaptation. However, he was unable to support the production adequately, even with Walter Matthau's help (as the jealous Hungarian who shoots Charlie in the first place). Pat Boone's hindrance (as the bland pal) didn't help much, either.

In his third and final 1964 release, Tony joined with Natalie Wood (she in top billing) in *Sex and the Single Girl* (Warner Bros.), which owed its title but little else to the best selling advice book by Helen Gurley Brown. However, both Tony and Natalie lost the show to two old pros, Lauren Bacall and Henry Fonda, who fielded the slapstick humor situation with far more relaxed presence. As executed by Richard Quine, the ex-actor who had directed Tony in *So This Is Paris,* Natalie appeared as authoress Brown who involves herself with research on marital and pre-marital sex habits. (*The Chapman Report* Warner Bros., 1962, had been a more salacious, but far more entertaining exercise using a similar titillating ploy.) Tony is onscreen as a writer for a scandal-type magazine which is determined to refute all of Ms. Brown's startling findings. Bacall and Fonda are Tony's sophisti-

With Natalie Wood in *Sex and the Single Girl* (1964)

cated neighbors and are blessed with the choicest dialog and the funnier of the two marital problems.

Tony's next feature, *The Great Race* (Warner Bros., 1965), has chalked up over eleven million dollars in distributors' domestic rentals. When it is considered that the feature cost twelve million dollars to produce, the U.S.-Canadian rental figure loses its impressiveness. Critics such as Wilfrid Mifflin in *Films in Review* called it a "great bore," but Don Mersereau of *Boxoffice* predicted that it "surely is Oscar Award material." The truth lies somewhere in between these two views. Although nominated for Oscars in several technical categories, including best song, the film gained only one Award, that for best sound effects.

Six weeks were spent in Europe where exterior shots were made in Vienna and Paris. For the most part, however, the Blake Edwards-directed comedy was made in California, near or on all of the Warner Bros. acreage. The entire production consumed six months' time and emerged on the screen as a 163-minute marathon event.

Reunited with Natalie Wood and Jack Lemmon, Tony is "The Great Leslie" a man of immense virtue. (He is so virtuous that his eyes and teeth occasionally sparkle, thanks to special effects man Danny Lee.) Dressed in pure white to remind everyone that he is good, he is pitted against the most villainous, hissable, black-clothed scoundrel in all

With Jack Lemmon in *The Great Race* **(1965)**

Christendom, Professor Fate (Lemmon). They compete for the honors in a 1908 auto race from New York to Paris, which takes them and a feminist newspaper reporter (Wood), through antics likened to, and in emulation of, Mack Sennett, Laurel and Hardy, and Harold Lloyd. The race is won by Professor Fate, but only because The Great Leslie slows his vehicle before reaching the Eiffel Tower as a show of his love for newswoman Maggie DuBois (Wood).

Offscreen, however, there was anything but love between Tony and Natalie. "Natalie is too career-minded," Tony insisted to reporters. "There was a time she was warm and friendly. Today she seems more wrapped up in herself. Maybe she feels she doesn't need anyone else." When director Edwards was publicly queried if he had planned a party in celebration of the film's completion, he replied, "Sure. It'll be quite an occasion. Both Natalie and Tony are going to set each other on fire." Adding fuel to the dispute among three co-stars was the fight between both Tony and Lemmon for top billing, above Natalie's credit. When no reasonable agreement could be reached, Warners was forced to make up two sets of credits, and agreed also to alternate the male stars' names in publicity releases.

Still convinced that he was or could be or should be the American cinema's greatest farceur, Tony continued demanding and accepting all kinds of comedy roles. The spring of 1965 found Tony in Paris for the Hal B. Wallis production, *Boeing-Boeing* (Paramount, 1965) based

With Dany Saval, Jerry Lewis, and Suzanna Leigh in *Boeing-Boeing* (1965)

619

on the very popular Marc Camoletti sex farce which had done so well on the Continent but failed to woo audiences in either London or New York. Tony was unhappy about the on-location site, a city he had once liked. Mercurial Tony told Roderick Mann of the *London Express* that all he wanted was to go home. "All those romantic songs about Paris were written by Americans," he said. " 'April in Paris,' actually it's a rotten time to be here. Rains most of the time." Christine joined him in the rain to accompany him home, and he told Mann, "I can't tell you how happy I am with her. In America, women compete with men. It's impossible. But she's European and she likes being bossed. So I boss her. At home, I'm a benevolent despot. And the age differential is just right. I think all men should be locked up until they're thirty-five and then only allowed out to marry twenty-year-old girls."

The Wallis film, directed by John Rich, afforded Tony yet another opportunity to try his talent at fielding a different brand of comedy, for this was a drawing room sex farce of a much less slapstick nature than either *Sex and the Single Girl* or the earlier *Goodbye, Charlie.* The highly-promoted gimmick of this film was that Jerry Lewis, long separated from ex-partner Dean Martin, would be eschewing his usual funnyman role to play a "straight" part. Curtis and Lewis appeared as foreign correspondents based in Paris, with Tony's Bernard Lawrence devoting more time to a bevy of international airline stewardesses than to his typewriter. Lewis portrays his arch rival, Robert Reed, who tries to wangle a little loving of his own from any or all of Bernard's girls. Thelma Ritter, as Tony's wry housekeeper whose main function is to keep her boss on schedule with his rotation of girlfriends, steals the picture from both Curtis and Lewis. Once again, before this latest Tony Curtis feature could be released, the studio had to arbitrate the billing problem between Tony and Lewis. The beleaguered studio fell back on the remedy which Warners' had used for *The Great Race,* as well as the old Broadway trick of having the co-stars' names split, with Player A's first name on top-left, while Player B's last name is on top right, and the player A's last name on bottom left and player B's first name bottom right on the second line.

On July 12, 1966, Tony's fourth daughter was born in Los Angeles. The newest addition to the Curtis household, she was named Allegra.

Forty-one-year-old Tony, who had become plump around the waist and fuller in the face, kept on with his "comedy" film career. In *Not with My Wife, You Don't* (Warner Bros., 1966), Virna Lisi was his spouse and George C. Scott was the Air Force colonel whom he is convinced will steal away her affections. After a cameo in *Chamber of Horrors* (Warner Bros., 1966), a television series pilot that was released instead to theatres, it was comedy time again with *Arriverderci, Baby!* (Paramount, 1966). The tone here was black humor as Tony expertly kills off his guardian (Anna Quayle), his rich first wife (Zsa Zsa Gabor),

620

With Christine Kaufmann Curtis and their children Allegra and Alessandra
(October, 1966)

With George C. Scott in *Not with My Wife, You Don't* (1966)

and his wealthy second mate (Fenella Fielding). Through thick and thin (the latter describes the entertainment values of the piece), his true love is Baby (Nancy Kwan), his mistress-confidante. As he prepares to rid himself of wife number three (Rosanna Schiaffino) for a five-million-dollar inheritance, he discovers that she is penniless. But by then, she has learned of his scheme and decides to booby-trap his car; he had planned that her demise should occur in an identical fashion. Neither party can go through with it, though, and each realizes that money is not everything. He bids Baby goodbye as he enters a lazy, down-to-earth married life with a wife who takes in laundry and cooks his spaghetti.

Filmed in England, France, and Italy, *Arriverderci, Baby!* was Tony's best comedy in years. But by now, Tony—like that other Universal wunderkind of the 1950s, Rock Hudson—was considered a slightly passé commodity on the film market. It was now the era of Michael Caine, Peter O'Toole, Sean Connery, Richard Burton, and, of course, that perennial boxoffice champ, John Wayne.

In June, 1966, Tony purchased oil magnate Bill Keck's Holmby Hills Mediterranean-style mansion for $300,000. Situated on four acres of the most expensive land in California, the villa contained eighteen rooms and an Olympic-sized indoor pool inlaid with Byzantine tile. A six-car garage went along with the place to house his 1934 Rolls Royce, the 1937 Bentley, a vintage Duesenberg, a 1965 Excalibur SS, and a shiny new 1966 Lincoln Continental. With this mansion and cars, intended as investments, Tony explained to the press, "I have no intention of winding up broke. Nobody's going to take care of me if I don't do it myself." (He had earlier sold his Bel Air home for $345,000.) Parked in the drive area were a Mustang and several other Fords. "Surprising," he told columnist Sheilah Graham, "when you remember that Christine does not drive." Tony also began to diet, refusing to eat such foods as bleached flour, milk, coffee, ice cream, sugar, or margarine. He substituted honey for sugar and ate whole wheat bread only. After each careful meal he smoked a cigar! Maybe it was the automobiles, or maybe it was the money, but whatever it was, at age forty-two, in spite of a few gray hairs, Tony looked younger. Perhaps it was from knowing that his total package of films up to that time had grossed sixty million dollars at the boxoffice.

If *Arriverderci, Baby!* had been an uplift in his film career as a comedian, *Don't Make Waves* (MGM, 1967) was a decided flip in the opposite direction. He portrays a California swimming pool salesman whose pitches are dampened by the presence of luscious Claudia Cardinale, the mistress of his boss (Robert Webber). Howard Thompson of the *New York Times* called the shots on this one with a simple comment: "It's pretty awful."

Tony withdrew from the lead role in *The Night They Raided Min-*

With Claudia Cardinale in *Don't Make Waves* **(1967)**

sky's (United Artists, 1969) due to artistic differences with producer Norman Lear, and he was replaced by Elliott Gould. Then he did duty in a cameo role which was different from his previous appearances. Over a telephone, his voice is heard as that of stage actor Donald Baumgart who has suddenly been blinded and is replaced in a new Broadway show by Guy Woodhouse (John Cassavetes). Most of the inhabitants of the notorious Bramford Apartments in New York know that Baumgart's tragedy was induced by the coven of witches who live there, that Guy, in payment for the turn of "fate," has agreed to give his soul to the devil and to allow the latter to father Mrs. Woodhouse's (Mia Farrow) baby. Hence the premise for *Rosemary's Baby* (Paramount, 1968).

Months earlier, producer Robert Fryer had conducted an extensive search, screen-testing over 150 prospects for the key role of the psychopathic killer for his film interpretation of Gerold Frank's bestselling novel, *The Boston Strangler.* Tony wanted the prize role, but his agents could not convince either Fryer or Twentieth Century-Fox's production chief, Richard Zanuck, that he was capable of such serious drama.

Tony took matters into his own hands in December, 1967, by re-doing his face with putty wax on his nose, practically eliminating his long eye lashes, modifying his eyebrows, and straightening his hair. He then photographed his "new" face and rushed two dozen eight-by-ten prints to Richard Fleischer, the director of the film, who years before had directed Tony in *The Vikings*. These pictures resulted in a test, and in two days, he was signed at $30,000 a week to enact the title role of Albert DeSalvo in the true story of the man who strangled and mutilated thirteen New England women over the course of eighteen months. It was while he was in the preliminary throes of learning the script (by Edward Anhalt) that the public announcement was made of Tony's marital separation from Christine. "It's a brand-new ball game," he said as he frequented Hollywood's fanciest private discotheques dressed in bell bottom trousers, Edwardian vests, and strands of love beads around his neck. "And now I'm a bachelor again," he stated. "Why? The next I'm married three times. I'm beginning to sound like the Jewish Tommy Manville, and that throws me. Where is there a weakness in me? What do I do that can make a woman so frustrated and so angry and so uptight that she can't live with me?"

Christine, who obtained a Juarez, Mexico divorce on April 16, 1968, has said, "He was very rude. He would leave me at home, to sit around the house while he was out having a good time—I don't know who with at all." Christine was given custody of their two children.

Four days later, on April 20, 1968, at two o'clock in the morning at the Sahara Hotel in Las Vegas, Tony (age forty-three) was married to Leslie Allen (age twenty-three), a model whose home was in Newton,

With his new bride, Leslie Allen, at the Curtis Hollywood home (April 20, 1968)

Massachusetts. "I was a bit wild until I met Leslie," he confessed to the press. "Now I never feel I want to cheat or flirt. I have never known a woman who cares for me so much." The couple, in public, made no pretenses about their strong physical attraction for one another. Tony once explained it with, "It's love, man. Everyone should try loving someone as I do with Leslie. You can do it anyway you like. Stroke, nuzzle, any way at all, just as long as you love."

On the release of *The Boston Strangler* (Twentieth Century-Fox) in October, 1968, *Variety* commended him with: "Tony Curtis, trying to shake the light comedy image, is quite convincing, both in makeup and voice. He may well be able to alter again the course of his career, as he did in 1957 when, in *Sweet Smell of Success,* he effected a major image change." *New York* Magazine made the following comment: "In an actually intelligent and subtle performance, he climbs inside DeSalvo and makes himself astonishingly at home." The *Hollywood Reporter* found that "he surpasses the past excellence of *The Outsider* and *The Great Imposter* in depths of anguish and humiliation that scarcely betray the actor at work." The film, which suffered from an over-use of the split screen technique, was called a "triumph of taste and restraint" by *Variety.*

As the 116-minute feature relates, Albert DeSalvo terrorized Boston from June, 1962, until January, 1964, during which time he strangled

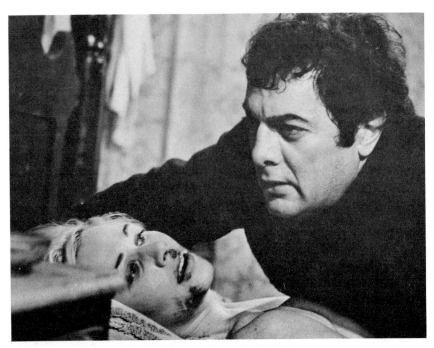

With Sally Kellerman in *The Boston Strangler* (1968)

thirteen women, each with a piece of her own garment, and then raped them. Although he confessed to all the murders, there was still insufficient evidence to indict him and, instead, he drew a life sentence for robbing and assaulting four women who lived to testify against him. DeSalvo, later was found stabbed to death in his Walpole, Massachusetts, prison cell on November 26, 1973. (This epilogue to his bizarre life was added as a voice-over postscript when the film was later televised in the Boston area.) Many felt that Tony should have been Oscar-nominated for his performance, in a year when Cliff Robertson *(Charly)* won the Best Actor Award.

Tony returned to comedy in *Those Daring Young Men in Their Jaunty Jalopies* (Paramount, 1969), a distillation of aspects from *Those Magnificent Men in Their Flying Machines* (Twentieth Century-Fox, 1966) and *The Great Race.* Like the latter picture, this film also deals with an auto endurance contest, but through Europe (with filming in England, France, and Italy by and with a team of international technicians). Tony appears as Chester Schofield, an American gambler and a partner in an English automobile plant, who enters the race with his partner, Terry-Thomas. It is spasmodically funny, but does not reach the slap-the-knee type of comedy of its inspirations. Two more intended laughing jags followed, in the form of *The Chastity Belt,* a.k.a., *On My Way to the Crusades I Met a Girl Who* (Warner Bros.-Seven Arts, 1969), which had a very scant release, and *Suppose They Gave a War and Nobody Came?* (Cinerama, 1970), both proving that a story *can* be told just in the title.

With Terry-Thomas and Eric Sykes in *Those Daring Young Men in Their Jaunty Jalopies* (1969)

With Monica Vitti in *La Cintura Di Castita* (*On My Way to the Crusades I Met a Girl Who . . .*) (1969)

With Suzanne Pleshette in *Suppose They Gave a War and Nobody Came?* (1970)

In Feburary, 1969, in Montreal, Tony received the Eleanor Roosevelt Humanitarian Award for the year in recognition of his efforts for charitable causes, and it was during this period that he "quit" smoking cigars, cigarettes, and pipe tobacco. At least, he persuaded the American Cancer Society that he had given up smoking, and an immediate campaign was launched in the hope of saving the world from a smoker's death. Tony was heard over radio in spot commercials sponsored by the American Cancer Society, as well as in similar television pleas. Soon, his name became synonymous with the words, "I Quit," and the Society distributed large, round, red campaign pins bearing the slogan. In a press conference in New York he claimed that his quitting tobacco had made him less argumentative and more sexy, but there were persistent rumors that he had been seen on the rooftops and in the men's room of television studios lighting up for a quick smoke between commercial tapings.

As he embarked for Europe in late 1969, he tossed several barbs at Hollywood in general and Universal Studios in particular which indicated that he was all too happy about leaving the country. He denounced the big studio system and said, "People in Hollywood are going to soothsayers now and to their mothers-in-law to ask if they should make a movie. I'm glad the picture business is on its ass. It'll result in fewer and better movies."

In Yugoslavia, he co-starred with Charles Bronson in the Gene Corman production, *You Can't Win 'Em All* (Columbia, 1970), a picture which was originally titled with the less appropriate *The Dubious Patriots.* In this half-baked adventure story, Tony and Bronson (in the latter's pre-major stardom days) are a pair of American soldiers of fortune at the end of World War I who turn up in Turkey at the time of the Ottoman Empire collapse. They have a great time tearing apart Greek, Turkish, and rebel forces and both fall for a Turkish miss (Michele Mercier) whom neither wins. The unsatisfying film ends on a note of perverse expectation, suggesting that a sequel might be in the offing. If there was to be one, director Peter Collinson made it quite clear that it would not be under his supervision, since he criticized both Tony and Bronson.

On Tony's return to the States, on the theory that he could be a man for all seasons if he so willed it, he ventured into a nightclub act at Caesar's Palace in Las Vegas, where he did little more than sing a few songs, mug a lot, and tell a few unmemorable anecdotes of Hollywood life. He devoted a greater amount of show time to shaking the hands of ringside fans. One Los Angeles critic referred to the debacle as a "crucifixion," while Ralph Pearl of the *Las Vegas Sun* wrote, "Tony Curtis, the Hollywood movie star, is not only a lousy movie actor, but he has come to Las Vegas, opened at Caesar's Palace and conclusively revealed that he is also a lousy café entertainer."

In late April, 1970, Tony arrived in London to discuss a television series with Sir Lew Grade, Britain's Mr. Show Business and founder of Associated Television, Ltd. At London's Heathrow Airport, Tony was arrested for possessing marijuana, which he admitted he had for his own use. He was fined the equivalent of $120 by a British court while the American Cancer Society directors back in New York huffed indignation through their clean lungs. A spokesman for the Society said, "It's terrible. People are quick to get suspicious and fed up and to think that Mr. Curtis didn't really mean what he said. We just don't know what to say." Rather than discuss the matter further, the Society withdrew the Curtis commercials from both radio and television.

Meanwhile, a humbled Tony quickly involved himself with the TV series, originally entitled "The Friendly Persuaders," which had Roger Moore (in his pre-James Bond stardom days) as co-star. "Look," Tony explained to interviewer Norma Lee Browning, "television is only a machine through which an actor works at his craft. I am in the business of making movies. . . . The only difference between a series for this machine called TV and the big movie screen is in the length of time it takes."

In the sixty-minute color series that premiered on September 18, 1971 (on NBC-TV network in the United States), Tony was a "self-polished" diamond from the Bronx, while dapper Moore portrayed a

With Roger Moore and Jenny Linden on the set of "The Persuaders" (1970)

rich British Lord. Anticipating a hit, Tony bought a $120,000 house on Chester Square in London. (He had earlier acquired an ancient palazzo on two hundred acres outside Rome and a ranch in Riverside, California.) With the announcement that his wife was expecting a child in December, Tony informed reporters, "I feel on top of the world. I feel like nineteen physically and mentally. I'm certainly not forty-five. I like being in Britain, too." But he added to that, "I'm particularly pleased that my next kid will be born here." The baby, Tony's first boy, was born on December 31, 1971, and was named Nicholas.

The teleseries, its title shortened to "The Persuaders," lasted two seasons in England, but just one in America. In France, both Tony and Moore were chosen Best Actors of the year; in Spain the series was named as the Best Foreign Telecast; and in Germany it was selected as the Best Dubbed Program. Tony revealed plans to make a film in London and another in Mexico, but neither project came about.

In 1972, he returned to California. In April, he sold his Bel Air mansion for a reported $900,000 and waited for offers of work. Then, Edward L. Rissien of Playboy Productions came along with the idea of Tony appearing with "special guest star" billing, in an ABC-TV "Movie-of-the-Week" entitled *The Third Girl from the Left* (October 16, 1973). In the weakly constructed telefeature, Tony plays Joey Jordan, a selfish but popular nightclub comic engaged for thirteen years to dancer Gloria Joyce (Kim Novak). She becomes attracted to a twenty-three-year-old college dropout (Michael Brandon). Later, when she is forced to make a choice between the two contrasting suitors, she decides to remain with Joey. Within his role, which received few positive press comments, Tony sang the song "Gloria."

On the domestic front, Tony obtained custody of Alexandra and Allegra, his daughters by Christine Kaufmann, through a court order in early 1973. Christine, who was then living in a rented room in Germany, said to newspeople "They're better off with Tony and his wife in America. They have a big house, a pool and every material thing they need." In February, he instigated proceedings to obtain legal custody of Kelly from Janet Leigh, and in June, he sought daughter Jamie, plus the return of $100,000 in child support payments which he alleged were spent by Miss Leigh for matters other than for the children's support. On May 2, 1973, a second son was born to Curtis and Leslie Allen. The new heir, born by Caesarian section at Cedars of Lebanon Hospital, was named Benjamin Anthony.

Then Tony made the announcement that he had signed to star (after Burt Reynolds turned the role down) in the David Merrick stage production, *The First Offenders,* co-authored and co-directed by Bruce Jay Friedman and Jacques Levy. The play was slated for an October, 1973 opening on Broadway at the Plymouth Theatre. Tony described the comedy's theme: "It's a triangle, two men and a girl, but the girl and

With Karen Valentine on "The Second Super Comedy Bowl" (CBS-TV, January 12, 1971)

With Kim Novak in *The Third Girl from the Left* (ABC-TV, October 16, 1973)

the man are both in love with the other man. I'm the object of their affections." When asked why he returned to the stage after more than twenty-five years, he explained to reporters, "There is no more Hollywood, really. And I liked this script when I read it. Besides, I will have the chance to do this as a movie later, if everything works out right."

But nothing did work out right. After five weeks of hectic rehearsal in New York, the show, now known as *Turtlenecks,* previewed in Detroit where the audience walk-outs per performance were estimated at from 117 to 400. It struggled through five weeks at Detroit's Fisher Theatre, however, and from there it went to Philadelphia for two weeks. The producers seemed to be asking for critical slams with the new title for the show, *The One-Night Stand.* In September, a few days before the comedy was scheduled to move on to Boston, producer Merrick closed it down. The audience reaction to the near sex onstage was expressed in such terms as "trash," "insulting," "filthy."

But Tony returned to New York smiling, and stated that he had hopes of publishing a couple of novels he had dashed off, *Julie Sparrow,* about a New York Jewish gangster, and *Kid Andrew Cody* about a midwest kid who goes to Hollywood. He said he was through with moviemaking, "If I had my way," he said, "I'd load all those Hollywood producers into a truck and drive them into the middle of the Pacific."

Apparently having burned all his professional bridges behind him, Tony, in January, 1974, became enthusiastic about making a new film, *Lepke,* for the AmeriEuro Pictures Corporation in Culver City, Cali-

In *Lepke* (1975)

632

fornia. "It's one of the best parts I ever had," he commented before going to California. "It's like starting all over again . . . it's what makes this business so stimulating."

During the filming of *Lepke* (Warner Bros., 1975) Tony's 71-year-old mother died on March 19, 1974, of a heart ailment at the Memorial Hospital in Culver City, California. Helen Schwartz was laid to rest at Hillside Memorial Cemetery a few days later.

In August, 1974, Tony was at work with Anne Bancroft in her television special, *Annie and the Hoods* (ABC-TV, November 27, 1974). Her "hoods" included bachelorhood, motherhood, childhood, adulthood, and Tony was with her in the sketch entitled "Womanhood." Also in the summer of 1974 he returned to Las Vegas where he headlined a magic show for four weeks.

Bent on increasing his film work, Tony joined the cast of Norman Rosemont's television production of *The Count of Monte Cristo* (NBC-TV, January 10, 1975). However, it was Richard Chamberlain who had the title role and it was Tony who played the villain, Mondego. Also in the cast was Tyrone Power's daughter Taryn. Reviewers and public alike were kind to this spirited two hour production, with most of the acting honors going to Chamberlain for his stylish portrayal. For some reason Tony persisted in emphasizing his New York accent, which jarred the credibility of the costumed proceedings. The Hollywood *Reporter* noted, "Tony Curtis is OK in beginning scenes but when he is a successful general he has a very embarrassing scene when he pompously over-acts at a hearing."

He was much more successful in television's *The Big Ripoff* (NBC-TV, March 11, 1975) a pilot for a projected mini-series. *Daily Variety* agreed that Tony was "ideally cast and convincing as the suave con man" who sets out to ripoff the kidnappers of a millionaire's wife.

It was also in March, 1975 that Tony sued independent producer Max J. Rosenberg for $75,000 claiming a breach of contract regarding a projected *The Man in the Iron Mask* movie that was to have been made in Italy in November, 1974. The star claimed he had agreed to a series of postponements, but the producer had never started filming. The sum demanded was for Curtis' ten weeks of shooting. The case has yet to be settled.

Meanwhile *Lepke* was distributed with less fanfare than it deserved. While the plotline and minor characterizations were banal, Tony offered a forthright performance as Louis "Lepke" Buchhalter who emerges from prison in 1919 at the age of twenty-two and continues a career of crime, becoming the mob leader of Brooklyn. Jaded reviewers on both sides of the Atlantic dismissed the film. The British *Monthly Film Bulletin* felt that the film "seems quite devoid of the kind of zest and enthusiasm that any number of B-grade variations on the theme have effortlessly attained." Unmentioned was that Tony had not looked so trim and earnest on screen in a long time, and that his characterization showed thoughtfulness, even if the film was hurt by the miscasting of Milton Berle (as Lepke's father-in-law) and others and producer-director Menahem Golan's attempt at a Jewish-flavored *The Godfather.*

On many occasions, Tony has gone full circle; first liking a field of endeavor, then hating it, and still later insisting he had always been enamored of the item in question. Such was the case with his "McCoy" series, based on the telefeature pilot, *The Big Ripoff.* Returning from Europe where he was vacationing with his wife and children, Curtis reported to his old home base, Universal, where the mini-series was to be shot. When asked what had made him change his mind about teleseries after "The Persuaders," the star insisted to reporter Dwight Newton of the San Francisco *Examiner*: "But it was nothing but successful in Europe. I made over $1.5 million on it. I own 25 percent." When asked if "McCoy" was geared to prove his appeal to American TV audiences, Curtis responded, "I couldn't care less that 'Persuaders' failed in America. This country is not the only place in town. In global terms, 600 million people have seen 'Persuaders.' " When Newton wondered again why Tony was doing "McCoy," the actor answered, "The American market is a big market. I have a deluxe product in a top-drawer spot. In two or three years, the amount of money generated can be incredible. But the really big money is in music. In Beverly Hills, people are lined up to buy the most expensive houses. All are in the music business." As a closing thought, Newton asked Tony if bad reviews bothered him. "It hurts me," said Curtis. "I don't like to get bum-rappers."

When Tony actually arrived on the Universal lot he was all smiles (he owns 1/3 of the series). As he later told Army Archerd of *Daily Variety:* "It was incredible to drive back there now—I was under contract 14 years and I left when I couldn't get outside rights. But—time heals all wounds. And besides, the people who were hassling me then are gone now."

Amazingly—especially to those who insisted that Tony had been washed up for good—"McCoy" has not faltered in the 1976 rating battles and Tony has acquired a renewed audience following. He has no ambition to be a director ("I enjoy the good life as a movie star") on his series.

Recently he grew a moustache for his role in the Elia Kazan-directed picture *The Last Tycoon* (Paramount, 1976). Robert De Niro has the title role as the Irving Thalberg-like movie producer, and besides Tony there are such other veterans in the cast as Ray Milland, Robert Mitchum, and Dana Andrews. Other possible projects that appeal to Tony are picture versions of *Line of Duty,* to be scripted by Ernest Tidyman, and *The Adventures of Omar Khayyam,* to be produced as a joint venture with Iranian backing.

Since there seems to be few topics on which Tony has *no* point of view, he is much in demand for interviews in all media. Recently, in talking with Hollywood columnist Marilyn Beck, he expressed his concern about his daughter Jamie (from his marriage to Janet Leigh). "She's doing all the wrong things," he insists. "Hiring a publicist, getting the glamor photos made, finding an agent to make her into an instant star. All that should come later, after she's mastered her craft. First you make a product, then you sell it." On television, it does not take much prompting to launch Tony on most any topic. At various times on TV (as well in other media) he has expressed his views on a wide variety of subjects.

On the Oscars: "[they] can take and shove it. George C. Scott and Marlon Brando were absolutely right in turning it down. Probably I'll never get the chance but I would certainly refuse to accept it."

On the reigning Hollywood gossip queens, Rona Barrett and Joyce Haber: "[they] are cancers on the rectum of the industry . . . vulgar, ugly broads."

On his ex-wives: "They've been obstreperous, very negative where the children were concerned. But isn't that how ex-wives are supposed to behave?"

Of his new series (which has allowed him to purchase his twelfth California home, this one a $280,000 abode in Bel Air): "I'm really privileged to be allowed to make four two-hour films for television is a mind-boggler. Really prestigious. Dee-lux. Check around town. If most actors get a commitment for *half* a film, they're ecstatic. For me to end up with such an incredible home-run deal is fabulous."

On reviews: "I read absolutely nothing about show biz. Don't want any part of that. I stiff-arm it. Don't even get the trade papers. Columnists don't call me because they know I'll reject them."

On keeping a wife: "When you get older you realize that a woman is much more than a love object. You have really got to divorce one from the other. Then you've got it."

On maturing: "At the beginning of my career, I was mindless. . . Satisfying physical needs, like eating and/or an affair with the leading lady of the moment, were my major concerns. What time has done is simplify my feelings about things. They're not as opulent as they used to be. Not so overt. By the time you reach 50, and you begin to see the final curtain and realize that today is not forever you'd better have reconciled your excesses or you're dead already."

On Universal Studios: "If I hadn't made a pain of myself, the bastards would have kept me in tits and sand movies forever."

On himself: "I try to be very candid and honest with everybody I deal with; I don't really like to be dishonest with anyone."

635

Feature Film Appearances
AS JAMES CURTIS

CRISS CROSS (Universal, 1949), 87 min.

Producer, Michel Kraike; director, Robert Siodmak; based on the novel by Don Tracy; screenplay, Daniel Fuchs; art directors, Bernard Herzbrun and Boris Leven; set decorators, Russell A. Gausman and Oliver Emert; music, Miklos Rozsa; assistant director, Fred Frank; makeup, Bud Westmore; costumes, Yvonne Wood; sound, Leslie I. Carey and Richard DeWesse; special effects, David S. Horsley; camera; Frank Palmer; editor, Ted J. Kent.

Burt Lancaster (Steve Thompson); Yvonne De Carlo (Anna); Dan Duryea (Slim Dundee); Stephen McNally (Pete Ramirez); Richard Long (Slade Thompson); Esy Morales (Orchestra Leader); Tom Pedi (Vincent); Percy Helton (Frank); Alan Napier (Finchley); Griff Barnett (Pop); Meg Randall (Helen); Joan Miller (The Lush); Edna M. Holland (Mrs. Thompson); John Doucette (Walt); Marc Krah (Mort); James O'Rear (Waxie); John "Skins" Miller (Midget); Robert Osterloh (Mr. Nelson); Vincent Renno (Headwaiter); Charles Wagenheim (Waiter); James (Tony) Curtis (Gigolo); Beatrice Roberts and Isabel Randolph (Nurses); Robert Winkler (Clark); Vitto Scotti (Track Usher); John Roy (Bartender); Timmy Hawkins (Boy).

AS ANTHONY CURTIS

CITY ACROSS THE RIVER (Universal, 1949), 90 min.

Producer, Maxwell Shane; associate producer, Ben Colman; director, Shane; based on the novel *The Amboy Dukes* by Irving Shulman; screenplay, Shane and Dennis Cooper; adaptation, Shulman; art directors, Bernard Herzbrun and Emrich Nicholson; set decorators, Russell A. Gausman, John Austin; music-music director, Walter Scharf; assistant director, Fred Frank; makeup, Bud Westmore; sound, Leslie I. Carey and Joe Lapis; special effects, David S. Horsley; camera, Maury Gertsman; editor, Ted J. Kent.

Stephen McNally (Stan Albert); Thelma Ritter (Mrs. Cusack); Luis Van Rooten (Joe Cusack); Jeff Corey (Lieutenant Macon); Sharon McManus (Alice Cusack); Sue England (Betty); Barbara Whiting (Annie Kane); Richard Benedict (Gaggsy Steens); Peter Fernandez (Frank Cusack); Al Ramsen (Benny Wilks); Joshua Shelley (Crazy Perrin); Anthony (Tony) Curtis (Mitch); Mickey Knox (Larry); Richard Jaeckel (Bull); Anabel Shaw (Jean Albert); Robert Osterloh (Mr. Bannon); Al Eben (Detective Kleiner); Sara Berner (Selma); Bert Conway (Mr. Hayes); Frank Cady (Shirley's Partner); Sandra Gould (Shirley); John Pickard (Detective); Judy Ann Nugent (Little Girl); Alfred Croce (Boy Dancer); Joe Draper (Policeman).

THE LADY GAMBLES (Universal, 1949), 99 min.

Producer, Michel Kraike; director, Michael Gordon; story, Lewis Meltzer and Oscar Saul; screenplay, Roy Huggins; adaptation, Halsted Welles; art director, Alexander Golitzen; set decorators, Russell A. Gausman and Ruby R. Levitt; music, Frank Skinner; assistant director, Frank Shaw; makeup, Bud Westmore and Bob Ewing; costumes, Orry-Kelly; sound, Leslie I. Carey and Corson Jowett; camera, Russell Metty; editor, Milton Carruth.

Barbara Stanwyck (Joan Boothe); Robert Preston (David Boothe); Stephen McNally (Corrigan); Edith Barrett (Ruth Phillips); John Hoyt (Dr. Rojac); Elliott Sullivan (Barky); John Harmon (Frenchy); Phil Van Zandt (Chuck); Leif Erickson (Tony); Curt Conway (Bank Clerk); Houseley Stevenson (Pawnbroker); Don Beddoe (Mr. Sutherland); Nana Bryant (Mrs. Sutherland); Anthony (Tony) Curtis (Bellboy); Peter Leeds (Hotel Clerk); Frank Moran (Murphy); Esther Howard (Cross Lady); John Indrisano (Bert); Polly Bailey (Woman at Slot Machine); Francis McDonald (Trainer); Rex Lease (Guide); Kenneth Cutler (Clerk); Al Bayne (Dice Shooter).

JOHNNY STOOL PIGEON (Universal, 1949), 76 min.

Producer, Aaron Rosenberg; director, William Castle; story, Henry Jordan; screenplay, Robert L. Richards; art directors, Bernard Herzbrun and Emrich Nicholson; set decorators, Russell A. Gausman and John Austin; music-music director, Milton Schwarzwald; assistant director, Jesse Hibbs; makeup, Bud Westmore; costumes, Orry-Kelly; sound, Leslie I. Carey and Richard De-Weese; special effects, David S. Horsley; camera, Maury Gertsman; editor, Ted J. Kent.

Howard Duff (George Morton); Shelley Winters (Terry); Dan Duryea (Johnny Evans); Anthony (Tony) Curtis (Joey Hyatt); John McIntire (Avery); Gar Moore (Sam Harrison); Leif Erickson (Pringle); Barry Kelley (McCandles); Hugh Reilly (Charlie); Wally Maher (Benson); Nacho Galindo (Martinez); Gregg Barton (Treasury Man); Robert Foulk (Pete); Duke York (Body Guard); Pat Shade (Bell Boy); Patricia Alphin (McCandles' Secretary); Charles Drake (Hotel Clerk); Ken Patterson (Dallas); Leslie Dennison (Canadian Undercover Man); Edwin Max (Carter); Grace Lenard (Woman Informer); Al Ferguson and Colin Kenny (Porters); Robert Kimball (Bartender); Robert O'Neil (Informer); Harry H. Evans (Federal Judge).

FRANCIS (Universal, 1949), 90 min.

Producer, Robert Arthur; director, Arthur Lubin; based on the novel by David Stern; screenplay, Stern; art directors, Bernard Herzbrun and Richard H. Riedel; set decorators, Russell A. Gausman and A. Roland Fields; music, Frank Skinner; assistant director, John Sherwood; makeup, Bud Westmore; costumes, Rosemary Odell; sound, Leslie I. Carey and Corson Jowett; special camera, David S. Horsley; camera, Irving Glassberg; editor, Milton Carruth.

Donald O'Connor (Peter Stirling); Patricia Medina (Maureen Gelder); ZaSu Pitts (Valerie Humpert); Ray Collins (Colonel Hooker); John McIntire (General Stevens); Eduard Franz (Colonel Plepper); Howland Chamberlin (Major Nadel); James Todd (Colonel Saunders); Robert Warwick (Colonel Carmichael); Frank Faylen (Sergeant Chillingbacker); Anthony (Tony) Curtis (Captain Jones); Mikel Conrad (Major Garber); Loren Tindall (Major Richards); Charles Meredith (Banker Munroe); Chill Wills (The Voice of Francis the Talking

Mule); Harry Harvey, Howard Negley, and Peter Prouse (Correspondents); Judd Holdren (Ambulance Man); Al Ferguson (Captain Dean); Roger Moore (M. C. Major).

WINCHESTER '73 (Universal, 1950), 92 min.
Producer, Aaron Rosenberg; director, Anthony Mann; based on the story by Stuart N. Lake; screenplay, Robert L. Richards and Borden Chase; art directors, Bernard Herzbrun and Nathan Juran; music director, Joseph Gershenson; camera, William Daniels; editor, Edward Curtiss.

James Stewart (Lin McAdam); Shelley Winters (Lola Manners); Dan Duryea (Waco Johnny Dean); Stephen McNally (Dutch Henry Brown); Millard Mitchell (Frankie "High Spade" Wilson); Charles Drake (Steve Miller); John McIntire (Joe Lamont); Will Geer (Wyatt Earp); Jay C. Flippen (Sergeant Wilkes); Rock Hudson (Young Bull); John Alexander (Jack Riker); Steve Brodie (Wesley); James Millican (Wheeler); Abner Biberman (Latigo Means); Anthony (Tony) Curtis (Doan); James Best (Crater); Gregg Martell (Mossman); Frank Chase (Cavalryman); Chuck Roberson (Long Tom); Carol Henry (Dudeen); Ray Teal (Marshal Noonan); Virginia Mullens (Mrs. Jameson); John Doucette (Roan Daley); Chief Yowlachie (Indian); Edmund Cobb (Target Watcher); Duke Yorke (First Man); Bud Osborne (Station Master); Ted Mapes (Bartender); John War Eagle (Indian Interpreter); Jennings Miles (Stage Coach Driver); Bonnie Kay Eddy (Betty Jameson).

SIERRA (Universal, 1950) C-83 min.
Producer, Michel Kraike; director, Alfred E. Green; based on the novel by Stuart Hardy; screenplay, Edna Anhalt; art directors, Bernard Herzbrun and Robert F. Boyle; music, Walter Scharf; camera, Russell Metty; editor, Ted J. Kent.

Wanda Hendrix (Riley Martin); Audie Murphy (Ring Hassard); Burl Ives (Lonesome); Dean Jagger (Jeff Hassard); Richard Rober (Big Mati); Anthony (Tony) Curtis (Brent Coulter); Houseley Stevenson (Sam Coulter); Elliott Reid (Duke Lafferty).

I WAS A SHOPLIFTER (Universal, 1950), 74 min.
Producer, Leonard Goldstein; director, Charles Lamont; story-screenplay, Irwin Gielgud; music director, Milton Schwarzwald; camera, Irving Glassberg; editor, Otto Ludwig.

Scott Brady (Jeff Andrews); Mona Freeman (Faye Burton); Andrea King (Ina Perdue); Anthony Curtis (Pepe); Charles Drake (Herb Klaxon); Gregg Martell (The Champ); Larry Keating (Harry Dunson); Robert Gist (Barkie Neff); Michael Raffetto (Sheriff Bascom); Rock Hudson (Bit).

AS TONY CURTIS

KANSAS RAIDERS (Universal, 1950), C-80 min.

Producer, Ted Richmond; director, Ray Enright; story-screenplay, Robert L. Richard; art directors, Bernard Herzbrun and Emrich Nicholson; music, Joseph Gershenson; camera, Irving Glassberg; editor, Milton Carruth.

Audie Murphy (Jesse James); Brian Donlevy (Quantrill); Marguerite Chapman (Kate Clarke); Scott Brady (Bill Anderson); Tony Curtis (Kit Dalton); Richard Arlen (Union Captain); Richard Long (Frank James); James Best (Cole Younger); John Kellogg (Red Leg Leader); Dewey Martin (James Younger); George Chandler (Willie); Charles Delaney (Pell); Richard Egan (First Lieutenant); Dave Wolfe (Tate); Mira McKinney (Woman); Sam Flint (Bank President); Buddy Roosevelt (Another Red Leg); Larry McGrath (Man in Crowd); Ed Peil, Sr. (Bank Teller).

THE PRINCE WHO WAS A THIEF (Universal, 1951), C-87 min.

Producer, Leonard Goldstein; director, Rudolph Mate; based on the story by Theodore Dreiser; screenplay, Gerald Drayson Adams, Aeneas MacKenzie; art directors, Bernard Herzbrun and Emrich Nicholson; music director, Hans J. Salter; camera, Irving Glassberg; editor, Edward Curtiss.

Tony Curtis (Julna); Piper Laurie (Tina); Everett Sloane (Yussef); Betty Garde (Mirna); Jeff Corey (Mokar); Peggie Castle (Princess Yasmin); Nita Bieber (Cahuena); Marvin Miller (Hakar); Donald Randolph (Mustapha); Hayden Rorke (Basra); Fred Graff (Zocco); Midge Ware (Sari); Carol Varga (Beulah); Susan Cabot (Girl); Milada Mladova (Dancer); King Donovan (Merat); Robert Rockwell (Bogo); James Vincent (Babu); Richard Morris (Taif); Jack Briggs (Officer); Nolan Leary (Dignitary); Frank Lackteen (Blind Beggar); Buddy Roosevelt (Merchant); George Magrill (Guard).

FLESH AND FURY (Universal, 1952), 82½ min.

Producer, Leonard Goldstein; director, Joseph Pevney; story, William Alland; screenplay, Bernard Gordon; art directors, Bernard Herzbrun and Emrich Nicholson; music, Hans J. Salter; camera, Irving Glassberg; editor, Virgil Vogel.

Tony Curtis (Paul Callan); Jan Sterling (Sonya Bartow); Mona Freeman (Ann Hollis); Wallace Ford (Jack Richardson); Connie Gilchrist (Ma Richardson); Katherine Locke (Mrs. Hollis); Harry Shannon (Mike Callan); Louis Jean Heydt (Andy Randolph); Nella Walker (Mrs. Hackett); Harry Guardino (Lou Callan); Joe Gray (Cliff); Harry Raven (Murphy); Ted Stanhope (Butler); Ken Patterson (Doctor Lester); Virginia Gregg (Claire); Grace Hayle (Mrs. Bien); Frank Wilcox (Business Man); Harry Cheshire (Dr. Gundling); Tommy Farrell (Rocky); George Eldredge (Dr. Buell); Bruce Richardson (Burns); Beatrice Gray (Mother); Edwin Parker (Man); Sam Pierce (Nash); Karl "Killer" Davis (Broadway Character); Ed Hinton (Cop); Sally Yarnell (Bit); Ed Hinkle (Student); Bryan Forbes (Fighter); Lucille Curtis (Maid).

NO ROOM FOR THE GROOM (Universal, 1952), 82 min.

Producer, Ted Richmond; director, Douglas Sirk; based on the novel *My True Love* by Darwin L. Teilhet; screenplay, Joseph Hoffman; art directors, Bernard Herzbrun and Richard H. Riedel; set decorators, Russell A. Gausman and Ruby R. Levitt; costumes, Bill Thomas; assistant directors, Fred Frank and George Lollier; dialog director, Jack Daniels; camera, Clifford Stine; editor, Russell Schoengarth.

Tony Curtis (Alvah Morrell); Piper Laurie (Lee Kingshead); Don De Fore (Herman Strouple); Spring Byington (Mamma Kingshead); Jack Kelly (Will Stubbins); Lillian Bronson (Aunt Elsa); Paul McVey (Dr. Trotter); Stephen Chase (Mr. Taylor); Lee Aaker (Donovan Murray); Frank Sully (Cousin Luke); James Parnell (Cousin Mike); Lee Turnbull (Cousin Pete); Dolores Mann (Cousin Susie); Fess Parker (Cousin Ben); Helen Noyes (Cousin Emmy); Janet Clark (Cousin Dorothy); Fred J. Miller (Cousin Henry); Lynne Hunter (Cousin Betty); Harold Lockwood, Catherine Howard, Lucille LaMarr and William O'Driscoll (Relatives); David Janssen (Soldier); Richard Mayer (Man on Street); Jack Daly (Customer at Bar).

SON OF ALI BABA (Universal, 1952), C-75 min.
Producer, Leonard Goldstein; director, Kurt Neumann; story-screenplay, Gerald Drayson Adams; art directors, Bernard Herzbrun and Emrich Nicholson; set decorators, Russell A. Gausman and John Austin; music director, Joseph Gershenson; choreography, Harold Belfer; camera, Maury Gertsman; editor, Virgil Vogel.

Tony Curtis (Kashma Baba); Piper Laurie (Kiki); Susan Cabot (Tala); William Reynolds (Mustafa); Hugh O'Brian (Hussein); Victor Jory (Caliph); Morris Ankrum (Ali Baba); Philip Van Zandt (Kareeb); Leon Belasco (Babu); Palmer Lee (Gregg Palmer) (Farouk); Barbara Knudson (Theda); Alice Kelley (Calu); Gerald Mohr (Captain Youssef); Milada Mladova (Zaza); Katherine Warren (Princess Karma); Robert Barrat (Commandant).

HOUDINI (Paramount, 1953), C-106 min.
Producer, George Pal; associate producer, Frank Freeman, Jr.; director, George Marshall; based on the book by Harold Kellock; screenplay, Philip Yordan; music, Roy Webb; art directors, Hal Pereira and Al Nozaki; set decorators, Sam Comer and Ray Moyer; assistant director, Michael D. Moore; technical advisor, Dunninger; costumes, Edith Head; sound, Harry Mills and Gene Garvin; special camera, Gordon Jennings; camera, Ernest Laszlo; editor, George Tomasini.

Tony Curtis (Houdini); Janet Leigh (Bess); Torin Thatcher (Otto); Angela Clarke (Mrs. Weiss); Stefan Schnabel (Prosecuting Attorney); Ian Wolfe (Fante); Sig Rumann (Schultz); Michael Pate (Dooley); Connie Gilchrist (Mrs. Schultz); Mary Murphy and Joanne Gilbert (Girls); Mabel Paige (Medium); Malcolm Lee Beggs (Warden); Frank Orth (White-haired Man); Barry Bernard (Inspector); Douglas Spencer (Sims); Peter Baldwin (Fred); Richard Shannon (Miner); Elsie Ames and Nick Arno (Entertainers); Esther Garber (Esther's Girl Friend); Norma Jean Eckart (Girl in Guillotine Act); Lewis Martin (Editor); Lawrence Ryle (German Judge); Cliff Clark (Barker); Jody Gilbert (Fat Girl); Edward Clark (Doorman); Grace Hayle (Woman who Screams).

THE ALL AMERICAN (Universal, 1953), 83 min.
Producer, Aaron Rosenberg; director, Jesse Hibbs; story-screenplay, D. D.

Beauchamp; art directors, Bernard Herzbrun and Eric Orbom; camera, Maury Gertsman; editor, Edward Curtiss.

Tony Curtis (Nick Bonelli); Lori Nelson (Sharon Wallace); Palmer Lee (Gregg Palmer) (Hunt Cameron); Mamie Van Doren (Susie Ward); Richard Long (Howard Carter); Herman Hickman (Jumbo); Paul Cavanagh (Professor Banning); Donald Randolph (David Carter); Barney Phillips (Clipper Colton); Jimmy Hunt (Whizzer); Douglas Kennedy (Tate Hardy); John Harmon (Bartender); Paul F. Smith (Smith); Stuart Whitman (Zip Parker); Morgan Jones (Casey); Frank Gifford (Stan Pomeroy); George Bozanic (McManus); Fortune Gordien (Gronski); Jim Hardy (Dutch Wilson); Malcolm Cassell (Louie); Myrna Hansen (Girl at Party); Bill Baldwin (Announcer); Bill Radovich (Joe); Harris Brown (Butler); Jim Sears (Dartmore Quarterback); Elmer Willhoite (Kenton); Douglas Deems (Usher).

FORBIDDEN (Universal, 1953), 85 min.
Producer, Ted Richmond; director, Rudolph Mate; story, William Sackheim; screenplay, Sackheim and Gil Doud; art directors, Bernard Herzbrun and Richard Riedel; camera, William Daniels; editor, Edward Curtiss.

Tony Curtis (Eddie Darrow); Joanne Dru (Christine Lawrence); Lyle Bettger (Justin Keit); Victor Sen Yung (Allan); Marvin Miller (Cliff Chalmer); Peter Mamakos (Sam); Mamie Van Doren (Singer); Mae Tai Sing (Soo Lee); Howard Chuman (Hon-Fai); Weaver Levy (Tang); Harold Fong (Wong); David Sharpe (Leon); Aen Ling Chow and Leemoi Chu (Girl Dealers); Alan Dexter (Barney); Barry Bernard (Black); Harry Lauter (Holly); Reginald Sheffield (Englishman); Alphonse Martell (Guest); Al Ferguson (Harbor Master); Jimmy Gray (Guard); Spencer Chan (Chin).

BEACHHEAD (United Artists, 1954), C-89 min.
Producer, Howard W. Koch; director, Stuart Heisler; based on the novel by Richard G. Hubler; screenplay, Richard Alan Simmons; music, Emil Newman and Arthur Lange; camera, Gordon Avil; editor, John F. Schreyer.

Tony Curtis (Burke); Frank Lovejoy (Sergeant Fletcher); Mary Murphy (Nina); Eduard Franz (Bouchard); Skip Homeier (Reynolds); John Doucette (Major Scott); Alan Wells (Biggerman); Sunshine Akira Fukunaga (Japanese Sailor); Dan Aoki (Sniper); Steamboat Mokuahi (Malanesian).

JOHNNY DARK (Universal, 1954), C-85 min.
Producer, William Alland; director, George Sherman; screenplay, Franklin Coen; art directors, Bernard Herzbrun and Robert Boyle; camera, Carl Guthrie; editor, Edward Curtiss.

Tony Curtis (Johnny Dark); Piper Laurie (Liz Kent); Don Taylor (Duke Benson); Paul Kelly (Jim Scott); Ilka Chase (Abbie Binns); Sidney Blackmer (James Fielding); Ruth Hampton (Miss Border-to-Border); Russell Johnson (Emory); Joseph Sawyer (Svenson); Robert Nichols (Smitty); Pierre Watkin (E. J. Winston); Ralph Montgomery (Morgan); William Leslie (Phil Clark); Brett Halsey (Co-driver); Scat Man Crothers (Himself); Vernon Rich (Ross); Robert Bice (Guard); Byron Kane (Reno Radio Announcer); Emily Belser (Waitress);

Don Mitchell (Announcer); Rick Burgess (Elevator Operator); John McKee (Patrolman).

THE BLACK SHIELD OF FALWORTH (Universal, 1954), C-99 min.

Producer, Robert Arthur; associate producer, Melville Tucker; director, Rudolph Mate; based on the novel *Men of Iron* by Howard Pyle; screenplay, Oscar Brodney; music supervisor, Joseph Gershenson; art director, Alexander Golitzen; camera, Irving Glassberg; editor, Ted J. Kent.

Tony Curtis (Myles Falworth); Janet Leigh (Lady Anne); David Farrar (Earl of Alban); Barbara Rush (Meg Falworth); Herbert Marshall (Earl of Mackworth); Rhys Williams (Diccon Bowman); Daniel O'Herlihy (Prince Hal); Torin Thatcher (Sir James); Ian Keith (King Henry IV); Patrick O'Neal (Walter Blunt); Craig Hill (Francis Gascoyne); Doris Lloyd (Dame Ellen); Leonard Mudie (Friar Edward); Maurice Marsac (Count de Vermois); Leo Britt (Sir Robert); Charles FitzSimons (Giles); Gary Montgomery (Peter); Claud Allister (Sir George); Robin Camp (Roger Ingoldsby).

SO THIS IS PARIS (Universal, 1954), C-96 min.

Producer, Albert J. Cohen; director, Richard Quine; story, Ray Buffum; screenplay, Charles Hoffman; assistant directors, William Holland and George Lollier; music, Tony Sherrell and Phil Mooney; music supervisor, Joseph Gershenson; choreography, Gene Nelson and Lee Scott; art directors, Alexander Golitzen and Eugene Lourie; gowns, Rosemary Odell; camera, Maury Gertsman; editor, Virgil Vogel

Tony Curtis (Joe Maxwell); Gloria De Haven (Colette D'Avril [Jane Mitchell]); Gene Nelson (Al Howard); Corinne Calvet (Suzanne Sorel); Paul Gilbert (Davey Jones); Allison Hayes (Carmen); Myrna Hansen (Ingrid); Christiane Martel (Christiane); Ann Codee (Grand'mere Marie); Arthur Gould-Porter (Albert); Roger Etienne (Pierre Deshons); Lizette Guy (Jeannine); Michelle Ducasse (Simone); Maithe Iragui (Cecile); Lucien Plauzoles (Eugene); Numa Lapeyre (Charlot); Pat Horn (Dancer); Regina Dombek (Miss Photo Flash); Jean De Briac (Mr. Sorel); Rolfe Sedan (Cab Driver); Andre Villon (Gendarme); Marcel De La Brosse (Headwaiter); Carlos Albert (Mailman).

SIX BRIDGES TO CROSS (Universal, 1955), 96 min.

Producer, Aaron Rosenberg; director, Joseph Pevney; based on the article "They Stole $2,500,000—And Got Away with It" by Joseph Dineen; screenplay, Sidney Boehm; art directors, Alexander Golitzen and Robert Clatworthy; song, Jeff Chandler and Henry Mancini; music director, Joseph Gershenson; assistant directors, Ronnie Rondell and Marsh Green; gowns, Jay Morley, Jr.; camera, William Daniels; editors, Russell Shoengarth and Verna MacCurran.

Tony Curtis (Jerry Florea); Julia Adams (Ellen Gallagher); George Nader (Edward Gallagher); Jay C. Flippen (Vincent Concannon); Kendall Clark (Sanborn); Sal Mineo (Jerry Florea as a Boy); Jan Merlin (Andy Norris); Richard Castle (Skids Radzievich); William Murphy (Red Flanagan); Kenny Roberts (Red Flanagan as a Boy); Peter Avramo (Hymie Weiner); Hal Conklin (Jerry's Attorney); Don Keefer (Sherman); Harry Bartell (Father Bonelli); Tito

Vuolo (Angie); Ken Patterson (Inspector J. L. Walsh); Paul Dubov (Bandit Leader); Peter Leeds (Harris); James F. Stone (George Russell); Howard Wright (Judge); Elizabeth Kerr (Governess); Charles Victor (Clerk); Carl Frank (Judge Manning); Grant Gordon (Dr. Moreno); Di Di Roberts, Doris Meade, and Harold W. Miller (Jail Visitors); John J. Muldoon (Radio Dispatcher).

THE PURPLE MASK (Universal, 1955), C-82 min.
Producer, Howard Christie; director, H. Bruce Humberstone; based on the play *Le Chevalier Au Masques* by Paul Armont, Jean Manoussi; screenplay, Oscar Brodney; adaptation, Charles Latour; art directors, Alexander Golitzen and Eric Orbom; music director, Joseph Gershenson; assistant directors, Joseph E. Kenny and Phil Bowles; costumes, Bill Thomas; camera, Irving Glassberg; editor, Ted J. Kent.

Tony Curtis (Rene); Colleen Miller (Laurette); Dan O'Herlihy (Brisquet); Gene Barry (Captain Laverne); Angela Lansbury (Madame Valentine); George Dolenz (Marcel Cadonal); John Hoyt (Rochet); Donald Randolph (Majolin); Robert Cornthwaite (Napoleon); Stephen Bekassy (Baron De Morleve); Paul Cavanagh (Duc de Latour); Myrna Hansen (Constance); Allison Hayes (Irene); Betty Jane Howarth (Yvonne); Carol Milletaire (Edouard); Gene Darcy (De Morsanne); Robert Hunter (De Vivanne); Richard Avonde (Roger); Glase Lohman (Raoul); Diane Dubois (Sabine); Jane Easton (Marie); Richard Richonne (Passerby); Everett Glass (Father Brochard); Jean De Briac (Count De Chauvac); Adrienne D'Ambricourt (Madame Anais); George Bruggeman (French Officer); Albert Godderis (Old Servant).

THE SQUARE JUNGLE (Universal, 1955), 80 min.
Producer, Albert Zugsmith; director, Jerry Hopper; story-screenplay, George Zuckerman; art directors, Alexander Golitzen and Alfred Sweeney; music, Heinz Roemheld; music director, Joseph Gershenson; assistant directors, Frank Shaw and Willard Kirklam; camera, George Robinson; editor, Paul Weatherwax.

Tony Curtis (Eddie Quaid [Packy Glennon]); Pat Crowley (Julie Walsh); Ernest Borgnine (Bernie Browne); Paul Kelly (Jim McBreede); Jim Backus (Pat Quaid); Leigh Snowden (Lorraine Evans); John Day (Al Gorski); David Janssen (Jack Lindsay); John Marley (Tommy Dillon); Barney Phillips (Dan Selby); Joe Vitale (Tony Adamson); Wendell Niles (Chicago Ring Announcer); Kay Stewart (Mrs. Gorski); Frank Marlowe (Rip Kane); Frankie Van and Walter J. Ekwert, (Seconds); Joe Louis (Himself); Carmen McRae (Singer); Clancy Cooper (Mike Walsh); Jesse Kirkpatrick (The Boss); Frank Moran (Referee); Dennis Moore (Bit); Barry Regan (Bartender); Jimmy Cross (Hawker).

TRAPEZE (United Artists, 1956), C-105 min.
Producer, James Hill; director, Sir Carol Reed; based on the novel *The Killing Frost* by Max Catto; adaptation, Liam O'Brien; screenplay, James R. Webb; art director, Rino Mondellini; assistant directors, Dick McWhorter, Michael Romanoff, and Robert Gendre; music, Malcolm Arnold; wardrobe, Frank Salvi and Gladys De Segonzac; camera, Robert Krasker; editor, Bert Bates.

Burt Lancaster (Mike Ribble); Tony Curtis (Tino Orsini); Gina Lollobrigida (Lola); Katy Jurado (Rosa); Thomas Gomez (Bouglione); Johnny Puleo (Max the Dwarf); Minor Watson (John Ringling North); Gerald Landry (Chikki); J. P. Kerrien (Otto); Sidney James (Snake Man); Gabrielle Fontan (Old Woman); Pierre Tabard (Paul); Gamil Ratab (Stefan); Michel Thomas (Ringmaster); and: Edward Hagopian, Eddie Ward, Sally Marlowe, Fay Alexander, The Arriolas, Mme. Felco Cipriano, The Codreanos, The Gimma Boys, and Simpion Bouglione.

THE RAWHIDE YEARS (Universal, 1956), C-85 min.
Producer, Stanley Rubin; director, Rudolph Maté; based on the novel by Norman A. Fox; adaptation, Robert Presnell, Jr. and D. D. Beauchamp; screenplay, Earl Felton; assistant directors, John Sherwood and Terry Nelson; music director, Joseph Gershenson; music, Frank Skinner and Hans J. Salter; songs, Peggy Lee and Laurindo Almeida; Frederick Herbert and Arnold Hughes; costumes, Bill Thomas; art directors, Alexander Golitzen and Richard H. Riedel; camera, Irving Glassberg; editor, Russell Schoengarth.

Tony Curtis (Ben Matthews); Colleen Miller (Zoe); Arthur Kennedy (Rick Harper); William Demarest (Brand Comfort); William Gargan (Marshal Sommers); Peter Van Eyck (Andre Boucher); Minor Watson (Matt Comfort); Robert Wilke (Neal); Donald Randolph (Carrico); Trevor Bardette (Captain); Chubby Johnson (Gif Lessing); James Anderson (Deputy Wade); Robert Foulk (Mate); Leigh Snowden (Miss Vanilla Bissell); Don Beddoe (Frank Porter); Malcolm Atterbury (Paymaster); Charles Evans (Colonel Swope); I. Stanford Jolley (Man); Rex Lease (Card Player); Chuck Roberson (Johnny); Marlene Felton (Miss Dal-Marie Smith); Clarence Lung (Chinese Stewart); Lane Bradford (Pirate).

MISTER CORY (Universal, 1957), C-92 min.
Producer, Robert Arthur; director, Blake Edwards; story, Leo Rosten; screenplay, Edwards; art directors, Alexander Golitzen and Eric Orbom; music supervisor, Joseph Gershenson; assistant director, Ronnie Rondell; gowns, Bill Thomas; special camera, Clifford Stone; camera, Russell Metty; editor, Edward Curtiss.

Tony Curtis (Cory); Martha Hyer (Abby Vollard); Charles Bickford (Biloxi); Kathryn Grant (Jen Vollard); William Reynolds (Alex Wyncott); Russ Morgan (Ruby Matrobe); Henry Daniell (Earnshaw); Willis Bouchey (Mr. Vollard); Joan Banks (Lola); Louise Lorimer (Mrs. Vollard); Harry Landers (Andy); Dick Crockett (The Cook); Hylton Socher (Bellboy); Glen Kramer (Ronnie Chambers); Paul Bryar (Dealer); George Eldredge (Guest); Charles Horvath (Truck Driver); Jack Gargan (Golfer); Dick Monda (Boy); Billy Eagle (Vendor); Anna Stein (Bit).

THE SWEET SMELL OF SUCCESS (United Artists, 1957), 96 min.
Executive producer, Harold Hecht; producer, James Hill; director, Alexander Mackendrick; based on the novel by Ernest Lehman; screenplay, Lehman and Clifford Odets; music, Elmer Bernstein; songs, Chico Hamilton and Fred

Katz; art director, Edward Carrere; camera, James Wong Howe.

Burt Lancaster (J. J. Hunsecker); Tony Curtis (Sidney Falco); Susan Harrison (Susan Hunsecker); Marty Milner (Steve Dallas); Sam Levene (Frank D'Angelo); Barbara Nichols (Rita); Jeff Donnell (Sally); Joseph Leon (Robard); Edith Atwater (Mary); Emile Meyer (Harry Kello); Joe Frisco (Herbie Temple); David White (Otis Elwell); Lawrence Dobkin (Leo Bartha); Lurene Tuttle (Mrs. Bartha); Queenie Smith (Mildred Tam); Autumn Russell (Linda); Jay Adler (Manny Davis); Lewis Charles (Al Evans).

THE MIDNIGHT STORY (Universal, 1957), 89 min.

·Producer, Robert Arthur; director, Joseph Pevney; story, Edwin Blum; screenplay, Blum and John Robinson; assistant director, Joseph E. Kenny; art directors, Alexander Golitzen and Eric Orbom; music director, Joseph Gershenson; special camera, Clifford Stine; camera, Russell Metty; editor, Ted J. Kent.

Tony Curtis (Joe Martini); Marisa Pavan (Anna Malatesta); Gilbert Roland (Sylvio Malatesta); Jay C. Flippen (Sergeant Jack Gillen); Argentina Brunetti (Mama Malatesta); Ted de Corsia (Lieutenant Kilrain); Richard Monda (Peanuts Malatesta); Kathleen Freeman (Rosa Cuneo); Herbert Vigram (Charlie Cuneo); Peggy June Maley (Veda Pinelli); John Cliff (Father Giuseppe); Russ Conway (Sergeant Sommers); Chico Vejar (Frankie Pellatrini); Tito Vuolu (Grocer); Helen Wallace (Mother Catherine); James Hyland (Frank Wilkins.

British release title: **Appointment with a Shadow.**

THE VIKINGS (United Artists, 1958), C-114 min.

Producer, Jerry Bresler; director, Richard Fleischer; based on the novel by Edison Marshall; adaptation, Dale Wasserman; screenplay, Calder Willingham; assistant director, Andre Smagghe; music, Mario Nascimbene; production designer, Harper Goff; animation prolog, UPA Pictures, Inc.; second unit director, Elmo Williams; makeup, John O'Gorman and Neville Smallwood; sound, Joe de Bretagne; camera, Jack Cardiff; editorial supervisor, Williams.

Kirk Douglas (Einar); Tony Curtis (Eric); Ernest Borgnine (Ragnar); Janet Leigh (Morgana); James Donald (Egbert); Alexander Knox (Father Goodwin); Frank Thring (Aella); Maxine Audley (Enid); Eileen Way (Kitala); Edric Connor (Sandpiper); Dandy Nichols (Bridget); Per Buckhoj (Bjorm); Almut Berg (Pigtails).

KINGS GO FORTH (United Artists, 1958), 109 min.

Producer, Frank Ross; associate producer, Richard Ross; director, Delmer Daves; based on the novel by Joe David Brown; screenplay, Merle Miller; music, Elmer Bernstein; art director, Fernando Carrere; camera, Daniel L. Fapp; editor, William Murphy.

Frank Sinatra (Sam Loggins); Tony Curtis (Britt Harris); Natalie Wood (Monique Blair); Leora Dana (Mrs. Blair); Karl Swenson (Colonel); Ann Codee

(Mme. Brieux); Jackie Berthe (Jean Francoise); Marie Isnard (Old Woman with Wine); Jazz Combo: Pete Candoli (Trumpet); Red Norvo (Vibraphone); Mel Lewis (Drums); Richie Kamuca (Tenor Sax); Red Wooten (Bass); Jimmy Weible (Guitar).

THE DEFIANT ONES (United Artists, 1958), 97 min.

Producer-director, Stanley Kramer; screenplay, Nathan E. Douglas and Harold Jacob Smith; production designer, Rudolph Sternad; music, Ernest Gold; song, William C. Handy and Chris Smith; art director, Fernando Carrere; set decorator, Joe Kish; costumes, Joe King; assistant director, Paul Helmick; makeup, Don Cash; special effects, Alex Weldon; camera, Sam Leavitt; editor, Frederic Knudtson.

Tony Curtis (John "Joker" Jackson); Sidney Poitier (Noah Cullen); Cara Williams (The Woman); Theodore Bikel (Sheriff Max Muller); Charles McGraw (Captain Frank Gibbons); Lon Chaney, Jr. (Big Sam); King Donovan (Solly); Claude Akins (Mac); Lawrence Dobkin (Editor); Whit Bissell (Lou Gans); Carl Switzer (Angie); Kevin Coughlin (The Kid).

THE PERFECT FURLOUGH (Universal, 1958), C-93 min.

Producer, Robert Arthur; director, Blake Edwards; screenplay, Stanley Shapiro; art director, Alexander Golitzen; set decorators, Russell A. Gausman and Oliver Emert; costumes, Bill Thomas; music, Frank Skinner; music supervisor, Joseph Gershenson; song, Skinner, Diane Lampert, and Richard Loring; makeup, Bud Westmore; assistant directors, Frank Shaw and Terry Nelson; camera, Phil Lathrop; editor, Milton Carruth.

Tony Curtis (Corporal Paul Hodges); Janet Leigh (Lieutenant Vicki Loren); Keenan Wynn (Harvey Franklin); Linda Cristal (Sandra Roca); Elaine Stritch (Liz Baker); Marcel Dalio (Henri); Les Tremayne (Colonel Leland); Jay Novello (Rene); King Donovan (Major Collins); Gordon Jones and Dick Crockett (M.P.s); Alvy Moore (Private Marvin Brewer); Lilyan Chauvin (French Nurse); Troy Donahue (Sergeant Nickles); Eugene Borden (French Doctor); Marcel Rousseau (Magistrate); James Lanphier (Assistant Hotel Manager); Roger Etienne (Bellboy); Manuel Paris (Doorman); Phil Harvey (Captain Morgan); Hugh Lawrence (Captain Johnson); Vernon Rich (Middle Aged Man); Carleton Young (Major Morrow); Sheila Keddy (Mrs. Appleton); Peter Camlin (Winemaker); Albert Carrier (Hairdresser); Genevieve Aumont (Pregnant Woman); Karen Scott (French Waitress); Gail Bonney (Spinster); Frankie Darro (Man in Cast); Jack Chefe (Maitre d'); Scotty Groves (Medic); Vic Romito (Reporter).

British release title: **Strictly for Pleasure.**

SOME LIKE IT HOT (United Artists, 1959), 120 min.

Producer, Billy Wilder; associate producers, Doane Harrison and I. A. L. Diamond; director, Wilder; suggested by a story by R. Thoeren and M. Logan; screenplay, Wilder and Diamond; music, Adolph Deutsch; song supervisor, Matty Malneck; assistant director, Sam Nelson; makeup, Emile LaVigne; art director, Ted Haworth; set decorator, Edward G. Boyle; wardrobe, Bert Henrikson; Miss Monroe's gowns, Orry-Kelly; sound, Fred Lau; special effects, Milt Rice; camera, Charles Lang, Jr.; editor, Arthur Schmidt.

Marilyn Monroe (Sugar); Tony Curtis (Joe [Josephine]); Jack Lemmon (Jerry [Daphne]); George Raft (Spats Colombo); Pat O'Brien (Mulligan); Joe E. Brown (Osgood Fielding III); Nehemiah Persoff (Little Bonaparte); Joan Shawlee (Sue); Billy Gray (Poliakoff); George E. Stone (Toothpick Charlie); Dave Barry (Beinstock); Mike Mazurki, Harry Wilson (Spats' Henchman); Beverly Wills (Dolores); Barbara Drew (Nellie); Edward G. Robinson, Jr. (Johnny Paradise).

OPERATION PETTICOAT (Universal, 1959), C-124 min.
Producer, Robert Arthur; director, Blake Edwards; suggested by a story by Paul King, Joseph Stone; screenplay, Stanley Shapiro and Maurice Richlin; art directors, Alexander Golitzen and Robert E. Smith; set decorators, Russell A. Gausman and Oliver Emert; gowns, Bill Thomas; makeup, Bud Westmore; music, David Rose; color consultant, Henri Jaffa; assistant director, Frank Shaw; sound, Leslie I. Carey and Vernon W. Cramer; special camera, Clifford Stine; camera, Russell Harlan; editors, Ted J. Kent and Frank Gross.

Cary Grant (Admiral Matt Sherman); Tony Curtis (Lieutenant Nick Holden); Joan O'Brien (Dolores Crandall); Dina Merrill (Barbara Duran); Arthur O'Connell (Tostin); Gene Evans (Molumphrey); Robert F. Simon (Captain J. B. Henderson); George Dunn (The Prophet); Richard Sargent (Stovall); Virginia Gregg (Major Edna Howard); Robert Gist (Watson); Gavin MacLeod (Hunkle); Dick Crockett (Harmon); Clarence Lung (Ramon); Madlyn Rhue (Lieutenant Claire Reid); Marion Ross (Lieutenant Ruth Colfax); Nicky Blair (Kraus); John Morley (Williams); Robert Hoy (Reiner); Frankie Darro (Dooley); Tony Pastor, Jr. (Fox); Leon Lontoc (Filipino Farmer); Alan Dexter (Navy Chief); Vi Ingraham (Pregnant Filipino Woman); Trusi Faiivae (Witch Doctor).

WHO WAS THAT LADY? (Columbia, 1960), 115 min.
Producer, Norman Krasna; director, George Sidney; based on the play *Who Was That Lady I Saw You With?* by Krasna; screenplay, Krasna; assistant director, David Silver; music, Andre Previn; song, Sammy Cahn and James Van Heusen; gowns, Jean Louis; art director, Edward Haworth; set decorator, James M. Crowe; makeup, Ben Lane; sound, Charles J. Rich and James Flaster; camera, Harry Stradling; editor, Viola Lawrence.

Tony Curtis (David Wilson); Dean Martin (Michael Haney); Janet Leigh (Ann Wilson); James Whitmore (Harry Powell); John McIntire (Bob Doyle); Barbara Nichols (Gloria Coogle); Larry Keating (Parker); Larry Storch (Orenov); Simon Oakland (Belka); Joi Lansing (Florence Coogle); Barbara Hines (Girl); Marion Javits (Miss Melish); Michael Lane (Glinka); Kam Tong (Lee Wong); William Newell (Schultz); Mark Allen (Joe Bendix); Snub Pollard (Tattoo Artist).

THE RAT RACE (Paramount, 1960), C-105 min.
Producers, William Perlberg and George Seaton; director, Robert Mulligan;

based on the play by Garson Kanin; screenplay, Kanin; music, Elmer Bernstein; costumes, Edith Head; art directors, Hal Pereira and Tambi Larsen; set decorators, Sam Comer and Frank McKelvy; assistant director, Richard Caffey; makeup, Wally Westmore; color consultant, Richard Mueller; sound, Hugo Grenzbach and Winston Leverett; special camera effects, John P. Fulton; process camera, Farciot Edouart; camera, Robert Burks; editor, Alma Macrorie.

Tony Curtis (Pete Hammond, Jr.); Debbie Reynolds (Peggy Brown); Jack Oakie (Mac); Kay Medford (Soda); Don Rickles (Nellie); Joe Bushkin (Frankie); Gerry Mulligan (Gerry); Sam Butera (Carl); Marjorie Bennett (Edie); Norman Fell (Phone Repairman); Lisa Drake (Toni); Hal K. Dawson (Man).

SPARTACUS (Universal, 1960), C-190 min.
Executive producer, Kirk Douglas; producer, Edward Lewis; director, Stanley Kubrick; based on the novel by Howard Fast; screenplay, Dalton Trumbo; music-music conductor, Alex North; production designer, Alexander Golitzen; art director, Eric Orbom; set decorators, Russell A. Gausman and Julia Heron; main titles designer, Saul Bass; historical-technical advisor, Vittorio Nino Novarese; wardrobe, Peruzzi; Miss Simmons' costumes, Bill Thomas; makeup, Bud Westmore; assistant director, Marshall Green; sound, Waldon O. Watson, Joe Lapis, Murray Spivack, and Ronald Pierce; camera, Russell Metty; additional camera, Clifford Stone; editor, Robert Lawrence; assistant editors, Robert Schulte and Fred Chulak.

Kirk Douglas (Spartacus); Laurence Olivier (Crassus); Jean Simmons (Varinia); Tony Curtis (Antoninus); Charles Laughton (Gracchus); Peter Ustinov (Batiatus); John Gavin (Julius Caesar); Nina Foch (Helena); Herbert Lom (Tigranes); John Ireland (Crixus); John Dall (Glabrus); Charles McGraw (Marcellus); Joanna Barnes (Claudia); Harold J. Stone (David); Woody Strode (Draba); Peter Brocco (Ramon); Paul Lambert (Giannicus); Nicholas Dennis (Dionysus); Robert J. Wilke (Guard Captain); Frederic Worlock (Laelius); John Hoyt (Roman Officer); Dayton Lummis (Symmachus); Jo Summers (Slave Girl); Dale Van Sickel (Trainer); Ted De Corsia (Legionary); Hallene Hill (Beggar Woman); Edwin Parker (Middle Aged Slave); Paul Kruger (Roman Senator); Jack Perkins (Gladiator); Bob Burns (Pirate); Judy Erwin (Child); Chuck Courtney, Tap Canutt, and Joe Canutt (Soldiers).

PEPE (Columbia, 1960), C-195 min.
Producer, George Sidney; associate producer, Jacques Gelman; director, Sidney; based on the play *Broadway Zauber* by Ladislas Bush-Fekete; screen story, Leonard Spigelgass and Sonya Levien; screenplay, Dorothy Kingsley and Claude Binyon; assistant director, David Silver; art director, Ted Haworth; set decorator, William Kiernan; music supervisor-background score, Johnny Green; special musical material, Sammy Cahn, Roger Eden; songs, Andre Previn and Dory Langdon; Hans Wittstatt and Langdon; Previn; and Augustin Lara and Langdon; choreography, Eugene Loring and Alex Romero; makeup, Ben Lane; gowns, Edith Head; camera, Joe MacDonald; editors, Viola Lawrence and Al Clark.

Cantinflas (Pepe); Dan Dailey (Ted Holt); Shirley Jones (Suzie Murphy); Carlos Montalban (Auctioneer); Vicki Trickett (Lupita); Matt Mattox (Dancer);

Hank Henry (Manager); Suzanne Lloyd (Carmen); Carlos Rivas (Carlos); Stephen Bekassy (Jewelry Salesman); Carol Douglas (Waitress); Francisco Reguerra (Priest); Joe Hyams (Charro); Joey Bishop, Michael Callan, Maurice Chevalier, Charles Coburn, Richard Conte, Bing Crosby, Tony Curtis, Bobby Darin, Sammy Davis, Jr., Jimmy Durante, Zsa Zsa Gabor, the voice of Judy Garland, Greer Garson, Hedda Hopper, Ernie Kovacs, Peter Lawford, Janet Leigh, Jack Lemmon, Dean Martin, Jay North, Kim Novak, Andre Previn, Donna Reed, Debbie Reynolds, Edward G. Robinson, Cesar Romero, Frank Sinatra, Billie Burke, Ann B. Davis, William Demarest, Jack Entratter, Colonel E. E. Fogelson, Jane Robinson, and Bunny Waters (Guest Stars); Shirley DeBurgh (Senorita Dancer); Steve Baylor and John Burnside (Parking Lot Attendants); James Bacon (Bartender); Jimmy Cavanaugh (Dealer); Jeanne Manet (French Woman); Robert B. Williams (Immigration Officer); Bonnie Green (Dancer); Lela Bliss (Dowager); Ray Walker (Assistant Director); David Landfield (Announcer's Voice); Margie Nelson (Patron); Dorothy Abbott, Kenner C. Kemp, Steve Carruthers, Jim Waters, and Billy Snyder (Bits); Fred Roberto (Cashier).

THE GREAT IMPOSTER (Universal, 1960), 112 min.

Producer, Robert Arthur; director, Robert Mulligan; based on the book by Robert Crichton; screenplay, Liam O'Brien; art director, Alexander Golitzen; set decorator, Julia Heron; music, Henry Mancini; music supervisor, Joseph Gershenson; makeup, Bud Westmore; assistant directors, Joseph Kenny and Charles Scott, Jr.; sound, Waldon O. Watson and Frank Wilkinson; camera, Robert Burks; editor, Frederic Knudtson.

Tony Curtis (Ferdinand Waldo Demara, Jr.); Karl Malden (Father Devlin); Edmond O'Brien (Captain Glover); Arthur O'Connell (Warden Chandler); Gary Merrill (Pa Demara); Joan Blackman (Catherine Lacey); Raymond Massey (Abbott Donner); Robert Middleton (Brown); Jeanette Nolan (Ma Demara); Sue Ane Langdon (Eulalie); Larry Gates (Cardinal); Mike Kellin (Thompson); Frank Gorshin (Barney); Cindi Wood (WAC Lieutenant); Robert Crawford (Fred Demara, Jr.); Richard Sargent (Hotchkiss); Ward Ramsey (Executive Officer Howard); Doodles Weaver (Farmer); Philip Ahn (Hun Kin); Harry Carey, Jr. (Dr. Joseph Mornay); Jerry Paris (Defense Lieutenant); Herbert Rudley (Senior Officer).

THE OUTSIDER (Universal, 1961), 108 min.

Producer, Sy Bartlett; director, Delbert Mann; based on the book *The Hero of Iwo Jima* by William Bradford Huie; screenplay, Stewart Stern; music-music conductor, Leonard Rosenman; music supervisor, Joseph Gershenson; art directors, Alexander Golitzen and Edward B. Haworth; set decorator, Oliver Emert; assistant director, Ray Gosnell; sound, Waldon O. Watson and Joe Lapis; camera, Joseph La Shelle; editor, Marjorie Fowler.

Tony Curtis (Ira Hamilton Hayes); James Franciscus (Jim Sorenson); Bruce Bennett (Major General Bridges); Gregory Walcott (Sergeant Kiley); Vivian Nathan (Nancy Hayes); Vincent Edwards (George); Miriam Colon (Anita); Edmond Hashim (Jay Morago); Paul Comi (Sergeant Boyle); Stanley Adams (Noomie); Wayne Heffley (Corporal Johnson); Ralph Moody (Uncle); Jeff Silver (McGruder); James Beck (Tyler); Forrest Compton (Bradley); Peter Homer,

Sr. (Mr. Alvarez); Mary Patton (Chairlady); Charley Stevens (Joseph Hayes); Ray Daley (Gagnon); Ronald Trujillo (Kenny Hayes); Walter Woolf King (Ci-. vilian); Al Hodge (Colonel); Kathleen Mulqueen (Mrs. Sorensen); John War Eagle (Mr. Goode); Gertrude Michael (Clubwoman); Ted Bessell (Kid); Gregory Fio Rito (David); Lynda Day (Kim); Jody Johnston (Jane); Tom Sherlock (Assistant); Riley Hill (Delivery Man).

TARAS BULBA (United Artists, 1962), C-122 min.
Producer, Harold Hecht; associate producer, Alexander Whitelaw; director, J. Lee Thompson; based on the book by Nikolai Gogol; screenplay, Waldo Salt, Karl Tunberg; art director, Edward Carrere; set decorator, William Calvert; music, Franz Waxman; song, Waxman and Mack David; orchestrator, Leonid Raab; costumes, Norma Koch; makeup, Frank McCoy, Emile Lavigne, and Daniele Strispeke; assistant director, Tom Shaw; sound, Stan Cooley, Bert Mallberg; special effects, Fred Wolff and Barney Wolff; special camera effects, Howard A. Anderson and Russ Lawson; camera, Joseph MacDonald; editors, William Reynolds, Gene Milford, Eda Warren, and Folmar Blangsted.

Tony Curtis (Andrei Bulba); Yul Brynner (Taras Bulba); Christine Kaufmann. (Natalie Dubrov); Sam Wanamaker (Filipenko); Brad Dexter (Shilo); Guy Rolfe (Prince Grigory); Perry Lopez (Ostap Bulba); George Macready (Governor); Ilka Windish (Sophia Bulba); Vladimir Sokoloff (Old Stephan); Vladimir Irman (Grisha Kubenkoi); Daniel Ocko (Ivan Mykola); Abraham Sofaer (Abbot); Mickey Finn (Korzh); Martine Milner (Redheaded Girl); Syl Lamont (Kimon Kandor); Jack Raine (Mayor); Marvin Goux (Brother Bartholomew).

40 POUNDS OF TROUBLE (Universal, 1962), C-106 min.
Producer, Stan Margulies; director, Norman Jewison; screenplay, Marion Hargrove; music, Mort Lindsay; songs, Lindsay and Sydney Shaw; art directors, Alexander Golitzen and Robert Clatworthy; set decorator, Ruby Levitt; makeup, Bud Westmore; costumes, Rosemary Odell; assistant directors, Tom Shaw, Terry Morse, Jr., and Carl Beringer; sound, Waldon O. Watson and Frank McWhorter; camera, Joseph MacDonald; editor, Marjorie Fowler.

Tony Curtis (Steve McCluskey); Phil Silvers (Bernie Friedman); Suzanne Pleshette (Chris Lockwood); Claire Wilcox (Penny Piper); Larry Storch (Floyd); Howard Morris (Julius); Stubby Kaye (Cranston); Edward Andrews (Herman); Mary Murphy (Liz McCluskey); Warren Stevens (Swing); Kevin McCarthy (Blanchard); Tom Reese (Bassett); Steve Gravers (Daytime); Karen Steele (Bambi); Gregg Palmer (Piper); Gerald Gordon (District Attorney); Sharon Farrell (Dolores); Charles Horvath (Stooge); Nicky Blair (Desk Clerk); Hallene Hill (Slot Machine Player); Jack LaRue (Nick the Greek); Jim Bannon (The Westerner); Charles Victor (Madison Avenue Type); Ruth Robinson (Little Old Lady); Tito Memminger (Room Clerk); Ramon Martinez (Indian Chief); Syl Lamont (Bellboy); Croftt Brook (Lawyer).

THE LIST OF ADRIAN MESSENGER (Universal, 1963), 98 min.
Producer, Edward Lewis; director, John Huston; based on the novel by Philip MacDonald; screenplay, Anthony Veiller; music supervisor, Joseph Gershenson; music, Jerry Goldsmith; art directors, Stephen Grimes and

George Webb; set decorator, Oliver Emert; makeup, Bud Westmore; assistant directors, Tom Shaw and Terry Morse, Jr.; sound, Waldon O. Watson and Frank Wilkinson; camera, Joseph MacDonald; editors, Terry Morse and Hugh Fowler.

George C. Scott (Anthony Gethryn); Dana Wynter (Lady Jocelyn Bruttenholm); Clive Brook (Marquis of Gleneyre); Herbert Marshall (Sir Wilfred Lucas); Jacques Roux (Raoul Le Borg); Bernard Archard (Inspector Pike); Gladys Cooper (Mrs. Karoudjian); Walter Anthony Huston (Derek); John Merivale (Adrian Messenger); Marcel Dalio (Max); Anita Sharpe-Bolster (Shopkeeper); Noel Purcell (Farmer); John Huston (Fox Hunter); Mona Lillian (Proprietress); Tony Curtis (Italian); Kirk Douglas (George Brougham); Burt Lancaster (Woman); Robert Mitchum (Jim Slattery); Frank Sinatra (Gypsy Stableman).

CAPTAIN NEWMAN, M.D. (Universal, 1963), C-126 min.
Producer, Robert Arthur; director, David Miller; based on the novel by Leo Rosten; screenplay, Richard L. Breen and Phoebe and Henry Ephron; second unit director, Robert D. Webb; assistant director, Phil Bowles; art directors, Alexander Golitzen and Alfred Sweeney; set decorator, Howard Bristol; costumes, Rosemary Odell; makeup, Bud Westmore; music, Frank Skinner; music supervisor, Joseph Gershenson; sound, Waldon O. Watson and William Russell; camera, Russell Metty; editor, Alma Macrorie.

Gregory Peck (Captain Josiah J. Newman); Tony Curtis (Corporal Jackson Laibowitz); Angie Dickinson (Lieutenant Francie Corum); Bobby Darin (Corporal Jim Tompkins); Eddie Albert (Colonel Norval Algate Bliss); Larry Storch (Corporal Gavoni); Jane Withers (Lieutenant Grace Blodgett); Dick Sargent (Lieutenant Alderson); Syl Lamont (Sergeant Kipp); James Gregory (Colonel Edgar Pyser); Robert Duvall (Captain Paul Cabot Winston); Bethel Leslie (Mrs. Paul Cabot Winston); Robert F. Simon (Lieutenant Colonel Larrabee); Paul Carr (Werbel); Vito Scotti (Major Alfredo Fortuno); Crahan Denton (Major General Snowden); Gregory Walcott (Captain Howard); Charles Briggs (Gorkow); Steve Marlo, George Lake, and Ken Swofford (Patients); Mike Trikilis and Nick Bon Tempi (Italian P.O.W.s); Penny Santon (Blue Grotto Waitress); Ann Doran (Mrs. Pyser); Alice Backes (WAC); John Hart (Officer); Buzz Henry, Chuck Roberson, Ronnie Rondell and Howard Curtis (Stuntmen); Haig Sakajian (Pilot).

WILD AND WONDERFUL (Universal, 1964), C-88 min.
Producer, Harold Hecht; director, Michael Anderson; based on a story by Dorothy Crider; screen story, Richard M. Powell, Phillip Rapp; screenplay, Larry Markes, Michael Morris, and Waldo Salt; art directors, Alexander Golitzen and Edward S. Haworth; set decorator, Ruby Levitt; Miss Kaufmann's gowns, Valentino; costume designer, Rosemary Odell; makeup, Bud Westmore; assistant director, L. C. McCardle; music, Morton Stevens; music supervisor, Joseph Gershenson; poodle trainer, Frank Weatherwax; sound, Weldon O. Watson and Joseph Lapis; camera, Joseph La Shelle; editor, Gene Milford.

Tony Curtis (Terry Williams); Christine Kaufmann (Giselle Ponchon); Larry Storch (Rufus Gibbs); Marty Ingels (Doc Bailey); Jacques Aubuchon (Papa Ponchon); Pierre Olaf (Jacquet); Cliff Osmond (Hercule); Fifi D'Orsay (Simone); Marcel Hillaire (Inspector Duvivier); Monsieur Cognac (The Dog);

651

Jules Munshin (Rousseleau); Sarah Marshall (Pamela); Marcel Dalio (Dr. Reynard); Vito Scotti (Andre); Steven Geray (Bartender); Stanley Adams (Mayor); Shelly Manne (Musician); Maurice Marsac (Announcer); Guy De Vestel (Gustav).

GOODBYE, CHARLIE (20th Century-Fox, 1964), C-117 min.

Producer, David Weisbart; director, Vincente Minnelli; based on the play by George Axelrod; screenplay, Harry Kurnitz; music, Andre Previn; song, Previn and Dory Langdon; orchestrator, Al Woodbury; art directors, Jack Martin Smith and Richard Day; set decorators, Walter M. Scott and Keogh Gleason; makeup, Ben Nye; costumes, Helen Rose; assistant director, David Hall; sound, W. D. Flick, Elmer Raguse; special camera effects, L. B. Abbott and Emil Kosa, Jr.; camera, Milton Krasner; editor, John W. Holmes.

Tony Curtis (George Tracy); Debbie Reynolds (Charlie Sorel, the Woman); Pat Boone (Bruce Minton); Walter Matthau (Sir Leopold Sartori); Joanna Barnes (Janie); Laura Devon (Rusty); Ellen McRae (Burstyn) (Franny); Martin Gabel (Morton Craft); Roger Carmel (Inspector); Harry Madden (Charlie the Male); Myrna Hansen (Starlet); Michael Romanoff (Patron); Michael Jackson (Himself); Anthony Eustrel (Butler); Donna Michelle (Guest on Yacht); Jerry Dunphy (TV Newscaster); Carmen Nisbet and Sydney Guilaroff (Patrons at Beauty Salon); Jack Richardson (Party Guest); Rudy Hansen and Edward Wermel (Germans in Bistro); Natalie Martinelli (Italian Girl).

SEX AND THE SINGLE GIRL (Warner Bros., 1964), C-114 min.

Producer, William T. Orr; director, Richard Quine; based on the book by Helen Gurley Brown; story, Joseph Hoffman; screenplay, Joseph Heller and David R. Schwartz; music, Neal Hefti; orchestrator, Art Morton; costumes, Edith Head and Norma Norell; assistant directors, Charles L. Hansen and Micheky McCardle; art director, Cary O'Dell; set decorator, Edward G. Boyle; makeup, Gordon Bau; sound, M. A. Merrick; camera, Charles Lang; editor, David Wages.

Tony Curtis (Bob Weston); Natalie Wood (Helen Brown); Henry Fonda (Frank); Lauren Bacall (Sylvia); Mel Ferrer (Rudy); Fran Jeffries (Gretchen); Leslie Parrish (Susan); Edward Everett Horton (The Chief); Larry Storch (Motorcycle Cop); Stubby Kaye (Helen's Cabbie); Howard St. John (Randall); Otto Kruger (Dr. Anderson); Max Showalter (Holmes); William Lanteau (Sylvester); Helen Kleeb (Hilda); Count Basie and His Orchestra (Themselves); Barbara Bouchet (Frannie); Taggart Casey (Guard); Fredd Wayne (Production Man); Paddi O'Hara (Strange Woman); Cheerio Meredith (Elderly Woman); Frank Baker (Pretzel Vendor); Edmund Glover (Dr. Chickering); Helen Kleeb (Hilda).

THE GREAT RACE (Warner Bros., 1965), C-163 min.

Producer, Martin Jurow; associate producer, Dick Crockett; director, Blake Edwards; story, Edwards, Arthur Ross; screenplay, Ross; assistant directors, Mickey McCardle, Jack Cunningham, and Dick Landry; production designer, Fernando Carrere; set decorator, George James Hopkins; choreography, Hermes Pan; music, Henry Mancini; songs, Mancini and Johnny Mercer; costumes, Donfeld; titles, DePatie-Freleng; sound, M. A. Merrick; special effects, Danny Lee; special camera effects, Linwood Dunn and James Gordon; camera, Russell Harlan; second unit camera, Harold Wellman; editor, Ralph W. Winters.

Tony Curtis (The Great Leslie); Jack Lemmon (Professor Fate); Natalie Wood (Maggie DuBois); Peter Falk (Max); Keenan Wynn (Hezekiah); Arthur O'Connell (Henry Goodbody); Vivian Vance (Hester Goodbody); Dorothy Provine (Lily Olay); Larry Storch (Texas Jack); Ross Martin (Baron Rolfe Von Stuppe); George Macready (General Kuhster); Marvin Kaplan (Frisbee); Hal Smith (Mayor of Boracho); Denver Pyle (Sheriff); William Bryant (Baron's Guard); Ken Wales (Baron's Guard); J. Edward McKinley (Chairman); Art Stewart (Man); Maria Schroeder (Woman in Tobelsk); Patricia King and Joyce Nizzari (Women in Western Scene); Greg Benedict and Chuck Hayward (Soldiers); Francis McDonald (Russian); Dick Alexander (Extra).

BOEING-BOEING (Paramount, 1965), C-102 min.

Producer, Hal B. Wallis; associate producer, Paul Nathan; director, John Rich; based on the play by Marc Camoletti; screenplay, Edward Anhalt; art directors, Hal Pereira and Walter Tyler; music, Neal Hefti; assistant director, Daniel J. McCauley; costumes, Edith Head; camera, Lucien Ballard; editors, Warren Low and Archie Marshek.

Tony Curtis (Bernard Lawrence); Jerry Lewis (Robert Reed); Christiane Schmidtmer (Lisa Berger); Dany Saval (Jacqueline Grieux); Suzanna Leigh (Vicky Hawkins); Thelma Ritter (Bertha); Lomax Study (Pierre); Eugene Borden, Peter Camlin, Roger Etienne, and George Dee (Cab Drivers); Francoise Ruggieri (French Taxi Driver); Robert Tafur (Elegant Gentleman); Nai Bonet (Air India Hostess); Mimi Dega (Wife); Victor Dunlop (Husband); Lucien Lanvin (French Waiter); Albert d'Arno and Maurice St. Clair (Maitre d's); Louise Lawson and Julie Parrish (Pretty Girls).

NOT WITH MY WIFE, YOU DON'T (Warner Bros., 1966), C-118 min.

Producer, Norman Panama; associate producer, Joel Freeman; director, Panama; story, Panama and Melvin Frank; screenplay, Panama, Larry Gelbart, and Peter Barnes; production designer, Edward Carrere; set decorator, George James Hopkins; title designer-visual consultation, Saul Bass and Associates; music/music conductor, Johnny Williams; song, Williams and Johnny Mercer; choreography, Shela Hackett; Miss Lisi's wardrobe, Edith Head; makeup, Gordon Bau; aviation liaison, H. Mahaddie; assistant director, Jack Aldworth; sound, Stanley Jones; camera, Charles Lang; European camera, Paul Beeson; editor, Aaron Stell.

Tony Curtis (Tom Ferris); Virna Lisi (Julie Ferris); George C. Scott ("Tank" Martin); Carroll O'Connor (General Parker); Richard Eastham (General Walters); Eddie Ryder (Sergeant Gilroy); George Tyne (Sergeant Dogerty); Ann Doran (Doris Parker); Donna Danton (Nurse Sally Ann); Natalie Core (Lillian Walters).

CHAMBER OF HORRORS (Warner Bros., 1966), C-99 min.

Producer, Hy Averback; associate producer, Jim Barnett; director, Averback; story, Ray Russell and Stephen Kandel; screenplay, Kandel; music, William Lava; art director, Art Loel; set decorator, William L. Kuehl; makeup, Gordon Bau; assistant director, Sam Schneider; sound, M. A. Merrick; camera, Richard Kline; editor, David Wages.

Patrick O'Neal (Jason Cravette); Cesare Danova (Anthony Draco); Wilfrid Hyde-White (Harold Blount); Laura Devon (Marie Champlair); Patrice Wymore (Vivian); Suzy Parker (Barbara Dixon); Tun Tun (Senor Pepe de Reyes); Philip Bourneuf (Inspector Strudwick); Jeannette Nolan (Mrs. Ewing Perryman); Marie Windsor (Madame Corona); Wayne Rogers (Sergeant Albertson); Vinton Haworth (Judge Randolph); Inger Stratton (Gloria); Richard O'Brien (Dr. Cobb); Berry Kroeger (Chun Sing); Charles Seel (Dr. Hopewell); Ayllene Gibbons (Barmaid); Tony Curtis (Card Player).

ARRIVERDERCI, BABY! (Paramount, 1966), C-100 min.
Producer-director, Ken Hughes; suggested by the story *The Careful Man* by Richard Deming; screenplay, Hughes and Ronald Harwood; second unit director, Richard Taylor; assistant director, Colin Brewer; art director, Seamus Flannery; set decorator, Patrick McLoughlin; makeup, George Frost and Eric Allwright; costumes, Elizabeth Haffenden and Joan Bridge; Miss Schiaffino's gowns, Pierre Balmain; music/music conductor, Dennis Farnom; additional music, Tibor Kunstler and The Plainsman; sound, John Mitchell; camera, Denys Coop; editor, John Shirley.

Tony Curtis (Nick Johnson); Rosanna Schiaffino (Francesca de Rienzi); Lionel Jeffries (Parker); Zsa Zsa Gabor (Gigi); Nancy Kwan (Baby); Fennella Fielding (Lady Fawcett); Anna Quayle (Aunt Miriam); Warren Mitchell (Conte de Rienzi/Maximilian); Mischa Auer (Romeo); Noel Purcell (Captain O'Flannery); Alan Gifford (American Brasshat); Joseph Furst (German Brasshat); Eileen Way (Dressmaker); John Brandon and Windsor Davies (Radio Engineers); Henri Vidon (Priest); Raymond Young (Photographer). Mark Lester (Bit).

DON'T MAKE WAVES (MGM, 1967), C-97 min.
Producers, John Calley and Martin Ransohoff; associate producer, Julian Bercovici; director, Alexander Mackendrick; based on the novel *Muscle Beach* by Ira Wallach; screenplay, Wallach and George Kirgo; adaptation, Maurice Richlin; music/music conductor, Vic Mizzy; title song, Jim McGuinn and Chris Hillman; art directors, George W. Davis and Edward Carfagno; set decorators, Henry Grace and Charles S. Thompson; sky-diving sequences, Leigh Hunt; assistant directors, Carl Beringer and Erich Von Stroheim, Jr.; makeup, William Tuttle; costumes, Donfeld; sound, Franklin Milton; camera, Philip H. Lathrop; editors, Rita Rowland and Thomas Stanford.

Tony Curtis (Carlo Cofield); Claudia Cardinale (Laura Califatti); Sharon Tate (Malibu); Robert Webber (Rod Prescott); Joanna Barnes (Diane Prescott); David Draper (Harry Hollard); Mort Sahl (Sam Lingonberry); Edgar Bergen (Madame Lavinia); Jim Backus and Henny Backus (Themselves); Ann Elder (Millie Gunder); Chester Yorton (Ted Gunder); Marc London (Fred Barker); Mary Grace Canfield (Seamstress); Dub Taylor (Electrician); Julie Payne (Helen); Paul Barselow (Pilot); Eduardo Tirella (Decorator).

ROSEMARY'S BABY (Paramount, 1968), C-136 min.

Producer, William Castle; associate producer, Dona Holloway; director, Roman Polanski; based on the novel by Ira Levin; screenplay, Polanski; production designer, Richard Sylbert; art director, Joel Schiller; set decorator, Robert Nelson; music, Christopher Komeda; makeup, Allan Snyder; costumes, Anthea Sylbert; assistant director, Daniel J. McCauley; sound, Harold Lewis; process camera, Farciot Edouart; camera, William Fraker; editors, Sam O'Steen and Bob Wyman.

Mia Farrow (Rosemary Woodhouse); John Cassavetes (Guy Woodhouse); Ruth Gordon (Mrs. Minnie Castevet); Sidney Blackmer (Roman Castevet); Maurice Evans (Hutch); Ralph Bellamy (Dr. Sapirstein); Angela Dorian (Terry Fionoffrio); Patsy Kelly (Laura-Louise); Elisha Cook, Jr. (Mr. Nicklas); Emmaline Henry (Elisa Dunstan); Marianne Gordon (Joan Jellico); Charles Grodin (Dr.Hill); Hanna Landy (Grace Cardiff); Phillip Leeds (Dr. Shand); Hope Summers (Mrs. Gilmore); Tony Curtis (Voice of Donald Baumgart); William Castle (Man at Phone Booth); Bill Baldwin (Salesman); George Savalas (Workman); Marilyn Harvey (Dr. Sapirstein's Receptionist); Patricia O'Neal (Mrs. Wees); Walter Baldwin (Mr. Wees); Almira Sessions (Mrs. Sabatini); Wendy Wagner (Tiger); Duke Fishman (Man); Al Szathmary (Taxi Driver); John Halloran (Mechanic).

THE BOSTON STRANGLER (20th Century-Fox, 1968), C-116 min.

Producer, Robert Fryer; associate producer, James Cresson; director, Richard Fleischer; based on the book by Gerold Frank; screenplay, Edward Anhalt; technical advisors, John S. Bottomly and Phillip J. Di Natale; assistant director, David Hall; art directors, Jack Martin Smith and Richard Day; set decorators, Walter M. Scott, Stuart A. Reiss, and Raphael Bretton; incidental music coordinator, Lionel Newman; sound, Don Bassman and David Dockendorf; costumes, Travilla; makeup, Dan Striepeke; split screen images, Fred Harpman; special camera effects, L. B. Abbott, Art Cruickshank, and John C. Caldwell; camera, Richard H. Kline; editor, Marion Rothman.

Tony Curtis (Albert DeSalvo); Henry Fonda (John S. Bottomly); George Kennedy (Phillip J. Di Natale); Mike Kellin (Julian Soshnick); Hurt Hatfield (Terence Huntley); Murray Hamilton (Frank McAfee); Jeff Corey (John Asgeirsson); Sally Kellerman (Dianne Cluny); William Marshall (Edward W. Brooke); George Voskovec (Peter Hurkos); Leora Dana (Mary Bottomly); Carolyn Conwell (Irmgard DeSalvo); Jeanne Cooper (Cloe); Austin Willis (Dr. Nagy); Lara Lindsay (Bobbie Eden); George Furth (Lyonel Brumley); Richard X. Slattery (Ed Willis); William Hickey (Eugene T. Rourke); Eve Collyer (Ellen Ridgeway); Alex Dreier (News Commentator); Elizabeth Bauer (Harriet Fordin); John Cameron Swayze (TV.Commentator); Marie Thomas (Gloria); Enid Markey (Edna); James Brolin (Sergeant Lisi); William Traylor (Arne Carr).

THOSE DARING YOUNG MEN IN THEIR JAUNTY JALOPIES (Paramount, 1969), C-130 min.

Producer, Ken Annakin; associate producer, Basil Keys; director, Annakin; Paris sequence director, Sam Itzkovitch; screenplay, Annakin and Jack Davies, Annakin; production designer, Ted Haworth; art directors, Elven Frederix and Erik Bjork; set decorator, Dario Simoni; titles designer, Ronald Searle; makeup, Amato Garbini; music-song, Ron Goodwin; assistant director, Giorgio Gentili; sound, John Brommage and David Hawkins; special effects, Dick Parker; camera, Gabor Pogany, Walter Wottitz, and Bert Palmgren; editor, Peter Taylor.

Tony Curtis (Chester Schofield); Susan Hampshire (Betty); Terry-Thomas (Sir Cuthbert Ware-Armitage); Eric Sykes (Perkins); Gert Frobe (Schnickel); Peter Cook (Major Digby Dawlish); Dudley Moore (Lieutenant Kit Barrington); Bourvil (Monsieur Dupont); Jack Hawkins (Count Levionovitch); Peer Schmidt (Otto); Walter Chiari (Angelo Pincelli); Lando Buzzanca (Marcello Agosti); Marie Dubois (Pasquale); Derren Nesbitt (Waleska); Nicholas Phipps (Golfer); Richard Wattis (Gold Club Secretary); Michael Trubshawe (German Rally Official).

British release title: **Monte Carlo or Bust.**

LA CINTURA DI CASTITA (THE CHASTITY BELT) (a.k.a., **ON MY WAY TO THE CRUSADES I MET A GIRL WHO . . .**, Warner Bros. 7 Arts, 1969), C-110 min. (English language edition: 74 min.).
Producer, Francesco Mazzei; director, Pasquale Festa Campanile; story, Ugo Liberatore; screenplay, Luigi Magni and Larry Gelbart; art director, Piero Poletto; music/music director, Riz Ortolani; costumes, Danilo Donati; titles-animation, Studio Favali; sound, Aurelio Verona; camera, Carlo Di Palma; editors, Gabrio Astori and Charles Nelson.

Tony Curtis (Guerrando da Montone); Monica Vitti (Boccadoro); Hugh Griffith (Sultan of Bari); John Richardson (Dragone); Nino Castelnuovo (Marculfo); Ivo Garrani (Duke of Pandolfo); Francesco Mule, Franco Sportelli, Umberto Raho, Leopoldo Trieste, and Gabriella Giorgelli (Bits).

SUPPOSE THEY GAVE A WAR AND NOBODY CAME? (Cinerama, 1970), C-100 min.
Producer, Fred Engel; associate producer, J. Paul Popkin; director, Hy Averback; story, Hal Captain; screenplay, Captain and Don McGuire; assistant director, Jack Aldworth; second unit director, Paul Baxley; art director, Jack Polin; set decorator, Jim Payne; music, Jerry Fielding; song, Fielding and David McKechnie; technical advisor, Major Paul Lacy; sound, Everett Hughes; special effects, Larry Hampton and George Peckham; camera, Burnett Guffey; aerial camera, Jack Willoughby; editor, John F. Burnett.

Brian Keith (Nace); Tony Curtis (Shannon Gambroni); Ernest Borgnine (Sheriff Harve); Ivan Dixon (Sergeant Jones); Suzanne Pleshette (Ramona); Tom Ewell (Billy Joe Davis); Bradford Dillman (Captain Myerson); Arthur O'Connell (Mr. Kruft); John Fiedler (Major Purvis); Don Ameche (Colonel Flanders); Robert Emhardt (Lester Calhoun); Maxine Stuart (Zelda); Christopher Mitchum (Alturi); Pamela Britton (Sergeant Graham); Grady Sutton (Reverend Dinwood); Eddie Firestone (Deputy Goulash); Janet E. Clark (Mrs. Davis); Paula Stewart and Carolyn Williamson (Girlfriends); John James Bannon and Vincent Howard (Military Police); Stanley W. Barrett (Green Beret).

YOU CAN'T WIN 'EM ALL (Columbia, 1970), C-99 min.

Producer, Gene Corman; associate producer, Harold Buck; director, Peter Collinson; screenplay, Leo V. Gordon; second unit director, Skeets Kelly; assistant director, Scott Wodehouse; art director, Seamus Flannery; music, Bert Kaempfert; music director, Muir Mathieson; sound, Barrie Copeland; camera, Kenneth Higgins; editor, Ray Poulton.

Tony Curtis (Adam Dyer); Charles Bronson (Josh Corey); Michele Mercier (Aila); Gregoire Aslan (Osman Bey); Fikret Hakan (Colonel Elci); Salih Guney (Captain Enver); Patrick Magee (The General); Tony Bonner (Reese); John Acheson (Davis); John Alderson (U. S. Major); Horst Jansen (Woller); Leo Gordon (Bolek); Reed De Rouen (U. S. Chief Petty Officer); Jenia Halil (Madam); Suna Keskin (Girl in Cafe).

THE THIRD GIRL FROM THE LEFT (ABC-TV, 1973), C-90 min.

Producer, Ron Roth; director, Peter Medak; screenplay, Dory Previn; songs, Previn; music supervisor, Nikolas Venet; music arranger, James E. Bond, Jr.; choreography, Miriam Nelson; art director, Frank Arrigo; Miss Novak's wardrobe, Bill Thomas; camera, Gayne Rescher; editor, Jim Benson.

Kim Novak (Gloria); Michael Brandon (David); George Furth (Zimmy); Tony Curtis (Joey); Michael Conrad (Hugh); Bern Hoffman (Len); Jenifer Shaw (Gaye); Louis Guss (Murray); Barbi Benton (Melanie); Anne Ramsey (Madeline); Larry Bishop (Bedford).

THE COUNT OF MONTE CRISTO (NBC-TV, 1975), C-120 min.

Producer, Norman Rosemont; director, David Greene; based on the novel by Alexandre Dumas; teleplay, Sidney Carroll; music, Allyn Ferguson; camera, Aldo Tonti; editor, Gene Milford.

Richard Chamberlain (Edmond Dantes/The Count of Monte Cristo); Louis Jourdan (Villefort); Trevor Howard (Abbe Faria); Donald Pleasence (Danglars); Tony Curtis (Mondego); Kate Nelligan (Mercedes); Dominic Guard (Albert Mondego); with: Taryn Power, Harold Bromley, Alessio Orano, Ralph Michael, Dominic Barto, Isabelle de Valvert, Carlo Puri, Antony Dawson, David Mills, Franco Mazzieri, Angelo Infanti.

THE BIG RIPOFF (NBC-TV, 1975), C-90 min.

Producers, Roland Kibbee and Dean Hargrove; director, Hargrove; teleplay, Kibbee and Hargrove; sound, Harold Lewis; camera, Bill Butler; editor, Robert L. Kimble.

Tony Curtis (McCoy); Brenda Vaccaro (Brenda); Larry Hagman (Darnell); John Dehner (Bishop); Lynn Borden (Grace Bishop); Morgan Woodward (Kelso); Roscoe Lee Browne (Silky); Jay Verela (Lieutenant Claypool); Jane Goodnow Gillett (Virginia); Nate Esformes (Art); Len Lesser (Phil); Fuddle Bagley (Notch); and: Carl Mathis Craig, Trina Parks, Billy Varga, Ted Christy, Ed Peck, Priscilla Pointer, Jack Krupnick, Linda Gray, Jefferson Kibbee, Barry

Cahill, Lucille Meredith, Manuel DePina, James V. Christy, Carol Ann Susi, Robert Gibbons, Ben Gage, John Francis.

LEPKE (Warner Bros., 1975); C-100 min.

Executive producer, Yoram Globus; producer-director, Menahem Golam; story, Wesley Lau; screenplay, Lau and Tamar Hoffs; assistant director, Fred Miller; production designer, Jack Degovia; set decorator, Vincent Cresciman; music, Ken Wannberg; costumes, Jodie Tillen; stunt co-ordinator, George P. Wilbur; sound effects, Paul Hockman; special effects, Cliff Wenger; camera, Andrew Davis; editor, Dov Hoenig and Aaron Stell.

Tony Curtis (Louis "Lepke" Buchalter); Anjanette Comer (Bernice Meyer); Michael Callan (Robert Kane); Warren Berlinger (Gurrah Shapiro); Gianni Russo (Albert Anastasia); Vic Tayback (Lucky Luciano); Mary Wilcox (Marion); Milton Berle (Mr. Meyer); Jack Ackerman (Little Augie); Louis Guss (Max Rubin); Vaughn Meader (Walter Winchell); Lillian Adams (Mama Meyer); Albert Cole (Gross); Zitto Kazan (Kid Twist Reles); Johnny Silver (Schwartz); J. S. Johnson (Mendy Weiss); Simmy Bow (Tannenbaum); John Durren (Dutch Schultz); Barry Miller (Young Lepke); Jon Ian Jacobs (Big Hesh); Matt Greene (Skinny); Richard C. Adams (Thomas Dewey); Sam Solomon (Butcher); Jeannine Brown (Prostitute); Raymond Cavaleri (Gino); Norman Pauker (Rabbi); Ida Mae McKenzie (Mrs. Shea); Jack Tesler (Feldman); Joseph Kim (Lin Phoo); Casey Morgan (Young Gurrah); Wesley Lau, Jim Hayes (Detectives); Guy Christopher (Reporter); Marco Goldstein (Cantor); Crane Jackson (Judge); To Castronova (Policeman); Robin Chesler (Sarah); Josef Behrens (Violinist).

THE LAST TYCOON (Paramount, 1976), C-

Producer, Sam Spiegel; director, Elia Kazan; based on the novel by F. Scott Fitzgerald; screenplay, Harold Pinter; assistant directors, Danny McCauley, Ron Wright; production designer, Gene Callahan; set decorator, Jerry Wunderlich; costumes, Anna Hill Johnstone; sound, Larry Jost; camera, Victor Kemper.

With: Robert De Niro, Tony Curtis, Robert Mitchum, Jeanne Moreau, Jack Nicholson, Donald Pleasence, Ray Milland, Dana Andrews, Ingrid Boulting, Theresa Russell, Anjelica Huston, Peter Strauss.

about the authors and researchers

JAMES ROBERT PARISH, New York-based free-lance writer, was born in Cambridge, Massachusetts. He attended the University of Pennsylvania and graduated as a Phi Beta Kappa with a degree in English. A graduate of the University of Pennsylvania Law School, he is a member of the New York Bar. As president of Entertainment Copyright Research Co., Inc., he headed a major researching facility for the film and television industries. Later he was a film interviewer-reviewer for film trade papers. He has been responsible for such reference volumes as *The American Movies Reference Book: The Sound Era*, and *The Emmy Awards: A Pictorial History*. He is the author of *The Fox Girls, The Paramount Pretties, The RKO Gals, Hollywood's Great Love Teams, Elvis!* and co-author of such books as *The Great Spy Pictures, The MGM Stock Company* and *Film Directors' Guide: The U.S.* Mr. Parish is a film reviewer for several national magazines.

DON E. STANKE was born in St. Paul, Minnesota. He has spent most of his adult life in or near San Francisco, California, where he worked for a number of years for the *San Francisco Examiner*. A long-standing film enthusiast, Don has been interviewing screen personalities and writing biographical articles on movie players for years; his work has appeared in such publications as *Films in Review, Film Fan Monthly*, and *Filmograph*. He is employed as office manager by the CGR Medical Corporation in the San Leandro, California district office. With James Robert Parish, he co-authored *The Glamour Girls* and *The Debonairs*.

T. ALLAN TAYLOR, godson of the late Margaret Mitchell, has long been active in book publishing and is currently the production manager of a leading abstracting and technical indexing service. He was the editor of *The Fox Girls, The RKO Gals, The Debonairs, The Glamour Girls, The Great Western Pictures*, and other volumes.

EARL ANDERSON, a native of San Francisco, was educated at San Francisco State College (B.A.) and the University of Washington (M.A.). Over the years he has contributed career articles on Marion Davies, Wallace Beery, Gladys Cooper, and others to *Films in Review*. Since 1960 he has been the assistant to the director of the California Palace of the Legion of Honor, where he has written museum bulletins devoted to aspects of the collection and has organized film series devoted to Irene Dunne, Mary Pickford, and the Western film.

Since an early age, Brooklynite JOHN ROBERT COCCHI has been viewing and collating data on motion pictures and is now regarded as one of America's most thorough film researchers. He is the New York editor of *Boxoffice* magazine. He was research associate on *The American Movies Reference Book, The Fox Girls, Good Dames, The MGM Stock Company: The Golden Era, The Great Gangster Pictures* and many other books. He is the author of his own Western film quiz book. He has co-founded one of Manhattan's leading film societies and has written cinema history articles for such journals as *Film Fan Monthly* and *Screen Facts.*

MICHAEL R. PITTS has been the entertainment editor of the *Anderson* (Ind.) *Daily Bulletin* and holds a B.A. in history and a M.A. in journalism from Ball State University. He has been published in numerous cinema journals and is the co-author of *The Great Spy Pictures, Film Directors Guide: The U.S., The Great Gangster Pictures,* and has contributed to such books as *The Debonairs.*

New York-born FLORENCE SOLOMON attended Hunter College and then joined Ligon Johnson's copyright research office. Later she was appointed director research at Entertainment Copyright Research Co., Inc. and is presently a reference supervisor at ASCAP's Index Division in Manhattan. Ms. Solomon has collaborated on such works as *The American Movies Reference Book, TV Movies, The Great Movie Series, Vincent Price Unmasked,* and others. She is the niece of the sculptor, the late Sir Jacob Epstein.

EDWARD MICHAEL CONNOR was born in Willimansett, Massachusetts. He later moved to New York where he joined the staff of the Pius Xth School of Liturgical Music. Still later he was a choir trainer. He joined the National Board of Review in 1954 and the National Catholic Office for Motion Pictures in 1959. He has contributed articles on the cinema to *Films in Review, Screen Facts,* and *Screen Careers,* and for years was musical editor of *Films in Review.* He is the author of *Prophecy for Today* and *Recent Apparitions of Our Lady.* Mr. Connor has contributed to both *The Great Gangster Pictures* and *The Great Western Pictures.*

Index

*Page Numbers in italics indicate
photographs of the listed subjects*

661

662

663

664

665

668

669